Reformation Roots

L T H

THE LIVING THEOLOGICAL HERITAGE

OF THE UNITED CHURCH OF CHRIST

Barbara Brown Zikmund

Series Editor

L T H

VOLUME TWO

Reformation Roots

Edited by John B. Payne

The Pilgrim Press

Cleveland, Ohio

The Pilgrim Press, Cleveland, Ohio 44115

Printed in the United States of America on acid-free paper

02 01 00 99 98 97 5 4 3 2 1

Library of Congress Cataloging-in-Publication Data
The living theological heritage of the United Church of Christ /
Barbara Brown Zikmund, series editor.
p. cm.
Includes bibliographical references and index.
Contents: v. 1. Ancient and Medieval Legacies / edited by Reinhard Ulrich
ISBN 0-8298-1064-1 (v. 1 : alk. paper)
1. United Church of Christ—Doctrines—History.
2. Theology, Doctrinal—History.
3. United Church of Christ—History.
I. Zikmund, Barbara Brown.

vol. 1, Ancient and Medieval Legacies ISBN 0-8298-1064-1
vol. 2, Reformation Roots ISBN 0-8298-1143-5
vol. 3, Colonial and National Beginnings ISBN 0-8298-1109-5
vol. 4, Consolidation and Expansion ISBN 0-8298-1110-9
vol. 5, Outreach and Diversity ISBN 0-8298-1111-7
vol. 6, Growing Toward Unity ISBN 0-8298-1112-5
vol. 7, United and Uniting ISBN 0-8298-1113-3

Contents

The Living Theological Heritage of the United Church of Christ

Remember me, O LORD, when you show favor to your people; help me when you deliver them; that I may see the prosperity of your chosen ones, that I may rejoice in the gladness of your nation, that I may glory in your heritage.

Psalm 106:4–5 (NRSV)

The United Church of Christ is a microcosm of the history of Christian theology. Although the UCC was not officially "born" until 1957, it draws upon a long-standing and rich theological legacy. A living theological heritage has shaped, and continues to support, its common life.

Unfortunately, a perception exists that the UCC is without any roots, that it is unsure about its faith. Lutherans quote the works of Martin Luther; Methodists revere the ideas of John Wesley; Episcopalians have the divines of the Church of England. But members of the United Church of Christ often seem uncertain about their theological heritage and identity.

The United Church of Christ was created out of a mid-twentieth-century ecumenical passion to heal the divisions of the Christian church. Its focus was on the future, not on the past. Nevertheless it has a remarkable theological and historical legacy. This volume, and others in this series, offers resources from Congregational Christian history and German Evangelical and Reformed traditions, along with many hidden histories, to leaders and members of the United Church of Christ and to the wider society. We hope that these materials will strengthen the denomination and inform those seeking a better understanding of the past and present life of the UCC.

For example, New England Congregationalism leaned on the theological insights of key English separatist thinkers in the late sixteenth and early seventeenth centuries. Participants in American frontier religion developed six theological principles to guide their Christian witness. The theological work of John Nevin and Philip Schaff shaped and reshaped the German Reformed church. German Evangelical immigrants brought with them a theology forged by a European "church union" movement. Few people know this heritage, and when they look for more information, it is difficult to find the sources.

For the past ten years the Office for Church Life and Leadership and the Board for Homeland Ministries of the United Church of Christ have been working on the Living Theological Heritage of the United Church of Christ. They designed this series of seven volumes to enable the United Church of Christ to recover its theological past and strengthen contemporary faith and practice. They offer the series to the churches and their members to enable them to move beyond their theological inferiority complex and to claim their heritage.

• • •

The series brings together key materials that undergird UCC faith and practice. A team of thirteen editors, guided by an editorial board of seven, present these volumes as a "quarry" of resources to be mined by the churches for years to come.

The design of each volume does three things:

First, it gathers together important materials that have shaped the theological identity of the United Church of Christ—ancient Christological discourses, sixteenth-century treatises by Reformation theologians, the Heidelberg Catechism, writings and sermons from colonial Congregationalism, the Cambridge Platform, mission statements, popular hymns, prayers, official ecumenical materials, resolutions from wider church meetings, minority reports, and even protest literature. Some of the materials are obvious and known, some are fugitive, and some are new discoveries. The editors chose all of them, from the first century to the twentieth century, not simply because they are part of the historical record, but because the editors believe these documents have shaped the theological identity of the UCC.

Second, each volume contains brief introductions to individual documents or groups of source materials, giving the reader background information needed to understand what is printed. Who wrote it? When was it written? Why was it written? What was the result? These document introductions help make the materials understandable "in and of themselves."

Third, each volume has one or more introductory essays to highlight broader insights and theological interpretations of the materials. Obviously any selection of documents can distort by highlighting some things and excluding others, but the editors have attempted to make the selections as inclusive as possible. The introductory essays, written by the editors, weave the materials into meaningful patterns and gather up the collective wisdom of the UCC to make it more accessible in the present.

• • •

The Living Theological Heritage of the United Church of Christ has seven volumes.

Volume 1, *Ancient and Medieval Legacies*, grounds the theological life of the United Church of Christ in the search for unity and theological clarity within the ancient and medieval church. As a Protestant denomination, why should the UCC concern itself with pre-Reformation theology and history? Because not to begin with the early church betrays its understanding of Christian unity. This volume explores the themes of unity ("united"), ecclesiology ("church"), and Christology ("Christ") from the time of Jesus to the Reformation. It highlights the fact that the United Church of Christ stands in a long line of faithful Christians who have sought to understand and name their faith from the first century to the present.

Volume 2, *Reformation Roots*, explores the theological legacies of the United Church of Christ found in the sixteenth-century Protestant Reformation. From reformers like Erasmus, Zwingli, Luther, Calvin, English separatists, and the irenic leaders of the Palatinate, the UCC has forged its theological core. Volume 2 provides a collection of Reformation materials especially meaningful to the United Church of Christ.

Volume 3, *Colonial and National Beginnings*, examines the development of early Congregationalism and German Reformed theology. It lifts up the ideas and concerns that motivated colonial thinking and demonstrates how they evolved with the migration and increasing diversity of the population.

Volume 4, *Consolidation and Expansion*, documents the story of the Christians and the German Evangelicals on the American frontier and tracks later developments in Congregational and German Reformed history. It illustrates how the Christian movement brought together Methodists from North Carolina, Baptists from New England, and Presbyterians from Kentucky. It reveals the contributions of German Evangelicals on the Mississippi frontier. At the same time, it follows the development of German Reformed and Congregational faith and practice as the nation matured and people migrated west.

Volume 5, *Outreach and Diversity*, brings together a mix of materials flowing from the mission outreach of all of these groups. It also explores the experiences of minority and immigrant communities. The call to evangelize, educate, and serve stretched the theological mind of those groups that later created the UCC. African American contributions, encounters with indigenous peoples, social witness, and new immigrants raised new theological issues and encouraged a pattern of theological engagement with the world.

Volume 6, *Growing Toward Unity*, celebrates the long-standing commitment of the UCC to an ecumenical vision and the search for Christian unity. It steps back from the complex history of peoples and ideas documented in the earlier volumes to examine the vision of Christian unity that eventually gave birth to the United Church of Christ. It is a theological heritage that takes the prayer of Jesus "that they might all be one" seriously.

Volume 7, *United and Uniting*, documents the evolution of United Church of Christ's theological identity since 1957. It looks at almost four decades of UCC life and gathers up its theological treasures. It recognizes that the theological journey of the UCC has been wide ranging, one that has produced a distinctive living theological heritage. It also invites the UCC to become more theologically self-conscious.

• • •

We hope that *The Living Theological Heritage of the United Church of Christ* will enable those who are members of the UCC to find new courage to speak with pride about their UCC faith and theological inheritance and give those who are not members of the church a clear understanding of this unique community of Christians.

BARBARA BROWN ZIKMUND
Series Editor

Reformation Roots

The Protestant Reformation is foundational to the United Church of Christ's theological heritage. Three of the major traditions of the UCC—the Reformed, the Evangelical, and the Congregational—are directly linked to the beginnings of the Reformation in sixteenth-century Europe. The Christian movement, which originated in the early nineteenth century, sprang from several denominations connected to the Reformation: Methodists in Virginia and North Carolina were descendants of John Wesley's eighteenth-century revival within the Church of England; Baptists in New England had links to the seventeenth-century Baptist movement in England; and Presbyterians in Kentucky looked to John Calvin's reforms as they had developed in sixteenth-century Scotland under John Knox.

In fact, the United Church of Christ is unusual because it is the only denomination that can claim so many strands of the Reformation tradition as its own—Lutheran, Reformed, Scottish Presbyterian, and English Puritan. The UCC debt to the Protestant Reformation is especially strong in those traditions of the United Church of Christ that continue to use Reformation confessions and catechisms in local worship and confirmation education. For instance, congregations that were once part of the Reformed Church in the United States used the Heidelberg Catechism in confirmation education; some former Reformed congregations continue to do so. Likewise, congregations that have roots in the Evangelical Synod of North America feel closely tied to the Lutheran and Reformed union in Prussia, which took place in 1817, and which is known in contemporary Germany as the Evangelical Church of the Union. These Evangelical congregations regularly make use of Luther's Small Catechism and the Augsburg Confession as well as the Heidelberg Catechism.

Congregationalists are often aware of the English Reformation roots of their ancestors who came to the shores of New England in the early 1600s, but they are sometimes not cognizant of the influence of the Westminster Confession on their tradition. Even the members of the Christian movement, who eschewed all denominational labels and creeds (wishing to build their faith and practice on the Bible alone), owe their exclusive commitment to Scripture and to the doctrine of the priesthood of all believers to teachings of the sixteenth-century Reformation.

Since the sixteenth century, all of these United Church of Christ traditions have been shaped and reshaped by the rise of modern science, the rationalism of the Enlightenment, the liberalism of the nineteenth century, and the rise of literary and historical criticism of the Bible. Of course there have been, and still are, many Protestants, especially among the so-called evangelicals, or conservatives, who have resisted these influences. They reject science, liberalism, and historical criticism, viewing them as threats to their convictions about the biblical account of creation or particular miracles.

The Protestant Reformation can be conceived of as the birth of the modern world, but it was also the last phase of the middle ages. The Reformation was a religious revolution that led to the breakup of medieval Christendom —promoting religious pluralism, centralized monarchies, increased control of the state over the church, and the secularization of church lands. At the same time, the Protestant Reformation was very medieval in its outlook. For the Protestant reformers, religious things still counted heavily, contrasting sharply with the increasing secularization of the modern world. Not only are Luther's views concerning the reality of the devil alien to many modern Christians, but so are his harsh attitudes toward the peasants' uprising in 1525 and toward the Jews. The persecution of the Anabaptists by Zwingli's Zurich and the burning of Servetus by Calvin's Geneva run against the grain of the modern tolerant mind, even if religious toleration in many places of the world is still more an ideal than a reality.

In spite of certain Reformation beliefs and practices that repel us, contemporary Christians can learn from the reformers' struggles of faith. Christians in the time of the Reformation were not saints or paragons of virtue, but human beings with anxieties and foibles who in the midst of their wrestlings were able, by God's grace, to give rise to original and powerful expressions of faith that still inspire and instruct. All Protestants, and especially all members of the United Church of Christ, are indebted to the sixteenth-century Reformers for insisting on the centrality of Scripture, the priesthood of all believers, and justification by faith.

The Church on the Eve of the Reformation

The state of the church on the eve of the Protestant Reformation is variously assessed. It was once argued that the late medieval church was so corrupt that it was ripe for reform. The situation of the clergy—those in local settings and those with responsibility for oversight—was characterized by simony (the purchase of church offices), pluralism (the holding of more than one ecclesiastical office), absenteeism (the neglect of pastoral duties), concubinage (the cohabitation of a woman with a cleric), and ignorance. These widespread abuses, according to many scholars, explain the emergence of Martin Luther and the need for reform.

Other historians acknowledge these abuses but do not think they were so perverse that the Reformation was inevitable. Indeed, some interpreters insist that there was no special decline in the morality of the clergy. Instead there were rising expectations on the part of an educated laity. The state of the parish clergy actually may have been on the upswing, due to improved education and the introduction of handbooks that provided standards for behavior.

That there was an intense and general anticlericalism on the eve of the Reformation probably has some basis. Clergy, from pope to local priests, were perceived as holding too much power—not only religious but economic and political. The pope was not simply the spiritual leader of western European Christendom, he was also the prince of a particular kingdom in Italy, the Papal States. As a territorial prince, the pope acted to defend and expand papal territory by diplomacy and conquest. Furthermore, as the pope sought to increase control over the jurisdiction of the church, he presided over a court that was overburdened by administrative and legal services. To support his activities as a territorial prince and as the administrator of a demanding bureaucracy, the pope needed more and more income.

The popes increased their income in various ways. Representatives of the papacy sold church offices to the highest bidder, levied higher taxes (such as *annates*, or the first year's income from an ecclesiastical office), and marketed *indulgences* (forgiveness of the penance for one's sin, granted by popes or bishops). In Germany, where resentment against Rome was widespread on account of these papal monetary schemes, the people became increasingly dissatisfied. The Renaissance popes, such as Innocent VIII, Alexander VI, and Julius II of the late fifteenth and early sixteenth centuries, had a reputation for squalor and shame with their practice of nepotism (appointing nephews and bastard children to church offices) and their support of a luxurious court. Even when these same Renaissance popes patronized the magnificent artistic creations of such greats as Raphael and

Michelangelo, they were perceived as so involved with secular affairs that they were unable to fulfill their office as the chief shepherd of the church.

The pope and other clergy were also resented because of the power and special political and economic privileges they possessed. Many bishops and abbots acted as secular princes, controlling large amounts of property and exacting tithes from the people. As dispensers of the channels of grace (the sacraments), priests had considerable spiritual and social power. Through the sacrament of penance (the confessional), priests learned of aberrant behavior, bestowed absolution after hearing confession, and prescribed proper penance. In the Mass, only priests could handle holy things. The cup was not made available to the laity. Priestly words of consecration ("This is my body") caused the bread and the wine to be changed into the very body and blood of Christ (a process known as *transubstantiation*). Many clergy intensified lay resentment by charging for confessions, burials, and masses for the dead.

In addition, there were many more priests than were needed. In Cologne, for example, there were six thousand priests out of forty thousand inhabitants. Desiderius Erasmus, the great Christian humanist, complained that the "huge herd of clergy" served "the cause of their stomach rather than the cause of the Gospel." Furthermore, clergy were resented because of the special privileges they enjoyed. They were immune from the criminal justice system and taxation, yet they carried on commercial or farming enterprises that competed with those of merchants and farmers who had to pay taxes. Finally, the sexual mores of clergy, especially their holding of concubines, left them open to charges of hypocrisy since they were seen as scarcely practicing what they preached.

Religious Devotion

Late medieval piety was shaped by a preoccupation with the specter of death occasioned by famine, war, and most especially the plague (called the Black Death), which wiped out one-third of the population of Europe in the mid-fourteenth century (and continued to break out sporadically all over Europe into the seventeenth century). The Dance of Death was frequently depicted in late medieval art: Death as a skeleton danced among its victims —the gay courtier, the wealthy merchant, the fat monk or priest, as well as the lowly peasant. None escaped Death's all-pervasive presence. Books on the *ars moriendi* (the art of dying), such as the fifteenth-century English translation *The Book of the Craft of Dying*, were common (see vol. 2:37–49).

Intimately connected with anxiety about death was great concern about divine judgment. In late medieval piety, Christ was perceived as a righteous judge condemning miserable sinners. One artistic representation of Christ as judge shows him sitting on a rainbow with a lily in one ear and a sword in the other—the lily symbolized his mercy, the sword was a sign of his wrath. All the more fearsome were pictures of Christ sitting on a rainbow with swords in both ears—signifying pure judgment.

If Christ was divine judge, it is no wonder that worship of Mary, the one who intercedes with her son to bestow mercy on sinners, was extremely important in the late middle ages. Devotion to Mary found expression in abundant representations of Mary in late medieval art, in sermons and liturgies dedicated to Mary, and in frequent pilgrimages to the sacred shrines of the virgin.

Overwhelmed by death and impending doom, Christians intensified their religious devotion. All of Europe was saturated with popular piety on the eve of the Reformation. Marian devotion and the veneration of saints and their relics increased. Christians made pilgrimages to shrines dedicated to the virgin, to Our Lady of Walsingham in England, and to other saints, such as St. James at Compostela in Spain or St. Thomas à Becket at Canterbury in England. Devotees wanted to see and touch the relics of saints. Frederick the Wise, the elector of Saxony and a supporter of Luther, maintained a huge collection of relics.

Another aspect of piety that needed reform was the selling of indulgences. In church practice, an indulgence is the partial or complete removal of temporal punishment for sin, granted by the church to those whose guilt has already been forgiven. Indulgences are closely related to the sacrament of penance, which has three parts: (1) contrition, or remorse for sin; (2) private confession to a priest and divine absolution through the priest; and (3) works of satisfaction done by the forgiven sinner. The first two parts of penance remove the guilt and the threat of eternal punishment. The third part occurs when the forgiven sinner does works of satisfaction or penance to compensate for offenses committed against God, the church, or a neighbor. Traditionally, works of satisfaction were prayers, fasting, and almsgiving. They reduced the temporal punishment each sinner had to endure in purgatory, a place of cleansing from light sins where everyone went before being admitted to heaven.

Indulgences became a form of satisfaction in the third part of penance. One could obtain an indulgence by some pious work, such as going on a pilgrimage or, increasingly in the late Middle Ages, making a gift to the church. With an indulgence, it was possible to reduce the works of satisfaction needed to compensate for offenses committed against God, the church, or a neighbor. Indulgences, however, had nothing to do with one's ultimate status before God. They did not bring forgiveness of sin. They did not change the human need for forgiveness.

Unfortunately, it was easy for the popular mind to become confused about indulgences. Some church leaders solicited gifts with promises that guilt and punishment were forgiven. This selling of indulgences was grounded in the theological concept of a "treasury house of merit" set forth by Clement VI in a bull, *Unigenitus* (*Only Begotten*), in 1342. It stated that because of the "superfluity" of merits accumulated by Christ, Mary, and the saints, there is an abundance of grace that the church is able to dispense to the faithful to partially or completely remove temporal punishment for sins. In 1476 Pope Sixtus IV extended the application of indulgences to purgatory. A diligent Christian could obtain indulgences for dead relatives or friends to lessen their time in purgatory.

Officially, the church insisted that the purchase of indulgences did not *ensure* that a loved one would be released from purgatory, but rather that indulgences were a kind of prayer of intercession. Unfortunately, it was easy for traffickers in indulgences to confuse the faithful by promising—as did Johann Tetzel (or Tezel), a popular indulgence preacher known by Martin Luther in Saxony—that "as soon as the penny in the box rings, the soul out of purgatory springs." The practice of and teachings about indulgences led Luther to speak out in protest in his famous Ninety-Five Theses.

Critics question the overly externalized, ceremonial religious observances that were so popular with laity in the late Middle Ages. It is clear, however, that these religious practices were genuine expressions of lay piety. In the end, this deep hunger for the divine on the part of the masses was not adequately satisfied by the ministries and theology of the late medieval church.

The thirst for a deeper, more spiritual piety was also nourished by important mystical movements on the edge of the institutional church in the thirteenth and fourteenth centuries. Many pious Christians followed the lead of a highly speculative Dominican, Meister Eckhart (also spelled Eckhardt or Eckart or Eckehart), and his follower (see vol. 1:442–451). Others looked to Johannes Tauler, Heinrich Suso, and the Friends of God. According to Eckhart and his followers, the mystical quest begins with the recognition that a divine spark is embedded in the core of the soul, which makes union with God possible. Before that union is actualized, however, a long process of spiritual discipline is required. Rapturous union with the divine comes only after the purgation of fleshly desires and through concentrated contemplation.

The sacraments are not rejected by the mystics, but their practice pales alongside experiences of divine immediacy. The Friends of God produced an important devotional classic that was later published by Martin Luther in 1516 as the *Theologia Germanica* (*German Theology*; see vol. 1:474–77).

The Brothers of the Common Life in fifteenth-century Netherlands were not mystics, but they successfully promoted a simple, inward piety that sought to conform to the life and teachings of Jesus in the Gospels. Members lived together in study, labor, and prayer without permanent vows. Eventually the Brothers reshaped the monastic system, leading to reform in the Netherlands and northern Germany. The most well-known product of this Modern Devotion movement (*Devotio Moderna*) is the classic devotional booklet by Thomas à Kempis, *The Imitation of Christ* (see vol. 2:51–68).

Theology

Theology in the middle ages is often called *scholastic*. This refers to the teaching that took place in the schools—at first the cathedral and monastic schools, and then the universities. More particularly, *scholasticism* refers to the method of teaching in theology and philosophy that uses a dialectical method of question and answer. The motto of the scholastics was set forth by Anselm of Canterbury (see vol. 1:376–79): *fides quaerens intellectum* (faith seeking understanding). The scholastics sought through the exercise of reason to reach a better comprehension of the articles of faith.

Late medieval scholasticism was divided into three chief schools: Thomism, after the great thirteenth-century Dominican scholastic St. Thomas Aquinas (1224 or 1225–74; see vol. 1:380–409); Scotism, after the Franciscan John Duns Scotus (c. 1266–1308); and Occamism, after the Franciscan William of Occam (c. 1285–c. 1349). On the eve of the Reformation, the most important exponent of Occamism was Gabriel Biel (c. 1420–95). The Thomists and the Scotists were said to belong to the *via antiqua* (the old way), whereas the Occamists belonged to the *via moderna* (the new, or modern, way).

Scholastics of the *via antiqua* were *realists*; that is, they thought that universals are truly real. From their point of view, for example, there exists a universal reality such as humankind, exemplified in individual human beings. On the other hand, the adherents of the *via moderna* were *nominalists*. They did not believe that universals exist in reality. Universals are concepts of the mind or terms or names (*nomina*) used in propositions by humans to describe similarities between things. What is real is not a generic humanity, but only individual human beings. Occamism favored the radical singularity and particularity of reality. It is important to realize that Occamism was the dominant theological school on the eve of the sixteenth-century Reformation.

Although all Occamists were nominalists, not all nominalists were Occamistic in their theology, or at least in their doctrines of salvation. The Occamists were relatively optimistic about the role of human beings in the process of salvation. They thought that human beings could make a small contribution toward their own redemption. If human beings tried their very best on the basis of the gifts provided by God at creation, they could produce a kind of half merit known as a *merit of fitness*, which God would reward, not because of the works themselves, but because of the covenant established by God with human beings. God has promised to reward human beings who make the first step in the direction of their own salvation. God provides justifying grace in response, and that enables humans to reach full merit and become truly worthy of eternal life (a *merit of worthiness*). This doctrine appeared to some of its opponents as Pelagian (that early-church heresy arguing that human beings could earn their salvation by their own efforts; see vol. 1:213–25).

Gregory of Rimini (d. 1358) opposed the Occamist position on humanity and salvation. He was a nominalist, but he was more Augustinian in his theory of salvation than was Occam. He and other scholastics, who belonged to an Augustinian renaissance in the late Middle Ages, stressed (more than did the Occamists) the sinfulness of humankind and the utter dependence of human beings on the free, sovereign grace of God. At the very moment of the Reformation, Luther's predecessor in the chair of theology at Wittenberg and his superior in the Augustinian monastery, John (or Johann or Johannes) von Staupitz, very much adhered to Augustinian understandings of humanity's sin, God's prevenient grace, and the utter dependence of humans on God's predestination (see vol. 2:69–85).

The scholastics did not dispute about speculative matters as much as about matters concerning the ultimate destiny of human beings—issues of justification and predestination and the role of God and humanity in both.

Luther's struggle for faith was concerned with these issues. Luther reported that he once belonged to the school of Occam, but that under the influence of Gregory of Rimini and his own mentor, Staupitz, as well as through his own reading of Augustine, he came to embrace an Augustinian position. Like his contemporary, Ulrich (or Huldrych or Huldreich) Zwingli, Luther also recovered St. Paul's teachings on sin, law, and grace in Romans and Galatians. In so doing, Luther, along with Zwingli, participated in an Augustinian and Pauline renaissance in the late Middle Ages. Although later the mature Luther and Zwingli came to differ from Augustine in certain ways, the influence of medieval theology on Reformation thinking is extremely important (see vol. 1:184–225).

Late Medieval Reform Movements

Prior to the sixteenth century, there had been several significant movements of protest and reform, some of which continued right up to the eve of the Protestant Reformation. First, there was *conciliarism*, which sought to bring about the calling of a church council to resolve the crisis of the Great Schism (a period from 1378 to 1417 when there were two rival popes, one at Rome and the other at Avignon in southern France). The papacy had moved from Rome to Avignon in 1309 and remained there until 1377. It returned to Rome, but with the election of the next pope in 1378, the French cardinals withdrew their allegiance to the Roman pope and elected a rival at Avignon. Eventually there were three contenders for the papal office.

Conciliarist theologians Pierre d'Ailly and John (or Jean) Gerson (see vol. 1:478–87) called for the restoration of unity and the renewal of the church in head and members. Their program to restore unity was finally achieved at the Council of Constance (1414–18; see vol. 1:510–21) when, after the deposition or resignation of the Avignon and Roman popes as well as a third pope elected at the Council of Pisa in 1409, a new pope, Martin V, was elected. At Constance, the conciliarists passed a decree (*Sacrosancta*) claiming that the church acting through councils had its authority directly from Christ and that popes were subject to the actions of councils.

As dramatic as these events appear, conciliarists were not radical reformers. They promoted the joint rule of the church by pope and council. They justified action against the authority of the pope only when the pope acted for the destruction rather than the edification of the church. Their call for the reformation of the church in head and members did not in the end succeed. In fact, conciliarism damaged its own cause when, at the Council of Basel (1431–49), the council deposed a clearly legitimate pope, Eugene (or Eugenius) IV, and elected Duke Amadeus VIII of Savoy. Not surprisingly, in 1460 Pope Pius II declared, in an encyclical entitled *Execrabilis*, that appeals over the head of a pope to a council were heretical.

Conciliarism continued to make its case, however, as evidenced by the calling of the Council of Pisa (1511–12) by Italian cardinals opposing Pope Julius II. The pope responded by calling his own council, the Fifth Lateran Council. Although conciliarism continued to be promoted by some concerned church leaders as a possible response to the Protestant Reformation of the sixteenth century, it was no longer the potent force it had been in the early fifteenth century.

Conciliarism, while detested by the papacy, was not deemed heretical. Other pre-sixteenth-century reform movements, however, were condemned as heretical, and their leaders and participants were severely persecuted. For example, the leader of the Hussite movement in Bohemia, John Huss (or Jan Hus), was burned at the stake by the Council of Constance in 1415 (see vol. 1:500–21). Inspired by the writings of John Wycliffe (also spelled Wyclif, Wickliffe or Wiclif), an English theologian at Oxford who died in 1384, Huss opposed the right of sinful clergy to retain the priestly office with its economic privileges. His railings against indulgences and the corruption of prelates caused him to be summoned to the Council of Constance for a hearing and trial. Supposedly, Huss had been granted a safe conduct by the emperor, but in the end he was condemned and killed by the very council that was trying to reform the church. His execution led to a popular rebellion in Bohemia that produced a fourfold program of reform (outlined in the *Four Articles of Prague*, 1420) calling for free preaching, an end to the practice of withholding the communion cup from the laity, limitations on the clergy's ability to own worldly possessions, and the punishment of priests who committed public sins.

The Hussite movement further split into two groups, the radical Taborites and the more moderate Utraquists, who advocated that the laity receive both kinds (i.e., bread and wine) in the Eucharist. The Utraquists, joined by Catholic forces, conquered in battle the radical Taborites in 1434 and entered into an agreement with the Council of Basel that recognized a weakened version of the Prague Articles. On the eve of the sixteenth century, the Utraquists had official status in Bohemia as a church alongside the Catholics.

Another Hussite splinter group, known as the Unity of the Brethren, originated in 1457–58. This reforming community never had legal status in fifteenth-century Bohemia, but three centuries later, it was granted land in eastern Germany (Herrnhut) by Nikolaus Ludwig Graf von Zinzendorf and became known as the Moravian Brethren, with Zinzendorf as its bishop.

The Lollards were an English heretical movement of the late fourteenth century, similar to the Hussites. They followed the reforming thought of John Wycliffe, who late in his career as an academic at Oxford adopted increasingly radical ideas, such as the primacy of Scripture; the denial of the authority of the pope (he even called the pope the antichrist); the concept of the true church as the invisible society of the elect headed by Christ, rather than a visible institution headed by the pope; and the rejection of the dogma of transubstantiation (see vol. 1:488–95). Like Huss, Wycliffe was critical of corrupt clergy and argued that clergy who were bad stewards of their offices should forfeit them. In spite of his radical ideas, Wycliffe, unlike John Huss, lived out his days in England and died a peaceful death.

Wycliffe's followers, known as Lollards as early as 1387, kept his teachings alive through preaching and written sermons passed from one to another. They produced the first English translation of the Bible. As a popular underground movement among townspeople, artisans, merchants, and gentry (especially in East Anglia, but also in the Midlands and London), they cultivated the ground on which later Reformation thinking would grow.

Another medieval heretical reform movement that set the stage for the sixteenth-century Protestant Reformation was the Waldenses. The Waldenses were followers of Peter Waldo (or Valdes), a merchant of Lyons in the late twelfth century who adopted apostolic poverty and who ran afoul of the ecclesiastical authorities because of his unauthorized preaching. He and his followers continued to preach, and the movement spread rapidly all over Europe. The Waldenses emphasized the Bible and led a simple life of poverty in imitation of the apostles. They rejected some of the sacraments and the doctrine of purgatory, and they were strongly critical of the moral and spiritual abuses of the church. After centuries of persecution, by the end of the fifteenth century they survived in isolated Alpine valleys connecting France and Italy. Through contacts with the French/Swiss reformers Guillaume (or William) Farel and John Calvin in sixteenth-century Geneva, the Waldenses embraced Swiss Protestant (Genevan) patterns of liturgy and ecclesiastical organization.

A final force for reform that shaped the sixteenth-century church was Renaissance humanism. This movement began in Italy in the early fourteenth century and spread to northern Europe. *Humanism* then did not mean a focus on human values to the exclusion of the divine, in spite of the fact that humanists stressed the freedom and dignity of humans. Renaissance humanism, especially in northern Europe, was very religious. The appellation referred to the study of the humanities—grammar, rhetoric, literature, history, and moral philosophy as studied in ancient Greece and Rome by Plato, Aristotle, Cicero, Quintilian, Ovid, Plutarch, and others. The humanists thought of themselves as bringing about a rebirth (renaissance) of those studies they thought would lead to a more cultivated, a more complete and moral humanity. They criticized the scholastic learning for its barbarous Latin as well as for its concern for logic and metaphysics, which they did not consider pertinent to human living.

Christian humanists in the sixteenth century, such as the well-known scholar Desiderius Erasmus, were students of Christian literature (the Bible and the writings of the early church). They saw this literature as the basis for all reform in church and society. Their motto was "back to the sources." Out of their intense philological study of Scripture and early Christian writings, they published new editions of those writings, taking advantage of the recently invented printing press. The most important result of their work for the Protestant Reformation was a more accurate edition of the New Testament, prepared by Erasmus and printed in 1516. His criticism of the Latin Vulgate on the basis of the Greek text seemed to many to threaten the authority of the medieval church.

For example, the traditional Latin Vulgate translation of Matthew 3:2 ("Repent for the kingdom of heaven is at hand") was "Do penance" (*Agite poenitentiam*), seemingly endorsing the medieval sacrament of penance. Erasmus, however, in his annotation on the passage, pointed out that the original Greek word *metanoiete* means "come to your senses" or "repent." One year later, in 1517, Martin Luther probably made use of Erasmus's annotation when he wrote in his Ninety-Five Theses that "the word penance cannot be properly understood as referring to the sacrament of penance, i.e., confession and satisfaction, as administered by the clergy." In 1522, when Luther translated the New Testament into German, he made extensive use of Erasmus's 1519 edition of the New Testament.

Erasmus offered a critique through humor as well as through careful textual scholarship. In his famous *Praise of Folly* and his *Colloquies*, he used stinging satire to belittle ignorant and degenerate monks and priests, thereby fanning the flames of anticlericalism. He also criticized superstitious laypersons who thought they could gain salvation by kissing relics or buying indulgences. His *Paraclesis*, or *Exhortation* (to the study of Christian philosophy), was an introduction to his New Testament edition, setting forth the essence of his intellectual, moral, and spiritual reform program (see vol. 2:86–97).

The reform proposals by Erasmus and other Christian humanists, however, had limited appeal since they were directed primarily to the intellectual elite. Erasmus called for the translation of Christian Scripture into all languages, but he never produced anything but Latin editions nor wrote anything in the language of the people. Pre-sixteenth-century reform movements—the conciliarists, Hussites, Lollards, Waldenses, mystics, Brothers of the Common Life, and Christian humanists—were irritants but posed no real threat to the medieval church. They focused on particular points in need of reform, but they failed to provide a comprehensive program for change. Each (except for Wycliffe and Huss) had a limited appeal that did not center on doctrinal reform, which was the principal thrust of the Protestant Reformation.

Reformation in Germany and Switzerland: Lutheran and Reformed Roots of the United Church of Christ

Martin Luther and the German Reformation

On October 31, 1517, Martin Luther nailed his Ninety-Five Theses, protesting the sale of indulgences, on the door of the Wittenberg castle church. With this act, the public phase of the Protestant Reformation began, although it did not become a mass movement until the early 1520s. Before the Reformation was a public event, however, it was a private struggle in the heart and mind of an Augustinian monk trying to work out his salvation with fear and trembling.

Born on November 10, 1483, Martin Luther (son of a prosperous miner, Hans, and his wife, Margarethe) attained a fine education at a series of grammar schools and was sent off to the University of Erfurt to prepare for a career in law. He earned his B.A. and M.A. there in 1502 and 1505, but shortly after entering law school he made an abrupt change; he entered the monastery of the Eremites of St. Augustine and began an intensive quest for a gracious God.

Driven by an acute sense of his own sin, Luther's conscience refused to be assuaged by any of the medieval paths to salvation. He tried the path of self-denying works such as prayer, fasting, and self-beatings, but he could never be sure whether he had done enough works or the right works. He found that the sacraments of the church did not help, for when he made confession to the priest or took communion, he could never be sure that his sin had been truly cleansed. He failed to find the mystical hope for union with God fulfilling, for he, unlike the mystics, did not perceive within his soul a divine ground or spark that could serve as a starting point that might lead to such a union.

Occamism, the scholastic school of theology in which he was trained, held out a promise: Do the best that you can, and God will not deny grace. Occamism optimistically taught that a person, using his or her own pure natural powers, could love God above all things and produce a kind of half merit that would dispose the person to receive justifying grace that, in turn, would make it possible to act so as fully to merit eternal life. Luther tried, but he found that he could not on his own love God with his whole heart and mind and strength. In fact, he found that he hated the God who demanded such love but failed to provide him the ability to meet the demand.

Eventually, Luther, helped by his Augustinian mentor, John von Staupitz, turned away from his scholastic teachers toward the theology of Augustine and the Bible, especially the letters of Paul. Augustine and Paul acknowledged the pervasive power of human sin but emphasized the freedom and sovereignty of divine grace. The solution to his spiritual crises, as he reported it toward the end of his life, was the message of grace found in Rom. 1:17: "For in it the righteousness of God is revealed through faith for faith; as it is written, 'The one who is righteous will live by faith.'"

Luther explained that he "beat importunately upon Paul at that place" by "meditating day and night" on the words until he broke through to a new insight. Whereas he had previously thought of *righteousness* as God's active righteousness by which God punishes sinners, Luther came to an understanding, after his long struggle with the text, that "the righteousness of God" is God's passive righteousness (identified elsewhere as Christ's righteousness) that God bestows on sinners through faith. Through this justification by faith, Luther felt that he "was altogether born again and had entered paradise itself through open gates." This insight not only resolved his own faith crisis, but it became the rule by which he judged most of the current church doctrine and practice as wrong because they were characterized by works righteousness.

Luther's private reformation became public when he composed the Ninety-Five Theses, which called into question the extravagant claims about indulgences being made by roving preachers, especially Johann Tetzel, in the neighborhood of Wittenberg. Luther objected to their promises of what a later Lutheran, Dietrich Bonhoeffer, called "cheap grace." In Thesis Ninety-Five, Luther wrote, "Let them thus be more confident of entering heaven through many tribulations rather than through a false assurance of peace."

Luther's theses were also a gentle criticism of the power of the papacy. After the theses were published and widely circulated (a development not intended by Luther), he gained considerable notoriety and support because of his supposed critique of the papacy and the ecclesiastical hierarchy, despite the fact that such criticism had not been Luther's original intent.

By the summer of 1519, when Luther debated with papal representative John Eck (Johann Eck) at Leipzig, the issue had expanded to embrace the authority of the church, specifically the authority of the pope. Luther argued that not only can papal decrees err, but so also can church councils. He insisted that Scripture was the one safe ground of authority. Luther's widely publicized and bold words at Leipzig further stirred up support and admiration, including that of Ulrich Zwingli, who had already been making his own way toward reform in Zurich, Switzerland. At several points before the famous confrontation with Emperor Charles V in April 1521 at the Diet of Worms, Luther declared his primary allegiance to the teaching of Scripture as over against human wisdom. Luther's cause became an ever more popular one, in spite of (or even because of) the fact that he was declared a heretic by a papal bull in 1520 and an enemy of the empire after the Diet of Worms.

Luther's own writings expanded the grievances against Rome and increased the demand for reform. Between 1517 and 1520, Luther produced thirty tracts and treatises. Over three hundred thousand copies of his writings, printed on the newly available printing presses, were everywhere in northern Europe. In 1520, Luther's *The Freedom of a Christian* spelled out the implications for the Christian life of his newly discovered doctrine of justification by faith alone (see vol. 2:98–120). Some persons interpreted his words about Christian freedom as having to do with social and political liberty. Leaders of the grassroots Peasants' War in 1525 expected Luther to support their demands for a more just society. Luther was clear, however, in his *Admonition to Peace*, a response to the peasants' Twelve Articles, that the gospel of Christian freedom was not to be confused with any political or social program.

Luther's cause was propagated not merely by his own works but also by the writings of many other clerics, such as Carlstadt, Osiander, Bugenhagen, Flacius, Brenz, and Eberlin von Gunzburg. The writings of the laity were less influential, but they show how ordinary people appropriated and propagated the Reformation message. Hans Sachs, the famous Meistersinger of Nuremberg, and Argula von Grumbach, a poor noblewoman of Bavaria, show strong partisanship for the evangelical cause. Von Grumbach entered the fray in 1523 by publishing a letter to the University of Ingolstadt defending Arsacius Seehofer, a student with sympathies for Luther's teaching, who had been accused of doctrinal errors (see vol. 2:574–84). Like other lay pamphleteers, von Grumbach and Seehofer were reluctant to be dubbed *Lutherans*. Hans Sachs delivered a sharp critique of the abuses of the Catholic Church even as he shared his concern about the abuse of the principle of Christian freedom among the followers of Luther (see vol. 2:585–602).

Katherine (Katharina) Schütz Zell, the wife of Matthew Zell, pastor at Strasbourg, strongly defended clerical marriage and otherwise promoted evangelical ideas in the 1520s. In the mid-1530s she edited and published a new version of a hymnbook of the Bohemian Brethren with a spirited preface, which shows her interest in fostering popular piety by the singing of lively, biblically sound hymns (see vol. 2:603–8).

The Reformation message was popularized through literary and artistic pamphlets, sermons, ballads, cartoons, and caricatures, including verses with accompanying illustrations for those who could not read. Hans Sachs wrote several verses attached to woodcuts published as broadsides, such as one depicting the papacy as the seven-headed beast of the Book of Revelation.

Throughout the first half of the sixteenth century, Reformation ideas spread rapidly. Many towns and cities in northern, central, and southern Germany embraced the Reformation cause as a mass movement. In other places, whole territories were brought to the Reformation when their princes converted to the Lutheran faith (beginning with East Prussia in 1525 and concluding with the Electoral Palatinate in 1546).

As Reformation ideas spread and took hold, there were increasing needs for new forms to express Protestant faith and practice: services of worship, catechisms, church orders, and confessions of faith. A large number of such ecclesiastical forms and ordinances were created. Luther wrote a new formula of Mass and Communion in 1523 (see vol. 2:121–36) and his Small Catechism in 1529 (see vol. 2:140–59). The Augsburg Confession (1530) was composed principally by Philip Melanchthon, Luther's younger colleague (see vol. 2:160–95). Luther wrote many hymns in German, drawing on familiar folk tunes and composing some himself. His "Out of the Depths I Cry to Thee" (see vol. 2:137–39) is revered not only within the Lutheran tradition but also in the United Church of Christ.

Zwingli and the Swiss Reformation

The Reformation in Switzerland ran a parallel course with that in Germany. Ulrich Zwingli, born just seven weeks after Luther on January 1, 1484, was the principal originator of Reformed, as distinguished from Lutheran, Protestantism. Beginning in Zurich, Reformed Protestantism spread throughout Switzerland, southern Germany, France, Holland, England, and Scotland. Through English Puritanism and Scottish Presbyterianism, it influenced Congregationalists and Presbyterians in colonial America. In America's middle and southern colonies, it continued in the life of Dutch and German Reformed settlers.

Zwingli was the founder of the Swiss Reformed tradition, but his role in shaping Reformed Protestantism was eventually eclipsed, after his untimely death, by his successor, Henry (or Heinrich) Bullinger (1504–75), and later by a reformer named John Calvin in the city of Geneva. Born in humble circumstances as one of eleven children at Wildhaus in eastern Switzerland, Zwingli was blessed by the support of a rich uncle who enabled him to study humanism and scholasticism at the universities of Basel and Vienna.

Zwingli was greatly influenced by the writings of Desiderius Erasmus. He made for himself a pocketbook edition of Erasmus's Greek New Testament and virtually memorized it. In the course of his ministry, however—first as the pastor in Glarus, then in Einseideln, and finally in Zurich—he became more and more persuaded by Augustine and Paul and their understandings of human depravity and God's grace. Although his personal struggle was not as intense as Luther's, Zwingli arrived at the same convictions about the sovereignty of God's grace, justification by faith, and Scripture as the sole authority for faith and practice.

Zwingli applied scriptural principles in a more thorough manner than Luther, and from the very beginning Zwingli's theology had more of a social and political dimension. As a pastor and a Swiss patriot, he was disturbed by the involvement of poor Swiss soldiers in mercenary service, which led not only to the loss of lives but also contributed to the corruption of their souls. He preached on matters of faith and personal sins but also on the ills of society. Zwingli's Sixty-Seven Articles highlight his deep concern for social justice, an important dimension of Reformed Protestantism from the sixteenth century to the present (see vol. 2:196–204).

When on January 1, 1519, Zwingli became the people's priest at the Great Minster Cathedral in Zurich, he gained an important platform for his evangelical ideas. Under his preaching and that of his colleagues, his new ideas inspired many members of the community to agitate for reform. They decided to do away with all ecclesiastical regulations that they considered *Menschensatzungen*, human laws or teachings without scriptural warrant. For example, the requirement to fast during Lent was broken in 1522 when several persons ate sausages in the home of the local printer, Froschauer. Present on this occasion, Zwingli defended those who broke the law but did not himself take part. Clerical celibacy also came under attack. Zwingli joined ten other clergy who petitioned the bishop "to allow priests to marry or at least wink at their marriage." Although they did not receive permission, many of the priests married anyway, including Zwingli, who married a widow of nine years, Anna Reinhart.

Things moved along fairly swiftly in Zurich despite the fact that Zwingli did not favor immediate revolution. He was wary of turmoil, stressing that consideration should be shown to the weak. In this respect, he was very similar to Luther, who had argued for moderation in 1522 and put a halt to the iconoclastic disturbances taking place in Wittenberg under the leadership of Andrew Carlstadt (Andreas Karlstadt or Karolostadt).

In Zurich on January 29, 1523, a public forum concerning religious innovations (usually called the First Disputation) took place before the town council and about six hundred citizens. At the invitation of the council, the bishop of Constance, who had responsibility for Zurich, sent a delegation. Zwingli prepared a document known as the Sixty-Seven Articles.

Whether the articles were considered as theses for debate or merely as summary statements of Zwingli's faith is not clear. In any case, no debate concerning these articles took place. The disputation belabored the question of tradition versus Scripture, old customs versus innovations, and the right of the council of Zurich to take things into its own hands and make changes in church matters. (Town councils in Switzerland and southern Germany had for some time exercised a considerable amount of control over the religious life of their communities.)

A second disputation in October 1523 concerned images (i.e., pictures, statues, and stained glass windows) and the Mass, but the council refused to make a final decision concerning their status. Some of Zwingli's followers became very disturbed by the delay and by Zwingli's acquiescence in it. They wanted immediate reformation. These radicals, later known as Anabaptists, eventually split with Zwingli. They rejected his position on the role of the council in bringing about reform and insisted that the church should consist of only truly faithful and holy believers—not all members of the community. They also insisted on the baptism of believers, instead of the baptism of infants, as the true sign of initiation into the church. Recent scholarship has shown, however, that not all Anabaptists favored the separation of church and state. Some hoped to win whole villages and territories to their point of view. The mature position of these Swiss Brethren is summarized in the 1527 Schleitheim Confession (see vol. 2:214–23).

The final act of the Zurich Reformation was the abolition of the Mass and its replacement with a simple Zwinglian liturgy on Maundy Thursday 1525 (see vol. 2:205–13). By this time, Zwingli had rejected the doctrine of transubstantiation, which holds that the bread and wine are literally transformed into the body and blood of Christ during the Mass. He had also come to oppose Luther's view that the body and blood are present in, with, and under the bread and the wine (later called the doctrine of consubstantiation).

As early as 1524, Zwingli adopted a symbolic, spiritual understanding of Christ's presence in the Eucharist. Although Zwingli and Luther carried on a vigorous debate, there was no meeting of the minds on the subject, not even at the famous Marburg Colloquy of 1529, called by Prince Philip of Hesse (see vol. 2:224–47). There, Luther and Zwingli affirmed fourteen common articles of belief, but they could not agree on the matter of God's presence in the Eucharist. Their disagreement led to the division of sixteenth-century Protestantism into two camps, Reformed and Lutheran. Only in very recent years have new ecumenical conversations between Reformed and Lutheran theologians produced an emerging Protestant consensus. The

United Church of Christ, with its Reformed and Lutheran roots, has played an important role in this dialogue, which is outlined in the document *A Common Calling: The Witness of Our Reformation Churches in North America Today* (1993).

Having failed to obtain an alliance with the Lutherans against the Catholics led by Charles V, Zwingli feared that Zurich was vulnerable to the Catholic Hapsburgs in the north and to the Catholic Swiss forest cantons in the south. When Zurich applied economic sanctions against the Catholic cantons, they marched against Zurich. A battle at Kappel (1531) ensued, and Zwingli, as chaplain, was killed. Henry Bullinger was chosen as Zwingli's successor.

If Zwingli was the prophet of Zurich's Reformation, Bullinger was its great organizer and theological leader. He exercised major responsibility for three important Swiss confessions: the First Helvetic Confession (1536); the Consensus of Zurich (1549), which explored the meaning of the Eucharist in collaboration with Calvin; and the Second Helvetic Confession (1566), which, apart from the Heidelberg Catechism (1563), stands as the most important Reformed confession of the sixteenth century. Both the Heidelberg Catechism and the Second Helvetic Confession became primary confessional statements within the Hungarian Reformed Church.

Bullinger was more influential than Calvin on English Protestantism under Edward VI (king from 1547–53) and for about thirty years under Elizabeth I. His *Decades*, a series of fifty doctrinal sermons, was widely circulated among English clergy. Decade One, of the Word of God, is a good example of his thinking on this fundamental theme of Reformation theology (see vol. 2:248–65).

Calvin and the Genevan Reformation

Before Zwingli's death, the Swiss Reformation, on the model of Zurich, had spread to other Swiss cities, such as Bern (1528) and Basel (1529). A reformer from Basel, John (Johannes) Oecolampadius, was another important figure in Swiss Protestantism. A gentle, learned man, he had assisted Erasmus with his New Testament edition and with new editions of early church writings. A close friend of Zwingli, he provided theological arguments from ancient Christian authors to support Zwingli's eucharistic arguments and stood by Zwingli's side at Marburg. The news of Zwingli's death was such a shock to Oecolampadius that he succumbed to an illness from which he never recovered.

Oecolampadius was the first of the Swiss reformers to propose that a pastoral discipline should be exercised by the church independent from the legal sanctions and penalties of a magistrate.

With assistance from the city of Bern, Reformation ideas soon spread to Geneva, although at that time Geneva was not a member of the Swiss confederacy. By 1532, a successful French reformer named William (or Guillaume) Farel was evangelizing in Geneva. In spite of considerable Catholic opposition, on May 21, 1536, Farel and Pierre Viret (a later reformer in the nearby city of Lausanne) succeeded in persuading the town council to adopt the Word of God as the standard for religious life in Geneva. The stage was set for the arrival of a greater French reformer, John Calvin, two months later.

John Calvin (1509–64) was a leader in the second generation of Protestant reformers. Luther and Zwingli were already twenty-five years old when Calvin was born on July 10, 1509, in Noyon, Picardy. Calvin's father, a notary for the cathedral chapter, sent his son to Paris to study for the priesthood. Once there, however, after several years of arts courses, Calvin became a budding humanist scholar. Calvin's father then directed him to study law at the University of Orleans and later at Bourges. When his father died in 1531, Calvin returned to Paris to study languages and literature, but not without completing his law degree. Like Zwingli and other reformers such as Martin Bucer and Philip Melanchthon, Calvin was imbued with Erasmian humanism. Devoted to the classics, Latin and Greek, he followed Erasmus in describing the gospel as Christian philosophy.

Calvin's conversion to the evangelical, or Protestant, faith is clouded in obscurity. Although he later stated that God "subdued my heart to docility by a sudden conversion," it is probable that his conversion was not a single event but a process, since that was the way he generally described conversion experiences.

We do know that Calvin was part of an evangelical humanist movement in Paris. On November 1, 1533, his friend Nicholas Cop, the rector of the University of Paris, delivered a controversial address blending together reform ideas from Erasmus and Luther. His sermon aroused such a tempest that Cop and Calvin fled Paris. After about a year of unsettled life in France, Calvin followed his friend to Basel, at that time a center of printing and scholarship and a hotbed of Erasmian humanism. In Basel in 1536, Calvin published the first edition of his monumental theological treatise entitled *Institutes of the Christian Religion*. Although the 1536 edition of his book was only a fraction of its final 1559 size, the work was on its way to becoming one of the most important Protestant expositions of the Christian faith ever written. The first edition of the *Institutes* shows that Calvin had become a Protestant, producing a text that Ford Lewis Battles, a translator of the text, calls "the kernel" of Calvin's Reformation faith (see vol. 2:266–71).

After a trip to Paris on family business, Calvin headed for Strasbourg. Forced to make a detour around battles between the French and imperial armies, he came by accident to Geneva. In Geneva, William Farel challenged Calvin by a fearful curse to leave the safe haven of his studies and enter the rough-and-tumble world of church reform. Struck with terror, Calvin could not resist Farel's summons.

Calvin wasted no time in presenting his reform program to the town council. He insisted on a confession of faith, the Geneva Confession (see vol. 2:272–79), a catechism, communion at least once a month, and church discipline to prepare people for communion. At the time, the town council allowed communion only once a quarter. The leadership of Geneva rejected the kind of discipline that Calvin and Farel desired, namely, the right of the city's pastors to excommunicate impenitent sinners.

It was not long before disagreements with the Geneva town council concerning the acceptance of several Bernese ceremonial customs and the council's continuing objections to proposed disciplines for the loose-living city caused the city to send Calvin and Farel into exile. Calvin returned to Basel, hoping to resume his scholarly career. His leisure, however, was soon interrupted, this time by a call from Martin Bucer, chief reformer of Strasbourg. Bucer invited Calvin to come to Strasbourg to serve as pastor to a congregation of French refugees. While there, Calvin was further influenced by the thought of Bucer.

Strasbourg, a sixteenth-century imperial free city subject directly to the emperor, was an important Reformation center in its own right. Although influences from Wittenberg and Zurich existed side by side in Strasbourg, the city charted its own course between Lutheran and Zwinglian positions. Matthew Zell, the preacher at the local cathedral, had preached reforming sermons as early as 1521. As already noted, his wife, Katherine Schütz, quickly joined the growing chorus calling for reform. Zell was followed by Wolfgang Capito, Caspar Hedio, and Martin Bucer, all of whom arrived in Strasbourg in 1523. Their evangelical preaching aroused considerable popular support, so much so that from the mid-1520s on, the city embraced many Reformation ideas and practices. One of the most important and influential developments was the Strasbourg Liturgy, generally credited to Martin Bucer.

The Strasbourg Liturgy, in its final 1539 form (see vol. 2:280–94), had considerable influence on Calvin's liturgy (see vol. 2:295–307) and on later Reformed liturgies. Calvin was impressed by the singing of the Psalms in Strasbourg and tried his hand at putting some of them into French verse himself. Later he suppressed his efforts in favor of the work of a French poet, Clément Marot. An interesting example of Calvin's versification of Psalm 46 was later translated into English by Ford Lewis Battles (see vol. 2:308–11).

Bucer also influenced Calvin in other ways, especially by persuading him to take a wife, Idelette de Bure, the widow of an Anabaptist convert. Bucer's Augustinian and Lutheran convictions about the sovereignty of God's grace and the depravity of humanity further shaped Calvin's thinking. Influenced by Bucer's careful exegesis of Scripture, Calvin published a commentary on Romans in 1540 that owed a great deal to Bucer's massive 1536 work on Romans. While at Strasbourg from 1540 to 1541, Calvin joined Bucer and Melanchthon at colloquies with Catholics at Hagenau, Worms, and Regensburg. Bucer strengthened Calvin's insistence that ecclesiastical discipline needed to be independent of the magistrate. Such reform around discipline was never accomplished by Bucer in Strasbourg, but it was achieved later by Calvin in Geneva.

Although he had been invited back by the magistrate, Calvin returned to Geneva with considerable trepidation in 1541. Immediately he moved to bring about reform, but it was not easy. The Ecclesiastical Ordinances of Geneva (see vol. 2:312–26) show how Calvin initially compromised with the council on many issues important to him—such as the frequency of communion and the right of the church consistory (pastors and elders) to exercise independent discipline. Not until 1555 did the consistory have the right to impose sanctions and excommunication independent of the magistrate.

After 1555 Calvin exercised considerable influence on the life of Geneva, yet he was never the dictator he has sometimes been depicted as being. Under his leadership Geneva became an unparalleled center for Reformed Protestantism. His reputation was most tarnished by the tragic execution of Michael Servetus, the Spanish anti-Trinitarian, who, as one scholar has put it, was drawn in 1553 to Geneva "as a moth to the flame." Condemned as a heretic, Servetus probably would have suffered the same fate anywhere else in sixteenth-century Europe. Calvin believed that Servetus was a heretic, yet he at least tried unsuccessfully to have Servetus executed by a less painful method than burning at the stake. In 1903, a group of admirers of Calvin tried to make some amends by erecting an expiatory monument on the site of Servetus's martyrdom.

The German Reformed Church and the Heidelberg Catechism

The Rhine Palatinate, of which Heidelberg was the capital, remained unaffected by the Reformation until its prince, Frederick II, introduced Lutheran reforms in 1546. However, after Emperor Charles V defeated the Protestants shortly thereafter, Frederick held back, hesitant to push for full reformation. His strong Lutheran successor, Otto Heinrich (ruled 1556–59), brought in more thorough reforms. Finally, during the rule of Frederick III, called Frederick the Pious (ruled 1559–76), the Palatinate took on its unique religious character.

Frederick III began his reign as a moderate Lutheran of the Melanchthonian type. During his rule, however, the Palatinate became more and more Reformed, or Calvinistic. Frederick III attracted a number of important Reformed theologians from all over Europe to the University of Heidelberg, making it a major Reformed theological center. Caspar Olevianus (1536–87) came from Trier, and Zacharias Ursinus (1534–83) from Silesia.

Caspar Olevianus, like Calvin, had been a student of law at Paris, Orleans, and Bourges. During his studies in France, he was greatly moved by the persecution of the Huguenots. In the late 1550s, he went to Zurich, where he met Ursinus. Although Olevianus tried to stir up reform when he returned to his hometown of Trier, he was stoutly resisted by the archbishop and forced to flee. Later he was called to Heidelberg, where he served as a professor of theology, pastor of Holy Spirit Church, and an important member of the church council. In that capacity, Olevianus exercised a strong influence on the development of Protestantism in the Palatinate.

Zacharias Ursinus was born in 1534 at Breslau. In his student years, he studied with Melanchthon at Wittenberg and followed his mentor in 1557 to Worms, where a colloquy concerning the Eucharist took place. For several years, new controversy concerning the presence of Christ in the Eucharist had divided Protestants into several parties. Reformed Protestants, led by Bullinger and Calvin, reached an accord in the Zurich Consensus of 1549. Lutherans, however, remained split between the conservatives (advocates of the view that the real body and blood of Christ were present in, with, and under the elements of bread and wine) and the Philipists (followers of Melanchthon's vaguer understanding, which refused to be very specific about the mode of the so-called real presence). At Worms, Melanchthon tried to get the various factions to agree on some general formula, but without success.

After the colloquy, Ursinus made a trip to Zurich and Geneva. At Geneva he met Calvin, who presented him with some books. After visiting Paris, he returned to Breslau, where he took up a teaching position. At Melanchthon's death in 1560, Ursinus was invited to return to Wittenberg, but he declined. Instead, he went to Zurich and studied for several months with an important Italian reformer, Peter Martyr Vermigli. While he was in Zurich, if not before, Ursinus became convinced that the Swiss Reformed understanding of the Eucharist, as spelled out in the Zurich Consensus, was very similar to Melanchthon's understanding of the real presence. As Melanchthon's loyal disciple, he eagerly tried to promote consensus and peace during the rest of his short career.

In 1561, Ursinus was called to Heidelberg to teach. It was only one year after a local debate between representatives of both the Lutheran and Reformed views on the Eucharist had finally convinced Frederick III to embrace the Reformed understanding.

Frederick III was genuinely worried about the faith of his people. Out of his concern, he invited Ursinus and several other theologians to prepare a new catechism for his realm. The result was the Heidelberg Catechism (see vol. 2:327–58). Although the exact authorship of the catechism remains unclear, it is fairly certain that, even if it was a committee product, Ursinus had the principal hand in it.

The Heidelberg Catechism was intended as a confession of faith and as a manual for instruction. It became the most important guide for German Reformed people throughout central Europe, and it went with them when they emigrated to Pennsylvania, Virginia, and North Carolina in the eighteenth century. Its impact was felt even beyond the German Reformed Church as it became a chief theological standard for worldwide Reformed Protestantism and was translated into forty languages.

In 1563, the church order that resulted in the Heidelberg Catechism also issued a reformed worship order, later known as the Palatinate Liturgy (see vol. 2:359–76). This liturgy became the primary form of worship for German Reformed people in the United States and influenced later liturgies in that tradition.

The Dutch Reformed Tradition and the Canons of Dort

Another important confession of faith that influenced Reformed Protestantism (and the traditions of the United Church of Christ) appeared in the Canons of Dort in 1619 (see vol. 2:377–96). This doctrinal statement shaped the development of Reformed theology in the Netherlands and elsewhere.

Dutch Protestants, after a long struggle with Spanish Catholics, finally broke away from Spain to form the Dutch Republic in the early seventeenth century. They continued, however, to experience internal conflict. On the one side, an Arminian party, named after Jacobus Arminius, wanted to modify the Calvinistic doctrine of predestination to include some recognition of human freedom and responsibility. On the other side, the Gomarists, named after Francis Gomar, insisted on a strict predestination theology. The issues between the two parties were not only theological but also political.

The Synod of Dort in 1618–19 stayed with strict Calvinistic doctrine. It not only summarized classic Calvinism for German and Dutch Reformed people but also made important contributions to the development of English Congregationalism. Two key Congregational leaders—Separatist John Robinson and Non-separatist William Ames—were living in exile in Holland and attended the synod. Several theologians from the German Reformed Church were also delegates. The Canons of Dort thus became an important standard of faith among Congregationalists in England and New England, and within German Reformed churches in Pennsylvania as they leaned on Dutch Reformed friends during the colonial era.

The English Reformation

While its Lutheran and Reformed roots are found in the continental European Reformation, the Congregational and the Christian portion of United Church of Christ history is deeply grounded in the English Reformation. Congregationalism is linked to the Puritan protest within the English Reformation, whereas the Christian movement emerged in early nineteenth-century America among Baptists, Presbyterians, and Methodists, who themselves are rooted in the English Reformation.

The English Reformation was both a political and a religious event. The occasion for the break of the English church with Rome was Henry VIII's divorce from Catherine of Aragon, who had produced no male heir to the throne. Henry wanted to guarantee an orderly succession. When the pope refused to annul his marriage, two English Protestant leaders, Thomas Cranmer, archbishop of Canterbury, and Thomas Cromwell, the king's chief minister, approved his divorce from Catherine and blessed his marriage to Anne Boleyn. Henry also got the English Parliament to declare that any child of Henry and Anne would be accepted as the rightful heir to the English throne.

Furthermore, in 1534, Cromwell convinced the English Parliament to pass the Act of Supremacy. This act declared that the king was "the only supreme head on earth of the Church of England called Anglicana Ecclesia." In 1533, Cromwell had prepared the way for this declaration of ecclesiastical independence by pushing through Parliament the Act in Restraint of Appeals. This act argued that there was no reason for appeals from English courts to those of a foreign power—meaning from English ecclesiastical courts to the court at Rome—since England was a self-contained, self-sufficient realm presided over by the king.

Although Henry VIII refused to bow to the power of the pope and had himself declared head of the church in England, he considered himself a good Catholic, not a Protestant. Sir Thomas More and many other devout Christians in England could not see how one could be a Catholic but not a *Roman* Catholic. More was sent to his death for insisting that he was "the king's servant, but God's first."

Cranmer and Cromwell remained cautious in espousing their Protestant views but quietly moved England toward reform. In 1536, they promoted the passage of an injunction that required every parish to have an English Bible. An official translation, known as the Great Bible and based on the translations of William Tyndale (also spelled Tindal or Tindale) and Miles Coverdale, appeared in 1539. Tyndale and Coverdale had early sympathized with Lutherans in the 1520s. During the intervening years, Protestant writings and ideas from Bullinger's Zurich and Bucer's Strasbourg became more popular in England. In fact, during Henry VIII's final years, forces for reform had spread so widely that the king and his Catholic ministers tried in vain to rein them in.

Being openly Protestant, however, remained very dangerous. Anne Askew, a member of the reformist circle surrounding Henry's last queen, Catherine Parr, was convicted and executed for violating the king's Six Articles (passed in 1539). The first of the Six Articles required belief in the dogma of transubstantiation. Anne Askew's accounts of her examinations before the authorities were published by John Bale (see vol. 2:609–18) and by John Foxe in his *Actes and Monuments of these latter and perilous dayes touching matters of the Church*. Her story became a source of inspiration to Protestant women martyrs when Protestants endured renewed persecution under the Catholic Queen Mary I (Mary Tudor), who ruled from 1553 to 1558. Foxe's *Book of Martyrs*, as it was popularly called, exercised a profound influence on the development of English Puritanism.

After Henry's death in 1547, the rule of young Edward VI provided a more hospitable environment for reform. Under the king's protector, Edward Seymour, duke of Somerset, the first Book of Common Prayer was published (1549). It was devised chiefly by Thomas Cranmer and represented a compromise between the old and the new. When Somerset was replaced by John Dudley, the earl of Warwick and later the duke of Northumberland, the pace of reform quickened. Cranmer invited several Protestant theologians from the continent to come to England and assist with reform. So it was that Peter Martyr Vermigli and Martin Bucer became Regius Professors of Divinity at Oxford and Cambridge, respectively. Bucer made important suggestions for further revisions of the Book of Common Prayer. Eventually, Cranmer incorporated his suggestions and many others into his revision of the book, published in 1552 (see vol. 2:397–418).

Edward VI, never in good health, died in 1553. For English Protestants, this was a disastrous turn of events. At his death, his half sister, Mary, the daughter of Catherine of Aragon, became the queen. As a good Catholic, Mary I tried valiantly to reverse the Protestant tide. During her reign of terror, some three hundred Protestants were burned at the stake. Another eight hundred went into exile abroad, fleeing to Zurich, Frankfurt, and Geneva. Ironically, when the so-called Marian exiles returned to England during the rule of Elizabeth I, they pressed for even more radical reforms.

Most of the victims of Mary's persecution were artisans and laborers. Under duress, many laypersons acted courageously, like John Careless, a weaver, who wrote to his wife expressing deep faith (see vol. 2:615–18). The deaths of Protestants under Mary, recorded for posterity in Foxe's *Book of Martyrs*, led English Protestants to despise Roman Catholics for centuries to come. Fortunately for Protestantism in England, Mary's reign was brief. If it had been longer, some scholars are of the opinion that she might have been more successful, for they think that Protestantism was not yet deeply embedded in the hearts and minds of the English people.

The Elizabethan Settlement and the Rise of Puritanism

Mary died November 17, 1558, and only twelve hours later Reginald Pole, the archbishop of Canterbury and papal legate, also died. Suddenly, Elizabeth, Mary's moderately Protestant half sister, was queen. By January 1559, a new Act of Supremacy was passed. Under the new law, the queen was not the "head," but rather the "governor," of the church. Soon thereafter, Parliament passed the Act of Uniformity, requiring the use of the newly revised Book of Common Prayer and imposing strict penalties for violations.

This so-called Elizabethan Settlement pleased neither those on the right (partisans of the pope) nor those on the left (radical Protestants, known as Puritans). The Puritans were increasingly unhappy with the prescriptions about ceremonies and vestments in the new prayer book, which they regarded as papist remnants. They preferred John Knox's Form of Prayers, or Geneva Service Book (completed in 1556; see vol. 2:432–44), which was based on Calvin's liturgy. In practice, however, they avoided publicly flouting the law and simply adapted the Book of Common Prayer for their own use, following their Puritan convictions.

The Marian exiles returned to England with the Geneva Bible (1560), filled with Calvinistic introductions and marginal notes (see vol. 2:419–31). As the most popular translation of the Bible among English Protestants, it eventually made a significant impact on New England Puritanism.

Puritans resisted a number of provisions in the prayer book: kneeling for communion, using a ring in marriage, making the sign of the cross in baptism, and wearing vestments (such as the surplice and cope). Archbishop Matthew Parker, on behalf of the queen, issued the Advertisements of 1566, mandating uniformity in clerical dress and ceremonies. This action had considerable success in bringing about uniformity. It also had the effect of dividing officially appointed clergy from the leadership of the Puritan movement. Clergy appointed by the bishop could be controlled more easily than unofficial preachers, chaplains, and lecturers. After 1566, many clergy complied with the rules, and those who resisted were deprived of their positions. A few Puritan clergy went underground, forming illegal conventicles.

The Rise of Presbyterianism

The next phase in the conflict between Puritans and the established church focused on ecclesiology, that is, the nature of good church government. Before pressing for radical changes, however, in 1571 moderate Puritans urged Parliament to remove the most offensive ceremonies in the Book of Common Prayer and limit the number of articles in the Thirty-Nine Articles (a confession of faith adopted in 1559) that had to be accepted. The bishops, however, refused to accept any compromise and moved to enforce subscription to all of the articles, the entire prayer book, and the wearing of the surplice.

In 1570, a leading Puritan named Thomas Cartwright delivered a series of lectures at Cambridge University on church government. Basing his lectures on the Bible, especially the Acts of the Apostles, Cartwright argued that the New Testament pattern of church government was presbyterian; that is, the early church was ruled by elders representing the people, not by bishops. Furthermore, Cartwright argued that in the Bible, local communities of faith (congregations) elected their own pastors. Cartwright concluded that the contemporary church ought to follow the pattern of the New Testament.

Cartwright's radical views on ecclesiology were opposed by John Whitgift, vice chancellor of the university and later archbishop of Canterbury. Whitgift insisted that no precise form of polity (church government) could be found in Scripture. He was confident that the church could adopt whatever form of church government seemed most expedient. It was not long before Cartwright was removed from his chair as Lady Margaret Professor of Divinity and fled to Geneva.

The failure of Puritan efforts for moderate reform provoked calls for more radical measures. In 1572, John Field and Thomas Wilcox published a tract entitled *An Admonition to Parliament*, strongly attacking church leadership. Field and Wilcox were scathing in their criticism of establishment clergy and the archbishop's and commissary's courts. According to Field and Wilcox, the clergy—in their preaching, in their administration of the sacraments, and in their dress—blindly followed the prayer book, with its ceremonies contrary to the Word of God ("they toss psalms in most places like tennis balls"). The commissary's court, they wrote, is "but a petty little stinking ditch, that floweth out of that former great puddle, robbing Christ's church of lawful pastors, of watchful Seniors and Elders and careful Deacons." With the naming of these church officers, it was clear that Field and Wilcox advocated a presbyterian model of church government and discipline. Although their manifesto went further than most Puritans would go, especially the older ones, it formed a basis for growing criticism among younger Puritan clergy against the episcopal establishment.

The Rise of Separatism

While moderate and radical Puritans like Cartwright, Field, and Wilcox leveled their criticism at the established church, most Puritans thought that biblical reform of the church in worship, government, and discipline was possible. They did not advocate any formal break with the church they sought to purify. They continued to agitate while waiting for a full reformation to take place.

A small minority of zealous Puritans, however, were not content to tarry for the magistrate. Like the Anabaptists, who criticized early Lutheran and Reformed efforts at change, they called for immediate reform. They insisted that true Christians needed to separate from a corrupt church.

Some Separatist congregations had arisen in London in response to the enforcement of the Advertisements of 1566. One under the leadership of Richard Fitz, and another that met once in Plumbers' Hall, were quickly suppressed.

The first notable argument for a Separatist form of Congregationalism was made by a radical thinker named Robert Browne. Browne had embraced a representational, or presbyterian, view of church government during his education at Cambridge under Thomas Cartwright. By 1581, however, he had given up presbyterian views to make the case for Separatist Congregationalism. With his friend Robert Harrison, he organized a Separatist congregation in Norwich.

Browne viewed the church as a covenanted community. He argued that the church is "a company or number of Christians or believers which by a willing covenant made with their God are under the government of God and Christ." With this understanding of the church, the relationship between pastors, elders, and the people must be one of mutual consent and responsibility. Furthermore, understood this way, the church is a committed community totally separate from the world.

According to Browne, those in such a committed community needed to submit to rigorous church discipline to keep the community pure. Furthermore, because the church gathered as a covenantal community under the government of God and Christ, it was not subject to the Elizabethan ecclesial establishment. In his famous *A Treatise of Reformation without Tarying for Anie* (see vol. 2:461–79), Browne affirmed the queen's rightful civil authority but denied all royal rule over the church, which is governed by Christ alone. Since the magistrate had no authority to reform the church, Browne pleaded with Puritans not to "tarry for the magistrate." Although Browne's doctrine of the church as a covenanted community anticipated New England Congregationalism, his convictions about the true church changed in later years, and he returned to the Anglican communion in 1585.

In spite of the return of Browne to the established church and the death of Harrison, the Separatist cause did not die out. As a result of renewed persecutions led by John Whitgift, now archbishop of Canterbury, a new wave of Separatism was spawned. John Greenwood, a Puritan member of the clergy who had been deprived of his position in Norfolk by the archbishop, came to London and joined a group of Separatists. In 1587, he was arrested while reading Scripture at a meeting of his congregation. When his Separatist friend Henry Barrow visited Greenwood in jail, he too was arrested.

From prison, Greenwood and Barrow wrote letters and tracts criticizing the apostasy of the English church and pleading for the renewal of "covenant" by independent congregations until the magistrate brought about reform of the public enormities of the "false church." Unlike Browne, Barrow in particular considered the magistrate the one endowed by God with the authority to set the whole church aright. Another Separatist Puritan preacher named John Penry, from Wales, joined the same London congregation and, in 1593, came to the same end as Greenwood and Barrow—imprisonment and death.

Enduring the imprisonments and executions of its leaders, this London Separatist congregation survived and acquired new leaders. Francis Johnson became its pastor in 1592, and Henry Ainsworth its teacher in 1597. Eventually, Johnson rejoined his exiled congregation in Amsterdam, but not until he had spent some time in a London prison himself. The *Confession* of the London congregation, written in 1596, was greatly admired by John Robinson, pastor of the Separatist congregation known as the *pilgrims*, who eventually settled in Plymouth, Massachusetts.

Separatist Congregationalism: John Robinson

In 1603, when James VI of Scotland also became James I of England, English Puritans had high hopes that he would support their desires for reform in the English church. Scotland had adopted Presbyterianism as a national church some time earlier. Very quickly, Puritans submitted to the king the Millenary Petition, urging him to reform the church, its worship, the quality and preaching of its ministers, and its discipline. Although the petition stopped short of calling for the removal of episcopacy and the installation of presbyterian government, James was greatly disturbed by these requests. In 1604, he called a conference at Hampton Court at which he announced that he would not support the Puritan reform proposals. He further informed the Puritans that presbyterian polity would fly in the face of monarchy, stating, "No bishop, no king." Richard Bancroft, who was installed as the new archbishop of Canterbury, enforced with vigor new constitutions and canons requiring conformity.

In the midst of this situation, a new Separatist congregation under the leadership of a ruling elder, William Brewster of Scrooby (in the lower Trent Valley), began to consider other options. The congregation had split off from another Separatist congregation led by John Smyth in neighboring Gainsborough, and, after considerable harassment, both the Gainsborough and the Scrooby congregations fled to Amsterdam in 1608. Exile did not bring peace, however, and the Scrooby group, under the leadership of John Robinson, settled in Leyden (or Leiden) to get away from the rising controversy among Smyth, Johnson, and Ainsworth.

Smyth became increasingly radical, insisting that the people, rather than the elders, should rule the church, and advocating believer's, rather than infant, baptism. Ainsworth was won over to Smyth's views on church government, and he decided to leave Johnson's church.

John Robinson, by then pastor of the congregation in Leyden, had joined Brewster's congregation in 1606 after he was suspended from his position at St. Andrew's in Norwich. He had studied at Cambridge with the eminent

Puritan divine William Perkins, whose important treatise on preaching, the *Art of Prophesying*, influenced many Puritans (see vol. 2:445–60).

In 1610, Robinson wrote another important Puritan treatise, *A Justification of Separation from the Church of England*, in which he criticized the worship, ministry, and discipline of the established church and argued that Scripture justified a Separatist congregational polity. Within a few years, however, Robinson came halfway back from his radical Separatism, eventually agreeing with the views of the so-called Non-separatist Congregationalists, Henry Jacob and William Ames.

In 1620, some members of Robinson's Leyden congregation decided that they might find even greater religious freedom by emigrating to America. To that end, a small group of pilgrims, led by William Brewster, set sail for the New World to establish Plymouth Plantation, in what is now Massachusetts. Robinson planned to join them later, but he died in 1625 before he could make the voyage. Just before his death, he summarized his Congregational ecclesiology and defended the members of his congregation against disparaging accounts of their faith and behavior in his *A Just and Necessary Apology* (see vol. 2:492–520). This tract had been originally published in Latin in 1619.

Non-Separatist Congregationalism: William Ames and Henry Jacob

Not all Congregationalists approached the problems they had with the Church of England in the same way. Non-separatist Congregationalists largely agreed with the Separatists concerning the need for a covenanted church with purified worship, proper discipline, and congregational polity. This was the biblical model, they thought. They disagreed with the Separatists, however, as to whether it was necessary to make a clean break with the established church. In spite of their criticism of the church as a whole, especially its episcopal hierarchy, they thought that within the larger church there were particular enclaves that did voluntarily assemble under an implicit covenant. They affirmed these congregations as true, visible churches, and they considered ministers that had been called and ordained by these congregations to be true ministers.

Non-separatist Congregationalists refused to split off from the Church of England, which they still considered to be their source. They worked to reform the church from within according to the Congregational ideal, hoping that eventually their understanding of the true church would be accepted by the ecclesiastical authorities. In spite of the early Separatist thinking of John Robinson, some of whose parishioners left Leyden to settle in Plymouth, Congregationalism in New England ended up predominantly Non-separatist. Robinson had been persuaded by Ames and Jacob to pull back from his Separatist views. In the end, New England Congregationalists, whether from the Plymouth Colony or the Massachusetts Bay Colony, were in fundamental agreement about the nature of the true church.

The most important English leaders of Non-separatist Congregationalism in the early 1600s were William Ames and Henry Jacob. William Ames, author of *The Marrow of Theology* (see vol. 2:521–51), was the chief theologian of the group. In this treatise, Ames set forth the fundamental Puritan doctrine of the covenant of grace.

The importance of Henry Jacob in Non-separatist Congregationalism is reflected in the fact that early seventeenth-century Non-separatist Congregationalists were known as Jacobites. Henry Jacob did spend some time in exile in Holland, but he returned to England in 1616 to found a congregation in the Southwark section of London. This was the first Non-separatist Congregational church in England, and it represents the beginning of self-conscious Congregationalism. Henry Jacob's catechism, *Principles and Foundations of Christian Religion* (see vol. 2:480–91), is considered by scholar Champlin Burrage to be "the earliest completely developed Independent, or Congregational Puritan (Non-separatist) Catechism in existence."

Although clergy leaders shaped the principal ideas of the Puritan movement, it would have died on the vine if it had not been cultivated and propagated by devout laypersons. Lady Margaret Hoby was such a Puritan. Her diary (see vol. 2:619–35), written at the end of Elizabeth's reign and during the beginning of James' rule, provides a vivid glimpse into the religious activities of a dedicated Puritan woman and her household.

Continued Repression, Civil War, and the Westminster Confession

Charles I (ruled 1625–49), like his father, James I, was a firm believer in the divine right of kings, and he strongly resisted the efforts of the Puritan-controlled Parliament to gain more rights. With the assistance of his principal ecclesiastical adviser, William Laud (named bishop of London in 1628 and archbishop of Canterbury in 1633), Charles I continued to persecute the Puritans. Laud held to Arminian theology, believing that human beings cooperate with God in the work of salvation. He also was an Anglo-Catholic, favoring the divine right of bishops and the use of the Book of

Common Prayer throughout the land. Puritans, on the other hand, were orthodox Calvinists, convinced that there was nothing sinners could do to bring about their salvation except to wait on the grace of God. They were also opposed to the efforts of Laud to jam the prayer book down their throats. William Laud's moves against the Puritans were even more an anathema to them than the repression they suffered under James I.

By 1628, therefore, increasing numbers of Non-separatist Puritans sought to escape the harassment of Charles I and Bishop Laud by emigrating to America. Unlike the Separatists, the Puritans who settled in the Massachusetts Bay Colony under the leadership of John Winthrop, the future governor of that colony, and ministers such as John Cotton, Thomas Shepard, and Thomas Hooker did not understand themselves to be forsaking their original church. As Francis Higginson, an early colonist, is reported to have said: "We do not go to New England as Separatists from the Church of England, though we cannot be separate from the corruptions in it." These non-separating Congregationalists saw themselves as building a holy commonwealth, a city set on a hill for the eyes of the world, but especially for the eyes of England. New England was viewed as a model for a properly constituted church and state. Distant from an antagonistic government, Congregationalism assumed a new shape in the free space of America.

Back in England, the government increased its efforts to impose episcopacy and to require the use of the Book of Common Prayer in Scotland as well as England. The Scottish Presbyterians rebelled, and Charles I called on Parliament in April 1640 to support a war against them. Unfortunately for the king, the Parliament was controlled by Puritans, who were already irritated with the king because of his refusal to consider their grievances, so they denied his request. Things went badly for the king's armies. After two defeats by Scottish forces and a Scottish invasion of northern England, the king tried again to get Parliament's help in September 1640, when he convened the so-called Long Parliament (1640–53). This act created a dangerous situation for the king. Once convened, the Puritans in Parliament carried out their own revolution. They placed Archbishop Laud in the Tower of London and eventually executed him. When no compromise was to be reached between the king and Parliament in 1642, civil war broke out.

As the war progressed, Parliament moved ahead with religious reform. Early in 1643, it abolished episcopacy and, in July, convened an assembly at Westminster to deal with the religious conditions of the realm. Needing help on the battlefield, Parliament turned to Scotland for assistance. Before entering the fray, however, the Scots bargained for the Solemn League and Covenant, an agreement requiring the establishment of Presbyterianism in both countries.

By that time, Parliament was dominated by Presbyterians from both Scotland and England, along with a handful of Congregationalists and Episcopalians. Without the Scottish pressure, many English Puritan ministers would have settled for a modified form of episcopal polity. As it was, five leading Congregationalists, including Thomas Goodwin and Philip Nye, presented *An Apologetical Narration*, objecting to the imposition of Presbyterianism and pleading for toleration. Theologically, Congregationalists and Presbyterians held to a common faith. When the Westminster Assembly produced its famous Westminster Confession (see vol. 2:552–73), it became the formative statement of faith for worldwide Presbyterianism and, except for its sections on church government, for New England Congregationalism.

The wishes of the five so-called Dissenting Brethren (Congregational) were unexpectedly fulfilled when Oliver Cromwell, commander of the New Model Army, assumed control of the country. Cromwell was an Independent Congregationalist, opposed to either an Episcopal or a Presbyterian establishment. Through his military exploits, he gained increasing power against the king, the Irish, and the Scots. Taking over the government, he had Charles I beheaded in January 1649. After dismissing the Long Parliament in 1653, Cromwell established himself as England's lord protector. During Oliver Cromwell's protectorate, all religious groups were tolerated except for Catholics and Unitarians.

Religious toleration and government without a king did not last. When Cromwell died in 1658, his son ruled for a time, but the deceased king's son, Charles II, reinstituted monarchy, restored episcopacy, and required religious uniformity in 1660. Finally, in 1688 William and Mary assumed the throne during the so-called Glorious Revolution, and an Act of Toleration was passed. Only after 1689 were dissenters—that is, Congregationalists, Presbyterians, and Baptists, but not Catholics or Unitarians—guaranteed a measure of religious freedom.

The living theological heritage of the United Church of Christ has been shaped by many traditions and movements within the Protestant Reformation. The documents of these traditions and movements are of varied genres: treatises, confessions, catechisms, liturgies, sermons, hymns, letters, dialogues, meditations, diaries. These documents not only inform us about the faith and practice of the Reformation era; they also inspire and instruct us in our Christian believing and living today.

Acknowledgments

I wish to express my gratitude to the following persons for their assistance in the production of this volume: Kathleen Chesnut, for the typing and editing of several of the documents; Jan McDonald, for the typing of portions of the manuscript; Donna Kaplan, for typing corrections; Elsbeth Duke, for her translation of the Hans Sachs text; Nancy Payne, for her editorial assistance; and John von Rohr, for providing me with a manuscript copy of the first chapter from his *The Shaping of American Congregationalism* before its publication by The Pilgrim Press (1993).

PART I

Late Medieval and Renaissance Piety and Theology

1. The Book of the Craft of Dying

(c. mid-15th century)

Beginning in the fifteenth century, a new genre of literature developed, one concerning the ars moriendi, *the "art of dying." Its popularity was shaped by the widespread preoccupation with death that accompanied famines and wars, but especially the plagues of the late Middle Ages. In the middle of the fourteenth century, the so-called Black Death wiped out one-third of the population of Europe. Death touched everyone directly.*

The origin of literature concerning the art of dying dates from the time of the Council of Constance (1414–18). John (or Jean) Gerson, chancellor of the University of Paris and an important conciliarist, gave the impetus to the ars moriendi *with his treatise,* De arte moriendi, *which was the third part of his* Opus Tripartitum (Three-Part Work), *written about 1408.*

As a result of the plague, there were not enough priests. To serve the needs of the people, Latin texts on the ars moriendi *were translated into the vernacular to assist those who were dying and enable them to receive instruction and consolation even without a priest. The texts were written for the dying and for lay bystanders, who were encouraged to ask certain questions and admonish and pray with someone who was dying.*

Many vernacular texts on the art of dying were produced during the latter half of the fifteenth century. Some were based on a short block-print version of the Latin text, illustrated by eleven woodcuts. The prints depicted five temptations, in the form of demons, that attack a dying human being. In the prints, the demons are conquered by angels, saints,

---

SOURCE: Frances M. M. Comper, ed., *The Book of the Craft of Dying and Other Early English Tracts Concerning Death* (London: Longmans, Green and Co., 1917; New York: Arno Press, 1977).

and the Virgin Mary, who intercedes for the dying person. Thus those who could read very little, and even the illiterate, received instruction, admonition, and solace from these tracts.

The text offered here is a translation of an earlier Latin treatise most often called Tractatus de arte Moriendi. *It was written by an unknown author, probably in the mid-fifteenth century. As is characteristic of most texts on the art of dying, it had six parts: (1) a commendation of death and of the profitability of the art of dying or the knowledge of how to die well; (2) a description of the five chief temptations that beset the dying one—unbelief (especially unbelief in the church's teaching), despair, impatience, pride, and avarice; (3) two sets of* interrogations, *or catechetical questions, one from St. Anselm and the other from John Gerson, which test the dying one's faithfulness and depth of contrition, yet end with words of consolation and a plea for trust in the redemption of Christ's passion; (4) a series of admonitions to encourage the dying one to imitate Christ's passion and death, accompanied by a series of prayers; (5) counsel to the bystanders as to how they are to minister to the dying person; and (6) prayers to be offered by bystanders when a sick person is about to die.*

In contrast to the frightening artistic depictions of the Dance of Death and the Last Judgment, the message of texts on the ars moriendi *is primarily one of comfort rather than judgment, even as an unbelieving and unrepentant sinner is issued some stern warnings.*

Texts on the ars moriendi *remained unchanged in form and content until the sixteenth century, when they underwent changes due to the impact of Renaissance humanism, Protestantism, and Counter-Reformation Catholicism. Although modified by these movements, texts on the* ars moriendi *remained vibrant well into the seventeenth century, shaping reflections on death by Protestants in England and on the continent.*[1]

Chapter I

The First Chapter Is of Commendation of Death and of Cunning to [i.e. Knowing How to] Die Well

Though bodily death be most dreadful of all fearful things, as the Philosopher [Aristotle] saith in the third book of Ethics, yet spiritual death of the soul is as much more horrible and detestable, as the soul is more worthy and precious than the body; as the prophet David saith: . . . The death of the sinful man is worst of all deaths [Ps. 34:21]. But as the same prophet saith: . . . The death of the good man is ever precious in the sight of God [Ps. 116:15], what manner of bodily death that ever they die. And thou shalt understand also that not only the death of holy martyrs is so precious, but also the death of all other rightful and good Christian men; and furthermore the death, doubtless, of all sinful men: how long, and how wicked, and how cursed they have been all their life before, unto their last end that they die in—if they die in the state of very [true] repentance and contrition, and in the very faith, and virtue, and charity of Holy Church—is acceptable and precious in the sight of God. As Saint John saith in the Apocalypse [Rev. 14:13]: . . . Blessed be all dead men that die in God.

Chapter II

The Second Chapter Is of Men's Temptations that Die

Know all men doubtless, that men that die, in their last sickness and end, have greatest and most grievous temptations, and such as they never had before in all their life. And of these temptations five be most principal.

I. The First is of the faith, forasmuch as faith is fundament of all men's soul's-heal. . . .

Therefore the devil with all his might is busy to avert fully a man from the faith in his last end; or, if he may not, that he laboureth busily to make his doubt therein, or somewhat draw him out of the way or deceive him with some manner of superstitious and false errors or heresies. But every good Christian man is bound namely habitually, though he may not actually and intellectually apprehend them, to believe, and full faith and credence give, not only to the principal articles of the faith, but also to all holy writ in all manner things; and fully to obey the statutes of the church of Rome, and stably to abide and die in them. For as soon as he beginneth to err or doubt in any of them all, as soon he goeth out of the way of life, and his soul's heal. But wit thou well without doubt, that in this temptation, and in all other that follow after, the devil may not noy thee, nor prevail against no man, in no wise, as long as he hath use of his free will, and of reason well disposed, but if he will wilfully consent unto his temptation.

And therefore no very Christian man ought (not) to dread any of his illusions, or his false threatenings, or his feigned fearings. For as Christ himself saith in the gospel: . . . The devil is a liar, and a father of all leasings [John 8:44]. But manly, therefore, and stiffly and steadfastly abide and persevere; and die in the very faith and unity and obedience of our mother Holy Church.

And it is right profitable and good, as it is used in some religious, when a man is in agony of dying, with an high voice oft times to say the Creed before him, that he that is sick may be mortified in stableness of the faith; and fiends that may not suffer to hear it may be voided and driven away from him. Also to stableness of very faith should strengthen a sick man principally the stable faith of our holy Fathers, Abraham, Isaac, and Jacob. Also the perseverant abiding faith of Job, of Raab the woman, and Achor, and such other. And also the faith of the Apostles, and other martyrs, confessors, and virgins innumerable. For by faith all they that have been of old time before us—and all they be now and shall be hereafter—they all please, and have [pleased] and shall please God by faith. For as it is aforesaid: Withouten faith it is impossible to please God. . . .

II. The Second Temptation is Desperation; the which is against [the] hope and confidence that every man should have unto God.

For when a sick man is sore tormented and vexed, with sorrow and sickness of his body, then the devil is most busy to superadd sorrow to sorrow, with all [the] ways that he may, objecting his sins against him for to induce him into despair. . . .

Also the devil bringeth again into a man's mind that is in point of death specially those sins that he hath done, and was not shriven of, to draw him thereby into despair. But therefore should no man despair in no wise. For though any one man or woman had done as many thefts, or manslaughters, or as many other sins as be drops of water in the sea, and gravel stones in the strand, though he had never done penance for them afore, nor never had been shriven of them before—neither then might have time, to be shriven of them—yet should he never despair; for in such a case very contrition of heart within, with will to be shriven if time sufficed, is sufficient and accepted by God for to save him everlastingly: as the Prophet saith in the psalm: . . . Lord God, Thou wilt never despise a contrite heart and a meek [Ps. 51:17]. . . .

Therefore against despair, for to induce him that is sick and laboureth in his dying to very trust and confidence that he should principally have to God at that time, the disposition of Christ in the cross should greatly draw him. . . .

Therefore no man should despair of forgiveness, but fully have hope and confidence in God; for the virtue of hope is greatly commendable, and of great merit before God. . . .

Furthermore, that no sinful man should in no wise despair—have he sinned never so greatly, nor never so sore, nor never so oft, nor never so long continued therein—we have open ensample in Peter that denied Christ; in Paul that pursued Holy Church; in Matthew and Zaccheus, the publicans; in Mary Maudeleyn [Magdalen], the sinful woman, [in the woman] that was taken in avoutry [adultery]; in the thief that hung on the cross beside Christ; in Mary Egyptian; and in innumerable other grievous and great sinners.

III. The Third Temptation is Impatience; the which is against charity, by the which we be bound to love God above all things.

For they that be in sickness, in their death bed suffer passingly [surpassingly] great pain and sorrow and woe; and namely they that die not by nature and course of age—that happeth right seldom, as open experience teacheth men—but die often through an accidental sickness; as a fever, a postune [tumor], and such other grievous and painful and long sickness. The which many men, and namely those that be undisposed [unprepared] to die and die against their will and lack very charity, maketh so impatient and grutching [murmuring], that other while [at times] through woe and impatience, they become wood [mad] and witless, as it hath been seen in many men. And so by that it is open and certain that they that die in that wise fail and lack very charity. . . . Therefore that man that will die well, it is needful that he grutch [complain] not in no manner of sickness that falleth to him before his death, or in his dying—be it never so painful or grievous—long time [or short time] dying. . . . There shall no man have the kingdom of heaven that grutcheth and is impatient; and there may no man grutch that hath it. But as the great Clerk Albert[2] saith, speaking of very contrition: If a very contrite man offereth himself gladly to all manner afflictions of sickness and punishing of his sins, that he may thereby satisfy God worthily for his offences, much more then every sick man should suffer patiently and gladly his own sickness alone, that is lighter without comparison than many sicknesses that other men suffer; namely that sickness before a man's death is as a purgatory to him, when it is suffered as it ought; that is to understand, if it be suffered patiently, gladly, and with a free and a kind will of heart. For the same clerk Albert saith: We have need to have a free, kind will to God, not only in such things as be to our consolation, but also in such things as be to our affliction. . . .

This temptation of impatience fighteth against charity, and without charity may no men be saved. . . .

IV. The Fourth Temptation is Complacence, or pleasance of a man that he hath in himself; that is spiritual pride, with the which the devil tempteth and beguileth most religious, and devout and perfect men.

For when the devil seeth that he may not bring a man out of faith, nor may not induce him into despair, neither to impatience, then he assaileth him by complacence of himself, putting such manner temptations in his heart: O how stable art thou in the faith! how strong in hope! how sad in patience! O how many good deeds hast thou done! and such other thoughts. . . .

And therefore he that shall die must beware when he feeleth himself tempted with pride, that then he [low and] meek himself thinking on his sins: and that he wot never whether he be worthy everlasting love or hate, that is to say, salvation or damnation. Nevertheless, lest he despair, he must lift up his heart to God by hope, thinking and revolving stably that the mercy of God is above all His works, and that God is true in all His words, and that He is truth and righteousness that never beguileth, neither is beguiled, which be-hight [vowed]. . . . Every man should follow Saint Antony[3] to whom the devil said: Antony, thou hast overcome me; for when I would have thee up by pride, thou keptest thyself a-down by meekness; and when I would draw thee down by desperation, thou keptest thyself up by hope. Thus should every man do, sick and whole, and then is the devil overcome.

V. The Fifth [Temptation] that tempteth and grieveth most carnal men and secular men, that be in overmuch occupation, and business outward about temporal things; that is their wives, their children, their carnal friends, and their worldly riches, and other things that they have loved inordinately before.

For he that will die well and surely must utterly and fully put away out of his mind all temporal and outward things, and plenerly [fully] commit himself all to God. . . .

But it is to be noted well that the devil in all these temptations abovesaid may compel no man, nor in no manner of wise prevail against him for to consent to him—as long as a man hath the use of reason with him—but if he will wilfully consent unto him; that every good Christian man, and also every sinful man—be he never so great a sinner—ought to beware of above all things. For the Apostle saith: . . . God, he saith, is true, and will not suffer you to be tempted more than ye may bear; but He will give you such support in your temptations that ye may bear them [I Cor. 10:13]. . . .Therefore (let) every man, rightful and sinful, bow himself, and submit himself fully unto the mighty hand of God; and with His help he shall surely get and have the victory in all manner of temptations, evils, and sorrows, and of death thereto.

Chapter III

The Third Chapter Containeth the Interrogations that Should Be Asked of Them that Be in Their Death Bed, while They May Speak and Understand

Now follow the interrogations of them that draw to the death, while they have reason with them and their speech. For this cause if any man is not fully disposed to die, he may the better be informed and comforted [thereto]. And as Saint Anselm[4] the bishop saith and teacheth, these interrogations should be had unto them that be in that plight.

First ask him this:

Brother, art thou glad that thou shalt die in the faith of Christ?
The sick man answereth: Yea.
Knowest thou well that thou hast not done as thou shouldst have done?
He answereth: Yea.
Repentest thee thereof?
He answereth: Yea.
Hast thou full will to amend thee, if thou mightest have full space of life?
He answereth: Yea.
Believest thou fully that Our Lord Jesu Christ, God's Son, died for thee?
He sayeth: Yea.
Thankest thou Him thereof with all thine heart?
He answereth: Yea.
Believest thou verily that thou mayest not be saved but by Christ's [death and His] passion?
He answereth: Yea.

Then thank Him thereof ever, while thy soul is in thy body, and put all thy trust in His passion and in His death only, having trust in none other thing. To this death commit thee fully. In His death wrap all thyself fully; and if it come to thy mind, or by thine enemy it be put into thy mind, that God will deem thee, say thus:

Lord, I put the death of Our Lord Jesu Christ between me and mine evil deeds, between me and the judgment; otherwise will I not strive with Thee.

If He say: Thou hast deserved damnation; say thou again: The death of our Lord Jesu Christ I put between me and mine evil merits, and the merits of His worthy passion I offer for merits I should have had, and alas I have not. Say also: Lord, put the death of my Lord Jesu Christ between me and Thy righteousness.

Then let him say this thrice. . . . Into thine hands, Lord, I commit my soul. And let the covent [convent] say the same. And if he may not speak, let the covent—or they that stand about—say thus: . . . Into Thine hands, Lord, we commend his soul. And thus he dieth surely; and he shall not die everlastingly.

But though these interrogations abovesaid be competent and sufficient to religious and devout persons, nevertheless all Christian men, both secular and religious, after the doctrines of the noble Clerk the Chancellor of Paris,[5] in their last end should be examined, enquired, and informed, more certainly and clearly, of the state and the health of their souls.

I. And First thus: Believest thou fully all the principal articles of the faith; and also all Holy Scripture in all things, after the exposition of the holy and true doctors of Holy Church; and forsakest all heresies and errors and opinions damned by the Church; and art glad also that thou shalt die in the faith of Christ, and in the unity and obedience of Holy Church?

The sick man answering: Yea.

II. The Second Interrogation shall be this: Knowledgest thou that often times, and in many manner wises, and grievously, thou hast offended thy Lord God that made thee of nought? . . .

He answereth: Yea.

III. The Third Interrogation shall be this: Art thou sorry in heart of all manner of sins that thou hast done against the high Majesty, and the Love of God, and the Goodness of God; and of all the goodness that thou hast not done, and mightest have done; and of all graces that thou hast slothed—not only for dread of death, or any other pain, but rather more for love of God and His righteousness—and for thou hast displeased His great goodness and kindness; and for the due order of charity, by the which we be bound to love God above all things; and of all these things thou askest the forgiveness of God? Desirest thou also in thine heart to have very knowing of all thine offences and forgets that thou hast done against God, and to have special repentance of them all?

He answereth: Yea.

IV. The Fourth Interrogation shall be this: Purposeth thou verily, and art in full will, to amend thee if thou mightest live longer; and never to sin more, deadly, wittingly, and with thy will: and rather than thou wouldest offend God deadly any more, to leave and lose wilfully all earthly things, were they never so lief to thee, and also the life of thy body thereto? And furthermore thou prayest God that He give thee grace to continue in this purpose?

He answereth: Yea.

V. The Fifth Interrogation shall be this: Forgivest thou fully in thine heart all manner men that ever have done thee any manner harm or grievance unto this time, either in word or in deed, for the love and worship of Our Lord Jesu Christ, of Whom thou hopest of forgiveness thyself; and askest also thyself to have forgiveness of all [them thou hast offended in any] manner wise?

He answereth: Yea.

VI. The Sixth Interrogation shall be this: Wilt thou that all manner things that thou hast in any manner wise misgotten, be fully restored again—so much as thy mayst, and art bound, after the value of thy goods; and rather leave and forsake all the goods of the world, if thou mayst not in none other wise?

He answereth: Yea.

VII. The Seventh Interrogation shall be this: Believest thou fully that Christ died for thee, and that thou mayst never be saved but by the mercy of Christ's passion; and thankest thou God thereof with all thine heart, as much as thou mayst?

He answereth: Yea.

Whoso may verily, of very good conscience and truth, withouten any feigning, answer yea to the foresaid seven interrogations, he hath an evident argument enough of health of his soul, that, and he died so, he shall be of the number of them that shall be saved.

Whosoever is not asked of another of these seven interrogations when he is in such peril of death—for there be right few that have the cunning of this craft of dying—he must remember himself in his soul, and ask himself, and subtly feel and consider, whether he be so disposed as it is above said, or no. For without that a man be disposed in such wise finally, he may not doubtless be saved everlastingly.

And what man that is disposed as is abovesaid, let him commend and commit himself, all in fear, fully to the passion of Christ; and continually—as much as he may, and as his sickness will suffer him—think on the passion of Christ; for thereby all the devil's temptations and guiles be most overcome and voided.

Chapter IV

The Fourth Chapter Containeth an Instruction: With Certain Obsecrations [Supplications] to Them that Shall Die

FURTHERMORE, forasmuch as Saint Gregory[6] saith: Every doing of Christ is our instruction and teaching; therefore such things as Christ did dying on the cross, the same should every man do at his last end, after his cunning and power. And Christ did five things on the cross. . . .

First He prayed on the cross. So a sick man, that is in point of death, he should pray; namely in his heart, if he may not with his mouth. . . .

The second was He cried. So should every man in his dying cry strongly with the heart, not with the voice. For God taketh more heed of the desire of the heart than the crying of the voice. The crying of the heart to God is nought else but the great desiring of man to have foregiveness of his sins, and to have everlasting life.

The third was He wept. With His bodily eyes and with tears of the heart, in token that so should every man in His dying weep with tears of his heart, that is to say, verily repenting of all his misdeeds.

The fourth He commendeth His soul to God. So should every man in his end, saying thus in heart and mouth, if he may, and (if not) else in heart: Lord God, into Thine hands I commend my spirit; for truly Thou boughtest me dear.

The fifth was He gave up wilfully His spirit. So should every man in his death; that is to say, he should die wilfully, conforming fully therein his own will to God's will, as he is bound.

Chapter V

The Fifth Chapter Containeth an Instruction unto Them that Shall Die

But it is greatly to be noted, and to be taken heed of, that right seldom (that) any man—yea among religious and devout men—dispose themselves to death betimes as they ought. For every man weeneth himself to live long, and troweth not that he shall die in short time; and doubtless that cometh of the devil's subtle temptation. And often times it is seen openly that many men, through such idle hope and trust, have for-slothed themselves [lost themselves through sloth], and have died intestate, or unavised, or undisposed [unprepared], suddenly. And therefore every man that hath love and dread of God, and a zeal of [the heal of] man's soul, let him busily induce and warn every of his even christians that is sick, or in any peril of body or of soul, that principally and first, over all other things, and withouten delays and long tarryings, he diligently provide and ordain for the spiritual remedy and medicine of his soul. . . .

Therefore every sick man, and every other man that is in any peril, should be diligently induced and exhorted that he maketh himself, before all other things, peace with God; receiving spiritual medicines, that is to say the sacraments of Holy Church; ordaining and making his testament; and lawfully disposing for his household, and other needs, if he hath any to dispose for. And there should not be given first to no man too much hope of bodily heal. But the contrary thereof is now often times done of many men, into great peril of souls; and namely of them that actually and openly be drawing and in point hastily to die, for none of them will hear nothing of death.

And so as the great Clerk, the Chancellor of Paris [Gerson] saith: Often times by such a [vain and a] false cheering and comforting, and feigned behoting [promising] of bodily heal, and trusting thereupon, men run and fall into certain damnation everlastingly. And therefore a sick man should be counselled and exhorted to provide and procure himself his soul's heal by very contrition and confession—and if it be expedient for him, that shall greatly avail to his bodily heal; and so he shall be most quiet and sure. . . .

Therefore to every such man that is in such case and is come to his last end, is to be counselled busily that he labour, with reason of his mind after his power, to have ordinate and very repentance; that is to mean—notwithstanding the sorrow and grievance of sickness, and dread that he hath of hasty death—that he use reason as much as he may, and enforce himself to have, wilfully, full displeasing of all sin, for the due end and perfect intent that is for God; and withstand his evil natural inclining to sin, though he might live longer, and also the delectations of his sins before; and labour as much as he may to have a very displeasure of them, though it be never so short. And lest he fall into despair tell him, and arm him with such things as be said above, in the second part, of temptation of Desperation. Exhort him also that he be strong in his soul against other temptations that be put and told, also mightily and manly withstand them all; for he may not be compelled by the devil to consent to none of them all. Let him also be charged and counselled that he die as a very true Christian man, and in full belief. . . .

And if the sick man hath lost his speech, and yet he hath full knowledge of the interrogations that be made to him, or the prayers that be rehearsed before him, then only with some outer sign, or with consent of heart, let him answer thereto. Nevertheless it is greatly to be charged and hasted [urged] that the interrogations be made to him or he lose his speech; for if his answers be not likely, and seemeth not in all sides to be sufficient to full heal and perpetual remedy of his soul, then must he put thereto remedy and counsel in the best manner that it may be done.

Then there shall be told unto him plainly the peril that he should fall in, though he should and would be greatly a-feared thereof. It is better and more rightful that he be compunctious and repentant, with wholesome fear and dread, and so be saved, than that he be damned with flattering and false dissimulation; for it is too inconvenient and contrary to Christian religion, and too devil-like, that the peril of death and of soul—for any vain dread of a man, lest he were anything distroubled thereby—shall be hid from any Christian man or woman that should die. . . .

Also present to the sick the image of the crucifix; the which should evermore be about sick men, or else the image of our Lady, or of some other saint the which he loved or worshipped in his heal. Also let there be holy water about the sick; and spring [sprinkle] often times upon him, and the others that be about him, that fiends may be voided from him.

If all things abovesaid may not be done, for hastiness and shortness of time, then put forth prayers; and namely such as be directed to our Saviour, specially Our Lord Jesu Christ. When man is in point of death, and hasteth fast to this end, then should no carnal friends, nor wife, nor children, nor riches, nor no temporal goods, be reduced [brought back] unto his mind, neither be communed of before him; only as much as spiritual health and profit of the sick man asketh and requireth.

Chapter VI

The Sixth Chapter Containeth Prayers that Should Be Said upon Them that Be A-Dying of Some Man that Is about Them

Last of all it is to be known that the prayers that follow may be conveniently said upon a sick man that laboureth to his end. And if it is a religious person, then when the covent [convent] is gathered together with smiting of the table, as the manner is, then shall be said first the litany, with the psalms and orisons [prayers] that be used therewith. Afterward, if he live yet, let some man that is about him say the orisons that follow hereafter, as the time and opportunity will suffer. And they may be often rehearsed again to excite the devotion of the sick man—if he have reason and understanding with him.

But nevertheless this ought not to be done of necessity, as though he might not be saved but if it were done; but for the profit and devotion of the sick that laboureth to his endward it may, and it is well done, that it be done so. But among seculars that be sick let these prayers be said; as the devotion and disposition, and the profit of them and others that be about them ask and require, and as the time will suffice.

But alas there be full few, not only among seculars but also in diverse religious that have the cunning of this craft, and will be nigh and assist to them that be in point of death and departing out of this world; asking them, and exhorting and informing and praying for them, as it is abovesaid—namely when they that be in dying would not, or hope not, to die yet, and so the sick men's soul stand in great peril. . . .

[Here follow examples of several prayers, of which we provide one.]

Oratio [Prayer]

Into the hands of Thine endless and unquenchable mercy, holy Father, rightful and most beloved Father, we commend the spirit of our brother [sister], Thy servant, after the greatness of love that the holy soul of Thy Blessed Son commended Himself to Thee on the cross; praying entirely [sincerely] that for thilk inestimable charity that Thine Holy Godhead drew fully into Thyself that blessed soul of Thy Son, that now in his last hour Thou receive sweetly the spirit of our brother, Thy servant, in the same love. AMEN.

Notes

1. For analyses of the *ars moriendi*, see Sister Mary C. O'Connor, *The Art of Dying Well: The Development of the Ars Moriendi* (New York: Columbia University Press, 1942); Nancy Lee Beaty, *The Craft of Dying: A Study in the Literary Tradition of the Ars Moriendi in England* (New Haven: Yale University Press, 1970); and for a brief account, Carlos M. N. Eire, "Ars Moriendi," *The Westminster Dictionary of Christian Spirituality*, ed. Gordon S. Wakefield (Philadelphia: The Westminster Press, 1983) 21.

2. Saint Albert Magnus (the Great) (c. 1200–1280) was an outstanding Dominican theologian and philosopher and teacher of Thomas Aquinas.

3. Saint Antony or Anthony (c. 250–355) was the father of Christian monasticism, who lived at first as a hermit in the Egyptian desert before instructing and organizing monks who followed him.

4. Saint Anselm (1003/34–1109) is sometimes called the father of medieval theology (scholasticism) (see vol. 1:376–79). He wrote the earliest source taken over by the literature concerning the art of dying, *Admonitio morienti et de peccatis nimium formidati* ("A Friendly Admonitian to the Dying Person Who Is Excessively Frightened on account of His Sins").

5. Jean Gerson (1363–1429), the great conciliar theologian, mystic, and chancellor of the University of Paris (see vol. 1:69), wrote the principal source for the *ars moriendi*: *De arte moriendi*, the third part of his *Opus Tripartitum* ("Three part Work").

6. Saint Gregory or Gregory I, pope (590–604), called "the Great" because of his extraordinary accomplishments as administrator and as reformer of the church and society as well as of the liturgy.

2. *The Imitation of Christ*

(c. 1427)

Thomas à Kempis

The Imitation of Christ *is one of the most popular and influential devotional books ever written. Although its authorship has been disputed, most scholars agree that it was probably written by Thomas à Kempis (c. 1379–1471). The piety expressed in this little book grew out of the* Devotio Moderna *(Modern Devotion), an important spiritual movement founded by Gerard (or Geert) Groote (1340–84) in the Netherlands, which helped to renew the church from the late fourteenth and fifteenth centuries to the Protestant Reformation. This movement gave rise to the Brothers (and eventually the Sisters) of the Common Life. Congregations of brothers and sisters maintained a warm and disciplined religious life characterized by Bible reading, meditation, and prayer. Though they lived in poverty, chastity, and obedience, they were not bound by permanent vows. Beyond devotional activities, their chief occupation was copying manuscripts.*

The Devotio Moderna *also gave rise to a renewal of monasticism through the Windesheim congregations of the Canons Regular of St. Augustine, inspiring a deeper and more intense spirituality and discipline in the order.*

In 1406, Thomas from Kempen (à Kempis) entered a monastery on Mount St. Agnes, which had been established in 1389 under the direction of the two-year-old Windesheim community. He was subprior and novice master, and as such he was responsible for the spiritual formation of new recruits in the monastery.

SOURCE: William C. Creasy, ed., *A New Reading of the 1441 Autograph Manuscripts* (Macon, Ga.: Mercer University Press, 1989). Used by permission.

Thomas is thought to have completed the manuscript of the Imitation *by 1427, since there are two complete manuscripts with that date on them. A later manuscript from 1441 has his autograph, but there is no certain proof of his authorship because the manuscript may simply have been transcribed by him. However, because the style and the themes of the* Imitation *are duplicated in other writings by Thomas, most scholars accept him as the author.*

The Imitation of Christ *is divided into four books. The first book, "Useful Reminders," can be summed up in a line from the first chapter: "Let it be the most important thing we do, to reflect on the life of Jesus Christ." In this chapter and the others that follow, there is an implied criticism of scholastic learning, with its debates about theological topics like the doctrine of the Trinity. According to the* Imitation, *religion is more a matter of living than of thinking, at least thinking about speculative issues. In the second book, the author stresses that true devotion concerns the inner life—being "united with Christ in the very depths of your heart." It has to do with purity and simplicity of feelings and intentions, the joy of a Christian conscience, gratitude for God's grace, and the imitation of Christ's life and his suffering. The third book describes the inner comfort that results from being centered in Christ. The fourth book, "The Book on the Sacrament," lifts up the necessity of a proper eucharistic devotion for the sustaining of the Christian life.*

The simplicity of the language of this text directly touches the heart of believers and continues to commend itself to contemporary Christians.

Book 1
Useful Reminders

Chapter 1
Of the Imitation of Christ.

"Anyone who follows me shall not walk in darkness," says the Lord. These are the words of Christ, and by them we are reminded that we must imitate his life and his ways if we are to be truly enlightened and set free from the darkness of our own hearts. Let it be the most important thing we do, to reflect on the life of Jesus Christ.

Christ's teaching surpasses all the teachings of the saints, and the person who has his spirit will find hidden nourishment in his words. Yet many people, even after hearing scripture read so often, lack a deep longing for it, for they do not have the spirit of Christ. Anyone who wishes to understand Christ's words and to savor them fully should strive to become like him in every way.

What good does it do, then, to debate about the Trinity, if by a lack of humility you are displeasing to the Trinity? In truth, lofty words do not make a person holy and just, but a virtuous life makes one dear to God. I would much rather feel profound sorrow for my sins than to be able to define the theological term for it. If you knew the whole Bible by heart and the sayings of all the philosophers, what good would it all be without God's love and grace? Vanity of vanities and all is vanity, except to love God and to serve only him. This is the highest wisdom: to see the world as it truly is, fallen and fleeting; to love the world not for its own sake but for God's; and to direct all your effort toward achieving the kingdom of heaven.

So, it is vanity to seek material wealth that cannot last and to place your trust in it. It is also vanity to seek recognition and status. It is vanity to chase after what the world says you should want and to long for things you should not have, things that you will pay a high price for later on if you get them. It is vanity to wish for a long life and to care little about a good life. It is vanity to focus only on your present life and not to look ahead to your future life. It is vanity to live for the joys of the moment and not to seek eagerly the lasting joys that await you.

Often remembering that saying: "The eye is not satisfied with seeing, nor is the ear filled with hearing." Make every effort, then, to shift your affections from the things that you can see to the things you cannot see, for people who live in the world on its terms instead of on God's stain their conscience and lose God's grace.

Chapter 2

Of Having a Humble Opinion about Yourself.

Everyone naturally wishes to have knowledge, but what good is great learning unless it is accompanied by a feeling of deep awe and profound reverence toward God? Indeed, a humble farmer who serves God is better than a proud philosopher, who, neglecting himself, contemplates the course of the heavens. The person who truly knows himself seems common in his own eyes, and the good things that others may say about him do not change the way he thinks about himself. If I knew everything in the world and did not have love, what good would it do me before God, who will judge me by what I have done?

Calm that excessive thirst for knowledge, for there is great discord and deception in it. People who have great learning are often eager to appear wise, and they often wish others to recognize them as wise people. There are many things that you can know about, though, that are of little or no use to the soul, and a person is exceedingly foolish who reaches for anything that does not lead toward salvation. Endless reading and talk do not satisfy the soul, but a good life puts the mind at rest, and a clean conscience brings great confidence in God. The more you know and the better you know it, the greater is your responsibility for using your knowledge wisely.

So, do not think highly of yourself because of what you know about any art or science, but rather respect the knowledge that has been entrusted to you. If it seems to you that you know many things and that you are an expert in them, recognize nevertheless that there are many things that you do not know. Do not be high-minded, but admit your great ignorance. Why do you wish to think yourself better than others when you discover many people more learned and more practiced in God's ways than you are? If you want to learn something that will really help you, learn to see yourself as God sees you and not as you see yourself in the distorted mirror of your own self importance. This is the greatest and most useful lesson we can learn: to know ourselves for what we truly are, to admit freely our weaknesses and failings, and to hold a humble opinion of ourselves because of them. Not to dwell on ourselves and always to think well and highly of others is great wisdom and perfection.

If you should see another person sin openly or commit some grave wrong, still you should not think yourself a better person by comparison, for you do not know how long you may remain in a good state. We are all frail, but think no one more frail than yourself.

Chapter 3

Of the Teaching of Truth.

Happy is that person whom Truth itself teaches, not by figures of speech and eloquent language, but as it is itself. Our opinions and our understanding often lead us astray and offer us very little insight. What good is a brilliant argument about hidden and obscure matters when God does not judge us by our knowledge of such things? It is a great mistake for us to neglect useful and necessary things and to direct our thoughts to curious and harmful ones. Having eyes, we do not see. Why should we bother about clever arguments and subtle reasoning?

When the eternal Word speaks we are set free from countless theories and conjectures. All things spring from this one Word and all things speak of one Word, and this Word is the beginning, which also speaks to us. Without the Word, no one understands correctly or draws the right conclusions about anything. That person to whom all things are One and who draws all things to One and who sees all things in One may be steadfast in heart and rest peacefully in God.

O God, the Truth, make me one with you in endless love! I am often worn out by all that I read and hear; you are all that I want or desire. Let all teachers hold their peace. Let all creation be silent in your sight. You alone speak to me.

The more a person is at one with himself and inwardly undivided, the more varied and profound things does he understand without effort, for he receives the light of understanding from above. A pure, simple and steady spirit is not distracted by flitting about from one thing to another, for he does all things to the honor of God and tries in his heart to be free from all.

• • •

Chapter 25

Of Improving Our Lives.

Be watchful and diligent in God's service, and often think over why you chose to serve Christ in the first place. Was it not that you might live for God and become a spiritual person? Be fervent, then, in going forward, for you will soon receive the reward of your labors, and then there will be no more fear or sorrow in you. By working a little now, you will find great rest later; indeed, you will find endless joy. If you remain faithful and fervent in what you do, God will doubtless be faithful and generous in rewarding you. You must keep good hope of attaining the victory, but you must not become overconfident, lest you grow lazy or self-satisfied.

There was once a certain anxious man who, wavering often between fear and hope and exhausted with grief, prostrated himself in prayer in church before the altar. Turning these things in his mind, he said: "Oh, if only I knew that I shall persevere." On the spot, he heard the divine answer in his own heart: "What if you knew this? What would you do? Do now what you would do then, and you will be very safe." Soon after, having been comforted and strengthened, he gave himself up to God's will, and his anxious wavering stopped. He no longer feared for his future; instead, he sought to know God's will for accomplishing today's good works. "Hope in the Lord and do good," says the Prophet, "and dwell in the land, and you shall be fed with its riches."

There is one thing that keeps many people from gaining ground and from fervently striving to improve: the dread of difficulty, or more accurately, the effort of the struggle. Those people progress most in virtue—truly, they progress beyond all others—who make a valiant effort to overcome the things that are most troublesome to them, that work most against them. A person makes more progress and deserves fuller grace in those instances where he overcomes such obstacles completely and where he cleanses his spirit by doing so. But not everyone has the same amount to overcome and cleanse. Nevertheless, a person striving diligently to excel will make greater progress—even if he has more to overcome—than will another who is more even-tempered but less keen for virtues.

Two things especially lead to great improvement: the will to drag yourself from the things that will naturally harm you and the desire to pursue the good things that you need the most. You should also watch out for those things that irritate you in other people; when you see them in yourself, get rid of them. Turn everything to your advantage. If you see or hear good examples, imitate them. If you think something is reprehensible, be careful that you do not do the same thing; if you have done it, try to correct yourself quickly. As you watch others, so do they watch you. How joyful and sweet it is to see fervent and devout friends living together agreeably and being well-disciplined. How sad it is—and what a burden!—to see people stumbling along in confusion, not practicing their own vocation. How harmful it is for those same people to neglect the purpose of their calling and to shift their attention to affairs that are none of their concern.

Remember what you set out to do, and place before you the image of the Crucified. When you look into the life of Jesus Christ you may well be ashamed that you have not tried harder to be like him, even though you have followed the ways of God for a long time. A religious person who trains himself intently and devoutly in the holy life and Passion of the Lord will find everything he needs, and he will find it in abundance. He need not look beyond Jesus for anything better. Oh, if the crucified Jesus were to enter into our hearts, how quickly and fully would we be taught!

A fervent, religious person takes all things and bears them well, whatever they may be. A careless and lukewarm person has trouble on top of trouble and endures anguish from every side, because he lacks inner comfort and cannot find it anywhere else. An undisciplined person is open to grave ruin, and a person who looks only for ease and relaxation in life will be limited in his spiritual development, for one thing or another will always displease him.

How do so many other people make do, especially those who are constrained so tightly under monastic vows? They seldom go out, they live apart, they eat the poorest food, they dress coarsely, they work much, they speak little, they watch long, they rise early, they pray long, they read often and they keep control over themselves in every way. Look at the Carthusians, the Cistercians, and the monks and nuns of various religious orders. Every night they rise to sing psalms to the Lord. You should be ashamed of yourself for being so lazy while so many others are praising God even before the sun rises! Oh, if only there were nothing else to do but to praise the Lord our God with all our hearts and voices! Oh, if you never needed to eat or drink or sleep, but could always praise God and could be entirely free to strive after spiritual things; then, you would be much happier than you are now, enslaved as you are by all sorts of necessities. Oh, that there were not such necessities but only the spiritual nourishment of the soul, which, alas, we taste too seldom.

When you come to this, that you look for your comfort from nothing but God, then you begin to know God perfectly; then, too, will you be quite content no matter what happens; then, you will neither rejoice for much nor grieve for little, but will commit yourself wholly and confidently to God, for he means everything to you. To God, nothing passes away or dies, but all things live and all things serve him promptly at a nod.

Always think of the end and that lost time never returns. Without care and diligence you will never acquire virtue. If you begin to grow apathetic you will begin to do badly. But if you give yourself enthusiastically to your spiritual life, you will find great peace and feel the effort lighter through God's grace and the love of virtue. The person who loves God with all his heart and soul—and who faithfully and diligently acts on that love—is ready for anything. It is greater work to resist our weaknesses than it is to sweat at manual labor. The person who does not avoid small faults, little by little slips into greater ones. You will always be glad at evening if you have spent the day well. Watch over yourself, rouse yourself, chide yourself, and no matter what others may do, do not neglect yourself. The more self-disciplined you are, the more you will progress. Amen.

Here end useful reminders for the spiritual life.

Book 2

Suggestions Drawing One toward the Inner Life

Chapter 1

Of God Speaking within You.

"The kingdom of God is within you," says the Lord. Turn to the Lord with your whole heart, let him be the most important part of your life, and your soul will find rest. If you put God first, you will see his kingdom blossom within you, for the kingdom of God is living in peace and joy with the Holy Spirit, a thing not given to those who do not yearn for him with all their hearts. Christ will come to you and comfort you if you prepare a worthy place for him in your heart. All his glory and beauty lies within you, and he finds great delight in living there. He often visits the person who has a rich inner life, holding sweet conversation with him, granting delightful comfort, much peace and intimate friendship.

So get up, faithful soul, and prepare your heart for this Bridegroom so that he will want to come to you and live in your heart, for he says: "If anyone loves me he will keep my word, and we shall come to him, and we shall make our home with him." Make room for Christ, then, and place him at the center of your life. When he alone rests there, you will have great wealth, and he will be all you need. He will care for you, and he will provide for you faithfully in everything; you will not have to depend on anyone else, for people soon change and they fall short of your expectations before you know it. Only Christ remains constant forever, and he will stand by you to the very end.

Do not rely too heavily on other people, for, like all of us, they have their flaws and foibles. Even if you love someone very much, and that person has been a great blessing to you, do not be disappointed if sometimes the two of you disagree. Those who are your greatest help today may not be tomorrow; their needs change, and so do yours. Place all your trust in God; worship and love him. He will defend you and do what is best for you. This world is not your permanent home; wherever you may be you are a stranger, a pilgrim passing through. You will never find peace unless you are united with Christ in the very depths of your heart.

Why do you look around here to find peace when you do not really belong here? Your place is in heaven, and you should see everything else in terms of heaven. All things pass away, and you pass away with them, too. See that you do not cling to passing things, lest you become caught up in them and perish along with them.

Let your highest thoughts be with the Most High and your prayer be directed to Christ without ceasing. If you cannot contemplate high and heavenly things, rest your thoughts on Christ's Passion, and dwell freely on his Sacred Wounds. If you go for refuge to Jesus' Wounds and to the precious marks of his Passion with humility and love, you will feel great comfort in troubled times, you will not be too concerned about what other people think of you, and it will not be hard to put up with the humiliating things that they may say about you. Christ was also scorned by many people, and in his greatest need he was abandoned by his friends as others heaped insults on his head. Christ was willing to suffer and to be despised, and do you presume to complain of anything? Christ had those who did not like him and those who disagreed with him, and would you have everyone be your friends and supporters? How will your patience be rewarded if you meet with no hardships? If you never encounter opposition, how will you be Christ's friend?

Prop yourself up with Christ and for Christ if you wish to live with Christ. If just once you could perfectly enter the inner life of Jesus and experience a little of his passionate love, then you would not care at all about what you might gain or lose in life. You would even bear insults gladly, for the love of Jesus makes a person think of himself in a very humble way. A lover of Jesus and of truth, a genuinely spiritual person who is free from a troubled heart, can turn himself to God at any time, rise above himself, and rest joyfully in the Lord.

The person who understands all things as they are and not as they are said to be, is truly wise and is taught more by God than by others. The person who knows how to walk by an inner light is not overly influenced by his surroundings, and he needs neither special places nor special times for prayer. A person who can quickly focus inwardly is at one with himself, because he never completely loses himself in his outside affairs. He is not distracted by such things, nor does occasional necessary business sidetrack him, but he adjusts himself to such things as they come. The person whose inner life is well-ordered and set in place is not troubled by the strange and twisted things that people do. A person is hindered and distracted in life in proportion to the cares he clutters about himself.

If everything were right with you and if you were pure throughout, everything would work to your advantage. As it is, many things often make you unhappy and upset you because you have not successfully shifted your attention from yourself to God, nor have you let go of the things that the world has set in your path. Nothing so stains and entangles a person's heart as a love of material things that is tarnished by self-interest. If you could put aside all those distracting things that the world has to offer, you could then contemplate heavenly things and you would often experience a deep inner joy.

• • •

Chapter 7

Of Loving Jesus Above All Else.

That person is truly blessed who understands what it is to love Jesus and to serve him with deep humility. Jesus wishes to be loved above all things; everything else must come second. The love of anything other than Jesus is deceptive and fickle; the love of Jesus is faithful and enduring. The person who clings to anything other than Jesus falls with its falling; the person who embraces Jesus stands firm forever. Love Jesus and keep him as your friend. When all things fade he will not abandon you, nor will he allow you to perish in the end.

If necessary, you must be willing to let go of everything if Jesus asks it of you. Cling to him in life and in death, and trust yourself to his faithfulness. He alone can help you when all else fails. Your Beloved will not share you with others—that is his nature; he wants to be first in your heart, as you are in his. If you knew how to disentangle yourself from your own confused feelings, Jesus would gladly stay with you.

You will find that whatever hope you have placed in anything other than Jesus is nearly a total loss. Do not trust or lean upon a wind-blown reed, for all flesh is grass, and its glory, like the wild-flower's, will fade away. If you trust in appearances, you will quickly be deceived; if you look for comfort and gain in others, you will often be disappointed. If you seek Jesus in everything, you will surely find him, but if you seek yourself, self you will surely find, but to your own ruin. By not seeking Jesus, we hurt ourselves more than the whole world and all our enemies could hurt us.

Chapter 8

Of Intimate Friendship with Jesus.

When Jesus is with us, all is right with the world and nothing seems difficult; when he is missing, everything is hard. When Jesus does not speak to the heart, comfort is worthless; but if he speaks only one word, we feel great joy. Did not Mary Magdalen arise at once from where she was weeping when Martha said to her, "the Master is here and is calling for you"? Oh, happy hour when Jesus calls us from tears to spiritual joy!

How dry and hard you are without Jesus! How foolish and empty if you want anything other than Jesus! Is this not a greater loss than if you were to lose the whole world? What can the world offer you without Jesus? To be without Jesus is an unbearable hell, and to be with Jesus is a sweet paradise. If Jesus is with you no foe can harm you. The person who finds Jesus finds a good treasure—indeed, a good beyond all good; the person who loses Jesus loses a very great thing, more than the whole world. It is poverty to live without Jesus; it is wealth to live with him.

To know how to talk with Jesus is a great art, and to know how to cling to him is great wisdom. Be humble and peaceful and Jesus will be with you; be devout and quiet and he will remain with you. You will quickly drive him away and lose his grace, though, if you divert your attention to your own affairs at his expense. And if you drive him away and lose him, to whom will you fly, and who will you then seek as a friend? You cannot live well without a friend, and if Jesus is not your best friend, you will end up being heartbroken and desolate. You act foolishly, then, if you center your life on anything else. It is better to have the whole world against us than to hurt Jesus.

So, from among all those dear to you let Jesus alone be especially loved. Love all things for Jesus' sake, but love Jesus for his own sake. Of all the friends you will find, you should love Jesus Christ in a unique way, for he is the only one who will be good and faithful to the end. Through him and in him love friends and foes alike, and pray that each one may come to know and love him.

Never wish to be more highly praised or more loved than others, for this belongs to God alone who has no equal. Do not wish that anyone should love you and only you, and do not make the same mistake yourself; rather, let Jesus be at the center of all your friendships. Be pure and free of heart, and do not be wrapped up in any other person to the exclusion of Jesus. You should bring a pure, unfettered heart to God if you wish to be free and to see how delightful the Lord is. And truly you will never arrive at this, unless his grace guides you and draws you, so that seeing all things in relation to God, you may be united to him in everything you do.

When the grace of God comes to you, then you are strong in all things, and when it leaves, you become poor and weak, left, as it were, to be beaten and kicked about. You should not be dejected, nor should you despair at this; rather, you should stand with a steady mind toward the will of God and endure whatever comes to you for the praise of Jesus Christ. After winter comes summer, after night the day returns, after a storm comes great calm.

• • •

Chapter 12

Of the Royal Road of the Holy Cross.

To many people this saying seems harsh: "Deny yourself, take up your cross and follow Jesus." But it will be much harsher to hear that final word: "Depart from me, you accursed, into everlasting fire." They who gladly hear and follow the word of the cross now will have nothing to fear later on when they hear of eternal damnation. This sign of the cross will be in the heavens when the Lord comes to judge. Then all the servants of the cross who, in life, conformed themselves to the Crucified Lord, will approach Christ the Judge with great confidence.

Why then are you afraid to take up the cross, the way that leads to the kingdom of God? In the cross is salvation; in the cross is life; in the cross is protection; in the cross is heavenly sweetness; in the cross is strength of mind; in the cross is spiritual joy; in the cross is supreme virtue; in the cross is perfect holiness. There is no salvation for the soul nor hope for eternal life, except in the cross.

So take up your cross and follow Jesus, and you will go on to eternal life. He went before you carrying his cross, and on the cross he died for you, that you too may carry your cross, and that you too may die on the cross. If you die with him, you will live with him. If you join him in suffering, you will join him in glory. Listen closely. Everything is founded on the cross, and everything consists in dying on it, and there is no other road to life and to true inner peace than the road of the holy cross and of our daily dying to ourselves. Walk where you will, seek where you will, and you will find no loftier way above nor safer way below than the way of the holy cross.

Plan as you like and arrange everything as best you can, yet you will always encounter some suffering whether you want to or not. Go wherever you will, you will always find the cross. Either you will feel physical pain or spiritual pain. Sometimes God will leave you, and sometimes a neighbor will upset you; even worse, you will sometimes be a burden to yourself! You can find neither remedy nor comfort which can free you or relieve you, but you must bear it as long as God wishes. God wants you to learn to endure troubles without comfort, to submit yourself totally to him, and to become more humble through adversity.

No one feels in his heart what Christ felt in his Passion, except the person who suffers as he did. So, the cross is always ready and waits for you everywhere. You cannot escape it no matter where you run, for wherever you go you are burdened with yourself, and wherever you go, there you are. Look up, look down; look out, look in. Everywhere you will find the cross, and you must endure patiently if you wish to have inner peace and gain eternal life.

If you bear your cross willingly, it will carry you and lead you to your desired goal where suffering will end, but that cannot happen here. If you bear your cross unwillingly, you will make a greater burden for yourself—and you must still carry it, in any case. If you fling aside one cross, you will certainly find another and, perhaps, a heavier one.

Do you expect to escape what no one has ever avoided? What saint was there in the world without crosses and afflictions? Not even our Lord Jesus Christ spent one hour without the anguish of his Passion as long as he lived. It was necessary that Christ should suffer and rise again from the dead and so enter into his glory. So why do you seek another way, different from the royal road, which is the way of the holy cross?

Christ's entire life was a cross and a martyrdom, and will you look for rest and happiness? You are deluded if you look for anything other than affliction, for our entire mortal life is surrounded by crosses. And the more we progress in the spiritual life, the heavier our crosses will be, for the pain of our separation from God increases in proportion to our love of God.

But one who bears many crosses is not without some comfort, for he knows the great rewards that will come to him by patiently accepting God's will. At the same time that he bends under the weight of his cross, his burden is changed into divine comfort, for he knows that God will reward him for his efforts. And the more a person's body is weakened by affliction, the more his spirit is strengthened by inner grace. Sometimes, through the love of conforming himself to Christ's cross, a person is so comforted by his trials and afflictions that he does not want to be without them, for he believes that the more and heavier burdens he can bear for Christ, the more acceptable he will become to him. For such a person, patiently living out God's will becomes a blessing.

It is not our strength but Christ's grace which can and does accomplish such great things in us. Christ's grace enables us to embrace warmly those things from which we naturally recoil. It is not in our nature to bear the cross, to love the cross, to discipline ourselves, to avoid seeking praise, to suffer insults willingly, to think humbly of ourselves, to appear humble to others, to endure adversity and loss, and not to seek prosperity as our first goal. If you take a look at yourself, you will see that you can do none of this alone, but if you confide in the Lord, he will give you heavenly strength and all that you have chosen to do will become easier. You will not even fear your enemy, the devil, if you are armed with faith and sealed with the cross of Christ.

So, as a good and faithful servant of Christ, brace yourself to bear the Lord's cross with valor; out of love for you he was nailed to it. Be ready to bear many hardships and every kind of misfortune, for you will surely experience them wherever you are and wherever you may try to hide. It must be so. There is no way to avoid it; you can only endure it patiently. Drink lovingly of the chalice of the Lord if you wish to be his friend and to share his life. Leave all divine comforts to God; let him deal with them as he chooses. As for you, be ready to bear up under afflictions and consider them to be great consolations. For even if you were to endure all the world's suffering all by yourself, it would still be nothing compared to the future glory that only a little suffering would earn for you.

When you have come to this, that enduring pain and sorrow for Christ's sake is sweet and pleasing to you, then think that all is well with you, for you have found paradise on earth. As long as suffering is hard for you and you seek to avoid it, all will go wrong with you, and the very trouble that you run from will hound you wherever you go. If you resign yourself to what must be—that is, that we must all suffer and die—you will feel much better, and you will find peace. Even if you were caught up to the third heaven with St. Paul, that would be no guarantee that you will not suffer adversity. "I shall show him," said Jesus, "how much he must suffer for my name." So, it remains for you to suffer if you wish to love Jesus and to serve him always.

If only you were worthy of enduring something for the name of Jesus! What great glory would be yours! How much joy would you give to God's saints! What an example you would be to your neighbor! For everyone praises a willingness to endure hardships, but only a few are willing to do it. So, you gladly ought to suffer a little for Christ; many people suffer much heavier things for the world.

Know for certain that you must lead a life that focuses less and less on yourself. The less self-centered you become, the more you become centered in God. You are not fit to understand heavenly things unless you resign yourself to bearing adversities for Christ. Nothing is more pleasing to God, and nothing is better for you in this world than to be willing to suffer for Christ. If you had the choice, you would choose to suffer adversities for Christ than to be comforted and put at ease, for you would be more like Christ, more like all the saints. Our worth and our spiritual progress do not rest on warm feelings and God-given comforts, but rather on patiently enduring great calamities and trials.

If there had been anything better, anything more suited or more useful to our salvation than suffering, Christ surely would have pointed it out to us by his word and example. For the disciples who followed him and for all those who wish to follow him, he clearly urges carrying the cross, saying: "If anyone would come after me, let him deny himself and take up his cross and follow me." So, let all your reading and studying end on this note: to enter the kingdom of God, we must endure many hardships.

Here end suggestions drawing one toward the inner life.

Book 3
Of Inner Comfort

• • •

Chapter 21
That We Should Rest in God above All Else.

Disciple:

O my soul, above all things and in all things always rest in the Lord, for he is the eternal rest of the saints.

Grant me most sweet and loving Jesus, to rest in you above every other creature, above all health and beauty, above all glory and honor, above all power and dignity, above all knowledge and precise thought, above all wealth and talent, above all joy and exultation, above all fame and praise, above all sweetness and consolation, above all hope and promise, above all merit and desire, above all gifts and favors you give and shower upon me, above all happiness and joy that the mind can understand and feel, and finally, above all angels and archangels, above all the hosts of heaven, above all things visible and invisible, and above all that is not you, my God.

You, O Lord, my God, you are supreme above all things. You alone are most high, you alone are most powerful, you alone are self-sufficient and complete, you alone are most sweet and delightful, you alone are most beautiful and loving, you alone are most noble and glorious above all things. In you all good exists perfectly and at once; it always was and it always will be. Therefore, whatever you give me, other than yourself, or whatever you reveal or promise to me is far too little, is not enough, as long as I do not see you or fully embrace you. My heart cannot truly rest nor be fully content, if it does not rise above all gifts and all created things and rest in you.

O my most beloved spouse, Jesus Christ, most pure lover, Lord of all creation, who will give me the wings of true freedom to fly to you and to rest in you? Oh, when shall I be free to see how sweet you are, my Lord God? When shall I find myself so completely absorbed in you that for love of you I shall not be conscious of myself but of you alone, beyond all ability to understand or to measure and in a way unique to me?

But now I often lament and bear my unhappiness with a heavy heart, for many evils befall me in this valley of tears. They often upset me, sadden me and cast a dark shadow over me. They often get in the way and distract me, allure and entangle me, so that I cannot freely come to you nor enjoy the happy embraces that always await the blessed spirits.

Let my sighs and great loneliness upon this earth move you, O Jesus, splendor of eternal glory, comfort of the wandering soul. My mouth falls silent before you; my silence speaks to you. How long will my Lord delay in coming? Let him come to me, his poor servant, and make me happy. Let him stretch forth his hand and deliver me from all distress, I who am so greatly in need of compassion.

Come, come. Without you no day or hour will be happy, for you are my joy, and without you my table is empty. I am miserable. I am as one imprisoned and loaded down with heavy chains until you revive me with the light of your presence and set me free and turn your kind face upon me. Others may go their own way, but nothing else delights me nor shall delight me except you, my God, my hope and my eternal salvation. I shall not be silent nor will I cease to pray until your grace returns to me and you speak to me in the depths of my heart.

Jesus:

My dear friend, I am here. See, I have come to you because you have invited me. Your tears and your soul's longing, your humility and your grief-stricken heart have moved me and brought me to you.

Disciple:

O Lord, I called you and longed to enjoy you, and I am prepared to give up everything for you. You first inspired me to seek you; therefore, may you be blessed, Lord, you who have granted this favor to your servant, according to your abundant mercy. What more does your servant have to say in your presence except that he should humble himself before you, remembering always his own shortcomings and unworthiness? There is no one like you among all the wonders of heaven and earth. Your works are exceedingly good, your judgments are true, and by your providence you govern the universe. Praise, therefore, and glory to you, O Wisdom of the Father. Let my mouth, my soul and all creation praise and bless you.

• • •

Book 4
The Book on the Sacrament

• • •

Chapter 3
How It Is Helpful to Receive Communion Often.

Disciple:

Look, Lord! I come to you so that your gift may help me and so that I may delight in your holy banquet, which you, O God, in your sweetness have prepared for us. You see, you are all that I can or should desire; you are my salvation and redemption, my hope and my strength, my honor and my glory. Therefore, give joy to the soul of your servant this day, for to you, Lord Jesus, I lift up my soul.

Now I wish to receive you with devotion and reverence; I long to bring you into my house, so that like Zacchaeus, I may be worthy of your blessing and may be numbered among the children of Abraham. My soul deeply yearns for your Body; my heart longs to be one with you. Give yourself to me and that will be enough, for no comfort satisfies me apart from you. I cannot live without you; without you, I an unable to exist. Therefore, I must come to you often and receive you as the medicine of my salvation, lest, deprived of this heavenly food, I should faint on my journey through life. In just this way, most merciful Jesus, while you were preaching to the people and healing various diseases, you once said: "I am unwilling to send them home with nothing to eat, lest they faint on the way." Treat me as you treated them, you who have left yourself in this Sacrament for the comfort of your faithful ones, for you are the sweet refreshment of the soul, and whoever shall partake of you worthily shall inherit and share in eternal glory.

It is most necessary for me, who waver and sin so often and who so quickly become lazy and falter, that by frequent prayers and confessions and by receiving your Holy Body, I may renew, purify, and enkindle myself.

If I stay away from you too long, I may fall away from my holy resolve. Because we are so attracted to the values of this world, we continually drift away from you, and unless divine medicine is brought to us quickly, we soon find ourselves lost and alone. Holy Communion draws us back to you and comforts us in your goodness.

If I am so often careless and lukewarm when I go to Holy Communion or celebrate Mass, what would happen if I did not receive this medicine or seek your help? Though I may not be in the proper frame of mind to celebrate or attend Mass daily, still I should try to receive the divine mysteries at suitable times and make myself a participant in so great a grace. The faithful soul's chief comfort, while far away from you and traveling through life, is remembering God often and receiving the Lord with great devotion.

Oh, the marvelous goodness and kindness that you show to us that you, Lord God, creator and giver of life, lower yourself to come to such a poor soul, and with the fullness of your divinity and humanity satisfy her hunger! O happy mind and blessed soul that deserves to receive you, the Lord God, with devotion, and in receiving you is filled with spiritual joy! Oh, how great a lord the soul receives! What a beloved guest she brings into her home! What a sweet companion she greets! What a faithful friend she welcomes! What a beautiful and noble spouse she embraces! I love you beyond all loves and beyond all desires!

My sweet beloved, let heaven and earth and all their array be silent in your presence, for whatever they have of loveliness and worth, they are all your gifts. They can never rise to the splendor of your name, whose wisdom is beyond all measure.

• • •

3. Eternal Predestination and Its Execution in Time

(1517)

John von Staupitz

John (or Johann or Johannes) von Staupitz (1460 or 1469–1524) is best known for his connection with Martin Luther. He was Luther's superior in the Order of the Hermits of St. Augustine at Wittenberg and preceded Luther at the university as professor of theology. During Luther's spiritual crisis, Staupitz was Luther's confessor, offering helpful counsel.

Staupitz, like Luther, was born in Saxony, but of more aristocratic parents. He was educated at Leipzig, Cologne, and Tübingen. As a member of the Augustinian order, a mendicant (begging) order that he joined in Munich, Staupitz was in 1497 made prior of the cloister in Tübingen. At Leipzig and Cologne, Staupitz studied the scholastic ideas of Thomas Aquinas, but in Tübingen his studies focused on nominalist theology as taught by Wendelin Steinbach, a disciple of Gabriel Biel, who was a well-known nominalist theologian greatly influenced by William of Occam.

In spite of this training in nominalist theology, Staupitz remained unconvinced by its teaching on humanity and salvation. Biel and Steinbach, like Occam, taught that human beings play an important role in their own salvation. Although they rejected the Pelagian view that human beings can earn their own salvation purely by their own efforts, they had great difficulty accepting Augustine. In his anti-Pelagian writings,

---

SOURCE: H. A. Oberman, ed., *Forerunners of the Reformation: The Shape of Late Medieval Thought*, trans. Paul L. Nyhus (New York: Holt, Rinehart and Winston, 1966). Used by permission of Henry Holt & Co.

Augustine had stressed the incapacity of sinful human beings to bring about their own salvation, insisting that the sovereignty of God's grace required a doctrine of eternal predestination.

These modern Pelagians, as their more strict Augustinian opponents called them, argued that salvation was by divine grace combined with a human role in the process. Biel and Steinbach upheld the doctrine of a covenant of works. They argued that God has contracted with human beings to grant them justifying grace, provided they do their very best, using their pure natural powers to love God above all things. Such effort on the part of humans is called a merit of fitness, *a kind of half merit, by which they become appropriately disposed to receive God's justifying grace. Humans do not earn their salvation on account of this merit. They require a full merit, the* merit of worthiness, *for that, and they can produce such a merit only after they have received justifying grace. God has contracted to give sinful human beings the gift of eternal life only after they have produced the merit of worthiness. Staupitz rejected this doctrine of salvation with its optimistic view of humanity in favor of a more strictly Augustinian position, which stressed human sin and the role of divine grace from the beginning to the end of the process of salvation.*

After Staupitz spent two years as prior of the cloister at Munich, the elector prince of Saxony, Frederick the Wise, invited him to become professor of Bible at the newly founded university in Wittenberg. Staupitz was also made vicar-general of his order, the Reformed Congregation of the Hermits of St. Augustine, a division of the Augustinian order known as Observants because of their strict adherence to the monastic rule. Conventional Augustinians were more lax in their adherence to the rule, and in Saxony, Staupitz sought, unsuccessfully, to merge the two groups.

Recognizing that his work as vicar-general was so heavy, Staupitz soon asked that a promising younger theologian take his place as professor of Bible at the university. In 1508, Martin Luther, who was a member of the strict order of Augustinians, had come from Erfurt to Wittenberg to study theology, and within two years he was teaching ethics. Staupitz urged Luther to get his doctorate in theology, and in 1512 he completed his degree and became Staupitz's successor.

While Luther was a student in Wittenberg, Staupitz became his counselor as well as his teacher, providing support during Luther's inner spiritual struggles over whether he was truly accepted by God. At Erfurt, Luther had been taught the nominalist Occamist understanding that through his own powers he could take the first step in the direction of his own salvation, that on his own he could love God above all things. In his own experience, however, Luther believed himself to be a sinner unable to make this first step and therefore condemned to hell. During this period of torment, Staupitz provided much needed solace and tried to convince Luther that the temptations besetting him were the signs of God's purpose for his life. At the same time, Staupitz, as a strict Augustinian, helped point Luther away from the teachings of Occam and Biel and encouraged him to read the writings of Augustine and Paul on sin and grace.

Staupitz agreed with the nominalists that the relation between God and humanity was one of covenant. It was, however, not a covenant of works but of grace. God's covenant was not a bilateral one with mutual indebtedness between God and humans; God's covenant was a unilateral one whereby God takes the initiative to establish it and acts to fulfill it for humankind by divine action in Jesus Christ. The offer of God's grace is not dependent on human works, but is free and unconditional. With Augustine, as found in his anti-Pelagian writings, Staupitz taught a doctrine of predestination whereby God freely chooses human beings for salvation.

This position contrasted with that of the Occamists, who taught that any predestination of persons for salvation is dependent on God's foreknowledge of their merits. God foreordains to salvation only those who make the right use of their free will. Staupitz felt that such a position undercuts God's free, sovereign grace. Salvation, according to Staupitz, comes as a result of God's grace revealed in Jesus Christ from beginning to end. His treatise Eternal Predestination and Its Execution in Time *presents Staupitz's thinking on this subject.*

Luther was greatly assisted by Staupitz's theology, even as he read other Augustinians, such as Gregory of Rimini, who argued with the Occamists in the fourteenth century. Luther also studied Augustine directly and read the letters of Paul. Luther reports that it was through the study of Romans in particular that his breakthrough occurred and his spiritual and theological crisis was resolved.

Staupitz and Luther were very close during Luther's early years in Wittenberg. They did not agree on all matters, however, especially when Luther began his protests against church practices and theology. In 1520 Staupitz left Wittenberg, resigning his post as vicar-general of the Augustinians, and joined the Benedictines in Salzburg, becoming an abbot there in 1522. In the end, Staupitz rejected the theology of his former protégé.

Staupitz is important not only because he had a close relationship to Luther, but also because his theology is an example of late medieval reform based on the recovery of a radical Augustinianism. Luther, Zwingli, Calvin, and other reformers all participated in this Augustinian renaissance.[1]

I. The Goal of Creation and Redemption

God is the creator of heaven and earth and all things contained in them. Each individual work is full of the glory of the Lord. He himself knows all there is to know, and perceives it in the mirror of eternity, and grasps the past, present, and future all at once. No thought escapes Him nor is any work hidden from Him. Not by chance, therefore, but by His bidding did He fashion the universe. With His wisdom He adorned and made attractive each and every thing so that each was very good but not, however, the best. It is impossible for the creature to be the best, since to be a creature means to tend toward nothingness, and to return to nothingness unless upheld by the One Who created him.

Indeed, goodness is not possible unless it be given by the Best, nor can it have any meritorious power unless done by the grace of the Best. Hence the Lord has made all things in and for Himself, whether by creation He provides for life or by redemption for good life. For just as He creates all things in such a fashion that their existence might derive from Him, so also He restores the fallen ones that their goodness and righteousness derive from Him. As the Lord says according to Scripture, "I, I am He who blots out your transgression for My own sake, and I will not remember your sins" (Isa. 43:25).

Since God is infinite perfection, and nothing better than He can be conceived, nothing more or less, nothing further is required than praise, honor, and glory. In order that we might know and love God, He has made the saints relate all His marvelous acts which He, the omnipotent Lord, has established in His everlasting glory. To the degree He is known He is loved, and to the degree He is loved He is praised. Therefore, the goal of creation and restoration is the praise of the Creator and Redeemer.

II. The Utility of Praising God

Provided one praises in the proper manner, the praise of God is never without beneficial effect. By praising God, immense in Himself, we make Him great in us, and by comparison with Him we reduce the created universe to its own proportions, to nothingness. Thus we prepare a worthy habitation for God and we erect a temple for the Holy Spirit, full of God and empty of all creatureliness. And so it happens that we, who have our origins outside ourselves (*extra nos*), cease to be what we were and begin to be what we were not. For surely by nature we were children of wrath but by grace we are children of God. We were cursed in Adam, but we are blessed in the promised Son.

Nothing, therefore, is more felicitous for the creature than to return with praise to his origin, to abandon himself and approach God. Nor can anyone praise God worthily without reducing himself to nothing. Hence, the more one is freed from himself the more felicitous it is for him. Indeed, eternally felicitous is he who does not cease to praise God.

For this purpose the Spirit of the Lord comes to our hearts saying, "How lovely is thy dwelling place, O Lord of hosts, My soul longs, yea, faints for the courts of the Lord, My heart and flesh sing for joy, they jump (*extra se*) to the living God" (Ps. 84:1, 2). And a little farther this is added, "Blessed are those who dwell in Thy house, ever singing they shall praise Thee" (Ps. 84:4).

Nor should this be forgotten, namely, that praise is required from the mouth and heart of every rational creature for the gifts of the whole creation which are put at man's disposal and were created for his benefit. But man should praise God most of all for the gifts personally given to him, so that amid this accumulation of gifts, man's responsibility grows, since they put the recipient under obligation.

III. The Deficiency of Man's Praise Without Christ

Just as we do not love unknown things and insufficiently love that which we insufficiently know, so we are unable to praise that which we do not know at all and have no reason to love. Nor can we worthily praise that which we can see only dimly and love only half-heartedly. Since, however, no one knows the Father except the Son and the man to whom the Son wishes to reveal Him, no one can rightly praise God who does not believe and confess Christ to be the true Son of God. He who sees Him sees the Father, since the Father is in the Son, and the Son in the Father. Now he sees in faith, but ultimately he will see face to face, just as he himself is seen.

That Christ is believed, acknowledged, and worshiped as the Son of God is not due to flesh and blood but rather to revelation by the Heavenly Father. Those who believe in Him are already saved in hope, since we are able "to comprehend with all the saints what is the breadth and length and height and depth, and to know the love of Christ which surpasses knowledge that we may be filled with the fullness of God" (Eph. 3:18, 19).

Undoubtedly it is necessary for him who desires to praise God rightly to know in what ways God wants to be praised and ought to be honored. There are four principal ways. First, we ought to acknowledge God as omnipotent, of infinite power and majesty. This is the "breadth," which transcends all measure and dimension. A second confession is necessary, that is, that God's wisdom cannot be measured; it stretches from pole to pole and establishes a perfect harmony in all things. This is the "length," which must be comprehended by anyone who wants to praise God rightly. Thirdly—more necessary than these—is to understand the sublimity of the infinite mercy of God and that His compassion overshadows all His other works [the "height"]. Nor should the fourth be forgotten, that is, that His justice is infinite and inflexible and His judgments are unfathomable [the "depth"].

These are the "unsearchable riches of Christ, the mystery hidden for ages in God, who created all things that through the Church the manifold wisdom of God might now be made known to the principalities and powers in the heavenly places. This was according to the eternal purpose which He had realized in Christ Jesus our Lord, in whom we have boldness and confidence of access through our faith in Him" (Eph. 3:8–12).

From the preceding we conclude that if we are to fulfill our debt of praise to God we must know Him, and we cannot know Him if we do not know Christ, because the sublimity of God's mercy is not seen, indeed, *cannot* be seen apart from Christ (*extra Christum*). The guardians of truth among the Jews perceived this when they established the rule that no one with the exception of the Messiah was allowed to use the four letters of the Hebrew name for God, so that neither in writing nor in thought could anyone articulate the name God apart from the Messiah. This was most appropriate, since only in Christ are the four previously stated incomprehensible conditions found all together.

IV. The Predestination of the Saints

From the foregoing it is clear, I think, that it is impossible to praise God without knowledge and love of Him. Nor is it possible to praise God worthily without absolutely certain knowledge of Him, which is attainable only through faith in Christ. For faith means just this, that where knowledge fails and scientific proof is out of the question, nothing remains except faith, hope, and love.

Since faith in Christ is so necessary that without it, it is impossible to please God, and since we are unable to acquire faith by our own means, it is clear that what flesh and blood does not reveal is, doubtless, a gift of God and not the result of our works. Therefore, let no one pride himself that it is because of his merits that he is enrolled among the faithful and let no one claim for nature what properly belongs to grace.

If, however, you attribute your election to nature, and accept your heritage from Adam, you are left, not with faith, hope, and love but with a half-dead man, lame, weakened by wounds, and powerless to perform even his natural tasks, to say nothing of those works which are beyond us and which transcend our every faculty, namely to know God as the Three in One, and to know the Son of God, God of God, Light of Light, who was incarnate, suffered, was crucified, and died.

For even our Augustine, notwithstanding the great reach of his natural insight, had no idea of the depths of mystery of the Incarnation. Therefore, it is most certain that no one can attain to true faith in Christ by his or anyone else's natural insights.

Originally God decided that for His praise and glory men should be created and that all corporeal things should be put at his disposal, but soon the nothingness of His creature came to light. Left to his own devices this creature could not avoid slipping, falling, and reverting to nothingness in his very existence, in his natural capacities, and in his natural actions. And it proved to be even less possible for him not to be deficient in morally good actions.

In order that the whole plan of creation should not be frustrated, there has been ordained preservation by divine power for nature and for free will the grace of the divine Incarnation; and thus natural life is upheld by preservation, a morally good life is sustained by grace, and both by God Himself. Accordingly, before the creation of the world it was determined that no one would be able to do morally good works without the grace of Christ.

Because mercy and justice contribute equally to the praise of the Almighty it has been decreed that some should be elected and predestined to conformation with the image of the Son of God and to faith in our Lord Jesus Christ (Rom. 8:29). But those who do not have faith are judged already (John 3:18).

This [election] is the first grace which precedes nature and works. No one elicits or merits this grace, nor is this grace due to merits foreknown by God, nor to good use of reason in the future foreseen by God, nor to merits already performed. Rather, the sole source of this grace is the most kind and generous will of God.

Once this first grace is given, other graces follow one by one without fail, and Christ is put under obligation to save the elect. That is exactly what He said to Zacchaeus, "It is necessary that I stay in thy house" (Luke 19:5), implying that even this Israelite, this son of Abraham, was elected according to promise. Necessity in the same sense of the word led to Christ's passion, crucifixion, and death for sinners.

These now are the eternal decrees, but beware lest you think you can order them chronologically, for you are limited by the deficiency of human speech. The earthly language that comes from earth is limited to earthly things.

I now ask, faithful soul, that you consider well the things that have been said; truly, you also shall experience this truth which Christ himself taught, namely that "the highest joy on earth is to know that your name is written in heaven" (Luke 10:20).

V. The Call to Faith and Salvation

Paul, illustrious doctor of the Church, tongue of Christ, and the most direct disciple of the most Holy Trinity said: "Those whom He predestined He Himself also called." He did not stay, "He *had* them called" (Rom. 8:30). Many are called by "the light that has arisen over us," others by the law, by prophets, by gifts, by tribulations, by Apostles or preachers of the faith. But not all are elected. However, those who are freely predestined are called without fail in their lifetime unto faith by God's powerful will. For indeed this is not done by Moses nor by the prophets nor by the Apostles, but by God Himself Who speaks to the heart.

Concerning this call the Son said, "No one comes to Me unless the Heavenly Father draws him" (John 6:44). Paul also preached this in an excellent manner: "I planted, Apollos watered, but God gave the growth" (1 Cor. 3:6). For indeed he who plants is nothing, nor he who waters, but He who gives the growth, that is God, is all.

Provided the exterior call is efficacious, then you could certainly say that all who are called will doubtless be justified. For just as God is committed to call all who are predestined, so He is committed to justify all who are called. This is not a natural obligation but an obligation of grace which the Apostle fully appreciates when he says, "He who did not spare His own Son but gave Him up for us all, will He not also give us all things with Him?" (Rom. 8:32).

For just as the knowledge of natural things flows from the knowledge of the first principle, so also each individual grace flows from the grace of predestination. In this and through this, as I have indicated above, Christ has been made the servant of our salvation and "has come into the world not to be ministered to but to minister and to give His life as a ransom for many" (Mark 10:45).

Hence the well-known saying attributed to our own Augustine is by no means defensible in the way in which it is put: "If you are not predestined make yourself predestined." For the gifts and call of God are not the result of penitence. How and by what means God calls men in the Spirit is known to the Spirit of God, which searches the very depths of God, and perhaps to the spirit of the man who is called.

VI. Justification of the Sinner

Those whom He called He also justified. From the beginning God created man righteous and good according to the image and likeness of Christ and in conformity with Christ Who is the luster of the glory of God and the form of His substance. Man has, however, by his own free will involved himself in endless questions, and from that time has fallen and, alas, continues to fall.

First, as you know, man began to question why God had commanded him to abstain from one tree of paradise, while all the others were at his disposal. He pondered whether perhaps it had rotten fruit which looked horrible or tasted bitter. But he saw that the forbidden fruit would be good to eat and was beautiful to the eye and that it was, so to see, delicious. The coldly calculating serpent insinuated himself into the thoughts of an innocent woman, since he knew well that the good of mankind, and indeed of every creature, consists in obedience to God alone. He raised the question of why God had commanded not to eat of the forbidden fruit, and when the wretched woman was caught in the first question a whole infinity of questions followed.

When she had heard that this was a tree of the knowledge of good and evil she did not want to be subject to God but rather she wanted to be like Him. Wrapped up in herself she broke the commandment and rejected obedience, whereby she was brought to naught and to subservience to the devil, the world, and the flesh. Damned to eternal death she was cast into such great misery that she became her own hell, perpetually tortured. She had neither the knowledge nor the will to be freed from this, let alone to free herself.

Oh woeful wretchedness! And worse, we bear this accursed damnation with joy, and serve sin with glee. But the hand of the Lord is not shortened —no, rather the earth is full of the mercy of the Lord and it reaches up to the heavens. Through eternity it was and is and shall be. As the prophet said, "The Lord is good, His mercy is everlasting" (Ps. 100:5). Hence sin is less able to harm us than grace is able to benefit us.

Therefore, God owes to the elect not only the call but also justification. That is, justification by which transgression is reshaped into true obedience to God. This happens at that moment when the sinner's eyes are opened again by the grace of God so that he is able to know the true God by faith. Then his heart is set afire so that God becomes pleasing to him. Both of these are nothing but grace, and flow from the merits of Christ, be they foreseen or already displayed. Our works do not, nor can they, bring us to this state, since man's nature is incapable of knowing or wanting or doing good. For this barren man God is sheer fear.

The sinner is justified by regeneration when he is reborn through water and the Holy Spirit. This is not a carnal but a spiritual birth, since that which is born of the flesh is flesh and that which is born of the spirit is spirit. He is reborn "not of blood nor of the will of flesh nor of the will of man but of God" (John 1:13). He is reborn not by necessity but by God's free election, for the Spirit breathes where He will.

He is reborn unto heaven, therefore necessarily not to himself but to Christ. Indeed "no one ascended into heaven except He Who descended from heaven, the Son of man who is in heaven" (John 3:13). He is reborn unto Christ, not unto his own righteousness. Because "just as Moses lifted up the serpent in the wilderness, so the Son of man must be lifted up in order that those who believe in Him might not perish but have eternal life" (John 3:14–15). In this regeneration God is the father, the will is the mother, and the seed is the means by which the merits of our Lord Jesus Christ sprout forth.

Where these three come together a son of God is born, justified, and made alive through faith active in love: that is to say, active through the fire of our love, set afire by the love of Him who is the only perpetual fire, coming down from heaven. All other fires have lost their spell. This fire makes God pleasing and acceptable to us, so that not only what is contrary to God but also that which is not God becomes displeasing to us. This fire is the grace which makes acceptable (*gratia gratum faciens*). It does not, as many people say, make man acceptable to God, since election itself has already done this; rather, it makes God alone pleasing and acceptable to man through the love which restores the obedience stolen by concupiscence. Through this love we are and live upright and just, not for ourselves but for God.

VII. The Elect on the Way to Glory

After the justification of the sinner his progress to glory follows without fail. This progress of the justified ends in the state of glory of the saints at that time when God most generously gives the eternal reward to each one according to his labors. And faith declares that those who do good works go forth into eternal life and those who do evil, into eternal fire. No one receives less than he merits but often more.

The Scriptures say that our perdition comes from ourselves and our salvation comes from God alone. And the Gospel says that just as the branches do not bear fruit unless they abide on the vine, so we do not bear fruit unless we abide in Christ. Those who abide in Christ and Christ in them bear much fruit. St. Paul, the most profound of all, says clearly in his writings that *we* do not live and even less do *we* work but Christ lives in us. From these and other passages wise men conclude that God rewards only His own work, knowing that He Himself gives grace and glory.

Scripture is clear concerning the first grace of justification, but regarding eternal life the diversity of witness raises some doubt. However, it ought to be remembered that God is the universal, principal, and most immediate cause of each individual thing and the prime agent of all actions. Therefore, though there are different kinds of work, it is one God who works all in all.

Thus it is God's work to make heat in the fire, it is He Who laughs in those who laugh, cries in those who cry, whinnies in the horse, roars in the lion; these works flow from nature. And there are greater works than these, namely, to know, to choose, and to do, but even these works still flow from nature, though from human nature. Therefore, all these natural works fall short of deserving eternal reward.

God accomplishes other works in us, works informed by faith that is alive and active in love. These works are more His than ours, for in justification love is poured into man, his will is set afire by the exceedingly great love of God and he receives the grace by which God becomes pleasing to him. As I said above, we call this the grace that makes acceptable not us to God but Him to us. For by the grace of predestination we are made acceptable to God. Then certainly this fire kindled by the heavenly flame does not die down but surges up until it reaches its origin, the love of God, the very place of the aforementioned eternal fire. This place is Jesus Christ, God and man. Since all works which flow from this fire go out from Christ and return to Christ, therefore these works are in a very true sense the works of Christ. But they are executed by men and they are finite; they are only imputed to God.

Still other works are the works performed by Christ Himself, the personal actions and suffering of our Lord Jesus Christ which He did and sustained for our salvation. Such are the works of the infinite Divine Person.

If now it is asked whether Christ is obliged to reward our good works with eternal life or, to say it more emphatically, whether God is bound to give Himself for our works, I answer "No" with regard to the first kind of works [that is, the natural works]. Christ is not bound to do this because those works take place outside of faith active in love and do not deserve to be called good works.

As regards the second kind, in view of the fact that these are the works of a finite person they are finite by nature. Therefore it is impossible to found upon them a righteousness of infinite merit to which an infinite reward is due. If, then, God decreed to give himself as reward for such works, this is grace and not justice.

We ought not to doubt, however, the merits of Christ [that is, the third kind], knowing, as we do, that He is both God and man and that His claim to be equal with God was not presumptuous. Therefore the merits of Christ entitle us to enter the eternal kingdom. It is with regard to the call of the elect soul to this kingdom that God has said: "Come quickly to me, my friend, my dear one, my dove." He went on to say: "[Settle down] within the holes in the rock," that is, "in the wounds of Christ"[2] (Song of Sol. 2:14) and "in the open cave," that is, "in the opening to the heart of Christ," whence the power of the sacraments bursts forth; and then added: "Show me your face, and make your voice heard in my ears, your voice will be sweet and your face beautiful."

VIII. The Works of the Justified Man

The man who is predestined, called, and justified surely does not live his life without good conduct and holy works. The justified man cannot but love. He loves God above all things and his neighbor according to the law. He has a love which is impatient with idleness. But granted by grace, this love brings Christ into the heart and in Christ obedience, contrition, and righteousness and thus a renewal of life. Christ is put on and Adam is cast out. He magnifies the life of Christ and damns the life of Adam, with its disobedience, iniquity, and self-indulgence. Those things that had characterized Adam he does not imitate, he hates them; and spontaneously he begins to follow the goodness, obedience, and resignation of Christ, so that just as through grace he holds Christ in his heart, so even more abundantly he strives to show Him in his action.

From Adam we inherit self-love, self-interested love, a distorted sense of values, blindness in judgment, and thus wickedness in works. From Christ comes love of God to the point of disregard for one's self, love of justice to the point of disregard of one's own life, clarity of judgment to the point of realization of our own stupidity, and hence goodness in our works.

Our hearts are fired to do these things by the inestimable love of God Who offered up to a most shameful death Christ burning with love for us.

Our hearts are fired to the works of Adam by the accursed concupiscence, through which true goodness becomes odious to us, the contrived things seem delightful, the eternal things are without savor, temporal things do not satisfy, the inner life is not considered; only external things console.

Thus our thinking is enslaved and our will is bound, so that all wisdom of the world, all intelligence, knowledge, and prudence become so subservient to concupiscence that it seems they were meant to serve only its purposes.

Quite rightly, therefore, is the wisdom of this world, even its highest achievement, deemed folly by God. Indeed, what serves concupiscence cannot be elevated to the knowledge of God, for he who begins with self-love cannot get beyond himself. Therefore, human acts performed without faith in Christ (*extra fidem Christi*) cannot serve God but only mammon. Hence I shall not even consider such works but pass them by as useless, not to say, impediments to salvation.

Rather let me now turn to those works we do in Christ renewed by grace, works that issue from the love of God and are directed to it. These works are not self-centered but Christ-centered. The mind is rededicated to God, the works start to become good and now possess characteristics of goodness which they never had without faith (*extra fidem*). These works display love which makes faith alive, faith which without works is said to be dead (James 2:26) and indeed is dead. No predestined adult ever dies without having performed such works, because they issue from God and return to God. They please the Most High and are graciously accepted as worthy of eternal reward.

Far more exalted are the merits of Christ Himself, His actions, sufferings, and death, for by nature He was and is the Son of God. His merits are given to us to be ours and on them we found and build our firm hope, for we know our hope is firmly founded on them. Only Christ's own merits can one call merit of full worthiness (*meritum condigni*). They are sufficient alone to save all Christianity or indeed the whole world. Through them the little children are saved and sometimes those still in the womb are sanctified. Through them guilt is absolved, and punishment is mitigated and remitted.

Since justification is due to grace and not to nature, since acceptation of works performed in grace is grace, and since it is again grace that the merits of Christ are made ours, it is appropriate to attribute the whole Christian life to grace. And thus the claim for man, namely, that he is master over his works from beginning to the end, is destroyed. So, therefore, the origin of the works of Christian life is predestination, its means is justification, and its aim is glorification or thanksgiving—all these are the achievements not of nature but of grace.

IX. The Marriage of Christ and the Christian

Perhaps you would like me now to state briefly how the merits of Christ really become ours. As you know, between Christ and the Christian there is a true, nay the truest, marriage of which our earthly marriage is the sacrament, and but a shadow in comparison with the sacred marriage of Christ [with the Church]. Hence the uprightness of human marriage consists in conformity to the true marriage of Christ and the Church. For, as the Apostle said: “Husbands, love your wives just as Christ loved the Church” (Eph. 5:25).

In human marriage there are two in one flesh. In the marriage with Christ there are no longer two, but there is one flesh—Christ and the Christian are one flesh, one spirit. And just as Christ left his father and mother to join his spouse, the Christian, so the Christian leaves father and mother to join Christ.

For the following reason, however, the contract between Christ and the Christian differs greatly from that between man and wife. The contract between man and wife requires that each one gives himself to the other, so that the man belongs to the woman and the woman to the man by free consent, and man has power over the body of woman as woman has over the body of man. But they wield no power over each other’s spirit, nor does the one have the other as a servant. Rather, they are partners and help each other in procreation. The marriage claim which the spouses have on each other is therefore limited and not all-embracing.

The contract between Christ and the Church is consummated thus: “I accept you as Mine, I accept you as My concern, I accept you into Myself.” And conversely the Church, or the soul, says to Christ, “I accept You as mine, You are my concern, I accept You into myself.” In other words Christ says, “The Christian is My possession, the Christian is My concern, the Christian is I”; so the spouse responds, “Christ is my possession, Christ is my concern, Christ is I.”

The first vow is the same as human marital vows, but the other two transcend them. By virtue of the first vow the Christian receives that which every spouse ought to give the other according to matrimonial law. By virtue of the second the Christian receives all the benefits, none excluded, that come to him from Christ himself; and by virtue of the third vow he is Christ as much as he is himself.

The first vow: Concerning the betrothal to Christ and the marriage with Him the prophets Isaiah and Jeremiah have spoken and David has sung: “He has set His tabernacle in the sun and He Himself comes as a bridegroom to His marriage bed. He exults like a giant as He goes on His way.

His going out is from the highest heaven and His meeting with the heights of it" (Ps. 19:4–6).

The second vow: Regarding "His concern with me and not with himself," the bride has explicitly said, "My beloved is my concern and I am His" (Song of Sol. 2:16; 6:2). I am His by right and He is mine by grace. And later she said more modestly, "I am my beloved's and His desire is toward me" (Song of Sol. 7:10). And Isaiah says, "Unto us a Child is born, unto us a Son is given" (Isa. 9:6).

The third vow: Concerning His becoming one with us, all Scriptures agree that Christ is in us and we in Him, especially where Christ said that He gave himself up for His disciples so that they might be one. To which he added, "I am in them, as You, O Father, are in Me, so that they might be completely one" (John 17:23).

From all this it follows that all things which Christ, the Incarnate Word, possesses, He makes ours by the assumption of human nature. He has given us all things for our salvation, as Scripture says: God, Who did not spare His own Son but delivered Him up for us all, will He not surely give us all things with Him?" (Rom. 8:32).

Finally, if Christ is I, I have a claim to heaven, I have hope, and I glory in that hope which belongs to the children of God; and more than that I also glory in all things which directly or indirectly foster hope.

• • •

XI. The Transference of Our Sin to Christ

If you think that the mercy of the Lord has not been given its due by showing how He justifies us through His own righteousness and how He did not shun marriage with sinners, you must realize that He goes even further. He makes our sins His own. Just as the Christian is just through the righteousness of Christ, so Christ is unrighteous and sinful through the guilt of the Christian.

Whereas the Jew would say "blasphemy" and the Greek "madness" the believer says, "You are right." The Jew is affronted, the Greek ridicules, the believer rejoices. Thus "we preach Christ crucified, a stumbling block to Jews and folly to Gentiles, but to those who are called, both Jews and Greeks, Christ, the power and wisdom of God" (1 Cor. 1:23–24). For it pleased God to overcome strength by weakness, to subjugate wisdom by foolishness, to condemn righteousness by sin "so that no one might take pride in himself before God" (1 Cor. 1:29).

For the time being let us be silent about other issues and let us see whether He who is sinless by nature can be convicted as a sinner. He stands clearly convicted by his own confession: "God, my God, why have You forsaken me? Why are You so far from helping me who is involved in transgressions?" (Ps. 22:1).

How can these be Your words, dearest Jesus? I see the answer clearly: God has placed upon You the iniquity of all and You alone are the Lamb of God Who bears the sins of the world. You are like the two goats at one and the same time. In Your human nature You are sacrificed by lot to the Lord for sin; as immortal God You live in eternity and hence are like the goat that was sent out. They put on Your head all the iniquities of the sons of Israel and all their trespasses and sins. You were sent forth into a barren land where no one dwells except God.

You are that matchless Spouse that is my possession, that is my concern, that is I. Therefore, You are mine and everything You have is my own and I am Yours and whatever there is in me is Your own. And because we are one, things which are Yours become mine while yet remaining Yours, and, likewise, things which are mine become Yours while at the same time they remain mine.[3]

Therefore I am righteous because of Your righteousness and a sinner because of my guilt.[4] You are a sinner because of my guilt and righteous because of Your own righteousness. By the same token, I am strong through Your power but weakened by my own feebleness. You are weakened by my feebleness and strong in Your own power. I am wise in Your wisdom and foolish in my stupidity. You are wise in Your wisdom and foolish in my stupidity.

• • •

XXIV. Self-resignation for the Benefit of the Church and the Praise of God

The last sign of true faith is the gift of healing, which spiritually seen is the mutual assistance Christians give each other, since they are united in Christ, in one Spirit and one Baptism. The sole purpose of this mutual aid is the increase of the praise of God. If it furthers this purpose to yield our merits to others, we should be prepared to abandon everything that nature and grace have bestowed upon us, even Christ Himself.

"See, with this apex of obedience and resignation, man powerfully created out of nothing and mercifully redeemed from sin, reduced to nothingness by himself, return to his origin with constant praise, through Jesus Christ our Lord."

Notes

1. See David C. Steinmetz, *Reformers in the Wings* (Philadelphia: Fortress Press, 1971), 18–29; Steinmetz, *Luther and Staupitz: An Essay in the Intellectual Origins of the Reformation* (Durham, N.C.: Duke University Press, 1980); and Heiko A. Oberman, *Masters of the Reformation* (Cambridge: Cambridge University Press, 1981), 75–91.

2. In his note here, Oberman points out that Luther reported that Staupitz directed him to give up his speculative concern about predestination and to focus on the wounds of Christ, in which "predestination is grasped and found, nowhere else." This was advice that Luther passed on to persons he counseled who were agitated by the same concern.

3. Oberman indicates Staupitz's independence of the medieval tradition that considered guilt and righteousness to be two successive stages, whereas for Staupitz "they are two aspects of the life in Christ." Oberman judges this to be "the closest parallel in pre-Reformation documents to Luther's *simul iustus et peccator* [at once sinner and justified]."

4. Compare Luther's *The Freedom of a Christian* (see vol. 2:105–6), where Luther uses the marriage analogy in a similar manner as Staupitz does here to depict the "happy exchange" that takes place between Christ and the believer.

4. Paraclesis

(1516)

Desiderius Erasmus

Renaissance humanism, which first emerged in fourteenth-century Italy, was an intellectual movement intent on renewing the study of the liberal arts (grammar, rhetoric, literature, history, moral philosophy) in order to bring about a more cultivated and complete humanity. Humanists revered the writings of classical antiquity, both Greek and Latin. Many humanists, especially those in northern Europe, wanted to revive interest not only in classical antiquity, but also in early Christianity. These Christian humanists cultivated a new appreciation of the Bible and of the writers of the early church (such as Jerome, Augustine, and Chrysostom), hoping to stimulate reform in church and society.

Desiderius Erasmus (c. 1466–1536) was the most important representative of Christian humanism. He was a great classical scholar, editing, translating, and publishing Greek and Latin authors. He culled proverbs from these authors for his own adages, interpreting classical sayings to make them more meaningful for his own day. For instance, Dulce bellum inexpertis, or "Sweet is war to those who have not experienced it," allowed him to write about the fruitlessness and the horrors of war. Although Erasmus was a scholar, he was also a popularizer of the classics. He wanted to make them available to all persons to help them become more educated and moral human beings.

Erasmus was also a Christian theologian, a biblical and textual scholar who edited, translated, and interpreted the New Testament and

---

SOURCE: John C. Olin, ed., *Christian Humanism and the Reformation: Selected Writings of Erasmus*, 2d ed. (New York: Fordham University, 1975). Used by permission.

ancient Greek and Latin church writings. As with the classics, he wanted the New Testament to be known and used by ordinary Christians. In the Paraclesis *(*Exhortation*), an introduction to his 1516 edition of the New Testament, he writes that "Christ wishes His mysteries published as openly as possible. I would that even the lowliest women read the Gospels and the Pauline Epistles, . . . that the farmer sing some portion of them at the plow, the weaver hum some parts of them to the movement of his shuttle, the traveler lighten the weariness of the journey with stories of this kind."*

Erasmus did not consider his classical scholarship and his Christian witness to be in conflict. He believed that the philosophy of Christ had much in common with the classics. "[W]hat else is the philosophy of Christ, which he himself calls a rebirth, than the restoration of human nature originally well formed? By the same token, although no one has taught this more perfectly and effectively than Christ, nevertheless one may find in the books of the pagans very much which does agree with His teaching."

The Protestant reformers were mixed in their response to Erasmus. Ulrich Zwingli agreed with his positive assessment of the writings of ancient Greece and Rome. For Martin Luther, however, Erasmus's call for the reform of church and society based on the teachings of the New Testament and early church writings did not go far enough. Luther was persuaded that Christian humanism, even though committed to the removal of the moral and spiritual abuses of the church, was not concerned enough with the reformation of doctrine.

The major impact of Erasmus's thought on the Protestant reformers came through his work on the New Testament. Between 1516 and 1535 he produced five Latin editions of the New Testament with Greek text. His fresh Latin translations, which in many places revised the centuries-old Vulgate text, and his expanding annotations explaining the reasons for his changes in translation and his interpretations of the text were used by all the reformers. Luther relied on Erasmus's 1519 edition of the New Testament when he made his German translation at the Wartburg castle in 1522.

The Greek text of Erasmus's edition, called the textus receptus*, or the "received text," lies behind all early English translations of the New Testament, from William Tyndale's version in 1525 to the King James Version in 1611. It was not until the Revised Version of 1881 that new manuscript traditions materially affected English translations. Tyndale's translation also leaned on Erasmus's Latin translation and, in an interesting way, influenced the development of Congregationalism. This* *is because Erasmus translated the Greek word* ekklesia *(church) into the Latin word* congregatio, *which Tyndale in turn translated into the English word* congregation.

While his New Testament edition was intended for a scholarly audience, his Paraphrases on the New Testament *(1517–1524), especially as translated into the vernacular, had a more popular appeal. They were widely read in both the Continental and English Reformations. Erasmus's* Paraclesis *captures the essence of his Christian humanism.*

Paraclesis

The illustrious Lactantius Firmianus, good reader, whose eloquence Jerome especially admires, as he begins to defend the Christian religion against the pagans desires especially an eloquence second only to Cicero's be given him, thinking it wrong, I believe, to want an equal eloquence.[1] But I indeed might heartily wish, if anything is to be gained by wishes of this kind, so long as I exhort all men to the most holy and wholesome study of Christian philosophy and summon them as if with the blast of a trumpet, that an eloquence far different from Cicero's be given me: an eloquence certainly much more efficacious, if less ornate than his. Or rather [I might wish for that kind of eloquence], if such power of speech was ever granted anyone, as the tales of the ancient poets not entirely without cause attributed to Mercury, who as if with a magic wand and a divine lyre induces sleep when he wishes and likewise snatches sleep away, plunging whom he wished into hell and again calling them forth from hell; or as the ancient tales assigned to Amphion and Orpheus, one of whom is supposed to have moved hard rocks, the other to have attracted oaks and ashes with a lyre; or as the Gauls ascribed to their Ogmius, leading about whither he wished all men by little chains fastened to their ears from his tongue; or as fabled antiquity attributed to Marsyas; or really, lest we linger too long on fables, as Alcibiades imputed to Socrates and old comedy to Pericles, an eloquence which not only captivates the ear with its fleeting delight but which leaves a lasting sting in the minds of its hearers, which grips, which transforms, which sends away a far different listener than it had received. One reads that the noble musician Timotheus, singing Doric melodies, was wont to rouse Alexander the Great to a desire for war. Nor were they lacking in former times who considered nothing more effective than the entreaties which the Greeks call *epodes*. But if there were any such kind of incantation anywhere, if there were any power of song which truly could inspire, if any Pytho truly swayed the heart, I would desire that it be at hand for me so that I might convince all of the most wholesome truth of all. However, it is more desirable that Christ Himself, whose business we are about, so guide the strings of our lyre that this song might deeply affect and move the minds of all, and, in fact, to accomplish this there is no need for the syllogisms and exclamations of the orators. What we desire is that nothing may stand forth with greater certainty than the truth itself, whose expression is the more powerful, the simpler it is.

And in the first place it is not pleasing to renew at the present time this complaint, not entirely new but, alas, only too just—and perhaps never more just than in these days—that when men are devoting themselves with such ardent spirit to all their studies, this philosophy of Christ alone is derided by some, even Christians, is neglected by many, and is discussed by a few, but in a cold manner (I shall not say insincerely). Moreover, in all other branches of learning which human industry has brought forth, nothing is so hidden and obscure which the keenness of genius has not explored, nothing is so difficult which tremendous exertion has not overcome. Yet how is it that even those of us who profess to be Christian fail to embrace with the proper spirit this philosophy alone? Platonists, Pythagoreans, Academics, Stoics, Cynics, Peripatetics, Epicureans not only have a deep understanding of the doctrines of their respective sects, but they commit them to memory, and they fight fiercely in their behalf, willing even to die rather than abandon the defense of their author. Then why do not we evince far greater spirit for Christ, our Author and Prince? Who does not judge it very shameful for one professing Aristotle's philosophy not to know that man's opinion about the causes of lightning, about prime matter, about the infinite? And neither does this knowledge render a man happy, nor does the lack of it render him unhappy. And do not we, initiated in so many ways, drawn by so many sacraments to Christ, think it shameful and base to know nothing of His doctrines, which offer the most certain happiness to all? But what purpose is served to exaggerate the matter by controversy, since it is what I might call a kind of wicked madness to wish to compare Christ with Zeno or Aristotle and His teaching with, to put it mildly, the paltry precepts of those men? Let them magnify the leaders of their sect as much as they can or wish. Certainly He alone was a teacher who came forth from heaven, He alone could teah certain doctrine, since it is eternal wisdom, He alone, the sole author of human salvation, taught what pertains to salvation, He alone fully vouches for whatsoever He taught, He alone is able to grant whatsoever He has promised. If anything is brought to us from the Chaldeans or Egyptians, we desire more eagerly to examine it because of the fact that it comes from a strange world, and part of its value is to have come from far off; and oftentimes we are anxiously tormented by the fancies of an insignificant man, not to say an impostor, not only to no avail but with great loss of time (I am not adding a more serious note, for the matter as it stands is most serious). But why does not such a desire also excite Christian minds who are convinced—and it is a fact—that this teaching has come not from Egypt or Syria but from heaven itself? Why do not all of us ponder within ourselves that this must be a new and wonderful kind of philosophy since, in order to transmit it to mortals, He who was God became man, He who was immortal became mortal, He who was in the heart of the Father descended to earth? It must be a great matter, and in no sense a commonplace one, whatever it is, because that wondrous Author came to teach after so many families of distinguished philosophers, after so many remarkable prophets. Why, then, out of pious curiosity do we not investigate, examine, explore each tenet? Especially since this kind of wisdom, so extraordinary that once for all it renders foolish the entire wisdom of this world, may be drawn from its few books as from the most limpid springs with far less labor than Aristotle's doctrine is extracted from so many obscure volumes, from those huge commentaries of the interpreters at odds with one another—and I shall not add with how much greater reward. Indeed, here there is no requirement that you approach equipped with so many troublesome sciences. The journey is simple, and it is ready for anyone. Only bring a pious and open mind, possessed above all with a pure and simple faith. Only be docile, and you have advanced far in this philosophy. It itself supplies inspiration as a teacher which communicates itself to no one more gladly than to minds that are without guile. The teachings of the others, besides the fact that they give hope of a false happiness, drive off the natural talents of many by the very difficulty, it is clear, of their precepts. This doctrine in an equal degree accommodates itself to all, lowers itself to the little ones, adjusts itself to their measure, nourishing them with milk, bearing, fostering, sustaining them, doing everything until we grow in Christ. Again, not only does it serve the lowliest, but it is also an object of wonder to those at the top. And the more you shall have progressed in its riches, the more you shall have withdrawn it from the shadow of the power of any other. It is a small affair to the little ones and more than the highest affair to the great. It casts aside no age, no sex, no fortune or position in life. The sun itself is not as common and accessible to all as is Christ's teaching. It keeps no one at a distance, unless a person, begrudging himself, keeps himself away.

Indeed, I disagree very much with those who are unwilling that Holy Scripture, translated into the vulgar tongue, be read by the uneducated, as if Christ taught such intricate doctrines that they could scarcely be understood by very few theologians, or as if the strength of the Christian religion consisted in men's ignorance of it. The mysteries of kings, perhaps, are better concealed, but Christ wishes his mysteries published as openly as possible. I would that even the lowliest women read the Gospels and the Pauline Epistles. And I would that they were translated into all languages so that they could be read and understood not only by Scots and Irish but also by Turks and Saracens. Surely the first step is to understand in one way or another. It may be that many will ridicule, but some may be taken captive. Would that, as a result, the farmer sing some portion of them at the plow, the weaver hum some parts of them to the movement of his shuttle, the traveller lighten the weariness of the journey with stories of this kind! Let all the conversations of every Christian be drawn from this source. For in general our daily conversations reveal what we are. Let each one comprehend what he can, let him express what he can. Whoever lags behind, let him not envy him who is ahead; whoever is in the front rank, let him encourage him who follows, not despair of him. Why do we restrict a profession common to all to a few? For it is not fitting, since Baptism is common in an equal degree to all Christians, wherein there is the first profession of Christian philosophy, and since the other sacraments and at length the reward of immortality belong equally to all, that doctrines alone should be reserved for those very few whom today the crowd call theologians or monks, the very persons whom, although they comprise one of the smallest parts of the Christian populace, yet I might wish to be in greater measure what they are styled. For I fear that one may find among the theologians men who are far removed from the title they bear, that is, men who discuss earthly matters, not divine, and that among the monks who profess the poverty of Christ and the contempt of the world you may find something more than worldliness. To me he is truly a theologian who teaches not by skill with intricate syllogisms but by a disposition of mind, by the very expression and the eyes, by his very life that riches should be disdained, that the Christian should not put his trust in the supports of this world but must rely entirely on heaven, that a wrong should not be avenged, that a good should be wished for those wishing ill, that we should deserve well of those deserving ill, that all good men should be loved and cherished equally as members of the same body, that the evil should be tolerated if they cannot be corrected, that those who are stripped of their goods, those who are turned away from possessions, those who mourn are blessed and should not be deplored, and that death should even be desired by the devout, since it is nothing other than a passage to immortality. And if anyone under the inspiration of the spirit of Christ preaches this kind of doctrine, inculcates it, exhorts, incites, and encourages men to it, he indeed is truly a theologian, even if he should be a common laborer or weaver. And if anyone exemplifies this doctrine in his life itself, he is in fact a great doctor. Another, perhaps, even a non-Christian, may discuss more subtly how the angels understand, but to persuade us to lead here an angelic life, free from every stain, this indeed is the duty of the Christian theologian.

But if anyone objects that these notions are somewhat stupid and vulgar, I should respond to him only that Christ particularly taught these rude doctrines, that the Apostles inculcated them, that however vulgar they are, they have brought forth for us so many sincerely Christian and so great a throng of illustrious martyrs. This philosophy, unlettered as it appears to these very objectors, has drawn the highest princes of the world and so many kingdoms and peoples to its laws, an achievement which the power of tyrants and the erudition of philosophers cannot claim. Indeed I do not object to having that latter wisdom, if it seems worthwhile, discussed among the educated. But let the lowly mass of Christians console themselves certainly with this title because, whether the Apostles knew or other Fathers understood these subtleties or not, they surely didn't teach them. If princes in the execution of their duties would manifest what I have referred to as a vulgar doctrine, if priests would inculcate it in sermons, if schoolmasters would instill it in students rather than that erudition which they draw from the fonts of Aristotle and Averroës, Christendom would not be so disturbed on all sides by almost continuous war, everything would not be boiling over with such a mad desire to heap up riches by fair means or foul, every subject, sacred as well as profane, would not be made to resound everywhere with so much noisy disputation, and, finally, we would not differ from those who do not profess the philosophy of Christ merely in name and ceremonial. For upon these three ranks of men principally the task of either renewing or advancing the Christian religion has been placed: on the princes and the magistrates who serve in their place, on the bishops and their delegated priests, and on those who instruct the young eager for all knowledge. If it happen that they, having laid aside their own affairs, should sincerely cooperate in Christ, we should certainly see in not so many years a true and, as Paul says, a genuine race of Christians everywhere emerge, a people who would restore the philosophy of Christ not in ceremonies alone and in syllogistic propositions but in the heart itself and in the whole life. The enemies of the Christian name will far more quickly be drawn to the faith of Christ by these weapons than by threats or arms. In the conquest of every citadel nothing is more powerful than the truth itself. He is not a Platonist who has not read the works of Plato; and is he a theologian, let alone a Christian, who has not read the literature of Christ? Who loves me,

Christ says, keeps my word, a distinguishing mark which He himself prescribed. Therefore, if we are truly and sincerely Christian, if we truly believe in Him who has been sent from Heaven to teach us that which the wisdom of the philosophers could not do, if we truly expect from Him what no prince, however powerful, can give, why is anything more important to us than His literature? Why indeed does anything seem learned that is not in harmony with His decrees? Why in the case of this literature that should be revered do we also allow ourselves, and I shall say almost to a greater extent than do the secular interpreters in the case of the imperial laws or the books of the physicians, to speak whatever comes to mind, to distort, to obscure? We drag heavenly doctrines down to the level of our own life as if it were a Lydian rule, and while we seek to avoid by every means appearing to be ignorant and for this reason gather in whatever is of account in secular literature, that which is of special value in Christian philosophy I shall not say we corrupt, but—and no one can deny it—we restrict to a few, although Christ wished nothing to be more public. In this kind of philosophy, located as it is more truly in the disposition of the mind than in syllogisms, life means more than debate, inspiration is preferable to erudition, transformation is a more important matter than intellectual comprehension. Only a very few can be learned, but all can be Christian, all can be devout, and—I shall boldly add—all can be theologians.

Indeed, this philosophy easily penetrates into the minds of all, an action in especial accord with human nature. Moreover, what else is the philosophy of Christ, which He himself calls a rebirth, than the restoration of human nature originally well formed? By the same token, although no one has taught this more perfectly and more effectively than Christ, nevertheless one may find in the books of the pagans very much which does agree with His teaching. There was never so coarse a school of philosophy that taught that money rendered a man happy. Nor has there ever been one so shameless that fixed the chief good in those vulgar honors and pleasures. The Stoics understood that no one was wise unless he was good; they understood that nothing was truly good or noble save real virtue and nothing fearful or evil save baseness alone. According to Plato, Socrates teaches in many different ways that a wrong must not be repaid with a wrong, and also that since the soul is immortal, those should not be lamented who depart this life for a happier one with the assurance of having led an upright life. In addition, he teaches that the soul must be drawn away from the inclinations of the body and led to those which are its real objectives although they are not seen. Aristotle has written in the *Politics* that nothing can be a delight to us, even though it is not in any way despised, except virtue alone. Epicurus also acknowledges that nothing in man's life can bring delight unless the mind is conscious of no evil, from which awareness true pleasure gushes forth as from a spring. What shall we say of this, that many—notably Socrates, Diogenes, and Epictetus—have presented a good portion of His teaching? But since Christ both taught and presented the same doctrine so much more fully, is it not a monstrous thing that Christians either disregard or neglect or even ridicule it? If there are things that belong particularly to Christianity in these ancient writers, let us follow them. But if these alone can truly make a Christian, why do we consider them as almost more obsolete and replaced than the Mosaic books? The first step, however, is to know what He taught; the next is to carry it into effect. Therefore, I believe, anyone should not think himself to be Christian if he disputes about instances, relations, quiddities, and formalities with an obscure and irksome confusion of words, but rather if he holds and exhibits what Christ taught and showed forth. Not that I condemn the industry of those who not without merit employ their native intellectual powers in such subtle discourse, for I do not wish anyone to be offended, but that I think, and rightly so, unless I am mistaken, that that pure and genuine philosophy of Christ is not to be drawn from any source more abundantly than from the evangelical books and from the Apostolic Letters, about which, if anyone should devoutly philosophize, praying more than arguing and seeking to be transformed rather than armed for battle, he would without a doubt find that there is nothing pertaining to the happiness of man and the living of his life which is not taught, examined, and unraveled in these works. If we desire to learn, why is another author more pleasing than Christ himself? If we seek a model for life, why does another example take precedence for us over that of Christ himself? If we wish some medicine against the troublesome desires of the soul, why do we think the remedy to be more at hand somewhere else? If we want to arouse a soul that is idle and growing listless by reading, where, I ask, will you find sparks equally alive and efficacious? If the soul seems distracted by the vexations of this life, why are other delights more pleasing? Why have we steadfastly preferred to learn the wisdom of Christ from the writings of men than from Christ himself? And He, since He promised to be with us all days, even unto the consummation of the world, stands forth especially in this literature, in which He lives for us even at this time, breathes and speaks, I should say almost more effectively than when He dwelt among men. The Jews saw and heard less than you see and hear in the books of the Gospels, to the extent that you make use of your eyes and ears, whereby this can be perceived and heard.

And what kind of a situation is this, I ask? We preserve the letters written by a dear friend, we kiss them fondly, we carry them about, we read them again and again, yet there are many thousands of Christians who, although they are learned in other respects, never read, however, the evangelical and apostolic books in an entire lifetime. The Mohammedans hold fast to their doctrines, the Jews also today from the very cradle study the books of Moses. Why do not we in the same way distinguish ourselves in Christ? Those who profess the way of life of Benedict hold, study, absorb a rule written by man, and by one nearly uneducated for the uneducated. Those who are in the Augustinian order are well versed in the rule of their founder. The Franciscans reverence and love the little traditions of their Francis, and to whatever corner of the earth they go, they carry them with them; they do not feel safe unless the little book is on their person. Why do these men attribute more to a rule written by man than does the Christian world to its rule, which Christ delivered to all and which all have equally professed in baptism? Finally, although you may even cite a thousand rules, can anything be holier than this? And I wish that this may come to pass: just as Paul wrote that the law of Moses was not full of glory compared with the glory of the Gospel succeeding it, so may all Christians hold the Gospels and Letters of the Apostles as so holy that in comparison with them these other writings do not seem holy. What others may wish to concede to Albert the Great, to Alexander, to Thomas, to Egidio, to Richard, to Occam, they will certainly be free, as far as I am concerned, to do, for I do not want to diminish the fame of anyone or contend with the studies of men that are now of long standing.[2] However learned these may be, however subtle, however seraphic, if they like, yet they must admit that the former are the most tried and true. Paul wishes that the spirits of those prophesying be judged whether they are of God. Augustine, reading every kind of book with discretion, asks nothing more than a just hearing also for his own works. But in this literature alone [i.e., Holy Scripture] what I do not comprehend, I nevertheless revere. It is no school of theologians who has attested to this Author for us but the Heavenly Father Himself through the testimony of the divine voice, and He has done this on two occasions: first at the Jordan at the time of the Baptism, then on Mount Tabor at the Transfiguration. "This is my beloved Son," He says, "in whom I am well pleased; hear Him" [Matt. 3:17; 17:5]. O solid and truly irrefragable authority, as the theologians say! What is this phrase, "Hear Him"? Certainly He is the one and only teacher, let us be the disciples of Him alone. Let each one extol in his studies his own author as much as he will wish, this utterance has been said without exception of Christ alone. A dove first descended on Him, the confirmation of the Father's testimony. Peter next bears His spirit, to whom the highest Pastor three times entrusted the feeding of His sheep, feeding them without a doubt, however, on the food of Christian doctrine [John 21:15 ff.]. This spirit was born again, as it were, in Paul, whom He himself called a "chosen vessel" and an extraordinary herald of His name [Acts 9:15]. What John had drawn from that sacred font of His heart, he expressed in his own writings. What, I pray, is like this in Scotus (I do not wish that this remark be taken as a pretext for abuse), what is like this in Thomas? Nevertheless, I admire the talents of the one, and I also revere the sanctity of the other. But why do not all of us apply ourselves to philosophy in these authors of such great value? Why do we not carry them about on our persons, have them ever in our hands? Why do we not hunt through these authors, thoroughly examine them, assiduously investigate them? Why devote the greater part of life to Averroës rather than to the Gospels? Why spend nearly all of life on the ordinances of men and on opinions in contradiction with themselves? The latter, in fact, may now be the views of the more eminent theologians, if you please; but certainly the first steps of the great theologian in the days to come will be in these authors [of Holy Scripture].

Let all those of us who have pledged in baptism in the words prescribed by Christ, if we have pledged sincerely, be directly imbued with the teachings of Christ in the midst of the very embraces of parents and the caresses of nurses. For that which the new earthen pot of the soul first imbibes settles most deeply and clings most tenaciously. Let the first lispings utter Christ, let earliest childhood be formed by the Gospels of Him whom I would wish particularly presented in such a way that children also might love Him. For as the severity of some teachers causes children to hate literature before they come to know it, so there are those who make the philosophy of Christ sad and morose, although nothing is more sweet than it. In these studies, then, let them engage themselves until at length in silent growth they mature into strong manhood in Christ. The literature of others is such that many have greatly repented the effort expended upon it, and it happens again and again that those who have fought through all their life up to death to defend the principles of that literature, free themselves from the faction of their author at the very hour of death. But happy is that man whom death takes as he meditates upon this literature [of Christ]. Let us all, therefore, with our whole heart covet this literature, let us embrace it, let us continually occupy ourselves with it, let us fondly kiss it, at length let us die in its embrace, let us be transformed in it, since indeed studies are transmuted into morals. As for him who cannot pursue this course (but who cannot do it, if only he wishes?), let him at least reverence this literature enveloping, as it were, His divine heart. If anyone shows us the footprints of Christ, in what manner, as Christians, do we prostrate ourselves, how we adore them! But why do we not venerate instead the living and breathing likeness of Him in these books? If anyone displays the tunic of Christ, to what corner of the earth shall we not hasten so that we may kiss it? Yet were you to bring forth His entire wardrobe, it would not manifest Christ more clearly and truly than the Gospel writings. We embellish a wooden or stone statue with gems and gold for the love of Christ. Why not, rather, mark with gold and gems and with ornaments of greater value than these, if such there be, these writings which bring Christ to us so much more effectively than any paltry image? The latter represents only the form of the body—if indeed it represents anything of Him—but these writings bring you the living image of His holy mind and the speaking, healing, dying, rising Christ himself, and thus they render Him so fully present that you would see less if you gazed upon Him with your very eyes.

Notes

1. Lactantius Firmianus was an early fourth-century Christian writer, the author of a defense of the Christian faith entitled *Institutiones divinae*. He had a reputation for great eloquence.

2. The names are those of medieval theologians: Albert the Great, Alexander of Hales, Thomas Aquinas, Egidio of Rome, Richard of St. Victor, and William of Occam.

PART II

Reformation in Germany, Switzerland, and the Netherlands

Martin Luther and the German Reformation

5. *The Freedom of a Christian*

(1520)

Martin Luther

In the summer of 1520 Martin Luther (1483–1546) wrote three Reformation manifestos: An Address to the Christian Nobility of the German Nation, A Prelude Concerning the Babylonian Captivity of the Church, and The Freedom of a Christian. *In the first, Luther gave expression to German grievances against Rome and called on the ruling class of Germany to initiate reform, since the leaders of the church seemed unwilling or unable to do so. The second treatise attacked the authority of the papacy, even describing the papacy as the antichrist. In it, Luther insisted on the authority of Scripture alone, and he concluded that according to Scripture, there are not seven sacraments, but three: Holy Baptism, Holy Eucharist, and penance.*

The third treatise of 1520, The Freedom of a Christian, *was of a much different character and style. Opening with a conciliatory letter to Pope Leo X, Luther wrote an inspirational booklet of devotion, describing "the whole of Christian life in a brief form." In this document, Luther sets forth clearly and persuasively his positions on faith, justification by faith, Christian freedom, love and good works, and the priesthood of all*

SOURCE: *Luther's Works: Career of the Reformer*, vol. 31, ed. Harold J. Grimm (Philadelphia: Fortress Press, 1957). Used by permission of Augsburg Fortress Publishers.

believers. The Freedom of a Christian *captures the center of Luther's Reformation faith, which he summarizes eloquently in its conclusion: "We conclude, therefore, that a Christian lives not in himself, but in Christ and in his neighbor. Otherwise he is not a Christian. He lives in Christ through faith, in his neighbor through love. By faith he is caught up beyond himself into God. By love he descends beneath himself into his neighbor."*

Many people have considered Christian faith an easy thing, and not a few have given it a place among the virtues. They do this because they have not experienced it and have never tasted the great strength there is in faith. It is impossible to write well about it or to understand what has been written about it unless one has at one time or another experienced the courage which faith gives a man when trials oppress him. But he who has had even a faint taste of it can never write, speak, meditate, or hear enough concerning it. It is a living "spring of water welling up to eternal life," as Christ calls it in John 4 [:14].

As for me, although I have no wealth of faith to boast of and know how scant my supply is, I nevertheless hope that I have attained to a little faith, even though I have been assailed by great and various temptations; and I hope that I can discuss it, if not more elegantly, certainly more to the point, than those literalists and subtle disputants have previously done, who have not even understood what they have written.

To make the way smoother for the unlearned—for only them do I serve—I shall set down the following two propositions concerning the freedom and the bondage of the spirit:

A Christian is a perfectly free lord of all, subject to none.
A Christian is a perfectly dutiful servant of all, subject to all.

These two theses seem to contradict each other. If, however, they should be found to fit together they would serve our purpose beautifully. Both are Paul's own statements, who says in 1 Cor. 9 [:19], "For though I am free from all men, I have made myself a slave to all," and in Rom. 13 [:8], "Owe no one anything, except to love one another." Love by its very nature is ready to serve and be subject to him who is loved. So Christ, although he was Lord of all, was "born of woman, born under the law" [Gal. 4:4], and therefore was at the same time a free man and a servant, "in the form of God" and "of a servant" [Phil. 2:6–7].

Let us start, however, with something more remote from our subject, but more obvious. Man has a twofold nature, a spiritual and a bodily one. According to the spiritual nature, which men refer to as the soul, he is called a spiritual, inner, or new man. According to the bodily nature, which men refer to as flesh, he is called a carnal, outward, or old man, of whom the Apostle writes in 2 Cor. 4 [:16], "Though our outer nature is wasting away, our inner nature is being renewed every day." Because of this diversity of nature the Scriptures assert contradictory things concerning the same man, since these two men in the same man contradict each other, "for the desires of the flesh are against the Spirit, and the desires of the Spirit are against the flesh," according to Gal. 5 [:17].

First, let us consider the inner man to see how a righteous, free, and pious Christian, that is, a spiritual, new, and inner man, becomes what he is. It is evident that no external thing has any influence in producing Christian righteousness or freedom, or in producing unrighteousness or servitude. A simple argument will furnish the proof of this statement. What can it profit the soul if the body is well, free, and active, and eats, drinks, and does as it pleases? For in these respects even the most godless slaves of vice may prosper. On the other hand, how will poor health or imprisonment or hunger or thirst or any other external misfortune harm the soul? Even the most godly men, and those who are free because of clear consciences, are afflicted with these things. None of these things touch either the freedom or the servitude of the soul. It does not help the soul if the body is adorned with the sacred robes of priests or dwells in sacred places or is occupied with sacred duties or prays, fasts, abstains from certain kinds of food, or does any work that can be done by the body and in the body. The righteousness and the freedom of the soul require something far different since the things which have been mentioned could be done by any wicked person. Such works produce nothing but hypocrites. On the other hand, it will not harm the soul if the body is clothed in secular dress, dwells in unconsecrated places, eats and drinks as others do, does not pray aloud, and neglects to do all the above-mentioned things which hypocrites can do.

Furthermore, to put aside all kinds of works, even contemplation, meditation, and all that the soul can do, does not help. One thing, and only one thing, is necessary for Christian life, righteousness, and freedom. That one thing is the most holy Word of God, the gospel of Christ, as Christ says, John 11 [:25], "I am the resurrection and the life; he who believes in me, though he die, yet shall he live"; and John 8 [:36], "So if the Son makes you free, you will be free indeed"; and Matt. 4 [:4], "Man shall not live by bread alone, but by every word that proceeds from the mouth of God." Let us then consider it certain and firmly established that the soul can do without anything except the Word of God and that where the Word of God is missing there is no help at all for the soul. If it has the Word of God it is rich and lacks nothing since it is the Word of life, truth, light, peace, righteousness, salvation, joy, liberty, wisdom, power, grace, glory, and of every incalculable blessing. This is why the prophet in the entire Psalm [119] and in many other places yearns and sighs for the Word of God and uses so many names to describe it.

On the other hand, there is no more terrible disaster with which the wrath of God can afflict men than a famine of the hearing of his Word, as he says in Amos [8:11]. Likewise there is no greater mercy than when he sends forth his Word, as we read in Psalm 107 [:20]: "He sent forth his word, and healed them, and delivered them from destruction." Nor was Christ sent into the world for any other ministry except that of the Word. Moreover, the entire spiritual estate—all the apostles, bishops, and priests—has been called and instituted only for the ministry of the Word.

You may ask, "What then is the Word of God, and how shall it be used, since there are so many words of God?" I answer: The Apostle explains this in Romans 1. The Word is the gospel of God concerning his Son, who was made flesh, suffered, rose from the dead, and was glorified through the Spirit who sanctifies. To preach Christ means to feed the soul, make it righteous, set it free, and save it, provided it believes the preaching. Faith alone is the saving and efficacious use of the Word of God, according to Rom. 10 [:9]: "If you confess with your lips that Jesus is Lord and believe in your heart that God raised him from the dead, you will be saved." Furthermore, "Christ is the end of the law, that every one who has faith may be justified" [Rom. 10:4]. Again, in Rom. 1 [:17], "He who through faith is righteous shall live." The Word of God cannot be received and cherished by any works whatever but only by faith. Therefore it is clear that, as the soul needs only the Word of God for its life and righteousness, so it is justified by faith alone and not any works; for if it could be justified by anything else, it would not need the Word, and consequently it would not need faith.

This faith cannot exist in connection with works—that is to say, if you at the same time claim to be justified by works, whatever their character—for that would be the same as "limping with two different opinions" [1 Kings 18:21], as worshiping Baal and kissing one's own hand [Job 31:27–28], which, as Job says, is a very great iniquity. Therefore the moment you begin to have faith you learn that all things in you are altogether blameworthy, sinful, and damnable, as the Apostle says in Rom. 3 [:23], "Since all have sinned and fall short of the glory of God," and, "None is righteous, no, not one; . . . all have turned aside, together they have gone wrong"

[Rom. 3:10–12]. When you have learned this you will know that you need Christ, who suffered and rose again for you so that, if you believe in him, you may through this faith become a new man in so far as your sins are forgiven and you are justified by the merits of another, namely, of Christ alone.

Since, therefore, this faith can rule only in the inner man, as Rom. 10 [:10] says, "For man believes with his heart and so is justified," and since faith alone justifies, it is clear that the inner man cannot be justified, freed, or saved by any outer work or action at all, and that these works, whatever their character, have nothing to do with this inner man. On the other hand, only ungodliness and unbelief of heart, and no outer work, make him guilty and a damnable servant of sin. Wherefore it ought to be the first concern of every Christian to lay aside all confidence in works and increasingly to strengthen faith alone and through faith to grow in the knowledge, not of works, but of Christ Jesus, who suffered and rose for him, as Peter teaches in the last chapter of his first Epistle [1 Pet. 5:10]. No other work makes a Christian. Thus when the Jews asked Christ, as related in John 6 [:28], what they must do "to be doing the work of God," he brushed aside the multitude of works which he saw they did in great profusion and suggested one work, saying, "This is the work of God, that you believe in him whom he has sent" [John 6:29]; "for on him has God the Father set his seal" [John 6:27].

Therefore true faith in Christ is a treasure beyond comparison which brings with it complete salvation and saves man from every evil, as Christ says in the last chapter of Mark [16:16]: "He who believes and is baptized will be saved; but he who does not believe will be condemned." Isaiah contemplated this treasure and foretold it in chapter 10: "The Lord will make a small and consuming word upon the land, and it will overflow with righteousness" [cf. Isa. 10:22]. This is as though he said, "Faith, which is a small and perfect fulfillment of the law, will fill believers with so great a righteousness that they will need nothing more to become righteous." So Paul says, Rom. 10 [:10], "For man believes with his heart and so is justified."

Should you ask how it happens that faith alone justifies and offers us such a treasure of great benefits without works in view of the fact that so many works, ceremonies, and laws are prescribed in the Scriptures, I answer: First of all, remember what has been said, namely, that faith alone, without works, justifies, frees, and saves; we shall make this clearer later on. Here we must point out that the entire Scripture of God is divided into two parts: commandments and promises. Although the commandments teach things that are good, the things taught are not done as soon as they are taught, for the commandments show us what we ought to do but do not give us the power to do it. They are intended to teach man to know himself, that through them he may recognize his inability to do good and may despair of his own ability. That is why they are called the Old Testament and constitute the Old Testament. For example, the commandment, "You shall not covet" [Exod. 20:17], is a command which proves us all to be sinners, for no one can avoid coveting no matter how much he may struggle against it. Therefore, in order not to covet and to fulfil the commandment, a man is compelled to despair of himself, to seek the help which he does not find in himself elsewhere and from someone else, as stated in Hosea [13:9]: "Destruction is your own, O Israel: your help is only in me." As we fare with respect to one commandment, so we fare with all, for it is equally impossible for us to keep any one of them.

Now when a man has learned through the commandments to recognize his helplessness and is distressed about how he might satisfy the law—since the law must be fulfilled so that not a jot or tittle shall be lost, otherwise man will be condemned without hope—then, being truly humbled and reduced to nothing in his own eyes, he finds in himself nothing whereby he may be justified and saved. Here the second part of Scripture comes to our aid, namely, the promises of God which declare the glory of God, saying, "If you wish to fulfil the law and not covet, as the law demands, come, believe in Christ in whom grace, righteousness, peace, liberty, and all things are promised you. If you believe, you shall have all things; if you do not believe, you shall lack all things." That which is impossible for you to accomplish by trying to fulfil all the works of the law—many and useless as they all are—you will accomplish quickly and easily through faith. God our Father has made all things depend on faith so that whoever has faith will have everything, and whoever does not have faith will have nothing. "For God has consigned all men to disobedience, that he may have mercy upon all," as it is stated in Rom. 11 [:32]. Thus the promises of God give what the commandments of God demand and fulfil what the law prescribes so that all things may be God's alone, both the commandments and the fulfilling of the commandments. He alone commands, he alone fulfills. Therefore the promises of God belong to the New Testament. Indeed, they are the New Testament.

Since these promises of God are holy, true, righteous, free, and peaceful words, full of goodness, the soul which clings to them with a firm faith will be so closely united with them and altogether absorbed by them that it not only will share in all their power but will be saturated and intoxicated by them. If a touch of Christ healed, how much more will this most tender spiritual touch, this absorbing of the Word, communicate to the soul all things that belong to the Word. This, then, is how through faith alone without works the soul is justified by the Word of God, sanctified, made true, peaceful, and free, filled with every blessing and truly made a child of God, as John 1 [:12] says: "But to all who . . . believed in his name, he gave power to become children of God."

From what has been said it is easy to see from what source faith derives such great power and why a good work or all good works together cannot equal it. No good work can rely upon the Word of God or live in the soul, for faith alone and the Word of God rule in the soul. Just as the heated iron glows like fire because of the union of fire with it, so the Word imparts its qualities to the soul. It is clear, then, that a Christian has all that he needs in faith and needs no works to justify him; and if he has no need of works, he has no need of the law; and if he has no need of the law, surely he is free from the law. It is true that "the law is not laid down for the just" [1 Tim. 1:9]. This is that Christian liberty, our faith, which does not induce us to live in idleness or wickedness but makes the law and works unnecessary for any man's righteousness and salvation.

This is the first power of faith. Let us now examine also the second. It is a further function of faith that it honors him whom it trusts with the most reverent and highest regard since it considers him truthful and trustworthy. There is no other honor equal to the estimate of truthfulness and righteousness with which we honor him whom we trust. Could we ascribe to a man anything greater than truthfulness and righteousness and perfect goodness? On the other hand, there is no way in which we can show greater contempt for a man than to regard him as false and wicked and to be suspicious of him, as we do when we do not trust him. So when the soul firmly trusts God's promises, it regards him as truthful and righteous. Nothing more excellent than this can be ascribed to God. The very highest worship of God is this that we ascribe to him truthfulness, righteousness, and whatever else should be ascribed to one who is trusted. When this is done, the soul consents to his will. Then it hallows his name and allows itself to be treated according to God's good pleasure for, clinging to God's promises, it does not doubt that he who is true, just, and wise will do, dispose, and provide all things well.

Is not such a soul most obedient to God in all things by this faith? What commandment is there that such obedience has not completely fulfilled? What more complete fulfillment is there than obedience in all things? This obedience, however, is not rendered by works, but by faith alone. On the other hand, what greater rebellion against God, what greater wickedness, what greater contempt of God is there than not believing his promise? For what is this but to make God a liar or to doubt that he is truthful?—that is, to ascribe truthfulness to one's self but lying and vanity to God? Does not a man who does this deny God and set himself up as an idol in his heart? Then of what good are works done in such wickedness, even if they were the works of angels and apostles? Therefore God has rightly included all things, not under anger or lust, but under unbelief, so that they who imagine that they are fulfilling the law by doing the works of chastity and mercy required by the law (the civil and human virtues) might not be saved. They are included under the sin of unbelief and must either seek mercy or be justly condemned.

When, however, God sees that we consider him truthful and by the faith of our heart pay him the great honor which is due him, he does us that great honor of considering us truthful and righteous for the sake of our faith. Faith works truth and righteousness by giving God what belongs to him. Therefore God in turn glorifies our righteousness. It is true and just that God is truthful and just, and to consider and confess him to be so is the same as being truthful and just. Accordingly he says in 1 Sam. 2 [:30], "Those who honor me I will honor, and those who despise me shall be lightly esteemed." So Paul says in Rom. 4 [:3] that Abraham's faith "was reckoned to him as righteousness" because by it he gave glory most perfectly to God, and that for the same reason our faith shall be reckoned to us as righteousness if we believe.

The third incomparable benefit of faith is that it unites the soul with Christ as a bride is united with her bridegroom. By this mystery, as the Apostle teaches, Christ and the soul become one flesh [Eph. 5:31–32]. And if they are one flesh and there is between them a true marriage—indeed the most perfect of all marriages, since human marriages are but poor examples of this one true marriage—it follows that everything they have they hold in common, the good as well as the evil. Accordingly the believing soul can boast of and glory in whatever Christ has as though it were its own, and whatever the soul has Christ claims as his own. Let us compare these and we shall see inestimable benefits. Christ is full of grace, life, and salvation. The soul is full of sins, death, and damnation. Now let faith come between them and sins, death, and damnation will be Christ's, while grace, life, and salvation will be the soul's; for if Christ is a bridegroom, he must take upon himself the things which are his bride's and bestow upon her the things that are his. If he gives her his body and very self, how shall he not give her all that is his? And if he takes the body of the bride, how shall he not take all that is hers?

Here we have a most pleasing vision not only of communion but of a blessed struggle and victory and salvation and redemption. Christ is God and man in one person. He has neither sinned nor died, and is not condemned, and he cannot sin, die, or be condemned; his righteousness, life, and salvation are unconquerable, eternal, omnipotent. By the wedding ring of faith he shares in the sins, death, and pains of hell which are his bride's. As a matter of fact, he makes them his own and acts as if they were his own and as if he himself had sinned; he suffered, died, and descended into hell that he might overcome them all. Now since it was such a one who did all this, and death and hell could not swallow him up, these were necessarily swallowed up by him in a mighty duel; for his righteousness is greater than the sins of all men, his life stronger than death, his salvation more invincible than hell. Thus the believing soul by means of the pledge of its faith is free in Christ, its bridegroom, free from all sins, secure against death and hell, and is endowed with the eternal righteousness, life, and salvation of Christ its bridegroom. So he takes to himself a glorious bride, "without spot or wrinkle, cleansing her by the washing of water with the word" [cf. Eph. 5:26–27] of life, that is, by faith in the Word of life, righteousness, and salvation. In this way he marries her in faith, steadfast love, and in mercies, righteousness, and justice, as Hos. 2 [:19–20] says.

Who then can fully appreciate what this royal marriage means? Who can understand the riches of the glory of this grace? Here this rich and divine bridegroom Christ marries this poor, wicked harlot, redeems her from all her evil, and adorns her with all his goodness. Her sins cannot now destroy her, since they are laid upon Christ and swallowed up by him. And she has that righteousness in Christ, her husband, of which she may boast as of her own and which she can confidently display alongside her sins in the face of death and hell and say, "If I have sinned, yet my Christ, in whom I believe, has not sinned, and all his is mine and all mine is his," as the bride in the Song of Solomon [2:16] says, "My beloved is mine and I am his." This is what Paul means when he says in 1 Cor. 15 [:57], "Thanks be to God, who gives us the victory through our Lord Jesus Christ," that is, the victory over sin and death, as he also says there, "The sting of death is sin, and the power of sin is the law" [1 Cor. 15:56].

From this you once more see that much is ascribed to faith, namely, that it alone can fulfill the law and justify without works. You see that the First Commandment, which says, "You shall worship one God," is fulfilled by faith alone. Though you were nothing but good works from the soles of your feet to the crown of your head, you would still not be righteous or worship God or fulfill the First Commandment, since God cannot be worshiped unless you ascribe to him the glory of truthfulness and all goodness which is due him. This cannot be done by works but only by the faith of the heart. Not by the doing of works but by believing do we glorify God and acknowledge that he is truthful. Therefore faith alone is the righteousness of a Christian and the fulfilling of all the commandments, for he who fulfills the First Commandment has no difficulty in fulfilling all the rest.

But works, being inanimate things, cannot glorify God, although they can, if faith is present, be done to the glory of God. Here, however, we are not inquiring what works and what kind of works are done, but who it is that does them, who glorifies God and brings forth the works. This is done by faith which dwells in the heart and is the source and substance of all our righteousness. Therefore it is a blind and dangerous doctrine which teaches that the commandments must be fulfilled by works. The commandments must be fulfilled before any works can be done, and the works proceed from the fulfillment of the commandments [Rom. 13:10], as we shall hear.

That we may examine more profoundly that grace which our inner man has in Christ, we must realize that in the Old Testament God consecrated to himself all the first-born males. The birthright was highly prized for it involved a twofold honor, that of priesthood and that of kingship. The first-born brother was priest and lord over all the others and a type of Christ, the true and only first-born of God the Father and the Virgin Mary and true king and priest, but not after the fashion of the flesh and the world, for his kingdom is not of this world [John 18:36]. He reigns in heavenly and spiritual things and consecrates them—things such as righteousness, truth, wisdom, peace, salvation, etc. This does not mean that all things on earth and in hell are not also subject to him—otherwise how could he protect and save us from them?—but that his kingdom consists neither in them nor of them. Nor does his priesthood consist in the outer splendor of robes and postures like those of the human priesthood of Aaron and our present-day church; but it consists of spiritual things through which he by an invisible service intercedes for us in heaven before God, there offers himself as a sacrifice, and does all things a priest should do, as Paul describes him under the type of Melchizedek in the Epistle to the Hebrews [Heb. 6–7]. Nor does he only pray and intercede for us but he teaches us inwardly through the living instruction of his Spirit, thus performing the two real functions of a priest, of which the prayers and the preaching of human priests are visible types.

Now just as Christ by his birthright obtained these two prerogatives, so he imparts them to and shares them with everyone who believes in him according to the law of the above-mentioned marriage, according to which the wife owns whatever belongs to the husband. Hence all of us who believe in Christ are priests and kings in Christ, as 1 Pet. 2 [:9] says: "You are a chosen race, God's own people, a royal priesthood, a priestly kingdom, that you may declare the wonderful deeds of him who called you out of darkness into his marvelous light."

The nature of this priesthood and kingship is something like this: First, with respect to the kingship, every Christian is by faith so exalted above all things that, by virtue of a spiritual power, he is lord of all things without exception, so that nothing can do him any harm. As a matter of fact, all things are made subject to him and are compelled to serve him in obtaining salvation. Accordingly Paul says in Rom. 8 [:28], "All things work together for good for the elect," and in 1 Cor. 3 [:21–23], "All things are yours whether . . . life or death or the present or the future, all are yours; and you are Christ's . . ." This is not to say that every Christian is placed over all things to have and control them by physical power—a madness with which some churchmen are afflicted—for such power belongs to kings, princes, and other men on earth. Our ordinary experience in life shows us that we are subjected to all, suffer many things, and even die. As a matter of fact, the more Christian a man is, the more evils, sufferings, and deaths he must endure, as we see in Christ the first-born prince himself, and in all his brethren, the saints. The power of which we speak is spiritual. It rules in the midst of enemies and is powerful in the midst of oppression. This means nothing else than that "power is made perfect in weakness" [2 Cor. 12:9] and that in all things I can find profit toward salvation [Rom. 8:28], so that the cross and death itself are compelled to serve me and to work together with me for my salvation. This is a splendid privilege and hard to attain, a truly omnipotent power, a spiritual dominion in which there is nothing so good and nothing so evil but that it shall work together for good to me, if only I believe. Yes, since faith alone suffices for salvation, I need nothing except faith exercising the power and dominion of its own liberty. Lo, this is the inestimable power and liberty of Christians.

Not only are we the freest of kings, we are also priests forever, which is far more excellent than being kings, for as priests we are worthy to appear before God to pray for others and to teach one another divine things. These are the functions of priests, and they cannot be granted to any unbeliever. Thus Christ has made it possible for us, provided we believe in him, to be not only his brethren, co-heirs, and fellow-kings, but also his fellow-priests. Therefore we may boldly come into the presence of God in the spirit of faith [Heb. 10:19, 22] and cry "Abba, Father!" pray for one another, and do all things which we see done and foreshadowed in the outer and visible works of priests.

He, however, who does not believe is not served by anything. On the contrary, nothing works for his good, but he himself is a servant of all, and all things turn out badly for him because he wickedly uses them to his own advantage and not to the glory of God. So he is no priest but a wicked man whose prayer becomes sin and who never comes into the presence of God because God does not hear sinners [John 9:31]. Who then can comprehend the lofty dignity of the Christian? By virtue of his royal power he rules over all things, death, life, and sin, and through his priestly glory is omnipotent with God because he does the things which God asks and desires, as it is written, "He will fulfill the desire of those who fear him; he also will hear their cry and save them" [cf. Phil. 4:13]. To this glory a man attains, certainly not by any works of his, but by faith alone.

From this anyone can clearly see how a Christian is free from all things and over all things so that he needs no works to make him righteous and save him, since faith alone abundantly confers all these things. Should he grow so foolish, however, as to presume to become righteous, free, saved, and a Christian by means of some good work, he would instantly lose faith and all its benefits, a foolishness aptly illustrated in the fable of the dog who runs along a stream with a piece of meat in his mouth and, deceived by the reflection of the meat in the water, opens his mouth to snap at it and so loses both the meat and the reflection.[1]

You will ask, "If all who are in the church are priests, how do these whom we now call priests differ from laymen?" I answer: Injustice is done those words "priest," "cleric," "spiritual," "ecclesiastic," when they are transferred from all Christians to those few who are now by a mischievous usage called "ecclesiastics." Holy Scripture makes no distinction between them, although it gives the name "ministers," "servants," "stewards" to those who are now proudly called popes, bishops, and lords and who should according to the ministry of the Word serve others and teach them the faith of Christ and the freedom of believers. Although we are all equally priests, we cannot all publicly minister and teach. We ought not do so even if we could. Paul writes accordingly in 1 Cor. 4 [1], "This is how one should regard us, as servants of Christ and stewards of the mysteries of God."

That stewardship, however, has now been developed into so great a display of power and so terrible a tyranny that no heathen empire or other earthly power can be compared with it, just as if laymen were not also Christians. Through this perversion the knowledge of Christian grace, faith, liberty, and of Christ himself has altogether perished, and its place has been taken by an unbearable bondage of human works and laws until we have become, as the Lamentations of Jeremiah [1] say, servants of the vilest men on earth who abuse our misfortune to serve only their base and shameless will.

To return to our purpose, I believe that it has now become clear that it is not enough or in any sense Christian to preach the works, life, and words of Christ as historical facts, as if the knowledge of these would suffice for the conduct of life; yet this is the fashion among those who must today be regarded as our best preachers. Far less is it sufficient or Christian to say nothing at all about Christ and to teach instead the laws of men and the decrees of the fathers. Now there are not a few who preach Christ and read about him that they may move men's affections to sympathy with Christ, to anger against the Jews, and such childish and effeminate nonsense. Rather ought Christ to be preached to the end that faith in him may be established that he may not only be Christ, but be Christ for you and me, and that what is said of him and is denoted in his name may be effectual in us. Such faith is produced and preserved in us by preaching why Christ came, what he brought and bestowed, what benefit it is to us to accept him. This is done when that Christian liberty which he bestows is rightly taught and we are told in what way we Christians are all kings and priests and therefore lords of all and may firmly believe that whatever we have done is pleasing and acceptable in the sight of God, as I have already said.

What man is there whose heart, upon hearing these things, will not rejoice to its depth, and when receiving such comfort will not grow tender so that he will love Christ as he never could by means of any laws or works? Who would have the power to harm or frighten such a heart? If the knowledge of sin or the fear of death should break in upon it, it is ready to hope in the Lord. It does not grow afraid when it hears tidings of evil. It is not disturbed when it sees its enemies. This is so because it believes that the righteousness of Christ is its own and that its sin is not its own, but Christ's, and that all sin is swallowed up by the righteousness of Christ. This, as has been said above, is a necessary consequence on account of faith in Christ. So the heart learns to scoff at death and sin and to say with the Apostle, "O death, where is thy victory? O death, where is thy sting? The sting of death is sin, and the power of sin is the law. But thanks be to God, who gives us the victory through our Lord Jesus Christ" [1 Cor. 15:55–57]. Death is swallowed up not only in the victory of Christ but also by our victory, because through faith his victory has become ours and in that faith we also are conquerors.

Let this suffice concerning the inner man, his liberty, and the source of his liberty, the righteousness of faith. He needs neither laws nor good works but, on the contrary, is injured by them if he believes that he is justified by them.

Now let us turn to the second part, the outer man. Here we shall answer all those who, offended by the word "faith" and by all that has been said, now ask, "If faith does all things and is alone sufficient unto righteousness, why then are good works commanded? We will take our ease and do no works and be content with faith." I answer: not so, you wicked men, not so. That would indeed be proper if we were wholly inner and perfectly spiritual men. But such we shall be only at the last day, the day of the resurrection of the dead. As long as we live in the flesh we only begin to make some progress in that which shall be perfected in the future life. For this reason the Apostle in Rom. 8 [:23] calls all that we attain in this life "the first fruits of the Spirit" because we shall indeed receive the greater portion, even the fullness of the Spirit, in the future. This is the place to assert that which was said above, namely, that a Christian is the servant of all and made subject to all. Insofar as he is free he does no works, but insofar as he is a servant he does all kinds of works. How this is possible we shall see.

Although, as I have said, a man is abundantly and sufficiently justified by faith inwardly, in his spirit, and so has all that he needs, except insofar as this faith and these riches must grow from day to day even to the future life; yet he remains in this mortal life on earth. In this life he must control his own body and have dealings with men. Here the works begin; here a man cannot enjoy leisure; here he must indeed take care to discipline his body by fastings, watchings, labors, and other reasonable discipline and to subject it to the Spirit so that it will obey and conform to the inner man and faith and not revolt against faith and hinder the inner man, as it is the nature of the body to do if it is not held in check. The inner man, who by faith is created in the image of God, is both joyful and happy because of Christ in whom so many benefits are conferred upon him; and therefore it is his one occupation to serve God joyfully and without thought of gain, in love that is not constrained.

While he is doing this, behold, he meets a contrary will in his own flesh which strives to serve the world and seeks its own advantage. This the spirit of faith cannot tolerate, but with joyful zeal it attempts to put the body under control and hold it in check, as Paul says in Rom. 7 [:22–23], "For I delight in the law of God, in my inmost self, but I see in my members another law at war with the law of my mind and making me captive to the law of sin," and in another place, "But I pommel my body and subdue it, lest after preaching to others I myself should be disqualified" [1 Cor. 9:27], and in Galatians [5:24], "And those who belong to Christ Jesus have crucified the flesh with its passions and desires."

In doing these works, however, we must not think that a man is justified before God by them, for faith, which alone is righteousness before God, cannot endure that erroneous opinion. We must, however, realize that these works reduce the body to subjection and purify it of its evil lusts, and our whole purpose is to be directed only toward the driving out of lusts. Since by faith the soul is cleansed and made to love God, it desires that all things, and especially its own body, shall be purified so that all things may join with it in loving and praising God. Hence a man cannot be idle, for the need of his body drives him and he is compelled to do many good works to reduce it to subjection. Nevertheless the works themselves do not justify him before God, but he does the works out of spontaneous love in obedience to God and considers nothing except the approval of God, whom he would most scrupulously obey in all things.

In this way everyone will easily be able to learn for himself the limit and discretion, as they say, of his bodily castigations, for he will fast, watch, and labor as much as he finds sufficient to repress the lasciviousness and lust of his body. But those who presume to be justified by works do not regard the mortifying of the lusts, but only the works themselves, and think that if only they have done as many and as great works as are possible, they have done well and have become righteous. At times they even addle their brains and destroy, or at least render useless, their natural strength with their works. This is the height of folly and utter ignorance of Christian life and faith, that a man should seek to be justified and saved by works and without faith.

In order to make that which we have said more easily understood, we shall explain by analogies. We should think of the works of a Christian who is justified and saved by faith because of the pure and free mercy of God, just as we would think of the works which Adam and Eve did in Paradise, and all their children would have done if they had not sinned. We read in Gen. 2 [:15] that "The Lord God took the man and put him in the garden of Eden to till it and keep it." Now Adam was created righteous and upright and without sin by God so that he had no need of being justified and made upright through his tilling and keeping the garden; but, that he might not be idle, the Lord gave him a task to do, to cultivate and protect the garden. This task would truly have been the freest of works, done only to please God and not to obtain righteousness, which Adam already had in full measure and which would have been the birthright of us all.

The works of a believer are like this. Through his faith he has been restored to Paradise and created anew, has no need of works that he may become or be righteous; but that he may not be idle and may provide for and keep his body, he must do such works freely only to please God. Since, however, we are not wholly recreated, and our faith and love are not yet perfect, these are to be increased, not by external works, however, but of themselves.

A second example: A bishop, when he consecrates a church, confirms children, or performs some other duty belonging to his office, is not made a bishop by these works. Indeed, if he had not first been made a bishop, none of these works would be valid. They would be foolish, childish, and farcical. So the Christian who is consecrated by his faith does good works, but the works do not make him holier or more Christian, for that is the work of faith alone. And if a man were not first a believer and a Christian, all his works would amount to nothing and would be truly wicked and damnable sins.

The following statements are therefore true: "Good works do not make a good man, but a good man does good works; evil works do not make a wicked man, but a wicked man does evil works." Consequently it is always necessary that the substance or person himself be good before there can be any good works, and that good works follow and proceed from the good person, as Christ also says, "A good tree cannot bear evil fruit, nor can a bad tree bear good fruit" [Matt. 7:18]. It is clear that the fruits do not bear the tree and that the tree does not grow on the fruits, also that, on the contrary, the trees bear the fruits and the fruits grow on the trees. As it is necessary, therefore, that the trees exist before their fruits and the fruits do not make trees either good or bad, but rather as the trees are, so are the fruits they bear; so a man must first be good or wicked before he does a good or wicked work, and his works do not make him good or wicked, but he himself makes his works either good or wicked.

Illustrations of the same truth can be seen in all trades. A good or a bad house does not make a good or a bad builder; but a good or a bad builder makes a good or a bad house. And in general, the work never makes the workman like itself, but the workman makes the work like himself. So it is with the works of man. As the man is, whether believer or unbeliever, so also is his work—good if it was done in faith, wicked if it was done in unbelief. But the converse is not true, that the work makes the man either a believer or an unbeliever. As works do not make a man a believer, so also they do not make him righteous. But as faith makes a man a believer and righteous, so faith does good works. Since, then, works justify no one, and a man must be righteous before he does a good work, it is very evident that it is faith alone which, because of the pure mercy of God through Christ and in his Word, worthily and sufficiently justifies and saves the person. A Christian has no need of any work or law in order to be saved since through faith he is free from every law and does everything out of pure liberty and freely. He seeks neither benefit nor salvation since he already abounds in all things and is saved through the grace of God because in his faith he now seeks only to please God.

Furthermore, no good work helps justify or save an unbeliever. On the other hand, no evil work makes him wicked or damns him; but the unbelief which makes the person and the tree evil does the evil and damnable works.

Hence when a man is good or evil, this is effected not by the works, but by faith or unbelief, as the Wise Man says, "This is the beginning of sin, that a man falls away from God" [cf. Sirach 10:14–15], which happens when he does not believe. And Paul says in Heb. 11 [:6], "For whoever would draw near to God must believe. . . ." And Christ says the same: "Either make the tree good, and its fruit good; or make the tree bad, and its fruit bad" [Matt. 12:33], as if he would say, "Let him who wishes to have good fruit begin by planting a good tree." So let him who wishes to do good works begin not with the doing of works, but with believing, which makes the person good, for nothing makes a man good except faith, or evil except unbelief.

• • •

Let this suffice concerning works in general and at the same time concerning the works which a Christian does for himself. Lastly, we shall also speak of the things which he does toward his neighbor. A man does not live for himself alone in this mortal body to work for it alone, but he lives also for all men on earth; rather, he lives only for others and not for himself. To this end he brings his body into subjection that he may the more sincerely and freely serve others, as Paul says in Rom. 14 [:7–8], "None of us lives to himself, and none of us dies to himself. If we live, we live to the Lord, and if we die, we die to the Lord." He cannot ever in this life be idle and without works toward his neighbors, for he will necessarily speak, deal with, and exchange views with men, as Christ also, being made in the likeness of men [Phil. 2:7], was found in form as a man and conversed with men, as Baruch 3 [:38] says.

Man, however, needs none of these things for his righteousness and salvation. Therefore he should be guided in all his works by this thought and contemplate this one thing alone, that he may serve and benefit others in all that he does, considering nothing except the need and the advantage of his neighbor. Accordingly the Apostle commands us to work with our hands so that we may give to the needy, although he might have said that we should work to support ourselves. He says, however, "that he may be able to give to those in need" [Eph. 4:28]. This is what makes caring for the body a Christian work, that through its health and comfort we may be able to work, to acquire, and lay by funds with which to aid those who are in need, that in this way the strong member may serve the weaker, and we may be sons of God, each caring for and working for the other, bearing one another's burdens and so fulfilling the law of Christ [Gal. 6:2]. This is a truly Christian life. Here faith is truly active through love [Gal. 5:6], that is, it finds expression in works of the freest service, cheerfully and lovingly done, with which a man willingly serves another without hope of reward; and for himself he is satisfied with the fullness and wealth of his faith.

Accordingly Paul, after teaching the Philippians how rich they were made through faith in Christ, in which they obtained all things, thereafter teaches them, saying, "So if there is any encouragement in Christ, any incentive of love, any participation in the Spirit, any affection and sympathy, complete my joy by being of the same mind, having the same love, being in full accord and of one mind. Do nothing from selfishness or conceit, but in humility count others better than yourselves. Let each of you look not only to his own interests, but also to the interests of others" [Phil. 2:1–4]. Here we see clearly that the Apostle has prescribed this rule for the life of Christians, namely, that we should devote all our works to the welfare of others, since each has such abundant riches in his faith that all his other works and his whole life are a surplus with which he can by voluntary benevolence serve and do good to his neighbor.

As an example of such life the Apostle cites Christ, saying, "Have this mind among yourselves, which you have in Christ Jesus, who, though he was in the form of God, did not count equality with God a thing to be grasped, but emptied himself, taking the form of a servant, being born in the likeness of men. And being found in human form he humbled himself and became obedient unto death" [Phil. 2:5–8]. This salutary word of the Apostle has been obscured for us by those who have not at all understood his words, "form of God," "form of a servant," "human form," "likeness of men," and have applied them to the divine and the human nature. Paul means this: Although Christ was filled with the form of God and rich in all good things, so that he needed no work and no suffering to make him righteous and saved (for he had all this eternally), yet he was not puffed up by them and did not exalt himself above us and assume power over us, although he could rightly have done so; but, on the contrary, he so lived, labored, worked, suffered, and died that he might be like other men and in fashion and in actions be nothing else than a man, just as if he had need of all these things and had nothing of the form of God. But he did all this for our sake, that he might serve us and that all things which he accomplished in this form of a servant might become ours.

So a Christian, like Christ his head, is filled and made rich by faith and should be content with this form of God which he has obtained by faith; only, as I have said, he should increase this faith until it is made perfect. For this faith is his life, his righteousness, and his salvation: it saves him and makes him acceptable, and bestows upon him all things that are Christ's, as has been said above, and as Paul asserts in Gal. 2 [:20] when he says,

"And the life I now live in the flesh I live by faith in the Son of God." Although the Christian is thus free from all works, he ought in this liberty to empty himself, take upon himself the form of a servant, be made in the likeness of men, be found in human form, and to serve, help, and in every way deal with his neighbor as he sees that God through Christ has dealt and still deals with him. This he should do freely, having regard for nothing but divine approval.

He ought to think: "Although I am an unworthy and condemned man, my God has given me in Christ all the riches of righteousness and salvation without any merit on my part, out of pure, free mercy, so that from now on I need nothing except faith which believes that this is true. Why should I not therefore freely, joyfully, with all my heart, and with an eager will do all things which I know are pleasing and acceptable to such a Father who has overwhelmed me with his inestimable riches? I will therefore give myself as a Christ to my neighbor, just as Christ offered himself to me; I will do nothing in this life except what I see is necessary, profitable, and salutary to my neighbor, since through faith I have an abundance of all good things in Christ."

Behold, from faith thus flow forth love and joy in the Lord, and from love a joyful, willing, and free mind that serves one's neighbor willingly and takes no account of gratitude or ingratitude, of praise or blame, of gain or loss. For a man does not serve that he may put men under obligations. He does not distinguish between friends and enemies or anticipate their thankfulness or unthankfulness, but he most freely and most willingly spends himself and all that he has, whether he wastes all on the thankless or whether he gains a reward. As his Father does, distributing all things to all men richly and freely, making "his sun rise on the evil and on the good" [Matt. 5:45], so also the son does all things and suffers all things with that freely bestowing joy which is his delight when through Christ he sees it in God, the dispenser of such great benefits.

• • •

See, according to this rule the good things we have from God should flow from one to the other and be common to all, so that everyone should "put on" his neighbor and so conduct himself toward him as if he himself were in the other's place. From Christ the good things have flowed and are flowing into us. He has so "put on" us and acted for us as if he had been what we are. From us they flow on to those who have need of them so that

I should lay before God my faith and my righteousness that they may cover and intercede for the sins of my neighbor which I take upon myself and so labor and serve in them as if they were my very own. That is what Christ did for us. This is true love and the genuine rule of a Christian life. Love is true and genuine where there is true and genuine faith. Hence the Apostle says of love in 1 Cor. 13 [:5] that "it does not seek its own."

We conclude, therefore, that a Christian lives not in himself, but in Christ and in his neighbor. Otherwise he is not a Christian. He lives in Christ through faith, in his neighbor through love. By faith he is caught up beyond himself into God. By love he descends beneath himself into his neighbor. Yet he always remains in God and in his love, as Christ says in John 1 [:51], "Truly, truly, I say to you, you will see heaven opened, and the angels of God ascending and descending upon the Son of man."

Enough now of freedom. As you see, it is a spiritual and true freedom and makes our hearts free from all sins, laws and commands, as Paul says, 1 Tim. 1[:9], "The law is not laid down for the just." It is more excellent than all other liberty, which is external, as heaven is more excellent than earth. May Christ give us this liberty both to understand and to preserve. Amen.

Finally, something must be added for the sake of those for whom nothing can be said so well that they will not spoil it by misunderstanding it. It is questionable whether they will understand even what will be said here. There are very many who, when they hear of this freedom of faith, immediately turn it into an occasion for the flesh and think that now all things are allowed them. They want to show that they are free men and Christians only by despising and finding fault with ceremonies, traditions, and human laws; as if they were Christians because on stated days they do not fast or eat meat when others fast, or because they do not use the accustomed prayers, and with upturned nose scoff at the precepts of men, although they utterly disregard all else that pertains to the Christian religion. The extreme opposite of these are those who rely for their salvation solely on their reverent observance of ceremonies, as if they would be saved because on certain days they fast or abstain from meats, or pray certain prayers; these make a boast of the precepts of the church and of the fathers, and do not care a fig for the things which are of the essence of our faith. Plainly, both are in error because they neglect the weightier things which are necessary to salvation, and quarrel so noisily about trifling and unnecessary matters.

How much better is the teaching of the Apostle Paul who bids us take a middle course and condemns both sides when he says, "Let not him who eats despise him who abstains, and let not him who abstains pass judgment on him who eats" [Rom. 14:3]. Here you see that they who neglect and disparage ceremonies, not out of piety, but out of mere contempt, are reproved, since the Apostle teaches us not to despise them. Such men are puffed up by knowledge. On the other hand, he teaches those who insist on the ceremonies not to judge the others, for neither party acts toward the other according to the love that edifies. Wherefore we ought to listen to Scripture which teaches that we should not go aside to the right or to the left [Deut. 28:14] but follow the statutes of the Lord which are right, "rejoicing the heart" [Ps. 19:8]. As a man is not righteous because he keeps and clings to the works and forms of the ceremonies, so also will a man not be counted righteous merely because he neglects and despises them.

Our faith in Christ does not free us from works but from false opinions concerning works, that is, from the foolish presumption that justification is acquired by works. Faith redeems, corrects, and preserves our consciences so that we know that righteousness does not consist in works, although works neither can nor ought to be wanting; just as we cannot be without food and drink and all the works of this mortal body, yet our righteousness is not in them, but in faith; and yet those works of the body are not to be despised or neglected on that account. In this world we are bound by the needs of our bodily life, but we are not righteous because of them. "My kingship is not of this world" [John 18:36], says Christ. He does not, however, say, "My kingship is not here, that is, in this world." And Paul says, "Though we live in the world we are not carrying on a worldly war" [2 Cor. 10:3], and in Gal. 2 [:20], "The life I now live in the flesh I live by faith in the Son of God." Thus what we do, live, and are in works and ceremonies, we do because of the necessities of this life and of the effort to rule our body. Nevertheless we are righteous, not in these, but in the faith of the Son of God.

Hence the Christian must take a middle course and face those two classes of men. He will meet first the unyielding, stubborn ceremonialists who like deaf adders are not willing to hear the truth of liberty [Ps. 58:4] but, having no faith, boast of, prescribe, and insist upon their ceremonies as means of justification. Such were the Jews of old, who were unwilling to learn how to do good. These he must resist, do the very opposite, and offend them boldly lest by their impious views they drag many with them into error. In the presence of such men it is good to eat meat, break the fasts, and for the sake of the liberty of faith do other things which they regard as the greatest of sins. Of them we must say, "Let them alone; they are blind guides." According to this principle Paul would not circumcise Titus when the Jews insisted that he should [Gal. 2:3], and Christ excused the apostles when they plucked ears of grain on the sabbath [Matt. 12:1–8]. There are many similar instances. The other class of men whom a Christian will meet are the simple-minded, ignorant men, weak in the faith, as the Apostle calls them, who cannot yet grasp the liberty of faith, even if they were willing to do so [Rom. 14:1]. These he must take care not to offend. He must yield to their weakness until they are more fully instructed. Since they do and think as they do, not because they are stubbornly wicked, but only because their faith is weak, the fasts and other things which they consider necessary must be observed to avoid giving them offense. This is the command of love which would harm no one but would serve all men. It is not by their fault that they are weak, but by that of their pastors who have taken them captive with the snares of their traditions and have wickedly used these traditions as rods with which to beat them. They should have been delivered from these pastors by the teachings of faith and freedom. So the Apostle teaches us in Romans 14: "If food is a cause of my brother's falling, I will never eat meat" [cf. Rom 14:21 and 1 Cor. 8:13]; and again, "I know and am persuaded in the Lord Jesus that nothing is unclean in itself; but it is unclean for any one who thinks it unclean" [Rom. 14:14].

For this reason, although we should boldly resist those teachers of traditions and sharply censure the laws of the popes by means of which they plunder the people of God, yet we must spare the timid multitude whom those impious tyrants hold captive by means of these laws until they are set free. Therefore fight strenuously against the wolves, but for the sheep and not also against the sheep. This you will do if you inveigh against the laws and the lawgivers and at the same time observe the laws with the weak so that they will not be offended, until they also recognize tyranny and understand their freedom. If you wish to use your freedom, do so in secret, as Paul says, Rom. 14 [:22], "The faith that you have, keep between yourself and God"; but take care not to use your freedom in the sight of the weak. On the other hand, use your freedom constantly and consistently in the sight of and despite the tyrants and the stubborn so that they also may learn that they are impious, that their laws are of no avail for righteousness, and that they had no right to set them up.

• • •

Since human nature and natural reason, as it is called, are by nature superstitious and ready to imagine, when laws and works are prescribed, that righteousness must be obtained through laws and works; and further, since they are trained and confirmed in this opinion by the practice of all earthly lawgivers, it is impossible that they should of themselves escape from the slavery of works and come to a knowledge of the freedom of faith. Therefore there is need of the prayer that the Lord may give us and make us *theodidacti*, that is, those taught by God [John 6:45], and himself, as he has promised, write his law in our hearts; otherwise there is no hope for us. If he himself does not teach our hearts this wisdom hidden in mystery [1 Cor. 2:7], nature can only condemn it and judge it to be heretical because nature is offended by it and regards it as foolishness. So we see that it happened in the old days in the case of the apostles and prophets, and so godless and blind popes and their flatterers do to me and to those who are like me. May God at last be merciful to them and to us and cause his face to shine upon us that we may know his way upon earth [Ps. 67:1–2], his salvation among all nations, God, who is blessed forever [2 Cor. 11:31]. Amen.

Note

1. One of Aesop's Fables.

6. Formula of Mass and Communion for the Church at Wittenberg

(1523)

MARTIN LUTHER

Martin Luther's (1483–1546) views on worship were a creative mixture of his convictions about Christian freedom and his own conservatism. On the one hand, Luther held that a Christian lives in faith, without requiring external forms or rites. He or she is free to use external forms or not. On the other hand, a Christian is also a sinner, standing in need of the regular inspiration and nurture of Word and sacrament. For this reason, a Christian, characterized not only by faith but by love, gladly submits to forms for the sake of his or her neighbor to aid in the neighbor's spiritual growth.

Luther took a conservative position on liturgy, at first retaining the Latin language in the Mass and keeping many elements of Catholic worship. He was more concerned about the preaching and teaching of the Word than about liturgy. While he was in exile at the Wartburg castle in 1521, however, his more radical colleague Andreas Carlstadt (or Karlstadt or Karolostadt) introduced a new liturgy in Wittenberg, and Luther was forced to deal with the liturgical issue.

Within a year, in response to the pleading of his friend Nicholas Hausman, the pastor in Zwickau, Luther composed his own order of service and wrote a rationale for evangelical worship. He insisted that Latin should remain the language of the Mass, enriched by a sermon delivered in the vernacular and by the singing of German hymns. After

---

SOURCE: Bard Thompson, ed., *Liturgies of the Western Church* (Cleveland: The World Publishing Co., 1961). Used by permission of Harcourt, Brace & Company.

several more German liturgies appeared in Germany and Switzerland, Luther wrote a German liturgy in 1526.

In the preface to Luther's German Mass, however, Luther still insisted that the Latin service needed to be kept, even though a German service was needed for "unlearned lay folk" in small towns and villages. Although Luther opposed the excessive ceremonialism of the Roman Mass, he retained many of its forms. Unlike some evangelicals, he argued for the purification and simplification of the Mass, not its destruction, keeping such elements as the introit, the Kyrie Eleison *("Lord have mercy"), the* Gloria *("Glory to God in the highest"), the collect, the epistle and gospel lessons for designated Sundays of the church year, the gradual (an anthem sung between the epistle and the gospel lessons), the alleluia, and the creed. The offering and the canon of the Mass, however, he expunged, arguing that they "reeked" of sacrifice.*

For Luther, the Mass as sacrifice was abominable, because it turned worship into a work that the priest offered to God to appease God's wrath and to obtain God's favor. Worship, he wrote, is not a work presented by human beings to God; it is a gracious deed accomplished by God on behalf of humanity. Luther also feared that the sacrifice of the Mass threatened the uniqueness of Christ's sacrifice on the cross.

Although Luther threw out all phrases suggesting sacrifice, he retained many things in the communion portion of the service: the sursum corda *("Lift up your hearts"), an abbreviated preface ("It is truly right and meet . . ."), the* Sanctus *("Holy, holy, holy . . .") and the* Benedictus *("Blessed is he who comes . . ."). He even retained the elevation (the lifting up of the cup), lest the weak be offended by its sudden removal. Likewise, he kept the Lord's Prayer, the* pax *("The peace of the Lord be with you always"), and the* Agnus Dei *("Lamb of God"). The heart of the communion service remained the words of institution.*

Luther's preservation of so many elements of the Latin Mass emphasizes his view of worship as communal and historical, connecting the faithful through the ages. He repudiated private masses and rejected excessive celebrations in honor of the saints.

Unlike some of the more radical sixteenth-century reformers, Luther did not believe that Christian worship was grounded only in Scripture. The Word governs the liturgy, but Scripture, according to Luther, should not become a new law prescribing exactly how worship ought to be carried on.

In his evangelical freedom, Luther rejected certain elements in the Roman Mass and made some important changes. He modified the epistle and gospel lessons, which he believed were geared too much to works.

He moved the position of the Sanctus, he paraphrased the Lord's Prayer, he insisted on communion in both kinds (bread and wine), and finally, with his introduction of German hymns, he encouraged worship to be more truly the work of the people. The Formula of Mass and Communion for the Church at Wittenberg *is the most important of Luther's writings on the liturgy.*[1]

To the Venerable in Christ D. Nicholas Hausman Bishop of the Church at Zwickau in Christ blessed. Mart. Luther.

Grace and peace in Christ he wishes (him). Thus far I have tried by means of books and sermons among the people to call their hearts away from godless opinions of ceremonies, thinking I would be doing something Christian and salutary if I would be the cause whereby the abomination, which Satan has set up in the holy place through the man of sin, might be removed without violence. Therefore, I have undertaken nothing either by force or command; nor have I changed old things for new, always being hesitant and fearful on account of those souls weak in the faith from whom the old and accustomed is not to be taken away suddenly or among whom a new and untried method of worshiping God is to be introduced; and especially on account of those light and fastidious spirits who, without faith, without reason, like unclean swine, rush wildly about and rejoice only in the novel, and as soon as the novelty has worn off forthwith become disgusted with it. A species of men than whom, as in other things, nothing is more troublesome than their sort; so, too, in sacred things they are most troublesome and intolerable. Nevertheless, even though I am moved with wrath, I am compelled to suffer them unless I would desire to have the Gospel itself taken away from the public.

But now since there is hope that the hearts of many have been enlightened and strengthened by the grace of God, and since the matter itself demands that the scandals be removed from the Kingdom of Christ, something must be dared in the name of Christ. For it is right that we provide for the few, lest while we fear constantly the levity and abuse of some others we provide for none at all, and while we wish to guard against the future scandals of such as these, we strengthen all of their abominations. Therefore, most excellent Nicolas, since you have requested it so frequently, we will busy ourself concerning some pious form of saying Mass (as they say) and of administering Communion. And thus will we do: we will no longer rule hearts by word of doctrine only, but we will put our hand to it also, and make that effective in the public administration; nevertheless, prejudicing no one, nor forbidding any one to embrace or follow some other method. Indeed we beg through Christ, from the heart, if something better shall be revealed to those who are in advance of us in these things, that they command us to be silent so that by common work we may aid the common cause.

In the first place we assert, it is not now, nor has it ever been, in our mind to abolish entirely the whole formal cultus of God, but to cleanse that which is in use, which has been vitiated by most abominable additions, and to point out a pious use. For this cannot be denied, that masses and the communion of bread and wine are a rite divinely instituted by Christ, which was observed, first under Christ Himself, then under the apostles, most simply and piously and without any additions. But so many human inventions have been added to it in course of time, that nothing of the mass and communion has come down to our age except the name.

Now the additions of the early fathers, who are said to have prayed one or two psalms in a subdued voice before blessing the bread and wine, were commendable: such Athanasius and Cyprian were thought to have been. Then they who added *Kyrie Eleison*, these also pleased; for we read that under Basil the Great *Kyrie Eleison* was in public use by the whole people. Now the reading of the *Epistles* and *Gospels* was and is necessary, unless it be a fault to read them in a language which is not understood by the common people. Afterward when chanting began, the psalms were changed into the *Introit*: then the Angelic Hymn was added, the *Gloria in excelsis et in terra pax*; also the *Graduals* and *Alleluia* and *Nicene Creed*, the *Sanctus*, *Agnus Dei* and *Communio*. All these are such as cannot be censured, especially those which are sung as *de tempore* or Lord's Day uses. These days only testify to ancient purity, the Canon excepted.

But when there was license to add and to change as it suited anyone, then because of the tyranny of avarice and sacerdotal ambition, those altars and images of Baal and all gods began to be placed in the temple of the Lord by our impious kings, that is, the bishops and pastors (shepherds). Here impious Ahaz took away the brazen altar and erected another brought from Damascus. But I am speaking about the Canon, that mangled and abominable thing gathered from much filth and scum. Then the Mass began to be a sacrifice; the Offertories and paid-for prayers were added; then Sequences and Proses were inserted in the *Sanctus* and the *Gloria in excelsis*. Then the Mass began to be a priestly monopoly, exhausting the wealth of the whole world, deluging the whole earth like a vast desert with rich, lazy, powerful and lascivious celibates. Then came masses for the dead, for travelers, for riches, and who can name the titles alone for which the Mass was made a sacrifice?

Nor do they cease to add to the Canon today: now it is for these feasts, then for others; now these *actiones*, then other *communicantes* are approved. And I will keep quiet about the *memores*, the commemoration of the living and of the dead, not yet brought to its end. And what shall I say of the external additions, vestments, vessels, candles, palls; then the organ and everything musical; images? There is scarcely one of the handicrafts in all the world, which does not contribute a great part of its activity to, and derive its gain from, the Mass.

Therefore, let these be passed by, and also let them pass—all such abominations being revealed by the Gospel—until they be entirely abolished. In the meanwhile we will test all things; what is good, we will retain. But in this book we omit saying that the Mass is (not)[2] a sacrifice or a good work, because we have taught about it sufficiently at other places. We accept it as Sacrament, or Testament, or Blessing as in Latin, or Eucharist as in Greek, or the Table of the Lord, or the Lord's Supper, or the Lord's Memorial, or Communion, or by whatever pious name you please, so long as it be not polluted by the name of sacrifice or work; and we will set forth the rite according to which, as it seems to us, it should be used.

In the first place, we approve and preserve the introits for the Lord's Day and for the Festivals of Christ, such as Easter, Pentecost, Nativity, although we prefer the Psalms from which they were taken as of old; but now we agree to the received usage. But if any desire to approve the introits for Apostles' Days, for Feasts of the Virgin and of other saints, we do not condemn this, if they have been chosen from Psalms and other Scriptures. We, of Wittenberg, seek to celebrate only on Lord's Days and on Festivals of the Lord, abrogating completely the festivals of all of the saints; or if there is anything worthy in them we think they should be referred to in the Lord's Day preaching. We regard the Festivals of the Purification and of the Annunciation as Festivals of Christ, like the Epiphany and the Circumcision. In place of the Festivals of St. Stephen and of St. John, the Evangelist, it pleases us to use the office of the Nativity. Let the Festivals of the Holy Cross be anathema. Let others act according to their own consciences, or according to the infirmity of others—whatever the Spirit may suggest.

In the second place, we accept *Kyrie Eleison* as it has been used customarily, with the various melodies for the different seasons, together with the Angelic Hymn, *Gloria in excelsis*, which follows; nevertheless its use rests on the judgment of the bishop, or, how often he desires its omission.

In the third place, the *Oratio* (prayer), or Collect which follows, if it is pious (and those appointed for the Lord's Days usually are), should be preserved in its accustomed use; but there should be but one. After this the Epistle lesson. Certainly the time has not yet come to attempt revision here, as nothing ungodly is read. But something seems to be needed, since those parts of the Epistles of Paul in which faith is taught are rarely read, but most frequently those parts dealing with morals and exhortations. While the originator of the Epistles seems to have been a singularly unlearned and superstitious friend of works, the office required the rather that, for the greater part, those sections in which faith in Christ is taught, be appointed. This certainly may be seen more frequently in the Gospels, whoever has been the originator of those lessons. But in the meantime vernacular preaching will supply this lack. If it shall come to pass in the future that Mass shall be celebrated in the vernacular (which may Christ grant!), attention must be given so that Epistles and Gospels, chosen from the best and more weighty parts of these writings, be read in the Mass.

In the fourth place, the *Gradual* of two verses, likewise with the *Alleluia*, or both, should be sung as the bishop decides. But the *Quadragesima Graduals* and the like, which are longer than two verses, any one who wishes may sing these in his own home. In church, we do not wish to extinguish the spirit of the faithful with tedious things. It is not fitting to distinguish the Quadragesima, or the Greater Week, or the Feria Sexta, with rites other than those customary elsewhere, lest we seem to banter and ridicule Christ further with half a mass and the one part of the Sacrament. For *Alleluia* is the perpetual voice of the Church, just as the memorial of His (Christ's) passion and victory is perpetual.

In the fifth place, we allow no *Sequences* or *Proses*, unless it please the bishop to use the short one for the Nativity of Christ, *Grates nunc omnes*. Nor are there hardly any which are redolent of the Spirit save those of the Holy Spirit: *Sancti Spiritus* and *Veni Sancte Spiritus*, which one may sing after breakfast or at Vespers or at Mass (if the bishop pleases).

In the sixth place, the *Gospel* lection follows, where we prohibit neither candles nor censing. But we do not demand this; let this be free.

In the seventh place, the custom of singing the Nicene Creed is not displeasing. Likewise concerning vernacular preaching, we are of the opinion that it does not matter whether this is done after the *Symbolum* or before the Introit of the Mass, although there is a reason why it might be more aptly done before Mass, because the Gospel is the voice calling in the wilderness and bidding unbelievers to faith.

The Mass indeed should be the use of the Gospel and also the Communion of the Table of the Lord, which certainly belongs to the faithful and is fitting to be celebrated privately; but nevertheless that reason does not bind us who are free, especially because all things which are done in the Mass up to the *Symbolum* are ours and are free, not exacted by God, on which account they do not necessarily pertain to the Mass.

In the eighth place, there follows that complete abomination, into the service of which all that precedes in the Mass has been forced, whence it is called *Offertorium*, and on account of which nearly everything sounds and reeks of oblation. In the midst of these things those words of life and salvation[3] have been placed, just like in times past the ark of the Lord was placed in the temple of idols next to Dagon. And there is no Israelite there who is able either to approach or lead back the ark, until it has made its enemies infamous, smiting them on the back with eternal shame, and has compelled them to send it away, which is a parable for the present time. Therefore repudiating all those things which smack of sacrifice and of the Offertory, together with the entire *Canon*, let us retain those things which are pure and holy, and then we will order our Mass in this fashion.

I. During the Creed or after the Canon,[4] let bread and wine be prepared in the customary way for consecration. Except that I am not yet fixed in my mind as to whether or not water should be mixed with the wine, although I rather incline to the preparation of pure wine, because the indication strikes me as wrong which Isaiah advances in Chapter I, "Your wine," he says, "is mixed with water." For pure wine symbolizes beautifully the purity of the teaching of the Gospel. Then, too, nothing has been poured out for us save the blood of Christ only, unmixed with ours, of which we make commemoration here. Neither can the dream of those stand who say that our union with Christ is here symbolized, the commemoration of which union we do not make here. Nor are we united before the shedding of His blood, otherwise at the same time we would be celebrating the pouring out of our own blood with the blood of Christ for ourselves. Nevertheless in opposition to liberty, I will not introduce a superstitious law. Christ will not care very much about this, nor are these matters worthy of contention. Enough foolish contention over this has been engaged in by the Roman and Greek Churches as also in many other matters. And because some assert that blood and water flowed from the side of Christ, that does not prove anything. For that water signifies something other than what they wish to be signified by that mixed water. Nor was that mixed with the blood. Moreover the figure proves nothing, and the example does not stand; hence as a human invention it is held to be free.

II. The bread and the wine having been prepared, then let the order be in this manner: The Lord be with you. Response: And with thy spirit. Lift up (your) hearts. Response: Let us lift them to the Lord. Let us give thanks unto our Lord God. Response: It is meet and right. It is truly meet and right, just and salutary for us to give thanks to Thee always and everywhere, Holy Lord, Father Almighty, Eternal God, through Christ our Lord.

III. Then . . . Who the day before He suffered took bread, giving thanks, broke and gave to His disciples, saying, Take, eat. This is my body, which is given for you.

Similarly also the cup, after He supped, saying, This cup is the new testament in my blood which is poured out for you and for many in remission of sins. As often as ye shall do this, do it in memory of me.

I wish these words of Christ, allowing a moderate pause after the Preface, to be recited in the same tone of voice in which the Lord's Prayer is sung at another place in the Canon; so that it will be possible for those standing by to hear, although in all these things liberty is allowed to pious minds to recite these words either silently or audibly.

IV. The Consecration ended, let the choir sing the *Sanctus*, and when the *Benedictus* is sung, let the bread and chalice be elevated according to the rite in use up to this time, chiefly on account of the infirm who might be greatly offended by the sudden change in this more noted rite in the Mass, especially where they have been taught through vernacular sermons what is sought by this elevation.

V. After this the Lord's Prayer is read. Thus: Let us pray: Taught by thy saving precepts, etc., omitting the prayer following: Deliver us, we beseech, with all signs, which they were wont to make over the host and with the host over the chalice; nor shall the host be broken or mixed in the chalice. But immediately after the Lord's Prayer shall be said, The Peace of the Lord, etc., which is, so to speak, a public absolution of the sins of the communicants, truly the Gospel voice announcing remission of sins, the one and most worthy preparation for the Lord's Table, if it be apprehended by faith and not otherwise than though it came forth from the mouth of Christ Himself. On account of this I wish it to be announced with face turned to the people, as the bishops were accustomed to do, which is the sole vestige of the ancient bishops left among our bishops.

VI. Then let him communicate himself first, then the people; in the meanwhile let the *Agnus Dei* be sung. But if he should desire to pray the prayer, O Lord Jesus Christ, Son of the living God, who according to the will of the Father, etc., before communing, he will not pray wrongly, only change the singular number to the plural, *ours* and *us* for mine and *me*. Likewise the prayer, The Body of the Lord, etc., guard *my* soul, or *thy* soul unto life eternal. And the Blood, of *our* Lord, guard *thy* soul unto life eternal.

VII. If he desires to sing the Communion let it be sung. But in place of the *ad complendam* or final collect which so frequently savors of sacrifice, let this prayer be read in the same tone: What we have taken with the mouth, O Lord. This one also may be read: Thy Body, O Lord, which we have received, etc., changing to the plural number. Who livest and reignest, etc. The Lord be with you, etc. In place of the *Ite missa*, let *Benedicamus domino* be said, adding Alleluia according to its own melodies where and when it is desired; or *Benedicamus* may be borrowed from Vespers.

VIII. Let the customary Benediction be given. Or take that from Numbers 6, which the Lord Himself arranged and ordered: *The Lord Bless us and guard us: May He show us His face and be merciful to us; The Lord turn His face to us and give us peace. Or that in Psalm 96, May God, our God, bless us: May God bless us and all the ends of the earth fear Him. Amen.* I believe Christ used something of this kind when, ascending into heaven, He blessed His disciples.

And this, too, should be free to the bishop, namely, by what order he may desire either to receive or to administer both species. For assuredly he may consecrate both bread and wine consecutively before he receives the bread; or between the consecration of the bread and wine he may communicate with the bread both himself and as many as desire it, and thereupon consecrate the wine and at length give to all to drink of it. After which manner Christ seems to have acted, as the words of the Gospel reveal, where He commanded to eat the bread before He blessed the cup. Then is said expressly: Likewise also the cup after He supped. Thus you perceive the cup was blessed only after eating the bread. But this quite new rite will not permit the doing of those things following the Consecration about which we spoke above, unless they should be changed.

This is the way we think about the Mass, but at the same time taking care in all such matters lest we make binding things which are free, or compel those to sin who either would do some other thing or omit certain things; only let them keep the Words of Consecration uncorrupted, and let them do this in faith. For these should be the usages of Christians, that is of children of the free woman, who observe these things voluntarily and from the heart, changing them as often as and in whatever manner they might wish. Wherefore it is not right that one should either require or establish some indispensable form as a law in this matter, by which he might ensnare or vex consciences. Whence also we find no complete example of this use in the ancient fathers and in the primitive Church, save only in the Roman Church. But if they have appointed something as a law in this matter, it should not be observed; because these things neither can nor should be bound by laws. Then, even if different people make use of different rites, let no one either judge or despise the other; but let each one abound in his own opinion, and let them understand and know even if they do differently; and let each one's rite be agreeable to the other, lest diverse opinions and sects yield diverse uses, just as happened in the Roman Church. For external rites, even if we are not able to do without them—just as we cannot do without food and drink—nevertheless, do not commend us to God, just as food does not commend us to God. But faith and love commend us to God. Wherefore let this word of Paul govern here: The kingdom of God is not food and drink, but righteousness, peace and joy in the Holy Spirit. Thus no rite is the Kingdom of God, but faith within you, etc.

We have passed by vestments. But we think about these as we do about other uses; we permit them to be used without restraint, only let pomp and the excess of splendor be absent. For neither are you the more acceptable if you should consecrate in vestments; nor are you the less acceptable if you should consecrate without vestments. For vestments do not commend us to God. But I do not wish them to be consecrated or blessed—as if they were about to be something sacred as compared with other garments—except by that general benediction, by which it is taught that every good creature of God is sanctified through word and prayer; otherwise it would be an utter superstition and impiety, introduced through the abominations of the pontiffs, as also other things.

Concerning the Communion of the People

We have said these foregoing things about the Mass and the office of the minister or bishop; now we will speak about the custom of communicating the people, on account of whom chiefly this Supper of the Lord was instituted and is called by that name. For as it is most absurd for a minister of the Word to act so foolishly as to publish the Word in public ministration where there is no hearer, and to cry aloud to himself alone amid rocks and woods and in the open air, so it is most wrong if ministers make ready and adorn the common Supper of the Lord where there would be no guests who would eat and drink, and they alone, who ought to minister to others, would eat and drink at an empty table and in an empty sanctuary. Wherefore if we wish truly to prize the institution of Christ, no private Mass should be left remaining in the Church, unless in this connection either infirmity or necessity should be tolerated for a time.

Moreover the custom is to be preserved here which is observed in connection with baptism; namely, that notice must first be given to the bishop, by those who are about to commune, that they request to be communicated with the Lord's Supper, so that he may be able to know both their names and manner of life. Then let him not admit those seeking, unless they should give a reason for their faith; and being questioned, should answer, whether they understand what the Supper of the Lord is; what it stands for; and of what they wish to become partakers by its use; to wit, if they are able to recite the Words of Consecration from memory and explain that they come because of the consciousness of sin, or the fear of death, or, troubled by some other evil of the temptation of the flesh, of the world, of the devil, they hunger and thirst for that word and sign of grace and salvation from the Lord Himself through the ministry of the bishop by which they may be consoled and comforted, such as Christ out of priceless love gave and instituted in this Supper when He said: Take and eat, etc.

But I think it will be sufficient if this questioning and investigation of him who seeks to be communicated is done once a year. Indeed it is possible that the one who seeks may be so understanding that he should be questioned either once only in his entire life, or in fact never. For through this custom we desire to guard against this: that the worthy and unworthy do not rush blindly to the Supper of the Lord, as we have seen done in the Roman Church hitherto, where nothing else is sought but to be communicated. Of faith, of comfort, of the whole use and fruits of the Supper absolutely neither mention nor consideration of these has had a place. Indeed they have concealed the very Words of Consecration, that is, the Bread of Life Itself, forcing this with vast zeal, yea, with highest frenzy, in order that communicants should perform a good work by their own merit, and that they should not nourish and strengthen faith through the goodness of Christ. But those who are not able to answer after the manner mentioned above, we desire such wholly excluded and banished from the communion of this Supper, as being without the wedding garment.

Then when the bishop has perceived that they understand these things, he should also watch this, whether they evidence this faith and knowledge in life and conduct—for Satan also both perceives all these things and is able to talk about them—that is, if he should see some fornicator, adulterer, drunkard, gamester, usurer, slanderer, or one made infamous by some manifest crime, let him be excluded absolutely from this Supper, unless by evident proof he shall have witnessed that his life has been changed. For the Supper should not be denied those who sometimes fall away and return, sorrowing over the lapse; indeed we should realize that the Supper was instituted especially on account of just such as these so that they may be refreshed and strengthened; for we all offend in many things; and we carry each other's burdens while we also mutually burden ourselves. But I am speaking of those contemptuous ones who sin shamelessly and without fear, yet, nevertheless, boast glorious things about the Gospel.

Then when Mass is celebrated, it is fitting that those about to be communicated gather together by themselves in one place and in one group. For to this end the altar was invented, also the choir. Not that standing here or there matters anything with God or adds anything to faith, but that it is necessary that they be seen and known openly, both by those who commune and those who do not commune; thus then their lives may be the better observed and proven and made known. For participation in this Supper is part of the confession by which they confess before God and angels and men that they are Christians. Therefore care must be taken lest they carry off the Supper stealthily, and then mingled with others it is not known whether they live well or badly. However, I do not wish this to be made a law here, but to point out this—what honorable and fitting (thing) may be performed freely by free Christians.

Now concerning private confession before communion. I still think as I have taught heretofore, namely, that it is neither necessary nor to be demanded; nevertheless it is useful and not to be despised, since the Lord neither required this Supper as necessary or established it by law, but left it free to everyone, saying, As often as you do this, etc. So concerning the preparation for the Supper, we think that preparing oneself by fasting and prayers is a matter of liberty. Certainly it behooves us to approach in soberness of mind and earnestly and diligently, whether you fast nothing at best or pray ever so little. In truth, I say, moderation in drinking, not that superstitious practice of the papists;[5] but moderation, lest you belch drunkenly and become sluggish and dull from a distended belly. For the best preparation is, as I have said, a soul moved and vexed by sins, death, temptations, and hungering and thirsting for healing and strength. Whatever of these things is true, these are the concern of the bishop and it rests with him that he may teach the people.

This now remains to be considered, whether both forms, [that is, both bread and wine] as they call them, should be ministered to the people. So here I say, Now that the Gospel has been inculcated among us these two whole years, at the same time sufficient indulgence also has been granted to infirmity. Hereafter one must act according to that saying of Paul: He who is ignorant, let him be ignorant. For it does not matter, if they, who for so long a time have not known the Gospel, do not receive again neither of the two forms, lest perchance bearing with infirmity perpetually may nourish obstinacy and result in proscription contrary to the Gospel. Wherefore simply according to the institution of Christ, let both forms be both sought and ministered. Those who do not desire this, let them have their way; and let nothing be ministered to them. For we point out this form of the Mass to those to whom it is known in some part. But those who have not heard as yet, or who have ability to know, it is not yet possible to offer them any counsel concerning this matter.

Nor should this matter be delayed at all in order that they may call together a Council, in which this may again by sanctioned as allowable. We have the law of Christ and we do not want either to be hindered by or to hear a Council in those matters which manifestly are of the Gospel. Yea, we say more. And if by chance a Council would decide and permit this, then least of all do we want to partake of both forms; nay, on the contrary, then first in contempt both of the Council and its statute, we would wish to partake either of one or neither, but never of both; and we would hold those to be wholly anathema who would partake of both on the authority of such Council and statute. Do you wonder at this and ask the reason? Hear!—if you know the bread and wine were instituted by Christ, and both are to be received by all, as the Gospel and Paul testify most clearly, and as the adversaries themselves are forced to admit; nevertheless you do not dare to believe and trust Him so that you receive, but you dare to receive if men decide this in a Council:—then are you not preferring men to Christ? Do you not extol sinful men above Him who is named and worshiped, God? Do you not trust in the words of men more than in the words of God? Nay rather, do you not utterly distrust the words of God and believe only the words of men? Moreover, how great is such hatred and denial of the most high God? What idolatry then can equal your religious obedience of a Council of men? Should you not the rather die a thousand times? Should you not the rather receive one or no form, than receive under such sacrilegious obedience and apostasy from the faith?

Therefore let them stop talking about their councils continually; but let them do this first, let them replace their sacrilege with the divine glory; let them confess that with Satan their master they have held back one form; that they have lifted themselves up above God; that they have condemned the Word, and destroyed so many people through so many ages; and let them do penance for this unspeakable tyranny of inhumanity and impiety. Then let them solemnly declare that we have done right when on our part and even against their dogmas we have taught and received both forms and have not waited for their Council, and let them give thanks because we refused to follow their perdition and abomination. After they have done this, we will be willing and well-disposed to honor and welcome their Council and ordinance. In the meantime should they not do this, but continue to demand that we await their authorization (for our action), we will listen to nothing; but we will continue both to teach and to do things which are opposed to them; in particular, those things which we know are especially displeasing to them. For what do they exact by this diabolical demand save that we exalt them above God, their words above His words, and erect the abominable monsters of their spectres as idols in the place of God, when we want the whole world to be put under God and made subject to Him.

I also wish as many of the songs as possible to be in the vernacular, which the people should sing during Mass either immediately after the *Gradual*, and immediately after the *Sanctus* and *Agnus dei*. For who doubts that once upon a time all the people sang these, which now only the choir sings or responds when the bishop is consecrating? But these songs may be ordered by the bishops in this manner, they may be sung either right after the Latin songs, or on alternate days, now Latin, now the vernacular, until the entire Mass shall be made vernacular. But poets are wanting among us,—or they are not known as yet,—who can put together pleasingly pious and spiritual songs, as Paul calls them, which are worthy to be used by all the people in the Church of God. In the meantime it is proper to sing this after communion: *Gott sey gelobet und gebenedeyet der uns selber hatt gespeyset*, [God be praised and blessed is he who has fed us], etc.; omitting this small part: *Und das heylige sacramente, an unserm letzten ende, aus des geweyeten priesters hende*, [And the holy sacrament, at our end, from the ordained priest's hands], which was added by someone of the cult of St. Barbara, who, holding the sacrament during his whole life as of little value, in death hopes, without faith, by this good work to enter into life. For both the meter and the manner of the music prove this part of the song is superfluous. In addition to that, this is good: *Nu bitten wyr den heyligen geist* [Now we beseech the Holy Spirit]. Also: *Eyn kindelin so lobelich* [A little child so praiseworthy]. For you will not find many, which in some respect taste of a dignified spirit. I say this, so that if there are any German poets, they may be moved to and work out, pious poems for us.

Let these things said concerning the mass and communion suffice for the time being; other matters, use and the thing itself will teach; only let the Word of God be announced in the church actively and faithfully. For that which some require so strongly, namely, that all these things be proved by the Scriptures and the example of the fathers, does not disturb us greatly; because we have said above, that in these matters liberty ought to rule, and it is not allowable to captivate Christian consciences either by laws or orders. For this reason the Scriptures define nothing of these things but permit the liberty of the spirit to abound according to its own perception in the matter, according to the fitness of places, times, and persons. Indeed the examples of the fathers are in part unknown; those which really are known are so varied that nothing definite can be established about them, evidently because they themselves used their own liberty. And even if they would be altogether definite and simple, nevertheless they could not impose upon us either law or necessity of imitating them.

In connection with the rest of the days, which we call *feriae* [festivals], I see nothing which cannot be continued, only discontinue the Mass; for Matins of three lessons and the Hours, including Vespers and *Compline de tempore*, excluding the *feriae* of saints, are nothing other than words of divine Scripture. And it is fitting, nay necessary, that the boys be accustomed to reading and hearing the Psalms and lections of Holy Scripture. But if anything here ought to be made new, the prolixity of things can be changed according to and at the will of the bishop; however after this fashion, that three Psalms be appointed for Matins, three for Vespers, together with one or two Responsories. These matters cannot be ordered better than at the will of the bishop whose duty it is to choose the best of the Responsories and Antiphons and to appoint their use from Lord's Day to Lord's Day throughout the week, so that neither excessive repetition of the same things cause aversion, nor too much variety and multitudinous singing and reading generate weariness of spirit. But let the entire Psalter, divided in parts, remain in use and the entire Scriptures, divided into lections, let this be preserved in the ears of the Church.

Here, too, must be noted what I have suggested elsewhere, in order that this singing may not be a matter merely of tongue and of speech, or without sense like the sound of a pipe or harp. Therefore, daily lections must be appointed, one for the morning in the New or Old Testament, another for Vespers in one or the other testament with vernacular exposition. This rite is an ancient one, as is proven by both the custom itself and the word *Homilia* in Matins, and *Capitulum* in Vespers and the other Hours, namely, that the Christians, as often as they gathered together, read something and then it was interpreted in the vernacular, after the custom which St. Paul describes in I Corinthians 14. Then when more evil times came, when prophets and interpreters were wanting, only this voice was left remaining after the lections and capitula, *Deo gratias*. Then in place of the interpretation, lections, psalms and hymns were multiplied and other things also in this wearying verbosity and superabundance. Although the hymns and *Te deum laudamus* bear testimony to this as does *Deo gratias* also, namely, that after the expositions and homilies they praised God and gave Him thanks for the true revelation of the Word of God. Such also I wish our vernacular songs to do.

This much, O best Nicolas, I have for you in writing about the rites and ceremonies of our Wittenberg church, already partly instituted and, Christ willing, to be completed at an early day; which example, if it pleases you and others, you may imitate. If not, we will give place to your wisdom, being prepared to accept what is more fitting from you and any others. Let it not frighten either you or any others because that sacrilegious Tophet still persists in our Wittenberg, which is impious and wretched gain to the princes of Saxony; I speak of the Church of All Saints.[6] For by the mercy of God there is antidote aplenty among us through the abundance of the Word of God, so that the pest, weary and faint in its own corner, may not be a pestilence to any save itself. And there are scarcely three or four swine and gourmands in that same house of perdition who worship that wealth; to all others and at the same time to all the people, it is a notable cause of loathing and an abomination.

Nor is it allowed to proceed against them by force or command, as you know it is not fitting for Christians to fight save with the power of the sword of the Spirit. For in this way I hold the people back daily, otherwise that house, now, for a long time, the House of All Saints,—nay rather the House of All Devils,—would be known by some other name in the earth. But I have not exercised the power of the Spirit, which God has given us, against that, patiently bearing that reproach, if perchance God may give them penitence; meanwhile I am content, because our house, which more truly is the House of All Saints, may reign here and stand as a tower of Lebanon against the House of All Devils. Thus we torment Satan with the Word, although he simulates a laugh; but Christ will grant that his hope will fail him and that he will be overthrown with all beholding.

Pray for me, O holy one of God.
Grace be with you and with all yours. Amen.

Notes

1. See *Liturgies of the Western Church*, ed. Bard Thompson (Cleveland: World Publishing, 1961), 95–104, and *Works of Martin Luther*, trans. Paul Z. Strodach, vol. 6 (Philadelphia: Muhlenberg Press, 1932), 67–81.

2. This word omitted in the original print.

3. Luther means the Words of Institution.

4. The Latin here is *post Canonem*. Probably a printer's error for *Concionem*, "sermon."

5. Luther means rigorous fasting.

6. In the Castle Church of All Saints, there was an enormous treasure of relics collected by Luther's prince, Frederick the Wise.

7. Hymn: "Out of the Depths I Cry to Thee"

(1523)

MARTIN LUTHER

Congregational singing, in the language of the people, was an important consequence of the Protestant Reformation. Although there had been congregational singing in German during religious pilgrimages, for special occasions, at festivals of the church year, and even, to some extent, at mass, all of this was tolerated rather than encouraged by the official church. From the sixteenth century on, Protestantism gave great impetus to congregational singing in Latin and in the vernacular. As congregational services of worship became more widespread, hymns were a major means of lay participation.

Martin Luther (1483–1546) recognized the power of congregational singing and did more than any other reformer to strengthen congregational worship through hymns. As a well-educated member of the clergy, Luther had received a classical musical education in grammar school and at university. He deepened his knowledge of music in connection with Johann Walter, the first Protestant cantor to set Lutheran chorales in polyphony in 1524. His association with George Rhau, the greatest publisher of music in the sixteenth century, was also important.

Luther not only knew a great deal about music, he loved it. He regarded music as a wonderful gift given to humanity before the Fall (human sinfulness), and as deserving the highest praise next to the Word of God. Music's primary functions, according to Luther, were to praise God, to aid in the expression of Christian devotion, and to educate

---

SOURCE: *Hymnal of the Evangelical and Reformed Church* (St. Louis: Eden Publishing House, 1941).

people in the gospel, helping with its propagation. Although he was not opposed to the use of musical instruments in worship, he believed that the primary means for carrying out these purposes was the singing of the human voice.

Luther continued to encourage the use of Latin hymns. Beginning in 1523, his Formula of Mass and Communion for the Church at Wittenberg *(see vol. 2:134) promoted the congregational singing of German songs and encouraged their production by German poets. Toward the end of the same year, Luther wrote George Spalatin, the court secretary chaplain to Frederick the Wise, asking him to turn some of the Psalms into verse. Luther indicated that he was asking others to do the same, and somewhat later he tried his own hand at hymn writing. The hymn* Aus Tiefer Not *(Out of the depths) is based on Psalm 130. Its four stanzas with melody have their foundation in the Strasburg hymnal of 1525. As one of the earliest of Luther's hymns, it gives a vivid expression of his religious devotion. "Out of the Depths I Cry to Thee" appeared in the Evangelical and Reformed Church* Hymnal *of 1941 in a translation derived from the* New Congregational Hymnbook *of 1859.*[1]

Out of the depths I cry to Thee;
Lord, hear me, I implore Thee;
Bend down Thy gracious ear to me,
Let my prayer come before Thee!
On my misdeeds in mercy look,
O deign to blot them from Thy book,
Or who can stand before Thee?

Thy sovereign grace and boundless love
Make Thee, O Lord, forgiving;
My purest thoughts and deeds but prove,
Sin in my heart is living:
None guiltless in Thy sight appear,
All who approach Thy throne must fear,
And humbly trust Thy mercy.

Thou canst be merciful while just,
This is my hope's foundation;
On Thy redeeming grace I trust,
Grant me, then, Thy salvation.
Shielded by Thee, I stand secure;
Thy word is firm, Thy promise sure,
And I rely upon Thee.

Where'er the greatest sins abound,
By grace they are exceeded;
Thy helping hand is always found
With aid, where aid is needed:
Thy hand, the only hand to save,
Will save the sinner from the grave,
And pardon his transgression. Amen.

Note

1. See Ulrich S. Leupold, "Liturgies and Hymns," in *Luther's Works*, vol. 53 (Philadelphia: Fortress Press, 1965), 221–22.

8. Small Catechism

(1529)

MARTIN LUTHER

Martin Luther (1483–1546) had been concerned about catechetical instruction for some time prior to the publication of the Small Catechism and the Large Catechism (called by Luther the German Catechism) in 1529. He regularly preached catechetical sermons and urged friends to prepare a catechism for children. Unfortunately, no catechism was forthcoming, and Luther became increasingly appalled by the ignorance he observed in electoral Saxony and Meissen during his visits in late 1528. He thus decided to write one himself, producing a Large Catechism for pastors and a Small Catechism for the uneducated and for children.

Although several Protestant catechisms had been prepared early in the Reformation, Luther's Small Catechism is often seen as the beginning of catechesis in the modern sense. It had enormous influence on all subsequent catechisms, both Protestant and Catholic. It was incorporated into Lutheran church orders and confessional statements in the sixteenth century, and it has remained a basis for catechetical instruction in Lutheran churches right up to the present.[1]

Luther's Small Catechism also became an important catechetical and confessional document for German immigrants in the German Evangelical history of the United Church of Christ. In 1934, when the German Evangelical Synod of North America merged with the Reformed Church in the United States to create the Evangelical and Reformed Church, Luther's Small Catechism, the Heidelberg Catechism (see vol. 2:327–58),

---

SOURCE: Theodore G. Tappert, ed., *Book of Concord* (Philadelphia: Fortress Press, 1959). Used by permission of Augsburg Fortress Publishers.

and the Augsburg Confession (see vol. 2:160–95) were claimed as "authoritative interpretations of the essential truth taught in the Holy Scriptures."[2] *Still later, in the United Church of Christ constitution and bylaws (approved in 1961), the Evangelical and Reformed Church and the National Council of the Congregational Christian Churches accepted Luther's Small Catechism and other theological legacies "without break in their respective historic continuities and traditions."*

Preface

Grace, mercy, and peace in Jesus Christ, our Lord, from Martin Luther to all faithful, godly pastors and preachers.

The deplorable conditions which I recently encountered when I was a visitor[3] constrained me to prepare this brief and simple catechism or statement of Christian teaching. Good God, what wretchedness I beheld! The common people, especially those who live in the country, have no knowledge whatever of Christian teaching, and unfortunately many pastors are quite incompetent and unfitted for teaching. Although the people are supposed to be Christian, are baptized, and receive the holy sacrament, they do not know the Lord's Prayer, the Creed, or the Ten Commandments, they live as if they were pigs and irrational beasts, and now that the Gospel has been restored they have mastered the fine art of abusing liberty.

How will you bishops answer for it before Christ that you have so shamefully neglected the people and paid no attention at all to the duties of your office? May you escape punishment for this! You withhold the cup in the Lord's Supper and insist on the observance of human laws, yet you do not take the slightest interest in teaching the people the Lord's Prayer, the Creed, the Ten Commandments, or a single part of the Word of God. Woe to you forever!

I therefore beg of you for God's sake, my beloved brethren who are pastors and preachers, that you take the duties of your office seriously, that you have pity on the people who are entrusted to your care, and that you help me to teach the catechism to the people, especially those who are young. Let those who lack the qualifications to do better at least take this booklet and these forms and read them to the people word for word in this manner:

In the first place, the preacher should take the utmost care to avoid changes or variations in the text and wording of the Ten Commandments, the Creed, the Lord's Prayer, the sacraments, etc. On the contrary, he should adopt one form, adhere to it, and use it repeatedly year after year. Young and inexperienced people must be instructed on the basis of a uniform, fixed text and form. They are easily confused if a teacher employs one form now and another form—perhaps with the intention of making improvements—later on. In this way all the time and labor will be lost.

This was well understood by our good fathers, who were accustomed to use the same form in teaching the Lord's Prayer, the Creed, and the Ten Commandments. We, too, should teach these things to the young and unlearned in such a way that we do not alter a single syllable or recite the catechism differently from year to year. Choose the form that pleases you, therefore, and adhere to it henceforth. When you preach to intelligent and educated people, you are at liberty to exhibit your learning and to discuss these topics from different angles and in such a variety of ways as you may be capable of. But when you are teaching the young, adhere to a fixed and unchanging form and method. Begin by teaching them the Ten Commandments, the Creed, the Lord's Prayer, etc., following the text word for word so that the young may repeat these things after you and retain them in their memory.

If any refuse to receive your instructions, tell them that they deny Christ and are no Christians. They should not be admitted to the sacrament, be accepted as sponsors in Baptism, or be allowed to participate in any Christian privileges. On the contrary, they should be turned over to the pope and his officials, and even to the devil himself. In addition, parents and employers should refuse to furnish them with food and drink and should notify them that the prince is disposed to banish such rude people from his land.

Although we cannot and should not compel anyone to believe, we should nevertheless insist that the people learn to know how to distinguish between right and wrong according to the standards of those among whom they live and make their living. For anyone who desires to reside in a city is bound to know and observe the laws under whose protection he lives, no matter whether he is a believer or, at heart, a scoundrel or knave.

In the second place, after the people have become familiar with the text, teach them what it means. For this purpose, take the explanations in this booklet, or choose any other brief and fixed explanations which you may prefer, and adhere to them without changing a single syllable, as stated above with reference to the text. Moreover, allow yourself ample time, for it is not necessary to take up all the parts at once. They can be presented one at a time. When the learners have a proper understanding of the First Commandment, proceed to the Second Commandment, and so on. Otherwise they will be so overwhelmed that they will hardly remember anything at all.

In the third place, after you have thus taught this brief catechism, take up a large catechism[4] so that the people may have a richer and fuller understanding. Expound every commandment, petition, and part, pointing out their respective obligations, benefits, dangers, advantages, and disadvantages, as you will find all of this treated at length in the many books written for this purpose. Lay the greatest weight on those commandments or other parts which seem to require special attention among the people where you are. For example, the Seventh Commandment, which treats of stealing, must be emphasized when instructing laborers and shopkeepers, and even farmers and servants, for many of these are guilty of dishonesty and thievery. So, too, the Fourth Commandment must be stressed when instructing children and the common people in order that they may be encouraged to be orderly, faithful, obedient, and peaceful. Always adduce many examples from the Scriptures to show how God punished and blessed.

You should also take pains to urge governing authorities and parents to rule wisely and educate their children. They must be shown that they are obliged to do so, and that they are guilty of damnable sin if they do not do so, for by such neglect they undermine and lay waste both the kingdom of God and the kingdom of the world and are the worst enemies of God and man. Make very plain to them the shocking evils they introduce when they refuse their aid in the training of children to become pastors, preachers, notaries, etc., and tell them that God will inflict awful punishments on them for these sins. It is necessary to preach about such things. The extent to which parents and governing authorities sin in this respect is beyond telling. The devil also has a horrible purpose in mind.

Finally, now that the people are freed from the tyranny of the pope, they are unwilling to receive the sacrament and they treat it with contempt. Here, too, there is need of exhortation, but with this understanding: No one is to be compelled to believe or to receive the sacrament, no law is to be made concerning it, and no time or place should be appointed for it. We should so preach that, of their own accord and without any law, the people will desire the sacrament and, as it were, compel us pastors to administer it to them. This can be done by telling them: It is to be feared that anyone who does not desire to receive the sacrament at least three or four times a year despises the sacrament and is no Christian, just as he is no Christian who does not hear and believe the Gospel. Christ did not say, "Omit this," or "Despise this," but he said, "Do this, as often as you drink it," etc. [1 Cor. 11:25]. Surely he wishes that this be done and not that it be omitted and despised. "*Do* this," he said.

He who does not highly esteem the sacrament suggests thereby that he has no sin, no flesh, no devil, no world, no death, no hell. That is to say, he believes in none of these, although he is deeply immersed in them and is held captive by the devil. On the other hand, he suggests that he needs no grace, no life, no paradise, no heaven, no Christ, no God, nothing good at all. For if he believed that he was involved in so much that is evil and was in need of so much that is good, he would not neglect the sacrament in which aid is afforded against such evil and in which such good is bestowed. It is not necessary to compel him by any law to receive the sacrament, for he will hasten to it of his own accord, he will feel constrained to receive it, he will insist that you administer it to him.

Accordingly you are not to make a law of this, as the pope has done. All you need to do is clearly to set forth the advantage and disadvantage, the benefit and loss, the blessing and danger connected with this sacrament. Then the people will come of their own accord and without compulsion on your part. But if they refuse to come, let them be, and tell them that those who do not feel and acknowledge their great need and God's gracious help belong to the devil. If you do not give such admonitions, or if you adopt odious laws on the subject, it is your own fault if the people treat the sacrament with contempt. How can they be other than negligent if you fail to do your duty and remain silent. So it is up to you, dear pastor and preacher! Our office has become something different from what it was under the pope. It is now a ministry of grace and salvation. It subjects us to greater burdens and labors, dangers and temptations, with little reward or gratitude from the world. But Christ himself will be our reward if we labor faithfully. The Father of all grace grant it! To him be praise and thanks forever, through Christ, our Lord. Amen.

[I]
The Ten Commandments in the plain form in which the head of the family shall teach them to his household[5]

The First

"You shall have no other gods."[6]

What does this mean?

Answer: We should fear, love, and trust in God above all things.

The Second

"You shall not take the name of the Lord your God in vain."

What does this mean?

Answer: We should fear and love God, and so we should not use his name to curse, swear, practice magic, lie, or deceive, but in every time of need call upon him, pray to him, praise him, and give him thanks.

The Third

"Remember the Sabbath day, to keep it holy."

What does this mean?

Answer: We should fear and love God, and so we should not despise his Word and the preaching of the same, but deem it holy and gladly hear and learn it.

The Fourth

"Honor your father and your mother."

What does this mean?

Answer: We should fear and love God, and so we should not despise our parents and superiors, nor provoke them to anger, but honor, serve, obey, love, and esteem them.

The Fifth

"You shall not kill."

What does this mean?

Answer: We should fear and love God, and so we should not endanger our neighbor's life, nor cause him any harm, but help and befriend him in every necessity of life.

The Sixth

"You shall not commit adultery."

What does this mean?

Answer: We should fear and love God, and so we should lead a chaste and pure life in word and deed, each one loving and honoring his wife or her husband.

The Seventh

"You shall not steal."

What does this mean?

Answer: We should fear and love God, and so we should not rob our neighbor of his money or property, nor bring them into our possession by dishonest trade or by dealing in shoddy wares, but help him to improve and protect his income and property.

The Eighth

"You shall not bear false witness against your neighbor."

What does this mean?

Answer: We should fear and love God, and so we should not tell lies about our neighbor, nor betray, slander, or defame him, but should apologize for him, speak well of him, and interpret charitably all that he does.

The Ninth

"You shall not covet your neighbor's house."

What does this mean?

Answer: We should fear and love God, and so we should not seek by craftiness to gain possession of our neighbor's inheritance or home, nor to obtain them under pretext of legal right, but be of service and help to him so that he may keep what is his.

The Tenth

"You shall not covet your neighbor's wife, or his manservant, or his maidservant, or his ox, or his ass, or anything that is your neighbor's."

What does this mean?

Answer: We should fear and love God, and so we should not abduct, estrange, or entice away our neighbor's wife, servants, or cattle, but encourage them to remain and discharge their duty to him.

Conclusion

What does God declare concerning all these commandments?

Answer: He says, "I the Lord your God am a jealous God, visiting the iniquity of the fathers upon the children to the third and the fourth generation of those who hate me, but showing steadfast love to thousands of those who love me and keep my commandments."

What does this mean?

Answer: God threatens to punish all who transgress these commandments. We should therefore fear his wrath and not disobey these commandments. On the other hand, he promises grace and every blessing to all who keep them. We should therefore love him, trust in him, and cheerfully do what he has commanded.

[II]
The Creed in the plain form in which the head of the family shall teach it to his household

The First Article: Creation

"I believe in God, the Father almighty, maker of heaven and earth."

What does this mean?

Answer: I believe that God has created me and all that exists; that he has given me and still sustains my body and soul, all my limbs and senses, my reason and all the faculties of my mind, together with food and clothing, house and home, family and property; that he provides me daily and abundantly with all the necessities of life, protects me from all danger, and preserves me from all evil. All this he does out of his pure, fatherly, and divine goodness and mercy, without any merit or worthiness on my part. For all of this I am bound to thank, praise, serve, and obey him. This is most certainly true.

The Second Article: Redemption

"And in Jesus Christ, his only son, our Lord: who was conceived by the Holy Spirit, born of the virgin Mary, suffered under Pontius Pilate, was crucified, dead, and buried: he descended into hell, the third day he rose from the dead, he ascended into heaven, and is seated on the right hand of God, the Father almighty, whence he shall come to judge the living and the dead."

What does this mean?

Answer: I believe that Jesus Christ, true God, begotten of the Father from eternity, and also true man, born of the virgin Mary, is my Lord, who has redeemed me, a lost and condemned creature, delivered me and freed me from all sins, from death, and from the power of the devil, not with silver and gold but with his holy and precious blood and with his innocent sufferings and death, in order that I may be his, live under him in his kingdom, and serve him in everlasting righteousness, innocence, and blessedness, even as he is risen from the dead and lives and reigns to all eternity. This is most certainly true.

The Third Article: Sanctification

"I believe in the Holy Spirit, the holy Christian church, the communion of saints, the forgiveness of sins, the resurrection of the body, and the life everlasting. Amen."

What does this mean?

Answer: I believe that by my own reason or strength I cannot believe in Jesus Christ, my Lord, or come to him. But the Holy Spirit has called me through the Gospel, enlightened me with his gifts, and sanctified and preserved me in true faith, just as he calls, gathers, enlightens, and sanctifies the whole Christian church on earth and preserves it in union with Jesus Christ in the one true faith. In this Christian church he daily and abundantly forgives all my sins, and the sins of all believers, and on the last day he will raise me and all the dead and will grant eternal life to me and to all who believe in Christ. This is most certainly true.

[III]
The Lord's Prayer in the plain form in which the head of the family shall teach it to his household.

Introduction

"Our Father who art in heaven."

What does this mean?

Answer: Here God would encourage us to believe that he is truly our Father and we are truly his children in order that we may approach him boldly and confidently in prayer, even as beloved children approach their dear father.

The First Petition

"Hallowed be thy name."

What does this mean?

Answer: To be sure, God's name is holy in itself, but we pray in this petition that it may also be holy for us.

How is this done?

Answer: When the Word of God is taught clearly and purely and we, as children of God, lead holy lives in accordance with it. Help us to do this, dear Father in heaven! But whoever teaches and lives otherwise than as the Word of God teaches, profanes the name of God among us. From this preserve us, heavenly Father!

The Second Petition

"Thy kingdom come."

What does this mean?

Answer: To be sure, the kingdom of God comes of itself, without our prayer, but we pray in this petition that it may also come to us.

How is this done?

Answer: When the heavenly Father gives us his Holy Spirit so that by his grace we may believe his holy Word and live a godly life, both here in time and hereafter forever.

The Third Petition

"Thy will be done, on earth as it is in heaven."

What does this mean?

Answer: To be sure, the good and gracious will of God is done without our prayer, but we pray in this petition that it may also be done by us.

How is this done?

Answer: When God curbs and destroys every evil counsel and purpose of the devil, of the world, and of our flesh which would hinder us from hallowing his name and prevent the coming of his kingdom, and when he strengthens us and keeps us steadfast in his Word and in faith even to the end. This is his good and gracious will.

The Fourth Petition

"Give us this day our daily bread."

What does this mean?

Answer: To be sure, God provides daily bread, even to the wicked, without our prayer, but we pray in this petition that God may make us aware of his gifts and enable us to receive our daily bread with thanksgiving.

What is meant by daily bread?

Answer: Everything required to satisfy our bodily needs, such as food and clothing, house and home, fields and flocks, money and property; a pious spouse and good children, trustworthy servants, godly and faithful rulers, good government; seasonable weather, peace and health, order and honor; true friends, faithful neighbors, and the like.

The Fifth Petition

"And forgive us our debts, as we also have forgiven our debtors."

What does this mean?

Answer: We pray in this petition that our heavenly Father may not look upon our sins, and on their account deny our prayers, for we neither merit nor deserve those things for which we pray. Although we sin daily and deserve nothing but punishment, we nevertheless pray that God may grant us all things by his grace. And assuredly we on our part will heartily forgive and cheerfully do good to those who may sin against us.

The Sixth Petition

"And lead us not into temptation."

What does this mean?

Answer: God tempts no one to sin, but we pray in this petition that God may so guard and preserve us that the devil, the world, and our flesh may not deceive us or mislead us into unbelief, despair, and other great and shameful sins, but that, although we may be so tempted, we may finally prevail and gain the victory.

The Seventh Petition

"But deliver us from evil."

What does this mean?

Answer: We pray in this petition, as in a summary, that our Father in heaven may deliver us from all manner of evil, whether it affect body or soul, property or reputation, and that at last, when the hour of death comes, he may grant us a blessed end and graciously take us from this world of sorrow to himself in heaven.

Conclusion

"Amen."

What does this mean?

Answer: It means that I should be assured that such petitions are acceptable to our heavenly Father and are heard by him, for he himself commanded us to pray like this and promised to hear us. "Amen, amen" means "Yes, yes, it shall be so."

[IV]

The Sacrament of Holy Baptism in the plain form in which the head of the family shall teach it to his household

First

What is Baptism?

Answer: Baptism is not merely water, but it is water used according to God's command and connected with God's Word.

What is this Word of God?

Answer: As recorded in Matthew 28:19, our Lord Christ said, "Go therefore and make disciples of all nations, baptizing them in the name of the Father and of the Son and of the Holy Spirit."

Second

What gifts or benefits does Baptism bestow?

Answer: It effects forgiveness of sins, delivers from death and the devil, and grants eternal salvation to all who believe, as the Word and promise of God declare.

What is this Word and promise of God?

Answer: As recorded in Mark 16:16, our Lord Christ said, "He who believes and is baptized will be saved; but he who does not believe will be condemned."

Third

How can water produce such great effects?

Answer: It is not the water that produces these effects, but the Word of God connected with the water, and our faith which relies on the Word of God connected with the water. For without the Word of God the water is merely water and no Baptism. But when connected with the Word of God it is a Baptism, that is, a gracious water of life and a washing of regeneration in the Holy Spirit, as St. Paul wrote to Titus [3:5–8], "He saved us by the washing of regeneration and renewal in the Holy Spirit, which he poured out upon us richly through Jesus Christ our Saviour, so that we might be justified by his grace and become heirs in hope of eternal life. The saying is sure."

Fourth

What does such baptizing with water signify?

Answer: It signifies that the old Adam in us, together with all sins and evil lusts, should be drowned by daily sorrow and repentance and be put to death, and that the new man should come forth daily and rise up, cleansed and righteous, to live forever in God's presence.

Where is this written?

Answer: In Romans 6:4, St. Paul wrote, "We were buried therefore with him by baptism into death, so that as Christ was raised from the dead by the glory of the Father, we too might walk in newness of life."

[V]
Confession and Absolution
How Plain People Are to Be Taught to Confess

What is confession?

Answer: Confession consists of two parts. One is that we confess our sins. The other is that we receive absolution or forgiveness from the confessor as from God himself, by no means doubting but firmly believing that our sins are thereby forgiven before God in heaven.

What sins should we confess?

Answer: Before God we should acknowledge that we are guilty of all manner of sins, even those of which we are not aware, as we do in the Lord's Prayer. Before the confessor, however, we should confess only those sins of which we have knowledge and which trouble us.

What are such sins?

Answer: Reflect on your condition in the light of the Ten Commandments: whether you are a father or mother, a son or daughter, a master or servant; whether you have been disobedient, unfaithful, lazy, ill-tempered, or quarrelsome; whether you have harmed anyone by word or deed; and whether you have stolen, neglected, or wasted anything, or done other evil.

Please give me a brief form of confession.

Answer: You should say to the confessor: "Dear Pastor, please hear my confession and declare that my sins are forgiven for God's sake."

"Proceed."

"I, a poor sinner, confess before God that I am guilty of all sins. In particular I confess in your presence that, as a manservant or maidservant, etc., I am unfaithful to my master, for here and there I have not done what I was told. I have made my master angry, caused him to curse, neglected to do my duty, and caused him to suffer loss. I have also been immodest in word and deed. I have quarreled with my equals. I have grumbled and sworn at my mistress, etc. For all this I am sorry and pray for grace. I mean to do better."

A master or mistress may say: "In particular I confess in your presence that I have not been faithful in training my children, servants, and wife to the glory of God. I have cursed. I have set a bad example by my immodest language and actions. I have injured by neighbor by speaking evil of him, overcharging him, giving him inferior goods and short measure." Masters and mistresses should add whatever else they have done contrary to God's commandments and to their action in life, etc.

If, however, anyone does not feel that his conscience is burdened by such or by greater sins, he should not worry, nor should he search for and invent other sins, for this would turn confession into torture,[7] he should simply mention one or two sins of which he is aware. For example, "In particular I confess that I once cursed. On one occasion I also spoke indecently. And I neglected this or that," etc. Let this suffice.

If you have knowledge of no sin at all (which is quite unlikely), you should mention none in particular, but receive forgiveness upon the general confession which you make to God in the presence of the confessor.

Then the confessor shall say: "God be merciful to you and strengthen your faith. Amen."

Again he shall say: "Do you believe that the forgiveness I declare is the forgiveness of God?"

Answer: "Yes, I do."

Then he shall say: "Be it done for you as you have believed [Matt. 8:13]. According to the command of our Lord Jesus Christ, I forgive you your sins in the name of the Father and of the Son and of the Holy Spirit. Amen. Go in peace" [Mark 5:34; Luke 7:50; 8:48].

A confessor will know additional passages of the Scriptures with which to comfort and to strengthen the faith of those whose consciences are heavily burdened or who are distressed and sorely tried. This is intended simply as an ordinary form of confession for plain people.

[VI]

The Sacrament of the Altar in the plain form in which the head of the family shall teach it to his household

What is the Sacrament of the Altar?

Answer: Instituted by Christ himself, it is the true body and blood of our Lord Jesus Christ, under the bread and wine, given to us Christians to eat and to drink.

Where is this written?

Answer: The holy evangelists Matthew, Mark, and Luke, and also St. Paul, write thus: "Our Lord Jesus Christ, on the night when he was betrayed, took bread, and when he had given thanks, he broke it, and gave it to the disciples and said, 'Take, eat; this is my body which is given for you. Do this in remembrance of me.' In the same way also he took the cup, after supper, and when he had given thanks he gave it to them, saying, 'Drink of it, all of you. This cup is the new covenant in my blood, which is poured out for many for the forgiveness of sins. Do this, as often as you drink it, in remembrance of me'" [1 Cor. 11:23–25; Matt. 26:26–28; Mark 14:22–24; Luke 22:19, 20].

What is the benefit of such eating and drinking?

Answer: We are told in the words "for you" and "for the forgiveness of sins." By these words the forgiveness of sins, life, and salvation are given to us in the sacrament, for where there is forgiveness of sins, there are also life and salvation.

How can bodily eating and drinking produce such great effects?

Answer: The eating and drinking do not in themselves produce them, but the words "for you" and "for the forgiveness of sins." These words, when accompanied by the bodily eating and drinking, are the chief thing in the sacrament, and he who believes these words has what they say and declare: the forgiveness of sins.

Who, then, receives this sacrament worthily?

Answer: Fasting and bodily preparation are a good external discipline, but he is truly worthy and well prepared who believes these words: "for you" and "for the forgiveness of sins." On the other hand, he who does not believe these words, or doubts them, is unworthy and unprepared, for the words "for you" require truly believing hearts.

[VII]

Morning and Evening Prayers

How the head of the family shall teach his household to say morning and evening prayers

In the morning, when you rise, make the sign of the cross and say, "In the name of God, the Father, the Son, and the Holy Spirit. Amen."

Then kneeling or standing, say the Apostles' Creed and the Lord's Prayer. Then you may say this prayer:

"I give Thee thanks, heavenly Father, through thy dear Son Jesus Christ, that Thou has protected me through the night from all harm and danger. I beseech Thee to keep me this day, too, from all sin and evil, that in all my thoughts, words, and deeds I may please Thee. Into thy hands I commend my body and soul and all that is mine. Let thy holy angel have charge of me, that the wicked one may have no power over me. Amen."

After singing a hymn (possibly a hymn on the Ten Commandments) or whatever your devotion may suggest, you should go to your work joyfully.

In the evening, when you retire, make the sign of the cross and say, "In the name of God, the Father, the Son, and the Holy Spirit. Amen."

Then, kneeling or standing, say the Apostles' Creed and the Lord's Prayer. Then you may say this prayer:

"I give Thee thanks, heavenly Father, through thy dear Son Jesus Christ, that Thou has this day graciously protected me. I beseech Thee to forgive all my sin and the wrong which I have done. Graciously protect me during the coming night. Into thy hands I commend my body and soul and all that is mine. Let thy holy angels have charge of me, that the wicked one may have no power over me. Amen."

Then quickly lie down and sleep in peace.

[VIII]
Grace at Table
How the head of the family shall teach his household to offer blessing and thanksgiving at table

Blessing before Eating

When children and the whole household gather at the table, they should reverently fold their hands and say:

"The eyes of all look to Thee, O Lord, and Thou givest them their food in due season. Thou openest thy hand; Thou satisfiest the desire of every living thing" [Ps. 145:15, 16].

(It is to be observed that "satisfying the desire of every living thing" means that all creatures receive enough to eat to make them joyful and of good cheer. Greed and anxiety about food prevent such satisfaction.)

Then the Lord's Prayer should be said, and afterwards this prayer:

"Lord God, heavenly Father, bless us, and these thy gifts which of thy bountiful goodness Thou hast bestowed on us, through Jesus Christ our Lord. Amen."

Thanksgiving after Eating

After eating, likewise, they should fold their hands reverently and say:

"O give thanks to the Lord, for he is good; for his steadfast love endures forever. He gives to the beasts their food, and to the young ravens which cry. His delight is not in the strength of the horse, nor his pleasure in the legs of a man; but the Lord takes pleasure in those who fear him, in those who hope in his steadfast love" [Ps. 106:1; 136:26; 147:9–11].

Then the Lord's Prayer should be said, and afterwards this prayer:

"We give Thee thanks, Lord God, our Father, for all thy benefits, through Jesus Christ our Lord, who lives and reigns forever. Amen."

[IX]
Table of Duties
Consisting of certain passages of the Scriptures, selected for various estates and conditions of men, by which they may be admonished to do their respective duties

Bishops, Pastors, and Preachers

"A bishop must be above reproach, married only once, temperate, sensible, dignified, hospitable, an apt teacher, no drunkard, not violent but gentle, not quarrelsome, and no lover of money. He must manage his own household well, keeping his children submissive and respectful in every way. He must not be a recent convert," etc. [1 Tim. 3:2–6].

Duties Christians Owe Their Teachers and Pastors[8]

"Remain in the same house, eating and drinking what they provide, for the laborer deserves his wages" [Luke 10:7]. "The Lord commanded that those who proclaim the gospel should get their living by the gospel" [1 Cor. 9:14]. "Let him who is taught the word share all good things with him who teaches. Do not be deceived; God is not mocked" [Gal. 6:6, 7]. "Let the elders who rule well be considered worthy of double honor, especially those who labor in preaching and teaching; for the scripture says, 'You shall not muzzle an ox when it is treading out the grain,' and 'The laborer deserves his wages'" [1 Tim. 5:17, 18]. "We beseech you, brethren, to respect those who labor among you and are over you in the Lord and admonish you, and to esteem them very highly in love because of their work. Be at peace among yourselves" [1 Thess. 5:12, 13]. "Obey your leaders and submit to them; for they are keeping watch over your souls, as men who will have to give account. Let them do this joyfully, and not sadly, for that would be of no advantage to you" [Heb. 13:17].

Governing Authorities

"Let every person be subject to the governing authorities. For there is no authority except from God, and those that exist have been instituted by God. Therefore he who resists the authorities resists what God has appointed, and those who resist will incur judgment. He who is in authority does not bear the sword in vain; he is the servant of God to execute his wrath on the wrongdoer" [Rom. 13:1–4].

Duties Subjects Owe to Governing Authorities

"Render therefore to Caesar the things that are Caesar's, and to God the things that are God's" [Matt. 22:21]. "Let every person be subject to the governing authorities. Therefore one must be subject, not only to avoid God's wrath but also for the sake of conscience. For the same reason you also pay taxes, for the authorities are ministers of God, attending to this very thing. Pay all of them their dues, taxes to whom taxes are due, revenue to whom revenue is due, respect to whom respect is due, honor to whom honor is due" [Rom. 13:1, 5–7]. "I urge that supplications, prayers, intercessions, and thanksgivings be made for all men, for kings and all who are in high positions, that we may lead a quiet and peaceable life, godly and respectful in every way" [1 Tim. 2:1, 2]. "Remind them to be submissive to rulers and authorities, to be obedient, to be ready for any honest work" [Titus 3:1]. "Be subject for the Lord's sake to every human institution, whether it be to the emperor as supreme, or to governors as sent by him to punish those who do wrong and to praise those who do right" [1 Pet. 2:13, 14].

Husbands

"You husbands, live considerately with your wives, bestowing honor on the woman as the weaker sex, since you are joint heirs of the grace of life, in order that your prayers may not be hindered" [1 Pet. 3:7]. "Husbands, love your wives, and do not be harsh with them" [Col. 3:19].

Wives

"You wives, be submissive to your husbands, as Sarah obeyed Abraham, calling him lord. And you are now her children if you do right and let nothing terrify you" [1 Pet. 3:1, 6].

Parents

"Fathers, do not provoke your children to anger, lest they become discouraged, but bring them up in the discipline and instruction of the Lord" [Eph. 6:4; Col. 3:21].

Children

"Children, obey your parents in the Lord, for this is right. 'Honor your father and mother' (this is the first commandment with a promise) 'that it may be well with you and that you may live long on the earth'" [Eph. 6:1–3].

Laborers and Servants, Male and Female

"Be obedient to those who are your earthly masters, with fear and trembling, with singleness of heart, as to Christ; not in the way of eye-service, as men-pleasers, but as servants of Christ, doing the will of God from the heart, rendering service with a good will as to the Lord and not to men, knowing that whatever good anyone does, he will receive the same again from the Lord, whether he is a slave or free" [Eph. 6:5–8].

Masters and Mistresses

"Masters, do the same to them, and forbear threatening, knowing that he who is both their Master and yours is in heaven, and that there is no partiality with him" [Eph. 6:9].

Young Persons in General

"You that are younger, be subject to the elders. Clothe yourselves, all of you, with humility toward one another, for 'God opposes the proud, but gives grace to the humble.' Humble yourselves therefore under the mighty hand of God, that in due time he may exalt you" [1 Pet. 5:5, 6].

Widows

"She who is a real widow, and is left all alone, has set her hope on God and continues in supplications and prayers night and day; whereas she who is self-indulgent is dead even while she lives" [1 Tim. 5:5, 6].

Christians in General

"The commandments are summed up in this sentence, 'You shall love your neighbor as yourself'" [Rom. 13:9]. "I urge that supplications, prayers, intercessions, and thanksgivings be made for all men" [1 Tim. 2:1].

Let each his lesson learn with care
And all the household well will fare.

Notes

1. See Denis Janz, *Three Reformation Catechisms: Catholic, Anabaptist, Lutheran Texts and Studies in Religion*, vol. 13 (New York: Edwin Mellen Press, 1982), 14.

2. See David Dunn et al., *A History of the Evangelical and Reformed Church* (New York: Pilgrim Press, 1990), 293.

3. Luther made visitations of congregations in electoral Saxony and Meissen between October 22, 1528, and January 9, 1529.

4. Luther here refers not only to his own Large Catechism but also to other treatments of the traditional parts of the catechism. See the reference to "many books" in the next sentence.

5. Latin title: *Small Catechism for the Use of Children in School. How, in a Very Plain Form, Schoolmasters Should Teach the Ten Commandments to Their Pupils.*

6. The Nuremberg editions of 1531 and 1558 read: "I am the Lord your God. You shall have no other gods before me." In some editions since the sixteenth century, "I am the Lord your God" was printed separately as an introduction to the entire Decalogue. The Ten Commandments are from Exod. 20:2–17 and Deut. 5:6–21.

7. Luther was here alluding to the medieval practice of confession.

8. This section and the next one were not prepared by Luther, but were later taken up into the Small Catechism, probably with Luther's consent.

9. The Augsburg Confession

(1530)

The Augsburg Confession emerged out of the political and ecclesiastical ferment of Germany in the late 1520s and 1530. At the Diet of Worms (a meeting held in the city of Worms) in April 1521, Martin Luther stood before the young, staunchly Catholic Emperor Charles V and refused to recant his Protestant beliefs. He was declared a heretic and became an outlaw of the empire. From that moment on, any person who associated with Luther fell under imperial ban, risking arrest and having their property confiscated.

Fortunately for the Lutheran movement, Charles V was overly preoccupied with foreign affairs from 1521 to 1529, dealing with a French conflict at his western border and worrying about the Turks on the eastern edge of the empire. This political vacuum gave Reformation ideas a great deal of room in which to grow. Since the emperor was not able to attend the key meetings that immediately followed Worms, no action was taken to enforce the decree of Worms.

In fact, those who attended the Diet of Speyer in 1526 decided that any crucial religious issues should be referred to a church council to meet in one and a half years. Until that time, each estate should conduct itself "as it trusts itself to be responsible before God and the imperial majesty."

At a second Diet of Speyer in 1529, the Catholic estates, which were in the majority, reversed the permissive decree of the previous Diet of Speyer and moved to enforce the decree of the Diet of Worms. They resolved that further changes in Catholic custom should cease. A small minority of estates that had embraced Lutheran reforms protested, and from that time

---

SOURCE: Theodore G. Tappert, ed., *Book of Concord* (Philadelphia: Fortress Press, 1959). Used by permission of Augsburg Fortress Publishers.

on those who disagreed with the Catholic position or leadership were called Protestants.

As the situation became more chaotic, Charles V was increasingly worried about keeping a united front against the Turks. He resolved to preside personally over the next diet, scheduled for Augsburg in April 1530, inviting princes and representatives from the empire's cities to come to Augsburg to settle religious differences through discussion.

In preparation for the Augsburg meeting, Frederick the Wise, Elector of Saxony, asked the theologians in Wittenberg to prepare an account of their faith and of the changes in practice adopted in Saxony. A statement of doctrine, known as the Schwabach Articles, had already been written by the Saxon theologians in the summer of 1529, but this statement was not acceptable to the emperor. Changes in practice had been set forth in the so-called Torgau Articles in March 1530.

As the meeting approached, Philip Melanchthon (1497–1560), Luther's younger colleague, was commissioned to lead the delegation of Lutheran theologians at Augsburg. Luther, who was still an outlaw of the empire, remained a short distance away at the Castle Coburg and kept in constant touch with those at the meeting.

The Augsburg Confession, predominantly written by Melanchthon, consists of two parts: "Articles of Faith and Doctrine" (I–XXI), and "Articles about Matters in Dispute, in Which an Account Is Given of the Abuses which Have Been Corrected" (XXII–XXVIII). The Articles of Faith and Doctrine built upon the Schwabach Articles. The sections dealing with matters of dispute borrowed from the Torgau Articles. Melanchthon was a moderate who wanted to heal the divisions of the church and convince the emperor that Lutheran faith and practice was truly catholic. While holding firm to article IV, "Justification," Melanchthon glossed over certain differences with the Catholics, such as the papacy, purgatory, invocation of the saints, and transubstantiation, but stressed the fundamental disagreements between Lutherans and Anabaptists, and between Lutherans and Zwinglians.

There were substantial editorial changes made in the draft of the confession right up to the last minute. Although Luther indicated his approval of the confession as a whole, he had some reservations that it was too irenic.[1]

The Augsburg Confession quickly became the most important symbol of the Lutheran movement, and it remains so today. It was later accepted as an important historical confession by the Evangelical Synod of North America, and today it continues as part of the testimony of faith for the United Church of Christ.[2]

A Confession of Faith Presented in Augsburg by certain Princes and Cities to His Imperial Majesty Charles V in the Year 1530

Psalm 119:46
"I will also speak of thy testimonies before kings, and shall not be put to shame."

Preface

Most serene, most mighty, invincible Emperor, most gracious Lord:

A short time ago Your Imperial Majesty graciously summoned a diet of the empire to convene here in Augsburg. In the summons Your Majesty indicated an earnest desire to deliberate concerning matters pertaining to the Turk, that traditional foe of ours and of the Christian religion, and how with continuing help he might effectively be resisted. The desire was also expressed for deliberation on what might be done about the dissension concerning our holy faith and the Christian religion, and to this end it was proposed to employ all diligence amicably and charitably to hear, understand, and weigh the judgments, opinions, and beliefs of the several parties among us, to unite the same in agreement on one Christian truth, to put aside whatever may not have been rightly interpreted or treated by either side, to have all of us embrace and adhere to a single, true religion and live together in unity and in one fellowship and church, even as we are all enlisted under one Christ. Inasmuch as we, the undersigned elector and princes and our associates, have been summoned for these purposes, together with other electors, princes, and estates,[3] we have complied with the command and can say without boasting that we were among the first to arrive.

In connection with the matter pertaining to the faith and in conformity with the imperial summons, Your Imperial Majesty also graciously and earnestly requested that each of the electors, princes, and estates should commit to writing and present, in German and Latin, his judgments, opinions, and beliefs with reference to the said errors, dissensions, and abuses. Accordingly, after due deliberation and counsel, it was decided last Wednesday that, in keeping with Your Majesty's wish, we should present our case in German and Latin today (Friday).[4] Wherefore, in dutiful obedience to Your Imperial Majesty, we offer and present a confession of our pastors' and preachers' teaching and of our own faith, setting forth how and in what manner, on the basis of the Holy Scriptures, these things are preached, taught, communicated, and embraced in our lands, principalities, dominions, cities, and territories.

If the other electors, princes, and estates also submit a similar written statement of their judgments and opinions, in Latin and German, we are prepared, in obedience to Your Imperial Majesty, our most gracious lord, to discuss with them and their associates, in so far as this can honorably be done, such practical and equitable ways as may restore unity. Thus the matters at issue between us may be presented in writing on both sides, they may be discussed amicably and charitably, our differences may be reconciled, and we may be united in one, true religion, even as we are all under one Christ and should confess and contend for Christ. All of this is in accord with Your Imperial Majesty's aforementioned summons. That it may be done according to divine truth we invoke almighty God in deepest humility and implore him to bestow his grace to this end. Amen.

If, however, our lords, friends, and associates who represent the electors, princes, and estates of the other party do not comply with the procedure intended by Your Imperial Majesty's summons, if no amicable and charitable negotiations take place between us, and if no results are attained, nevertheless we on our part shall not omit doing anything, in so far as God and conscience allow, that may serve the cause of Christian unity. Of this Your Imperial Majesty, our aforementioned friends (the electors, princes, and estates), and every lover of the Christian religion who is concerned about these questions will be graciously and sufficiently assured from what follows in the confession which we and our associates submit.

In the past Your Imperial Majesty graciously gave assurance to the electors, princes, and estates of the empire, especially in a public instruction at the diet in Spires in 1526, that for reasons there stated Your Imperial Majesty was not disposed to render decisions in matters pertaining to our holy faith but would diligently urge it upon the pope to call a council. Again, by means of a written instruction at the last diet in Spires a year ago, the electors, princes, and estates of the empire were, among other things, informed and notified by Your Imperial Majesty's viceroy (His Royal Majesty of Hungary and Bohemia, etc.) and by Your Imperial Majesty's orator and appointed commissioners, that Your Imperial Majesty's viceroy, administrators, and councilors of the imperial government (together with the absent electors, princes, and representatives of the estates) who were assembled at the diet convened in Ratisbon [1527] had considered the proposal concerning a general council and acknowledged that it would be profitable to have such a council called. Since the relations between Your Imperial Majesty and the pope were improving and were progressing toward a good, Christian understanding,[5] Your Imperial Majesty was sure that the pope would not refuse to call a general council, and so Your Imperial Majesty graciously offered to promote and bring about the calling of such a general council by the pope, along with Your Imperial Majesty, at the earliest opportunity and to allow no hindrance to be put in the way.

If the outcome should be such as we mentioned above, we offer in full obedience, even beyond what is required, to participate in such a general, free, and Christian council as the electors, princes, and estates have with the highest and best motives requested in all the diets of the empire which have been held during Your Imperial Majesty's reign. We have at various times made our protestations and appeals concerning these most weighty matters, and have done so in legal form and procedure. To these we declare our continuing adherence, and we shall not be turned aside from our position by these or any following negotiations (unless the matters in dissension are finally heard, amicably weighed, charitably settled, and brought to Christian concord in accordance with Your Imperial Majesty's summons) as we herewith publicly witness and assert. This is our confession and that of our associates, and it is specifically stated, article by article, in what follows.

Articles of Faith and Doctrine

I. [God][6]

We unanimously hold and teach, in accordance with the decree of the Council of Nicaea, that there is one divine essence, which is called and which is truly God, and that there are three persons in this one divine essence, equal in power and alike eternal: God the Father, God the Son, God the Holy Spirit. All three are one divine essence, eternal, without division, without end, of infinite power, wisdom, and goodness, one creator and preserver of all things visible and invisible. The word "person" is to be understood as the Fathers employed the term in this connection, not as a part or a property of another but as that which exists of itself.

Therefore all the heresies which are contrary to this article are rejected. Among these are the heresy of the Manichaeans,[7] who assert that there are two gods, one good and one evil; also that of the Valentinians,[8] Arians,[9] Eunomians,[10] Mohammedans,[11] and others like them; also that of the Samosatenes,[12] old and new, who hold that there is only one person and sophistically assert that the other two, the Word and the Holy Spirit, are not necessarily distinct persons but that the Word signifies a physical word or voice and that the Holy Spirit is a movement induced in creatures.

II. [Original Sin]

It is also taught among us that since the fall of Adam all men who are born according to the course of nature are conceived and born in sin. That is, all men are full of evil lust and inclinations from their mothers' wombs and are unable by nature to have true fear of God and true faith in God. Moreover, this inborn sickness and hereditary sin is truly sin and condemns to the eternal wrath of God all those who are not born again through Baptism and the Holy Spirit.

Rejected in this connection are the Pelagians[13] and others who deny that original sin is sin, for they hold that natural man is made righteous by his own powers, thus disparaging the sufferings and merit of Christ.

III. [The Son of God]

It is also taught among us that God the Son became man, born of the virgin Mary, and that the two natures, divine and human, are so inseparably united in one person that there is one Christ, true God and true man, who was truly born, suffered, was crucified, died, and was buried in order to be a sacrifice not only for original sin but also for all other sins and to propitiate God's wrath. The same Christ also descended into hell, truly rose from the dead on the third day, ascended into heaven, and sits on the right hand of God, that he may eternally rule and have dominion over all creatures, that through the Holy Spirit he may sanctify, purify, strengthen, and comfort all who believe in him, that he may bestow on them life and every grace and blessing, and that he may protect and defend them against the devil and against sin. The same Lord Christ will return openly to judge the living and the dead, as stated in the Apostles' Creed.

IV. [Justification]

It is also taught among us that we cannot obtain forgiveness of sin and righteousness before God by our own merits, works, or satisfactions, but that we receive forgiveness of sin and become righteous before God by grace, for Christ's sake, through faith, when we believe that Christ suffered for us and that for his sake our sin is forgiven and righteousness and eternal life are given to us. For God will regard and reckon this faith as righteousness, as Paul says in Romans 3:21–26 and 4:5.

V. [The Office of the Ministry]

To obtain such faith God instituted the office of the ministry, that is, provided the Gospel and the sacraments. Through these, as through means, he gives the Holy Spirit, who works faith, when and where he pleases, in those who hear the Gospel. And the Gospel teaches that we have a gracious God, not by our own merits but by the merit of Christ, when we believe this.

Condemned are the Anabaptists and others who teach that the Holy Spirit comes to us through our own preparations, thoughts, and works without the external word of the Gospel.

VI. [The New Obedience]

It is also taught among us that such faith should produce good fruits and good works and that we must do all such good works as God has commanded, but we should do them for God's sake and not place our trust in them as if thereby to merit favor before God. For we receive forgiveness of sin and righteousness through faith in Christ, as Christ himself says, "So you also, when you have done all that is commanded you, say, 'We are unworthy servants'" [Luke 17:10]. The Fathers also teach thus, for Ambrose says, "It is ordained of God that whoever believes in Christ shall be saved, and he shall have forgiveness of sins, not through works but through faith alone, without merit."[14]

VII. [The Church]

It is also taught among us that one holy Christian church will be and remain forever. This is the assembly of all believers among whom the Gospel is preached in its purity and the holy sacraments are administered according to the Gospel. For it is sufficient for the true unity of the Christian church that the Gospel be preached in conformity with a pure understanding of it and that the sacraments be administered in accordance with the divine Word.[15] It is not necessary for the true unity of the Christian church that ceremonies, instituted by men, should be observed uniformly in all places. It is as Paul says in Eph. 4:4, 5, "There is one body and one Spirit, just as you were called to the one hope that belongs to your call, one Lord, one faith, one baptism."

VIII. [What the Church Is]

Again, although the Christian church, properly speaking, is nothing else than the assembly of all believers and saints, yet because in this life many false Christians, hypocrites, and even open sinners remain among the godly, the sacraments are efficacious even if the priests who administer them are wicked men, for as Christ himself indicated, "The Pharisees sit on Moses' seat" [Matt. 23:2].

Accordingly the Donatists[16] and all others who hold contrary views are condemned.

IX. [Baptism]

It is taught among us that Baptism is necessary and that grace is offered through it. Children, too, should be baptized, for in Baptism they are committed to God and become acceptable to him.

On this account the Anabaptists who teach that infant Baptism is not right are rejected.

X. [The Holy Supper of Our Lord]

It is taught among us that the true body and blood of Christ are really present in the Supper of our Lord under the form of bread and wine and are there distributed and received. The contrary doctrine is therefore rejected.

XI. [Confession]

It is taught among us that private absolution should be retained and not allowed to fall into disuse. However, in confession it is not necessary to enumerate all trespasses and sins, for this is impossible. Ps. 19:12, "Who can discern his errors?"

XII. [Repentance]

It is taught among us that those who sin after Baptism receive forgiveness of sin whenever they come to repentance, and absolution should not be denied them by the church. Properly speaking, true repentance is nothing else than to have contrition and sorrow, or terror, on account of sin, and yet at the same time to believe the Gospel and absolution (namely, that sin has been forgiven and grace has been obtained through Christ), and this faith will comfort the heart and again set it at rest. Amendment of life and the forsaking of sin should then follow, for these must be the fruits of repentance, as John says, "Bear fruit that befits repentance" [Matt. 3:8].

Rejected here are those who teach that persons who have once become godly cannot fall again.[17]

Condemned on the other hand are the Novatians[18] who denied absolution to such as had sinned after Baptism.

Rejected also are those who teach that forgiveness of sin is not obtained through faith but through the satisfactions made by man.

XIII. [The Use of the Sacraments]

It is taught among us that the sacraments were instituted not only to be signs by which people might be identified outwardly as Christians, but that they are signs and testimonies of God's will toward us for the purpose of awakening and strengthening our faith. For this reason they require faith, and they are rightly used when they are received in faith and for the purpose of strengthening faith.

XIV. [Order in the Church]

It is taught among us that nobody should publicly teach or preach or administer the sacraments in the church without a regular call.

XV. [Church Usages]

With regard to church usages that have been established by men, it is taught among us that those usages are to be observed which may be observed without sin and which contribute to peace and good order in the church, among them being certain holy days, festivals, and the like. Yet we accompany these observances with instruction so that consciences may not be burdened by the notion that such things are necessary for salvation. Moreover it is taught that all ordinances and traditions instituted by men for the purpose of propitiating God and earning grace are contrary to the Gospel and the teaching about faith in Christ. Accordingly monastic vows and other traditions concerning distinctions of foods, days, etc., by which it is intended to earn grace and make satisfaction for sin, are useless and contrary to the Gospel.

XVI. [Civil Government]

It is taught among us that all government in the world and all established rule and laws were instituted and ordained by God for the sake of good order, and that Christians may without sin occupy civil offices or serve as princes and judges, render decisions and pass sentence according to imperial and other existing laws, punish evildoers with the sword, engage in just wars, serve as soldiers, buy and sell, take required oaths, possess property, be married, etc.

Condemned here are the Anabaptists who teach that none of the things indicated above is Christian.[19]

Also condemned are those who teach that Christian perfection requires the forsaking of house and home, wife and child, and the renunciation of such activities as are mentioned above. Actually, true perfection consists alone of proper fear of God and real faith in God, for the Gospel does not teach an outward and temporal but an inward and eternal mode of existence and righteousness of the heart. The Gospel does not overthrow civil authority, the state, and marriage but requires that all these be kept as true orders of God and that everyone, each according to his own calling, manifest Christian love and genuine good works in his station of life. Accordingly Christians are obliged to be subject to civil authority and obey its commands and laws in all that can be done without sin. But when commands of the civil authority cannot be obeyed without sin, we must obey God rather than men [Acts 5:29].

XVII. [The Return of Christ to Judgment]

It is also taught among us that our Lord Jesus Christ will return on the last day for judgment and will raise up all the dead, to give eternal life and everlasting joy to believers and the elect but to condemn ungodly men and the devil to hell and eternal punishment.

Rejected, therefore, are the Anabaptists who teach that the devil and condemned men will not suffer eternal pain and torment.[20]

Rejected, too, are certain Jewish opinions which are even now making an appearance and which teach that, before the resurrection of the dead, saints and godly men will possess a worldly kingdom and annihilate all the godless.[21]

XVIII. [Freedom of the Will]

It is also taught among us that man possesses some measure of freedom of the will which enables him to live an outwardly honorable life and to make choices among the things that reason comprehends. But without the grace, help, and activity of the Holy Spirit man is not capable of making himself acceptable to God, of fearing God and believing in God with his whole heart, or of expelling inborn evil lusts from his heart. This is accomplished by the Holy Spirit, who is given through the Word of God, for Paul says in 1 Cor. 2:14, "Natural man does not receive the gifts of the Spirit of God."

In order that it may be evident that this teaching is no novelty, the clear words of Augustine on free will are here quoted from the third book of his *Hypognosticon*:[22] "We concede that all men have a free will, for all have a natural, innate understanding and reason. However, this does not enable them to act in matters pertaining to God (such as loving God with their whole heart or fearing him), for it is only in the outward acts of this life that they have freedom to choose good or evil. By good I mean what they are capable of by nature: whether or not to labor in the fields, whether or not to eat or drink or visit a friend, whether to dress or undress, whether to build a house, take a wife, engage in a trade, or do whatever else may be good and profitable. None of these is or exists without God, but all things are from him and through him. On the other hand, by his own choice man can also undertake evil, as when he wills to kneel before an idol, commit murder, etc."

XIX. [The Cause of Sin]

It is taught among us that although almighty God has created and still preserves nature, yet sin is caused in all wicked men and despisers of God by the perverted will. This is the will of the devil and of all ungodly men; as soon as God withdraws his support, the will turns away from God to evil. It is as Christ says in John 8:44, "When the devil lies, he speaks according to his own nature."

XX. [Faith and Good Works]

Our teachers have been falsely accused of forbidding good works. Their writings on the Ten Commandments, and other writings as well, show that they have given good and profitable accounts and instructions concerning true Christian estates and works. About these little was taught in former times, when for the most part sermons were concerned with childish and useless works like rosaries, the cult of saints, monasticism, pilgrimages, appointed fasts, holy days, brotherhoods, etc. Our opponents no longer praise these useless works so highly as they once did, and they have also learned to speak now of faith, about which they did not preach at all in former times. They do not teach now that we become righteous before God by our works alone, but they add faith in Christ and say that faith and works make us righteous before God. This teaching may offer a little more comfort than the teaching that we are to rely solely on our works.

Since the teaching about faith, which is the chief article in the Christian life, has been neglected so long (as all must admit) while nothing but works was preached everywhere, our people have been instructed as follows:

We begin by teaching that our works cannot reconcile us with God or obtain grace for us, for this happens only through faith, that is, when we believe that our sins are forgiven for Christ's sake, who alone is the mediator who reconciles the Father. Whoever imagines that he can accomplish this by works, or that he can merit grace, despises Christ and seeks his own way to God, contrary to the Gospel.

This teaching about faith is plainly and clearly treated by Paul in many passages, especially in Eph. 2:8, 9, "For by grace you have been saved through faith; and this is not your own doing, it is the gift of God—not because of works, lest any man should boast," etc.

That no new interpretation is here introduced can be demonstrated from Augustine, who discusses this question thoroughly and teaches the same thing, namely, that we obtain grace and are justified before God through faith in Christ and not through works. His whole book, *De spiritu et litera* (On the Spirit and the Letter), proves this.

Although this teaching is held in great contempt among untried people, yet it is a matter of experience that weak and terrified consciences find it most comforting and salutary. The conscience cannot come to rest and peace through works, but only through faith, that is, when it is assured and knows that for Christ's sake it has a gracious God, as Paul says in Rom. 5:1, "Since we are justified by faith, we have peace with God."

In former times this comfort was not heard in preaching, but poor consciences were driven to rely on their own efforts, and all sorts of works were undertaken. Some were driven by their conscience into monasteries in the hope that there they might merit grace through monastic life. Others devised other works for the purpose of earning grace and making satisfaction for sins. Many of them discovered that they did not obtain peace by such means. It was therefore necessary to preach this doctrine about faith in Christ and diligently to apply it in order that men may know that the grace of God is appropriated without merits, through faith alone.

Instruction is also given among us to show that the faith here spoken of is not that possessed by the devil and the ungodly, who also believe the history of Christ's suffering and his resurrection from the dead, but we mean such true faith as believes that we receive grace and forgiveness of sin through Christ.

Whoever knows that in Christ he has a gracious God, truly knows God, calls upon him, and is not, like the heathen, without God. For the devil and the ungodly do not believe this article concerning the forgiveness of sin, and so they are at enmity with God, cannot call upon him, and have no hope of receiving good from him. Therefore, as has just been indicated, the Scriptures speak of faith but do not mean by it such knowledge as the devil and ungodly men possess. Heb. 11:1 teaches about faith in such a way as to make it clear that faith is not merely a knowledge of historical events but is a confidence in God and in the fulfillment of his promises. Augustine also reminds us that we should understand the word "faith" in the Scriptures to mean confidence in God, assurance that God is gracious to us, and not merely such a knowledge of historical events as the devil also possesses.

It is also taught among us that good works should and must be done, not that we are to rely on them to earn grace but that we may do God's will and glorify him. It is always faith alone that apprehends grace and forgiveness of sin. When through faith the Holy Spirit is given, the heart is moved to do good works. Before that, when it is without the Holy Spirit, the heart is too weak. Moreover, it is in the power of the devil, who drives poor human beings into many sins. We see this in the philosophers who undertook to lead honorable and blameless lives; they failed to accomplish this, and instead fell into many great and open sins. This is what happens when a man is without true faith and the Holy Spirit and governs himself by his own human strength alone.

Consequently this teaching concerning faith is not to be accused of forbidding good works but is rather to be praised for teaching that good works are to be done and for offering help as to how they may be done. For without faith and without Christ human nature and human strength are much too weak to do good works, call upon God, have patience in suffering, love one's neighbor, diligently engage in callings which are commanded, render obedience, avoid evil lusts, etc. Such great and genuine works cannot be done without the help of Christ, as he himself says in John 15:5, "Apart from me you can do nothing."

XXI. [The Cult of Saints]

It is also taught among us that saints should be kept in remembrance so that our faith may be strengthened when we see what grace they received and how they were sustained by faith. Moreover, their good works are to be an example for us, each of us in his own calling. So His Imperial Majesty may in salutary and godly fashion imitate the example of David in making war on the Turk, for both are incumbents of a royal office which demands the defense and protection of their subjects.

However, it cannot be proved from the Scriptures that we are to invoke saints or seek help from them. "For there is one mediator between God and men, Christ Jesus" [1 Tim. 2:5], who is the only saviour, the only highpriest, advocate, and intercessor before God [Rom. 8:34]. He alone has promised to hear our prayers. Moreover, according to the Scriptures, the highest form of divine service is sincerely to seek and call upon this same Jesus Christ in every time of need. "If anyone sins, we have an advocate with the Father, Jesus Christ the righteous" [1 John 2:1].

This is just about a summary of the doctrines that are preached and taught in our churches for proper Christian instruction, the consolation of consciences, and the amendment of believers. Certainly we should not wish to put our own souls and consciences in grave peril before God by misusing his name or Word, nor should we wish to bequeath to our children and posterity any other teaching than that which agrees with the pure Word of God and Christian truth. Since this teaching is grounded clearly on the Holy Scriptures and is not contrary or opposed to that of the universal Christian church, or even of the Roman church (in so far as the latter's teaching is reflected in the writings of the Fathers), we think that our opponents cannot disagree with us in the articles set forth above. Therefore, those who presume to reject, avoid, and separate from our churches as if our teaching were heretical, act in an unkind and hasty fashion, contrary to all Christian unity and love, and do so without any solid basis of divine command or Scripture. The dispute and dissension are concerned chiefly with various traditions and abuses. Since, then, there is nothing unfounded or defective in the principal articles and since this our confession is seen to be godly and Christian, the bishops should in all fairness act more leniently, even if there were some defect among us in regard to traditions, although we hope to offer firm grounds and reasons why we have changed certain traditions and abuses.

Articles about Matters in Dispute, in Which an Account Is Given of the Abuses Which Have Been Corrected

From the above it is manifest that nothing is taught in our churches concerning articles of faith that is contrary to the Holy Scriptures or what is common to the Christian church. However, inasmuch as some abuses have been corrected (some of the abuses having crept in over the years and others of them having been introduced with violence), we are obliged by our circumstances to give an account of them and to indicate our reasons for permitting changes in these cases in order that Your Imperial Majesty may perceive that we have not acted in an unchristian and frivolous manner but have been compelled by God's command (which is rightly to be regarded as above all custom) to allow such changes.

XXII. [Both Kinds in the Sacrament]

Among us both kinds are given to laymen in the sacrament. The reason is that there is a clear command and order of Christ, "Drink of it, all of you" [Matt. 26:27]. Concerning the chalice Christ here commands with clear words that all should drink of it.

In order that no one might question these words and interpret them as if they apply only to priests, Paul shows in 1 Cor. 11:20ff. that the whole assembly of the congregation in Corinth received both kinds. This usage continued in the church for a long time, as can be demonstrated from history and from writings of the Fathers. In several places Cyprian mentions that the cup was given to laymen in his time.[23] St. Jerome also states that the priests who administered the sacrament distributed the blood of Christ to the people.[24] Pope Gelasius himself ordered that the sacrament was not to be divided.[25] Not a single canon can be found which requires the reception of only one kind. Nobody knows when or through whom this custom of receiving only one kind was introduced, although Cardinal Cusanus mentions when the use was approved.[26] It is evident that such a custom, introduced contrary to God's command and also contrary to the ancient canons, is unjust. Accordingly it is not proper to burden the consciences of those who desire to observe the sacrament according to Christ's institution or to compel them to act contrary to the arrangement of our Lord Christ. Because the division of the sacrament is contrary to the institution of Christ, the customary carrying about of the sacrament in processions is also omitted by us.[27]

XXIII. [The Marriage of Priests]

Among all people, both of high and of low degree, there has been loud complaint throughout the world concerning the flagrant immorality and the dissolute life of priests who were not able to remain continent and who went so far as to engage in abominable vices. In order to avoid such unbecoming offense, adultery, and other lechery, some of our priests have entered the married state. They have given as their reason that they have been impelled and moved to take this step by the great distress of their consciences, especially since the Scriptures clearly assert that the estate of marriage was instituted by the Lord God to avoid immorality, for Paul says, "Because of the temptation to immorality, each man should have his own wife" (1 Cor. 7:3), and again, "It is better to marry than to be aflame with passion" (1 Cor. 7:9). Moreover, when Christ said in Matt. 19:11, "Not all men can receive this precept," he indicated that few people have the gift of living in celibacy, and he certainly knew man's nature. God created man as male and female according to Gen. 1:27. Experience has made it all too manifest whether or not it lies in human power and ability to improve or change the creation of God, the supreme Majesty, by means of human resolutions or vows without a special gift or grace of God. What good has resulted? What honest and chaste manner of life, what Christian, upright, and honorable sort of conduct has resulted in many cases? It is well known what terrible torment and frightful disturbance of conscience many have experienced on their deathbeds on this account, and many have themselves acknowledged this. Since God's Word and command cannot be altered by any human vows or laws, our priests and other clergy have taken wives to themselves for these and other reasons and causes.

It can be demonstrated from history and from the writings of the Fathers that it was customary for priests and deacons to marry in the Christian church of former times. Paul therefore said in 1 Tim. 3:2, "A bishop must be above reproach, married only once." It was only four hundred years ago that the priests in Germany were compelled by force to take the vows of celibacy.[28] At that time there was such serious and strong resistance that an archbishop of Mayence[29] who had published the new papal decree was almost killed during an uprising of the entire body of priests. The decree concerning celibacy was at once enforced so hastily and indecently that the pope at the time not only forbade future marriages of priests but also broke up the marriages which were of long standing. This was of course not only contrary to all divine, natural, and civil law, but was also utterly opposed and contrary to the canons which the popes had themselves made and to the decisions of the most renowned councils.[30]

Many devout and intelligent people in high station have expressed similar opinions and the misgiving that such enforced celibacy and such prohibition of marriage (which God himself instituted and left free to man) never produced any good but rather gave occasion for many great and evil vices and much scandal. As his biography shows, even one of the popes, Pius II, often said and allowed himself to be quoted as saying that while there may well have been some reasons for prohibiting the marriage of clergymen, there were now more important, better, and weightier reasons for permitting them to be married. There is no doubt that Pope Pius, as a prudent and intelligent man, made this statement because of grave misgivings.

In loyalty to Your Imperial Majesty we therefore feel confident that, as a most renowned Christian emperor, Your Majesty will graciously take into account the fact that, in these last times of which the Scriptures prophesy, the world is growing worse and men are becoming weaker and more infirm.

Therefore it is most necessary, profitable, and Christian to recognize this fact in order that the prohibition of marriage may not cause worse and more disgraceful lewdness and vice to prevail in German lands. No one is able to alter or arrange such matters in a better or wiser way than God himself, who instituted marriage to aid human infirmity and prevent unchastity.

The old canons also state that it is sometimes necessary to relax severity and rigor for the sake of human weakness and to prevent and avoid greater offense.

In this case relaxation would certainly be both Christian and very necessary. How would the marriage of priests and the clergy, and especially of the pastors and others who are to minister to the church, be of disadvantage to the Christian church as a whole? If this hard prohibition of marriage is to continue longer, there may be a shortage of priests and pastors in the future.

As we have observed, the assertion that priests and clergymen may marry is based on God's Word and command. Besides, history demonstrates both that priests were married and that the vow of celibacy has been the cause of so much frightful and unchristian offense, so much adultery, and such terrible, shocking immorality and abominable vice that even some honest men among the cathedral clergy and some of the courtiers in Rome have often acknowledged this and have complained that such vices among the clergy would, on account of their abomination and prevalence, arouse the wrath of God. It is therefore deplorable that Christian marriage has not only been forbidden but has in many places been swiftly punished, as if it were a great crime, in spite of the fact that in the Holy Scriptures God commanded that marriage be held in honor. Marriage has also been highly praised in the imperial laws and in all states in which there have been laws and justice. Only in our time does one begin to persecute innocent people simply because they are married—and especially priests, who above all others should be spared—although this is done contrary not only to divine law but also to canon law. In 1 Tim. 4:1, 3 the apostle Paul calls the teaching that forbids marriage a doctrine of the devil. Christ himself asserts that the devil is a murderer from the beginning [John 8:44]. These two statements fit together well, for it must be a doctrine of the devil to forbid marriage and then to be so bold as to maintain such a teaching with the shedding of blood.

However, just as no human law can alter or abolish a command of God, neither can any vow alter a command of God. St. Cyprian therefore offered the counsel that women who were unable to keep their vows of chastity should marry. He wrote in his eleventh letter, "If they are unwilling or unable to keep their chastity, it is better for them to marry than to fall into the fire through their lusts, and they should see to it that they do not give their brothers and sisters occasion for offense."[31]

In addition, all the canons show great leniency and fairness toward those who have made vows in their youth—and most of the priests and monks entered into their estates ignorantly when they were young.

XXIV. [The Mass]

We are unjustly accused of having abolished the Mass. Without boasting, it is manifest that the Mass is observed among us with greater devotion and more earnestness than among our opponents. Moreover, the people are instructed often and with great diligence concerning the holy sacrament, why it was instituted, and how it is to be used (namely, as a comfort for terrified consciences) in order that the people may be drawn to the Communion and Mass. The people are also given instruction about other false teachings concerning the sacrament. Meanwhile no conspicuous changes have been made in the public ceremonies of the Mass, except that in certain places German hymns are sung in addition to the Latin responses for the instruction and exercise of the people. After all, the chief purpose of all ceremonies is to teach the people what they need to know about Christ.

Before our time, however, the Mass came to be misused in many ways, as is well known, by turning it into a sort of fair, by buying and selling it, and by observing it in almost all churches for a monetary consideration. Such abuses were often condemned by learned and devout men even before our time. Then when our preachers preached about these things and the priests were reminded of the terrible responsibility which should properly concern every Christian (namely, that whoever uses the sacrament unworthily is guilty of the body and blood of Christ) [1 Cor. 11:27], such mercenary Masses and private Masses, which had hitherto been held under compulsion for the sake of revenues and stipends, were discontinued in our churches.

At the same time the abominable error was condemned according to which it was taught that our Lord Christ had by his death made satisfaction only for original sin, and had instituted the Mass as a sacrifice for other sins. This transformed the Mass into a sacrifice for the living and the dead, a sacrifice by means of which sin was taken away and God was reconciled. Thereupon followed a debate as to whether one Mass held for many people merited as much as a special Mass held for an individual. Out of this grew the countless multiplication of Masses, by the performance of which men expected to get everything they needed from God. Meanwhile faith in Christ and true service of God were forgotten.

Demanded without doubt by the necessity of such circumstances, instruction was given so that our people might know how the sacrament is to be used rightly. They were taught, first of all, that the Scriptures show in many places that there is no sacrifice for original sin, or for any other sin, except the one death of Christ. For it is written in the Epistle to the Hebrews that Christ offered himself once and by this offering made satisfaction for all sin [Heb. 9:28; 10:10, 14]. It is an unprecedented novelty in church doctrine that Christ's death should have made satisfaction only for original sin and not for other sins as well. Accordingly it is to be hoped that everyone will understand that this error is not unjustly condemned.

In the second place, St. Paul taught that we obtain grace before God through faith and not through works. Manifestly contrary to this teaching is the misuse of the Mass by those who think that grace is obtained through the performance of this work, for it is well known that the Mass is used to remove sin and obtain grace and all sorts of benefits from God, not only for the priest himself but also for the whole world and for others, both living and dead.

In the third place, the holy sacrament was not instituted to make provision for a sacrifice for sin—for the sacrifice has already taken place—but to awaken our faith and comfort our consciences when we perceive that through the sacrament grace and forgiveness of sin are promised us by Christ. Accordingly the sacrament requires faith, and without faith it is used in vain.

Inasmuch, then, as the Mass is not a sacrifice to remove the sins of others, whether living or dead, but should be a Communion in which the priest and others receive the sacrament for themselves, it is observed among us in the following manner: On holy days, and at other times when communicants are present, Mass is held and those who desire it are communicated. Thus the Mass is preserved among us in its proper use, the use which was formerly observed in the church and which can be proved by St. Paul's statement in 1 Cor. 11:20ff. and by many statements of the Fathers. For Chrysostom reports how the priest stood every day, inviting some to Communion and forbidding others to approach.[32] The ancient canons also indicate that one man officiated and communicated the other priests and deacons, for the words of the Nicene canon read, "After the priests the deacons shall receive the sacrament in order from the bishop or priest."[33]

Since, therefore, no novelty has been introduced which did not exist in the church from ancient times, and since no conspicuous change has been made in the public ceremonies of the Mass except that other unnecessary Masses which were held in addition to the parochial Mass, probably through abuse, have been discontinued, this manner of holding Mass ought not in fairness be condemned as heretical or unchristian. In times past, even in large churches where there were many people, Mass was not held on every day that the people assembled, for according to the Tripartite History, Book 9, on Wednesday and Friday the Scriptures were read and expounded in Alexandria, and otherwise these services were held without Mass.[34]

XXV. [Confession]

Confession has not been abolished by the preachers on our side. The custom has been retained among us of not administering the sacrament to those who have not previously been examined and absolved. At the same time the people are carefully instructed concerning the consolation of the Word of absolution so that they may esteem absolution as a great and precious thing. It is not the voice or word of the man who speaks it, but it is the

Word of God, who forgives sin, for it is spoken in God's stead and by God's command. We teach with great diligence about this command and power of keys and how comforting and necessary it is for terrified consciences. We also teach that God requires us to believe this absolution as much as if we heard God's voice from heaven, that we should joyfully comfort ourselves with absolution, and that we should know that through such faith we obtain forgiveness of sins. In former times the preachers who taught much about confession never mentioned a word concerning these necessary matters but only tormented consciences with long enumerations of sins, with satisfactions, with indulgences, with pilgrimages and the like. Many of our opponents themselves acknowledge that we have written about and treated of true Christian repentance in a more fitting fashion than had been done for a long time.

Concerning confession we teach that no one should be compelled to recount sins in detail, for this is impossible. As the psalmist says, "Who can discern his errors?" [Ps. 19:12]. Jeremiah also says, "The heart is desperately corrupt; who can understand it?" [Jer. 17:9]. Our wretched human nature is so deeply submerged in sins that it is unable to perceive or know them all, and if we were to be absolved only from those which we can enumerate we would be helped but little. On this account there is no need to compel people to give a detailed account of their sins. That this was also the view of the Fathers can be seen in Dist. I, *De poenitentia*, where these words of Chrysostom are quoted: "I do not say that you should expose yourself in public or should accuse yourself before others, but obey the prophet who says, 'Show your way to the Lord' [Ps. 37:5]. Therefore confess to the Lord God, the true judge, in your prayer, telling him of your sins not with your tongue but in your conscience."[35] Here it can be clearly seen that Chrysostom does not require a detailed enumeration of sins. The marginal note in *De poenitentia*, Dist. 5, also teaches that such confession is not commanded by the Scriptures but was instituted by the church. Yet the preachers on our side diligently teach that confession is to be retained for the sake of absolution (which is its chief and most important part), for the consolation of terrified consciences, and also for other reasons.

XXVI. [The Distinction of Foods]

In former times men taught, preached, and wrote that distinctions among foods and similar traditions which had been instituted by men serve to earn grace and make satisfaction for sin. For this reason new fasts, new ceremonies, new orders, and the like were invented daily, and were ardently and urgently promoted, as if these were a necessary service of God by means of which grace would be earned if they were observed and a great sin committed if they were omitted. Many harmful errors in the church have resulted from this.

In the first place, the grace of Christ and the teaching concerning faith are thereby obscured, and yet the Gospel earnestly urges them upon us and strongly insists that we regard the merit of Christ as something great and precious and know that faith in Christ is to be esteemed far above all works. On this account St. Paul contended mightily against the law of Moses and against human tradition so that we should learn that we do not become good in God's sight by our works but that it is only through faith in Christ that we obtain grace for Christ's sake. This teaching has been almost completely extinguished by those who have taught that grace is to be earned by prescribed fasts, distinctions among foods, vestments, etc.

In the second place, such traditions have also obscured the commands of God, for these traditions were exalted far above God's commands. This also was regarded as Christian life: whoever observed festivals in this way, prayed in this way, fasted in this way, and dressed in this way was said to live a spiritual and Christian life. On the other hand, other necessary good works were considered secular and unspiritual: the works which everybody is obliged to do according to his calling—for example, that a husband should labor to support his wife and children and bring them up in the fear of God, that a wife should bear children and care for them, that a prince and magistrates should govern land and people, etc. Such works, commanded by God, were to be regarded as secular and imperfect, while traditions were to be given the glamorous title of alone being holy and perfect works. Accordingly there was no end or limit to the making of such traditions.

In the third place, such traditions have turned out to be a grievous burden to consciences, for it was not possible to keep all the traditions, and yet the people were of the opinion that they were a necessary service of God. Gerson writes that many fell into despair on this account, and some even committed suicide, because they had not heard anything of the consolation of the grace of Christ. We can see in the writings of the summists and canonists how consciences have been confused, for they undertook to collate the traditions and sought mitigations to relieve consciences, but they were so occupied with such efforts that they neglected all wholesome Christian teachings about more important things, such as faith, consolation in severe trials, and the like. Many devout and learned people before our time have also complained that such traditions caused so much strife in the church that godly people were thereby hindered from coming to a right knowledge of Christ. Gerson and others have complained bitterly about this.[36] In fact, Augustine was also displeased that consciences were burdened with so many traditions, and he taught in this connection that they were not to be considered necessary observances.[37]

Our teachers have not taught concerning these matters out of malice or contempt of spiritual authority, but dire need has compelled them to give instruction about the aforementioned errors which have arisen from a wrong estimation of tradition. The Gospel demands that the teaching about faith should and must be emphasized in the church, but this teaching cannot be understood if it is supposed that grace is earned through self-chosen works.

It is therefore taught that grace cannot be earned, God cannot be reconciled, and sin cannot be atoned for by observing the said human traditions. Accordingly they should not be made into a necessary service of God. Reasons for this shall be cited from the Scriptures. In Matt. 15:1–20 Christ defends the apostles for not observing the customary traditions, and he adds, "In vain do they worship me, teaching as doctrines the precepts of men" [Matt. 15:9]. Since he calls them vain service, they must not be necessary. Thereupon Christ says, "Not what goes into the mouth defiles a man" [Matt. 15:11]. Paul also says in Rom. 14:17, "The kingdom of God does not mean food and drink," and in Col. 2:16 he says, "Let no one pass judgment on you in questions of food and drink or with regard to a festival," etc. In Acts 15:10, 2 Peter says, "Why do you make trial of God by putting a yoke upon the neck of the disciples which neither our fathers nor we have been able to bear? But we believe that we shall be saved through the grace of the Lord Jesus, just as they will." Here Peter forbids the burdening of consciences with additional outward ceremonies, whether of Moses or of another. In 1 Tim. 4:1, 3 such prohibitions as forbid food or marriage are called a doctrine of the devil, for it is diametrically opposed to the Gospel to institute or practice such works for the purpose of earning forgiveness of sin or with the notion that nobody is a Christian unless he performs such services.

Although our teachers are, like Jovinian,[38] accused of forbidding mortification and discipline, their writings reveal something quite different. They have always taught concerning the holy cross that Christians are obliged to suffer, and this is true and real rather than invented mortification.

They also teach that everybody is under obligation to conduct himself, with reference to such bodily exercise as fasting and other discipline, so that he does not give occasion to sin, but not as if he earned grace by such works. Such bodily exercise should not be limited to certain specified days but should be practiced continually. Christ speaks of this in Luke 21:34, "Take heed to yourselves lest your hearts be weighed down with dissipation," and again, "This kind of demon cannot be driven out by anything but fasting and prayer" [Mark 9:29]. Paul said that he pommeled his body and subdued it [1 Cor. 9:27], and by this he indicated that it is not the purpose of mortification to merit grace but to keep the body in such a condition that one can perform the duties required by one's calling. Thus fasting in itself is not rejected, but what is rejected is making a necessary service of fasts on prescribed days and with specified foods, for this confuses consciences.

We on our part also retain many ceremonies and traditions (such as the liturgy of the Mass and various canticles, festivals, and the like) which serve to preserve order in the church. At the same time, however, the people are instructed that such outward forms of service do not make us righteous before God and that they are to be observed without burdening consciences, which is to say that it is not a sin to omit them if this is done without causing scandal. The ancient Fathers maintained such liberty with respect to outward ceremonies, for in the East they kept Easter at a time different from that in Rome.[39] When some regarded this difference as divisive of the church, they were admonished by others that it was not necessary to maintain uniformity in such customs. Irenaeus said, "Disagreement in fasting does not destroy unity in faith,"[40] and there is a statement in Dist. 12 that such disagreement in human ordinances is not in conflict with the unity of Christendom.[41] Moreover, the Tripartite History, Book 9, gathers many examples of dissimilar church usages and adds the profitable Christian observation, "It was not the intention of the apostles to institute holy days but to teach faith and love."[42]

XXVII. [Monastic Vows]

In discussing monastic vows it is necessary to begin by considering what opinions have hitherto been held concerning them, what kind of life was lived in the monasteries, and how many of the daily observances in them were contrary not only to the Word of God but also to papal canons. In the days of St. Augustine monastic life was voluntary. Later, when true discipline and doctrine had become corrupted, monastic vows were invented, and the attempt was made to restore discipline by means of these vows as if in a well-conceived prison.

In addition to monastic vows many other requirements were imposed, and such fetters and burdens were laid on many before they had attained an appropriate age.

Many persons also entered monastic life ignorantly, for although they were not too young, they had not sufficiently appreciated or understood their strength. All of those who were thus ensnared and entangled were pressed and compelled to remain, in spite of the fact that even the papal canons might have set many of them free. The practice was stricter in women's convents than in those of men, though it would have been seemly to show more consideration to women as the weaker sex. Such severity and rigor displeased many devout people in the past, for they must have seen that both boys and girls were thrust into monasteries to provide for their maintenance. They must also have seen what evils came from this arrangement, what scandals and burdened consciences resulted. Many people complained that in such a momentous matter the canons were not strictly adhered to. Besides, monastic vows gained such a reputation, as is well known, that many monks with even a little understanding were displeased.

It was claimed that monastic vows were equal to Baptism, and that by monastic life one could earn forgiveness of sin and justification before God. What is more, they added that monastic life not only earned righteousness and godliness, but also that by means of this life both the precepts and the counsels included in the Gospel were kept, and so monastic vows were praised more highly than Baptism. They also claimed that more merit could be obtained by monastic life than by all other states of life instituted by God—whether the office of pastor and preacher, of ruler, prince, lord, or the like, all of whom serve in their appointed calling according to God's Word and command without invented spirituality. None of these things can be denied, for they are found in their own books.

Furthermore, those who were thus ensnared and inveigled into a monastery learned little about Christ. Formerly the monasteries had conducted schools of Holy Scripture and other branches of learning which are profitable to the Christian church, so that pastors and bishops were taken from monasteries. But now the picture is changed. In former times people gathered and adopted monastic life for the purpose of learning the Scriptures, but now it is claimed that monastic life is of such a nature that thereby God's grace and righteousness before God are earned. In fact, it is called a state of perfection and is regarded as far superior to the other estates instituted by God. All this is mentioned, without misrepresentation, in order that one may better grasp and understand what our teachers teach and preach.

For one thing, it is taught among us with regard to those who desire to marry that all those who are not suited for celibacy have the power, right, and authority to marry, for vows cannot nullify God's order and command. God's command in 1 Cor. 7:2 reads, "Because of the temptation to immorality, each man should have his own wife and each woman her own husband." It is not alone God's command that urges, drives, and compels us to do this, but God's creation and order also direct all to marriage who are not endowed with the gift of virginity by a special act of God. This appears from God's own words in Gen. 2:18, "It is not good that the man should be alone; I will make him a helper fit for him."

What objection may be raised to this? No matter how much one extols the vow and the obligation, no matter how highly one exalts them, it is still impossible to abrogate God's command. Learned men say that a vow made contrary to papal canons is not binding. How much less must be their obligation, lawfulness, and power when they are contrary to God's command!

If there were no reasons which allowed annulment of the obligation of a vow, the popes could not have dispensed and released men from such obligation, for no man has the right to cancel an obligation which is derived from divine law. Consequently the popes were well aware that some amelioration ought to be exercised in connection with this obligation and have often given dispensations, as in the case of the king of Aragon[43] and many others. If dispensations were granted for the maintenance of temporal interests, how much more should dispensations be granted for necessities of men's souls!

Why, then, do our opponents insist so strongly that vows must be kept without first ascertaining whether a vow is of the proper sort? For a vow must involve what is possible and voluntary and must be uncoerced. Yet it is commonly known to what an extent perpetual chastity lies within human power and ability, and there are few, whether men or women, who have taken monastic vows of themselves, willingly, and after due consideration. Before they came to a right understanding they were persuaded to take monastic vows, and sometimes they have been compelled and forced to do so. Accordingly it is not right to argue so rashly and insistently about the obligation of vows inasmuch as it is generally conceded that it belongs to the very nature and character of a vow that it should be voluntary and should be assumed only after due consideration and counsel.

Several canons and papal regulations annul vows that are made under the age of fifteen years.[44] They hold that before this age one does not possess sufficient understanding to determine or arrange the order of one's whole future life. Another canon concedes still more years to human frailty, for it prohibits the taking of monastic vows before the eighteenth year.[45] On the basis of this provision most monastics have excuse and reason for leaving their monasteries inasmuch as a majority of them entered the cloister in their childhood, before attaining such age.

Finally, although the breaking of monastic vows might be censured, it would not follow that the marriage of those who broke them should be dissolved. For St. Augustine says in his *Nuptiarum* (On Marriage), Question 27, Chapter I, that such a marriage should not be dissolved,[46] and St. Augustine is no inconsiderable authority in the Christian church, even though some have subsequently differed from him.

Although God's command concerning marriage frees and releases many from monastic vows, our teachers offer still more reasons why monastic vows are null and void. For all service of God that is chosen and instituted by men to obtain righteousness and God's grace without the command and authority of God is opposed to God and the holy Gospel and contrary to God's command. So Christ himself says in Matt. 15:9, "In vain do they worship me, teaching as doctrines the precepts of men." St. Paul also teaches everywhere that one is not to seek for righteousness in the precepts and services invented by men but that righteousness and godliness in God's sight come from faith and trust when we believe that God receives us into his favor for the sake of Christ, his only Son.

It is quite evident that the monks have taught and preached that their invented spiritual life makes satisfaction for sin and obtains God's grace and righteousness. What is this but to diminish the glory and honor of the grace of Christ and deny the righteousness of faith? It follows from this that the customary vows were an improper and false service of God. Therefore they are not binding, for an ungodly vow, made contrary to God's command, is null and void. Even the canons teach that an oath should not be an obligation to sin.

St. Paul says in Gal. 5:4, "You are severed from Christ, you who would be justified by the law; you have fallen away from grace." In the same way, those who would be justified by vows are severed from Christ and have fallen away from God's grace, for they rob Christ, who alone justifies, of his honor and bestow this honor on their vows and monastic life.

One cannot deny that the monks have taught and preached that they were justified and earned forgiveness of sins by their vows and their monastic life and observances. In fact, they have invented a still more indecent and absurd claim, namely, that they could apply their good works to others. If one were inclined to count up all these claims for the purpose of casting them into their teeth, how many items could be assembled which the monks themselves are now ashamed of and wish had never occurred! Besides all this, they persuaded the people that the invented spiritual estate of the orders was Christian perfection. Certainly this is exaltation of works as a means of attaining justification. Now, it is no small offense in the Christian church that the people should be presented with such a service of God, invented by men without the command of God, and should be taught that such a service would make men good and righteous before God. For righteousness of faith, which should be emphasized above all else in the Christian church, is obscured when man's eyes are dazzled with this curious angelic spirituality and sham of poverty, humility, and chastity.

Besides, the commands of God and true and proper service of God are obscured when people are told that monks alone are in a state of perfection. For this is Christian perfection: that we fear God honestly with our whole hearts, and yet have sincere confidence, faith, and trust that for Christ's sake we have a gracious, merciful God; that we may and should ask and pray God for those things of which we have need, and confidently expect help from him in every affliction connected with our particular calling and station in life; and that meanwhile we do good works for others and diligently attend to our calling. True perfection and right service of God consist of these things and not of mendicancy or wearing a black or gray cowl, etc. However, the common people, hearing the state of celibacy praised above all measure, draw many harmful conclusions from such false exaltation of monastic life, for it follows that their consciences are troubled because they married. When the common man hears that only mendicants are perfect, he is uncertain whether he can keep his possessions and engage in business without sin. When the people hear that it is only a counsel[47] not to take revenge, it is natural that some should conclude that it is not sinful to take revenge outside of the exercise of their office. Still others think that it is not right at all for Christians, even in the government, to avenge wrong.

Many instances are also recorded of men who forsook wife and child, and also their civil office, to take shelter in a monastery. This, they said, is fleeing from the world and seeking a life more pleasing to God than the other. They were unable to understand that one is to serve God by observing the commands God has given and not by keeping the commands invented by men. That is a good and perfect state of life which has God's command to support it; on the other hand, that is a dangerous state of life which does not have God's command behind it. About such matters it was necessary to give the people proper instruction.

In former times Gerson censured the error of the monks concerning perfection and indicated that it was an innovation of his time to speak of monastic life as a state of perfection.[48]

Thus there are many godless opinions and errors associated with monastic vows: that they justify and render men righteous before God, that they constitute Christian perfection, that they are the means of fulfilling both evangelical counsels and precepts, and that they furnish the works of supererogation which we are not obligated to render to God. Inasmuch as all these things are false, useless, and invented, monastic vows are null and void.

XXVIII. [The Power of Bishops]

Many and various things have been written in former times about the power of bishops, and some have improperly confused the power of bishops with the temporal sword. Out of this careless confusion many serious wars, tumults, and uprisings have resulted because the bishops, under pretext of the power given them by Christ, have not only introduced new forms of worship and burdened consciences with reserved cases[49] and violent use of the ban, but have also presumed to set up and depose kings and emperors according to their pleasure. Such outrage has long since been condemned by learned and devout people in Christendom. On this account our teachers have been compelled, for the sake of comforting consciences, to point out the difference between spiritual and temporal power, sword, and authority, and they have taught that because of God's command both authorities and powers are to be honored and esteemed with all reverence as the two highest gifts of God on earth.

Our teachers assert that according to the Gospel the power of keys or the power of bishops is a power and command of God to preach the Gospel, to forgive and retain sins, and to administer and distribute the sacraments. For Christ sent out the apostles with this command, "As the Father has sent me, even so I send you. Receive the Holy Spirit. If you forgive the sins of any, they are forgiven; if you retain the sins of any, they are retained" [John 20:21–23].

This power of keys or of bishops is used and exercised only by teaching and preaching the Word of God and by administering the sacraments (to many persons or to individuals, depending on one's calling). In this way are imparted not bodily but eternal things and gifts, namely, eternal righteousness, the Holy Spirit, and eternal life. These gifts cannot be obtained except through the office of preaching and of administering the holy sacraments, for St. Paul says, "The gospel is the power of God for salvation to everyone who has faith" [Rom. 1:16]. Inasmuch as the power of the church or of bishops bestows eternal gifts and is used and exercised only through the office of preaching, it does not interfere at all with government or temporal authority. Temporal authority is concerned with matters altogether different from the Gospel. Temporal power does not protect the soul, but with the sword and physical penalties it protects body and goods from the power of others.

Therefore, the two authorities, the spiritual and the temporal, are not to be mingled or confused, for the spiritual power has its commission to preach the Gospel and administer the sacraments. Hence it should not invade the function of the other, should not set up and depose kings, should not annul temporal laws or undermine obedience to government, should not make or prescribe to the temporal power laws concerning worldly matters. Christ himself said, "My kingship is not of this world" [John 18:36], and again, "Who made me a judge or divider over you?" [Luke 12:14]. Paul also wrote in Phil. 3:20, "Our commonwealth is in heaven," and in 2 Cor. 10:4, 5, "The weapons of our warfare are not worldly but have divine power to destroy strongholds and every proud obstacle to the knowledge of God."

Thus our teachers distinguish the two authorities and the function of the two powers, directing that both be held in honor as the highest gifts of God on earth.

In cases where bishops possess temporal authority and the sword, they possess it not as bishops by divine right, but by human, imperial right, bestowed by Roman emperors and kings for the temporal administration of their lands. Such authority has nothing at all to do with the office of the Gospel.

According to divine right, therefore, it is the office of the bishop to preach the Gospel, forgive sins, judge doctrine and condemn doctrine that is contrary to the Gospel, and exclude from the Christian community the ungodly whose wicked conduct is manifest. All this is to be done not by human power but by God's Word alone. On this account parish ministers and churches are bound to be obedient to the bishops according to the saying of Christ in Luke 10:16, "He who hears you hears me." On the other hand, if they teach, introduce, or institute anything contrary to the Gospel, we have God's command not to be obedient in such cases, for Christ says in Matt. 7:15, "Beware of false prophets." St. Paul also writes in Gal. 1:8, "Even if we, or an angel from heaven, should preach to you a gospel contrary to that which we preached to you, let him be accursed," and in 2 Cor. 13:8, "We cannot do anything against the truth, but only for the truth." Again Paul refers to "the authority which the Lord has given me for building up and not for tearing [Priests] down" [2 Cor. 13:10]. Canon law requires the same in Part II, Question 7, in the chapters "Sacerdotes" and "Oves" [they].[50]

St. Augustine also writes in his reply to the letters of Petilian that one should not obey even regularly elected bishops if they err or if they teach or command something contrary to the divine Holy Scriptures.[51]

Whatever other power and jurisdiction bishops may have in various matters (for example, in matrimonial cases and in tithes),[52] they have these by virtue of human right. However, when bishops are negligent in the performance of such duties, the princes are obliged, whether they like to or not, to administer justice to their subjects for the sake of peace and to prevent discord and great disorder in their lands.

Besides, there is dispute as to whether bishops have the power to introduce ceremonies in the church or establish regulations concerning foods, holy days, and the different orders of the clergy. Those who attribute such power to bishops cite Christ's saying in John 16:12, 13, "I have yet many things to say to you, but you cannot bear them now. When the Spirit of truth comes, he will guide you into all the truth." They also cite the example in Acts 15:20, 29, where the eating of blood and what is strangled was forbidden. Besides, they appeal to the fact that the Sabbath was changed to Sunday—contrary, as they say, to the Ten Commandments. No case is appealed to and urged so insistently as the change of the Sabbath, for thereby they wish to maintain that the power of the church is indeed great because the church has dispensed from and altered part of the Ten Commandments.

Concerning this question our teachers assert that bishops do not have power to institute or establish anything contrary to the Gospel, as has been indicated above and as is taught by canon law throughout the whole of the ninth Distinction.[53] It is patently contrary to God's command and Word to make laws out of opinions or to require that they be observed in order to make satisfaction for sins and obtain grace, for the glory of Christ's merit is blasphemed when we presume to earn grace by such ordinances. It is also apparent that because of this notion human ordinances have multiplied beyond calculation while the teaching concerning faith and righteousness of faith has almost been suppressed. Almost every day new holy days and new fasts have been prescribed, new ceremonies and new venerations of saints have been instituted in order that by such works grace and everything good might be earned from God.

Again, those who institute human ordinances also act contrary to God's command when they attach sin to foods, days, and similar things and burden Christendom with the bondage of the law, as if in order to earn God's grace there had to be a service of God among Christians like the Levitical service, and as if God had commanded the apostles and bishops to institute it, as some have written. It is quite believable that some bishops were misled by the example of the law of Moses. The result was that countless regulations came into being—for example, that it is a mortal sin to do manual work on holy days (even when it does not give offense to others), that it is a mortal sin to omit the seven hours,[54] that some foods defile the conscience, that fasting is a work by which God is reconciled, that in a reserved case sin is not forgiven unless forgiveness is secured from the person for whom the case is reserved, in spite of the fact that canon law says nothing of the reservation of guilt but speaks only about the reservation of ecclesiastical penalties.

Where did the bishops get the right and power to impose such requirements on Christendom to ensnare men's consciences? In Acts 15:10 St. Peter forbids putting a yoke on the neck of the disciples. And St. Paul said in 2 Cor. 10:8 that authority was given for building up and not for tearing down. Why, then, do they multiply sins with such requirements?

Yet there are clear passages of divine Scripture which forbid the establishment of such regulations for the purpose of earning God's grace or as if they were necessary for salvation. Thus St. Paul says in Col. 2:16, "Let no one pass judgment on you in questions of food and drink or with regard to a festival or a new moon or a sabbath. These are only a shadow of what is to come; but the substance belongs to Christ." Again in Col. 2:20–23, "If with Christ you died to the regulations of the world, why do you live as if you still belonged to the world? Why do you submit to regulations, 'Do not handle, Do not taste, Do not touch' (referring to things which all perish as they are used), according to human precepts and doctrines? These have an appearance of wisdom." In Titus 1:14 St. Paul also forbids giving heed to Jewish myths or to commands of men who reject the truth.

Christ himself says concerning those who urge human ordinances on people, "Let them alone; they are blind guides" [Matt. 15:14]. He rejects such service of God and says, "Every plant which my heavenly Father has not planted will be rooted up" [Matt. 15:13].

If, then, bishops have the power to burden the churches with countless requirements and thus ensnare consciences, why does the divine Scripture so frequently forbid the making and keeping of human regulations? Why does it call them doctrines of the devil? Is it possible that the Holy Spirit warned against them for nothing?

Inasmuch as such regulations as have been instituted as necessary to propitiate God and merit grace are contrary to the Gospel, it is not at all proper for the bishops to require such services of God. It is necessary to preserve the teaching of Christian liberty in Christendom, namely, that bondage to the law is not necessary for justification, as St. Paul writes in Gal. 5:1, "For freedom Christ has set us free; stand fast, therefore, and do not submit again to a yoke of slavery." For the chief article of the Gospel must be maintained, namely, that we obtain the grace of God through faith in Christ without our merits; we do not merit it by services of God instituted by men.

What are we to say, then, about Sunday and other similar church ordinances and ceremonies? To this our teachers reply that bishops or pastors may make regulations so that everything in the churches is done in good order, but not as a means of obtaining God's grace or making satisfaction for sins, nor in order to bind men's consciences by considering these things necessary services of God and counting it a sin to omit their observance even when this is done without offense. So St. Paul directed in 1 Cor. 11:5 that women should cover their heads in the assembly. He also directed that in the assembly preachers should not all speak at once, but one after another, in order [1 Cor. 14:30].

It is proper for the Christian assembly to keep such ordinances for the sake of love and peace, to be obedient to the bishops and parish ministers in such matters, and to observe the regulations in such a way that one does not give offense to another and so that there may be no disorder or unbecoming conduct in the church. However, consciences should not be burdened by contending that such things are necessary for salvation or that it is a sin to omit them, even when no offense is given to others, just as no one would say that a woman commits a sin if without offense to others she goes out with uncovered head.

Of like character is the observance of Sunday, Easter, Pentecost, and similar holy days and usages. Those who consider the appointment of Sunday in place of the Sabbath as a necessary institution are very much mistaken, for the Holy Scriptures have abrogated the Sabbath and teach that after the revelation of the Gospel all ceremonies of the old law may be omitted. Nevertheless, because it was necessary to appoint a certain day so that the people might know when they ought to assemble, the Christian church appointed Sunday for this purpose, and it was the more inclined and pleased to do this in order that the people might have an example of Christian liberty and might know that the keeping neither of the Sabbath nor of any other day is necessary.

There are many faulty discussions of the transformation of the law, of the ceremonies of the New Testament, and of the change of the Sabbath, all of which have arisen from the false and erroneous opinion that in Christendom one must have services of God like the Levitical or Jewish services and that Christ commanded the apostles and bishops to devise new ceremonies which would be necessary for salvation. Such errors were introduced into Christendom when the righteousness of faith was no longer taught and preached with clarity and purity. Some argue that although Sunday must not be kept as of divine obligation, it must nevertheless be kept as almost of divine obligation, and they prescribe the kind and amount of work that may be done on the day of rest. What are such discussions but snares of conscience? For although they undertake to lighten and mitigate human regulations, yet there can be no moderation or mitigation as long as the opinion remains and prevails that their observance is necessary. And this opinion will remain as long as there is no understanding of the righteousness of faith and Christian liberty.

The apostles directed that one should abstain from blood and from what is strangled. Who observes this prohibition now? Those who do not observe it commit no sin, for the apostles did not wish to burden consciences with such bondage but forbade such eating for a time to avoid offense. One must pay attention to the chief article of Christian doctrine, and this is not abrogated by the decree [i.e., in Acts 15:28–29].

Scarcely any of the ancient canons are observed according to the letter, and many of the regulations fall into disuse from day to day even among those who observe such ordinances most jealously. It is impossible to give counsel or help to consciences unless this mitigation is practiced, that one recognizes that such rules are not to be deemed necessary and that disregard of them does not injure consciences.

The bishops might easily retain the obedience of men if they did not insist on the observance of regulations which cannot be kept without sin. Now, however, they administer the sacrament in one kind and prohibit administration in both kinds. Again, they forbid clergymen to marry and admit no one to the ministry unless he first swears an oath that he will not preach this doctrine, although there is no doubt that it is in accord with the holy Gospel. Our churches do not ask that the bishops should restore peace and unity at the expense of their honor and dignity (though it is incumbent on the bishops to do this, too, in case of need), but they ask only that the bishops relax certain unreasonable burdens which did not exist in the church in former times and which were introduced contrary to the custom of the universal Christian church. Perhaps there was some reason for introducing them, but they are not adapted to our times. Nor can it be denied that some regulations were adopted from want of understanding. Accordingly the bishops ought to be so gracious as to temper these regulations inasmuch as such changes do not destroy the unity of Christian churches. For many regulations devised by men have with the passing of time fallen into disuse and are not obligatory, as papal law itself testifies. If, however, this is impossible and they cannot be persuaded to mitigate or abrogate human regulations which are not to be observed without sin, we are bound to follow the apostolic rule which commands us to obey God rather than men [Acts 5:29].

St. Peter forbids the bishops to exercise lordship as if they had power to coerce the churches according to their will [1 Peter 5:2]. It is not our intention to find ways of reducing the bishops' power, but we desire and pray that they may not coerce our consciences to sin. If they are unwilling to do this and ignore our petition, let them consider how they will answer for it in God's sight, inasmuch as by their obstinacy they offer occasion for division and schism, which they should in truth help to prevent.

Conclusion

These are the chief articles that are regarded as controversial. Although we could have mentioned many more abuses and wrongs, to avoid prolixity and undue length we have indicated only the principal ones. The others can readily be weighed in the light of these. In the past there have been grave complaints about indulgences, pilgrimages, and misuse of the ban. Parish ministers also had endless quarrels with monks about the hearing of confessions, about burials, about sermons on special occasions, and about countless other matters. All these things we have discreetly passed over for the common good in order that the chief points at issue may better be perceived.

It must not be thought that anything has been said or introduced out of hatred or for the purpose of injuring anybody, but we have related only matters which we have considered it necessary to adduce and mention in order that it may be made very clear that we have introduced nothing, either in doctrine or in ceremonies, that is contrary to Holy Scripture or the universal Christian church. For it is manifest and evident (to speak without boasting) that we have diligently and with God's help prevented any new and godless teaching from creeping into our churches and gaining the upper hand in them.

In keeping with the summons, we have desired to present the above articles as a declaration of our confession and the teaching of our preachers. If anyone should consider that it is lacking in some respect, we are ready to present further information on the basis of the divine Holy Scripture.

Your Imperial Majesty's most obedient servants:

JOHN, duke of Saxony, elector
GEORGE, margrave of Brandenburg
ERNEST, duke of Lüneburg
PHILIP, landgrave of Hesse
JOHN FREDERICK, duke of Saxony
FRANCIS, duke of Lüneburg
WOLFGANG, prince of Anhalt
Mayor and council of Nuremberg
Mayor and council of Reutlingen

Notes

1. See Leif Grane, *The Augsburg Confession: A Commentary*, trans. John Rasmussen (Minneapolis: Augsburg, 1987), 11–20, and *Book of Concord,* ed. Theodore G. Tappert (Philadelphia: Muhlenberg Press, 1959), 23–24.
2. See David Dunn et al., *A History of the Evangelical and Reformed Church* (New York: Pilgrim Press, 1990), 283, 293.
3. The diets, or parliamentary assemblies of the empire, were made up of the seven princes who were called "electors," of the other princes, and of representatives of the free cities. The notes that follow (except those in brackets) are those of Tappert based on the German edition.
4. At the last minute the presentation was postponed from Friday (June 24) to Saturday (June 25).
5. The peace of Barcelona (1529) was followed by an alliance (1529) and the coronation of the emperor in February 1530.
6. The titles of some articles, here enclosed in square brackets, were inserted in and after 1533.

7. A religion based on Persian dualism combined with Christian and other elements, founded in the third century by Mani and named after him.

8. Gnostics of the second century who took their name from Valentinus.

9. Followers of Arius who were condemned at the Council of Nicaea in 325 and who held that Jesus was a highly exalted creature and quite distinct in substance from God.

10. Followers of Eunomius, an extreme Arian of the late fourth century.

11. The Reformers frequently referred to Mohammedanism as an anti-Trinitarian heresy.

12. Followers of Paul of Samosata, who taught in the third century that Jesus was a human being specially endowed by the Spirit.

[13. Followers of Pelagius, who at the beginning of the fifth century rejected the Augustinian doctrine of an inherited depravity and that of a special empowerment of grace in order to be able to accomplish God's law and attain salvation. Luther and Melanchthon charged certain of the medieval scholastic theologians with Pelagianism.]

14. Ambrosiaster, *The First Epistle to the Corinthians*, 1:4.

[15. For the significance of this sentence for the Lutheran and Reformed dialogue in the twentieth century, see *A Common Calling*, ed. Keith Nickle and Timothy F. Lull (Minneapolis: Augsburg Fortress, 1993), 32–34.]

[16. Rigorists of the fourth and fifth centuries in North Africa who had broken away from the Catholic Church because of the failure of some bishops to remain faithful under persecution. They rejected the validity of the baptism and ordination of the Catholic Church and thought of their church as alone holy.]

[17. The Anabaptists were perfectionists who insisted that converts lead holy lives after baptism. See George H. Williams, *The Radical Reformation*, 3d ed. (Kirkville, Mo.: Sixteenth Century Publishers, 1992), 434.]

[18. Rigorists in Rome who denied reconciliation to those who were guilty of grave sins, such as apostasy under the persecution of Decius, 250–251.]

[19. Many, but not all, Anabaptists refused to assume civil office and bear the sword. See James M. Stayer, *Anabaptists and the Sword*, 2d ed. (Law-rence, Kans.: Coronado Press, 1972).]

[20. Hans Denck was one Anabaptist who taught universal salvation. See Williams, *The Radical Reformation*, 254, 258.]

21. Incited by Hans Hut and some Jews in Worms, Melchior Rinck predicted that the millennium would be ushered in during Easter 1530.

22. *Hypomnesticon contra Pelagianos et Coelestinianos*, III, 4, 5, ascribed to Augustine in older collections of his works.

23. Cyprian, *Epistle 57*.

24. Jerome, *Commentary on Zephaniah*, 3.

25. Gratian, *Decretum*, Part III, *De consecratione*, dist. 2, chap. 12.

26. Nicholas of Cusa (1401–64), *Epistle III to the Bohemians*, refers the authorization for the withdrawal of the cup to the Fourth Lateran Council, 1215.

27. Reference is to the observance of the Corpus Christi festival on the Thursday following Trinity Sunday. The Evangelical princes refused to participate in the Corpus Christi procession in Augsburg on June 16, 1530. Even "carrying the sacrament across the street" was later forbidden.

28. Although the requirement of celibacy was frequently asserted and practiced in earlier centuries, it was not until the end of the eleventh century that it was

generally enforced by Pope Gregory VII. At that time, most of the priests in Germany were still married.

29. Siegfried of Mayence at synods in Erfurt and Mayence in 1075.

30. Gratian, *Decretum*, part I, dist. 82, chap. 2–5; also dist. 84, chap. 4. The Council of Nicaea refused to require celibacy; see Evagrius, *Ecclesiastical History*, I, 11.

31. Cyprian, *Epistles*, 62, 2. The text refers to the numbering of Cyprian's letters adopted by Erasmus.

32. Chrysostom, Homily 3 in *Epistle to the Ephesians*, chap. 1.

33. Canon 18 of the Council of Nicaea.

34. *The Tripartite Ecclesiastical History* by the Roman monk Cassiodorus (480–570) was the principal book of church history used in the late Middle Ages, and it quotes here from Socrates, *Ecclesiastical History*, V, 22.

35. Gratian, *Decretum*, part II, chap. 33, q. 3, *De poenitentia*, dist. I, c. 87:4. The quotation is from Chrysostom, Homily 31, in *Epistle to the Hebrews*.

36. John Gerson, *The Spiritual Life*, lectio 2.

37. Augustine, *Epistle 54* to Januarius, 2:2.

38. The Reformers were here misled by Jerome's slanderous misrepresentation of Jovinian, a Roman ascetic of the fourth century who contended against the monastic teaching about merits and the stages of ethical perfection, but not against "mortification and discipline."

39. In Asia Minor, Easter was observed on the Jewish Passover, while in the West, as in Palestine and Egypt, it was observed on the Sunday following.

40. In Eusebius, *Ecclesiastical History*, V, 24, 13.

41. Gratian, *Decretum*, part 1, dist. 12, chap. 10.

42. Cassiodorus, *Tripartite Ecclesiastical History*, IX, 38, quoting from Socrates, *Ecclesiastical History*, V, 22.

43. Ramiro II, a monk, was released from his vows after the death of his childless brother so that he might assume the throne.

44. Gratian, *Decretum*, part II, chap. 20, q. 1, c. 10.

45. Ibid., chap. 5.

46. Augustine, *De bono viduitatis*, chap. 9.

[47. That is, a Gospel commandment that applies only to those who "would be perfect" (Matt. 19:21), not a precept demanded of all Christians. Such a distinction between the commandments would lead to the idea of two levels of morality, one for ordinary Christians and a second for monks.]

48. Among many other places, see John Gerson, *Evangelical Counsels, in Opera*, II, 680.

49. Cases in which absolution was reserved for bishops or the pope.

50. Gratian, *Decretum*, part II, q. 7, c. 8, 13.

51. Augustine, *The Unity of the Church*, 11, 28.

52. The payment to the church of one-tenth of the gross income from all lands and industries was required since the early Middle Ages.

53. Gratian, *Decretum*, part I, dist. 9, c. 8ff.

54. The canonical hours, or seven daily hours of prayer, prescribed for monastics and others.

Zwingli and the Swiss Reformation

10. Sixty-Seven Articles

(1523)

ULRICH ZWINGLI

After serving parishes in Glarus and Einsiedeln, Ulrich (or Huldrych or Huldreich) Zwingli (1484–1531) was chosen as people's priest at the Great Cathedral in Zurich in 1519. Zwingli was an enthusiastic disciple of Desiderius Erasmus; inspired by Erasmus's biblical scholarship, Zwingli copied out by hand the Greek text of the Pauline epistles from Erasmus's New Testament and virtually memorized it. Zwingli's library contained more writings of Erasmus than of any other contemporary. Under Erasmus's influence, he emphasized preaching directly from the Greek New Testament, applying the text not only to the individual lives of parishioners, but also to the reform of the church and society. Like Erasmus, Zwingli was impressed by the directness of Matt. 11:28–30, "Come unto me all ye who labor and are heavy laden," and applied this text to a simple Christianity of faith and deeds freed from burdensome ecclesiastical ceremonies and regulations.

After coming to Zurich, Zwingli moved beyond the teachings of Erasmus to take a position closer to that of Martin Luther. He became increasingly concerned about the sinfulness of humanity and the central importance of the cross of Christ. Zwingli probably came to such new understandings as he increased his knowledge of Paul's letters and became more familiar with the writings of Augustine, who dwelt on the doctrine of original sin and the sovereignty of divine grace. In spite of this shift, Zwingli remained deeply indebted to Erasmus throughout his career.[1]

SOURCE: Samuel Macauley Jackson, ed., *Selected Works*, with introduction by Edwards Peters (Philadelphia: University of Pennsylvania Press, 1972). Used by permission.

Zwingli's preaching, grounded in the Bible, spoke out forthrightly on religious, moral, and political topics. He preached that there was no scriptural warrant for many common practices, such as the invocation of the saints, required fasting during Lent, and celibacy. His bold preaching stirred up opposition from the upholders of the old customs in Zurich and from the bishop of Constance, in whose diocese Zurich lay. Zwingli himself did not want turmoil. He did not favor reform by revolution, but by education and governmental action.

The town council, out of a concern for public peace and to provide Zwingli with a public forum in which to give an account of his faith and defend himself against charges of heresy, called for a public meeting to be held at the Zurich courthouse on January 29, 1523. Clergy from Zurich and the surrounding countryside were invited to the meeting. The bishop of Constance was asked to come or to send a representative.

As it worked out, the bishop did send a delegation led by John Faber. For this occasion, Zwingli prepared his Sixty-Seven Articles, or conclusions, to stimulate scholarly debate. They were "summary statements of previous sermons" and an "account of faith."[2]

In the end, no debate on these articles took place. The meeting ended up becoming a hearing on whether Zwingli was guilty of heresy. The articles, however, stand as a good summary of Zwingli's beliefs at this time. Written in an apologetic manner, they state from the outset that Scripture and Christ form the basic foundation of his teachings.

In Articles 1–16, Zwingli argues that all faith and practice must square with the teachings of Scripture as centered in Christ. The next articles explain the polemical consequences of this standpoint as applied to church belief and custom. The concluding articles show how Zwingli thought that the gospel was concerned not just with personal salvation, but with the salvation of the whole community—religious and civil.

In the articles dealing with the magistrate, to whom Zwingli ascribes a major role in the community, Zwingli deals with social and political ethics, especially the connection between the laws of the community, grounded in divine will, and the plight of the oppressed. On this matter, some scholars note a difference between Luther and Zwingli. "Luther sees before him the troubled angefochtenen *(human beings) and proclaims to them* solus Christus *(Christ alone) and* Christus pro me *(Christ for me). Zwingli sees before him mendacious and self-seeking human beings and the disruption of their social life."*[3]

At the end of the meeting, Zwingli was exonerated of heresy. Furthermore, both the pro-Zwingli and the anti-Zwingli parties were ordered to cease charging each other with heresy, and their preachers were com-

manded to preach according to Scripture. Despite a formal agreement on the scriptural principle, which had been reached by the council before the January 1523 meeting,[4] *no specific program based on Zwingli's articles was adopted.*

In fact, the debate ended up virtually ignoring Zwingli's articles. It focused on issues such as Scripture versus tradition, the recent innovations in Zurich versus the old customs, and the right of a town council, rather than a church council, to sit in judgment. On this last issue, Zwingli contended that "within this room is without doubt a Christian assembly." What was intended as a hearing became in fact "the first evangelical General Synod."[5]

The articles and opinions below, I, Ulrich Zwingli, confess to have preached in the worthy city of Zurich as based upon the Scriptures which are called inspired by God, and I offer to protect and conquer with the said articles, and where I have not now correctly understood said Scriptures I shall allow myself to be taught better, but only from said Scriptures.

I. All who say that the Gospel is invalid without the confirmation of the Church err and slander God.

II. The sum and substance of the Gospel is that our Lord Jesus Christ, the true Son of God, has made known to us the will of his heavenly Father, and has with his innocence released us from death and reconciled God.

III. Hence Christ is the only way to salvation for all who ever were, are and shall be.

IV. Who seeks or points out another door errs, yea, he is a murderer of souls and a thief.

V. Hence all who consider other teachings equal to or higher than the Gospel err, and do not know what the Gospel is.

VI. For Jesus Christ is the guide and leader, promised by God to all human beings, which promise was fulfilled.

VII. That he is an eternal salvation and head of all believers, who are his body, but which is dead and can do nothing without him.

VIII. From this follows first that all who dwell in the head are members and children of God, and that is the church or communion of the saints, the bride of Christ, *Ecclesia catholica*.

IX. Furthermore, that as the members of the body can do nothing without the control of the head, so no one in the body of Christ can do the least without his head, Christ.

X. As that man is mad whose limbs (try to) do something without his head, tearing, wounding, injuring himself; thus when the members of Christ undertake something without their head, Christ, they are mad, and injure and burden themselves with unwise ordinances.

XI. Hence we see in the clerical (so-called) ordinances, concerning their splendor, riches, classes, titles, laws, a cause of all foolishness, for they do not also agree with the head.

XII. Thus they still rage, not on account of the head (for that one is eager to bring forth in these times from the grace of God,) but because one will not let them rage, but tries to compel them to listen to the head.

XIII. Where this (the head) is hearkened to one learns clearly and plainly the will of God, and man is attracted by his spirit to him and changed into him.

XIV. Therefore all Christian people shall use their best diligence that the Gospel of Christ be preached alike everywhere.

XV. For in the faith rests our salvation, and in unbelief our damnation; for all truth is clear in him.

XVI. In the Gospel one learns that human doctrines and decrees do not aid in salvation.

About the Pope

XVII. That Christ is the only eternal high priest, wherefrom it follows that those who have called themselves high priests have opposed the honor and power of Christ, yea, cast it out.

About the Mass

XVIII. That Christ, having sacrificed himself once, is to eternity a certain and valid sacrifice for the sins of all faithful, wherefrom it follows that the mass is not a sacrifice, but is a remembrance of the sacrifice and assurance of the salvation which Christ has given us.

XIX. That Christ is the only mediator between God and us.

About the Intercession of the Saints

XX. That God desires to give us all things in his name, whence it follows that outside of this life we need no mediator except himself.

XXI. That when we pray for each other on earth, we do so in such fashion that we believe that all things are given to us through Christ alone.

About Good Works

XXII. That Christ is our justice, from which follows that our works in so far as they are good, so far they are of Christ, but in so far as they are ours, they are neither right nor good.

Concerning Clerical Property

XXIII. That Christ scorns the property and pomp of this world, whence from it follows that those who attract wealth to themselves in his name slander him terribly when they make him a pretext for their avarice and wilfullness.

Concerning the Forbidding of Food

XXIV. That no Christian is bound to do those things which God has not decreed, therefore one may eat at all times all food, wherefrom one learns that the decree about cheese and butter is a Roman swindle.

About Holiday and Pilgrimage

XXV. That time and place is under the jurisdiction of Christian people, and man with them, wherefrom is learnt that those who fix time and place deprive the Christians of their liberty.

About Hoods, Dress, Insignia

XXVI. That God is displeased with nothing so much as with hypocrisy; whence is learnt that all is gross hypocrisy and profligacy which is mere show before men. Under this condemnation fall hoods, insignia, plates, etc.

About Order and Sects

XXVII. That all Christian men are brethren of Christ and brethren of one another, and shall create no father (for themselves) on earth. Under this condemnation fall orders, sects, brotherhoods, etc.

About the Marriage of Ecclesiasts

XXVIII. That all which God has allowed or not forbidden is righteous, hence marriage is permitted to all human beings.

XXIX. That all who are called clericals sin when they do not protect themselves by marriage after they have become conscious that God has not enabled them to remain chaste.

About the Vow of Chastity

XXX. That those who promise chastity [outside of matrimony] take foolishly or childishly too much upon themselves, whence is learnt that those who make such vows do wrong to the pious being.

About the Ban

XXXI. That no special person can impose the ban upon any one, but the Church, that is the congregation of those among whom the one to be banned dwells, together with their watchman, i.e., the pastor.

XXXII. That one may ban only him who gives public offence.

About Illegal Property

XXXIII. That property unrighteously acquired shall not be given to temples, monasteries, cathedrals, clergy or nuns, but to the needy, if it cannot be returned to the legal owner.

About Magistry

XXXIV. The spiritual (so-called) power has no justification for its pomp in the teaching of Christ.

XXXV. But the lay has power and confirmation from the deed and doctrine of Christ.

XXXVI. All that the spiritual so-called state claims to have of power and protection belongs to the lay, if they wish to be Christians.

XXXVII. To them, furthermore, all Christians owe obedience without exception.

XXXVIII. In so far as they do not command that which is contrary to God.

XXXIX. Therefore all their laws shall be in harmony with the divine will, so that they protect the oppressed, even if he does not complain.

XL. They alone may put to death justly, also, only those who give public offence (if God is not offended let another thing be commanded).

XLI. If they give good advice and help to those for whom they must account to God, then these owe to them bodily assistance.

XLII. But if they are unfaithful and transgress the laws of Christ they may be deposed in the name of God.

XLIII. In short, the realm of him is best and most stable who rules in the name of God alone, and his is worst and most unstable who rules in accordance with his own will.

About Prayer

XLIV. Real petitioners call to God in spirit and truly, without great ado before men.

XLV. Hypocrites do their work so that they may be seen by men, also receive their reward in this life.

XLVI. Hence it must always follow that church song and outcry without devoutness, and only for reward, is seeking either fame before the men or gain.

About Offence

XLVII. Bodily death a man should suffer before he offend or scandalize a Christian.

XLVIII. Who through stupidness or ignorance is offended without cause, he should not be left sick or weak, but he should be made strong, that he may not consider as a sin which is not a sin.

XLIX. Greater offence I know not than that one does not allow priests to have wives, but permits them to hire prostitutes. Out upon the shame!

About Remittance of Sin

L. God alone remits sin through Jesus Christ, his Son, and alone our Lord.

LI. Who assigns this to creatures detracts from the honor of God and gives it to him who is not God; this is real idolatry.

LII. Hence the confession which is made to the priest or neighbor shall not be declared to be a remittance of sin, but only a seeking for advice.

LIII. Works of penance coming from the counsel of human beings (except the ban) do not cancel sin; they are imposed as a menace to others.

LIV. Christ has borne all our pains and labor. Hence whoever assigns to works of penance what belongs to Christ errs and slanders God.

LV. Whoever pretends to remit to a penitent being any sin would not be a vicar of God or St. Peter, but of the devil.

LVI. Whoever remits any sin only for the sake of money is the companion of Simon and Balaam, and the real messenger of the devil personified.

About Purgatory

LVII. The true divine Scriptures know naught about purgatory after this life.

LVIII. The sentence of the dead is known to God only.

LIX. And the less God has let us know concerning it, the less we should undertake to know about it.

LX. That man earnestly calls to God to show mercy to the dead I do not condemn, but to determine a period of time therefor (seven years for a mortal sin), and to lie for the sake of gain, is not human, but devilish.

About the Priesthood

LXI. About the consecration which the priests have received in late times the Scriptures know nothing.

LXII. Furthermore, they know no priests except those who proclaim the word of God.

LXIII. They command honor should be shown, i.e., to furnish them with food for the body.

About the Cessation of Misusages

LXIV. All those who recognize their errors shall not be allowed to suffer, but to die in peace, and thereafter arrange in a Christian manner their bequests to the Church.

LXV. Those who do not wish to confess, God will probably take care of. Hence no force shall be used against their body, unless it be that they behave so criminally that one cannot do without that.

LXVI. All the clerical superiors shall at once settle down, and with unanimity set up the cross of Christ, not the money-chests, or they will perish, for I tell thee the ax is raised against the tree.

LXVII. If any one wishes conversation with me concerning interest, tithes, unbaptized children or confirmation, I am willing to answer.

Let no one undertake here to argue with sophistry or human foolishness, but come to the Scriptures to accept them as the judge (*foras cares!* [apart from them there is nothing] the Scriptures breathe the Spirit of God), so that the truth either may be found, or if found, as I hope, retained. Amen.

Thus may God rule.

The basis and commentary of these articles will soon appear in print.

Notes

1. See Ulrich Gäbler, *Huldrych Zwingli: His Life and Work*, trans. Ruth C. L. Gritsch (Philadelphia: Fortress Press, 1986), 34.

2. See Heiko A. Oberman, *Masters of the Reformation*, trans. Dennis Martin (Cambridge: Cambridge University Press, 1981), 211.

3. See Gottfried W. Locher, *Huldrych Zwingli in neuer Sicht* (Zurich: Zwingli Verlag, 1969), 269, quoted in Gäbler, 67.

4. Oberman, 194.

5. Ibid., 230.

11. Action or Use of the Lord's Supper

(1525)

ULRICH ZWINGLI

After the disputation of January 29, 1523, the pace of reform in Zurich quickened under the impact of Ulrich (or Huldrych or Huldreich) Zwingli's (1484–1531) preaching. His preaching followed the main themes that he had set forth in the Sixty-Seven Articles (see vol. 2:196–204). Although a second disputation was held October 26–28, 1523, where the subject of images and the Mass came up for debate, a definitive decision concerning them was delayed. Radical reformers, who later came to be known as Anabaptists, complained that reform was not proceeding quickly enough. Zwingli preached against the veneration of pictures and statues as violating the first and second commandments. He felt that pictures and statues obscured the sharp distinction between the Creator and creature, which was a cardinal principle of his theology.

After some hesitation, the Zurich town council decreed on June 15, 1524, that all images should be abolished. In an orderly manner, paintings on the walls of churches were whitewashed and all statues of the saints, all gold and silver utensils, and all crucifixes were removed. In late 1524 and early 1525, the monasteries were dissolved, and church property was secularized. Their accumulated wealth was used to help the poor.

The last vestige of the old religion to disappear in Zurich was the Mass, no doubt because of its centrality to faith and piety. Zwingli had already rejected the Mass as a sacrifice in the eighteenth of his Sixty-Seven Articles. He wrote that it "is not a sacrifice, but is a remembrance of the sacrifice and assurance of salvation which Christ has given us." By late 1524, Zwingli also repudiated the Catholic doctrine that bread and

---

SOURCE: Bard Thompson, ed., *Liturgies of the Western Church* (Cleveland: The World Publishing Co., 1961). Used by permission of Harcourt, Brace & Company.

wine changed into the very body and blood of Christ when the words of consecration were spoken by a priest (transubstantiation). Zwingli adopted a symbolic understanding of the words of institution. "This is my body," he judged, should be interpreted as meaning "This signifies my body."

Under the influence of Zwingli's views, other pastors gave up the Mass or at least greatly altered it. These irregularities around the Mass led Zwingli and other pastors to appeal to the town council on the Tuesday of Holy Week, April 11, 1525, for a ruling. The next day, the council voted by a small majority to abolish the Mass and ordered that a simpler Zwinglian service of the Eucharist be introduced. The first service of worship following the new model took place the next day, Maundy Thursday. In place of beautiful silver and gold utensils, there were simple wooden cups and plates. Instead of priests clothed in elaborate ecclesiastical vestments, there were ministers dressed in simple black academic gowns. Instead of priests facing the altar in the chancel, ministers stood behind the table in the nave, facing the congregation. The Eucharist was not a priestly event but a communal act of the people. The elements were passed from person to person. If anyone was offended, he or she could receive the bread and wine directly from the minister.

Other changes were made to emphasize the communal nature of the service. Congregational recitation replaced singing by the choir. Zwingli was a gifted musician, but he opposed the use of instrumental or vocal music in the service because he felt it distracted from the true spirituality of worship. Zwingli's service replaced belief in the transubstantiation of the elements with an emphasis on the transformation of the whole people of God into Christ's body.[1]

Zwingli's service was new, yet it contained several traditional elements: the Gloria *("Glory to God on high"), the* Agnus Dei *("O Lord God, thou Lamb of God"), "The Lord be with you," the Apostles' Creed in a German version, the* Benedictus *("Blessed be the name of the Lord"), and "Depart in peace." At the center of the whole liturgy was the sermon preceding the communion, making the epistle and gospel lessons extremely dominant in the communion liturgy. John 6:63, "It is the spirit that gives life, the flesh is of no avail," was central in Zwingli's Eucharistic theology. The sermon was so important that Zwingli limited the Lord's Supper to four times a year: Christmas, Easter, Pentecost, and autumn. The autumn celebration was either September 11 (the feast day of the patron saints of Zurich, Felix and Regula) or November 1 (All Saints' Day). In all cases, Zwingli insisted that the Eucharist was a communal act of thanksgiving, contemplation, and remembrance to be carried out with simplicity and dignity.*[2]

To all who believe in Christ: We who administer God's Word and are Pastors in Zurich offer Grace and Peace from God.

Dearly beloved brethren, after a long time of error and darkness, we rejoice at the true way and light which God, our heavenly Father, has disclosed to us through His grace. And we esteem it so much more highly, we receive and embrace it with such exceeding desire, because there has been so much destructive and dangerous error. Though innumerable deceptions have occurred till now, to the detriment of faith and love, it still appears to us that not the least of them occurred in the abuse of this Supper. After a long captivity, we have reclaimed the Supper and re-established it in its proper use—by the help of God we hope—just as the children of Israel recovered the Passover lamb in the time of Hezekiah and Josiah the Kings. So much for the Supper itself. Concerning the ceremonies which go with it, some people might suppose that we have perhaps done too much, others that we have done too little. In this matter, however, every congregation may hold its own opinion, for we do not wish to quarrel with anyone on this account. No doubt, all believers are well aware of how much damage and apostasy from God have resulted heretofore from the great mass of ceremonies. We therefore think it best to prescribe as little ceremonial and churchly custom as we can for our people's use of this Supper—which is also a ceremony, but instituted by Christ—lest we yield again, in time, to the old error. Nevertheless, to keep the action from being performed wholly without life and shape, and to make some concession to human weakness, we have authorized such ceremonies for the action—as appointed here—which we have deemed beneficial and appropriate to enhance in some degree the spiritual memorial of the death of Christ, the increase of faith and brotherly love, the reformation of life, and the prevention of the vices of the human heart.

But at the same time, we have no wish at all to condemn the additional ceremonies of other churches—singing and such—for perhaps they are suitable for them and beneficial to their devotion; for we hope that all pastors everywhere are constantly diligent to serve the Lord and to win many people.

We are also prepared, in keeping with divine ordinances, to exclude from this Supper all those who defile the body of Christ with intolerable stains and blemishes, because a communion of Christians and a pure, devout life ought to follow this memorial of Christ's passion and thanksgiving for His death. In what manner this shall be done will be explained in a separate booklet, since time is not left to do it now.

The grace of Christ be with you all.

A Preface

That Christ's Supper is seriously abused has been brought out quite strongly and clearly from the Word of God for a long time: therefore, it will be necessary to remove from it everything which does not conform to the divine Word.

This memorial is a thanksgiving and a rejoicing before Almighty God for the benefit which He has manifested to us through His Son; and whoever appears at this feast, meal or thanksgiving bears witness that he belongs to those who believe that they are redeemed by the death and blood of our Lord Jesus Christ: Therefore, on Maundy Thursday, the young people who now desire to come faithfully and in the knowledge of God and His Word and to celebrate this thanksgiving and Supper, shall repair to the nave of the church, between the choir and the transept-aisle, males to the right, females to the left; and the other people shall stay in the archway, the gallery, and other places. And while the Sermon takes place, unleavened bread and wine shall be placed upon a table in the front of the nave. And then the intent and action of Christ—the way He instituted this memorial—shall be recited clearly, intelligibly, and in German (as follows hereafter). Thereupon the bread shall be carried round by the designated servers on broad wooden plates from one seat to the next—to allow each person to break off a morsel or mouthful with his hand and eat it. In the same fashion, they shall go round with the wine, so that no one need move from his place.

And when that is done, praise and thanks shall be offered to God, with clear and distinct words, in a loud, intelligible voice. Then the whole multitude and congregation shall say "Amen" at the end of the service.—On Good Friday, people of middle age shall assemble at the aforesaid place in the nave, and the thanksgiving shall take place in the same way, the men and women separated, as above.—On Easter Day, the old folk likewise.

The plates and cups are of wood, that pomp may not come back again.

And we shall use this order, so long as it pleases our churches, four times a year: at Easter, Pentecost, autumn, and Christmas.

Action or Use of the Lord's Supper
A Memorial or Thanksgiving of Christ
As It Will Be Begun in Zurich
At Easter in the Year 1525.

The overseer or pastor turns toward the people and prays the following prayer with a loud, clear voice:

A Prayer

O Almighty, Eternal God, whom all creatures rightly honor, worship and praise as their Lord, Creator and Father: grant us poor sinners that with real constancy and faith we may perform thy praise and thanksgiving, which thine only begotten Son, our Lord and Savior Jesus Christ, hath commanded the faithful to do in memory of His death; through the same Jesus Christ, thy Son, our Lord, who liveth and reigneth with thee in unity with the Holy Spirit, God for ever and ever. Amen.

The server or Lector says the following in a loud voice:

The Lection is found in the first Epistle of Paul to the Corinthians, the eleventh chapter.

"When ye come together therefore into one place [v. 20] . . . For he that eateth and drinketh unworthily, that is, improperly and not as one ought, eateth and drinketh judgment and damnation to himself, not discerning the Lord's body" [v. 29].

Here the servers say with the whole church:

Praise be to God.

Now the pastor begins the first verse of the following hymn of praise, and then the people—men and women—say the verses alternately, one after the other.

The pastor:	Glory be to God on high!
The men:	And peace on earth!
The women:	To men, a right will!
The men:	We praise thee, we bless thee.
The women:	We worship thee, we glorify thee.
The men:	We give thanks to thee for thy great glory and goodness, O Lord God, heavenly King, Father Almighty!
The women:	O Lord, thou only-begotten Son, Jesus Christ, and the Holy Ghost.
The men:	O Lord God, thou Lamb of God, Son of the Father, thou that takest away the sin of the world, have mercy upon us!
The women:	Thou that takest away the sin of the world, receive our prayer!

The men:	Thou that sittest at the right hand of the Father, have mercy upon us.
The women:	For thou only art holy.
The men:	Thou only art the Lord.
The women:	Thou only, O Jesus Christ, with the Holy Ghost, art most high in the glory of God the Father.
Men and women:	Amen.

Now the deacon or lector says:

The Lord be with you.

The people respond:

And with thy spirit.

The lector says the following:

The following Lection from the Gospel is found in John, the sixth chapter.

The people respond:

Praise be to God.

Now the lector begins as follows:

"Verily, verily, I say unto you, He that believeth and trusteth in me hath everlasting life. I am the bread of life [vs. 47, 48] . . . It is the spirit that quickeneth; the flesh profiteth nothing: the words that I speak unto you, they are spirit, and they are life" [v. 63].

Then the lector kisses the book and says:

Praise and thanks be to God. He willeth to forgive all our sins according to his holy Word.

The people say:

Amen!

Now the first server begins the first line:

I believe in one God,

The men:	In the Father Almighty.
The women:	And in Jesus Christ, his only-begotten Son, our Lord.
The men:	Who was conceived by the Holy Ghost.
The women:	Born of the Virgin Mary.
The men:	Suffered under Pontius Pilate, was crucified, dead and buried.
The women:	He decended into hell.
The men:	The third day he rose again from the dead.
The women:	He ascended into heaven.
The men:	And sitteth on the right hand of God the Father Almighty.
The women:	From thence he shall come to judge the quick and the dead.
The men:	I believe in the Holy Ghost.
The women:	The holy, universal Christian Church, the Communion of Saints.
The men:	The forgiveness of sins.
The women:	The resurrection of the body.
The men:	And the life everlasting.
Men and women:	Amen.

Then the server says:

Dear brothers, in keeping with observance and institution of our Lord Jesus Christ, we now desire to eat the bread and drink the cup which He has commanded us to use in commemoration, praise and thanksgiving that He suffered death for us and shed His blood to wash away our sin. Wherefore, let everyone call to mind, according to Paul's word, how much comfort, faith and assurance he has in the same Jesus Christ our Lord, lest anyone pretend to be a believer who is not, and so be guilty of the Lord's death. Neither let anyone commit offense against the whole Christian communion, which is the body of Christ.

Kneel, therefore, and pray:

Our Father, which art in heaven, hallowed be thy name. Thy kingdom come. Thy will be done, in earth as it is in heaven. Give us our daily bread. Forgive us our debt, as we forgive our debtors. And lead us not into temptation, but deliver us from evil.

The people say:

Amen.

Now the server prays further as follows:

O Lord, God Almighty, who by thy Spirit hast brought us together into thy one body, in the unity of faith, and hast commanded that body to give thee praise and thanks for thy goodness and free gift in delivering thine only begotten Son, our Lord Jesus Christ, to death for our sins: grant that we may do the same so faithfully that we may not, by any pretense or deceit, provoke thee who art the truth which cannot be deceived. Grant also that we may live as purely as becometh thy body, thy family and thy children, so that even the unbelieving may learn to recognize thy name and glory. Keep us, Lord, that thy name and glory may never be reviled because of our lives. O Lord, ever increase our faith, which is trust in thee, thou who livest and reignest, God for ever and ever. Amen.

The Way Christ Instituted This Supper

The server reads as follows:

"On the night in which He was betrayed and given up to death, Jesus took bread; and when he had given thanks, he brake it, and said, take, eat; this is my body: do this in remembrance of me. After the same manner also, he took the cup after supper, said thanks, and gave it to them, saying, Drink ye all of this: this cup is the new testament in my blood. This do ye, as oft as ye do it, in remembrance of me. For as often as ye shall eat this bread and drink this cup, ye should shew forth and glorify the Lord's death."

Then the designated servers carry round the unleavened bread, from which each one of the faithful takes a morsel or mouthful with his own hand, or has it offered to him by the server who carries the bread around. And when those with the bread have proceeded so far that everyone has eaten his small piece, the other servers then follow with the cup, and in the same manner give it to each person to drink. And all of this takes place with such honor and propriety as well becomes the Church of God and the Supper of Christ.

Afterwards, the people having eaten and drunk, thanks is given according to the example of Christ, by the use of Psalm 112;[3] *and the shepherd or pastor begins:*

The pastor:	Praise, O ye servants of the Lord, Praise the name of the Lord.
The men:	Blessed be the name of the Lord, from this time forth and for evermore.

The women:	From the rising of the sun unto the going down of the same the Lord's name is highly praised.
The men:	The Lord is exalted above all nations and His glory above the heavens.
The women:	Who is like unto the Lord our God, who sitteth so high and bendeth down to have care for the things in heaven and earth?
The men:	He raiseth up the humble out of the dust and lifteth the poor out of the filth,
The women:	That He may set him with princes, with the princes of his people.
The men:	He maketh the barren woman of the house to be a mother, who has the joy of children.

Then the pastor says:

We give thee thanks, O Lord, for all thy gifts and blessings: thou who livest and reignest, God for ever and ever.

The people respond:

Amen.

The pastor says:

Depart in peace.

Notes

1. See Markus Jenny, *Die Einheit des Abendmahlgottesdienstes bei den elsässischen und schweizerischen Reformatoren, Studien zur Dogmengeschichte und systematischen Theologie*, vol. 23 (Zurich: Zwingli Verlag, 1968), 62.

2. See Fritz Büsser, *Huldrych Zwingli, Reformation als prophetischer Auftrag* (Göttingen: Musterschmidt, 1973), 81–87; Ulrich Gäbler, *Huldrych Zwingli: His Life and Work*, trans. Ruth C. L. Gritsch (Philadelphia: Fortress Press, 1986), 105–8; Gottfried W. Locher, *Die Zwinglische Reformation im Rahmen der europäischen Kirchengeschichte* (Göttingen: Vandenhoeck and Ruprecht, 1979), 145–47; and *Liturgies of the Western Church*, ed. Bard Thompson (Cleveland: World Publishing Company, 1961), 141–48.

3. Ps. 113:1–9. According to the Vulgate, 112 is the number.

12. The Schleitheim Confession of Faith

(1527)

Even though recent research emphasizes the multiple origins of Anabaptism, Swiss Anabaptists connected to Ulrich (or Huldrych or Huldreich) Zwingli (1484–1531) were a principal wing of this movement. The first Anabaptist congregation did not emerge in Switzerland until early 1525, but as early as October 1523 differences arose between Zwingli and some of his radical followers in and around Zurich. Conrad Grebel and Felix Manz, two of Zwingli's close disciples, were disturbed when Zwingli went along with a town council ruling that delayed the removal of the Mass and images. They wanted more immediate action.

Soon thereafter, these radicals took a position that the church ought to include only the faithful members, rejecting any understanding that the church could be run by political leaders and include all the citizens of a community. It was only logical for them also to repudiate infant baptism, which symbolized membership in a public Christian community.

In private conversations, Zwingli himself had raised some questions concerning infant baptism, but he was not prepared to break with the idea of a state church. Discussions between the two sides sought to overcome their differences, but the breach became an open one in January 1525 when the town council declared the Anabaptist position heretical and ordered the children of Anabaptists to be baptized. Families that refused this order were deported.

Zurich Anabaptists paid no attention, administering their first adult baptisms on January 25, 1525. Very soon an Anabaptist community was

---

SOURCE: John Wenger, ed., *Mennonite Quarterly Review* 19, no. 4 (October 1945): 247–53. Used by permission.

formed in Zollikon, a village outside of Zurich, and before long others were established in villages and towns in northeastern Switzerland.

The best summary of the teachings and practices of these Anabaptists, known as Swiss Brethren, is found in a confession of faith by Michael Sattler, adopted in 1527 at an Anabaptist conference at Schleitheim, a village near Schaffhausen in Switzerland. In this Schleitheim Confession of Faith, the way of the Swiss brothers and sisters is clearly distinguished from those reformers who supported a close relation between church and state.

More so than in previous writings, the articles of this confession stress not only such characteristic Anabaptist beliefs as adult baptism and communion as a fellowship meal eaten in remembrance of Christ's death, but also the importance of separation from the world. They disapprove of the swearing of an oath, the holding of public office, and the taking up of the sword. These separatist and pacifist positions were not so firmly held by some Anabaptists, however, such as Balthasar Hubmaier, who did not oppose a Christian's holding public office or using the sword.

The Swiss Anabaptist community understood itself here more self-consciously as a persecuted minority, whereas previously some Anabaptists attempted to convert whole villages or territories to their point of view. In addition, the Schleitheim Confession demonstrates how Anabaptists came to adopt stricter discipline within their own communities, especially through the use of the ban, a practice that further separated them from the worldly.[1]

As soon as Zwingli read the Schleitheim Confession, he wrote a response, found in the second part of his Refutation of the Tricks of the Anabaptists. *The Zurich reformer is not shown at his best in this response. In a convoluted argument filled with sarcasm, he accused the Anabaptists of numerous offenses: sectarianism; sedition; works righteousness and self-righteousness; immoderation in the administration of the ban; ignoring the Old Testament, with its covenant sign of circumcision as a scriptural basis for infant baptism, as well as the patristic evidence for the practice of infant baptism from apostolic times; misapplying the gospel injunction "resist not evil" to magistrates, when it really applied to private individuals; flying in the face of the clear witness of Scripture by denying the possibility of Christian magistrates; and finally, failing to understand that the prohibition of oaths does not apply to public oaths.*[2]

Already before the Schleitheim Confession and Zwingli's response, the Zurich government had adopted repressive measures against the Anabaptists. Felix Manz was drowned on January 5, 1527, in mockery of the most prominent Anabaptist symbol, adult baptism. In May of the same year, Michael Sattler was burned at the stake by Catholic authorities in Rottenburg, Germany.

It is unfortunate that Protestants who had originally been part of the same movement as Zwingli and who owed many of their ideas to the Zurich reformer met such a tragic end. The Zwinglians and the Anabaptists were, in the words of one Zwingli scholar, "brothers [and sisters] in Christ." In light of these common roots, it is encouraging to note that there are some recent signs of dialogue between Protestants in the Reformed tradition and Mennonites (who are the inheritors of the Anabaptist tradition).[3]

Brotherly Union of a Number of Children of God Concerning Seven Articles[4]

May joy, peace and mercy from our Father through the atonement of the blood of Christ Jesus, together with the gifts of the Spirit—Who is sent from the Father to all believers for their strength and comfort and for their perseverance in all tribulation until the end, Amen—be to all those who love God, who are the children of light, and who are scattered everywhere as it has been ordained of God our Father, where they are with one mind assembled together in one God and Father of us all: Grace and peace of heart be with you all, Amen.

Beloved brethren and sisters in the Lord: First and supremely we are always concerned for your consolation and the assurance of your conscience (which was previously misled) so that you may not always remain foreigners to us and by right almost completely excluded, but that you may turn again to the true implanted members of Christ, who have been armed through patience and knowledge of themselves, and have therefore again been united with us in the strength of a godly Christian spirit and zeal for God.

It is also apparent with what cunning the devil has turned us aside, so that he might destroy and bring to an end the work of God which in mercy and grace has been partly begun in us. But Christ, the true Shepherd of our souls, Who has begun this in us, will certainly direct the same and teach [us] to His honor and our salvation, Amen.

Dear brethren and sisters, we who have been assembled in the Lord at Schleitheim on the Border, make known in points and articles to all who love God that as concerns us we are of one mind to abide in the Lord as God's obedient children, [His] sons and daughters, we who have been and shall be separated from the world in everything, [and] completely at peace.

To God alone be praise and glory without the contradiction of any brethren. In this we have perceived the oneness of the Spirit of our Father and of our common Christ with us. For the Lord is the Lord of peace and not of quarreling, as Paul points out. That you may understand in what articles this has been formulated you should observe and note [the following].

A very great offense has been introduced by certain false brethren among us, so that some have turned aside from the faith, in the way they intend to practice and observe the freedom of the Spirit and of Christ. But such have missed the truth and to their condemnation are given over to the lasciviousness and self-indulgence of the flesh. They think faith and love may do and permit everything, and nothing will harm them nor condemn them, since they are believers.

Observe, you who are God's members in Christ Jesus, that faith in the Heavenly Father through Jesus Christ does not take such form. It does not produce and result in such things as these false brethren and sisters do and teach. Guard yourselves and be warned of such people, for they do not serve our Father, but their father, the devil.

But you are not that way. For they that are Christ's have crucified the flesh with its passions and lusts. You understand me well and [know] the brethren whom we mean. Separate yourselves from them for they are perverted. Petition the Lord that they may have the knowledge which leads to repentance, and [pray] for us that we may have constancy to persevere in the way which we have espoused, for the honor of God and of Christ, His Son, Amen.

The articles which we discussed and on which we were of one mind are these: 1. Baptism; 2. The Ban [Excommunication]; 3. Breaking of Bread; 4. Separation from the Abomination; 5. Pastors in the Church; 6. The Sword; and 7. The Oath.

First. Observe concerning baptism: Baptism shall be given to all those who have learned repentance and amendment of life, and who believe truly that their sins are taken away by Christ, and to all those who walk in the resurrection of Jesus Christ, and wish to be buried with Him in death, so that they may be resurrected with Him, and to all those who with this significance request it [baptism] of us and demand it for themselves. This excludes all infant baptism, the highest and chief abomination of the pope. In this you have the foundation and testimony of the apostles. Matt. 28, Mark 16, Acts 2, 8, 16, 19. This we wish to hold simply, yet firmly and with assurance.

Second. We are agreed as follows on the ban [i.e. excommunication]: The ban shall be employed with all those who have given themselves to the Lord, to walk in His commandments, and with all those who are baptized into the one body of Christ and who are called brethren or sisters, and yet who slip sometimes and fall into error and sin, being inadvertently overtaken. The same shall be admonished twice in secret and the third time openly disciplined or banned according to the command of Christ. Matt. 18. But this shall be done according to the regulation of the Spirit (Matt. 5) before the breaking of bread, so that we may break and eat one bread, with one mind and in one love, and may drink of one cup.

Third. In the breaking of bread we are of one mind and are agreed [as follows]: All those who wish to break one bread in remembrance of the broken body of Christ, and all who wish to drink of one drink as a remembrance of the shed blood of Christ, shall be united beforehand by baptism in one body of Christ which is the church of God and whose Head is Christ. For as Paul points out we cannot at the same time be partakers of the Lord's table and the table of devils; we cannot at the same time drink the cup of the Lord and the cup of the devil. That is, all those who have fellowship with the dead works of darkness have no part in the light. Therefore all who follow the devil and the world have no part with those who are called unto God out of the world. All who lie in evil have no part in the good.

Therefore it is and must be [thus]: Whoever has not been called by one God to one faith, to one baptism, to one Spirit, to one body, with all the children of God's church, cannot be made [into] one bread with them, as indeed must be done if one is truly to break bread according to the command of Christ.

Fourth. We are agreed [as follows] on separation: A separation shall be made from the evil and from the wickedness which the devil planted in the world; in this manner, simply that we shall not have fellowship with them [the wicked] and not run with them in the multitude of their abominations. This is the way it is: Since all who do not walk in the obedience of faith, and have not united themselves with God so that they wish to do His will, are a great abomination before God, it is not possible for anything to grow or issue from them except abominable things. For truly all creatures are in but two classes, good and bad, believing and unbelieving, darkness and light, the world and those who [have come] out of the world, God's temple and idols, Christ and Belial; and none can have part with the other.

To us then the command of the Lord is clear when He calls upon us to be separate from the evil and thus He will be our God and we shall be His sons and daughters.

He further admonishes us to withdraw from Babylon and the earthly Egypt that we may not be partakers of the pain and suffering which the Lord will bring upon them.

From all this we should learn that everything which is not united with our God and Christ cannot be other than an abomination which we should shun and flee from. By this is meant all popish and antipopish works and church services, meetings and church attendance, drinking houses, civic affairs, the commitments [made in] unbelief and other things of that kind, which are highly regarded by the world and yet are carried on in flat contradiction to the command of God, in accordance with all the unrighteousness which is in the world. From all these things we shall be separated and have no part with them for they are nothing but an abomination, and they are the cause of our being hated before our Christ Jesus, Who has set us free from the slavery of the flesh and fitted us for the service of God through the Spirit Whom He has given us.

Therefore there will also unquestionably fall from us the unchristian, devilish weapons of force—such as sword, armor and the like, and all their use [either] for friends or against one's enemies—by virtue of the word of Christ, Resist not [him that is] evil.

Fifth. We are agreed as follows on pastors in the church of God: The pastor in the church of God shall, as Paul has prescribed, be one who out-and-out has a good report of those who are outside the faith. This office shall be to read, to admonish and teach, to warn, to discipline, to ban in the church, to lead out in prayer for the advancement of all the brethren and sisters, to lift up the bread when it is to be broken, and in all things to see to the care of the body of Christ, in order that it may be built up and developed, and the mouth of the slanderer be stopped.

This one moreover shall be supported of the church which has chosen him, wherein he may be in need, so that he who serves the Gospel may live of the Gospel as the Lord has ordained. But if a pastor should do something requiring discipline, he shall not be dealt with except [on the testimony of] two or three witnesses. And when they sin they shall be disciplined before all in order that the others may fear.

But should it happen that through the cross this pastor should be banished or led to the Lord [through martyrdom] another shall be ordained in his place in the same hour so that God's little flock and people may not be destroyed.

Sixth. We are agreed as follows concerning the sword: The sword is ordained of God outside the perfection of Christ. It punishes and puts to death the wicked, and guards and protects the good. In the Law the sword was ordained for the punishment of the wicked and for their death, and the same [sword] is [now] ordained to be used by the worldly magistrates.

In the perfection of Christ, however, only the ban is used for a warning and for the excommunication of the one who has sinned, without putting the flesh to death—simply the warning and the command to sin no more.

Now it will be asked by many who do not recognize [this as] the will of Christ for us, whether a Christian may or should employ the sword against the wicked for the defense and protection of the good, or for the sake of love.

Our reply is unanimously as follows: Christ teaches and commands us to learn of Him, for He is meek and lowly in heart and so shall we find rest to our souls. Also Christ says to the heathenish woman who was taken in adultery, not that one should stone her according to the law of His Father (and yet He says, As the Father has commanded me, thus I do), but in mercy and forgiveness and warning, to sin no more. Such [an attitude] we also ought to take completely according to the rule of the ban.

Secondly, it will be asked concerning the sword, whether a Christian shall pass sentence in worldly dispute and strife such as unbelievers have with one another. This is our united answer: Christ did not wish to decide or pass judgment between brother and brother in the case of the inheritance, but refused to do so. Therefore we should do likewise.

Thirdly, it will be asked concerning the sword, Shall one be a magistrate if one should be chosen as such? The answer is as follows: They wished to make Christ king, but He fled and did not view it as the arrangement of His Father. Thus shall we do as He did, and follow Him, and so shall we not walk in darkness. For He Himself says, He who wishes to come after me, let him deny himself and take up his cross and follow me. Also, He Himself forbids the [employment of] force of the sword saying, The worldly princes lord it over them, etc., but not so shall it be with you. Further, Paul says, Whom God did foreknow He also did predestinate to be conformed to the image of His Son, etc. Also Peter says, Christ has suffered (not ruled) and left us an example, that ye should follow His steps.

Finally it will be observed that it is not appropriate for a Christian to serve as a magistrate because of these points: The government magistracy is according to the flesh, but the Christians' is according to the Spirit; their houses and dwelling remain in this world, but the Christians' are in heaven; their citizenship is in this world, but the Christians' citizenship is in heaven; the weapons of their conflict and war are carnal and against the flesh only, but the Christians' weapons are spiritual, against the fortification of the devil. The worldlings are armed with steel and iron, but the Christians are armed with the armor of God, with truth, righteousness, peace, faith, salvation and the Word of God. In brief, as is the mind of Christ toward us, so shall the mind of the members of the body of Christ be through Him in all things, that there may be no schism in the body through which it would be destroyed. For every kingdom divided against itself will be destroyed. Now since Christ is as it is written of Him, His members must also be the same, that His body may remain complete and united to its own advancement and upbuilding.

Seventh. We are agreed as follows concerning the oath: The oath is a confirmation among those who are quarreling or making promises. In the Law it is commanded to be performed in God's Name, but only in truth, not falsely. Christ, who teaches the perfection of the Law, prohibits all swearing to His [followers], whether true or false,—neither by heaven, nor by the earth, nor by Jerusalem, nor by our head,—and that for the reason which He shortly thereafter gives, For you are not able to make one hair white or black. So you see it is for this reason that all swearing is forbidden: we cannot fulfill that which we promise when we swear, for we cannot change [even] the very least thing on us.

Now there are some who do not give credence to the simple command of God, but object with this question: Well now, did not God swear to Abraham by Himself (since He was God) when He promised him that He would be with him and that He would be his God if he would keep His commandments,—why then should I not also swear when I promise to someone? Answer: Hear what the Scripture says: God, since He wished more abundantly to show unto the heirs the immutability of His counsel, inserted an oath, that by two immutable things (in which it is impossible for God to lie) we might have a strong consolation. Observe the meaning of this Scripture: What God forbids you to do, He has power to do, for everything is possible for Him. God swore an oath to Abraham, says the Scripture, so that He might show that His counsel is immutable. That is, no one can withstand nor thwart His will; therefore He can keep His oath. But we can do nothing, as is said above by Christ, to keep or perform [our oaths]: therefore we shall not swear at all [*nichts schweren*].

Then others further say as follows: It is not forbidden of God to swear in the New Testament, when it is actually commanded in the Old, but it is forbidden only to swear by heaven, earth, Jerusalem and our head. Answer: Hear the Scripture, He who swears by heaven swears by God's throne and by Him who sitteth thereon. Observe: it is forbidden to swear by heaven, which is only the throne of God: how much more is it forbidden [to swear] by God Himself! Ye fools and blind, which is greater, the throne or Him who sitteth thereon?

Further some say, Because evil is now [in the world, and] because man needs God for [the establishment of] the truth, so did the apostles Peter and Paul also swear. Answer: Peter and Paul only testify of that which God promised to Abraham with the oath. They themselves promise nothing, as the example indicates clearly. Testifying and swearing are two different things. For when a person swears he is in the first place promising future things, as Christ was promised to Abraham Whom we a long time afterwards received. But when a person bears testimony he is testifying about the present, whether it is good or evil, as Simeon spoke to Mary about Christ and testified, Behold this (child) is set for the fall and rising of many in Israel, and for a sign which shall be spoken against.

Christ also taught us along the same line when He said, Let your communication be Yea, yea; Nay, nay; for whatsoever is more than these cometh of evil. He says, Your speech or word shall be yea and nay. (However) when one does not wish to understand, he remains closed to the meaning. Christ is simply Yea and Nay, and all those who seek Him simply will understand His Word. Amen.

Dear brethren and sisters in the Lord: These are the articles of certain brethren who had heretofore been in error and who had failed to agree in the true understanding, so that many weaker consciences were perplexed, causing the Name of God to be greatly slandered. Therefore there has been a great need for us to become of one mind in the Lord, which has come to pass. To God be praise and glory!

Now since you have so well understood the will of God which has been made known by us, it will be necessary for you to achieve perseveringly, without interruption, the known will of God. For you know well what the servant who sinned knowingly heard as his recompense.

Everything which you have unwittingly done and confessed as evil doing is forgiven you through the believing prayer which is offered by us in our meeting for all our shortcomings and guilt. [This state is yours] through the gracious forgiveness of God and through the blood of Jesus Christ. Amen.

Keep watch on all who do not walk according to the simplicity of the divine truth which is stated in this letter from [the decisions of] our meeting, so that everyone among us will be governed by the rule of the ban and henceforth the entry of false brethren and sisters among us may be prevented.

Eliminate from you that which is evil and the Lord will be your God and you will be His sons and daughters.

Dear brethren, keep in mind what Paul admonishes Timothy when he says, The grace of God that bringeth salvation hath appeared to all men, teaching us that, denying ungodliness and worldly lusts, we should live soberly, righteously, and godly, in this present world; looking for that blessed hope, and the glorious appearing of the great God and our Saviour Jesus Christ; Who gave Himself for us, that He might redeem us from all iniquity, and purify unto Himself a people of His own, zealous of good works. Think on this and exercise yourselves therein and the God of peace will be with you.

May the Name of God be hallowed eternally and highly praised, Amen. May the Lord give you His peace, Amen.

The Acts of Schleitheim on the Border
[Canton Schaffhausen, Switzerland],
on Matthias' [Day],[5] Anno MDXXVII.

Notes

1. See Martin Haas, "Michael Sattler," in *Profiles of Radical Reformers*, ed. Hans-Jürgen Goertz (Scottdale, Pa.: Herald Press, 1982), 132–43.

2. See Ulrich Zwingli, "Refutation of the Tricks of the Anabaptists," in *Ulrich Zwingli 1484–1531: Selected Works*, ed. Samuel M. Jackson (Philadelphia: University of Pennsylvania Press, 1972), 177–219.

3. See Fritz Blanke, *Brothers in Christ* (Scottdale, Pa.: Herald Press, 1961), and Hans Georg von Berg et al., eds., "Mennonites and Reformed in Dialogue," *Studies from the World Alliance of Reformed Churches* 7 (1986).

4. The words in brackets are inserted by the translator to clarify the text. The words in parentheses are a part of the original text.

5. February 24.

13. The Marburg Colloquy

(1529)

The Marburg Colloquy was one of the most dramatic moments of the sixteenth-century Reformation, when Martin Luther (1483–1546) and Ulrich (or Huldrych or Huldreich) Zwingli (1484–1531), along with their colleagues, debated each other on their understanding of the Eucharist. Philip of Hesse, a Lutheran prince, invited the two reformers to come to his castle high on the hill in Marburg. Philip was interested in a political and military alliance to unite North German Lutherans and Swiss and South German Zwinglians. As the 1520s came to a close, Protestantism was threatened by the powerful forces of Catholic Holy Roman Emperor Charles V. Charles, recently free from entangling wars with the French and the Turks, felt that he needed to deal with the Protestant heresy in his empire.

Aware of this threat, Philip brought Luther and Zwingli together, hoping to forge a theological union that could provide the basis for a political alliance. Zwingli accepted the prince's invitation readily. Luther, however, came reluctantly.

At the colloquy, the two reformers agreed on fourteen articles of faith, but they disagreed sharply on the fifteenth article, the one dealing with the Eucharist. Not only was Philip unable to create a political alliance, but more significantly, the divisions between Luther and Zwingli became more rigid. After the Marburg Colloquy, continental Protestantism split along two major confessional lines: Lutheran and Reformed.

SOURCE: Donald J. Ziegler, ed., *Great Debates of the Reformation* (New York: Random House, 1969). Used by permission.

The Marburg Colloquy climaxed a eucharistic controversy that began between Luther and Zwingli in 1526. Although both reformers rejected the medieval doctrine of the sacrifice of the Mass, they differed on the question of how Christ was present in the Eucharist. Luther opposed the medieval dogma of transubstantiation (which held that the words of consecration transform the bread and the wine into the body and blood of Christ), but he continued to believe that the body and blood were present in, with, and under the bread and wine. Luther's understanding came to be called consubstantiation.

Zwingli felt that Luther was too catholic or papist. As early as November 1524 Zwingli had moved toward a more spiritualistic, symbolic understanding of the Eucharist. Relying on the biblical text John 6:63, "The spirit gives life, the flesh is of no avail," Zwingli rejected any affirmation that Christ was bodily present. Leaning on the work of the Dutch humanist Cornelius Hoen, he argued that the word is *in the words of institution, "This* is *my body," had the sense of* signifies*—This* signifies *my body. Furthermore, he insisted that according to Acts 1:2 and 9, Christ ascended bodily into heaven and therefore could not be bodily in the Eucharist.*

At the Marburg Colloquy and in the polemical writings leading up to the debate, Luther rejected Zwingli's exegesis of John 6. He adhered steadfastly to a literal interpretation of the words of institution, rejecting Zwingli's spiritualist reading of John 6 and insisting that Scripture intends no sharp demarcation between the physical and the spiritual. Luther asserted that Scripture shows that the Holy Spirit makes use of the bodily in the work of salvation—"the Word, water, Christ's body and his saints on earth."

Luther's response to Zwingli's argument that Christ could not be bodily present because he had already ascended to the right hand of God noted that the phrase "right hand of God" could more readily be given a metaphorical meaning—referring to Christ's almighty power—than could the words of institution.

The Marburg debate over the Eucharist also reveals major differences between Luther and Zwingli over Christology. Luther insisted on the complete unity of the divine and human in Christ. He adopted an ancient doctrine that emphasized the communication of the attributes; that is, on the basis of the union of the divine and human nature in Jesus Christ, what is normally ascribed to Christ's humanity can be ascribed to Christ's divinity, and vice versa. To Luther, this doctrine meant that the category of ubiquity could be applied to Christ, not only in his deity but in his humanity.

For Zwingli, however, such a doctrine was blasphemous because it confused the human and the divine, the creature and the Creator. Zwingli insisted that the two must be kept clearly distinct, even in Christ. Only in Christ's deity can Christ be present everywhere, and therefore only in Christ's deity can Christ be present in the Eucharist. As a human being, Jesus Christ can be in only one place at one time.[1]

The Marburg Colloquy took place October 1–3, 1529. Besides Luther and Zwingli, other participants were Philip Melanchthon, Luther's younger colleague at Wittenberg, who was more eager for rapprochement with the Catholics than with the Zwinglians; Johannes Oecolampadius, the reformer of Basel who shared Zwingli's view of the Eucharist; Martin Bucer (or Butzer), the reformer of Strasbourg who was interested in overcoming divisions, but who, unlike Melanchthon, desired reconciliation between the Wittenbergers and the Swiss. No transcript of the debate exists. The record of the debate, following the translation of Ziegler, rests on reports from several of the participants.[2]

Tensions and misunderstandings between Lutherans and Reformed Protestants have continued for the past four hundred years. Fortunately, in recent decades there have been new efforts to reach mutual understanding on issues that have divided them since Marburg. The United Church of Christ, which incorporates both Lutheran and Reformed legacies, has been an active participant in these efforts.[3]

THE HESSIAN CHANCELLOR FEIGE: My gracious prince and lord has summoned you for the express and urgent purpose of settling the dispute over the sacrament of the Lord's Supper. Although much has been written about the matter, it is the desire of my gracious prince and lord that no one display his own particular feelings, rather that everyone seek the glory of God, the common Christian welfare, and brotherly concord. And let everyone on both sides present his arguments in a spirit of moderation, as becomes such matters. My gracious prince and lord thanks you for coming here. Now then, Doctor Luther, you may proceed!

LUTHER: Noble prince, gracious lord! Undoubtedly the colloquy is well intentioned. Two years ago I rejected it because I knew that both sides had written enough and that no further arguments were left on either side. My mind was made up, and I wished it to remain so to the end of my days. I had no intention of writing anything further. But when my gracious prince and lord, Landgrave Philip, took up the matter at the Diet of Speyer, I then agreed: the pious wishes of the most excellent prince must be obeyed. Although I have no intention of changing my mind, which is firmly made up, I will nevertheless present the grounds of my belief and show where the others are in error.

I am happy to hold the colloquy. However, before we proceed to the Lord's Supper, I must take notice of several things that apparently are proclaimed from the churches of Zurich, Basel, and Strassburg and that obviously are in error, assuming that they are represented correctly in their writings. In Strassburg, so I have read, several have said that Arius, if one still had his writings, was more accurate in his teaching about the Trinity than St. Augustine or other orthodox fathers. They have so differentiated between the two natures of Christ that they have nearly made two persons out of one. Yet they say [with Christ, in John 5:56]: "He who eats my flesh"—in other words, that which is divine! Several deny that original sin can incur damnation. Several teach that baptism is not a sign of faith, but merely an outward symbol of belonging. They ascribe justification not to faith in Christ alone, but partly to our own powers as well. Yet my opponents accuse me of holding erroneous views about the spoken word and about the whole range of scriptural matters like purgatory and indeed many other points of Christian faith and Christian teaching. And so, without unanimity in these matters, it would be pointless to discuss the real significance of the Lord's Supper.

OECOLAMPADIUS: I am not aware that I have ever espoused the articles in question, which disagree with the teaching of Doctor Luther. The present colloquy has been announced as a comparison of our views on the Lord's Supper. So it seems appropriate to me that we debate this matter first. If we find, however, that any teachings on other matters are incorrect, I am quite willing to let each assume responsibility for his own errors.

ZWINGLI: I concur in this view, having of course spoken privately with Master Philip [Melanchthon] about the matter. My view on justification has been published in the pamphlet *On the Clarity and Certainty of the Word of God*. So let us now discuss the Lord's Supper, and at the end of our discussion we shall be most happy to talk about any and all other points of dispute.

LUTHER: Very well, so be it. But I affirm publicly that I do not concur with such publications, and I wish to make this known to forestall anyone at home saying that I dared not open my mouth.

Your basic contentions are these: In the last analysis you wish to prove that a body cannot be in two places at once, and you produce arguments about the unlimited body which are based on natural reason. I do not question how Christ can be God and man and how the two natures can be joined. For God is more powerful that all our ideas, and we must submit to his word.

Prove that Christ's body is not there where the Scripture says, "This is my body"! Rational proofs I will not listen to. Corporeal proofs, arguments based on geometrical principles I repudiate absolutely, like those [of the Swiss] that a door cannot be made into a gate or a fingerhold into a pillory [any more than the body of Christ can be interpreted as residing in two places at once]. God is beyond all mathematics, and the words of God are to be revered and carried out in awe. It is God who commands, "Take, eat, this is my body." I request, therefore, valid scriptural proof to the contrary.

Luther writes on the table in chalk, "This is my body," and covers the words with a velvet cloth.

Oecolampadius and Luther

OECOLAMPADIUS: The sixth chapter of John clarifies the other scriptural passages. Christ is not speaking there about a local presence. "The flesh is of no avail," he says [John 6:63]. It is not my intention to employ rational, or geometrical, arguments—neither am I denying the power of God—but as long as I have the complete faith I will speak from that. For Christ is risen; he sits at the right hand of God; and so he cannot be present in the bread. Our view is neither new nor sacrilegious, but is based on faith and Scripture.

It is from a physical to a spiritual repast that one must proceed. The Holy Scripture employs figurative language, metaphors, metonyms, and comparable terms, where the words mean something other than what they say. And so even the words "This is my body" may contain language that is figurative, like those that read, "John is Elijah" [Matt. 11:14], "The rock was Christ" [1 Cor. 10:4], "I am the true vine" [John 15:1], "The seed is the word of God" [Luke 8:11].

LUTHER: Oecolampadius has drawn several figures of speech from Holy Scripture, like "I am the vine"; and he argues for a spiritual repast, saying: "The fathers are on our side." To which I need only reply in brief: Many metaphors are found in Holy Scripture. This I grant. But that here—"This is my body"—a metaphor is presen—this you must prove. Do not tell us what we have long known! If it were proved that Christ had used the demonstrative to say "I am the vine," I would believe this as well. General statements permit the use of metaphor, but here [where Christ says "This is my body"] the demonstrative is used—positive proof—and so you must prove that a metaphor is used here! No one is ever about to do this.

How then is the physical repast excluded by the spiritual one in the statement, "The flesh is of no avail"? The fathers partially support your position, if we let it go unquestioned, this I grant. But how does this help you if you fail to prove that "body"—"This is my body"—means body in a figurative sense? Speak to the point, please, without digressing!

OECOLAMPADIUS: "I am the vine" is also demonstrative. This could be, could it not?!

LUTHER: I do not deny figurative speech, but you must prove that this is what we have here. It is not enough to say that these words—"This is my body"—could be interpreted in this way. You must prove that they must be so interpreted in a figurative sense.

Your argument is based upon a preconception, *ex petitione principii*! Just because Christ speaks in the sixth chapter of John about a spiritual repast, you conclude that there is no physical repast whatsoever. You want me to place my trust in this, which is no proof at all. And so my faith is strong because you have not proved your words. My text is priceless and full of authority. Agree with it!

This is what I find so annoying—that you don't prove what you are supposed to prove.

OECOLAMPADIUS: Well then! I shall prove that the words—"This is my body" —must be taken figuratively. Listen to John 6. (He reads John 6:48–63.) Christ is speaking here to the Jews and also to his disciples about the eating of his body and the drinking of his blood, and when they took him to mean a physical eating and shuddered at the thought, he replied: "It is the spirit that gives life, the flesh is of no avail" [v. 63]. From this, one ought to understand that he repudiated once for all the physical eating of his flesh; and it ought to follow that he neither could nor would maintain this repudiated view thereafter.

LUTHER: I repeat the passage from John. (He reads John 6:48–63.) It is your opinion that Christ moved away from the physical repast in his emphasis upon the spiritual repast. I reply that he wanted to teach the Jews of Capernaum that he should not be eaten like bread and meat in a bowl, like roast pork. When I partake of Christ in the bread, it is not in the vulgar sense, but as a gift of the Holy Spirit. Hence it is not a repast that is petty and repulsive, but one that is most holy. Man can still believe those words; the body of Christ is there.

OECOLAMPADIUS: I take your word for it: there is a double meaning, a twofold sense of the word of God. One is limited and physical; the other is most holy and spiritual. The limited meaning has reference to eating the flesh of Christ, which as you have pointed out, Doctor Luther, Christ emphatically rejected. But Christ has ordained that noble conception, that spiritual sense, which we teach.

LUTHER: I am well informed on the distinction between the two scriptural meanings. But I cannot and I will not tolerate your thrusting aside the physical meaning of the words of the Lord's Supper, for you do this without scriptural evidence and authority. Whatever you might fancy the words to mean in a physical sense, that fact remains that they are the work of the Highest Majesty. Nobody can deny this, and so it follows that nobody can disparage what is physical and petty. Forgiveness of sins, eternal life, and the rewards of heaven are certainly bound up with these things, which are physical and petty, to the end of revealing the power of God's word to physical beings. And for this reason one must never empty and limit their meanings, but must wholeheartedly treasure them as things that are spiritual and sublime.

OECOLAMPADIUS: You deem it an article of faith that Christ is in the bread, but this is an opinion, not a belief. It is evil to attribute too much to that which is physical. Listen to Augustine, *On Christian Doctrine*.

He reads a part from Book III, chapter 9 [where Augustine argues that the "signs" of the body and blood in the sacrament should be taken properly in "spiritual freedom," not restricted in "carnal servitude" by "limited" or "literal" understanding].

LUTHER: I return again to the words of the Lord's Supper. When I speak of the "body which is given for us," this is not "a limited understanding of the Scripture." Even if we were concerned only with the bread it would not be "a limited understanding of the Scripture." Indeed, to do the smallest thing at the command of the Master is spiritual. We baptize with plain water because we attach significance, not to the words themselves, but to their author. Because God is their author, one kisses the word. In the case, for example, of a prince ordering a horse to be shod, the horseshoe is something petty among petty things. Hunger —"Blessed are they who hunger" [Matt. 5:6]—is likewise unimportant in itself. So it is with the words, "baptize by water" [Matt. 28:19]. It is not to the water but to the Holy Spirit that we attribute the purification. As for the material element in itself, we are completely in accord. We treasure not the bread, but the word, and the one who utters it—Jesus Christ. It is like when the prince directs the servant to shoe the horse. Then the iron becomes a thing of value, when it is placed on the foot of the horse.

Treasure the cross! God often works wonders through unimportant things, as he did with Abraham when he was to sacrifice his son, as he did with Adam through a tree. Whenever we speak of Christ's body, we are speaking of the body at the right hand of the Father.

How much we would like to accept your view, but we cannot, for yours is a wanton misconception—I beg your pardon, gracious prince and lord! Those words—"This is my body"—hold me captive.

And if Augustine or other teachers also wish to interpret the signs, they ought to follow Christ and interpret as he interprets. If they do so, then one must rely on them and believe them. When they do not, then one must abandon the doctors and believe Christ. *One should not* believe them just because they are doctors.

Now you may speak!

OECOLAMPADIUS: The illustration that you give is acceptable to me. Luther is attempting to show that the word of God brings Christ into the bread.

LUTHER: This is correct. To illustrate: A prince orders a piece of iron turned into a horseshoe, and someone else attaches it to a thing of value. In this way something petty becomes important. So we come to understand the meaning of Christ.

OECOLAMPADIUS: And if we have a spiritual repast, why is a physical one necessary?

LUTHER: Your argument comes down to this: Because we have a spiritual repast, a physical one is not needed. I reply that in no way do we deny the spiritual repast, which we consistently teach and believe to be necessary. But from this it cannot be proved that the physical repast is useless or unnecessary. I do not inquire into whether it is necessary or not, for we are not here for this. It is written, "Take, eat, this is my body," and for this reason one must do it and believe it at all costs. One must do this! Otherwise I could not be baptized, I could not believe in Christ! In many ways he gives himself to us: in preaching, in baptism, as often as a brother needs consolation, in the sacrament. Again and again the body of Christ is eaten, as he himself commanded us to do. If he were to command me to eat dung, I would do so, assured that it were good for me. The servant doesn't brood over the wish of his lord. One must close his eyes.

OECOLAMPADIUS: Where is it written that we should move through the Scriptures with our eyes closed, Herr Doctor?

LUTHER: We could debate for a hundred years and nothing would come of it! Not until you have disposed of my text will I be satisfied. That one who spoke the words in the sixth chapter of John also spoke the words, "This is my body."

OECOLAMPADIUS: According to the sixth chapter of John, "The flesh is of no avail." Eating of the flesh is of no avail, but partaking of the spirit is; hence we must look for that which avails and respect the will of God. We insist upon this enlightened view of the Scriptures and upon the comparison of passage with passage. This is what Augustine does.

I stand by what I have said.

LUTHER: And I stand by my text.

Zwingli and Luther

ZWINGLI: It is a prejudice, a preconception, which keeps Doctor Luther from yielding his point. He refuses to yield until a passage is quoted that proves that the body in the Lord's Supper is figurative. It is the prejudice of a heretic somewhat reminiscent of Helvidius, who denied that Jesus was the only son of Mary because it was clearly stated [in John 7:3], "So his brothers said to him." One cannot reason thus from Scripture! Comparison of scriptural passages is always necessary. Although we have no scriptural passage that says, "This is the sign of the body," we still have proof that Christ dismissed the idea of a physical repast. Since it is our task here to investigate scriptural passages, and since the passage in John 6 moves away from the physical repast, we must therefore take it into account. From this it follows that Christ did not give himself in the Lord's Supper in a physical sense. And finally, you yourself have acknowledged that it is the spiritual repast that offers solace. And since we are agreed on this major question, I beg you for the love of Christ not to burden anyone with the crime of heresy because of these differences. The fathers certainly did not condemn one another in this way when they disagreed.

I return to the sixth chapter of John: "It is the spirit that gives life, the flesh is of no avail." By this he did not mean that the humanity of Christ was of no avail, for his humanity was the means of our redemption. It is wonderfully consoling to me whenever I reflect upon it: Christ assumed flesh like mine—this is wonderfully consoling. You proceed differently than the evangelist intended; your references to cutting up and chewing [Christ's body] are abnormal, and hence improper. "*Pos dynatai hemin houtos dounai ten sarka phagein*?" [How is he able to give us his flesh to eat?] I am reading [from the Greek text] because my memory might deceive me. *Esthiein, edere, comedere, manducare* [to eat] is one thing. There is nothing here about cutting up and chewing. John 6 [62] reads: "If you were to see me ascending to heaven," which Augustine takes as excluding the question of seeing the body ascend.[4] He had no desire to eat the "actual" body of Christ "in a physical sense." "It is the spirit that gives life" [John 6:63]. Flesh and spirit are opposites.

You spoke of taking the Scriptures literally. Much I agreed with, much I did not because it was perfectly childish, like saying, "If God commanded me to eat dung." The works that God commands are for our well-being. God is truth and light, and he leads us not into the darkness. Consequently he does not mean "This is my body" in a literal, actual, physical sense, which contradicts the Scriptures. It is the oracles of demons that are obscure, not the maxims of Christ. God does not work in this way. The soul is spiritual, the soul does not eat flesh. Spirit eats spirit.

Do not take offense at my words, for I desire your friendship, not the bitterness of your heart. I confront you willingly, Doctor Luther, and you, Master Philip.

LUTHER: I promise to control my feelings in deference to God and our gracious prince and lord. What is past is past. Let us look to the future! If we cannot agree on everything, we can still enter into fellowship—as we shall discuss in conclusion.

Respecting Helvidius, it can be proved from Scripture that "brother" can mean "cousin." But this is not to prove a figure of speech in "This is my body." What you mean by "eating" seems to include everything but eating. To you, "eating" means flesh, flesh. Assuming that you were right, it would still be pointless in this matter. If God were to place rotten or shriveled apples before me, I would eat them in a spiritual sense on the authority of his word. For wheresoever the word of God is, there we find a spiritual repast. When God speaks to us, then faith is required. This is what is meant by "eating." If he appends a physical sense to its meaning, then we must obey. We eat in faith this body, which is given for us. The mouth receives the body of Christ, the soul believes the words as it eats the body. If I were to take Christ's body in my arms, that would be "embracing." You have attached unusual meanings to things that are dear to me.

If you think that God does not confront us with the incomprehensible, then I cannot agree with you. The virginity of Mary, the forgiveness of sins, and many others like this are incomprehensible—even the words "This is my body." We read in the Psalms: "Thy way was through the sea, thy path through the great waters; yet thy footprints were unseen" [Ps. 77:19]. If we knew his way, then he would not be incomprehensible—he the miraculous!

ZWINGLI: It can be demonstrated from the Scripture that allusions are symbolical. Ezekiel, for example, was told to shave his head [Ezek. 5:1 ff.], and then it reads, "This is Jerusalem"—which is to say that this would happen to Jerusalem. Or, the passing of God over the houses "is the Passover" [Ezek. 12:27]—a corresponding use of figurative speech.

Luther refuses to recognize figures of speech like these and others that one encounters even in the Lord's Supper, when indeed many passages are found that belie his literal interpretation. There are those, however, like "the elder is the head, the prophet is the tail" [Isa. 9:14 ff.]. To the prophets, such prophecies are common, for Isaiah here the word "is" meaning "signifies." Since then it is necessary to collate doubtful passages with others, we must take the word "is" in the Lord's Supper to mean "signifies."

Luther is employing the rhetorical device of exaggeration against us at this point. His argument is weighty: If God commands, then you know that he has so commanded you! If God commands that his body be eaten in remembrance of him, then consequently we know that God is pleased when we do this. Luther is not talking about the inner meaning of the Scripture, which reveals to us the will of God, but about the literal meaning. We assert it to be impossible that God would command us to eat his flesh in a physical sense.

It is a game of words that we are playing. He insists that the spoken word adds something to the bread and wine, Melanchthon agreeing with me that something is only "signified" by the words. For us it is the "essence" of the words which adds something. I ask that we examine "the word" carefully, for it is full of meaning! For example, when a papist hears the word—the death of Christ is our justification—he fails to believe because he fails to catch its inner meaning. These words are only there for the purpose of "signifying" the will of the Father. You reject our meanings, we reject yours. "I shall not be visible to you" says Christ [John 12:8], hence he is not bodily present in the Lord's Supper.

It is not true that God confronts us with much that is incomprehensible. That Christ is truly God and man is well known to the faithful. In regard to

Mary, when she asked, "How can this be?" it was spoken, "The Holy Spirit will come upon you" [Luke 1:34 ff.]. Accordingly she understood the power of the living God, and this was sufficient for her. But here, in the sixth chapter of John, the young men were uncertain whether or not Jesus was speaking of a physical repast. So he spoke of a spiritual repast. This is clear.

You say, "Where the word of God is, there the feast of Christ is." The pope uses these words too and they accomplish nothing. The words of faith are what I believe! Christ taught nothing about the eating of the body. As far as understanding the words of the Lord's Supper is concerned, it is one thing to teach about them and another to understand them. Even when I eat pure bread, Luther says, as soon as the word is added to the element it becomes a sacrament. The word of whom? If spoken by a papist, then the element does not become a sacrament when the word is added. Therefore the words that are spoken must be understood and comprehended according to my belief, whereby a sacrament is a thing of inner significance, a sign used in communication. One must extend it to his brothers as a testament that Christ died for them. That the body is eaten in the mouth is a statement that utterly amazes me. If Christ is present, then he is there to sustain the soul, not the body. How can he reconcile opposites? You cannot overcome what I say with philosophy or rhetoric. Melanchthon has granted that the Jews did not understand the spiritual sense of Christ's words [cf. John 6:53 ff.]. Christ spoke to them in order to heal them, for they suffered from the malady of misunderstanding. I speak therefore from an understanding of the spiritual sense of the Scriptures, and when Luther interprets them differently, and ambiguously, then he does violence to the Scriptures. "The words that I speak are spirit and life" [John 6:63] means just this—"the words," that is, the form of expression. It is not a question of the spoken word.

LUTHER: You stray from the point, admonishing me for my rhetoric and refusing to tolerate my "exaggerations." As regards Ezekiel and Exodus, these are allegories; but there are many passages that have a demonstrative meaning, which do not mean "signify." I am not consciously interpreting the words ambiguously.

Briefly, in regard to Christ's words, we do not claim that the body becomes present when we speak the words. Rather we are speaking what Christ has instituted. The words are not ours, but those of the Master. It is at the command of his lord, for example, that the servant takes the horse to the pasture. If I were to say, "This is my body," it would be Luther's body—which belongs to the gallows! "Do this," it says [Luke 22:19], and by these words the hand of the priest becomes the hand of Christ. The mouth is not mine, the tongue is not mine, but they are Christ's, one and the same whether I am a boy or a knave. So it is too with baptism. "Go forth and baptize" [Matt. 28:19]—this is not my word, but God's. For example, when a prince attacks another with his soldiers, the fists of all become his fists. We do not admit these words as idle chatter. Christ says, "If you say to the mountain, 'Move hence to yonder place,' then it will move" [Matt. 17:20]. I refuse to debate the meaning of the word "is," for I am satisfied that Christ said it. The devil himself cannot make it otherwise. I do not require adherence to the words on my own authority, but on the authority and at the command of Christ.

Regarding the other argument—that Christ spoke of the well-established order of things in John 6—it was faith that he intended to speak about; and at one place [v. 70] he even spoke of a devil.

With respect to the soul eating the body of Christ, where the word of God is, there a spiritual repast must be, because faith is required. And if one doesn't have this, what's that to me? The physical body is there in the word. This is how it is. Faith, in short, means this: It is not for us to comment on the loving word of God, only when faith or the articles of faith are contradicted by an absurdity.

Regarding the Virgin Mary [when she was told in Luke 1:35], "The Holy Spirit will come upon you," she asked, "How can this be?" Abraham did likewise [Gen. 17:17] when Isaac was promised to him. It was hope against hope. At this point understanding ceases, for when I question, then I fall from faith, becoming a fool thereby in this regard.

If you interpret the Lord's Supper figuratively, why not do the same with these words—"He was taken up into heaven" [Mark 16:19]?

I call upon you as before: your basic contentions are shaky. Give way, and give glory to God!

ZWINGLI: And we call upon you to give glory to God and to quit begging the question! The issue at stake is this: Where is the proof of your position? I am willing to consider your words carefully—no harm meant! You're trying to outwit me. I stand by this passage in the sixth chapter of John [v. 63] and shall not be shaken from it. You'll have to sing another tune!

LUTHER: You're being obnoxious!

ZWINGLI (excitedly): Don't you believe that Christ was attempting in John 6 to help those who did not understand?

LUTHER: You're trying to dominate things! You insist on passing judgment! Leave that to someone else! "This is a hard saying," we read in John. The Jews were speaking of what was impossible and absurd. It is your point which must be proved, not mine. But let us stop this sort of thing. It serves no purpose.

ZWINGLI: It certainly does! It is for you to prove that the passage in John 6 speaks of a physical repast.

LUTHER: You express yourself poorly and make about as much progress as a cane standing in a corner. You're going nowhere.

ZWINGLI: No, no, no! This is the passage that will break your neck!

LUTHER: Don't be so sure of yourself. Necks don't break this way. You're in Hesse, not Switzerland.

Christ's body is deadly, poisonous, and devilish when eaten by one who is unworthy. Death, confinement, and matters of this sort are evil things; and yet, when they are joined by the word, they are beneficial.

I have noted so many times that not only do I not disdain or deny this spiritual repast, but that to the contrary I say and believe it to be particularly necessary. I do say, however, that the conclusion does not follow that this physical repast, instituted and presented by the Lord Jesus Christ, is not necessary, above all to the faithful who partake in both spiritual and physical respects. Much less does it follow, indeed it does not follow at all, that the true body of Christ cannot in any way be present in the Lord's Supper in a physical sense. It is there and it is necessary. For although the spirit does not itself partake of Christ's body in a physical sense, yet it receives and heeds the word as it partakes of the bread and wine.

ZWINGLI: You must excuse what I have just said. It is one of the expressions that we use.

LANDGRAVE PHILIP (nodding to Zwingli): I accept your apology. Herr Doctor Luther, do not take undue offense at this expression.

He rose and everybody went to lunch.

• • •

ZWINGLI: You contradict yourself. One moment you say the eating of the flesh of Christ is necessary, then at your discretion you say that it is not necessary.

LUTHER: I have said and I say again that Christ's flesh, when eaten by the unfaithful, is not only unnecessary but poisonous and deadly as well, the same being true of the word of God and of God himself. Further, as it is unnecessary and fatal to the unfaithful, so to the faithful it is necessary and beneficial, life in eternity. But even if it were unnecessary and pernicious in itself—which it is not—through the word it would still be beneficial to the life that is united with it.

ZWINGLI: I insist that the words of the Lord's Supper must be figurative. This is ever apparent, and even required by the article of faith: "taken up into heaven, seated at the right hand of the Father." Otherwise, it would indeed be absurd to look for him in the Lord's Supper at the same time that Christ is telling us that he is in heaven. One and the same body cannot possibly be in different places.

LUTHER: I ask you, why not accept a figure of speech in the words—"He ascended into heaven"—and let the text of the Lord's Supper stand as it is? A figure of speech would certainly be much easier to find in the word "heaven," since "heaven," as you know, is used with different meanings in Holy Scripture.

ZWINGLI: That word does not require a figure of speech.

LUTHER: Then neither do the others.

Oecolampadius, Luther, and Melanchthon

OECOLAMPADIUS: I am not yet satisfied with our discussion of John 6. I demand that we not insert distortions into Scripture. In John 3, Christ instructs Nicodemus that one must be born anew into the kingdom of God. This alone suffices to make the physical eating of Christ's body in the Lord's Supper unnecessary and unprofitable.

LUTHER: You are right that we may insert nothing into Scripture. But you must prove that we have inserted something. For this is the point that we have disputed with the pope. God has many ways and means of instilling, sustaining, and increasing our faith: through public or private teaching, baptism, partaking of the body of the Master. As to why his means are so numerous and varied, one may ponder this as he wishes. It is no concern of ours. He knows that is necessary and profitable for us. Hence the conclusion is ill-contrived and badly taken that, since rebirth makes heaven accessible, then Christ's body is not present or is superfluous in the Lord's Supper. To the contrary, it is precisely the renewed and reborn person who needs this Supper, one who can truly partake in faith.

OECOLAMPADIUS: In John 16 [28], Christ says, "I came from the Father and have come into the world; again, I am leaving the world and going to the Father." This passage excludes the presence of Christ's body in the Lord's Supper and forces one to concede the figure of speech in the words of the Master.

LUTHER: With which I contrast Luke 24 [44]: "These are my words which I spoke to you, while I was still with you." From this it is easy to recognize what Christ meant by the words [which you quoted]. He was leaving the world.

OECOLAMPADIUS: Listen to the other passage in John [16:7]: "It is to your advantage that I go away, for if I do not go away, the Counselor will not come to you." Since Christ says it is advantageous for him to go away, then undoubtedly his continued presence not only would serve no purpose, but would even pose a restriction. As Christ himself says, "If I do not go away, the Counselor will not come to you." From Romans 8[11], "He who raised Christ Jesus from the dead will give life to your mortal bodies," exactly the same conclusion follows: that we will be defeated and deprived of our hope for resurrection if we ascribe Christ's body to the bread. We must not rest our hope for resurrection upon the bread.

LUTHER: This hope is not removed or taken from us by the presence of Christ's body in the bread. On the contrary, it is thereby supported and strengthened, for the word is attended with the promise of grace. Faith proceeds from the presence of the body in the Lord's Supper and in heaven.

OECOLAMPADIUS: Luther continually stresses the same thing, as if we had pure bread without the word of God. The church is founded on the words, "You are the Son of the living God" [Matt. 16:16], not on the words, "This is my body" [Matt. 26:26].

LUTHER: It disturbs you that I hold fast to the words, "This is my body." I do so because they are sufficient for me. Prove the ones that you employ. I profess Christ in heaven, but I also profess Christ in the sacrament. I choose to infer from those words that Christ is in heaven and in the Lord's Supper. What is contrary to nature is no concern of mine as long as it is not contrary to faith.

We hold the flesh of Christ to be very, indeed to be absolutely, necessary. No text, no interpretation, no employment of human reasoning can take it away from us. If you wish to regard the flesh of Christ as unnecessary, then you may do so as far as I am concerned; the word of God is our support. But the word says, first of all, that Christ has a body—this I believe; second, that this same body rose to heaven and sits at the right hand of God—this too I believe. It says, further, that this same body is in the Lord's Supper and is given to us to eat. Likewise I believe this, for my Lord Jesus Christ can easily do what he wishes, and that he wishes to do this is attested by his own words. On these words I take my stand until Christ himself speaks otherwise.

OECOLAMPADIUS: Everybody can only be in one place, confined within limits.

LUTHER: Mathematical hairsplitting I will not listen to. God—this even the Aristotelians grant—can make a body be in one place alone or in several places at the same time or in no place at all; and he can make several be in one place at the same time. Therefore I wish to avoid distressing argumentation about whether the presence is real or not. This is no concern of mine. It is not arguments of this nature, based upon reason, but scriptural passages of clarity and certainty, that are called for. Nevertheless, if everybody wants this, I shall argue mathematics into the ground with you at the appointed time. I have already declared, however, that such argumentation will contribute nothing to this question. Here it is scriptural evidence that is needed.

OECOLAMPADIUS: In Matthew 26 [11], it says: "You will always have the poor with you [but you will not always have me]." From this it follows that Christ is always and everywhere present in his divinity, grace, and power. When, however, he says that he would be absent, it must be his human nature that is absent. But if his human nature were absent, then he cannot be present in the Lord's Supper in a bodily sense. Christ resembled us in all respects. As he is of the same nature as the Father in his divinity, so he is of the same nature as ourselves in his humanity. In this we agree: Christ is present in heaven as he is in the Lord's Supper.

LUTHER: Indeed, he is in baptism, in the Lord's Supper, in teaching, until the end of the world, until he comes. You may distinguish between humanity and divinity until that time—this is no concern of mine. "You always have the poor with you" [Matt. 26:11]—this is the best argument you have produced today, one which appears agreeable. He is present in the sacrament in the same bodily substance as when he was born of the Virgin. I shall not get involved in the matter of his being in heaven and in the bread. Here is a perfect analogy with faith, for here is faith in things that are not seen [Heb. 11:1], and a promise is also included. "You will not always have me" is the antithesis of those words. The poor are visible to you, you wash their feet, but you will not always have me. Corresponding to this, he says, of course [Luke 24:44], "These are my words which I spoke to you, while I was still with you." But if these words seem to you to stand in opposition to the words of the Lord's Supper, why not find a figure of speech in them rather than in the words of the Lord's Supper?

OECOLAMPADIUS: Don't cling so fast to Christ's humanity and flesh! Raise your thoughts to Christ's divinity!

LUTHER: I know God only as he became human, so I shall have him in no other way.

OECOLAMPADIUS: Also we say that we "do not know Christ after the flesh," for in the sacrament we know him after the spirit. If you are not a new creature [in Christ], then you know Christ after the flesh [2 Cor. 5:16–17].

MELANCHTHON: "Not after the flesh" means not after "our flesh."

LUTHER: Neither do we know him after the flesh. To know after the flesh means knowing in a physical sense, without spirit and without faith. We know him after the spirit, however, in the sense that we are certain in faith that Christ came for us, that he accomplished and suffered everything for us.

OECOLAMPADIUS: When Christ gave his body for us, truly he gave for us the body that he had, but he had one that could suffer and die. If this is so, then certainly it can be of no further use, which all the more requires the spiritual repast.

LUTHER: Partaking of the body of Christ can be of use because it involves the promise of forgiveness of sins. Since, however, every promise requires faith, and since faith is spiritual knowledge, then the bodily repast, if it is eaten in faith, must at the same time be eaten in spirit. That this body which is used in this manner is offered to me as a repast is sufficient for me. Whether it could die or live is no more a concern of mine than the kind of clothing Christ wore at the Last Supper. This is immaterial.

OECOLAMPADIUS: You refuse to grant a figure of speech in the Lord's Supper—and make a synecdoche out of it. In opposition to the view of the fathers, you introduce an innovation. So it is!

LUTHER: This is for God to decide. We compel no one, leaving it up to God. The synecdochic mode of expression is used so frequently, not only in Holy Scripture, but also in every kind of speech, that we cannot begin to do without it. It is present when the form of something involves the substance, and vice versa. For example, when a king says to the servant, "Bring me my sword," he really wants the scabbard brought along with it, even though he did not expressly command this in the words that he used. Or one speaks of the mug and means the beer. Hence the words "This is my body" are an encompassing mode of expression. The body is in the bread as the sword is in the scabbard. The text compels this mode of expression. Metaphor, however, obscures the main point—the body, that is, the figure of the body!—which is not the effect of synecdoche. It is for the sake of hairsplitters that synecdoche can be used. Another example: "He on whom you see the Spirit descend," it says [John 1:33]. He saw the dove in which the Holy Spirit was present. A figurative mode of expression obscures the essence and leaves the empty form. The synecdoche is not a comparison—no; this is here in this place and it is within that. So it is here: "This is my body."

Philip, you reply, for I have gotten tired.

OECOLAMPADIUS: The example of John 1 [33] should be taken differently. The dove signifies the Holy Spirit.

Zwingli, Luther, and Osiander[5]

ZWINGLI: Several things have been said about Christ's body in heaven, but not enough. In Romans 8 [3], it states, "God sent his own Son in the likeness of sinful flesh." In Philippians 2 [6 ff.]: "He lowered himself, taking the form of a servant, and was born in the likeness—*schemati*—(Melanchthon laughs) of a man." In Hebrews 2 [17]: "He had to be made like his brethren in every respect, though without sin." In Hebrews 4 [15]: "One who in every respect has been tempted as we are, yet without sinning." Thus he possessed the limitations of humanity. "As was the man of dust, so are those who are of the dust"—limited [1 Cor. 15:48]. I shall not allow the words to be passed over. "If Christ's body is above, then it must be in one place,"[6] Augustine says. If Christ's body is in different places and if we are supposed to resemble him, then our bodies must reside in several different places at the same time. If he resembles us in all respects, even being created in our likeness, and if we cannot be in several places, then he cannot do so either, precisely because he resembles us. We are not advancing anything new, for Augustine and Fulgentius think as we do. Luther says that Christ's body is omnipresent, hence something unlimited. Christ's body is in one place and cannot be in many places.

LUTHER: As regards the ancient fathers, we shall no doubt find that you speak about those on your side, we about those on ours. Regarding the words of Paul [Phil. 2:6 ff.]—"similar in all respects to a servant—*hexeis*—born in the likeness of a man"—does this mean therefore that Christ had a wife and little black eyes? And a permanent home in Germany? I will not here tolerate mathematically exact likenesses. Again you make a secondary issue into one of major importance. The passage can only demonstrate at most that the form of our body is similar to the body of Christ. It does not necessarily follow, however, that we also possess the power of his body, for this would require a special decree from God himself. I have discussed the matter of mathematical likenesses in my book,[7] which you have read without comprehension. I shall not debate mathematics any further, for I am not able to set down instructions on how it is in heaven and on earth. We have no intention of investigating such things. God is beyond all mathematics! Christ can make his body be nowhere, as he can make it be in one place. He is in the Lord's Supper, not in the sense of being in one place. You wish to draw a major conclusion from a secondary point. This is faulty reasoning; the Scripture means taking the form [of a servant] here—for a time.

ZWINGLI: It reads, "*Hos en morphe theou hyparchon.*" Likewise, "*morphen doulou labon*" [Phil. 2:6 ff.].

LUTHER: Read in German or Latin, not in Greek.

ZWINGLI: Pardon me for using the Greek Testament. For twelve years I have used it, having read the Latin version only once. *Morphe*, in the letter to the Philippians, signifies both the limited and the unlimited form. Christ is limited as we are limited.

LUTHER: Certainly. It is a matter of substance and form. God can make Christ's body be nowhere, and he can make it be in one place.

ZWINGLI: We speak too of a "sacramental" presence of the body of Christ, and by this we mean that the body of Christ is "represented" in the Lord's Supper.

LUTHER: You seek to describe a continuous presence of Christ's body in such a way as to remove the substance of the body from the bread, leaving us merely the empty form, even though the words of Christ read quite differently: "This is my body."

ZWINGLI: Oecolampadius and I further grant that God can of course make a body be in different places. But that he does this in the Lord's Supper, this is what we want proved. The Holy Scriptures always show us Christ in one particular place, as in the manger, in the temple, in the desert, on the cross, in the tomb, at the right hand of the Father. For this reason, I believe that he must always be in one particular place.

OSIANDER: With these references one can do no more than prove that Christ was in particular places at various times. That, however, he always and eternally is, indeed must be, in one particular place or a certain spot, and that he cannot be nowhere or in many places in ways which are natural and unnatural, as you say—this will never be proved by these passages.

ZWINGLI: I have proved that Christ was in one place. You prove in return that he is nowhere at all or in many places.

LUTHER: You expressed your willingness at the outset to prove that this cannot be, and that our understanding was false. It is your obligation to do this, and not to demand proof of us, for we are not obligated to you.

ZWINGLI: It would be outrageous if we affirmed, taught, and defended such an important article and yet were neither able nor willing to point to a single passage of Scripture!

LUTHER (raising the tablecloth): "This is my body"! Right here is our Scripture. You haven't torn it away from us yet like you promised to do. We need none other. My esteemed lords, as long as the text of my Lord Jesus Christ is there—*Hoc est corpus meum*—then truly I cannot pass over it, but must confess and believe that Christ's body is there.

ZWINGLI (immediately jumping up): So you too place Christ's body in the Lord's Supper in a spatial sense. You say, indeed, that Christ's body must be there—there, there! There—that is certainly an adverb of space.

LUTHER: I have simply quoted Christ's words and not expected such tricks in reasoning. If we mean to debate with such cunning, then I declare as before that I shall have nothing to do with mathematical reasoning; and I exclude and reject the adverb of space from the text of the Lord's Supper. The words read "This," not " 'there' is my body"! Whether he is there in space or outside of space is a question that I have no desire to raise. I prefer to do nothing here, since God has not yet revealed anything about it, and nothing can be proved by a mortal.

ZWINGLI: Must we then have just about everything your way?

Adjournment of the colloquy for dinner.

• • •

CHANCELLOR FEIGE: You were supposed "to seek ways and means of achieving harmony."

LUTHER: I know of no other way than for you to honor the word of God and believe as we do. I remain true to my faith and cannot yield.

OECOLAMPADIUS (or Zwingli?): We can neither comprehend nor believe that Christ's body is there.

LUTHER: I commend you to God and to his judgment. My thanks to you, Herr Oecolampadius, for presenting your case, not in a spirit of bitterness, but with friendliness. Also to you, Herr Zwingli, I express my thanks despite your expressions of bitterness. Please forgive me if I have spoken harshly to you. I am after all only flesh and blood. I should like to have had the matter settled to our mutual satisfaction.

OECOLAMPADIUS: I call upon the will of God to protect the poor church.

ZWINGLI: I call upon you, Doctor Luther, to forgive my bitterness. I have always desired your friendship a great deal, and I want it still. (With tears in his eyes) There are no others in Italy and France whom I would rather see.

LUTHER: Call upon God, that you may receive understanding.

OECOLAMPADIUS: Call upon him yourself, for you need it just as much as we!

The Strassburgers and Luther

JACOB STURM:[8] Noble prince, gracious lord! I had assumed that the colloquy was to be concerned with only one article of dispute. However, Doctor Luther said several things at the outset that could be taken to prejudice the city of Strassburg, namely that we do not preach correctly about the Trinity, and so on. If I were to say nothing about it and if one were to conclude from this colloquy that these matters had not been clarified, then I have it on the advice of two ministerial delegates here that not one but two quarrels would be taken home. Therefore I ask your grace to permit Martin Bucer to dispel doubts and to respond to the matter in question.

After short consultation BUCER[9] was given permission to express his viewpoint:

Very briefly I shall make known our view of the Trinity, of Christ, of justification, of baptism, and so on.

Further particulars are lacking. In conclusion BUCER said:

I request your testimony, Herr Doctor Luther, on whether we are teaching correctly.

LUTHER: Indeed no! I am neither your lord nor your judge. What you teach in Strassburg is no concern of mine. As long as you persist in not accepting my teaching, I cannot tolerate you as disciples. We have heretofore been sensitive of course to the fact that you prefer to propagate your teaching under our name. I have heard you just now, but I do not know whether you teach this at home or not, and so on. Therefore I shall not give testimony to you. You do not of course need it, for you boast everywhere that you have learned nothing from us. Of what use then would our testimony be? It is all too obvious that you have learned nothing from us. We would indeed be unwilling to have such disciples. I shall not be your teacher. You have my writings and my confession.

BUCER: I ask you—do you recognize me as a brother, or do you believe that I am in error? This I ask to the end of correcting my error.

LUTHER: As I am not your lord, not your judge, not even your teacher, so our spirit has nothing in common with your spirit. To the contrary, it is apparent that we are not of the same spirit. For we cannot be of the same spirit when on the one side the word of Christ is believed in innocent faith and on the other this same faith is censured, contested, slandered, and violated with all sorts of outrageous blasphemy. For this reason, as I have said before, we commend you to the judgment of God. Teach as you wish to be judged before God.

CHANCELLOR FEIGE: My gracious prince and lord would thank you for the pleasure that your presence has brought to his princely grace. For the present we shall retire. And if his princely grace again summons you, together or singly, let it not be an imposition. His princely grace wishes to encourage further deliberation. You must not always be so divided.

Notes

1. See John B. Payne, "Zwingli and Luther: The Giant vs. Hercules," *Christian History* 3, no. 1 (1984): 8–11, 33–35.

2. See Walther Köhler, "Das Marburger Religionsgespräch 1529. Versuch einer Rekonstruktion," *Schriften des Vereins für Reformationsgeschichte* 48 (1929), 7–38.

3. See James E. Andrews and Joseph A. Burgess, eds., *An Invitation to Action: The Lutheran-Reformed Dialogue, series 3, 1981–83* (Philadelphia: Fortress Press, 1984); William G. Rusch and Daniel F. Martensen, eds., *The Leuenberg Agreement and Lutheran-Reformed Relationship* (Minneapolis: Augsburg, 1989); and Keith F. Nickle and Timothy F. Lull, *A Common Calling*.

4. Augustine takes John 6:62 as meaning that "the Son of God was on earth in the flesh he had taken. The Son of man was in heaven in the unity of person." Tractate 27.4, *St. Augustine Tractates on the Gospel of John 11–27*, trans. John W. Rettig, *Fathers of the Church*, vol. 79 (Washington, D.C.: Catholic University Press, 1988), 279–80.

5. Andreas Osiander was a follower of Luther from St. Lawrence's Church at Nuremberg.

6. Augustine, Tractate on John 30.1, *Lectures or Tractates on the Gospel According to St. John, Nicene and PostNicene Fathers*, ed. Philip Schaff, vol. 7, 186.

7. That is, Luther's "Confession Concerning Christ's Supper," *Luther's Works*, ed. Helmut Lehmann, vol. 37 (Philadelphia, Fortress Press, 1971), 278ff.

8. Jacob Sturm was the leading magistrate of the city of Strassburg.

9. Martin Bucer was the leading theologian of Strassburg and a strong proponent of conciliation between Lutherans and Zwinglians.

14. Sermon One, Decade One: "Of the Word of God"

From *Decades*

(1549–51)

Heinrich Bullinger

Heinrich (or Henry) Bullinger (1504–75), the successor of Zwingli at Zurich, has been neglected in Reformation scholarship and lost to the memory of most Protestants. He was, however, along with John Calvin, the principal leader of Reformed Protestantism from 1531 until his death in 1575. His was an important role, both before and after Calvin. Calvin did not begin his ministry in Geneva until 1536, and he died in 1564.

Besides providing direction to the Reformation in Zurich following the city's defeat (and Zwingli's death) at the Second Battle of Kappel (1531), Bullinger played a key role in bringing about the unification of Swiss Protestantism.

Bullinger shared in the authorship of the Helvetic Confession (1536) and the Zurich Consensus (1549), showing significant agreement with Calvin, especially on the doctrine of the Eucharist. He was the primary author of the Second Helvetic Confession (1566), the culminating expression of his theology. Along with the Heidelberg Catechism (see vol. 2:327–58), this work was the most important confessional writing of Reformed Protestantism during the sixteenth century.

The Europewide impact of Bullinger's influence is shown in his massive correspondence. He exchanged letters with leaders of churches as far away as Poland, Hungary, and England. About one-seventh of his

---

SOURCE: *The Decades of Henry Bullinger*, ed. Thomas Harding, trans. H. I., *The First and Second Decades* (Cambridge: Cambridge University Press, 1849).

letters, numbering about twelve thousand, appear to have been written by Bullinger himself. In addition, he dedicated several of his writings to leading monarchs of Europe.[1]

Apart from the Second Helvetic Confession, Bullinger's most widely distributed and influential writing was probably his Decades, *a series of fifty doctrinal sermons in five groups of ten. Published in Latin in 1549–51, they were intended to provide instruction to students and pastors in the essentials of the evangelical faith. In design and structure, they are parallel to Calvin's* Institutes.

The Third and Fourth Decades were dedicated to Edward VI of England (ruled 1547–53), and the Fifth Decade was dedicated to Lord Henry Grey, the father of Lady Jane Grey, who read the Decades *as a young girl of fourteen and was so impressed that she entered into extensive correspondence with Bullinger.*

Although portions of the Decades *were available in English, the first complete translation was not published until 1577. Second and third editions appeared in 1584 and 1587. The translator was someone with the initials "H. I.," a "student in Divinitie" who has never been further identified. The translator writes in the preface that the purpose in making this translation is to assist in bringing about a more godly and educated clergy and to make clear and sound sermons available for use in worship services in parishes without learned, able preachers. He makes some defense against those Christians, presumably Puritans, who oppose all read sermons.*

The work was so highly regarded in the sixteenth-century Anglican Church that in 1586 the archbishop of Canterbury, John Whitgift, ordered every member of the clergy "under the degree of master of arts or the bachelor of law, and not licensed to be a public preacher, [to] . . . provide a Bible, Bullinger's Decades *in Latin or English, and a paper-book." A minister was expected to read a chapter of the Bible every day and write a summary of it in the notebook. Every week the minister was to read a sermon from the* Decades *and likewise record its main points in the notebook. Every quarter of the year preachers were expected to show their notebooks to an authorized member of the clergy for inspection. This directive was given to Anglican clergy to fend off attacks by Puritans about improperly educated clergy.*[2]

Sermon One of the First Decade explores the Word of God, a central theme not only in Bullinger's but in all Reformation theology. The translation of 1587 was later edited for the Parker Society by Thomas Harding.

Of the Word of God; the Cause of It; and How, and by Whom, It Was Revealed to the World

All the decrees of Christian faith, with every way how to live rightly, well, and holily, and finally, all true and heavenly wisdom, have always been fetched out of the testimonies, or determinate judgments, of the word of God; neither can they, by those which are wise men indeed, or by the faithful and those which are called by God to the ministry of the churches, be drawn, taught, or, last of all, soundly confirmed from elsewhere, than out of the word of God. Therefore, whosoever is ignorant what the word of God, and the meaning of the word of God is, he seemeth to be as one blind, deaf, and without wit, in the temple of the Lord, in the school of Christ, and lastly, in the reading of the very sacred scriptures. But whereas some are nothing zealous, but very hardly drawn to the hearing of sermons in the church; that springeth out of no other fountain than this, which is, because they do neither rightly understand, nor diligently enough weigh, the virtue and true force of the word of God. That nothing therefore may cause the zealous desirers of the truth and the word of God to stay on this point; but rather that that estimation of God's word, which is due unto it, may be laid up in all men's hearts; I will (by God's help) lay forth unto you, dearly beloved, those things which a godly man ought to think and hold, as concerning the word of God. And pray ye earnestly and continually to our bountiful God, that it may please him to give to me his holy and effectual power to speak, and to you the opening of your ears and minds, so that in all that I shall say the Lord's name may be praised, and your souls be profited abundantly.

First, I have to declare what the word of God is. *Verbum* in the scriptures, and according to the very property of the Hebrew tongue, is diversely taken. For it signifieth what thing soever a man will; even as among the Germans the word *ding* is most largely used. In St. Luke, the angel of God saith to the blessed virgin: "With God shall no word be unpossible" [Luke 1:37]; which is all one as if he had said, all things are possible to God, or to God is nothing unpossible. *Verbum* also signifieth a word uttered by the mouth of man. Sometime it is used for a charge, sometime for a whole sentence, or speech, or prophecy: whereof in the scriptures there are many examples. But when *verbum* is joined with any thing else, as in this place we call it *verbum Dei*, then is it not used in the same signification. For *verbum Dei*, "the word of God," doth signify the virtue and power of God: it is also put for the Son of God, which is the second person in the most reverend Trinity. For that saying of the holy evangelist is evident to all men, "The word was made flesh" [John 1:14]. But in this treatise of ours, the word of God doth properly signify the speech of God, and the revealing of God's will; first of all uttered in a lively-expressed voice by the mouth of Christ, the prophets and apostles; and after that again registered in writings, which are rightly called "holy and divine scriptures." The word doth shew the mind of him out of whom it cometh: therefore the word of God doth make declaration of God. But God of himself naturally speaketh truth; he is just, good, pure, immortal, eternal: therefore it followeth that the word of God also, which cometh out of the mouth of God, is true, just, without deceit and guile, without error or evil affection, holy, pure, good, immortal, and everlasting. For in the gospel saith the Lord, "Thy word is truth" [John 17:17]. And the apostle Paul saith, "The word of God is not tied" [2 Tim. 2:9]. Again, the scripture everywhere crieth: "The word of the Lord endureth for ever" [Isa. 40:8; 1 Pet. 1:25]. And Salomon saith: "Every word of God is purely cleansed. Add thou nothing to his words, lest peradventure he reprove thee, and thou be found a liar" [Prov. 30:5, 6]. David also saith: "The sayings of the Lord are pure sayings, even as it were silver cleansed in the fire, and seven times fined from the earth" [Ps. 12:6].

This you shall more fully perceive, dearly beloved, if I speak somewhat more largely of the cause or beginning, and certainty, of the word of God. The word of God is truth: but God is the only well-spring of truth: therefore God is the beginning and cause of the word of God. And here indeed God, since he hath not members like mortal men, wanteth also a bodily mouth: yet nevertheless, because the mouth is the instrument of the voice, to God is a mouth attributed. For he spake to men in the voice of a man, that is, in a voice easily understood of men, and fashioned according to the speech usually spoken among men. This is evidently to be seen in the things wherein he dealt with the holy fathers, with whom, as with our parents Adam and Eva, Noe, and the rest of the fathers, he is read to have talked many and oftentimes. In the mount Sina the Lord himself preached to the great congregation of Israel, rehearsing so plainly, that they might understand those ten commandments, wherein is contained every point of godliness. For in the fifth of Deuteronomy thus we read: "These words," meaning the ten commandments, "spake the Lord with a loud voice, from out of the midst of the fire, to the whole congregation" [Deut. 5:22]. And in the fourth chapter: "A voice of words you heard, but no similitude did you see beside the voice" [Deut. 4:8]. God verily used oftentimes the means of angels, by whose ministry he talked with mortal men. And it is very well known to all men, that the Son of God the Father, being incarnate, walked about in the earth; and, being very God and man, taught the people of Israel almost for the space of three years. But in times past, and before that the Son of God was born in the world, God, by little and little, made himself acquainted with the hearts of the holy fathers, and after that with the minds of the holy prophets; and last of all, by their preachings and writings, he taught the whole world. So also Christ our Lord sent the Holy Ghost, which is of the Father and the Son, into the apostles, by whose mouths, words, and writings he was known to all the world. And all these servants of God, as it were the elect vessels of God, having with sincere hearts received the revelation of God from God himself, first of all, in a lively expressed voice delivered to the world the oracles and word of God which they before had learned; and afterward, when the world drew more to an end, some of them did put them in writing for a memorial to the posterity. And it is good to know how, and by whom, all this was done: for by this narration the true cause, certainty, and dignity of the word of God doth plainly appear.

There are not extant to be seen the writings of any man, from the beginning of the world, until the time of Moses, which are come to our knowledge; although it be likely that that same ancient and first world was not altogether without all writings. For by St. Jude, the apostle, and brother of St. James, is cited the written prophecy of our holy father Enoch, which is read to have been the seventh from our father Adam [Jude 14, 15]. Furthermore, the writing, or history, of Job seemeth to have been set forth a great while before. But howsoever it is, all the saints in the church of God give to Moses, the faithful servant of God, the first place among the holy writers.

From the beginning therefore of the world, God, by his Spirit and the ministry of angels, spake to the holy fathers; and they by word of mouth taught their children, and children's children, and all their posterity, that which they had learned at the mouth of God; when they verily had heard it, not to the intent to keep it close to themselves, but also to make their posterity partakers of the same. For God oftentimes witnesseth, that "he will be the God of the fathers and of their seed evermore" [Gen. 17:7]. This is most plainly to be seen in the history of Adam, Noe, and Abraham, the first and great grandfathers. In the eighteenth of Genesis, verily, we read, that the angel of God, yea, and that more is, that even the Lord himself, did say to Abraham: "And shall I hide from Abraham what I mind to do? since of Abraham shall come a great and mighty people, and all the nations of the earth shall be blessed in him? And this I know, that he will command his children and his posterity after him, to keep the way of the Lord, and to do justice, judgment" [Gen. 18:17–19], and the rest. Abraham therefore, a faithful and zealous worshipper of God, did not (even as also those old fathers of the first world did not) wax negligent at all herein, but did diligently teach men the will and judgments of God: whereupon of Moses, yea, and of God himself, he is called a prophet [Gen. 20:7]. That devout and lively tradition of the fathers, from hand to hand, was had in use continually, even from the beginning of the world until the time of Moses.

Moreover, God of his goodness did provide that no age at any time should be without most excellent lights, to be witnesses of the undoubted faith, and fathers of great authority. For the world before the deluge had in it nine most excellent, most holy, and wise men; Adam, Seth, Enos, Kenam, Malaleel, Jared, Enoch, Methusalem, and Lamech. The chief of these, Adam and Methusalem, do begin and make an end of all the sixteen hundred and fifty-six years of the world before the deluge. For Adam lived nine hundred and thirty years [Gen. 5:5]: he dieth therefore the seven hundred and twenty-sixth year before the flood. And Methusalem lived nine hundred and sixty-nine years [Gen. 5:27]: he dieth in the very same year that the flood did overflow; and he lived together with Adam two hundred and forty-three years, so that of Adam he might be abundantly enough instructed as concerning the beginnings of things, as concerning God, the falling and restoring again of mankind, and all things else belonging to religion, even as he was taught of God himself. These two fathers, with the rest above named, were able sufficiently enough to instruct the whole age in the true salvation and right ways of the Lord.

After the deluge God gave to the world again excellent men, and very great lights. The names of them are Noe, Sem, Arphaxad, Sale, Heber, Palec, Reu, Saruch, Nachor, Thare, Abraham, Isaac, and Jacob. Here we have thirteen most excellent patriarchs, among whom the first two, Noe and Sem, are the chief; next to whom Abraham, Isaac, and Jacob, were more notable than the rest. Noe lived nine hundred and fifty years in all. He was six hundred years old when the flood drowned the world [Gen. 7:6]. He therefore saw and heard all the holy fathers of the first world before the deluge, three only excepted, Adam, Seth, and Enos. And also he lived many years together with the other, which had both seen and heard them; so that he could be ignorant in no point of those things which Adam had taught. Noe dieth (which is marvel to be told, and yet very true) in the forty-ninth year of Abraham's age. Sem, the son of Noah, lived many years with his father; for he lived in all six hundred years. He was born to Noah about ninety-six years before the deluge. He saw and heard, therefore, not only his father Noe and his grandfather Lamech, but also his great grandsire Methusalem, with whom he lived those ninety-six years before the deluge. Of him he might be informed of all those things which Methusalem had heard and learned of Adam and the other patriarchs. Sem dieth, after the death of Abraham, in the fifty-second year of Jacob, which was thirty-seven years after the death of Abraham, in the year one hundred and twelve of Isaac's age: so that Jacob, the patriarch, might very well learn all the true divinity of Sem himself, even as he had heard it of Methusalem, who was the third witness and teacher from Adam. Furthermore, Jacob the patriarch delivered to his children that which he received of God to teach to his posterity. In Mesopotamia there is born to Jacob his son Levi, and to him again is born Kahad, which both saw and heard Jacob. For Kahad lived no small number of years with his grandfather Jacob; for he is rehearsed in the roll of them which went with Jacob down into Egypt [Gen. 46:11]: but Jacob lived seventeen years with his children in Egypt. This Kahad is the grandfather of Moses, the father of Amram, from whom Moses did perfectly draw that full and certain tradition by hand, as concerning the will, commandments, and judgments of God, even as Amram his father had learned them of his father Kahad, Kahad of Jacob, Jacob of Sem, Sem of Methusalem and of Adam the first father of us all: so now that Moses is from Adam the seventh witness in the world. And from the beginning of the world to the birth of Moses are fully complete two thousand three hundred and sixty-eight years of the world. And whosoever shall diligently reckon the years, not in vain set down by Moses in Genesis and Exodus, he shall find this account to be true and right.

Now also it behoveth us to know those chief principles of that lively tradition, delivered by the holy fathers at the appointment of God, as it were from hand to hand, to all the posterity. The fathers taught their children that God, of his natural goodness, wishing well to mankind, would have all men to come to the knowledge of the truth, and to be like in nature to God himself, holy, happy, and absolutely blessed: and therefore that God, in the beginning, did create man to his own similitude and likeness, to the intent that he should be good, holy, immortal, blessed, and partaker of all the good gifts of God; but that man continued not in that dignity and happy state; but by the means of the devil, and his own proper fault, fell into sin, misery, and death, changing his likeness to God into the similitude of the devil. Moreover, that God here again, as it were, of fresh began the work of salvation, whereby mankind, being restored and set free from all evil, might once again be made like unto God; and that he meant to bring this mighty and divine work to pass by a certain middle mean, that is, by the Word incarnate. For as, by this taking of flesh, he joined man to God; so, by dying in the flesh, with sacrifice he cleansed, sanctified, and delivered mankind; and, by giving him his Holy Spirit, he made him like again in nature to God, that is, immortal, and absolutely blessed. And last of all, he worketh in us a willing endeavour aptly to resemble the property and conditions of him to whose likeness we are created, so that we may be holy both body and soul. They added moreover, that the Word should be incarnate in his due time and appointed age; and also, that there did remain a great day for judgment, wherein, though all men were gathered together, yet the righteous only should receive that reward of heavenly immortality.

So then, this is the brief sum of the holy father's tradition, which it is best to untwist more largely, and to speak of it more diligently, as it were by parts. First, therefore, the fathers taught, that the Father, the Son, and the Holy Ghost are one God in the most reverend Trinity, the maker and governor of heaven and earth and all things which are therein; by whom man was made, and who for man did make all things, and put all things under mankind, to minister unto him things necessary, as a loving Father and most bountiful Lord. Then they taught, that man consisted of soul and body, and that he indeed was made good according to the image and likeness of God; but that by his own fault, and egging forward of the devil, falling into sin, he brought into the world death and damnation, together with a web of miseries, out of which it cannot rid itself: so that now all the children of Adam, even from Adam, are born the sons of wrath and wretchedness; but that God, whose mercy aboundeth, according to his incomprehensible goodness, taking pity on the misery of mankind, did, even of his mere grace, grant pardon for the offence, and did lay the weight of the punishment upon his only Son, to the intent that he, when his heel was crushed by the serpent, might himself break the serpent's head [Gen. 3:15]: that is to say, God doth make a promise of seed, that is, of a Son, who, taking flesh of a peerless woman, (I mean, that virgin most worthy of commendations,) should by his death vanquish death and Satan, the author of death; and should bring the faithful sons of Adam out of bondage; yea, and that more is, should by adoption make them the sons of God, and heirs of life everlasting. The holy fathers, therefore, taught to believe in God, and in his Son, the redeemer of the whole world; when in their very sacrifices they did present his death, as it were an unspotted sacrifice, wherewith he meant to wipe away and cleanse the sins of all the world.

And therefore had they a most diligent eye to the stock and lineal descent of the Messias. For it is brought down, as it were by a line, from Adam to Noe, and from Noe by Sem even to Abraham himself: and to him again it was said, "In thy seed shall all the nations of the earth be blessed" [Gen. 22:18]: in which words the promise once made to Adam, as touching Christ the redeemer and changer of God's curse into blessing, is renewed and repeated again. The same line is brought down from Abraham by Isaac unto Jacob; and Jacob, being full of the Spirit of God, pointed out his son Juda to be the root of the blessed Seed, as it is to be seen in the forty-ninth of Genesis. Lastly, in the tribe of Juda the house of David was noted, out of which that seed and branch of life should come.

Moreover, the holy fathers taught, that God by a certain league hath joined himself to mankind, and that he hath most straitly bound himself to the faithful, and the faithful likewise to himself again. Whereupon they did teach to be faithful to God-ward, to honour God, to hate false gods, to call upon the only God, and to worship him devoutly. Furthermore, they taught, that the worship of God did consist in things spiritual, as faith, hope, charity, obedience, upright dealing, holiness, innocency, patience, truth, judgment, and godliness. And therefore did they reprehend naughtiness and sin, falsehood, lack of belief, desperation, disobedience, unpatientness, lying, hypocrisy, hatred, despiteful taunts, violence, wrong, unrighteous dealing, uncleanness, riotousness, surfeiting, whoredom, unrighteousness, and ungodliness. They taught, that God was a rewarder of good, but a punisher and revenger of evil. They taught, that the souls of men were immortal, and that the bodies should rise again in the day of judgment: therefore they exhorted us all so to live in this temporal life, that we do not leese [lose] the life eternal.

This is the sum of the word of God revealed to the fathers, and by them delivered to their posterity. This is the tradition of the holy fathers, which comprehendeth all religion. Finally, this is the true, ancient, undoubted, authentical, and catholic faith of the fathers.

Besides this, the holy fathers taught their children, and children's children, the account of the years from the beginning of the world, and also the true historical course, as well profitable as necessary, of things from the creation of the world even unto their own times; lest peradventure their children should be ignorant of the beginning and succession of worldly things, and also of the judgments of God, and examples of them which lived as well godly as ungodly.

I could declare unto you all this evidently, and in very good order, out of the first book of Moses, called Genesis, if it were not that thereby the sermon should be drawn out somewhat longer than the use is. But I suppose that there are few, or rather none at all, here present, which do not perceive that I have rehearsed this that I have said, touching the tradition of the ancient fathers, as it were word for word, out of the book of Genesis; so that now I may very well go forward in the narration which I have begun.

So then, whatsoever hitherto was of the fathers delivered to the world by word of mouth, and as it were from hand to hand, that was first of all put into writing by the holy man Moses, together with those things which were done in all the time of Moses' life, by the space of one hundred and twenty years. And that his estimation might be the greater throughout all the world, among all men, and in all ages; and that none should but know, that the writings of Moses were the very word of God itself; Moses was furnished, and as it were consecrated by God, with signs and wonders to be marvelled at indeed, which the almighty by the hand, that is, by the ministry of Moses, did bring to pass: and verily, he wrought them not in any corner of the world, or place unknown, but in Egypt, the most flourishing and renowned kingdom of that age.

Those miracles were greater and far more by many, than that they can be here rehearsed in few words: neither is it needful to repeat them, because you, dearly beloved, are not unskilful or ignorant of them at all. After that also, God by other means procured authority to Moses. For many and oftentimes God had communication with Moses; and amongst the rest of his talk said he: "Behold, I will come to thee in a thick cloud, that the people may hear me talking with thee, and may believe thee for evermore" [Exod. 19:9].

Neither was the Lord therewith content, but commanded Moses to call together all the people, six hundred thousand men, I say, with their wives and children. They are called out to the mount Sina, where God appeareth in a wonderful and terrible fashion; and he himself, preaching to the congregation, doth rehearse unto them the ten commandments. But the people, being terrified with the majesty of God, doth pray and beseech, that God himself would no more afterward preach to the congregation with his own mouth, saying, that it were enough, if he would use Moses as an interpreter to them, and by him speak to the church [Exod. 20:19]. The most high God did like the offer; and, after that, he spake to the people by Moses whatsoever he would have done. And for because that the people was a stiff-necked people, and by keeping company with idolaters in Egypt was not a little corrupted, Moses now began to set down in writing those things which the holy fathers by tradition had taught, and the things also which the Lord had revealed unto him. The cause why he wrote them was, lest peradventure by oblivion, by continuance of time, and obstinacy of a people so slow to believe, they might either perish, or else be corrupted. The Lord also set Moses an example to follow. For whatsoever God had spoken to the church in mount Sina, the same did he straightway after write with his own finger in two tables of stone, as he had with his finger from the beginning of the world written the same in the hearts of the fathers. Afterward also, in plain words, he commanded Moses to write whatsoever the Lord had revealed. Moses obeyed the Lord's commandment, and wrote them. The Holy Ghost, which was wholly in the mind of Moses, directed his hand as he writ. There was no ability wanting in Moses, that was necessary for a most absolute writer. He was abundantly instructed by his ancestors: for he was born of the holiest progeny of those fathers, whom God appointed to be witnesses of his will, commandments, and judgments; suppose Amram, Kahad, Jacob, Sem, Methusalem and Adam. He was able, therefore, to write a true and certain history, from the beginning of the world even until his own time.

Whereunto he added those things which were done among the people of God in his own life-time, whereof he was a very true witness, as one that saw and heard them. Yea, and that more is, whatsoever he did set forth in his books, that did he read to his people, and amongst so many thousands was there not one found which gainsayed that which he rehearsed: so that the whole consent and witness-bearing of the great congregation did bring no small authority to the writings of Moses.

Moses therefore contained in the five books, called the five books of Moses, an history from the beginning of the world, even unto his own death, by the space of two thousand four hundred and eighty-eight years: in which he declared most largely the revelation of the word of God made unto men, and whatsoever the word of God doth contain and teach: in which, as we have the manifold oracles of God himself, so we have most lightsome testimonies, sentences, examples, and decrees of the most excellent, ancient, holy, wise, and greatest men of the world, touching all things which seem to appertain to true godliness, and the way how to live well and holily. These books therefore found a ready prepared entrance of belief among all the posterity, as books which are authentical, and which of themselves have authority sufficient, and which, without gainsaying, ought to be believed of all the world. Yea, and that more is, our Lord Jesus Christ, the only-begotten Son of God, doth refer the faithful to the reading of Moses; yea, and that indeed in the chiefest points of our salvation: the places are to be seen, John v. Luke xvi. In the fifth of Matthew he saith: "Do not think that I am come to destroy the law and the prophets; for I am not come to destroy them, but to fulfil them. For, verily, I say unto you, though heaven and earth do pass, one jot or tittle of the law shall not pass, till all be fulfilled. Whosoever, therefore, shall undo one of the least of these commandments, and shall teach men so, he shall be called the least in the kingdom of heaven" [Matt. 5:17–19].

There have verily some been found, that have spoken against Moses, the servant of God. But God hath imputed that gainsaying as done against his divine majesty, and punished it most sharply. The proofs hereof are to be seen in Exod. xvi. and Numeri the xii. And first, of the people murmuring against Moses; then of Mary, Moses's sister, speaking against her brother. But to the people it was said: "Not against the ministers, but against the Lord, are your complaints" [Exod. 16:8]. As for Mary, she was horribly stricken with a leprosy [Num. 12:10; Miriam: Vulg. Maria]. Theotectus was stricken blind, and Theopompus fell to be mad, because he had unreverently touched the word of God.[3] For, although the word of God be revealed, spoken, and written by men, yet doth it not therefore cease to be that which indeed it is; neither doth it therefore begin to be the word of men, because it is preached and heard of men: no more than the king's commandment, which is proclaimed by the crier, is said to be the commandment of the crier. He despiseth God, and with God all the holy patriarchs, whosoever doth contemn Moses, by whom God speaketh unto us, and at whose hand we have received those things which the patriarchs from the beginning of the world by tradition delivered to the posterity. There is no difference between the word of God, which is taught by the lively expressed voice of man, and that which is written by the pen of man, but so far forth as the lively voice and writing do differ between themselves: the matter undoubtedly, the sense, and meaning, in the one and the other is all one. By this, dearly beloved, you have perceived the certain history of the beginning of the word of God.

Now let us go forward to the rest; that is, to add the history of the proceeding of the word of God, and by what means it shined ever and anon very clear and brightly unto the world. By and by, after the departure of the holy man Moses out of this world into heaven, the Lord of his bountifulness gave most excellent prophets unto his church, which he had chosen to the intent that by it he might reveal his word unto the whole world. And the prophets were to them of the old time, as at this day amongst us are prophets, priests, wise men, preachers, pastors, bishops, doctors or divines, most skilful in heavenly things, and given by God to guide the people in the faith. And he, whosoever shall read the holy history, will confess that there flourished of this sort no small number, and those not obscure, even till the captivity of Babylon. Amongst whom are reckoned these singular and excellent men, Phinees, Samuel, Helias [Elijah], Heliseus [Elisha], Esaias [Isaiah], and Jeremias. David and Salomon were both kings and prophets. In time of the captivity at Babylon, Daniel and Ezechiel were notably known. After the captivity flourished, among the rest, Zacharias the son of Barachias. Here have I reckoned up a few among many: who, although they flourished at sundry times, and that the one a great while after the other, yet did they all, with one consent, acknowledge that God spake to the world by Moses, who (God so appointed it) left to the church in the world a breviary of true divinity, and a most absolute sum of the word of God contained in writing. All these priests, divines, and prophets, in all that they did, had an especial eye to the doctrine of Moses. They did also refer all men, in cases of faith and religion, to the book of Moses. The law of Moses, which is indeed the law of God, and is most properly called *Thora*, as it were the guide and rule of faith and life, they did diligently beat into the minds of all men. This did they, according to the time, persons, and place, expound to all men. For all the priests and prophets, before the incarnation of Christ, did by word of mouth teach the men of their time godliness and true religion. Neither did they teach any other thing than that which the fathers had received of God, and which Moses had received of God and the fathers; and straightways after committing it to writing, did set it out to all us which follow, even unto the end of the world: so that now in the prophets we have the doctrine of Moses and tradition of the fathers, and them in all and every point more fully and plainly expounded and polished, being moreover to the places, times, and persons very fitly applied.

Furthermore, the doctrine and writings of the prophets have always been of great authority among all wise men throughout the whole world. For it is well perceived by many arguments, that they took not their beginning of the prophets themselves, as chief authors; but were inspired from God out of heaven by the Holy Spirit of God: for it is God, which, dwelling by his Spirit in the minds of the prophets, speaketh to us by their mouths. And for that cause have they a most large testimony at the hands of Christ, and his elect apostles. What say ye to this moreover, that God by their ministry hath wrought miracles and wonders to be marvelled at, and those not a few; that at the least by mighty signs we might learn that it is God, by whose inspiration the prophets do teach and write whatsoever they left for us to remember?

Furthermore, so many commonweals and congregations gathered together, and governed by the prophets according to the word of God, do shew most evident testimonies of God's truth in the prophets. Plato, Zeno, Aristotle, and other philosophers of the gentiles, are praised as excellent men. But which of them could ever yet gather a church to live according to their ordinances? And yet our prophets have had the most excellent and renowned commonweals or congregations, yea, and that more is, the most flourishing kingdoms in all the world under their authority. All the wise men in the whole world (I mean those which lived in his time) did reverence Salomon, a king and so great a prophet, and came unto him from the very outmost ends of the world. Daniel also had the preeminence among the wise men at Babylon, being then the most renowned monarchy in all the world. He was moreover in great estimation with Darius Medus, the son of Astyages or Assuerus, and also with Cyrus that most excellent king. And here it liketh me well to speak somewhat of that divine foreknowledge in our prophets, and most assured foreshewing of things which were to come after many years passed. And now, to say nothing of others, did not Esaias most truly foretell those things, which were afterward fulfilled by the Jews in our Lord Christ? Not in vain did he seem to them of old time to be rather an evangelist than a prophet foretelling things to come. He did openly tell the name of king Cyrus one hundred and threescore years, at the least, before that Cyrus was born [Isa. 44:28; 45:1]. Daniel also was called of them in the old time by the name of one which knew much. For he did foretell those things which are and have been done in all the kingdoms of the world almost, and among the people of God, from his own time until the time of Christ, and further until the last day of judgment, so plainly, that he may seem to have compiled a history of those things which then were already gone and past. All these things, I say, do very evidently prove, that the doctrine and writings of the prophets are the very word of God: with which name and title they are set forth in sundry places of the scriptures. Verily, Peter the apostle saith, "The prophecy came not in old time by the will of man: but holy men of God spake as they were moved by the Holy Ghost."

And although God did largely, clearly, plainly, and simply reveal his word to the world by the patriarchs, by Moses, by the priests and prophets; yet did he, in the last times of all, by his Son set it forth most clearly, simply, and abundantly to all the world. For the very and only-begotten Son of God the Father, as the prophets had foretold, descending from heaven, doth fulfil all whatsoever they foretold, and by the space almost of three years doth teach all points of godliness. For saith John: "No man at any time hath seen God; the only-begotten Son, which is in the bosom of the Father, he hath declared him" [John 1:18]. The Lord himself, moreover, saith to his disciples: "All things which I have heard of my Father have I made known to you" [John 15:15]. And again he saith: "I am the light of the world: whosoever doth follow me doth not walk in darkness, but shall have the light of life" [John 8:12]. Our Lord also did teach, that to him, which would enter into heaven and be saved, the heavenly regeneration was needful [John 3:5], because in the first birth man is born to death, in the second to life; but that that regeneration is made perfect in us by the Spirit of God, which instructeth our hearts in faith, I say, in faith in Christ, who died for our sins, and rose again for our justification [Rom. 4:25]. He taught that by that faith they which believe are justified; and that out of the same faith do grow sundry fruits of charity and innocency, to the bringing forth whereof he did most earnestly exhort them. He taught furthermore, that he was the fulfilling, or fulness, of the law and the prophets; and did also approve and expound the doctrine of Moses and the prophets. To doctrine he joined divers miracles and benefits, whereby he declared, that he himself was that light of the world, and the mighty and bountiful Redeemer of the world. And, to the intent that his doctrine and benefits might be known to all the world, he chose to himself witnesses, whom he called apostles, because he purposed to send them to preach throughout the world. Those witnesses were simple men, innocents, just, tellers of truth, without deceit or subtilties, and in all points holy and good; whose names it is very profitable often to repeat in the congregation. The names of the apostles are these: Peter and Andrew, James and John, Philip and Bartholomew, Thomas and Matthew, James the son of Alphe, and Judas his brother, whose surname was Thaddæus, Simon and Judas Iscariot, into whose room (because he had betrayed the Lord) came St. Matthias [Matt. 10:2–4; Acts 1:26]. These had he, by the space almost of three years, hearers of his heavenly doctrine, and beholders of his divine works. These, after his ascension into the heavens, did he, by the Holy Ghost sent down from heaven, instruct with all kind of faculties. For, as they were in the scriptures passing skilful, so were they not unskilful, or wanting eloquence, in any tongue. And, being once after this manner instructed, they depart out of the city of Jerusalem, and pass through the compass of the earth, preaching to all people and nations that which they had received to preach of the Saviour of the world and the Lord Jesus Christ. And when for certain years they had preached by word of mouth, then did they also set down in writing that which they had preached. For some, verily, writ an history of the words and deeds of Christ, and some of the words and deeds of the apostles. Other some sent sundry epistles to divers nations. In all which, to confirm the truth, they use the scripture of the law and the prophets, even as we read that the Lord oftentimes did. Moreover, to the twelve apostles are joined two great lights of the world; John Baptist, than whom there was never any more holy born of women [Matt. 11:11]; and the chosen vessel [Acts 9:15] Paul, the great teacher of the Gentiles [1 Tim. 2:7; 2 Tim. 1:11].

Neither is it to be marvelled at, that the forerunner and apostles of Christ had always very great dignity and authority in the church. For, even as they were the embassadors of the eternal King of all ages and of the whole world; so, being endued with the Spirit of God, they did nothing according to the judgment of their own minds. And the Lord by their ministry wrought great miracles, thereby to garnish the ministry of them, and to commend their doctrine unto us. And what may be thought of that, moreover, that by that word of God they did convert the whole world; gathering together, and laying the foundations of, notable churches throughout the compass of the world? Which verily by man's counsel and words they had never been able to have brought to pass. To this is further added, that they which once leaned to this doctrine, as a doctrine giving life, did not refuse to die: besides that, how many soever had their belief in the doctrine of the gospel, they were not afraid, through water, fire, and swords, to cut off this life, and to lay hand on the life to come. The faithful saints could in no wise have done these things, unless the doctrine which they believed had been of God.

Although therefore that the apostles were men, yet their doctrine, first of all taught by a lively expressed voice, and after that set down in writing with pen and ink, is the doctrine of God and the very true word of God. For therefore the apostle left this saying in writing: "When ye did receive the word of God which ye heard of us, ye received it not as the word of men, but, as it is indeed, the word of God, which effectually worketh in you that believe" [1 Thess. 2:13].

But now the matter itself and place require, that I gather also and plainly reckon up those books, wherein is contained the very word of God, first of all declared of the fathers, of Christ himself, and the apostles by word of mouth; and after that also written into books by the prophets and apostles. And in the first place verily are set the five books of Moses. Then follow the books of Josue, of Judges, of Ruth, two books of Samuel, two of Kings, two of Chronicles; of Esdras, Nehemias, and Hester one a-piece. After these come Job, David or the book of Psalms, Proverbs, Ecclesiastes, and Cantica [Song of Songs]. With them are numbered the four greater prophets, Esaias, Jeremias, Ezechiel, and Daniel: then the twelve lesser prophets, whose names are very well known: with these books the old Testament ended. The new Testament hath in the beginning the evangelical history of Christ the Lord, written by four authors, that is, by two apostles, Matthew and John; and by two disciples, Mark and Luke, who compiled a wonderful goodly and profitable book of the Acts of the Apostles. Paul to sundry churches and persons published fourteen epistles. The other apostles wrote seven which are called both canonical and catholic. And the books of the new Testament are ended with the Revelation of Jesus Christ, which he opened to the disciple whom he loved, John the evangelist and apostle; shewing unto him, and so to the whole church, the ordinance of God touching the church, even until the day of judgment. Therefore in these few and mean, not unmeasurable, in these plain and simple, not dark and unkemmed [unkempt] books, is comprehended the full doctrine of godliness, which is the very word of the true, living, and eternal God.

Also the books of Moses and the prophets through so many ages, perils, and captivities, came sound and uncorrupted even until the time of Christ and his apostles. For the Lord Jesus and the apostles used those books as true copies and authentical; which undoubtedly they neither would, nor could, have done, if so be that either they had been corrupted, or altogether perished. The books also, which the apostles of Christ have added, were throughout all persecutions kept in the church safe and uncorrupted, and are come sound and uncorrupted into our hands, upon whom the ends of the world are fallen. For by the vigilant care and unspeakable goodness of God, our Father, it is brought to pass, that no age at any time either hath or shall want so great a treasure.

Thus much hitherto have I declared unto you, dearly beloved, what the word of God is, what the beginning of it in the church was, and what proceeding, dignity, and certainty it had. The word of God is the speech of God, that is to say, the revealing of his good will to mankind, which from the beginning, one while by his own mouth, and another while by the speech of angels, he did open to those first, ancient, and most holy fathers; who again by tradition did faithfully deliver it to their posterity. Here are to be remembered those great lights of the world, Adam, Seth, Methusalem, Noe, Sem, Abraham, Isaac, Jacob, Amram, and his son Moses, who, at God's commandment, did in writing comprehend the history and traditions of the holy fathers, whereunto he joined the written law, and exposition of the law, together with a large and lightsome history of his own lifetime. After Moses, God gave to his church most excellent men, prophets and priests; who also, by word of mouth and writings, did deliver to their posterity that which they had learned of the Lord. After them came the only-begotten Son of God himself down from heaven into the world, and fulfilled all, whatsoever was found to be written of himself in the law and the prophets. The same also taught a most absolute mean how to live well and holily: he made the apostles his witnesses: which witnesses did afterwards first of all with a lively expressed voice preach all things which the Lord had taught them; and then, to the intent that they should not be corrupted, or clean taken out of man's remembrance, they did commit it to writing: so that now we have from the fathers, the prophets, and apostles, the word of God as it was preached and written.

These things had their beginning of one and the same Spirit of God, and do tend to one end, that is, to teach us men how to live well and holily. He that believeth not these men, and namely the only-begotten Son of God, whom, I pray you, will he believe? We have here the most holy, innocent, upright-living, most praiseworthy, most just, most ancient, most wise, and most divine men of the whole world and compass of the earth, and briefly, such men as are by all means without comparison. All the world cannot shew us the like again, although it should wholly a thousand times be assembled in councils. The holy emperor Constantine gathered a general council out of all the compass of the earth; thither came there together, out of all the world, three hundred and eighteen most excellent fathers: but they that are of the wisest sort will say, that these are not so much as shadows, to be compared to them, of whom we have received the word of God. Let us therefore in all things believe the word of God delivered to us by the scriptures. Let us think that the Lord himself, which is the very living and eternal God, doth speak to us by the scriptures. Let us for evermore praise the name and goodness of him, who hath vouchedsafe so faithfully, fully, and plainly to open to us, miserable mortal men, all the means how to live well and holily.

To him be praise, honour, and glory for evermore. Amen.

Notes

1. See Fritz Büsser, "Bullinger," *Theologische Realenzyklpädie*, ed. Gerhard Krause and Gerhard Muller, vol. 7 (Berlin: Walter de Gruyter, 1981), 375–87.

2. See G. W. Bromiley, ed., *Zwingli and Bullinger*, Library of Christian Classics, vol. 24 (Philadelphia: Westminster Press, 1953), 284; and Walter Hollweg, *Heinrich Bullingers Hausbuch, Beiträge zur Geschichte und Lehre der Reformierten Kirche*, ed. Paul Jacobs et al. (Giessen: Münchowsche Universitätsdruckerie, 1956), 34–35, 40–41, 142–68.

3. Theodectus was a rhetorician and tragedian in fourth-century Athens, and a contemporary of Theopompus, an orator and historian. Josephus reports that when Theodectus and Theopompus sought to write about the sacred books, the former was afflicted by God with blindness and the latter by madness for thirty days.. Flavius Josephus, *Antiquities of the Jews*, bk. 12, ch. 2, *The Life and Works of Flavius Josephus*, trans. William Whiston (Philadelphia: John C. Winston, 1957), 353–54.

Calvin and the Genevan Reformation

15. The Law

From Institution of the Christian Religion

(1536)

JOHN CALVIN

John Calvin's Institution of the Christian Religion *(more usually translated* Institutes*) ranks as one of the most important presentations of Christian doctrine ever written. It has exercised an enormous influence on the Reformed tradition.*

Originally written at Basel in 1535, when Calvin (1509–64) was only twenty-six years old, it was first published there in March 1536. Calvin fled to Basel from his native France in January 1535 to escape persecution against Protestants, generated by the placards affair. Documents attacking the Mass had been posted in many of the larger cities in France in October 1534. Soon thereafter a royal edict was issued against Lutherans. Calvin and many of his evangelical friends fled; at least one who remained was burned at the stake as a heretic.

Except for two prefaces—one in Latin, the other in French—that Calvin had written in early 1535 for the French translation of the Bible by his cousin, Pierre Olivetan, the Institutes of the Christian Religion was Calvin's first effort to write down many of the beliefs that had been fermenting in his mind for some time. The book had a twofold purpose: first, it was written to the French king, Francis I, to defend the persecuted evangelicals remaining in France. Calvin maintained that the evan-

---

SOURCE: John T. McNeill, ed., *Institution of the Christian Religion* (1536), translated and annotated by Ford Lewis Battles (Atlanta: John Knox Press, 1975). Used by permission of Westminster John Knox Press.

gelicals, not the papists, carried on the faith of the ancient, one, holy, catholic church. Second, Calvin's purpose was catechetical, "to hand on some rudiments" of the Christian religion to "our own Frenchmen in particular," who "were hungering and thirsting after Christ."

The word institutio *(institutes) is ambiguous. It can mean "manual" or "instruction" or "summary." It is a word used by ancient classical and early church writers, and also by contemporary humanists such as Erasmus, who had considerable influence on Calvin.*[1] *It is also clear that Martin Luther's Small Catechism (see vol. 2:140–59) shaped the outline of the* Institutes.[2]

Although its original form was a simple catechetical compendium of Christian doctrine, by the final edition in 1559 Calvin's Institutes *had become a weighty theological textbook five times its original size. Over time it also became more polemical in tone.*

The section on the law comes at the very beginning of the 1536 Institutes. *It sets forth in succinct form what Battles, the translator, has called "the kernel of Calvin's faith." Some scholars consider it a reflection on his personal conversion. How Calvin was converted to the evangelical persuasion is still debated by scholars, who disagree on its date, its duration (all at once or gradual?), and its content. Most likely, it was a process similar to the one he describes when discussing Christian conversion in general.*[3]

A. Knowledge of God

1. Nearly the whole of sacred doctrine consists in these two parts: knowledge of God and of ourselves. Surely, we ought for the present to learn the following things about God. To hold with sure faith, first that he is infinite wisdom, righteousness, goodness, mercy, truth, power and life [Bar. 3:12–14; James 1:17]. And all of these things, wherever seen, come from him [Prov. 16:4]. Secondly, that all things in heaven and on earth have been created for his glory [Ps. 148:1–14; Dan. 3:59–63]. To serve him for his nature's sake alone, to keep his rule, accept his majesty, and in obedience recognize him as Lord and King [Rom. 1:20]—all this is due him by right. Thirdly, that he is himself a just judge, and therefore, is going to take harsh vengeance upon those who have turned aside from his precepts, who have not followed his will through all things, who think, say and do things other than those that pertain to his glory [Ps. 7:9–11; Rom. 2:1–16]. Fourthly, that he is merciful and gentle, ready to receive the miserable and poor that

flee to his mercy and put their trust in him; prepared to spare and pardon, if any ask a favor of him; willing to succor and give aid, if any ask for his help; willing to save any who put all their trust in him and cleave to him [Ps. 103:3–4, 8–11; Isa. 55:6; Ps. 25:6–11; 85:5–7, 10].

B. Knowledge of Man

2. In order for us to come to a sure knowledge of ourselves, we must first grasp the fact that Adam, parent of us all, was created in the image and likeness of God [Gen. 1:26–27]. That is, he was endowed with wisdom, righteousness, holiness, and was so clinging by these gifts of grace to God that he could have lived forever in Him, if he had stood fast in the uprightness God had given him. But when Adam slipped into sin, this image and likeness of God was cancelled and effaced, that is, he lost all the benefits of divine grace, by which he could have been led back into the way of life [Gen. 3]. Moreover, he was far removed from God and became a complete stranger. From this it follows that man was stripped and deprived of all wisdom, righteousness, power, life, which—as has already been said—could be held only in God. As a consequence, nothing was left to him save ignorance, iniquity, impotence, death, and judgment [Rom. 5:12–21]. These are indeed the "fruits of sin" [Gal. 5:19–21]. This calamity fell not only upon Adam himself, but also flowed down into us, who are his seed and offspring. Consequently, all of us born of Adam are ignorant and bereft of God, perverse, corrupt, and lacking every good. Here is a heart especially inclined to all sorts of evil, stuffed with depraved desires, addicted to them, and obstinate toward God [Jer. 17:9]. But if we outwardly display anything good, still the mind stays in its inner state of filth and crooked perversity. The prime matter or rather the matter of concern for all rests in the judgment of God, who judges not according to appearance, nor highly esteems outward splendor, but gazes upon the secrets of the heart [1 Sam. 16:7; Jer. 17:10]. Therefore, however much of a dazzling appearance of holiness man may have on his own, it is nothing but hypocrisy and even an abomination in God's sight, since the thoughts of the mind, ever depraved and corrupted, lurk beneath.

3. Even though we have been so born that nothing is left for us to do which could be acceptable to God, nor has it been put in our power to please him—yet we do not cease to owe the very thing we cannot supply. Inasmuch as we are God's creatures, we ought to serve his honor and glory, and obey his commandments. And we are not allowed to excuse ourselves by claiming that we lack ability and, like impoverished debtors, cannot pay our debt. For the guilt that binds us is our own, arising from our own sin,

leaving us without the will or the capacity to do good [John 8:34–38; Rom. 7:15–25]. Now, since God justly avenges crimes, we must recognize that we are subject to the curse and deserve the judgment of eternal death. Indeed there is no one of us with either the will or the ability to do his duty.

C. The Law

4. For this reason Scripture calls us all "children of God's wrath" and declares we are hurtling to death and destruction [Eph. 2:1–3; Rom. 3:9–20]. To man is left no reason why he should seek in himself his righteousness, power, life, and salvation; for all these are in God only; cut off and separated from Him by sin [Hos. 13:4–9], man will find in himself only unhappiness, weakness, wickedness, death, in short, hell itself. To keep men from being ignorant of these things, the Lord engraved and, so to speak, stamped the law upon the hearts of all [Rom. 2:1–16]. But this is nothing but conscience, for us the witness within of what we owe God; it sets before us good and evil, thus accusing and condemning us, conscious as we are within ourselves that we have not discharged our duty, as was fitting. Yet man is swollen with arrogance and ambition and blinded by self-love. Consequently, he is unable to see himself and, as it were, to descend into himself, and confess his misery. Seeing our condition, the Lord has provided us with a written law to teach us what perfect righteousness is and how it is to be kept: that is, firmly fixed in God, we turn our gaze to him alone, and to him aim our every thought, yearning, act, or word. This teaching of righteousness clearly shows how far we have strayed from the right path. To this end also look all promises and curses, set forth for us in the law itself. For the Lord promises that, if anyone should perfectly and exactly fulfill by his effort whatever is commanded, he will receive the reward of eternal life [Lev. 18:5]. By this he undoubtedly points out to us that the perfection of life taught in the law is truly righteousness, is so considered with him, and would be worthy of such a reward if any could be found among men. But he pronounces a curse and announces the judgment of eternal death upon all who do not fully and without exception keep the whole righteousness of the law [Deut. 27:26; Gal. 3:10].

Surely by this punishment he constrains all men that ever were, are, or will be. Among them not one can be pointed out who is not a transgressor of the law. The law teaches us God's will, which we are constrained to fulfill and to which we are in debt; it shows us how we are able to carry out exactly nothing of what God has commanded us [Rom. 3:1; 7:7–25]. Consequently, it is clearly a mirror for us wherein we may discern and contemplate our sin and curse, just as we commonly gaze upon the scars and blemishes of our face in a mirror. Properly speaking, this very written law is but a witness of natural law, a witness which quite often arouses our memory, and instills in us the things we had not sufficiently learned, when natural law was teaching within. Now we are ready to understand what we are to learn from the law. God is the Creator, our Lord and Father. For this reason we owe him glory, honor, and love. Since, however, not one of us performs these duties, we all deserve the curse, judgment, in short, eternal death. Therefore we are to seek another way to salvation than the righteousness of our own works. This way is forgiveness of sins. Then, since it is not in our power or ability to discharge what we owe the law, we must despair of ourselves and must seek and await help from another quarter. After we descend to this humility and submission, the Lord will shine upon us, and show himself lenient, kindly, gentle, indulgent. For of him it is written: "he resists the proud, gives grace to the humble" [James 4:6; 1 Pet. 5:5]. And first, if we pray him to avert his wrath, and ask his pardon, he will without doubt grant it to us. Everything our sins deserved he forgives, and receives into grace.

D. God's Love in Christ

5. Then, if we implore his helping hand, surely we will be persuaded that, equipped with his protection, we will be able to do all things. He bestows upon us according to his own good will a new heart in order that we may will, and a new power, whereby we may be enabled to carry out his commandments [Ezek. 36:26]. And all these blessings he showers upon us for the sake of Jesus Christ our Lord, who—even though he was one God with the Father [John 1:1–14]—put on our flesh, to enter a covenant with us and to join us (far separated from God by our sins) closely to him [Isa. 53:4–11]. He also by the merit of his death paid our debts to God's justice, and appeased his wrath [Eph. 2:3–5]. He redeemed us from the curse and judgment that bound us, and in his body the punishment of sin, so as to absolve us from it [Col. 1:21–22]. Descending to earth, he brought with him all the rich heavenly blessings and with a lavish hand showered them upon us [John 1:14–16; 7:38; Rom. 8:14–17]. These are the Holy Spirit's gifts. Through him we are reborn, wrested from the power and chains of the devil, freely adopted as children of God, sanctified for every good work. Through him also—so long as we are held in this mortal body—there are dying in us the depraved desires, the promptings of the flesh, and everything the twisted and corrupt perversity of our nature brings forth. Through him we are renewed from day to day [2 Cor. 4:16], that we may walk in newness of life [Rom. 6:4] and live for righteousness.

6. God offers to us and gives us in Christ our Lord all these benefits, which include free forgiveness of sins, peace and reconciliation with God, the gifts and graces of the Holy Spirit. They are ours if we embrace and receive them with sure faith, utterly trusting and, as it were leaning upon divine goodness, not doubting that God's Word, which promises us all these things, is power and truth [Rom. 3:21–26; 5:1–11]. In short, if we partake of Christ, in Him we shall possess all the heavenly treasures and gifts of the Holy Spirit, which lead us into life and salvation. Except with a true and living faith, we will never grasp this. With it, we will recognize all our good to be in him, ourselves to be nothing apart from him; we will hold as certain that in him we become God's children and heirs of the heavenly kingdom [John 1:12; Rom. 8:14–17]. On the other hand, those who have no part in Christ, whatever their nature, whatever they may do or undertake, depart into ruin and confusion and into the judgment of eternal death; they are cast away from God and are shut off from all hope of salvation [John 3:18–20; 1 John 5:12]. This knowledge of ourselves and of our poverty and ruin teaches us to humble ourselves and cast ourselves before God and seek his mercy [Jer. 31:18–20]. Not from ourselves is the faith that furnishes us a taste of divine goodness and mercy, wherein God in his Christ has to do with us. Rather, it is God who is to be asked to lead us, unfeignedly repentant, to the knowledge of ourselves; to lead us, by sure faith, to the knowledge of his gentleness and of his sweetness, which he shows forth in his Christ in order that Christ as our leader, who is the only way to reach the Father, may bring us into eternal blessedness [Phil. 1:6; John 14:6; Rom. 5:1–11].

Notes

1. See William J. Bouwsma, *John Calvin: A Sixteenth Century Portrait* (New York: Oxford University Press, 1989), 17ff.

2. See Alexandre Ganoczy, *The Young Calvin*, trans. David Foxglover and Wade Provo (Philadelphia: Westminster Press, 1987), 137.

3. See *The Piety of John Calvin: An Anthology Illustrative of the Reformer*, ed. and trans. Ford Lewis Battles (Grand Rapids, Mich.: Baker, 1978), 43–48. Also see Bouwsma, 11, and Ganoczy, 241–66.

16. The Geneva Confession

(1536)

WILLIAM FAREL AND JOHN CALVIN

The year 1536 was a momentous one for John Calvin (1509–64). During this year he published the first edition of his famous Institutes of the Christian Religion, *and he became the ministerial leader of the church at Geneva, Switzerland. Calvin originally had no intention of going to Geneva. He had made a brief trip to northern Italy and was returning to Basel. He traveled to Paris to wind up his personal affairs and pick up his brother Antoine and his half sister, Marie. They were headed to Strasbourg. Unfortunately, the way was blocked by army troops, and they took a detour through Geneva.*

Originally, Calvin planned to stay just one night. That evening, however, he met William (Guillaume) Farel, a Frenchman, who with Pierre Viret had inaugurated Protestant reforms in Geneva two months earlier. Farel entreated Calvin to stay and work with him to consolidate Protestant reform in Geneva. Calvin refused, pleading his desire to remain free for his studies. Farel persisted, threatening Calvin with the divine curse if he refused to help. Calvin, who preferred the life of a scholar to the rough-and-tumble of church politics, reluctantly agreed to stay.

Calvin and Farel wasted little time in presenting a program of reform to the Geneva town council. They urged the adoption of a confession of faith that would be binding on all citizens. They argued that failure to subscribe to this confession ought to constitute grounds for excommunication.

SOURCE: *Calvin: Theological Treatises*, Library of Christian Classics, vol. 22, translated with introduction and notes by J. K. S. Reid (Philadelphia: Westminster Press, 1954). Used by permission of Westminster John Knox Press.

The Geneva Confession (its actual title is The Confession of Faith which all the citizens and inhabitants of Geneva and the subjects of the country must promise to keep and uphold) was submitted to the council November 10, 1536. Although it was adopted by the council soon thereafter, many Geneva citizens refused to subscribe to it.

The authorship of the Geneva Confession is disputed. Early biographers assumed that Calvin wrote it. Nineteenth-century editors of Calvin's collected works ascribed it to Farel. Others have concluded that the two reformers collaborated. There is no doubt that the Geneva Confession is a concise summary of the doctrine held in common by Calvin and Farel at the beginning of the Genevan Reformation.[1]

---

1. The Word of God

First we affirm that we desire to follow Scripture alone as rule of faith and religion, without mixing with it any other thing which might be devised by the opinion of men apart from the Word of God, and without wishing to accept for our spiritual government any other doctrine than what is conveyed to us by the same Word without addition or diminution, according to the command of our Lord.

2. One Only God

Following, then, the lines laid down in the Holy Scriptures, we acknowledge that there is one only God, whom we are both to worship and serve, and in whom we are to put all our confidence and hope: having this assurance, that in him alone is contained all wisdom, power, justice, goodness and pity. And since he is spirit, he is to be served in spirit and in truth. Therefore we think it an abomination to put our confidence or hope in any created thing, to worship anything else than him, whether angels or any other creatures, and to recognize any other Saviour of our souls than him alone, whether saints or men living upon earth; and likewise to offer the service, which ought to be rendered to him, in external ceremonies or carnal observances, as if he took pleasure in such things, or to make an image to represent his divinity or any other image for adoration.

3. The Law of God Alike for All

Because there is one only Lord and Master who has dominion over our consciences, and because his will is the only principle of all justice, we confess all our life ought to be ruled in accordance with the commandments of his holy law in which is contained all perfection of justice, and that we ought to have no other rule of good and just living, nor invent other good works to supplement it than those [corrected from "whose"] which are there contained, as follows: Exodus 20: "I am the Lord thy God, who brought thee," and so on.

4. Natural Man

We acknowledge man by nature to be blind, darkened in understanding, and full of corruption and perversity of heart, so that of himself he has no power to be able to comprehend the true knowledge of God as is proper, nor to apply himself to good works. But on the contrary, if he is left by God to what he is by nature, he is only able to live in ignorance and to be abandoned to all iniquity. Hence he has need to be illumined by God, so that he come to the right knowledge of his salvation, and thus to be redirected in his affections and reformed to the obedience of the righteousness of God.

5. Man by Himself Lost

Since man is naturally (as has been said) deprived and destitute in himself of all the light of God, and of all righteousness, we acknowledge that by himself he can only expect the wrath and malediction of God, and hence that he must look outside himself for the means of his salvation.

6. Salvation in Jesus

We confess then that it is Jesus Christ who is given to us by the Father, in order that in him we should recover all of which in ourselves we are deficient. Now all that Jesus Christ has done and suffered for our redemption, we veritably hold without any doubt, as it is contained in the Creed, which is recited in the Church, that is to say: I believe in God the Father Almighty, and so on.

7. Righteousness in Jesus

Therefore we acknowledge the things which are consequently given to us by God in Jesus Christ: first, that being in our own nature enemies of

God and subjects of his wrath and judgment, we are reconciled with him and received again in grace through the intercession of Jesus Christ, so that by his righteousness and guiltlessness we have remission of our sins, and by the shedding of his blood we are cleansed and purified from all our stains.

8. Regeneration in Jesus

Second, we acknowledge that by his Spirit we are regenerated into a new spiritual nature. That is to say that the evil desires of our flesh are mortified by grace, so that they rule us no longer. On the contrary, our will is rendered conformable to God's will, to follow in his way and to seek what is pleasing to him. Therefore we are by him delivered from the servitude of sin, under whose power we were of ourselves held captive, and by this deliverance we are made capable and able to do good works and not otherwise.

9. Remission of Sins Always Necessary for the Faithful

Finally, we acknowledge that this regeneration is so effected in us that, until we slough off this mortal body, there remains always in us much imperfection and infirmity, so that we always remain poor and wretched sinners in the presence of God. And, however much we ought day by day to increase and grow in God's righteousness, there will never be plenitude or perfection while we live here. Thus we always have need of the mercy of God to obtain the remission of our faults and offences. And so we ought always to look for our righteousness in Jesus Christ and not at all in ourselves, and in him be confident and assured, putting no faith in our works.

10. All Our Good in the Grace of God

In order that all glory and praise be rendered to God (as is his due), and that we be able to have true peace and rest of conscience, we understand and confess that we receive all benefits from God, as said above, by his clemency and pity, without any consideration of our worthiness or the merit of our works, to which is due no other retribution than eternal confusion. None the less our Saviour in his goodness, having received us into the communion of his son Jesus, regards the works that we have done in faith as pleasing and agreeable; not that they merit it at all, but because, not imputing any of the imperfection that is there, he acknowledges in them nothing but what proceeds from his Spirit.

11. Faith

We confess that the entrance which we have to the great treasures and riches of the goodness of God that is vouchsafed to us is by faith; inasmuch as, in certain confidence and assurance of heart, we believe in the promises of the Gospel, and receive Jesus Christ as he is offered to us by the Father and described to us by the Word of God.

12. Invocation of God Only and Intercession of Christ

As we have declared that we have confidence and hope for salvation and all good only in God through Jesus Christ, so we confess that we ought to invoke him in all necessities in the name of Jesus Christ, who is our Mediator and Advocate with him and has access to him. Likewise we ought to acknowledge that all good things come from him alone, and to give thanks to him for them. On the other hand, we reject the intercession of the saints as a superstition invented by men contrary to Scripture, for the reason that it proceeds from mistrust of the sufficiency of the intercession of Jesus Christ.

13. Prayer Intelligible

Moreover since prayer is nothing but hypocrisy and fantasy unless it proceed from the interior affections of the heart, we believe that all prayers ought to be made with clear understanding. And for this reason, we hold the prayer of our Lord to show fittingly what we ought to ask of him: Our Father which art in heaven, . . . but deliver us from evil. Amen.

14. Sacraments

We believe that the sacraments which our Lord has ordained in his Church are to be regarded as exercises of faith for us, both for fortifying and confirming it in the promises of God and for witnessing before men. Of them there are in the Christian Church only two which are instituted by the authority of our Saviour: Baptism and the Supper of our Lord; for what is held within the realm of the pope concerning seven sacraments, we condemn as fable and lie.

15. Baptism

Baptism is an external sign by which our Lord testifies that he desires to receive us for his children, as members of his Son Jesus. Hence in it there is represented to us the cleansing from sin which we have in the blood of Jesus Christ, the mortification of our flesh which we have by his death that we may live in him by his Spirit. Now since our children belong to such an alliance with our Lord, we are certain that the external sign is rightly applied to them.

16. The Holy Supper

The Supper of our Lord is a sign by which under bread and wine he represents the true spiritual communion which we have in his body and blood. And we acknowledge that according to his ordinance it ought to be distributed in the company of the faithful, in order that all those who wish to have Jesus for their life be partakers of it. In as much as the mass of the pope was a reprobate and diabolical ordinance subverting the mystery of the Holy Supper, we declare that it is execrable to us, an idolatry condemned by God; for so much is it itself regarded as a sacrifice for the redemption of souls that the bread is in it taken and adored as God. Besides there are other execrable blasphemies and superstitions implied here, and the abuse of the Word of God which is taken in vain without profit or edification.

17. Human Traditions

The ordinances that are necessary for the internal discipline of the Church, and belong solely to the maintenance of peace, honesty and good order in the assembly of Christians, we do not hold to be human traditions at all, in as much as they are comprised under the general command of Paul, where he desires that all be done among them decently and in order. But all laws and regulations made binding on conscience which oblige the faithful to things not commanded by God, or establish another service of God than that which he demands, thus tending to destroy Christian liberty, we condemn as perverse doctrines of Satan, in view of our Lord's declaration that he is honoured in vain by doctrines that are the commandment of men. It is in this estimation that we hold pilgrimages, monasteries, distinctions of foods, prohibition of marriage, confessions and other like things.

18. The Church

While there is one only Church of Jesus Christ, we always acknowledge that necessity requires companies of the faithful to be distributed in different places. Of these assemblies each one is called Church. But in as much as all companies do not assemble in the name of our Lord, but rather to blaspheme and pollute him by their sacrilegious deeds, we believe that the proper mark by which rightly to discern the Church of Jesus Christ is that his holy gospel be purely and faithfully preached, proclaimed, heard, and kept, that his sacraments be properly administered, even if there be some imperfections and faults, as there always will be among men. On the other hand, where the Gospel is not declared, heard, and received, there we do not acknowledge the form of the Church. Hence the churches governed by the ordinances of the pope are rather synagogues of the devil than Christian churches.

19. Excommunication

Because there are always some who hold God and his Word in contempt, who take account of neither injunction, exhortation nor remonstrance, thus requiring greater chastisement, we hold the discipline of excommunication to be a thing holy and salutary among the faithful, since truly it was instituted by our Lord with good reason. This is in order that the wicked should not by their damnable conduct corrupt the good and dishonour our Lord, and that though proud they may turn to penitence. Therefore we believe that it is expedient according to the ordinance of God that all manifest idolaters, blasphemers, murderers, thieves, lewd persons, false witnesses, sedition-mongers, quarrellers, those guilty of defamation or assault, drunkards, dissolute livers, when they have been duly admonished and if they do not make amendment, be separated from the communion of the faithful until their repentance is known.

20. Ministers of the Word

We recognize no other pastors in the Church than faithful pastors of the Word of God, feeding the sheep of Jesus Christ on the one hand with instruction, admonition, consolation, exhortation, deprecation; and on the other resisting all false doctrines and deceptions of the devil, without mixing with the pure doctrine of the Scriptures their dreams or their foolish imaginings. To these we accord no other power or authority but to conduct, rule, and govern the people of God committed to them by the same Word, in which they have power to command, defend, promise, and warn, and without which they neither can nor ought to attempt anything. As we receive the true ministers of the Word of God as messengers and ambassadors of God, it is necessary to listen to them as to him himself, and we hold their ministry to be a commission from God necessary in the Church. On the other hand we hold that all seductive and false prophets, who abandon the purity of the Gospel and deviate to their own inventions, ought not at all to be suffered or maintained, who are not the pastors they pretend, but rather, like ravening wolves, ought to be hunted and ejected from the people of God.

21. Magistrates

We hold the supremacy and dominion of kings and princes as also of other magistrates and officers, to be a holy thing and a good ordinance of God. And since in performing their office they serve God and follow a Christian vocation, whether in defending the afflicted and innocent, or in correcting and punishing the malice of the perverse, we on our part also ought to accord them honour and reverence, to render respect and subservience, to execute their commands, to bear the charges they impose on us, so far as we are able without offence to God. In sum, we ought to regard them as vicars and lieutenants of God, whom one cannot resist without resisting God himself; and their office as a sacred commission from God which has been given them so that they may rule and govern us. Hence we hold that all Christians are bound to pray God for the prosperity of the superiors and lords of the country where they live, to obey the statutes and ordinances which do not contravene the commandments of God, to promote welfare, peace and public good, endeavouring to sustain the honour of those over them and the peace of the people, without contriving or attempting anything to inspire trouble or dissension. On the other hand we declare that all those who conduct themselves unfaithfully towards their superiors, and have not a right concern for the public good of the country where they live, demonstrate thereby their infidelity towards God.

Note

1. See *Calvin: Theological Treatises*, translated with introduction and notes by J. K. S. Reid, *Library of Christian Classics*, vol. 22 (Philadelphia: Westminster Press, 1954), 25; and Francois Wendel, *Calvin: The Origins and Development of His Religious Thought*, trans. Philip Mairet (London: Collins, 1963), 52.

17. The Strasbourg Liturgy

(1539)

Martin Bucer

John Calvin had exercised his ministry in Geneva only a short time when the citizens recoiled against the discipline which Calvin and his colleague William Farel were seeking to impose on them. The town council especially resisted all efforts to impose excommunication upon obdurate sinners. Like the magistrates in other Protestant cities in Switzerland and South Germany, the Genevan council reserved that right to itself. The result was that in May 1538, the magistrate expelled Calvin and Farel from Geneva.

Calvin returned to Basel to resume his studies. Soon thereafter, however, another reformer named Martin Bucer invited Calvin to come to Strasbourg to minister to a growing congregation of French refugees. There Calvin came under the influence of the thought of Martin Bucer.

In this important Alsatian city, Martin Bucer (1491–1551), along with Matthew Zell and Wolfgang Capito, shaped the Protestant position. As an outstanding biblical scholar, Bucer made a deep impression on Calvin. He was also an important ecumenical theologian, as shown in his writings on the Eucharist and in his efforts to achieve rapprochement between Lutherans and Zwinglians and between Protestants and Catholics. Bucer participated in the 1529 Marburg Colloquy (a debate on the Eucharist between Luther and Zwingli) (see vol 2:225–47) and in the 1536 Wittenberg Concord (an agreement drawn up by Phillip Melanchthon between northern German Lutheran and southern German

---

SOURCE: Bard Thompson, ed., *Liturgies of the Western Church* (Cleveland: The World Publishing Co., 1961). Used by permission of Harcourt, Brace & Company.

cities). Bucer also took part, along with Melanchthon and Calvin, in colloquies between Catholics and Protestants at Hagenau, Worms, and Regensburg (1540–41).

Bucer was a supreme organizer of the church and a creative liturgist. His understandings of worship had considerable influence on Calvin. After 1549, when he moved to England, Bucer played a significant role in the development of the Book of Common Prayer. Especially through his liturgical work, Bucer made an important contribution to the Reformed tradition.

The earliest German service in Strasbourg was developed by Diobald Schwarz, an assistant to Matthew Zell, the first evangelical preacher in Strasbourg. Early in 1524 Schwarz created a German mass closely patterned after the Latin rite. Soon thereafter, Bucer, who had been in Strasbourg only since 1522, introduced more radical worship reforms. By 1526, the liturgy at Strasbourg was decidedly evangelical. The name Mass *was changed to* Lord's Supper. *Rejecting all understandings of the Mass as sacrifice, the* altar *became the* table. A minister, *rather than a* priest, *stood behind the table to offer communicants the elements across the table. Priestly vestments and added ceremonials were eliminated.*

In the Strasbourg Liturgy, the sermon assumed an important place within a service based on the continuous reading of Scripture (especially the Gospels), rather than on liturgical pericopes. The words of institution during the Eucharist section of the service used the exact biblical words from Paul and from the Gospels. There was a strong emphasis on congregational singing of the psalms, replacing the Kyrie Eleison *and the* Gloria. *Congregational psalm singing was a particular contribution of the Strasbourg service to the Reformed tradition.*

Further distinctive features of Strasbourg worship service were replacing the preface ("It is truly right and meet . . .") and the Sanctus *("Holy, holy, holy . . .") with the Great Prayer; placing the general confession and absolution (based on 1 Timothy 1) at the beginning of the service; and singing the Apostles' Creed after the sermon.*[1]

The 1539 service translated by Bard Thompson contains slight changes from the 1537 service, and includes important changes in the 1526 service: (1) it uses three possible forms of prayer of confession; (2) it uses other passages of Scripture besides the text from 1 Tim. 1:15 for the words of absolution and the authoritative declaration of the forgiveness of sins by the minister; (3) it contains a fourfold explanation of the meaning of the Eucharist and an exhortation following the sermon; (4) it provides for three alternative versions of the Great Prayer, each ending with the Lord's Prayer and preceding the words of institution; (5) it includes an addition to the words used at the administration of the sacraments ("Remember, believe and proclaim that Christ has died for you and gave himself to you as food and drink unto eternal life"), an addition missing in the 1539 edition but restored in 1541; and (6) it provides for three forms of thanksgiving after the communion act.[2]

A salient feature of these changes is the emphasis on the spiritual, real presence of Christ in the explanation concerning the Eucharist by the minister and in each of the versions of the Great Prayer: "The Lord truly offers and gives His holy and sanctifying body and blood to us in the Holy Supper, with the visible things of bread and wine, through the ministers of the Church." This understanding of the real presence was commonly held by Bucer, Melanchthon, and Calvin.

A second conspicuous feature of Bucer's eucharistic theology in the Strasbourg Liturgy is the emphasis on communion as a union with Christ and with one another, so that "He may live in us, and we in him." A third important characteristic of this liturgy is its focus on "the external ministry of the Church," which alone is authorized to pronounce absolution and administer the sacrament.

These themes of a true, objective presence of Christ, a genuine communion with Christ's body and blood, and an external ministry of the church were important in Bucer's theology in the 1530s. Some modifications on the Communion service may have occurred out of his negotiations with the Lutherans on the Eucharist, which culminated in the Wittenberg Concord of 1536. Bucer's emphasis on the importance of external ministry may also have been affected by conflicts with Anabaptists and spiritualists. These theological changes, however, could just as well have come from Bucer's more careful reading of ancient Christian writings.[3]

Psalter, with Complete Church Practice
Strassburg, MDXXXIX
Concerning the Lord's Supper, or Mass, and the Sermons[4]

First: there are three Sermons to be heard every day. In the morning at the time of early Mass, which is after 5 o'clock in winter and about 4 in summer, meetings are held in all parish churches, and so arranged that a person may surely be able to come to two of them. First at these services, the Public Confession of Sin is recited. It is followed by a Christian exhortation from Scripture. After that, an appropriate pause is observed for a special silent prayer, which the Minister brings to a close with a collect in keeping with the subject or according to the occasion and spirit, and then with the blessing. This is called The Morning Prayer.

Second: there is a Sermon in the cathedral every day about 8 o'clock, summer and winter.

Third: there is an evening Sermon in the cathedral at 4 o'clock in summer, or earlier if convenient, but at 3 in wintertime.

Since, alas, the holy days are always misused by the common people to do wicked things, and since there are scarcely any days on which God is more disgraced and profaned [corrected from prefaned], let us not insist that any holiday be kept the whole day except Sunday. It is desirable that that weekly day of rest might be kept holy by the worship of God. With regard to the other glorious days which commemorate the works of our redemption—such as the Incarnation and birth of our Lord Jesus, His Passion, Ascension and the like—these are observed in Sermons. Yet when those Sermons are over, no one is kept from his physical work. Moreover, the congregation is assisted daily by that which constitutes a true holiday, namely: Christian assemblies are held for the exercise of Word and prayer, and for the practice of spiritual works. But Christmas is generally a complete holiday, and a few other days as well.

This is how Sundays are kept. First, early morning prayer is conducted in the cathedral as usual. After that, about 6 o'clock, the Assistants hold a Sermon and exhortation for the domestic servants in the neighboring parish churches. Soon after, the congregation having assembled, the Pastor comes in and goes before the Altar-Table, which has been placed near the people, so that everyone may understand every word. And he begins the Common Worship with more or less the following words: he may add to it or abbreviate it according to the demands of time and occasion.

The Confession

Make confession to God the Lord, and let everyone acknowledge with me his sin and iniquity.

Almighty, eternal God and Father, we confess and acknowledge unto thee that we were conceived in unrighteousness and are full of sin and transgression in all our life. We do not fully believe thy Word nor follow thy holy commandments. Remember thy goodness, we beseech thee, and for thy Name's sake be gracious unto us, and forgive us our iniquity which, alas, is great.

Another Confession[5]

Almighty, eternal God and Father, we confess and acknowledge that we, alas, were conceived and born in sin, and are therefore inclined to all evil and slow to all good; that we transgress thy holy commandments without ceasing, and ever more corrupt ourselves. But we are sorry for the same, and beseech thy grace and help. Wherefore have mercy upon us, most gracious and merciful God and Father, through thy Son our Lord Jesus Christ. Grant to us and increase in us thy Holy Spirit, that we may recognize our sin and unrighteousness from the bottom of our hearts, attain true repentance and sorrow for them, die to them wholly, and please thee entirely by a new and godly life. Amen.

Another[6]

I poor sinner confess to thee, O Almighty, eternal, merciful God and Father, that I have sinned in manifold ways against thee and thy commandments.

I confess that I have not believed in thee, my one God and Father, but have put my faith and trust more in creatures than in thee, my God and Creator, because I have feared them more than thee. And for their benefit and pleasure, I have done and left undone many things in disobedience to thee and thy commandments.

I confess that I have taken thy holy Name in vain, that I have often sworn falsely and lightly by the same, that I have not always professed it nor kept it holy as I ought; but even more, I have slandered it often and grossly with all my life, words and deeds.

I confess that I have not kept thy Sabbath holy, that I have not heard thy holy Word with earnestness nor lived according to the same; moreover that I have not yielded myself fully to thy divine hand, nor rejoiced in thy work done in me and in others, but have often grumbled against it stoutly and have been impatient.

I confess that I have not honored my father and mother, that I have been disobedient to all whom, I justly owe obedience, such as father and mother, my superiors, and all who have tried to guide and teach me faithfully. I confess that I have taken life: that I have offended my neighbor often and grossly by word and deed, caused him harm, grown angry over him, borne envy and hatred toward him, deprived him of his honor and the like.

I confess that I have been unchaste. I acknowledge all my sins of the flesh and all the excess and extravagance of my whole life in eating, drinking, clothing and other things; my intemperance in seeing, hearing, speaking, etc., and in all my life; yea, even fornication, adultery and such.

I confess that I have stolen. I acknowledge my greed. I admit that in the use of my worldly goods I have set myself against thee and thy holy laws. Greedily and against charity have I grasped them. And scarcely, if at all, have I given of them when the need of my neighbor required it.

I confess that I have born false witness, that I have been untrue and unfaithful toward my neighbor. I have lied to him, I have told lies about him, and I have failed to defend his honor and reputation as my own.

And finally I confess that I have coveted the possessions and spouses of others. I acknowledge in summary that my whole life is nothing else than sin and transgression of thy holy commandments and an inclination toward all evil.

Wherefore I beseech thee, O heavenly Father, that, thou wouldst graciously forgive me these and all my sins. Keep and preserve me henceforth that I may walk only in thy way and live according to thy will; and all of this through Jesus Christ, thy dear Son, our Saviour. Amen.

An Absolution or Word of Comfort: 1 Tim. 1

This is a faithful saying, and worthy of all acceptation, that Christ Jesus came into the world to save sinners.

Let everyone, with St. Paul, truly acknowledge this in his heart and believe in Christ. Thus, in His name, I proclaim unto you the forgiveness of all your sins, and declare you to be loosed of them on earth, that you be loosed of them also in heaven, in eternity. Amen.

Sometimes he uses other passages which assure us of the forgiveness of sins and of Christ's ransom for our sin,

such as John 3 [16]
or in the forementioned place [John 3:35f.]
or Acts 10 [43]
or 1 John 2 [1f.]

Thereafter the church begins to sing a Psalm or hymn instead of the Introit; and sometimes the Kyrie eleison and the Gloria in excelsis.

When the singing is over, the Minister offers a short prayer for grace and a right spirit, that the Sermon and Word of God which are to follow may be heard with profit. The prayer is to this effect:

The Lord be with you.

Let us pray.

Almighty, gracious Father, forasmuch as our whole salvation depends upon our true understanding of thy holy Word, grant to all of us that our hearts, being freed from worldly affairs, may hear and apprehend thy holy Word with all diligence and faith, that we may rightly understand thy gracious will, cherish it, and live by it with all earnestness, to thy praise and honor; through our Lord Jesus Christ. Amen.

Then the church sings a Psalm or, if it is too long, several verses at the direction of the precentor [leader of congregational singing]. And the Minister goes to the pulpit and reads out of one of the Gospels as much as he proposes to expound in a single sermon, treating the book in succession. Since the Gospels have described the words and works of our Lord quite clearly, it is the custom of Sunday morning generally to preach from one of the Gospels, more than from other books; and they should be dealt with in their order, not as heretofore by picking out several pieces, often without particular skill, so that all the other things given in the Gospels have been withheld from the congregation. In the afternoon and at other hours, the other biblical books are also expounded.

Near the end of the Sermon, the Minister explains the action of the Lord's Supper and exhorts the people to observe the same with right faith and true devotion. This said exhortation usually contains four points:

The first: that, since the Lord now wishes to communicate his body and blood to us, we should reflect upon the fact that our body and blood—which means, our whole nature—are corrupted to all evil and thus to eternal death, so that they of themselves may nevermore share in the Kingdom of God. 1 Cor. 15.

The second: that to deliver us from such corruption, the eternal Word of God became flesh, so that there might be a holy flesh and blood: this is to say, a truly divine man, through whom the flesh and blood of us all would be restored and sanctified. And this happens as we truly eat and drink of His body and blood.

The third: that the Lord truly offers and gives His holy and sanctifying body and blood to us in the Holy Supper, with the visible things of bread and wine, through the ministry of the Church, as His holy Word declares: "Take and eat, this is my body which is given for you; Drink ye all of it, this is my blood which is shed for you for the forgiveness of sin." And we must accept this Word of the Lord with simple faith, and doubt not that He, the Lord Himself, is in the midst of us through the external ministry of the Church which He Himself has ordained for that purpose. Such does He proclaim to us with His own words: that the bread which we break may truly be, even for us, the communion of His body, and the cup with which we give thanks, the communion of His blood. 1 Cor. 10. But we must always diligently consider why the Lord thus imparts to us His holy, sanctifying communion in the holy sacrament: namely, that He may ever more live in us, and that we may be one body in Him our Head, even as we all partake here of one bread. 1 Cor. 10.

The fourth: that in this action, we keep the Lord's memorial and feast with true devotion and thankfulness, so that we always laud and praise Him in all our words and deeds, yea with our whole life, for all His benefits: for his Incarnation and bitter death whereby He has paid for our sin; for this blessed communion of His body and blood; that is, for Himself entire, who is true God and man, through whom alone we obtain the true and blessed life and live both here and in eternity.

When, however, the holy Supper is not held—as in the case of the neighboring parish churches where it is now observed but once a month (though in the cathedral, every Sunday)—but children are there to be baptized, the mystery of Baptism is explained and the people are exhorted to a truly sacred use of this holy sacrament.

At the conclusion of the Sermon, the people sing the Creed[7] *or else, according to the occasion, a Psalm or hymn. Thereafter, if the holy Supper is to be observed, the Minister stands behind the Table and speaks to the people.*

The Lord be with you.

Let us pray.

Then he leads the prayer, with these or similar words:

Almighty, merciful God and Father, thou who hast promised us though thy Son that whatsoever we ask of thee in His name thou wilt grant unto us, and hast also commanded us through thy Spirit to pray for those in authority and for all men: We do heartily beseech thee through Jesus Christ, thy most-beloved Son our Saviour, to enlighten with the knowledge of thy Gospel the hearts of our lord Emperor and King, all princes and nobles, and the magistrates and ruling body of this city, that they and all those in power may acknowledge thee as their sovereign and true Lord, serve thee with fear and trembling, and rule over us, who are the work of thy hand and the sheep of thy pasture, according to thy will and good pleasure.

Grant that all men everywhere may come to knowledge of the truth. Especially to this congregation, being assembled in thy name, send forth thy Holy Spirit, the Master and Teacher, who may write thy law upon our hearts, take away our blindness, and lead us to recognize our sin, which otherwise, alas, is death, and its baseness and shame is concealed. Make it vivid to us, O Lord, and enlighten our eyes that we may see the truth and recognize indeed that there is nothing in us except mere sin, death, hell and the deserved wrath of God, So, may we hunger and thirst after the rich well-spring of thy goodness and grace, and gratefully accept the same which thou hast delivered to us through thine only-begotten Son, who, having become like unto men and us poor sinners, suffered and died and rose from the dead, in order that He may save us from sin, death, and hell, and bring us to the resurrection and our inheritance of the Kingdom of God.

And grant us, O Lord and Father, that with true faith we may keep this Supper of thy dear Son, our Lord Jesus, as He hath ordained it, so that we verily receive and enjoy the true communion of His body and blood, of our Saviour Himself, who is the only saving bread of heaven. In this holy sacrament, He wishes to offer and give Himself so that He may live in us, and we in Him, being members of His body and serving thee fruitfully in every way to the common edification of thy Church, being set free from every passion of our evil, corrupted flesh, from all anger, vexation, envy, hatred, selfishness, lewdness, unchastity, and what more there may be of the damned work of the flesh: To the end that, by all means, we as thine obedient children may ever lift our hearts and souls unto thee in true childlike trust, and always call upon thee, saying as our only Master and Saviour, our Lord Jesus Christ, hath taught us:

Our Father . . .

Another Prayer[8]

Almighty, heavenly Father, thou hast promised us through thy Son, our Lord Jesus Christ, that whatsoever we ask in His name, thou wilt grant unto us, and hast commanded us to petition thee for all men, and especially for those in authority: we do therefore beseech thee, dear faithful Father, through thy Son our Saviour, for our lord Emperor and king, all princes and nobles, and also for the magistrates of this city. Grant thy Spirit and a godly fear unto those whom thou hast surely set over us as lords in thy stead, that they may administer their office to thine honor and according to thy will, in order that thy children everywhere may lead a calm and quiet life, in all godliness and propriety.

We pray thee moreover for all whose duty it is to proclaim thy holy Word and be pastors of thy Church. Grant them thy Word and Spirit that they may serve thee in such wise that all of thine elect may be gathered unto thee, and that those who already bear thy name and are counted as Christians may live agreeably to their call, to thy glory and the edification of thy Church.

We beseech thee also for those whom thou dost chasten through sickness and other adversity. Enable them to perceive thy gracious hand and accept thy discipline for their amendment, that in thy grace thou mayest also impart to them thy comfort and help.

We pray thee moreover for those who do not yet apprehend thy holy Gospel, but remain in error and depravity. Enlighten their eyes that they also may recognize thee as their God and Creator, and be converted to thy will.

Heavenly Father, we pray thee even for ourselves who are gathered here. Grant that we may be gathered in thy name. Drive from our hearts and souls all things which displease thee. Enable us to understand that we live and move and have our being in thee, also that our sins are so great and so abominable before thee that neither thy grace nor the life could have been restored to us except through the death of thy Son, our Lord Jesus Christ. Enable us to grasp by true faith that such love dost thou have for us that thou hast given thy dear Son in death for us, so that when we believe in Him we shall not perish but have everlasting life. Merciful God and Father, draw our hearts and souls to this thy Son, so that—as He presents Himself to us in His holy Gospel and sacraments, and bestows His body and blood that we who are corrupt in ourselves may live in Him—we may receive such a love as His with living faith and eternal gratitude, and therefore die to all evil more and more each day, grow and increase in all goodness, and lead our lives in all propriety, patience, and love toward our neighbor. Thereto doth our Lord call and incite us so kindly through His holy Gospel and the sacraments. Wherefore grant us, O heavenly Father, that we may now receive and enjoy the same in sincere faith to our salvation, and always as true and living members of Him who is our Lord and thy dear Son, and be through Him thy true and obedient children who ever call upon thee and pray to thee in a right spirit and from truly believing hearts: saying as He Himself hath taught us:

Our Father . . .

Another Prayer[9]

Almighty God, heavenly Father, thou hast promised us through thy dear Son, our Lord Jesus Christ, that whatsoever we ask of thee in His name thou wilt grant unto us. Thy very Son our Lord hath taught us, by Himself and by His beloved apostles, to assemble in His name, and hath promised to be there in the midst of us, and to procure and obtain for us at thy hand whatever we agree to ask of thee on earth. And especially hath He commanded us to pray for those whom thou hast set over us as magistrates and rulers; and then for all the desires both of thy people and of all men. Forasmuch as we have all come together, before thine eyes, to thy praise, and in the name of thy Son our Lord Jesus: we do heartily beseech thee, merciful God and Father, through thy most-beloved Son our only Saviour, graciously to forgive us all our sin and iniquity; and lift our hearts and souls unto thee that we may be able to beseech and implore thee with all our heart, according to thy will and pleasure which alone are righteous.

Wherefore we beseech thee, O heavenly Father, for our most gracious rulers, thy servants: our lord Emperor and King, and all the princes and nobles, and the magistrates of this city. Grant unto them thy holy and right-sovereign Spirit, and ever increase the same in them, that they may acknowledge thee in true faith as the King of all kings and Lord of all lords, and thy Son our Lord Jesus as Him to whom thou hast given all power in heaven and earth; and so may they rule over their subjects, the work of thy hand and the sheep of thy pasture, according to thy good pleasure, that we here and everywhere may lead a quiet, peaceful life in all godliness and propriety, and, being delivered from the fear of our enemies, serve thee in all righteousness and holiness.

Moreover we beseech thee, O faithful Father and Saviour, for all those whom thou hast established over thy faithful people as pastors and curates of souls, and to whom thou hast intrusted the ministration of thy holy Gospel. Grant them thy Holy Spirit and increase the same in them, that they will be found faithful, and will always serve thee in such wise that thy poor erring lambs everywhere will be gathered to Christ thy Son, their chief Shepherd and Bishop, and daily be raised up in Him unto all holiness and righteousness, to the eternal praise of thy name.

Merciful God and gracious Father, we beseech thee further for all mankind. As it is thy will to be known as a Saviour to all the world, draw to thy Son, our Lord Jesus, those who are still estranged from Him. And those whom thou hast drawn to Him and taught that through Him alone, our only Mediator, thou wilt pardon our sin and show every grace: grant that they may prosper daily in such knowledge, that, being filled with the fruit of all good works, they may live without scandal, to thy praise and the edification of their neighbor, and await with sure hope the advent and the day of thy Son our Lord. And those whom thou holdest in special discipline, whom thou dost visit and chasten with poverty, misery, sickness, imprisonment, and other adversity: O Father of mercy and Lord of all consolation, enable them to perceive thy gracious, fatherly hand, that they may turn their whole hearts to thee who alone dost chasten them, so that thou wilt comfort them as a Father and finally deliver them from all evil.

And to all of us here gathered before thee, in the name of thy Son and at His Table, grant, O God and Father, that we may truly and profoundly recognize the sin and depravity in which we were born, and into which we thrust ourselves deeper and deeper by our sinful life. And as there is nothing good in our flesh, yea, as our flesh and blood cannot inherit thy kingdom, grant that we may yield ourselves with all our heart in true faith to thy Son, our only Redeemer and Saviour. And since, for our sake, He hath not only sacrificed to thee His own body and blood upon the Cross for our sin, but also wishes to give them to us for food and drink unto eternal life, grant that we may now accept with entire longing and devotion His goodness and gift, and with right faith receive and enjoy His true body and true blood, yea, Himself our Saviour, true God and man, the only true bread of heaven: That we may live no more our sinful and depraved life, but that He in us and we in Him may live His holy, blessed and eternal life, being verily the partakers of the true and eternal testament, the covenant of grace, sure and certain that thou wilt be our gracious Father forever, who nevermore reckons our sins against us and makes all manner of provision for us in body and soul as thy dear children and heirs: so that we may at all times render praise and thanks to thee, and glorify thy holy name with all our words and deeds. Wherefore, O heavenly Father, grant that we may celebrate today the glorious and blessed memorial of thy dear Son our Lord, and shew forth His death, that we shall ever grow and be strengthened in faith to thee and in all good works. And so, greatly comforted, we do now and always call upon thee, our God and Father, and pray to thee as our Lord hath taught us to pray, saying:

Our Father . . .[10]

At the conclusion of this prayer, the Minister makes a short exhortation, if he has not done so at the end of the Sermon, to the effect that the Holy Supper is to be observed with true faith and meet devotion; and he explains this Mystery.

After such an exhortation and explanation, the Minister reads the words of the Lord, as the holy Evangelists and Paul have recorded them.

The Institution of the Lord's Supper

In the same night in which the Lord Jesus was betrayed, while they were eating, He took the bread, and brake it, and gave it to His disciples, and said:

Take, eat, this is my body which is given for you; do this in remembrance of me. In the same manner He also took the cup after the supper, gave thanks, and offered it to them, and said: Drink ye all of it; this is the new testament in my blood, which is shed for you and for many for the forgiveness of sins; this do ye, as oft as ye drink it, in remembrance of me.

Forthwith the Minister speaks in these words:

Believe in the Lord, and give eternal praise and thanks unto Him!

Herewith he distributes the bread and cup of the Lord, first saying these words:

Remember, believe and proclaim that Christ the Lord has died for you.

Thereupon the church sings "Gott sey gelobet" [God be Praised] or another Psalm appropriate to the occasion.

After the singing, he once again offers a prayer, in this wise:

The Lord be with you.

Let us pray.

Grant unto us, O heavenly Father, that the remembrance of our redemption may never leave our hearts, but that we may walk in Christ, the Light of the world, far removed from our foolish reason and blind wills, which are vain and injurious darkness; through Christ Jesus our Lord. Amen.

Almighty God, heavenly Father, we give thee eternal praise and thanks that thou hast been so gracious unto us poor sinners, having drawn us to thy Son our Lord Jesus, whom thou hast delivered to death for us and given to be our nourishment and our dwelling unto eternal life. Grant that we may never relinquish these things from our hearts, but ever grow and increase in faith to thee, which, through love, is effective of all good works. And so may our whole life be devoted to thy praise and the edification of our neighbor; through the same Jesus Christ, thy Son, our Lord. Amen.[11]

Another Thanksgiving

Almighty, gracious, heavenly Father, we give thee eternal praise and thanks that, through thy holy Gospel and Sacrament, thou hast again offered and presented to us thy most precious treasure: the true bread of heaven and food of eternal life, our Lord Jesus Christ. And we heartily beseech thee to grant that we may receive Him and partake of Him in true faith now and forever, and be so nourished by His flesh and blood that we may be set free from all evil and increase daily in all goodness, to thy glory; through the same Jesus Christ our Lord. Amen.

Another Thanksgiving

We give thee eternal praise and thanks, O heavenly Father, that thou hast drawn us poor sinners to thy dear Son, our Lord Jesus Christ, and hast again imparted to us His true communion. And we beseech thee, grant to us that this holy communion may always be effective and strong in us, so that in true faith, propriety, patience and love, sparing no diligence, we may lead a new and heavenly life wholly pleasing unto thee, to thy praise and honor and to the edification of our neighbor; through the same &c.

The Blessing: Num. in the 6 chap. The Lord bless you and keep you; the Lord make His face to shine upon you, and be gracious unto you; the Lord lift up His countenance upon you and give you peace.

Depart! The Spirit of the Lord go with you unto eternal life! Amen.

Following the meal on Sunday, there is another Sermon in the cathedral, before and after which the holy psalms are also sung and common prayer conducted. Shortly after this Sermon, the Minister holds instruction for the children in the cathedral, except in wintertime, namely, when the children might suffer on account of the cold. He explains to them the Ten Commandments, the Creed and the Lord's Prayer in succession, about which he asks them questions, and thus drills them in the knowledge of our Lord Jesus Christ.

A similar exercise is also held in the other parish churches at the time of Vesper Prayer, which comes after the two services. Psalms are sung at the beginning and the end, and the prayer is concluded with a collect which is directed to the subject of discussion. At this time, provision is also made for the observance of Holy Baptism, if children are present to be baptized.

Four times a year, congregational catechization takes place in all the parish churches, morning and afternoon. The common matters of our Christian religion are treated, and expounded with a short and simple explanation: the Articles of our holy Christian faith, the Ten Commandments and Lord's Prayer, the understanding of the holy sacraments, and whatever else may be fruitfully brought up in connection with the elementary instruction of our Christian religion within the allotted time.

Notes

1. See *Liturgies of the Western Church*, ed. Bard Thompson (Cleveland: World Publishing Company, 1961), 159–66; William D. Maxwell, *John Knox's Genevan Service Book, 1556* (Edinburgh: Oliver and Boyd, 1931), 27–32; and Hughes Oliphant Old, *The Patristic Roots of Reformed Worship* (Zurich: Theologischer Verlag, 1975), 39–42.

2. See Friedrich Hubert, *Die Strassburger liturgischen Ordnungen im Zeitalter der Reformation* (Göttingen: Vandenhoeck and Ruprecht, 1900), 71–74, 88–114.

3. See W. Peter Stephens, *The Holy Spirit in the Theology of Martin Bucer* (Cambridge: Cambridge University Press, 1970), 250–57; and Old, 80–87.

4. According to Bard Thompson, the editor of this version of the liturgy, his source is F. Hubert, *Die Strassburger liturgischen Ordnungen im Zeitalter der Reformation*. The following notes are those of Bard Thompson.

5. This Confiteor [Confession] was probably written by Bucer himself. It was the one that Calvin used. An enlarged, English version first appeared in John Knox's Genevan Service Book, 1556.

6. The third Confiteor is based upon the Ten Commandments, each of which prompts a paragraph of confession. Perhaps Bucer's use of the Commandments invited Calvin to introduce the singing of the Law in the first part of his own Strassburg liturgy.

7. The Apostles' Creed. Immediately after the Creed, the bread and wine were brought to the Table.

8. An alternate form. Bucer provided three alternates of the Great Prayer. The first was traditional in Strassburg. The second and third were added ca. 1536. It was the third that Calvin adopted with slight alterations.

9. See note 8.

10. Matt. 6:9–13, including the Matthean doxology.

11. Calvin's Post-Communion thanksgiving is an adaptation of this prayer. An expanded version is found in the *Book of Common Order*.

18. The Form of Church Prayers and Hymns with the Manner of Administering the Sacraments and Consecrating Marriage according to the Custom of the Ancient Church

(GENEVA, 1542; STRASBOURG, 1545)

JOHN CALVIN

The changes promoted by John Calvin (1509–64) when he first came to Geneva in 1536 were unpopular, and he was forced to leave Geneva in 1538. Eventually he went to Strasbourg to serve a congregation of French refugees. In Strasbourg he prepared a French liturgy, which, with a few modifications, was adopted in Geneva when he returned. The Genevan liturgy was later taken up by French Huguenot churches as well.[1]

Calvin's French liturgy was modeled after Martin Bucer's Strasbourg Liturgy (see vol. 2:280–94), itself a revision of earlier German Strasbourg services patterned after the Mass. Calvin's liturgy, therefore, is not an original creation, but a new look at the Mass informed by Scripture and the writers of the ancient church.[2]

Calvin borrowed and adapted material from Bucer's liturgy of 1537–39, in particular the second form of the prayer of confession, the third form of the Great Prayer, and the first prayer of thanksgiving after the supper. Calvin's Strasbourg service followed Bucer's by having a formula of absolution, which was not permitted in Geneva.

Calvin also affirmed Bucer's directive that preaching should be based on "the continuous reading of Scripture."[3] *Impressed by psalm singing in*

SOURCE: Bard Thompson, ed., *Liturgies of the Western Church* (Cleveland: The World Publishing Co., 1961). Used by permission of Harcourt, Brace & Company.

the Strasbourg German congregations, Calvin introduced psalm singing into his French service. He had earlier expressed a desire for the singing of psalms in the first edition of the Institutes *(see vol. 2:308–11).*

Already, back in 1536, he had also declared his view that the Eucharist should be celebrated at least once a week. He found that Bucer agreed with him, and he was pleased with that practice in the cathedral at Strasbourg. Unfortunately, when he returned to Geneva, the magistrate would not even permit his suggested compromise of holding the Eucharist once a month. As a result, the generally infrequent celebration of the Lord's Supper among congregations within the Reformed tradition would have had little support from the two principal designers of the service, Calvin and Bucer.

There are, however, some important differences between the liturgies of Calvin and Bucer. First, in Calvin's service, the creed (the Apostles' Creed) is a part of the celebration of the supper, whereas for Bucer it follows the sermon, coming before the Communion. Furthermore, the eucharistic prayer, which in Bucer's Strasbourg service was joined immediately with the prayer of intercession, is given its own position in Calvin's Communion service in both the Strasbourg and Geneva versions.

Calvin's liturgy connects church discipline with the Eucharist. Preceding the invitation to the supper, Calvin calls for the excommunication of all public sinners. This change was probably derived from Guillaume (or William) Farel's French Service Book *(1533), which took it from the Basel* Service Book *(1526) by John Oecolampadius, principal reformer of that city and the first sixteenth-century reformer to link church discipline and the sacraments.*[4]

Finally, the Reformed sursum corda *("Let us lift our spirits and our hearts on high where Jesus Christ is in the glory of his Father"), at the conclusion of the exhortation and before the distribution of the elements, comes from Farel, not Bucer.*[5] *This* sursum corda *is a prominent feature of later Reformed worship, including the Palatinate Liturgy (see vol. 2:359–76).*

According to the Genevan service, the essentials of worship are (1) gratitude, (2) a sense of unworthiness, and (3) obedience to the majestic, gracious God for God's gift of salvation. With Calvin and Bucer, worship is an act of God before it is ever an act of humanity. In fact, human worship in faith, gratitude, and obedience to God's acts in creation and redemption is made possible only by the work of the Holy Spirit. Worship is not so much an individual activity as a corporate celebration. For all these reasons, Calvin argued that the Communion ought to be celebrated as often as possible.

The Form of Church Prayers[6]

On working days, the Minister frames the sort of exhortation to prayer which may seem suitable to him, adapting it to the times and to the topic of his Sermon.

On Sunday morning [and on the day of prayers], the following form is generally used.

Our help is in the name of the Lord, who made heaven and earth. Amen.

Confession

My brethren, let each of you present himself before the face of the Lord, and confess his faults and sins, following my words in his heart.

O Lord God, eternal and almighty Father, we confess and acknowledge unfeignedly before thy holy majesty that we are poor sinners, conceived and born in iniquity and corruption, prone to do evil, incapable of any good, and that in our depravity we transgress thy holy commandments without end or ceasing: Wherefore we purchase for ourselves, through thy righteous judgment, our ruin and perdition. Nevertheless, O Lord, we are grieved that we have offended thee; and we condemn ourselves and our sins with true repentance, beseeching thy grace to relieve our distress. O God and Father most gracious and full of compassion, have mercy upon us in the name of thy Son, our Lord Jesus Christ. And as thou dost blot out our sins and stains, magnify and increase in us day by day the grace of thy Holy Spirit: that as we acknowledge our unrighteousness with all our heart, we may be moved by that sorrow which shall bring forth true repentance in us, mortifying all our sins, and producing in us the fruits of righteousness and innocence which are pleasing unto thee; through the same Jesus Christ &c. [our Lord. Amen.]

Strassburg only:

Now the Minister delivers some word of Scripture to console the conscience; and then he pronounces the Absolution in this manner:

Let each of you truly acknowledge that he is a sinner, humbling himself before God, and believe that the heavenly Father wills to be gracious unto him in Jesus Christ.

To all those that repent in this wise, and look to Jesus Christ for their salvation, I declare that the absolution of sins is effected, in the name of the Father, and of the Son, and of the Holy Spirit. Amen.

Now the Congregation sings the first table of the Commandments, after which the Minister says:

The Lord be with us. Let us pray to the Lord.

Heavenly Father, full of goodness and grace, as thou art pleased to declare thy holy will unto thy poor servants, and to instruct them in the righteousness of thy law, grant that it may also be inscribed and impressed upon our hearts in such wise, that in all our life we may endeavor to serve and obey none beside thee. Neither impute to us at all the transgressions which we have committed against thy law: that, perceiving thy manifold grace upon us in such abundance, we may have cause to praise and glorify thee through Jesus Christ, thy Son, our Lord. Amen.

Strassburg:

While the Congregation sings the rest of the Commandments, the Minister goes into the pulpit; and then he offers prayers of the type which follows. [7]

Geneva:

That done, a Psalm is sung by the Congregation. Then the Minister commences again to pray, beseeching God for the grace of His Holy Spirit, that His Word may be faithfully expounded to the honor of His name and the edification of the Church, and be received with such humility and obedience which it deserves. The form is left to the discretion of the Minister.

Collect for Illumination. Lesson and Sermon

At the end of the Sermon, the Minister, having made exhortations to prayer, commences in this manner:

Almighty God, heavenly Father, thou has promised to grant our requests which we make unto thee in the name of thy well-beloved Son, Jesus Christ our Lord: by whose teaching and that of His apostles we have also been taught to gather together in His name, with the promise that He will be in the midst of us, and will be our intercessor with thee, to obtain all those things for which we agree to ask on earth.

First we have thy commandment to pray for those whom thou hast established over us as rulers and governors; and then, for all the needs of thy people, and indeed of all mankind. Wherefore, with trust in thy holy doctrine and promises, and now especially that we are gathered here before thy face and in the name of thy Son, our Lord Jesus, we do heartily beseech thee, our gracious God and Father, in the name of our only Saviour and Mediator, to grant us the free pardon of our [faults and] offenses through thine infinite mercy, and to draw and lift up our thoughts and desires unto thee in such wise that we may be able to call upon thee with all our heart, yea agreeably to thy good pleasure and only-reasonable will.

Wherefore we pray thee, O heavenly Father, for all princes and lords, thy servants, to whom thou hast intrusted the administration of thy justice, and especially for the magistrates of this city. May it please thee to impart to them thy Spirit, who alone is good and truly sovereign, and daily stablish them in the same, that with true faith they may acknowledge Jesus Christ, thy Son, our Lord, to be the King of kings and Lord of lords, as thou hast given Him all power in heaven and earth. May they seek to serve Him and to exalt His kingdom in their government, guiding and ruling their subjects, who are the work of thy hands and the sheep of thy pasture, in accordance with thy good pleasure. So may all of us both here and throughout the earth, being kept in perfect peace and quietness, serve thee in all godliness and virtue, and being delivered and protected from the fear of our enemies, give praise unto thee all the days of our life.

We pray thee also, O faithful Father and Saviour, for all those whom thou hast ordained pastors of thy faithful people, to whom thou hast intrusted the care of souls and the ministry of thy holy Gospel. Direct and guide them by thy Holy Spirit, that they may be found faithful and loyal ministers of thy glory, having but one goal: that all the poor, wandering, and lost sheep be gathered and restored to the Lord Jesus Christ, the chief Shepherd and Prince of bishops, so that they may grow and increase in Him daily unto all righteousness and holiness. Wilt thou, on the contrary, deliver all the churches from the mouths of ravening wolves and from all mercenaries who seek their own ambition or profit, but never the exaltation of thy holy name alone, nor the salvation of thy flock.[8]

We pray thee now, O most gracious and merciful Father, for all men everywhere. As it is thy will to be acknowledged the Saviour of the whole world, through the redemption wrought by thy Son Jesus Christ, grant that those who are still estranged from the knowledge of Him, being in the darkness and captivity of error and ignorance, may be brought by the illumination of thy Holy Spirit and the preaching of thy Gospel to the straight way of salvation, which is to know thee, the only true God, and Jesus Christ whom thou hast sent. Grant that those whom thou hast already visited with thy grace and enlightened with the knowledge of thy Word may grow in goodness day by day, enriched by thy spiritual blessings: so that all together we may worship thee with one heart and one voice, giving honor and reverence to thy [Son Jesus] Christ, our Master, King, and Lawgiver.

Likewise, O God of all comfort, we commend unto thee all those whom thou dost visit and chasten with cross and tribulation, whether by poverty, prison, sickness, or banishment, or any other misery of the body or affliction of the spirit. Enable them to perceive and understand thy fatherly affection which doth chasten them unto their correction, that they may turn unto thee with their whole heart, and, having turned, receive full consolation and deliverance from every ill.

Finally, O God and Father, grant also to those who are gathered here in the name of thy Son Jesus, to hear His Word (and to keep His holy Supper),[9] that we may acknowledge truly, without hypocrisy, what perdition is ours by nature, what condemnation we deserve and heap upon ourselves from day to day by our unhappy and disordered life. Wherefore, seeing that there is nothing of good in us and that our flesh and blood cannot inherit thy kingdom, may we yield ourselves completely, with all our love and steadfast faith, to thy dear Son, our Lord, the only Saviour and Redeemer:

To the end that He, dwelling in us, may mortify our old Adam, renewing us for a better life, by which thy name, according as it is holy and worthy, may be exalted and glorified everywhere and in all places, and that we with all creatures may give thee true and perfect obedience, even as thine angels and heavenly messengers have no desire but to fulfil thy commandments. Thus may thy will be done without any contradiction, and all men apply themselves to serve and please thee, renouncing their own will and all the desires of their flesh. In this manner mayest thou have lordship and dominion over us all, and may we learn more and more each day to submit and subject ourselves to thy majesty. In such wise mayest thou be King and Ruler over all the earth, guiding thy people by the sceptre of thy Word and the power of thy Spirit, confounding thine enemies by the might of thy truth and righteousness. And thus may every power and principality which stands against thy glory be destroyed and abolished day by day, till the fulfillment of thy kingdom be manifest, when thou shalt appear in judgment.

Grant that we who walk in the love and fear of thy name may be nourished by thy goodness; and supply us with all things necessary and expedient to eat our bread in peace. Then, seeing that thou carest for us, we may better acknowledge thee as our Father and await all good gifts from thy hand, withdrawing our trust from all creatures, to place it entirely in thee and thy goodness.

And since in this mortal life we are poor sinners, so full of weakness that we fail continually and stray from the right way, may it please thee to pardon our faults by which we are beholden to thy judgment; and through that remission, deliver us from the obligation of eternal death in which we stand. Be pleased, therefore, to turn aside thy wrath from us, neither impute to us the iniquity which is in us; even as we, by reason of thy commandment, forget the injuries done to us, and instead of seeking vengeance, solicit the good for our enemies.

Finally, may it please thee to sustain us by thy power for the time to come, that we may not stumble because of the weakness of our flesh. And especially as we of ourselves are so frail that we are not able to stand fast for a single moment, while, on the other hand, we are continually beset and assailed by so many enemies—the devil, the world, sin, and our own flesh never ceasing to make war upon us—wilt thou strengthen us by thy Holy Spirit and arm us with thy grace, that we may be able to resist all temptations firmly, and persevere in this spiritual battle until we shall attain full victory, to triumph at last in thy kingdom with our Captain and Protector, Jesus Christ our Lord.

Geneva only:

On those days when the Lord's Supper is to be celebrated, that which follows is joined to the preceding:

And as our Lord Jesus has not only offered His body and blood once on the Cross for the remission of our sins, but also desires to impart them to us as our nourishment unto everlasting life, grant us this grace: that we may receive at His hands such a great benefit and gift with true sincerity of heart and with ardent zeal. In steadfast faith may we receive His body and blood, yea Christ Himself entire, who being true God and true man, is verily the holy bread and heaven which gives us life. So may we live no longer in ourselves, after our nature which is entirely corrupt and vicious, but may He live in us and lead us to the life that is holy, blessed and everlasting: whereby we may truly become partakers of the new and eternal testament, the covenant of grace, assured that it is thy good pleasure to be our gracious Father forever, never reckoning our faults against us, and to provide for us, as thy well-beloved children and heirs, all our needs both of body and soul. Thus may we render praise and thanks unto thee without ceasing and magnify thy name in word and deed.

Grant us, therefore, O heavenly Father, so to celebrate this day the blessed memorial and remembrance of thy dear Son, to exercise ourselves in the same, and to proclaim the benefit of His death, that, receiving new growth and strength in faith and in all things good, we may with so much greater confidence proclaim thee our Father and glory in thee. Amen.

When the Supper has been completed, this thanksgiving, or one similar, is used:

Heavenly Father, we offer thee eternal praise and thanks that thou hast granted so great a benefit to us poor sinners, having drawn us into the Communion of thy Son, Jesus Christ our Lord, whom thou hast delivered to death for us, and whom thou givest us as the meat and drink of life eternal. Now grant us this other benefit: that thou wilt never allow us to forget these things; but having them imprinted on our hearts, may we grow and increase daily in the faith which is at work in every good deed. Thus may we order and pursue all our life to the exaltation of thy glory and the edification of our neighbor; through the same Jesus Christ, thy Son, who in the unity of the Holy Spirit liveth and reigneth with thee, O God, forever. Amen.

Strassburg:

At the end a Psalm is sung, after which the Minister dismisses the Congregation, saying:

Geneva:

The blessing which is given at the departure of the people, according to our Lord's appointment. Num. 6.

The Lord bless you and keep you. The Lord make His face to shine upon you and be merciful unto you. The Lord lift up His countenance upon you and keep you in virtuous prosperity. Amen.

The Manner of Celebrating the Lord's Supper

It is proper to observe that on the Sunday prior to the celebration of the Lord's Supper, the following admonitions are made to the people: first, that each person prepare and dispose himself to receive it worthily and with such reverence that it deserves; second, that children may certainly not be brought forward unless they are well instructed and have made profession of their faith in church; third, that if strangers are there who may still be untaught and ignorant, they proceed to present themselves for private instruction. On the day of the Lord's Supper, the Minister touches upon it in the conclusion of his Sermon, or better, if there is occasion, preaches the whole Sermon about it, in order to explain to the people what our Lord wishes to say and signify by this mystery, and in what way it behooves us to receive it.

Strassburg:

Then, after the accustomed prayers have been offered, the Congregation, in making confession of the faith, sings the

Geneva:

Then, having made the prayers and the Confession of Faith (which is to testify in the name of the people that they all wish to live and die in

Apostles' Creed to testify that all wish to live and die in the Christian doctrine and religion. Meanwhile, the Minister prepares the bread and wine on the Table. Thereafter he prays in this fashion:

the Christian doctrine and religion), he says in a loud voice:

Strassburg only:

Inasmuch as we have made confession of our faith to testify that we are children of God, hoping therefore that He will take heed of us as a gracious Father, let us pray to Him, saying:

Heavenly Father, full of all goodness and mercy, as our Lord Jesus Christ has not only offered His body and blood once on the Cross for the remission of our sins, but also desires to impart them to us as our nourishment unto everlasting life, we beseech thee to grant us this grace: that we may receive at His hands such a great gift and benefit with true sincerity of heart and with ardent zeal. In steadfast faith may we receive His body and blood, yea Christ Himself entire, who, being true God and true man, is verily the holy bread of heaven which gives us life. So may we live no longer in ourselves, after our nature which is entirely corrupt and vicious, but may He live in us and lead us to the life that is holy, blessed and everlasting: whereby we may truly become partakers of the new and eternal testament, the covenant of grace, assured that it is thy good pleasure to be our gracious Father forever, never reckoning our faults against us, and to provide for us, as thy well-beloved children and heirs, all our needs both of soul and body. Thus may we render praise and thanks unto thee without ceasing, and magnify thy name in word and deed.

Grant us, therefore, O heavenly Father, so to celebrate this day the blessed memorial and remembrance of thy dear Son, to exercise ourselves in the same, and to proclaim the benefit of His death, that, receiving new growth and strength in faith and in all things good, we may with so much greater confidence proclaim thee our Father and glory in thee; through the same Jesus Christ, thy Son, our Lord, in whose name we pray unto thee, as He hath taught us.

Our Father which art in, etc.

Strassburg & Geneva:

Then the Minister says:

Let us hear how Jesus Christ instituted His holy Supper for us, as St.

Paul relates it in the eleventh chapter of First Corinthians:

I have received of the Lord, he says, that which I have delivered unto you: That the Lord Jesus, on the night in which He was betrayed, took bread: And when He had given thanks, He brake it and said, Take, eat, this is my body which is broken for you: this do in remembrance of me. After the same manner, when He had supped, He took the cup saying, This cup is the new testament in my blood: this do ye, as oft as ye shall drink it, in remembrance of me. For as often as ye eat this bread and drink this cup, ye do proclaim the Lord's death till He come. Therefore, whosoever shall eat this bread and drink of this cup unworthily shall be guilty of the body and blood of the Lord. But let a man examine himself and so let him eat of this bread and drink of this cup. For whosoever eateth and drinketh unworthily, taketh his own condemnation, not discerning the Lord's body.

We have heard, my brethren, how our Lord observed His Supper with His disciples, from which we learn that strangers and those who do not belong to the company of His faithful people must not be admitted. Therefore, following that precept, in the name and by the authority of our Lord Jesus Christ, I excommunicate all idolaters, blasphemers and despisers of God, all heretics and those who create private sects in order to break the unity of the Church, all perjurers, all who rebel against father or mother or superior, all who promote sedition or mutiny; brutal and disorderly persons, adulterers, lewd and lustful men, thieves, ravishers, greedy and grasping people, drunkards, gluttons, and all those who lead a scandalous and dissolute life. I warn them to abstain from this Holy Table, lest they defile and contaminate the holy food which our Lord Jesus Christ gives to none except they belong to His household of faith.

Moreover, in accordance with the exhortation of St. Paul, let every man examine and prove his own conscience to see whether he truly repents of his faults and grieves over his sins, desiring to live henceforth a holy life according to God. Above all, let him see whether he has his trust in the mercy of God and seeks his salvation wholly in Jesus Christ and, renouncing all hatred and rancor, has high resolve and courage to live in peace and brotherly love with his neighbors.

If we have this witness in our hearts before God, never doubt that He claims us as His children, and that the Lord Jesus addresses His Word to us, to invite us to His Table and to give us this holy Sacrament which He imparted to His disciples.

And yet, we may be conscious of much frailty and misery in ourselves, such that we do not have perfect faith, but are inclined toward defiance and unbelief, or that we do not devote ourselves wholly to the service of God and with such zeal as we ought, but have to fight daily against the lusts of our flesh. Nevertheless, since our Lord has granted us the grace of having

His Gospel graven on our hearts, so that we may withstand all unbelief, and has given us the desire and longing to renounce our own wishes, that we may follow His righteousness and His holy commandments: let us be assured that the sins and imperfections which remain in us will not prevent Him from receiving us and making us worthy partakers of this spiritual Table. For we do not come here to testify that we are perfect or righteous in ourselves: On the contrary, by seeking our life in Jesus Christ we confess that we are in death. Know, therefore, that this Sacrament is a medicine for the poor sick souls, and that the only worthiness which our Lord requires of us is to know ourselves sufficiently to deplore our sins, and to find all our pleasure, joy and satisfaction in Him alone.

Above all, therefore, let us believe those promises which Jesus Christ, who is the unfailing truth, has spoken with His own lips: He is truly willing to make us partakers of His body and blood, in order that we may possess Him wholly and in such wise that He may live in us and we in Him. And though we see but bread and wine, we must not doubt that He accomplishes spiritually in our souls all that He shows us outwardly by these visible signs, namely, that He is the bread of heaven to feed and nourish us unto eternal life. So, let us never be unmindful of the infinite goodness of our Saviour who spreads out all His riches and blessings on this Table, to impart them to us. For in giving Himself to us, He makes a testimony to us that all that He has is ours. Therefore, let us receive this Sacrament as a pledge that the virtue of His death and passion is imputed to us for righteousness, even as though we had suffered them in our own persons. May we never be so perverse as to draw away when Jesus Christ invites us so gently by His Word. But accounting the worthiness of this precious gift which He gives, let us present ourselves to Him with ardent zeal, that He may make us capable of receiving it.

To do so, let us lift our spirits and hearts on high where Jesus Christ is in the glory of His Father, whence we expect Him at our redemption. Let us not be fascinated by these earthly and corruptible elements which we see with our eyes and touch with our hands, seeking Him there as though He were enclosed in the bread or wine. Then only shall our souls be disposed to be nourished and vivified by His substance when they are lifted up above all earthly things, attaining even to heaven, and entering the Kingdom of God where He dwells. Therefore let us be content to have the bread and wine as signs and witnesses, seeking the truth spiritually where the Word of God promises that we shall find it.[10]

Strassburg:

That done, the Minister, having informed the people that they are

Geneva:

That done, the Ministers distribute the bread and the chalice to the to come to the holy Table in reverence, good order, and Christian humility, first partakes himself of the bread and wine, then administers it to the deacon, and subsequently to the whole congregation, saying:

people, having admonished them to come forward with reverence and in good order. Meanwhile some Psalms are sung; or some portion of Scripture is read, appropriate to the significance of the sacrament. At the conclusion, Thanksgiving is offered, as it has been stated.

Take, eat, the body of Jesus which has been delivered unto death for you.

Strassburg only:
And the deacon offers the cup, saying:

This is the cup of the new testament in the blood of Jesus which has been shed for you.

Meanwhile, the Congregation sings the Psalm: Louang' et Grâce [138 "Praise and Thanksgiving"].

Thanksgiving after the Supper

Heavenly Father, we offer thee eternal praise and thanks that thou hast granted so great a benefit to us poor sinners, having drawn us into the Communion of thy Son, Jesus Christ our Lord, whom thou hast delivered to death for us, and whom thou givest us as the meat and drink of life eternal. Now grant us this other benefit: that thou wilt never allow us to forget these things; but having them imprinted on our hearts, may we grow and increase daily in the faith which is at work in every good deed. Thus may we order and pursue all our life to the exaltation of thy glory and the edification of our neighbor; through the same Jesus Christ, thy Son, who in the unity of the Holy Spirit liveth and reigneth with thee, O God, forever. Amen.

After thanks has been given, the Canticle of Simeon is sung: Maintenant Seigneur Dieu [Now Lord God].

Then the Minister dismisses the Congregation by pronouncing the Benediction used on Sunday.

Notes

1. See James Hastings Nichols, *Corporate Worship in the Reformed Tradition* (Philadelphia: Westminster Press, 1968), 57.

2. See Hughes Oliphant Old, *The Patristic Roots of Reformed Worship* (Zurich: Theologischer Verlag, 1975), 119–30, 141–55, 339.

3. See Erwin Mülhaupt, *Die Predigt Calvins, ihre Geschichte, ihre Form und ihre religiösen Grundgedanken*, vol. 18 (Berlin: W. de Gruyter, 1931), cited in Old, 201, n. 2.

4. See Old, 272; and *Liturgies of the Western Church*, ed. Bard Thompson (Cleveland: World Publishing Company, 1961), 186.

5. See note 10.

6. Bard Thompson, the editor of this version of Calvin's liturgy, makes the following comments here: Both editions of Calvin's liturgy—Strassburg and Genevan—are given in *Calvini opera*, VI, 173–84. The Strassburg edition has been edited separately by Stephen A. Hurlbut in *The Liturgy of the Church of Scotland* (Charleston: St. Albans Press, 1954), 8–23. Where differences occur between the two texts, the Strassburg version is given in the left column.

7. According to Thompson, this is the example given:

Let us call upon our Heavenly Father, Father of all goodness and mercy, beseeching Him to cast the eye of His clemency upon us, His poor servants, neither impute to us the many faults and offenses which we have committed, provoking His wrath against us. But as we look into the face of the Son, Jesus Christ our Lord, whom He hath appointed Mediator between Himself and us, let us beseech Him, in whom is all fulness of wisdom and light, to vouchsafe to guide us by His Holy Spirit into the true understanding of His holy doctrine, making it productive in us of all the fruits of righteousness: to the glory and exaltation of His name, and to the instruction and edification of His Church. And let us pray unto Him in the name and favor of His well-beloved Son, Jesus Christ, as He hath taught us to pray, saying: Our Father, which art in heaven, etc.

Calvin employed several other Collects for Illumination. He derived the following from Bucer:

Almighty and gracious Father, since our whole salvation standeth in our knowledge of thy Holy Word, strengthen us now by thy Holy Spirit that our hearts may be set free from all worldly thoughts and attachments of the flesh, so that we may hear and receive that same Word, and, recognizing thy gracious will for us, may love and serve thee with earnest delight, praising and glorifying thee in Jesus Christ our Lord. Amen."

8. According to Thompson's note here, "This sentence, while not in the 1539 edition of Bucer's liturgy, is found in certain earlier and later editions of that liturgy."

9. According to Thompson's note here, "That which is enclosed by these two marks ( ) is not said except on the day of the Lord's Supper."

10. According to Thompson's note here, "This final paragraph of the Exhortation probably came from Farel's liturgy: *La Maniere et fasson*, edited by J. G. Baum (Strasbourg: Treuttel et Wurtz, 1859), 64–65."

19. Hymn: "For Us Our God Is Firm Support" (Psalm 46)

(1539)

John Calvin

As on many other subjects, John Calvin's (1509–64) views on music in worship stood between those of Zwingli and Luther. Whereas Zwingli was opposed to music altogether, Luther was eager that music be included in services of worship, even writing new words to use with secular tunes. Calvin struck a middle ground. He felt that music could be permitted in worship, but it had to be vocal, sung in unison, scriptural (that is, based on the psalms), and solemn and dignified, not rowdy or exuberant.

Shortly after coming to Geneva in 1536, Calvin introduced the singing of psalms into the Genevan service. He and his colleague Guillaume (or William) Farel thought that singing would add more inspiration and fervor to the services of worship. Most likely, Calvin had heard that worshipers in Strasbourg were singing psalms in worship. When Calvin later found himself in Strasbourg, he became all the more impressed with the singing of psalms in the German services and determined to introduce psalm singing into the French congregation where he was pastor. Calvin wrote French metrical versions of some of the psalms and set them to tunes provided by Strasbourg composers Mattheus Greiter and Wolfgang Dachstein. These psalms were published in a psalmbook in 1539 in Strasbourg.

In spite of this success, Calvin disparaged his own work as a poet of the psalms, much preferring the work of Clément Marot, a leading poet

---

SOURCE: *The Piety of John Calvin*, ed. Ford Lewis Battles, music ed. Stanley Tagg (Grand Rapids, Mich.: Baker Book House, 1978). Used by permission.

at the court of Francis I. Not surprisingly, Marot was invited to come to Geneva in 1542. By 1551 Calvin's texts were removed from the Genevan Psalter and replaced with texts by Marot and Theodore Beza,[1] *who would be Calvin's successor in Geneva.*

Beza exercised strong leadership among Reformed Protestants in Geneva and France. In 1562 the whole Psalter was set into French metrical verse, and much of it was sung to the music of Louis Bourgeois. The most famous of these musical psalms is the "Old Hundredth." In French its versification was written by Beza, and it was set to music by Bourgeois. Its memorable English version was written by William Kethe, "All People that on Earth Do Dwell," is a notable example of the way in which the Genevan Psalter influenced the English and Scottish Psalters.[2]

The versification of Psalm 46 by Calvin with music by Dachstein was translated into English by Ford Lewis Battles, with music arranged by Stanley E. Tagg. Psalm 46 was also the psalm on which Luther based his reformation hymn "A Mighty Fortress Is Our God." Luther appropriated the psalm in the light of his religious experience and his Christocentric theology. Calvin's poetic exposition is more objective and closer to the text of the psalm. Calvin's verse (and Battles's excellent translation) reflects his personal anxieties, but it also relays Calvin's sense of worship as solemn praise of God's majesty and glory. Calvin insisted that music, like worship, should be characterized as ceaseless prayer, containing majesty, gravity, and moderation.[3]

For us our God is firm support,
Stronghold and fortress, certain help,
Wherein our plight we shall possess
A present refuge, haven safe.
Whence firm assurance we will have,
Even when we will see the earth
Trembling and quaking, now removed,
Mountains now hiding in the sea.

While seas are loudly thundering,
As if with anger fierce they swell:
And lofty crags reverberate,
Are battered, toppled by the waves.

The chosen city of our God,
House to which He has given rain:
Gentle and clear her stream will be,
And ever gladden her abode.

While God the Lord is in her midst
Firm and unmoved,
unmoved she will remain:
To aid her in both time and place
From early morning
He will watch, He will watch.
All pagan nations storm,
all nations storm with rage,
Kingdoms have been in trouble thrown,
in trouble:
But our God, chastising with His voice
Makes in a moment them all calm.

God of the armies, leader, chief,
The God of Jacob is for us:
And our protector He will be
Against our adversaries all.
Come, raise your eyes then to behold,
Each one of you now strain to see
The marvels that your God has done
In overcoming all His foes.

Only our God by His decree
Can set at peace
the whole wide earth,
And unopposed can in the world
Cause every conflict,
cause conflict now to cease.
He it is who can break,
is who can break the bows,
Shatter the warrior's spear to bits,
He shatters;

To the chariots
He will put His torch
And let them fall consumed with fire.

Now be it known to every man
That God it is who must be feared;
Because of His tremendous power,
Throughout the world exalted be.
God, ruler over heaven's hosts,
For us will ever guardian be,
The God of Jacob will for us
Refuge provide, us e'er preserve.

Notes

1. See *The Piety of John Calvin*, ed. Ford Lewis Battles (Grand Rapids, Mich.: Baker, 1978), 139. The hymn "I Greet Thee, Who My Sure Redeemer Art" (*UCC Hymnal*, no. 144) is falsely ascribed to Calvin.

2. See Friedrich Blume, *Protestant Church Music: A History* (New York: W. W. Norton, 1974), 546.

3. For Calvin's expressions of anxiety concerning the violence of the sea (as in the second verse), see William Bouwsma, *John Calvin* (New York: Oxford University Press, 1988), 33.

20. Draft Ecclesiastical Ordinances

(1541)

John Calvin

While John Calvin (1509–64) was in Strasbourg, after being told in 1538 by the Genevan magistrate to leave, Geneva became more and more torn apart by factious fighting. By the fall of 1540, Calvin's supporters succeeded in persuading their opponents that Calvin was the only one who could bring order out of chaos.

In spite of their confidence, Calvin was very reluctant to return to Geneva. He later wrote, "Rather would I submit to death a hundred times than to that cross on which I had to perish a thousand times over."[1] *As months passed, however, he was persuaded to go back.*

Upon his return, Calvin was determined to bring about a new church order, namely the order of church government as "prescribed to us in the Word of God and as was used in the early Church." On the very day he arrived, September 13, 1541, he pressed the various city councils to establish a committee of pastors and members of the town council to draft a constitution for the church.

The original draft was composed rather quickly, but it took until November 20 before the revised Ecclesiastical Ordinances were approved by the General Council after passing through the Little Council, the Council of the Two Hundred. The magistracy was resistant to any suggestion that infringed on its rights. In fact, most of the revisions were made to preserve the authority of the civil power. For example, ministers were given power to elect persons to the office of

---

SOURCE: *Calvin: Theological Treatises*, Library of Christian Classics, vol. 22, translated with introduction and notes by J. K. S. Reid (Philadelphia: Westminster Press, 1954). Used by permission of Westminster John Knox Press.

pastor only after they had made the candidate known to the magistracy.[2] *Calvin wanted to continue the ancient custom of the imposition of hands in ordination, but due to the objections of the magistracy, he was forced to compromise.*[3] *Furthermore, the magistracy reserved to itself the final sentence of judgment in cases where crimes were committed by ministers.*[4]

Calvin believed that the Eucharist should be observed at least once a month, but the magistracy permitted the sacrament only four times a year.[5] *Calvin wanted the consistory, the body of ministers and elders, to exercise independent discipline in the church. He felt that the ministers should have the right to bar from the Eucharist any stubborn, unrepentant sinners, but the magistracy sharply curtailed that power in an additional article.*[6] *The town councils were unwilling to permit the ministers and elders to exercise any independent jurisdiction over spiritual matters, retaining that role for themselves. In fact, it took until 1555 before the political leadership of Geneva granted the church independent spiritual jurisdiction, including the authority to impose excommunication. Calvin's leadership in Geneva was crucial, but Geneva's political leaders were slow to give him what he wanted.*

The most influential portion of the Ecclesiastical Ordinances *is the first section, describing the fourfold ministry: pastors, doctors (teachers), elders, and deacons. Calvin derived this understanding of ministry from Martin Bucer;*[7] *it was later imitated by Reformed churches in France, Belgium, Holland, and Germany, and by Presbyterians in Scotland and England. German Reformed colonists, and some Congregationalists (whose offspring later created the United Church of Christ), ordered their ministry in this pattern when they came to Massachusetts and Pennsylvania in the seventeenth and eighteenth centuries.*

Added to the translation of the "Draft of the Ecclesiastical Ordinances," *by J. K. S. Reid, are the most important of his notes, which detail the changes in the text mandated by the magistracy. These changes are indicated in the notes, starting with note 8.*

Ecclesiastical Constitution[8]

There are four orders of office instituted by our Lord for the government of his Church.

First, pastors; then doctors; next elders; and fourth deacons.

Hence if we will have a Church well ordered and maintained we ought to observe this form of government.

As to the pastors, whom Scripture also sometimes calls elders and ministers, their office is to proclaim the Word of God, to instruct, admonish, exhort and censure, both in public and private, to administer the sacraments and to enjoin brotherly corrections along with the elders and colleagues.

Now in order that nothing happen confusedly in the Church, no one is to enter upon this office without a calling. In this it is necessary to consider three things, namely: the principal thing is the examination; then what belongs to the institution of the ministers; third, what ceremony or method of procedure it is good to observe in introducing them to office.

The examination contains two parts, of which the first concerns doctrine—to ascertain whether the candidate for ordination has a good and holy knowledge of Scripture; and also whether he be a fit and proper person to communicate it edifyingly to the people.

Further to avoid all danger of the candidate holding some false opinion, it will be good that he profess his acceptance and maintenance of the doctrine approved by the Church.

To know whether he is fit to instruct, it would be necessary to proceed by interrogation and by hearing him discuss in private the doctrine of the Lord.

The second part concerns life, to ascertain whether he is of good habits and conducts himself always without reproach. The rule of procedure in this matter which it is needful to follow is very well indicated by Paul.

There follows, to whom it belongs to institute Pastors

It will be good in this connection to follow the order of the ancient Church, for it is the only practice which is shown us in Scripture. The order is that ministers first elect such as ought to hold office;[9] afterwards that he be presented to the Council; and if he is found worthy the Council receive and accept him, giving him certification to produce finally to the people when he preaches, in order that he be received by the common consent of the company of the faithful. If he be found unworthy, and show this after due probation, it is necessary to proceed to a new election for the choosing of another.

As to the manner of introducing him, it is good to use the imposition of hands, which ceremony was observed by the apostles and then in the ancient Church, providing that it take place without superstition and without offence. But because there has been much superstition in the past and scandal might result, it is better to abstain from it because of the infirmity of the times.[10]

When he is elected, he has to swear in front of the Seigneury. Of this oath there will be a prescribed form, suitable to what is required of a minister.

Now as it is necessary to examine the ministers well when they are to be elected, so also it is necessary to have good supervision to maintain them in their duty.

First it will be expedient that all the ministers, for conserving purity and concord of doctrine among themselves, meet together one certain day each week, for discussion of the Scriptures; and none are to be exempt from this without legitimate excuse. If anyone be negligent, let him be admonished.

As for those who preach in the villages, throughout the Seigneury, they are to be exhorted to come as often as they are able. For the rest, if they default an entire month, it is to be held to be very great negligence, unless it is a case of illness or other legitimate hindrance.

If there appear difference of doctrine, let the ministers come together to discuss the matter. Afterwards, if need be, let them call the elders[11] to assist in composing the contention. Finally, if they are unable to come to friendly agreement because of the obstinacy of one of the parties, let the case be referred to the magistrate to be put in order.

To obviate all scandals of living, it will be proper that there be a form of correction[12] to which all submit themselves. It will also be the means by which the ministry may retain respect, and the Word of God be neither dishonoured nor scorned because of the ill reputation of the ministers. For as one is to correct those who merit it, so it will be proper to reprove calumnies and false reports which are made unjustly against innocent people.

But first it should be noted that there are crimes which are quite intolerable in a minister, and there are faults which may on the other hand be endured while direct fraternal admonitions are offered.

Of the first sort are:

. . . heresy, schism, rebellion against ecclesiastical order, blasphemy open and meriting civil punishment, simony and all corruption in presentations, intrigue to occupy another's place, leaving one's Church without lawful leave or just calling, duplicity, perjury, lewdness, larceny, drunkenness, assault meriting punishment by law, usury, games forbidden by the law and scandalous, dances and similar dissoluteness, crimes carrying with them loss of civil rights, crime giving rise to another separation from the Church.

Of the second sort are:

. . . Strange methods of treating Scripture which turn to scandal, curiosity in investigating idle questions, advancing some doctrine or kind or practice not received in the Church, negligence in studying and reading

the Scriptures, negligence in rebuking vice amounting to flattery, negligence in doing everything required by his office, scurrility, lying, slander, dissolute words, injurious words, foolhardiness and evil devices, avarice and too great parsimony, undisciplined anger, quarrels and contentions, laxity either of manner or of gesture and like conduct improper to a minister.[13]

In the case of the crimes which cannot at all be tolerated, if some accusation and complaint arise, let the assembly of ministers and elders investigate it, in order to proceed reasonably and according to whatever is discovered in judging the case, and then report judgment to the magistrate in order that if required the delinquent be deposed.[14]

In the case of the lesser vices which may be corrected by simple admonition, one is to proceed according to the command of our Lord, so that as a last step it come for ecclesiastical judgment.

To keep this discipline in operation, let the minIsters every three months take special notice whether there be anything to discuss among themselves, to remedy it as is reasonable.

Of the number, place and time of preachings

Each Sunday, there is to be sermon at St. Peter[15] and St. Gervais at break of day, and at the usual hour at the said St. Peter and St. Gervais.

At midday, there is to be catechism, that is, instruction of little children in all the three churches, the Magdalene, St. Peter and St. Gervais.

At three o'clock second sermon in[16] St. Peter and St. Gervais.

For bringing children to catechism, and for receiving the sacraments, the boundaries of the parishes should as far as possible be observed; that is, St. Gervais embracing what it had in the past, the Magdalene similarly, St. Peter what belonged formerly to St. Germain, St. Cross, Our Lady the New, and St. Legier.

Besides the two preachings which take place, on working days there will be a sermon at St. Peter three times a week, on Monday, Tuesday and Friday[17] one hour before beginning is made at the other places.

To maintain these charges and others pertaining to the ministry, it will be necessary to have five ministers and three coadjutors who will also be ministers, to aid and assist as necessity requires.

Concerning the second order, which we have called Doctors

The office proper to doctors is the instruction of the faithful in true doctrine, in order that the purity of the Gospel be not corrupted either by ignorance or by evil opinions. As things are disposed today, we always include under this title aids and instructions for maintaining the doctrine of God and defending the Church from injury by the fault of pastors and ministers. So to use a more intelligible word, we will call this the order of the schools.

The degree nearest to the minister and most closely joined to the government of the Church is the lecturer in theology, of which it will be good to have one in Old Testament and one in New Testament.

But because it is only possible to profit from such lectures if first one is instructed in the languages and humanities, and also because it is necessary to raise offspring for time to come, in order not to leave the Church deserted to our children, a college should be instituted for instructing children to prepare them for the ministry as well as for civil government.

For the first, a proper place ought to be assigned for both doing lessons and accommodating the children and others who would profit. There must be a man learned and expert in arranging both the house and the instruction, who is able also to lecture. He is to be chosen and remunerated on condition that he have under his charge lecturers both in languages and in dialectic, if it can be done. Likewise there should be some matriculated persons to teach the little children; and[18] these we hope shortly to appoint to assist the master.

All who are there will be subject like ministers to ecclesiastical discipline.

There need be no other school in the city for the little children, but let the girls have their school apart, as has hitherto been the case.

Let no one be received if he is not approved by the ministers[19] on their testimony, for fear of impropriety.

Concerning the third order which is that of Elders[20]

Their office is to have oversight of the life of everyone, to admonish amicably those whom they see to be erring or to be living a disordered life, and, where it is required, to enjoin fraternal corrections themselves and along with others.

In the present condition of the Church, it would be good to elect two of the Little Council, four of the Council of Sixty, and six of the Council of Two Hundred, men of good and honest life, without reproach and beyond suspicion, and above all fearing God and possessing spiritual prudence. These should be so elected that there be some in every quarter of the city, to keep an eye on everybody.[21]

The best way of electing them seems to be this, that[22] the Little Council suggest the nomination of the best that can be found and the most suitable; and to do this, summon the ministers to confer with them; after this they should present those whom they would commend to the Council of Two

Hundred, which will approve them. If it find them worthy,[23] let them take the special oath, whose form will be readily drawn up.[24] And at the end of the year, let them present themselves to the Seigneury for consideration whether they ought to be continued or changed. It is inexpedient that they be changed often without cause, so long as they discharge their duty faithfully.

The fourth order of ecclesiastical government, that is, the Deacons

There were always two kinds in the ancient Church, the one deputed to receive, dispense and hold goods for the poor, not only daily alms, but also possessions, rents and pensions; the other to tend and care for the sick and administer allowances to the poor. This custom we follow again now for we have procurators and hospitallers.[25]

The[26] number of procurators appointed for this hospital seems to us to be proper; but we wish that there be also a separate reception office, so that not only provisions be in time made better, but that those who wish to do some charity may be more certain that the gift will not be employed otherwise than they intend. And if the revenue assigned by their Lordships be insufficient, or should extraordinary necessity arise, the Seigneury will advise about adjustment, according to the need they see.

The election of both procurators and hospitallers is to take place like that of the elders; and in electing them the rule proposed by Paul for deacons is to be followed [1 Tim. 3; Titus 1].

With regard to the office[27] of procurator, we think the rules which have already been imposed on them by us are good, by means of which, in urgent affairs, and where there is danger in deferment, and chiefly when there is no grave difficulty or question of great expense, they are not obliged always to be meeting, but one or two can do what is reasonable in the absence of the others.

It will be their duty to watch diligently that the public hospital is well maintained, and that this be so both for the sick and the old people unable to work, widowed women, orphaned children and other poor creatures. The sick are always to be lodged in a set of rooms separate from the other people who are unable to work, old men, widowed women, orphaned children and the other poor.

Moreover, care for the poor dispersed through the city should be revived, as the procurators may arrange it.

Moreover, besides the hospital for those passing through which must be maintained, there should be some attention given to any recognized as worthy of special charity. For this purpose, a special room should be set aside to receive those who ought to be assisted by the procurators, which is to be reserved for this business.

It should above all be demanded that the families of the hospitallers be honourably ruled in accordance with the will of God, since they have to govern houses dedicated to God.The ministers[28] must on their side enquire whether there be any lack or want of anything, in order to ask and desire the Seigneury to put it in order. To do this, some of their company with the procurators should visit the hospital every three months, to ascertain if all is in order.

It would be good, not only for the poor of the hospital, but also for those of the city who cannot help themselves, that they have a doctor and a surgeon of their own[29] who should still practise in the city, but meanwhile be required to have care of the hospital and to visit the other poor.

As for the hospital for plague, it should be wholly separate and apart, and especially if it happen that the city be visited by this scourge of God.

For the rest, to discourage mendicancy which is contrary to good order, it would be well,[30] and we have so ordered it, that there be one of our officials at the entrance of the churches to remove from the place those who loiter; and if there be any who give offence or offer insolence to bring them to one of the Lords Syndic. Similarly for the rest of the time, let the Overseers of Tens take care that the total prohibition of begging be well observed.

Of the Sacraments[31]

Baptism is to take place at the time of Sermon, and should be administered only by ministers or coadjutors. The names of children with those of their parents are to be registered, that, if any be found a bastard, the magistrate may be informed.

The stone or baptismal font is to be near the pulpit, in order that there be better hearing for the recitation of this mystery and practice of baptism.

Only such strangers as are men of faith and of our communion are to be accepted as godparents, since others are not capable of making the promise to the Church of instructing the children as is proper.

Of the Supper

Since the Supper was instituted for us by our Lord to be frequently used, and also was so observed in the ancient Church until the devil turned everything upside down, erecting the mass in its place, it is a fault in need of correction, to celebrate it so seldom.[32]

Hence it will be proper that it be always administered in the city once a month, in such a way that every three months it take place in each parish. Besides, it should take place three times a year generally, that is to say at Easter, Pentecost and Christmas, in such a way that it be not repeated in the parish in the month when it should take place by turn.

The ministers are to distribute the bread in proper order and with reverence; and none are to give the chalice except the colleagues or deacons with the ministers. Hence there should not be a large number of vessels.

The tables should be beside the pulpit in order that the mystery be more conveniently set forth beside the tables.

It should be celebrated in the church at the most fitting time.

The Sunday before the celebration, intimation is to be made, in order that no child come before it has made profession of its faith as proved by examination by the Catechism, and also that all strangers and new-comers may be exhorted first to come and present themselves at the church, so that they be instructed and thus none approach to his own condemnation.

Of Marriage

After the announcement of the customary banns, the marriage ceremony is to take place as the parties require, whether Sunday or working day, provided it be at the beginning of Service. It is proper that one abstain from this on the day when the Supper is to be celebrated, in honour of the sacrament.

It will be good to introduce ecclesiastical songs, the better to incite the people to prayer and to praise God.

To begin with, little children are to be instructed; then in time all the Church will be able to follow.

With regard to differences in matrimonial cases, because it is not a spiritual matter but involved with civil affairs,[33] we remit these to their Lordships, desiring them nevertheless to be willing to set up a Consistory without delay to judge in such matters, to which, if it seem good to them, there could be joined some ministers as counsellors. Above all may it please them to appoint men to make ordinances which may be followed forthwith.

Of Burial

The dead are to be buried decently in the place appointed. The attendance and company are left to each man's discretion.

It will be good[34] that the carriers be warned by us[35] to discourage all superstitions contrary to the Word of God, not to do duty at too late an hour, and to make a report in the case of sudden death, in order to obviate all inconvenience that might thereby arise.

Moreover they are to do duty not earlier than twelve hours after death, and not later than twenty-four.

Of the Visitation of the Sick

There are many people negligent in comforting themselves in God by his Word when they are afflicted with sickness, and so many die without the admonition or teaching which is more salutary for a man then than at any other time. It will be good therefore that their Lordships ordain and make public that no one is to be totally confined to bed for three days without informing the minister, and that each be advised to call the ministers when they desire it in good time, in order that they be not diverted from the office which they publicly discharge in the Church. Above all it is to be commanded that parents, friends and attendants do not wait until the patient is about to die, for in this extremity consolation is in most cases hardly useful.

Of the Visitation of Prisoners

It will be good that their Lordships ordain[36] a certain day each week on which admonition be given to prisoners, to reprove and exhort them; and if it seem good to them,[37] let them depute someone of their company in order that no fraud be committed. If they have anyone in irons, whom it is not desirable to take out, if it seems good to them,[38] they could give entry to some minister to console him in their presence as above. For if one waits until they are about to die, they are often so preoccupied with fear of death, that they can neither receive nor listen. The day for doing this, it is decided, will be Saturday after dinner.

The Order to be observed in the case of little Children

All citizens and inhabitants are to bring or convey their children on Sundays at midday to Catechism, of which something has been said.

A definite formulary is to be composed by which they will be instructed, and on this, with the teaching given them, they are to be interrogated about what has been said, to see if they have listened and remembered well.

When a child has been well enough instructed to pass the Catechism, he is to recite solemnly the sum of what it contains, and also to make profession of his Christianity in the presence of the Church.

Before this is done, no child is to be admitted to receive the Supper; and parents are to be informed not to bring them before this time. For it is a very perilous thing, for children as for parents, to introduce them without good and adequate instruction; for which purpose this order is to be used.

In order that there be no mistake, let it be ordained that children who come to school assemble there before twelve o'clock, and that the masters conduct them in good order in each parish.

The fathers are to bring the others or have them conducted. In order that there be the less confusion, the distinction of parishes in this connection is to be observed as far as possible, as has been said above concerning the sacraments.

Those who contravene these regulations are to be called before the company of the elders, and, if they will not yield to good advice, they must be reported to their Lordships.[39]

To advise who do their duty and who do not, elders are to keep an eye over all to give warning.

Of the Order which is to be observed in the case of those in authority, for the maintenance of supervision in the Church

The elders, as already said, are to assemble once a week with the ministers, that is to say on Thursday morning, to see that there be no disorder in the Church and to discuss together remedies as they are required.

Because they have no compulsive authority or jurisdiction, may it please their Lordships, to give them one of their officials to summon those whom they wish to admonish.

If anyone refuse with contempt to comply, their office will be to inform their Lordships,[40] in order that remedy be applied.

There follows the list of persons whom the elders ought to admonish, and how one is to proceed.

If there be anyone who dogmatizes against the received doctrine, conference is to be held with him. If he listen to reason, he is to be dismissed without scandal or dishonour. If he be opinionative, he is to be admonished several times, until it is seen that measures of greater severity are needed. Then he is to be interdicted from the communion of the Supper and reported to the magistrate.

If anyone is negligent in coming to church, so that a noticeable contempt of the communion of the faithful is evident, or if any show himself contemptuous of the ecclesiastical order, he is to be admonished, and if he prove obedient dismissed in friendliness. If he persevere in his evil way, after being three times admonished, he is to be separated from the Church and reported.[41]

As for each man's conduct, for the correction of faults, proceedings should be in accordance with the order which our Lord commands.

Secret vices are to be secretly admonished; no one is to bring his neighbour before the Church to accuse him of faults that are not in the least notorious or scandalous, unless after having found him contumacious.

For the rest, those who despise particular admonitions by their neighbour are to be admonished anew by the Church; and if they will not at all come to reason or acknowledge their fault when convicted of it, they will be informed that they must abstain from the Supper until such time as they return in a better frame of mind.

As for vices notorious and public which the Church cannot dissimulate, if they are faults that merit admonition only, the duty of the elders[42] will be to summon those who are implicated to make friendly remonstrance to them in order that they make correction, and, if amendment is evident, to do them no harm. If they persevere in doing wrong, they are to be admonished repeatedly; and if even then there is no result, they are to be informed that, as despisers of God, they must abstain from the Supper until a change of life is seen in them.

As for crimes which merit not merely remonstrance in words but correction by chastisement, should any fall into them, according to the needs of the case, he must be warned that he abstain for some time from the Supper, to humble himself before God and to acknowledge his fault the better.

If any in contumacy or rebellion wish to intrude against the prohibition, the duty of the minister is to turn him back, since it is not permissible for him to be received at the Communion.

Yet all this should be done with such moderation, that there be no rigour by which anyone may be injured; for even the corrections are only medicines for bringing back sinners to our Lord.[43]

These regulations are to be not only for the city but also for the villages dependent upon the Seigneury.

Form of Oath prescribed for Ministers, July 17, 1542[44]

The form and fashion of oath and promise which ministers of the gospel, admitted and received in the city of Geneva, are to make before the Lord Syndic and Council of the said city runs as follows:

I promise and swear that in the ministry to which I am called I will serve faithfully before God, setting forth purely his Word for the edification of this Church to which he has bound me; that I will in no way abuse his doctrine to serve my carnal affections nor to please any living man; but that I will employ it with pure conscience in the service of his glory and for the profit of his people to which I am debtor.

I promise also and swear to defend the Ecclesiastical Ordinances as they are approved by the Little, the Great and the General Councils of this City, and, in the measure in which I am given charge of administering those that have come short, to acquit myself loyally, without giving place to hatred, or favour, or vengeance, or any other carnal feeling, and in general to do what is proper to a good and faithful minister.

Thirdly, I swear and promise to guard and maintain the honour and welfare of the Seigneury and the City, to take pains, so far as is possible for me, that the people continue in beneficial peace and unity under the government of the Seigneury, and to consent in no wise to those who would violate it.

Finally, I promise and swear to be subject to the polity and constitution of this City, to show a good example of obedience to all others, being for my part subject to the laws and the magistracy, so far as my office allows; that is to say without prejudice to the liberty which we must have to teach according to what God commands us and to do the things which pertain to our office. And in conclusion, I promise to serve the Seigneury and the people in such wise, so long as I be not at all hindered from rendering to God the service which in my vocation I owe him.

Notes

1. See *Letters of John Calvin*, ed. Jules Bonnet, trans. David Constable, vol. 1 (Philadelphia: Presbyterian Board of Education, 1858), 151.
2. See note 9.
3. See note 10.
4. See notes 13 and 14.
5. See note 32.
6. See note 43.
7. See François Wendel, *Calvin: The Origins and Development of His Religious Thought*, trans. Philip Mairet (London: Collins, 1963), 52.
8. Instead of the title, the following: In the Name of Almighty God, we, the Syndics of the Small and the Great Council with our people assembled at the sound of trumpet and great bell, according to our ancient customs, having considered that it is a thing worthy of commendation above all others, that the doctrine of the

Holy Church of our Lord be well preserved in purity and the Christian Church be duly maintained, that the youth be in the future faithfully instructed, the hospital kept in good condition for sustaining the poor, all of which cannot be done unless there be a certain rule and manner of life by which each estate attends to the duties of its office: For this reason it appeared good to us that the spiritual government such as our Lord showed and instituted by his Word should be reduced to good order and have place and be observed among us. Hence we have commanded and established to be followed and observed in our city and territory the Ecclesiastical Constitution which follows, seeing that it is taken from the gospel of Jesus Christ.

9. Add: having made it known to the Seigneury

10. The article runs: As to the manner of introduction, since the ceremonies of time past have been perverted into much superstition, because of the weakness of the times, it will suffice that a declaration be made by one of the ministers denoting the office to which ordination is being made; then that prayers and petitions be made, in order that the Lord give him grace to discharge it.

11. and the clerk at the Seigneury

12. correction of ministers, as will be later set forth

13. The rest of the article reads: If there are civil crimes, that is crimes which should be punished by the laws, should any ministers fall into them, the Seigneury is to take them in hand, and beyond the ordinary penalty they are accustomed to impose on others, deposition from office will be the punishment.

14. As to the other crimes of which the first investigation belongs to the ecclesiastical Consistory, the clerks or elders with the ministers are to be watchful for them. And if anyone is convicted of them, they are to make a report to the Council with their advice and judgment; thus the final sentence of punishment is to be reserved to the Seigneury.

15. Add: at the Magdalene

16. At three o'clock also in all the three parishes

17. For the end of the article: These sermons are to be heard one after another at such an hour that they can be finished before beginning elsewhere. If some extraordinary prayer for the necessity of the time is to be made, the order for Sunday will be observed.

18. this we wish and order to be done

19. by the ministers having first informed the Seigneury; and then let him again be presented to the Council along with their testimony, for fear of impropriety. The examination ought always to be conducted in the presence of two gentlemen of the Little Council.

20. who are to be sent or deputed by the Seigneury to the Consistory

21. Add: what we wish to be done.

22. Similarly, we have determined that the method of electing them will be such that

23. Add: after being approved

24. will be drawn up as for ministers.

25. And in order to avoid confusion, for we have procurators and hospitallers, one of the four procurators is to be receptionist at said the hospital for all its goods, and is to have a suitable wage, in order that he discharge his office properly.

26. The number of four procurators is to remain as it is, of whom one will have charge of reception, as has been said, so that the

27. and authority of the procurators, we affirm

28. and the assistants or elders with one of the Lords Syndic
29. at the expense of the city
30. The Seigneury should appoint some of its officers, and so we have ordained
31. Add sub-title: Of Baptism
32. Add: For the present, let it be advised and ordained that it always be administered four times in the year.
33. it will remain the business of the Seigneury. Nevertheless we have advised leaving to the Consistory the duty of hearing the parties, in order to report their advice to the Council. For assessing judgment, proper ordinances are to be set up, which will be followed henceforward.
34. we have further advised and ordained
35. before the Seigneury
36. Further we have ordained
37. And two of the Gentlemen of the Council are to be deputed to assist, in order that there be committed
38. when it seem good to the Council, it could
39. let report be made to the Seigneury
40. the Council
41. to the Seigneury.
42. of the assistants of the elders
43. additional article: All this is to take place in such a way that the ministers have no civil jurisdiction, nor use anything but the spiritual sword of the Word of God, as Paul commands them; nor is the Consistory to derogate from the authority of the Seigneury or ordinary justice. The civil power is to remain unimpaired. Even where there will be need to impose punishment or to constrain parties, the ministers with the Consistory having heard the parties and used such remonstrances and admonitions as are good, are to report the whole matter to the Council, which in their turn will advise sentence and judgment according to the needs of the case.
44. The editors of the *Corpus Reformatorum* comment as follows: "The draft proposed by the ministers in September 1541, in demanding that the pastor elected and accepted should take oath before the Seigneury, contented itself with saying that 'there would be a written form, suitable to what is required of a minister.' But the Ordinances as published on November 20 of the same year did not even give this reference: they only spoke as before of it being inserted at the place indicated. Apparently the revision continued to be cautious, as is expressly said of the oath to be exacted from members of the Consistory, whose imposition was decreed. 'They are to take a specific oath whose form will be readily drawn up,' says the draft: 'whose form will be drawn up as for the ministers' says the official text" (X/i, 31). *Corpus Reformatorum, vol. 38, part 1, Joannis Calvini Opera Quae Supersunt Omnia*, ed. Guilielmus Baum, Eduardus Cunitz, and Eduardus Reuss, vol. 10, part 1 (Braunsweig: Schwetschke and Son, 1871), 31, n. 1.
The document here, by the change it suffered on revision, is proved to be the Draft presented by Calvin to the Little Council.

The German Reformed Church and the Heidelberg Catechism

21. The Heidelberg Catechism

(1563)

Apart from the Bible, the Heidelberg Catechism was the primary document shaping the religious consciousness of the German Reformed Church in the eighteenth and nineteenth centuries. As a catechism and confession of faith among Reformed Protestants around the world, it has been translated into more than forty different languages.

The origins of the catechism are found in the sixteenth-century political and theological situation of the German region in central Europe known as the Palatinate. After 1546, the year of Martin Luther's death, Lutheran Protestantism dominated the area under Frederick II. In 1547, however, when the Catholic Emperor Charles V defeated Protestant forces in another area, Frederick II became very cautious in his support of Reformation ideas, not wishing to offend the emperor. His successor, Otto Heinrich (ruled 1556–59), a more vigorous Lutheran, sought to complete the work of reformation in his territories. In 1559 Heinrich was succeeded by Frederick III.

Frederick III, known as Frederick the Pious, began his reign as a moderate Lutheran, but gradually came to appreciate Reformed and Calvinist ideas. Like the moderate reformer Philip Melanchthon, he was devoted to peace and unity and greatly annoyed by the "squabble of the theologians." Melanchthon, who himself came from the Palatinate, continued to be respected there.

By the mid-sixteenth century, the squabble of the theologians in German principalities was intense. Arguments took place not only

---

SOURCE: *The Heidelberg Catechism*, trans. Allen O. Miller and M. Eugene Osterhaven (Philadelphia: United Church Press, 1962). Used by permission.

between Lutheran and Reformed leaders (whether Zwinglians or Calvinists), but also between Gnesio-Lutherans (Genuine Lutherans) and Philipists (followers of Melanchthon). As early as the 1530s, Melanchthon had taken a position independent from Luther on free will and the doctrine of the real presence in the Eucharist. Melanchthon's understanding of a spiritual, real presence differed from that of Luther, and was actually very close to that of John Calvin and Martin Bucer. Among Lutherans, Melanchthon's followers were known as Cryptocalvinists.

In the Palatinate church and at the University of Heidelberg, bitter conflicts arose between representatives of the Gnesio-Lutherans, who insisted on the true, substantial presence of the body and blood of Christ in, with, and under the bread and wine, and the Melanchthon-Calvinists, who argued for a personal union or communion with Christ through the use of the elements.

Frederick III was strongly influenced by theologians following Melanchthon and Reformed thinking. In December 1561 he ordered the celebration of the Eucharist according to the Reformed rite. Soon thereafter he invited Caspar Olevianus, a leading Reformed theologian, pastor, and superintendent of Holy Spirit Church, to come to Heidelberg. In 1561 he also invited a former student of Melanchthon at Wittenberg, Zacharias Ursinus, to join the theological faculty of the University of Heidelberg. Ursinus had studied with Melanchthon and at Zurich with Peter Martyr Vermigli, another important reformer. Ursinus became the chief Protestant thinker in the Palatinate until his death in 1583.

Concerned about keeping theological peace, early in 1562 Frederick III ordered the preparation of a new church order for his realm, including a new catechism to replace the many different catechisms then in use. In response, Ursinus produced two works: first, a detailed Latin textbook for theological students, known as the Major Catechism; and second, a short German catechism for the instruction of children, known as the Minor Catechism. The Minor Catechism had three divisions, similar to those found later in the Heidelberg Catechism: human misery, God's redemption of humans from misery, and human gratitude for this redemption.

The two catechisms were handed over to a commission of theologians, church leaders, and ministers for editorial revision. Instead of producing two works—a confessional norm and a popular catechism—the commission decided that there was a need for one unified work that could serve simultaneously as confession and catechism. Frederick III played a key role in the process, influencing the decision to include marginal proof texts from the Scripture. Biblical references without quotations are given here.

The final shape of the Heidelberg Catechism must be credited to Ursinus, who drew on his own works and on earlier Reformation catechisms. Some scholars also give credit to Olevianus, but it is now believed that Olevianus exercised little influence on its composition.[1]

---

1. Our Only Comfort

Lord's Day 1

1. What is your only comfort, in life and in death?

That I belong—body and soul, in life and in death (Rom. 14:8)—not to myself (1 Cor. 6:19–20) but to my faithful Savior, Jesus Christ (1 Cor. 3:23), who at the cost of his own blood (1 Peter 1:18–19) has fully paid for all my sins (1 John 1:7; 2:2) and has completely freed me from the dominion of the devil (1 John 3:8); that he protects me so well (John 6:35, 39) that without the will of my Father in heaven not a hair can fall from my head (Matt. 10:29–31); indeed, that everything must fit his purpose for my salvation (Rom. 8:28). Therefore, by his Holy Spirit, he also assures me of eternal life (2 Cor. 1:21–22), and makes me wholeheartedly willing and ready from now on to live for him (Rom. 8:14, 17).

2. How many things must you know that you may live and die in the blessedness of this comfort?

Three (Titus 3:3–8). First, the greatness of my sin and wretchedness (John 9:41). Second, how I am freed from all my sins and their wretched consequences (John 17:1–3). Third, what gratitude I owe to God for such redemption (1 Peter 2:9–10).

PART I

Man's Sin and Guilt—The Law of God

2. Our Human Guilt

Lord's Day 2

3. Where do you learn of your sin and its wretched consequences?

From the Law of God (Rom. 3:20).

4. What does the Law of God require of us?

Jesus Christ teaches this in a summary in Matthew 22:37–40: "YOU SHALL LOVE THE LORD YOUR GOD WITH ALL YOUR HEART, AND WITH ALL YOUR SOUL, AND WITH ALL YOUR MIND (Cf. Deut. 6:5). THIS IS THE GREAT AND FIRST COMMANDMENT. AND A SECOND IS LIKE IT, YOU SHALL LOVE YOUR NEIGHBOR AS YOURSELF (Cf. Lev. 19:18). ON THESE TWO COMMANDMENTS DEPEND ALL THE LAW AND THE PROPHETS" (Cf. Luke 10:27).

5. Can you keep all this perfectly?

No (Rom. 3:10, 23; 1 John 1:8), for by nature I am prone to hate God and my neighbor (Rom. 8:7).

Lord's Day 3

6. Did God create man evil and perverse like this?

No (Gen. 1:31). On the contrary, God created man good and in his image (Gen. 1:27), that is, in true righteousness and holiness (Eph. 4:24), so that he might rightly know God his Creator, love him with his whole heart, and live with him in eternal blessedness, praising and glorifying him (Rev. 21:3).

7. Where, then, does this corruption of human nature come from?

From the fall and disobedience of our first parents, Adam and Eve, in the Garden of Eden (Gen. 3:1–6); whereby our human life is so poisoned (Rom. 5:12) that we are all conceived and born in the state of sin (Ps. 51:5).

8. But are we so perverted that we are altogether unable to do good and prone to do evil?

Yes (Gen. 6:5; Isa. 53:6; Job. 14:4; John 3:6), unless we are born again through the Spirit of God (John 3:5).

Lord's Day 4

9. Is not God unjust in requiring of man in his Law what he cannot do?

No, for God so created man that he could do it (Gen. 1:31). But man, upon the instigation of the devil (John 8:44), by deliberate disobedience, has cheated himself and all his descendants out of these gifts (Rom. 5:12, 18–19).

3. The Judgment and the Grace of God

10. Will God let man get by with such disobedience and defection?

Certainly not, for the wrath of God is revealed from heaven, both against our inborn sinfulness and our actual sins (Rom. 1:18), and he will punish them according to his righteous judgment in time and in eternity, as he has declared: "Cursed be everyone who does not abide by all things written in the book of the Law, and do them" (Gal. 3:10).

11. But is not God also merciful?

God is indeed merciful (Exod. 34:6–7) and gracious, but he is also righteous (Exod. 20:5; Ps. 5:4–6). It is his righteousness which requires that sin committed against the supreme majesty of God be punished with extreme, that is, with eternal punishment of body and soul (Matt. 25:45–46).

PART II

Man's Redemption and Freedom–The Grace of God in Jesus Christ

4. Justification by Grace

Lord's Day 5

12. Since, then, by the righteous judgment of God we have deserved temporal and eternal punishment, how may we escape this punishment, come again to grace, and be reconciled to God?

God wills that his righteousness be satisfied (Exod. 23:7); therefore, payment in full must be made to his righteousness, either by ourselves or by another (Rom. 8:3–4).

13. Can we make this payment ourselves?

By no means. On the contrary, we increase our debt each day (Job 9:3; Rom. 2:4–5; Matt. 6:12).

14. Can any mere creature make the payment for us?

No one. First of all, God does not want to punish any other creature for man's debt (Ezek. 18:20; Heb. 2:14–15). Moreover, no mere creature can bear the burden of God's eternal wrath against sin and redeem others from it (Ps. 130:3; 49:7).

15. Then, what kind of mediator and redeemer must we seek?

One who is a true (1 Cor. 15:21) and righteous man (Isa. 53:9; Heb. 7:26; 2 Cor. 5:21) and yet more powerful than all creatures, that is, one who is at the same time true God (Isa. 9:6).

Lord's Day 6

16. Why must he be a true and righteous man?

Because God's righteousness requires (Rom. 5:12, 15) that man who has sinned should make reparation for sin, but the man who is himself a sinner cannot pay for others (1 Peter 3:18).

17. Why must he at the same time be true God?

So that by the power of his divinity he might bear as a man the burden of God's wrath (Isa. 53:8), and recover for us (Acts 2:23–24; John 3:16) and restore to us righteousness and life (John 3:16; 2 Cor. 5:21).

18. Who is this mediator who is at the same time true God and a true and perfectly righteous man?

Our Lord Jesus Christ (Matt. 1:23; Luke 2:11), who is freely given to us for complete redemption and righteousness (1 Cor. 1:30).

5. The Holy Trinity

19. Whence do you know this?

From the holy gospel, which God himself revealed in the beginning in the Garden of Eden (Gen. 3:14–15), afterward proclaimed through the holy patriarchs (Gen. 22:18; 49:10) and prophets (Heb. 1:1–2; Acts 10:43) and foreshadowed through the sacrifices and other rites of the Old Covenant (Heb. 9:13–15), and finally fulfilled through his own well-beloved Son (Gal. 4:4–5).

Lord's Day 7

20. Will all men, then, be saved through Christ as they became lost through Adam?

No. Only those who, by true faith, are incorporated into him and accept all his benefits (John 1:11–13; Rom. 11:17–20; Heb. 4:2; 10:39).

21. What is true faith?

It is not only a certain knowledge by which I accept as true all that God has revealed to us in his Word (John 17:3), but also a wholehearted trust which the Holy Spirit creates in me (Rom. 4:13, 16; Matt. 16:15–17; 2 Cor. 1:21–22) through the gospel (Rom. 1:16; 10:17), that, not only to others, but to me also God has given the forgiveness of sins, everlasting righteousness and salvation, out of sheer grace solely for the sake of Christ's saving work (Rom. 3:21–26).

22. What, then, must a Christian believe?

All that is promised us in the gospel (John 20:31), a summary of which is taught us in the articles of the Apostles' Creed, our universally acknowledged confession of faith.

23. What are these articles?

I BELIEVE IN GOD THE FATHER ALMIGHTY, MAKER OF HEAVEN AND EARTH;

AND IN JESUS CHRIST, HIS ONLY-BEGOTTEN SON, OUR LORD: WHO WAS CONCEIVED BY THE HOLY SPIRIT, BORN OF THE VIRGIN MARY; SUFFERED UNDER PONTIUS PILATE, WAS CRUCIFIED, DEAD, AND BURIED; HE DESCENDED INTO HELL, THE THIRD DAY HE ROSE AGAIN FROM THE DEAD; HE ASCENDED INTO HEAVEN AND SITS AT THE RIGHT HAND OF GOD THE FATHER ALMIGHTY; FROM THENCE HE SHALL COME TO JUDGE THE LIVING AND THE DEAD.

I BELIEVE IN THE HOLY SPIRIT; THE HOLY CATHOLIC CHURCH; THE COMMUNION OF SAINTS; THE FORGIVENESS OF SINS; THE RESURRECTION OF THE BODY; AND THE LIFE EVERLASTING.

Lord's Day 8

24. How are these articles divided?

Into three parts: The first concerns God *the Father* and our *creation*; the second, God *the Son* and our *redemption*; and the third, God *the Holy Spirit* and our *sanctification*.

25. Since there is only one Divine Being (Deut. 6:4), why do you speak of three, Father, Son, and Holy Spirit?

Because God has thus revealed himself in his Word, that these three distinct Persons are the one, true, eternal God (Matt. 3:16–17).

6. God the Father

Lord's Day 9

26. What do you believe when you say: "I believe in God the Father Almighty, Maker of heaven and earth"?

That the eternal Father of our Lord Jesus Christ, who out of nothing created heaven and earth with all that is in them (Ps. 90:1–2; Isa. 44:24), who also upholds and governs them by his eternal counsel and providence (Matt. 10:29), is for the sake of Christ his Son my God and my Father (Rom. 8:15–16). I trust in him so completely that I have no doubt that he will provide me with all things necessary for body and soul (Luke 12:22). Moreover, whatever evil he sends upon me in this troubled life he will turn to my good (Rom. 8:28), for he is able to do it, being Almighty God, and is determined to do it, being a faithful Father (Matt. 7:9–11).

Lord's Day 10

27. What do you understand by the providence of God?

The almighty and ever-present power of God (Acts 17:24–25) whereby he still upholds, as it were by his own hand, heaven and earth together with all creatures (Heb. 1:3), and rules in such a way that leaves and grass, rain and drought, fruitful and unfruitful years, food and drink (Acts 14:15–17), health and sickness (John 9:3), riches and poverty (Prov. 22:2), and everything else, come to us not by chance but by his fatherly hand (Eph. 1:11).

28. What advantage comes from acknowledging God's creation and providence?

We learn that we are to be patient in adversity (Rom. 5:3–4), grateful in the midst of blessing (Deut. 8:10), and to trust our faithful God and Father for the future, assured that no creature shall separate us from his love (Rom. 8:38–39), since all creatures are so completely in his hand that without his will they cannot even move (Acts 17:28).

7. God the Son

Lord's Day 11

29. Why is the Son of God called JESUS, which means SAVIOR?

Because he saves us from our sins (Matt. 1:21), and because salvation is to be sought or found in no other (Acts 4:12).

30. Do those who seek their salvation and well-being from saints, by their own efforts, or by other means really believe in the only Savior Jesus?

No. Rather, by such actions they deny Jesus, the only Savior and Redeemer, even though they boast of belonging to him (1 Cor. 1:12–13). It therefore follows that either Jesus is not a perfect Savior, or those who receive this Savior with true faith must possess in him all that is necessary for their salvation (Col. 1:19–20).

Lord's Day 12

31. Why is he called CHRIST, that is, the ANOINTED ONE?

Because he is ordained by God the Father and anointed with the Holy Spirit (Luke 3:21–22) to be *our chief Prophet* and *Teacher* (Acts 3:22), fully revealing to us the secret purpose and will of God concerning our redemption (John 1:18); to be *our only High Priest* (Heb. 7:17), having redeemed us by the one sacrifice of his body and ever interceding for us with the Father (Heb. 9:12, 28; Rom. 8:34); and to be *our eternal King*, governing us by his Word and Spirit, and defending and sustaining us in the redemption he has won for us (Luke 1:32–33; Zech. 9:9).

32. But why are you called a Christian?

Because through faith I share in Christ (Acts 11:26; 1 Cor. 12:27) and thus in his anointing (Acts 2:17), so that I may confess his name (Matt. 10:5, 32), offer myself a living sacrifice of gratitude to him (Rom. 12:1; 1 Peter 2:5, 9), and fight against sin and the devil with a free and good conscience throughout this life (1 Tim. 1:18–19) and hereafter rule with him in eternity over all creatures (2 Tim. 2:11–13).

Lord's Day 13

33. Why is he called GOD'S ONLY-BEGOTTEN SON, since we also are God's children?

Because Christ alone is God's own eternal Son (John 1:1–3, 14, 18), whereas we are accepted for his sake as children of God by grace (Eph. 1:5–6).

34. Why do you call him OUR LORD?

Because, not with gold or silver but at the cost of his blood (1 Peter 1:18–19), he has redeemed us body and soul from sin and all the dominion of the devil, and has bought us for his very own (1 Cor. 7:23).

Lord's Day 14

35. What is the meaning of: "Conceived by the Holy Spirit, born of the Virgin Mary"?

That the eternal Son of God, who is and remains true and eternal God (John 1:1), took upon himself our true manhood from the flesh and blood of the Virgin Mary (John 1:14) through the action of the Holy Spirit (Luke 1:35), so that he might also be the true seed of David (Rom. 1:1–3), like his fellow men in all things (Phil. 2:5–7), except for sin (Heb. 4:15).

36. What benefit do you receive from the holy conception and birth of Christ?

That he is our Mediator (1 Tim. 2:5–6), and that, in God's sight, he covers over with his innocence and perfect holiness the sinfulness in which I have been conceived (Rom. 4:7).

Lord's Day 15

37. What do you understand by the word "suffered"?

That throughout his life on earth, but especially at the end of it, he bore in body and soul the wrath of God against the sin of the whole human race (Isa. 53:12; 1 Peter 2:24), so that by his suffering, as the only expiatory sacrifice, he might redeem our body and soul from everlasting damnation, and might obtain for us God's grace, righteousness, and eternal life (Rom. 3:24–25).

38. Why did he suffer "under Pontius Pilate" as his judge?

That he, being innocent, might be condemned by an earthly judge (John 19:13–16), and thereby set us free from the judgment of God which, in all its severity, ought to fall upon us (Isa. 53:4–5).

39. Is there something more in his having been crucified than if he had died some other death?

Yes, for by this I am assured that he took upon himself the curse which lay upon me, because the death of the cross was cursed by God (Gal. 3:13).

Lord's Day 16

40. Why did Christ have to suffer "death"?

Because the righteousness and truth of God are such that nothing else could make reparation for our sins except the death of the Son of God (Heb. 2:9).

41. Why was he "buried"?

To confirm the fact that he was really dead (Acts 13:29).

42. Since, then, Christ died for us, why must we also die?

Our death is not a reparation for our sins (Rom. 7:24; Ps. 49:7), but only a dying to sin and an entering into eternal life (1 Thess. 5:9–10).

43. What further benefit do we receive from the sacrifice and death of Christ on the cross?

That by his power our old self is crucified, put to death, and buried with him (Rom. 6:6), so that the evil passions of our mortal bodies may reign in us no more (Rom. 6:12), but that we may offer ourselves to him as a sacrifice of thanksgiving (Rom. 12:1).

44. Why is there added: "He descended into hell"?

That in my severest tribulations I may be assured that Christ my Lord has redeemed me from hellish anxieties and torment by the unspeakable anguish, pains, and terrors which he suffered in his soul both on the cross and before (Isa. 53:5; Matt. 27:46).

Lord's Day 17

45. What benefit do we receive from "the resurrection" of Christ?

First, by his resurrection he has overcome death that he might make us share in the righteousness which he has obtained for us through his death (Rom. 4:24–25). Second, we too are now raised by his power to a new life

(Rom. 6:3–4). Third, the resurrection of Christ is a sure pledge to us of our blessed resurrection (Rom. 8:11).

Lord's Day 18

46. How do you understand the words: "He ascended into heaven"?

That Christ was taken up from the earth into heaven before the eyes of his disciples (Luke 24:50–51) and remains there on our behalf (Heb. 9:24) until he comes again to judge the living and the dead (Acts 1:11; 10:42).

47. Then, is not Christ with us unto the end of the world, as he has promised us? (Matt. 28:20)

Christ is true man and true God. As a man he is no longer on earth (John 17:11), but in his divinity, majesty, grace, and Spirit, he is never absent from us (John 14:18–19).

48. But are not the two natures in Christ separated from each other in this way, if the humanity is not wherever the divinity is?

Not at all; for since divinity is incomprehensible and everywhere present (Jer. 23:23–24), it must follow that the divinity is indeed beyond the bounds of the humanity which it has assumed, and is nonetheless ever in that humanity as well, and remains personally united to it (John 3:13; Col. 2:9).

49. What benefit do we receive from Christ's ascension into heaven?

First, that he is our Advocate in the presence of his Father in heaven (Rom. 8:34). Second, that we have our flesh in heaven as a sure pledge that he, as the Head, will also take us, his members, up to himself (John 14:2). Third, that he sends us his Spirit as a counterpledge (John 14:16–17) by whose power we seek what is above, where Christ is, sitting at the right hand of God, and not things that are on earth (Col. 3:1).

Lord's Day 19

50. Why is there added: "And sits at the right hand of God"?

Because Christ ascended into heaven so that he might manifest himself there as the Head of his Church (Eph. 1:20–23), through whom the Father governs all things (Matt. 28:18).

51. What benefit do we receive from this glory of Christ, our Head?

First, that through his Holy Spirit he pours out heavenly gifts upon us, his members (Acts 2:33; Eph. 4:8). Second, that by his power he defends and supports us against all our enemies (John 10:28).

52. What comfort does the return of Christ "to judge the living and the dead" give you?

That in all affliction and persecution I may await with head held high the very Judge from heaven who has already submitted himself to the judgment of God for me and has removed all the curse from me (Luke 21:28; Phil. 3:20); that he will cast all his enemies and mine into everlasting condemnation (Matt. 25:41–43), but he shall take me, together with all his elect, to himself into heavenly joy and glory (Matt. 25:34).

8. God the Holy Spirit

Lord's Day 20

53. What do you believe concerning "the Holy Spirit"?

First, that, with the Father and the Son, he is equally eternal God (Gen. 1:1–2; John 4:24); second, that God's Spirit is also given to me (Matt. 28:19), preparing me through a true faith to share in Christ and all his benefits (1 Cor. 6:17, 19), that he comforts me (Acts 9:31) and will abide with me forever (John 14:16).

Lord's Day 21

54. What do you believe concerning "the Holy Catholic Church"?

I believe that, from the beginning to the end of the world, and from among the whole human race (Gen. 26:3b–4; Rev. 5:9), the Son of God (Col. 1:18), by his Spirit and his Word (Isa. 59:21), gathers, protects, and preserves for himself, in the unity of the true faith (Acts 13:47–48; Eph. 4:3–6; 5:25–27), a congregation chosen for eternal life. Moreover, I believe that I am and forever will remain a living member of it eternally (John 10:28).

55. What do you understand by "the communion of saints"?

First, that believers one and all, as partakers of the Lord Christ, and all his treasures and gifts, shall share in one fellowship (1 Cor. 1:9; 12:4–7, 12–13). Second, that each one ought to know that he is obliged to use his gifts freely and with joy for the benefit and welfare of other members (1 Cor. 12:14, 21, 26–27; 13:4–5).

56. What do you believe concerning "the forgiveness of sins"?

That, for the sake of Christ's reconciling work (2 Cor. 5:19, 21), God will no more remember my sins nor the sinfulness with which I have to struggle all my life long (Jer. 31:34; Rom. 8:1–2); but that he graciously imparts to me the righteousness of Christ so that I may never come into condemnation (John 3:17–18).

Lord's Day 22

57. What comfort does "the resurrection of the body" give you?

That after this life my soul shall be immediately taken up to Christ, its Head (Luke 23:43), and that this flesh of mine, raised by the power of Christ, shall be reunited with my soul, and be conformed to the glorious body of Christ (1 Cor. 15:20, 42–46, 54; Job 19:25; 1 John 3:2; Phil. 3:21).

58. What comfort does the article concerning "the life everlasting" give you?

That, since I now feel in my heart the beginning of eternal joy (Rom. 14:17), I shall possess, after this life, perfect blessedness, which no eye has seen, nor ear heard, nor the heart of man conceived (1 Cor. 2:9), and thereby praise God forever (John 17:3).

9. True Faith

Lord's Day 23

59. But how does it help you now that you believe all this?

That I am righteous in Christ before God, and an heir of eternal life (Rom. 1:17; 5:1; John 3:36).

60. How are you righteous before God?

Only by true faith in Jesus Christ (Rom. 3:21–22). In spite of the fact that my conscience accuses me that I have grievously sinned against all the commandments of God, and have not kept any one of them (Rom. 3:9–10), and that I am still ever prone to all that is evil (Rom. 7:23), nevertheless, God, without any merit of my own (Titus 3:5), out of pure grace (Eph. 2:8), grants me the benefits of the perfect expiation of Christ (1 John 2:1–2), imputing to me his righteousness and holiness (Rom. 4:3–5) as if I had never committed a single sin nor had ever been sinful, having fulfilled myself all the obedience which Christ has carried out for me (Rom. 4:24), if only I accept such favor with a trusting heart (Rom. 3:24–25).

61. Why do you say that you are righteous by faith alone?

Not because I please God by virtue of the worthiness of my faith, but because the satisfaction, righteousness, and holiness of Christ alone are my righteousness before God (1 Cor. 1:30; 2:2), and because I can accept it and make it mine in no other way than by faith alone.

Lord's Day 24

62. But why cannot our good works be our righteousness before God, or at least a part of it?

Because the righteousness which can stand before the judgment of God must be absolutely perfect and wholly in conformity with the divine Law (Gal. 3:10). But even our best works in this life are all imperfect and defiled with sin (Isa. 64:6).

63. Will our good works merit nothing, even when it is God's purpose to reward them in this life, and in the future life as well?

This reward is not given because of merit, but out of grace (Luke 17:10).

64. But does not this teaching make people careless and sinful?

No, for it is impossible for those who are ingrafted into Christ by true faith not to bring forth the fruit of gratitude (Matt. 7:16–17; John 15:5).

10. The Holy Sacraments

Lord's Day 25

65. Since, then, faith alone makes us share in Christ and all his benefits, where does such faith originate?

The Holy Spirit creates it in our hearts (Eph. 2:8) by the preaching of the holy gospel (1 Peter 1:23, 25), and confirms it by the use of the holy Sacraments.

66. What are the Sacraments?

They are visible, holy signs and seals (Rom. 4:11) instituted by God in order that by their use he may the more fully disclose and seal to us the promise of the gospel, namely, that because of the one sacrifice of Christ accomplished on the cross he graciously grants us the forgiveness of sins and eternal life (Acts 2:38; 22:16; Matt. 26:28).

67. Are both the Word and the Sacraments designed to direct our faith to the one sacrifice of Jesus Christ on the cross as the only ground of our salvation?

Yes, indeed, for the Holy Spirit teaches in the gospel and confirms by the holy Sacraments that our whole salvation is rooted in the one sacrifice of Christ offered for us on the cross (Rom. 6:3; Gal. 3:27; 1 Cor. 11:26).

68. How many Sacraments has Christ instituted in the New Testament?

Two, holy Baptism and the holy Supper.

11. Holy Baptism

Lord's Day 26

69. How does holy Baptism remind and assure you that the one sacrifice of Christ on the cross avails for you?

In this way: Christ has instituted this external washing with water (Matt. 28:19) and by it has promised (Matt. 3:11) that I am as certainly washed with his blood and Spirit from the uncleanness of my soul and from all my sins, as I am washed externally with water which is used to remove the dirt from my body (1 Peter 3:21).

70. What does it mean to be washed with the blood and Spirit of Christ?

It means to have the forgiveness of sins from God, through grace, for the sake of Christ's blood which he shed for us in his sacrifice on the cross (Eph. 1:7), and also to be renewed by the Holy Spirit and sanctified as members of Christ, so that we may more and more die unto sin and live in a consecrated and blameless way (1 Cor. 6:11; Rom. 6:4).

71. Where has Christ promised that we are as certainly washed with his blood and Spirit as with the water of baptism?

In the institution of Baptism which runs thus: "GO THEREFORE AND MAKE DISCIPLES OF ALL NATIONS, BAPTIZING THEM IN THE NAME OF THE FATHER AND OF THE SON AND OF THE HOLY SPIRIT" (Matt. 28:19). "HE WHO BELIEVES AND IS BAPTIZED WILL

BE SAVED: BUT HE WHO DOES NOT BELIEVE WILL BE CONDEMNED" (Mark 16:16). This promise is also repeated where the Scriptures call baptism "the water of rebirth" (Titus 3:5) and the washing away of sins (Acts 22:16).

Lord's Day 27

72. Does merely the outward washing with water itself wash away sins?

No (Matt. 3:11; Eph 5:25b–26); for only the blood of Jesus Christ and the Holy Spirit cleanse us from all sins (1 John 1:7; 1 Cor. 6:11).

73. Then why does the Holy Spirit call baptism the water of rebirth and the washing away of sins?

God does not speak in this way except for a strong reason. Not only does he teach us by Baptism that just as the dirt of the body is taken away by water, so our sins are removed by the blood and Spirit of Christ (Rev. 7:14); but more important still, by the divine pledge and sign he wishes to assure us that we are just as truly washed from our sins spiritually as our bodies are washed with water (Gal. 3:27).

74. Are infants also to be baptized?

Yes, because they, as well as their parents, are included in the covenant and belong to the people of God (Gen. 17:7; Matt. 19:14). Since both redemption from sin through the blood of Christ and the gift of faith from the Holy Spirit are promised to these children no less than to their parents (Acts 2:38–39), infants are also by baptism, as a sign of the covenant, to be incorporated into the Christian church and distinguished from the children of unbelievers (Acts 10:47; 1 Cor. 7:14). This was done in the Old Covenant by circumcision (Cf. Gen. 17:9–14). In the New Covenant baptism has been instituted to take its place (Col. 2:11–13).

12. The Lord's Supper—Holy Communion

Lord's Day 28

75. How are you reminded and assured in the holy Supper that you participate in the one sacrifice of Christ on the cross and in all his benefits?

In this way: Christ has commanded me and all believers to eat of this broken bread, and to drink of this cup in remembrance of him. He has thereby promised (see Question 77 below) that his body was offered and broken on the cross for me, and his blood was shed for me, as surely as I see with my eyes that the bread of the Lord is broken for me, and that the cup is shared with me. Second, he has promised that he himself as certainly feeds and nourishes my soul to everlasting life with his crucified body and shed blood as I receive from the hand of the minister and actually taste the bread and the cup of the Lord which are given to me as sure signs of the body and blood of Christ.

76. What does it mean to eat the crucified body of Christ and to drink his shed blood?

It is not only to embrace with a trusting heart the whole passion and death of Christ, and by it to receive the forgiveness of sins and eternal life (John 6:35, 40, 6:53–54). In addition, it is to be so united more and more to his blessed body by the Holy Spirit dwelling both in Christ and in us (John 6:56) that, although he is in heaven (Acts 3:20–21) and we are on earth, we are nevertheless flesh of his flesh and bone of his bone (Eph. 5:30), always living and being governed by one Spirit, as the members of our bodies are governed by one soul (1 John 3:24b; Eph. 4:15–16).

77. Where has Christ promised that he will feed and nourish believers with his body and blood just as surely as they eat of this broken bread and drink of this cup?

In the institution of the Holy Supper which reads: THE LORD JESUS ON THE NIGHT WHEN HE WAS BETRAYED TOOK BREAD, AND WHEN HE HAD GIVEN THANKS, HE BROKE IT, AND SAID, "THIS IS MY BODY WHICH IS FOR YOU. DO THIS IN REMEMBRANCE OF ME." IN THE SAME WAY ALSO THE CUP, AFTER SUPPER, SAYING, "THIS CUP IS THE NEW COVENANT IN MY BLOOD. DO THIS, AS OFTEN AS YOU DRINK IT, IN REMEMBRANCE OF ME." FOR AS OFTEN AS YOU EAT THIS BREAD AND DRINK THE CUP, YOU PROCLAIM THE LORD'S DEATH UNTIL HE COMES (1 Cor. 11:23–26).

This promise is also repeated by the apostle Paul: WHEN WE BLESS "THE CUP OF BLESSING," IS IT NOT A MEANS OF SHARING IN THE BLOOD OF CHRIST? WHEN WE BREAK THE BREAD, IS IT NOT A MEANS OF SHARING THE BODY OF CHRIST? BECAUSE THERE IS ONE LOAF, WE, MANY AS WE ARE, ARE ONE BODY; FOR IT IS ONE LOAF OF WHICH WE ALL PARTAKE (1 Cor. 10:16–17).

Lord's Day 29

78. Do the bread and wine become the very body and blood of Christ?

No, for as the water in baptism is not changed into the blood of Christ, nor becomes the washing away of sins by itself, but is only a divine sign and confirmation of it, so also in the Lord's Supper (Matt. 26:26–29) the sacred bread does not become the body of Christ itself (1 Cor. 11:26–28), although, in accordance with the nature and usage of sacraments (1 Cor. 10:1–4), it is called the body of Christ.

79. Then why does Christ call the bread his body, and the cup his blood, or the New Covenant in his blood, and why does the apostle Paul call the Supper "a means of sharing" in the body and blood of Christ?

Christ does not speak in this way except for a strong reason. He wishes to teach us by it that as bread and wine sustain this temporal life so his crucified body and shed blood are the true food and drink of our souls for eternal life (John 6:51, 55). Even more, he wishes to assure us by this visible sign and pledge that we come to share in his true body and blood through the working of the Holy Spirit as surely as we receive with our mouth these holy tokens in remembrance of him (1 Cor. 10:16–17), and that all his sufferings and his death are our own as certainly as if we had ourselves suffered and rendered satisfaction in our own persons.

Lord's Day 30

80. What difference is there between the Lord's Supper and the papal Mass?

The Lord's Supper testifies to us that we have complete forgiveness of all our sins through the one sacrifice of Jesus Christ which he himself has accomplished on the cross once for all (Heb. 7:27; 9:12, 25–28); and that through the Holy Spirit we are incorporated into Christ (1 Cor. 6:17), who is now in heaven with his true body at the right hand of the Father (Heb. 1:3; 8:1) and is there to be worshiped (John 20:17; Acts 7:55–56; Col. 3:1). But the Mass teaches that the living and the dead do not have forgiveness of sins through the sufferings of Christ unless Christ is again offered for them daily by the priests; (and that Christ is bodily under the form of bread and wine and is therefore to be worshiped in them). Therefore the Mass is fundamentally a complete denial of the once for all sacrifice and passion of Jesus Christ (Heb. 9:25–26; 10:11–14) (and as such an idolatry to be condemned).

Note: *Question 80 is omitted in the first edition. The sections in parentheses were added for the first time in the third edition.*

13. Church Discipline

81. Who ought to come to the table of the Lord?

Those who are displeased with themselves for their sins (Matt. 5:3), and who nevertheless trust that these sins have been forgiven them and that their remaining weakness is covered by the passion and death of Christ (Ps. 103:2–3; Eph. 1:7), and who also desire more and more to strengthen their faith and improve their life (Matt. 5:5; Ps. 116:12–14). The impenitent and hypocrites, however, eat and drink judgment to themselves (1 Cor. 10:21; 11:28).

82. Should those who show themselves to be unbelievers and enemies of God by their confession and life be admitted to this Supper?

No, for then the covenant of God would be profaned and his wrath provoked against the whole congregation (1 Cor. 11:20, 26–29, 34). According to the ordinance of Christ and his apostles, therefore, the Christian church is under obligation, by the office of the keys, to exclude such persons until they amend their lives.

Lord's Day 31

83. What is the office of the keys?

The preaching of the holy gospel and Christian discipline. By these two means the kingdom of heaven is opened to believers and shut against unbelievers (Matt. 16:19; John 20:23).

84. How is the kingdom of heaven opened and shut by the preaching of the holy gospel?

In this way: The kingdom of heaven is opened when it is proclaimed and openly testified to believers, one and all, according to the command of Christ, that as often as they accept the promise of the gospel with true faith all their sins are truly forgiven them by God for the sake of Christ's gracious work. On the contrary, the wrath of God and eternal condemnation falls upon all unbelievers and hypocrites as long as they do not repent (Matt. 28:19; 16:19; John 20:21–23). It is according to this witness of the gospel that God will judge the one and the other in this life and in the life to come.

85. How is the kingdom of heaven shut and opened by Christian discipline?

In this way: Christ commanded that those who bear the Christian name in an unchristian way either in doctrine or in life should be given brotherly admonition. If they do not give up their errors or evil ways, notification is given to the church or to those ordained for this by the church. Then, if they do not change after this warning, they are forbidden to partake of the holy Sacraments and are thus excluded from the communion of the church and by God himself from the kingdom of Christ (Matt. 18:15–18; 1 Cor. 5:11–13). However, if they promise and show real amendment, they are received again as members of Christ and of the church (Luke 15:18).

PART III

Man's Gratitude and Obedience—New Life Through the Holy Spirit

14. Discipleship and Good Works

Lord's Day 32

86. Since we are redeemed from our sin and its wretched consequences by grace through Christ without any merit of our own, why must we do good works?

Because just as Christ has redeemed us with his blood he also renews us through his Holy Spirit according to his own image, so that with our whole life we may show ourselves grateful to God for his goodness (Rom. 6:13; 12:1) and that he may be glorified through us (Matt. 5:16; 1 Cor. 6:19–20); and further, so that we ourselves may be assured of our faith by its fruits (Matt. 7:17; Gal. 5:22–24) and by our reverent behavior may win our neighbors to Christ (1 Peter 3:1–2).

87. Can those who do not turn to God from their ungrateful, impenitent life be saved?

Certainly not! Scripture says, "Surely you know that the unjust will never come into possession of the kingdom of God. Make no mistake: no fornicator or idolater, none who are guilty either of adultery or of homosexual perversion, no thieves or grabbers or drunkards or slanderers or swindlers, will possess the kingdom of God" (1 Cor. 6:9–10) (N.E.B.).

Lord's Day 33

88. How many parts are there to the true repentance or conversion of man?

Two: the dying of the old self and the birth of the new (Rom. 6:4–6; 2 Cor. 5:17).

89. What is the dying of the old self?

Sincere sorrow over our sins and more and more to hate them and to flee from them (Rom. 8:13; 2 Cor. 7:10).

90. What is the birth of the new man?

Complete joy in God through Christ (Rom. 5:1) and a strong desire to live according to the will of God in all good works (Gal. 2:20).

91. But what are good works?

Only those which are done out of true faith (Rom. 14:20b, 22b–23), in accordance with the Law of God (1 Sam. 15:22), and for his glory (1 Cor. 10:31), and not those based on our own opinion or on the traditions of men (Deut. 12:32; Matt. 15:9).

Lord's Day 34

92. What is the Law of God?

God spoke all these words saying:

First Commandment

"I AM THE LORD YOUR GOD, WHO BROUGHT YOU OUT OF THE LAND OF EGYPT, OUT OF THE HOUSE OF BONDAGE. YOU SHALL HAVE NO OTHER GODS BEFORE ME."

Second Commandment

"YOU SHALL NOT MAKE YOURSELF A GRAVEN IMAGE, OR ANY LIKENESS OF ANYTHING THAT IS IN HEAVEN ABOVE, OR THAT IS IN THE EARTH BENEATH, OR THAT IS IN THE WATER UNDER THE EARTH; YOU SHALL NOT BOW DOWN TO THEM OR SERVE THEM; FOR I THE LORD YOUR GOD AM A JEALOUS GOD, VISITING THE INIQUITY OF THE FATHERS UPON THE CHILDREN TO

THE THIRD AND THE FOURTH GENERATION OF THOSE WHO HATE ME, BUT SHOWING STEADFAST LOVE TO THOUSANDS OF THOSE WHO LOVE ME AND KEEP MY COMMANDMENTS."

Third Commandment

"YOU SHALL NOT TAKE THE NAME OF THE LORD YOUR GOD IN VAIN; FOR THE LORD WILL NOT HOLD HIM GUILTLESS WHO TAKES HIS NAME IN VAIN."

Fourth Commandment

"REMEMBER THE SABBATH DAY, TO KEEP IT HOLY. SIX DAYS YOU SHALL LABOR, AND DO ALL YOUR WORK; BUT THE SEVENTH DAY IS A SABBATH TO THE LORD YOUR GOD; IN IT YOU SHALL NOT DO ANY WORK, YOU, OR YOUR SON, OR YOUR DAUGHTER, YOUR MANSERVANT, OR YOUR MAIDSERVANT, OR YOUR CATTLE, OR THE SOJOURNER WHO IS WITHIN YOUR GATES; FOR IN SIX DAYS THE LORD MADE HEAVEN AND EARTH, THE SEA, AND ALL THAT IS IN THEM, AND RESTED THE SEVENTH DAY; THEREFORE THE LORD BLESSED THE SABBATH DAY AND HALLOWED IT."

Fifth Commandment

"HONOR YOUR FATHER AND YOUR MOTHER, THAT YOUR DAYS MAY BE LONG IN THE LAND WHICH THE LORD YOUR GOD GIVES YOU."

Sixth Commandment

"YOU SHALL NOT KILL."

Seventh Commandment

"YOU SHALL NOT COMMIT ADULTERY."

Eighth Commandment

"YOU SHALL NOT STEAL."

Ninth Commandment

"YOU SHALL NOT BEAR FALSE WITNESS AGAINST YOUR NEIGHBOR."

Tenth Commandment

"YOU SHALL NOT COVET YOUR NEIGHBOR'S HOUSE; YOU SHALL NOT COVET YOUR NEIGHBOR'S WIFE, OR HIS MANSERVANT, OR HIS MAIDSERVANT, OR HIS OX, OR HIS ASS, OR ANYTHING THAT IS YOUR NEIGHBOR'S" (Exod. 20:1–17).

93. How are these commandments divided?

Into two tables (Exod. 34:28–29), the first of which teaches us in four commandments how we ought to live in relation to God; the other, in six commandments, what we owe to our neighbor (Matt. 22:37–39).

15. Love and Honor to God—The First Table of the Law

94. What does the Lord require in the first commandment?

That I must avoid and flee all idolatry (1 Cor. 10:5–14), sorcery, enchantments (Lev. 19:31), invocation of saints or other creatures (Matt. 4:10) because of the risk of losing my salvation. Indeed, I ought properly to acknowledge the only true God (John 17:3), trust in him alone (Jer. 17:5, 7), in humility (1 Peter 5:5–6) and patience (Heb. 10:36) expect all good from him only (James 1:17), and love (Deut. 6:5), fear (Deut. 6:2) and honor (Rev. 5:13) him with my whole heart. In short, I should rather turn my back on all creatures than do the least thing against his will (Matt. 10:37).

95. What is idolatry?

It is to imagine or possess something in which to put one's trust in place of or beside the one true God who has revealed himself in his Word (Gal. 4:8–9).

Lord's Day 35

96. What does God require in the second commandment?

That we should not represent (Acts 17:29) him or worship him in any other manner than he has commanded in his Word (1 Sam. 15:23).

97. Should we, then, not make any images at all?

God cannot and should not be pictured in any way. As for creatures, although they may indeed be portrayed, God forbids making or having any likeness of them in order to worship them, or to use them to serve him (Exod. 23:24; 34:13–14).

98. But may not pictures be tolerated in churches in place of books for unlearned people?

No, for we must not try to be wiser than God who does not want his people to be taught by means of lifeless idols (Heb. 2:18–20), but through the living preaching of his Word (2 Tim. 3:16–17).

Lord's Day 36

99. What is required in the third commandment?

That we must not profane or abuse the name of God by cursing (Lev. 24:11, 13, 16), by perjury (Lev. 19:12), or by unnecessary oaths (Matt. 5:37). Nor are we to participate in such horrible sins by keeping quiet and thus giving silent consent. In a word, we must not use the holy name of God except with fear and reverence (Ps. 99:3; Deut. 28:58) so that he may be rightly confessed (Matt. 10:32) and addressed (1 Tim. 2:8) by us, and be glorified in all our words and works (Col. 3:17).

100. Is it, therefore, so great a sin to blaspheme God's name by cursing and swearing that God is also angry with those who do not try to prevent and forbid it as much as they can?

Yes, indeed (Lev. 5:1); for no sin is greater or provokes his wrath more than the profaning of his name. That is why he commanded it to be punished with death (Lev. 24:15–16).

Lord's Day 37

101. But may we not swear oaths by the name of God in a devout manner?

Yes, when the civil authorities require it of their subjects, or when it is otherwise needed to maintain and promote fidelity and truth, to the glory of God and the welfare of our neighbor. Such oath-taking is grounded in God's Word (Deut. 6:13) and has therefore been rightly used by God's people under the Old and New Covenants (Cf. Gen. 21:24; 31:53–54; Josh. 9:15, 19; 1 Sam. 24:22; 2 Sam. 3:35; 1 Kings 1:28–30; Rom. 1:9; 2 Cor. 1:23).

102. May we also swear by the saints or other creatures?

No; for a lawful oath is a calling upon God, as the only searcher of hearts, to bear witness to the truth, and to punish me if I swear falsely (2 Cor. 1:23). No creature deserves such honor (Matt. 5:34–35).

Lord's Day 38

103. What does God require in the fourth commandment?

First, that the ministry of the gospel and Christian education be maintained (2 Tim. 2:2; 3:15), and that I diligently attend church, especially on the Lord's day (Lev. 23:3; Acts 2:42, 46), to hear the Word of God (Rom. 10:17; 1 Cor. 14:19), to participate in the holy Sacraments (1 Cor. 11:24), to call publicly upon the Lord (1 Tim. 2:1), and to give Christian service to those in need (1 Cor. 16:2). Second, that I cease from my evil works all the days of my life, allow the Lord to work in me through his Spirit, and thus begin in this life the eternal Sabbath (Isa. 66:23).

16. Love and Service of the Neighbor—The Second Table of the Law

Lord's Day 39

104. What does God require in the fifth commandment?

That I show honor, love, and faithfulness to my father and mother and to all who are set in authority over me; that I submit myself with respectful obedience to all their careful instruction and discipline (Eph. 6:1–4; Rom. 13:1–2); and that I also bear patiently their failures (Prov. 23:22; 1 Peter 2:18), since it is God's will to govern us by their hand (Col. 3:18–21).

Lord's Day 40

105. What does God require in the sixth commandment?

That I am not to abuse, hate, injure, or kill my neighbor, either with thought, or by word or gesture, much less by deed, whether by myself or through another (Matt. 5:21–22), but to lay aside all desire for revenge (Rom. 12:19); and that I do not harm myself or willfully expose myself to danger (Matt. 4:7). This is why the authorities are armed with the means to prevent murder (Rom. 13:4).

106. But does this commandment speak only of killing?

In forbidding murder God means to teach us that he abhors the root of murder, which is envy (Gal. 5:19–21), hatred (1 John 2:9), anger, and desire for revenge (Rom. 12:19), and that he regards all these as hidden murder (1 John 3:15).

107. Is it enough, then, if we do not kill our neighbor in any of these ways?

No; for when God condemns envy, hatred, and anger, he requires us to love our neighbor as ourselves (Matt. 22:39; 7:12), to show patience, peace, gentleness (Rom. 12:10), mercy (Matt. 5:7) and friendliness (Rom. 12:15–18) toward him, to prevent injury to him as much as we can (Matt. 5:45), also to do good to our enemies (Matt. 5:44; Rom. 12:20–21).

Lord's Day 41

108. What does the seventh commandment teach us?

That all unchastity is condemned by God (Gal. 5:19–21), and that we should therefore detest it from the heart (Jude 23), and live chaste and disciplined lives (1 Thess. 4:3–4), whether in holy wedlock or in single life (Heb. 13:4).

109. Does God forbid nothing more than adultery and such gross sins in this commandment?

Since both our body and soul are a temple of the Holy Spirit, it is his will that we keep both pure and holy. Therefore he forbids all unchaste actions, gestures, words (Eph. 5:3–4), thoughts, desires (Matt. 5:27–29), and whatever may excite another person to them (Eph. 5:18).

Lord's Day 42

110. What does God forbid in the eighth commandment?

He forbids not only the theft and robbery (1 Cor. 6:10) which civil authorities punish, but God also labels as theft all wicked tricks and schemes by which we seek to get for ourselves our neighbor's goods, whether by force or under the pretext of right (Luke 3:14), such as false weights (Prov. 11:1) and measures (Ezek. 45:10), deceptive advertising or merchandising (Prov. 12:22), counterfeit money, exorbitant interest (Luke 6:35), or any other means forbidden by God. He also forbids all greed (Luke 12:15) and misuse and waste of his gifts (Luke 16:1–2).

111. But what does God require of you in this commandment?

That I work for the good of my neighbor wherever I can and may, deal with him as I would have others deal with me (Matt. 7:12), and do my work well so that I may be able to help the poor in their need (Eph. 4:28).

Lord's Day 43

112. What is required in the ninth commandment?

That I do not bear false witness against anyone (Prov. 19:5), twist anyone's words (Ps. 15:3, 5), be a gossip or a slanderer (Rom. 1:29–30), or condemn anyone lightly without a hearing (Matt. 7:1). Rather I am required to avoid, under penalty of God's wrath, all lying and deceit as the works of the devil himself (John 8:44; Prov. 12:22; 13:5). In judicial and all other matters I am to love the truth, and to speak and confess it honestly (Eph. 4:25). Indeed, in so far as I am able, I am to defend and promote my neighbor's good name (1 Peter 4:8).

17. The Joy of the Righteous Man

Lord's Day 44

113. What is required in the tenth commandment?

That there should never enter our heart even the least inclination or thought contrary to any commandment of God, but that we should always hate sin with our whole heart and find satisfaction and joy in all righteousness (Rom. 7:7).

114. But can those who are converted to God keep these commandments perfectly?

No, for even the holiest of them make only a small beginning in obedience in this life (1 John 1:8; Rom. 7:14). Nevertheless, they begin with serious purpose to conform not only to some, but to all the commandments of God (Rom. 7:22; Jas. 2:10).

115. Why, then, does God have the ten commandments preached so strictly since no one can keep them in this life?

First, that all our life long we may become increasingly aware of our sinfulness (1 John 1:9), and therefore more eagerly seek forgiveness of sins and righteousness in Christ (Rom. 7:24–25). Second, that we may constantly and diligently pray to God for the grace of the Holy Spirit, so that more and more we may be renewed in the image of God, until we attain the goal of full perfection after this life (1 Cor. 9:24).

18. Prayer

Lord's Day 45

116. Why is prayer necessary for Christians?

Because it is the chief part of the gratitude which God requires of us (Ps. 50:14–15), and because God will give his grace and Holy Spirit only to those who sincerely beseech him in prayer without ceasing, and who thank him for these gifts (Matt. 7:7–8).

117. What is contained in a prayer which pleases God and is heard by him?

First, that we sincerely call upon the one true God, who has revealed himself to us in his Word (Ps. 145:18; John 4:24), for all that he has commanded us to ask of him (1 John 5:14). Then, that we thoroughly acknowledge our need and evil condition (Isa. 66:2) so that we may humble ourselves in the presence of his majesty (2 Chron. 7:14). Third, that we rest assured (Jas. 1:6) that, in spite of our unworthiness, he will certainly hear our prayer for the sake of Christ our Lord, as he has promised us in his Word (Matt. 7:8; John 14:13–14).

118. What has God commanded us to ask of him?

All things necessary for soul and body (Jas. 1:17; Matt. 6:33) which Christ the Lord has included in the prayer which he himself taught us.

119. What is the Lord's Prayer?

"OUR FATHER WHO ART IN HEAVEN, HALLOWED BE THY NAME. THY KINGDOM COME, THY WILL BE DONE, ON EARTH AS IT IS IN HEAVEN. GIVE US THIS DAY OUR DAILY BREAD; AND FORGIVE US OUR DEBTS, AS WE ALSO HAVE FORGIVEN OUR DEBTORS; AND LEAD US NOT INTO TEMPTATION, BUT DELIVER US FROM EVIL, FOR THINE IS THE KINGDOM AND THE POWER AND THE GLORY, FOREVER. AMEN" (Matt. 6:9–13).

19. Our Lord's Prayer

Lord's Day 46

120. Why has Christ commanded us to address God: "Our Father"?

That at the very beginning of our prayer he may awaken in us the child-like reverence and trust toward God which should be the motivation of our prayer, which is that God has become our Father through Christ and will much less deny us what we ask him in faith than our human fathers will refuse us earthly things (Matt. 7:9–11).

121. Why is there added: "who art in heaven"?

That we may have no earthly conception of the heavenly majesty of God (Jer. 23:23–24), but that we may expect from his almighty power all things that are needed for body and soul (Rom. 8:32).

Lord's Day 47

122. What is the first petition?

"Hallowed be they name." That is: help us first of all to know thee rightly (John 17:3), and to hallow, glorify, and praise thee in all thy works through which there shine thine almighty power, wisdom, goodness, righteousness, mercy, and truth (Ps. 119:137). And so order our whole life in thought, word, and deed that thy name may never be blasphemed on our account, but may always be honored and praised (Pss. 71:8; 115:1).

Lord's Day 48

123. What is the second petition?

"Thy kingdom come." That is: so govern us by thy Word and Spirit that we may more and more submit ourselves unto thee (Matt. 6:33; Ps. 119:5). Uphold and increase thy church (Ps. 51:18). Destroy the works of the devil, every power that raises itself against thee, and all wicked schemes thought up against thy holy Word (1 John 3:8), until the full coming of thy kingdom (Rev. 22:17) in which thou shalt be all in all (1 Cor. 15:20, 28).

Lord's Day 49

124. What is the third petition?

"Thy will be done, on earth, as it is in heaven." That is: grant that we and all men may renounce our own will (Matt. 16:24) and obey thy will, which alone is good, without grumbling (Luke 22:42), so that everyone may carry out his office and calling as willingly and faithfully (1 Cor. 7:24) as the angels in heaven (Ps. 103:20).

Lord's Day 50

125. What is the fourth petition?

"Give us this day our daily bread." That is: be pleased to provide for all our bodily needs (Ps. 104:27–28) so that thereby we may acknowledge that thou art the only source of all that is good (Acts 14:17), and that without thy blessing neither our care and labor nor thy gifts can do us any good (1 Cor. 15:58). Therefore, may we withdraw our trust from all creatures and place it in thee alone (Ps. 55:22).

Lord's Day 51

126. What is the fifth petition?

"And forgive us our debts, as we also have forgiven our debtors." That is: be pleased, for the sake of Christ's blood, not to charge to us, miserable sinners, our many transgressions, nor the evil which still clings to us (1 John 2:1–2). We also find this witness of thy grace in us, that it is our sincere intention heartily to forgive our neighbor (Matt. 6:14–15).

Lord's Day 52

127. What is the sixth petition?

"And lead us not into temptation, but deliver us from evil." That is: since we are so weak that we cannot stand by ourselves for one moment (John 15:5), and besides, since our sworn enemies, the devil (1 Peter 5:8), the world (John 15:19), and our own sin (Rom. 7:23), ceaselessly assail us, be pleased to preserve and strengthen us through the power of thy Holy Spirit so that we may stand firm against them, and not be defeated in this spiritual warfare (Matt. 26:41), until at last we obtain complete victory (1 Thess. 3:13; 5:23).

128. How do you close this prayer?

"For thine is the kingdom and the power and the glory, forever." That is: we ask all this of thee because, as our King, thou art willing and able to give us all that is good since thou hast power over all things (Rom. 10:12–13), and that by this not we ourselves but thy holy name may be glorified forever (John 14:13).

129. What is the meaning of the little word "Amen"?

Amen means: this shall truly and certainly be. For my prayer is much more certainly heard by God than I am persuaded in my heart that I desire such things from him (2 Cor. 1:20; 2 Tim. 2:13; Isa. 65:24).

Note

1. See Bard Thompson et al., *Essays on the Heidelberg Catechism* (Philadelphia: United Church Press, 1963), 8–30, 76–92; Derk Visser, *Zacharias Ursinus, The Reluctant Reformer: His Life and Times* (New York: United Church Press, 1983), 99–120; J. F. Gerhard Goeters, "Entstehung und Früh-geschichte des Katechismus," *Handbuch zum Heidelberger Katechismus*, ed. Lothar Coenen (Neukirchen-Vluyn: Neukirchener Verlag des Erziehungsvereins GmbH, 1963), 3–23.

22. The Palatinate Liturgy

(1563)

Along with the Heidelberg Catechism (see vol. 2:327–58), several forms of worship were issued in the new Church Order published in November 1563 in Heidelberg at the command of Frederick III (the Pious). It contained orders for common or church prayer on Sunday mornings, holy days, and fast days; an order for preparation for the Lord's Supper; and an order for the Lord's Supper itself. There were services for preaching on the catechism on Sunday and holy day afternoons, for preaching on workdays, and for morning and evening prayer on workdays.

The Lord's Supper was to be observed at least once a month and was preceded by a service of preparation on Saturday. Preaching services were to be held in the cities on Wednesdays and Fridays; on other workdays, morning and evening prayer was to take place.

As in all Reformation liturgies, preaching was central. The Heidelberg Catechism was supposed to shape all preaching, not simply the sermons in the Sunday afternoon services dedicated to catechetical preaching. In every service, the minister was expected to use the article of the catechism that was applicable to the topic of the sermon, which in turn was based on Scripture. The catechism further provided a proper doctrinal definition of the Lord's Supper, which was always preached about during the preparatory service.

The influence of the Heidelberg Catechism can be seen in other parts of services as well. For example, the order of the catechism (human

---

SOURCE: Bard Thompson, "The Palatinate Liturgy," *Theology and Life* 6, no. 1 (spring 1963): 49–63. Used by permission.

misery, human redemption, human gratitude) informs the prayer before the sermon. The same structure shapes the charge to the people in the questions at the beginning of the preparation for the Lord's Supper. It reappears in the self-examination that is part of the form for the celebration of the Lord's Supper. When young people come to communion for the first time, they are asked questions out of the catechism during the preparation for the Lord's Supper.

The Palatinate Liturgy was composed by a committee in which Zacharias Ursinus (1534–83) played a leading role. It is probable that Caspar Olevianus (1536–87) also made a substantial contribution to the liturgy, especially in the final paragraphs of the service of the Eucharist, which concern church discipline.[1]

Calvin's Form of Church Prayers *was one of the sources of the Palatinate Liturgy, but there were others: an earlier Palatinate order produced under Otto Heinrich; the Zurich order of 1535; and the order of the Church of the Strangers in London and Frankfurt, composed by a Polish Protestant named John Laski (or Johannes Alasco or à Lasco). The authors of the Palatinate Liturgy borrowed in some cases almost literally from some of these sources.*[2]

In North America, the Palatinate Liturgy became the primary form of worship of German Reformed congregations well into the nineteenth century. It was a major source for the Reformed Book of Worship *(1866) that succeeded it. Its influence is especially evident in the service of preparation for Holy Communion, based on the preparatory service in the 1563 liturgy. This service was later incorporated into the Evangelical and Reformed* Book of Worship *(1947) and* The Hymnal *(1941).*

A. Of Common Prayer[3]

Before the Sermon, especially in the morning on Sunday and holy days, and on fast days,[4] *the following prayer shall be delivered to the people, in which the Christian Congregation is explicitly reminded of the misery of man, and the saving grace of God is implored, so that hearts become humble and more desirous of receiving the Word of grace.*[5]

Grace, peace, and mercy . . . (1 Tim. 1:2).

Heavenly Father, eternal and merciful God, we confess and acknowledge before thy divine majesty that we are poor, miserable sinners, conceived and born in all sin and corruption, prone to every evil, unfit for any good; and that we, with our sinful life, transgress thy holy commandments without ceasing, whereby we provoke thy wrath against us, and, according to thy righteous judgment, purchase for ourselves eternal damnation. Nevertheless, O Lord, we suffer remorse and sorrow that we have provoked thee to anger; we condemn ourselves and our iniquities, and plead that thy grace may come to relieve our misery and distress. Wherefore have mercy upon us, O most gracious God and Father, and forgive us all our sin through the holy passion of thy dear Son, our Lord Jesus Christ. And vouchsafe to us hereafter the grace of thy Holy Spirit, who teaches us to recognize our unrighteousness with all our heart, so as to abhor ourselves: that sin may be mortified in us, and that we may arise to newness of life, wherein we may produce the perfect fruit of holiness and righteousness, which, for Christ's sake, is well-pleasing unto thee.[6]

Grant us also to understand thy Holy Word according to thy divine will, that we may learn thereof to place our whole trust in thee alone, and to draw away from all creatures: that even our Old Man with all his lusts may be crucified more and more each day, and that we may offer ourselves as a living sacrifice unto thee, to the honor of thy holy name and the edification of our neighbor; through our Lord Jesus Christ, who hath taught us to pray, saying:

Our Father . . .

On Sunday, after the morning Sermon,[7] *the Minister shall say:*

Beloved in the Lord, whereas we see in God's commandments, as in a mirror, how great and manifold are our sins, by which we merit both temporal and eternal punishment, let us heartily confess the same to our faithful Father. Therefore say with me:

I, poor sinner, confess before thee, my God and Creator, that I, alas, have sinned against thee grievously and in manifold ways: not alone by gross, outward sins, but much more by inward and inborn blindness, unbelief and doubt, despondence and impatience, pride and evil covetousness, secret envy, hatred and malice, and other wicked devices—as thou, my Lord and God, dost perceive in me, and I, alas, cannot sufficiently perceive. I repent of these things and grieve over them: And from the heart I implore grace through thy dear Son, Jesus Christ.[8]

Thereupon he shall proclaim the forgiveness of sins to the believers and the judgment of God to the impenitent, and shall say:

Harken now to the undoubted comfort of the grace of God which he doth promise in His Gospel to all that believe.

Thus saith the Lord Christ in the third chapter of John: God so loved the world that He gave His only-begotten Son, that all who believe in Him shall not perish, but have everlasting life.

Now, as many there be of you, who despair of themselves and their sins, and trust that their debts are completely forgiven to them through the merit of Christ alone, who resolve more and more to desist from sins, and to serve the Lord in true holiness and righteousness: To those (as they believe in the Son of the living God) I proclaim at God's command that they are released in heaven from all their sins (as He doth promise in His holy Gospel) through the perfect satisfaction of the most holy passion and death of our Lord Jesus Christ. Amen.

But as many there be among you, who still take pleasure in their sins and shame, or persist in sins against their conscience: To such I declare by the command of God that His wrath and judgment abideth upon them, all their sins being retained in heaven: And they can never be delivered from eternal damnation, except they repent.

Inasmuch as we do not doubt, but that our prayers are satisfied through the passion of Jesus Christ, and are acceptable unto God, let us heartily call upon Him and say:

Prayer after the Sermon

Almighty God, Maker of heaven and earth, we give thee thanks from the bottom of our hearts that thou hast created us, and hast preserved, nourished, and sustained us and our children to this day, and art yet willing to keep and govern us in the future. But especially do we thank thee that thou hast given us the knowledge of thy Son Jesus Christ, whom thou hast promised in Paradise, and hast forgiven our sins through His bitter suffering and death. And we beseech thee to renew us in the image of thy Son Jesus Christ, through the preaching of thy Word and the power of thy Holy Spirit, that in both body and soul we may live with thee forever, and give thee praise, for which we were at first created. And wilt thou defend us from Satan, lest he tear thy holy Word out of our hearts, as he did to our first parents Adam and Eve.

So long as thou willest to govern us in this life also through the hand of our civil authorities, who are thy servants, we do therefore beseech thee, thou who holdest their hearts in thy hand, to grant peace and concord to them all: to his imperial and royal majesty,[9] to all princes and lords, especially our most gracious Elector and Prince, Duke Frederick, Count Palatine, together with her electoral grace, his wife, to the young lord and ladies, councilors and officials (also to the illustrious Council of the city) and the honorable community of this place. Grant that they direct their whole government to the end that our Lord Jesus Christ, to whom thou hast given all power in heaven and earth, may reign over them and their subjects: that the poor people, who are the creatures of thy hand and the sheep of thy pasture, and for whom the Lord Jesus shed His blood, may be governed in all holiness and righteousness: likewise that we may show unto them, all becoming honor and loyalty for thy sake, and lead an honest, peaceful, and Christian life under their rule.

Grant thy blessing and benediction also to the fruit of the earth, that by this means we may know thee as a Father, source of all goodness and mercy.

Neither do we pray thee for ourselves alone, but for all men of the whole world, that thou wilt graciously have mercy upon them all together, but especially upon those who are our fellow members in the body of Christ and who suffer persecution by the Turks and the pope for the sake of thy truth. O Father of all grace, wilt thou restrain such fury of thine enemies who persecute thy Son in His members; and gird the persecuted with an invincible resolve and with the power of thy Holy Spirit, that they may receive with thanksgiving such persecution from thy hand, and in the midst of their tribulation experience that joy which passeth all understanding. Comfort and sustain all of the poor, the prisoners, the sick, the widows and orphans, the women with child, the troubled and tempted hearts; and grant them thy peace through our dear Lord Jesus Christ, who hath given us this undoubted promise: Verily, verily, I say unto you, Whatsoever ye shall ask the Father in my name, He will give it you. And then He hath instructed us to pray in this manner:

Our Father . . .

Or in this wise:

Almighty God, heavenly Father, who hast promised us that whatsoever we shall ask of thee in the name of thy dear Son Jesus Christ, thou will surely grant unto us: we beseech thee to act in us by thy Holy Spirit, that we may rightly know thee, and may hallow, adore and praise thee in all thy words, in which there radiates thine omnipotence, wisdom, goodness, righteousness, mercy and truth. Grant also that we may order our whole life, in thought, word and deed, that on our account, thy name may not be profaned, but honored and glorified.

Hallowed be thy name.

Rule us also by the sceptre of thy Word and the power of thy Holy Spirit, that we, with all men, may increasingly subject and yield ourselves to thy majesty. Preserve and increase thy Church, and destroy all the works of the Devil, and all false and evil designs which are devised against thy holy Word. Put thine enemies to shame by the might of thy truth and righteousness, so that every power which exalts itself against thine honor may be further overthrown and destroyed day by day, till the consummation of thy Kingdom be at hand, when thou shalt manifest thy glory in us at the Last Judgment, and be forever all in all.

Thy Kingdom come.

Grant also that we, with all men, may renounce our own will and all the lusts of our flesh, and, without argument, obey thy will which alone is good, so that every man may fulfil his office and calling as readily and faithfully as do the angels in heaven.

Thy will be done.

Wilt thou provide us, moreover, with every physical need, and grant us peace and good government, that we may perceive by these means that thou are the only source of all good, and a faithful Father who carest for His children, and that without thy blessing neither our trouble and labor nor yet thy mercies are able to prosper us. Wherefore we may withdraw our trust in all creatures, to place it in thee alone.

Give us this day our daily bread.

On account of the shed blood of Jesus Christ, reckon not to us poor sinners all our iniquities and debts, neither the corruption which ever clings to us: even as we find this testimony of thy grace in our hearts, that we sincerely forgive our neighbor and desire to attend his welfare.

Forgive us our debts . . .

And as we are indeed so weak in ourselves that we cannot stand fast for a moment, and thereto our sworn enemies, the devil, the world and our own flesh, do not cease to assail us, wilt thou uphold and strengthen us by the power of thy Holy Spirit, that we may firmly withstand these foes, and be not overcome in this spiritual battle, but remain steadfast till at length we obtain the full victory, and reign forever in thy Kingdom with thy Son, our Lord and Defender, Jesus Christ.

All these things we ask of thee, that thou, not we, mayest receive eternal praise. Thou canst do such things, for thou art Almighty God. And thou desirest to do them as a faithful Father, as surely as we beseech thee heartily for the same, through our Lord Jesus. Amen.

Our Father . . .

Praise ye the Lord with your song.

After the singing, let the Minister say:

The Lord bless you and keep you. The Lord make His face to shine upon you and be gracious unto you. The Lord lift up His countenance upon you and give you peace. Amen.

B. Of the Preparation for the Holy Supper[10]

The Lord's Supper shall be observed at least once a month in the towns, once every two months in the villages, and on Easter, Pentecost and Christmas in both places. Yet where the edification, custom, or need of the churches may necessitate, it is Christian and proper to observe it more often. And whenever it is determined to hold the Lord's Supper, notice shall always be given by the Minister to the Congregation of God a week beforehand, with an exhortation that the entire Congregation prepare itself for that occasion.

To that end he shall also admonish the parents and heads of families that in the meantime they instruct their children and other young folk whom they intend to bring to the Lord's Table for the first time, and that they point them out to the Minister after the Sermon on the forthcoming Saturday or some other preceding day convenient to the schedule of the church, so that they may receive further instruction.

On the Saturday before the Lord's Supper, the Preparatory Service shall be held. It is a Sermon on the true understanding of the sacrament, to which an introduction is found in both the Catechism[11] *and the Order for Holy Communion.*

At the end of the Sermon, the Minister shall admonish the people to remain, in order to hear further instruction and to make profession of their faith. Thereupon the Minister shall walk to the front of the Table, and shall first exhort those young people at hand, who have not previously gone to the Lord's Table, to present themselves and make profession of their faith. Then the Minister shall bid those who so identify themselves to recite, first, the articles of the Christian faith, the Ten Commandments, and the Lord's Prayer; thereafter he shall ask them questions from the Catechism about the Lord's Supper. Yet some of those present may not be able, out of timidity, to relate and recite such matters word for word in the usual way; but if they are not otherwise culpable, they shall be reminded by the Minister of the chief articles of the Christian faith, and, having made their profession, shall be admitted with the Congregation to the Lord's Supper.

When the examination has been completed, the Minister shall charge the people with the following trial and confession, in the form of questions:

The Word of God ascribes to us these three points: first our sins; second, our redemption; third, the gratitude which we owe God in return.[12] Therefore let each one hold before his eyes the sum of God's commandments, in which His will is charged to us, namely: Thou shalt love God with the whole soul, the whole mind, and all strength, and thy neighbor as thyself. But then, inasmuch as we have never kept any of these matters, we are shown, as in a mirror, our sins and misery, and finally even eternal damnation. Wherefore I ask you first whether you make such a confession with me before the face of God, and abhor yourselves on that account, and thirst after the righteousness and grace of Jesus Christ?

Answer: We do.

Second, do you likewise believe that God is not only merciful, but also just, who will not suffer sin to go unpunished; and that since no creatures could have endured such punishment for us, the only Son of God was sent into this world by the Father's mercy, and took upon Himself a true human body and soul, that He might bear for us, in our very flesh and blood, and punishment and wrath of God which we have deserved; and that according to the undoubted promise of the Gospel, this perfect satisfaction of the Son of God for our sin is granted to each one in particular who accepts it with hearty trust as his own; and that each one has the forgiveness of his sins, as surely as if he had never committed nor borne any sin, and henceforth is even counted righteous and holy before God, as though he himself had fulfilled all the righteousness which Jesus Christ, his Saviour, has accomplished for him and bestowed him by grace, apart from any personal merit—notwithstanding his unworthiness of all this, nor the many infirmities that yet remain in him, for all of the same are covered by the passion and obedience of Jesus Christ, till at last they are entirely removed.

Further, do you also believe that by means of His Holy Supper, with true warrants and seals, and through the action of the Holy Spirit in your[13] heart, Christ now again confirms to each among you this redemption He once promised and granted to you in Holy Baptism, to this effect: first, that His body was as surely offered for you on the Cross, and His blood shed for you, as you see with your eyes that the bread which the Lord calls His body is broken for you, and the cup of thanksgiving is offered unto you; second, that by the operation of the Holy Spirit, the Lord Christ Himself feeds and nourishes your hungry and contrite heart and weary soul with His crucified body and shed blood unto eternal life, as surely as you do receive from the Minister's hand, and do eat and drink by mouth, of the holy bread and cup of the Lord in remembrance of Him; and that therefore the passion and death of Christ is as certainly your own, as if you had suffered in your own body all that the Lord endured in His blessed body on your behalf. Then, for the sake of this comfort, the Lord Jesus instituted His Holy Supper in remembrance of Him, that we may celebrate it with heartfelt gratitude and joy, until He shall come in the clouds to deliver us wholly from the cross which we must patiently carry after Him in this vale of tears, and take us body and soul unto Himself in the eternal kingdom of His Father. Is this your faith?

Answer: It is.

Third, let each one also search his heart, whether he desires to be thankful to the Lord Christ all the rest of his life; whether he has heartily renounced all envy, hatred and bitterness, and has forgiven his neighbor, even as the Lord Jesus has forgiven us poor sinners many thousand times over; whether he firmly resolves, here in the Lord's presence, to hate all profanity, obscene words and acts, gluttony and drunkenness, and other sins so heartily, that, by the grace of God, he may nevermore commit the same throughout his life?

Answer: We do.

All who now find this in their heart should not doubt that they already possess the forgiveness of all their sins through the holy passion and death of Christ, and assuredly retain the same so long as they persevere in this understanding, notwithstanding the many infirmities which yet remain in them, but which are covered by the same passion and death of Christ. Wherefore, let each one who heartily desires this say:

Amen.

Fall on your knees and pray as the Lord hath taught us:

Our Father . . .

After the prayer, let the Minister say:

The God of peace sanctify you wholly. And may your whole spirit, soul and body be kept blameless unto the coming of our Lord Jesus Christ. He that calleth you is faithful, and He will also do it. Amen . . .

And should any person have a private concern, about which he would like to speak with his Minister, such an opportunity shall not be denied him.

C. Of the Lord's Holy Supper[14]

On those days when Holy Communion is to be celebrated, a Sermon shall be delivered on the Lord's death and on His Supper, in which the institution, order, reasons, profit and fruit of the Holy Supper shall be treated. And in this Sermon, the Minister shall study brevity for the sake of the subsequent Action, in which the Supper is sufficiently performed, directly after the completion of the Sermon and Sunday Prayer, as set forth below.

Then, before there is singing, the Minister of the Word shall read out the following exhortation—clearly, forcefully, and earnestly—by the Table at which the Supper is to be celebrated.

Form for the Celebration of the Holy Supper

Beloved in the Lord Jesus Christ, hear the Words of Institution of the Holy Supper of our Lord Jesus Christ, which the holy Apostle Paul records for us in the First Epistle to the Corinthians, at the eleventh chapter: I have received from the Lord that which I have delivered unto you. For the Lord Jesus, in the night in which He was betrayed, took bread, and giving thanks He brake it, and said, Take, eat: this is my body which is broken for you: this do in remembrance of me. After the same manner also He took the cup, after Supper, and said, This cup is the new testament in my blood: this do ye, as oft as ye drink it, in remembrance of me.

For as often as ye eat this bread, and drink this cup, ye shall proclaim the Lord's death till He comes. Now, whoever eats this bread or drinks the cup of the Lord unworthily, is guilty of the body and the blood of the Lord. But let a man examine himself, and so let him eat of that bread and drink of that cup. For he that eateth and drinketh unworthily eateth and drinketh judgment to himself, not discerning the Lord's body.

That we may now celebrate the Lord's Supper to our comfort, it is of necessity, above all, that we rightly examine ourselves beforehand, and second, that we direct the Supper to the end for which the Lord Christ appointed it, namely, in remembrance of Him.

True self-examination consists of these three parts. First, let each one reflect upon his sin and condemnation, that he may abhor and humble himself before God; for the wrath of God against sin is so great that, rather than suffer it to go unpunished, He hath punished the same in His dear Son Jesus Christ, by the bitter and shameful death of the Cross.

Second, let each one search his heart, whether he also believes this certain promise of God, that all of his sins are forgiven him, solely through the passion and death of Jesus Christ; and that the perfect righteousness of Christ is imputed and granted to him as his own, as though he himself in his own person had paid for all his sins and fulfilled all righteousness.

Third, let each one search his conscience, whether he is also disposed to show his gratitude unto the Lord God henceforth with his whole life, and to walk uprightly in His presence; likewise, whether he unfeignedly and heartily renounces all enmity, jealousy and hatred, and has an earnest determination to live hereafter in true love and unity with his neighbor.

Those, now, who are disposed, God will assuredly receive in grace and will recognize as worthy participants at the Table of His Son Jesus Christ.

But those on the contrary who do not perceive this testimony in their heart, eat and drink judgment to themselves. Wherefore, according to the command of Christ and the Apostle Paul, we warn all to abstain from the Lord's Table who know themselves afflicted with the following sins; and we declare unto them that they have no part in the Kingdom of Christ: all idolaters; all who invoke dead saints, angels, or other creatures; worshipers of images; all sorcerers and diviners who make the sign of the cross upon cattle and people and other things, and those who give credence to such signs; all who despise God and His Word and the holy sacraments; all blasphemers; all who desire to cause schism and sedition in Church or State; all perjurers; all who are disobedient to their parents and superiors; all murderers, contentious and quarrelsome persons who live in envy and hatred with their neighbors; all adulterers, fornicators, drunkards, thieves, usurers, robbers, gamblers, misers, and all who lead a scandalous life. Lest their judgment and damnation be the more severe, all of these persons, so long as they persist in such sins, should resolve to abstain from this food which Christ hath ordained solely for His believers.

But this is not charged to us, dear Christians, to discourage the contrite hearts of believers, as if none might go to the Lord's Supper except they were completely sinless. For we do not come to this Supper in order to show that we are perfect and righteous in ourselves. On the contrary, by seeking our life outside of ourselves, in Jesus Christ, we confess that we lie in the midst of death. Therefore, though we still find much infirmity and misery in ourselves—such that we do not have perfect faith, neither do we undertake to serve God as zealously as we ought, but have to fight daily against the weakness of our faith and the evil lusts of our flesh—nevertheless, since we profoundly deplore such infirmities through the grace of the Holy Spirit, and heartily desire to resist our unbelief and live according to all the commandments of God, we shall be sure and certain that no sin or weakness yet remaining in us against our will, can keep God from taking us into grace and so making us worthy participants of this heavenly food and drink.

In the second place, let us now consider to what end the Lord hath instituted His Supper for us, namely that we do this in remembrance of Him.

As we do so, we are to remember Him thus: first, by having perfect trust in our heart that our Lord Jesus Christ was sent into this world by the Father, according to the promises made to the Patriarchs in the beginning; that He took upon Himself our flesh and blood; that He endured for us on earth, from the beginning of His Incarnation till the end of His life, the wrath of God under which we must have perished eternally; and that He fulfilled complete obedience to the divine law, accomplishing righteousness on our behalf. Especially are we to remember Him when the burden of our sins and of God's wrath pressed from Him the bloody sweat in the Garden; when He was bound, that He might set us free; when afterward He suffered untold abuse, that we might never be put to shame. Innocent, He was condemned to death, that we might be acquitted before the tribunal of God. Indeed, He permitted His blessed body to be nailed on the Cross, that He might fasten thereon the indictment of our sins, and took upon Himself our condemnation, to replenish us with His benediction. And he humbled Himself, even in that deepest abuse of all, that hellish anguish of body and soul on the beams of the Cross, when He cried out with a loud voice, My God, my God, why hast thou forsaken me: that we might find acceptance with God and nevermore be forsaken of Him. Finally, by His death and the shedding of His blood, He sealed the new and eternal testament, the covenant of grace and reconciliation; as He said, It is finished.

That we might now firmly believe that we belong to this covenant of grace, the Lord Jesus took bread in His last Supper, and giving thanks He brake it, and gave it to His disciples, and said, Take and eat: this is my body which is given for you: this do in remembrance of me. After the same manner He took the cup after supper, gave thanks, and said, Take and drink ye all of it: this cup is the new testament in my blood, which is shed for you and for many, for the remission of sins: this do ye, as oft as ye drink it, in remembrance of me. Which is to say: as often as you eat this bread and drink this cup, you shall be reminded and assured by this means, as by a sure memorial and pledge, of my heartfelt love and faithfulness unto you. I give my body to die upon the timber of the Cross, and shed my blood for the sake of you who must otherwise have perished in eternal death; and I feed and nourish your hungry and thirsty souls unto eternal life with my same crucified body and shed blood, as truly as this bread is seen broken to each one, and to each this cup is given, and you do eat and drink of the same with your mouth in remembrance of me.

From this institution of the Holy Supper of our Lord Jesus Christ, we perceive that He directs our faith and trust to His perfect sacrifice, made once upon the Cross, as the sole basis and foundation of our salvation, when He became the true meat and drink of eternal life unto our hungry and thirsty souls. For by His death He hath taken away the cause of our perpetual hunger and grief—sin, in fact—and hath obtained for us the life-giving Spirit: that through the same Spirit who dwells in Christ the head, and in us His members, we might have true communion with Him, and be made partakers of all His benefits, of eternal life, righteousness, and glory.

Through the same Spirit, therefore, we also may be bound together as members of one body in true brotherly love, as the Holy Apostle saith: There is one bread, so we who are many are one body, because we all partake of one bread (1 Cor. 10:17). For as of many grains, one flour is ground and one bread is baked, as of many grapes pressed together, one wine and one draught flows and blends, likewise all we, being incorporated with Christ by true faith, shall be one body all together through brotherly love, for the sake of Christ our dear Saviour, who first loved us so dearly: And this we manifest not by word alone, but by deed to one another. Thereto may the Almighty and merciful Father of our Lord Jesus Christ assist us by His Holy Spirit. Amen.

Let us pray.

Merciful God and Father, we beseech thee to act upon our hearts by thy Holy Spirit in this Supper, at which we keep the glorious memorial of the bitter death of thy dear Son Jesus Christ, that with true faith we may ever more yield ourselves to Him, and that through the power of the Holy Spirit our weary and contrite hearts may be fed and quickened by His true body and blood, yea of Him who is true God and man, the only bread of heaven. Thus may we live no longer in our sins, but He in us and we in Him, and so truly partake of the new and eternal testament and covenant of grace, that we do not doubt that thou wilt be our gracious Father, nevermore reckoning our sins against us, but providing us all things for body and soul.[15] Grant us thy grace that we may cheerfully take up our cross, deny ourselves, confess our Saviour, and in all tribulations wait with head uplifted for our Lord Jesus Christ out of heaven, when He will make our mortal bodies like unto His transfigured and glorious body and take us to Himself in eternity. Amen.

Our Father . . .

Confirm us also, by this Holy Supper, in the universal and undoubted Christian faith, of which we make confession with mouth and heart, saying:

I believe in God . . .

That we may now be fed with Christ, the true bread of heaven, let us not cleave with our hearts to this external bread and wine, but lift up our hearts and faith into heaven, where Christ Jesus is our Intercessor at the right hand of His heavenly Father (where the articles of our Christian faith also direct us), and doubt not that through the action of the Holy Spirit, our souls shall be fed and nourished with His body and blood, as truly as we receive the holy bread and cup in remembrance of Him.[16]

Here the Minister shall break a piece of the bread of the Lord for each one, and shall administer it to him, saying:

The bread which we break is the communion of the body of Christ.

And the other Minister shall deliver the cup to him, saying:

The cup of blessing which we bless is the communion of the blood of Christ.

According to the number of communicants and the structure of each church, there shall either be singing while Communion is served, or several chapters of Scripture shall be read which are helpful to the remembrance of Christ's death, such as John 14–18 and Isaiah 53; and of these passages, the ones which are most appropriate and edifying to each church may be used.

At the completion of Communion, the Minister shall say:

Dearly beloved, as the Lord hath now fed our souls at His Table, let us praise His name with thanksgiving, each one saying in his heart:

Bless the Lord, O my soul, and all that is within me bless His holy name. Bless the Lord, O my soul, and forget not the goodness He hath done to me: Who forgiveth thee all thine iniquities, and healeth all thine infirmities; who redeemeth thy life from destruction; who crowneth thee with grace and loving-kindness (Ps. 103:1–4). The Lord is merciful, patient, and of great goodness. He doth not deal with us after our sins; nor reward us according to our offence. For as high as the heaven is above the earth, He sheweth mercy upon them that fear Him. As far as the rising of the sun is from the setting of the same, so far doth He put our transgressions from us. As a father pitieth his children, so the Lord pitieth them that fear Him. (Ps. 103:8, 10–13). Who did not spare His own Son, but delivered Him up for us all, and with Him give us all things (Rom. 8:32). Wherefore God sheweth His love toward us, in that while we were yet sinners, Christ died for us. According as we have been justified by His blood, much more shall we be saved from wrath by Him. For if while we were yet enemies we are reconciled to God by the death of His Son, much more, now that we are reconciled to Him, shall we be saved by His life (Rom. 5:8–10). Wherefore my mouth and heart shall publish the Lord's praise from this time forth forevermore. Amen.

Or in this wise:

Almighty, merciful God and Father, we give thee most hearty thanks that of thine infinite mercy, thou hast given us thine only-begotten Son to be our Mediator, the sacrifice for our sin, and the food and drink of eternal life, granting us true faith that we may become partakers of these thy benefits, and hast bidden thy dear Son Jesus Christ to institute His Holy Supper to strengthen us in the same. We beseech thee, O faithful God and Father, that by the operation of thy Spirit, thou wilt cause us to prosper in this memorial of our Lord Jesus Christ and proclamation of His death, for our daily increase in true faith and the saving communion of Christ; through the same Jesus Christ, thy beloved Son. Amen.

It pertains, however, to the true and godly administration and use of the holy sacraments, not only that they are observed in the manner ordained by God and to the end for which He appointed them, but also that they are not administered to such persons whom He has excluded from them. Thus, it is of necessity that Christian excommunication be exercised in the church, not by words alone, but by deed as well. That is, if there are some in the congregation who are guilty of blasphemous doctrine or grievous vices, they shall not be admitted to the Lord's Supper until they show amendment.

And urgent necessity requires that the Christian Church be set free from the intolerable mischief and dreadful tyranny of the popish bann, by which the pope and his crowd have cast everything under his feet. Thus, since we are obliged not only to root out and destroy that which is evil, but in its place to plant and build that which is good, it is no less urgent that a legitimate, Christian excommunication be maintained in the Christian congregation, according to the command of Christ in Matt. 18, and for the welfare and need of the church.

But lest this exclusion from the use of the sacraments fall into abuse and disorder, as in popery, such order and moderation shall be observed therein as prescribed by Christ and St. Paul. Above all, it is not vested in one or several ministers or other individuals, but rests in the entire Christian congregation, to which the ministers, as well as the humblest member of the church, are subject. For if every preacher at his pleasure should put under the bann whomever he wished, this would not be the bann instituted by Christ, but one devised by Antichrist.

Therefore in every locality, according to the convenience and need of the same, several honorable and god-fearing men shall be appointed from the congregation. On behalf, and in the name, of the whole congregation, and in connection with the ministers, they shall truly and earnestly exhort (once, twice, or three times, according to circumstances) such persons to amend their ways who are offensive either by dangerous errors of faith or by their lives, such as fornicators, misers, idolaters, slanderers, drunkards, or those who otherwise lead a disorderly life. And if they do not take heed of this, they shall be separated from the Christian congregation by the denial of the holy sacraments, until they promise and give proof of amendment. There shall also be a further ordinance concerning the procedure in this matter.

Notes

1. See Emil Sehling, ed., *Die Evangelischen Kirchenordnungen des XVI, Jahrhunderts Kurpfalz*, vol. 14 (Tübingen: J. C. B. Mohr, 1969), 44.

2. See Sehling, 45–46; G. Nordholt, "Die zum Katechismus gehörende Gestalt der Gemeinde und des Gottesdienstes (unter Berücksichtigung der kurpfälzischen Kirchenordnung)," in *Handbuch zum Heidelberger Katechismus*, ed. Lothar Coenen (Neukirchen-Vluyn: Neukirchener Verlag des Erziehungsvereins GmbH, 1963), 35; and James Hastings Nichols, *Corporate Worship in the Reformed Tradition* (Philadelphia: Westminster Press, 1968), 75–81.

3. From Wilhelm Niesel, ed., *Bekenntnisschriften und Kirchenordnungen* (Zurich: Evangelischer Verlag A. G. Zollikon-Zurich, 1938), 195–205.

4. **Order of Holy Days:** Holy days shall be kept in the same manner as Sunday. These holy days shall be observed: all Sundays, Christmas and the day following, New Year's day, Easter and the day following, Ascension day, Pentecost and the Monday following.

On Christmas and the day after, the basis of our salvation, namely the two natures in Christ with the benefit we obtain therefrom, shall be expounded in the narratives of the birth of Christ, as that is dealt with in the end of Part I and the beginning of Part II of the Catechism.

The Ministers in the towns are also permitted to begin to explain the narratives of the Passion on Invocavit Sunday and pursue the same until Easter, according to the convenience of each particular church.

On Easter and the Monday following, the narratives of Christ's resurrection shall be preached, so that the Christian congregation may receive good, basic instruction from the holy, divine Scripture upon the two principal articles of our Christian faith, namely, that Christ arose from the dead on the third day, and that we too shall arise from the dead.

The festival of Christ's ascension also has its narratives, as they are written in the Acts of the Apostles, chapter 1, and elsewhere. Upon them, we may teach and preach concerning those articles of our faith in which we profess that Christ has ascended into heaven, sitteth at the right hand of God, and from thence will come to judge the living and the dead.

On Pentecost and the Monday following, the second chapter in the Acts of the Apostles shall be the basis of preaching.

Niesel, ed., *Bekenntnisschriften und Kirchenordnungen*, 205; Thompson, "The Palatinate Liturgy," 49–51, n. 2.

5. **Of Ecclesiastical Singing and Clothing:** With reference to the singing of Psalms, the Apostle Paul admonishes that it be done not only with the mouth, but with the heart as well; and that all of it should be useful to the edification of the churches. But as the heart cannot praise God by that which it does not understand,

we herewith require that none other than German Psalms be sung in our churches. Furthermore, the Ministers shall use respectable and modest clothing in the discharge of their ecclesiastical duties, as well as at other times (*wie auch sonst*).

Niesel, ed., *Bekenntnisschriften und Kirchenordnungen*, 209; Thompson, "The Palatinate Liturgy," 51–52, n. 3.

6. According to Bard Thompson, the editor of the version reprinted here, "So far, this prayer is an adaptation of Calvin's form of confession. The following paragraph seems to correspond to Calvin's collect for illumination before the Sermon."

7. **Of Doctrine and Preaching:** Thus saith the Lord Jesus Christ in the seventeenth chapter of John: This is the life eternal, that they know thee, the only true God, and Jesus Christ whom thou hast sent.

In order to lead His chosen ones to this knowledge and to eternal life, the Lord Jesus Christ has appointed the preaching of repentence and forgiveness of sins. By such means (thus instituted because of our weakness, which could not endure the voice of God) the knowledge of God and the life everlasting may be commenced in our hearts here on earth: until we attain in heaven, without external means, to that perfection in which we shall behold God face to face.

As God reveals Himself in His Word, which is fully contained in the canonical books of the Old and New Testament, all sermons shall be drawn therefrom and based thereon, and shall be directed every time to the existing defects and faults of the people, according to the declaration of the holy Apostle Paul in 2 Tim 3:16. All Scripture inspired by God is profitable for doctrine, for reproof, for correction, for training in righteousness, that a man of God may be perfect, equipped for all good works.

And inasmuch as the Word of God tends to arrange doctrine to this effect: That first it leads men to knowledge of their sins and misery, then teaches them also how they are redeemed from all sins and misery, and third, how they are to be thankful to God for such redemption: therefore the preachers shall attend diligently to these three points in treating their text, and ever take care to use the medicine well, according to the necessity of wounded consciences. They should also know how to suit their sermons to the meagre and limited understanding of the common people, so that the article of the Catechism, to which the doctrine refers that the preacher is treating, may be introduced at the same time and intelligently impressed upon the people (*Also dass der Artickel des Catechismi darauff die Lehr so er für hat / sich lendet / mit eingeführet / vnd dem volck verstendtlich eingebildet werde*).

Neither shall the parsons take it upon themselves to expound any book apart from the Holy Scripture without the advice and previous knowledge of their Superintendents, who shall then supervise that the books of the New Testament, which are most fruitful to the common man and most edifying to the Church, are set forth and expounded, especially on Sunday.

Niesel, ed., *Bekenntnisschriften und Kirchenordunungen*, 142–43; Thompson, "The Palatinate Liturgy," 52–55, n. 6.

8. According to Thompson's note here, "This prayer comes verbatim from the Würtemberg liturgy of 1536. Cf. A. L. Richter, ed., *Die evangelischen Kirchenordnungen des 16. Jahrhunderts*, I, 268."

9. Ferdinand I, Holy Roman Emperor (d. 1564).

10. *Bekenntnisschriften und Kirchenordnungen*, 187–89.

11. That is, the Heidelberg Catechism (1563).

12. The threefold structure of the Heidelberg Catechism.

13. According to Thompson's note here, "For the sake of clarity, the pronouns in this passage which refer to the believer have been changed from the third person (he, his, him) to the second person (you, your)."

14. *Bekenntnisschriften und Kirchenordnungen*, 190–95.

15. According to Thompson's note here, "To this point, the prayer corresponds to the next-to-last paragraph of Calvin's Great Prayer."

16. Thompson points out that this is the Reformed *Sursum corda*, typical of the liturgies of Farel, Calvin, Knox, and Laski.

The Dutch Reformed Tradition and the Canons of Dort

23. The Canons of Dort

(1619)

The Synod of Dort (November 13, 1618, to May 9, 1619) represented "the conclusion of the Reformation of doctrine in the Reformed region."[1] It had a strong influence on the Dutch Reformed Church and also on other Reformed churches on the European continent, in England, and in the American colonies, including key traditions within the United Church of Christ—Congregationalists in New England and the German Reformed Church in Pennsylvania.

The Synod of Dort climaxed a long struggle between two ecclesiastical/political parties in the Netherlands. On one side was the Arminian party, named after Jacobus Arminius (1560–1609), who opposed the strict Calvinist doctrine of predestination and advocated religious toleration. Arminius was also a mild Erastian—that is, he approved of limited control of the church by the state. The chief leaders of the Arminian party just before and during the Synod of Dort were Simon Episcopius, Arminius's successor as professor of theology at Leiden; Johan Uytenbogaert, preacher at the Hague; Johan van Oldenbarnevelt, the Advocate of Holland; and Hugo Grotius, an outstanding scholar and jurist.

On the other side were a group of orthodox Calvinists led by Francis Gomar (his followers were called Gomarists). Gomar championed a strict doctrine of predestination, was strongly anti-Catholic, and favored the independence of the church from the state.

SOURCE: *Ecumenical Creeds and Reformed Confessions* (Grand Rapids, Mich.: CRC Publications, 1988). Used by permission.

In 1617 orthodox Calvinists were stoutly supported by Maurice of Orange (or Maurice of Nassau), Stadtholder of Holland and commander of the armies. Maurice had fought successfully for the independence of the northern states of the Netherlands from Spain and worked closely with Oldenbarnevelt. Over the years an antagonism had developed between Maurice and Oldenbarnevelt. Oldenbarnevelt was accused of high treason and executed four days after the end of the Synod of Dort for subversion of the country's religion and policy.

The Synod of Dort is most well known for its pronouncements on predestination over against the Arminian position earlier set forth in the 1610 Dutch Remonstrance to the States of Holland and West Friesland. Arminians after that date were called Remonstrants.

The Remonstrants summarized the strict Calvinist position in five articles, all of which they rejected: (1) That before Creation and the Fall, God predestined some people to eternal life and others to eternal damnation, without regard for righteousness or sin, obedience, or disobedience, but simply because it pleased God to show divine mercy to the former and divine justice to the latter. This was known as the supralapsarian *(beyond the Fall) view. (2) That in view of the Fall, God ordained that a certain part of the human race would be exempt from the consequences of the Fall and would be saved by free grace, but that the rest would be left in their condition of sin to their condemnation (the* sublapsarian *view). (3) That Christ died only for the elect, not for all human beings. (4) That grace is irresistible, so that the elect will be necessarily converted and given faith, but the necessary grace for conversion and faith will be withheld from the nonelect. (5) That those who have been granted divine grace can never lose it.*

Positively, the Remonstrants affirmed five articles: (1) That God has determined to save from the fallen human race those who by the grace of the Holy Spirit believe in Jesus Christ and who remain steadfast in this faith by this same grace. (2) That Christ died for all human beings, but his atoning sacrifice, although sufficient for all, is effective only for believers. (3) That human beings in their fallen state do not possess saving faith themselves, but must be regenerated by God in Christ through the Holy Spirit. (4) That human beings can bring about what is truly good only by grace, but they can resist grace. (5) That although Jesus Christ stands by believers in all trials and temptations, the Scriptures must be studied further to determine whether grace can be lost through negligence.

In 1611 the Remonstrants and their opponents, the Contraremonstrants, held a conference at the Hague to try to settle the conflict between them.

Instead of leading to a resolution, it actually deepened the division. After further conferences with no beneficial results, Maurice, a Contraremonstrant, was able to influence the naming of a preparatory commission to issue a call to convene a national synod—the Synod of Dort. The synod included not only representatives of the various provincial synods of the Netherlands, but also representatives from other Reformed churches in Europe, Great Britain, the Palatinate, Hesse, Bremen, Nassau, Emden, and Switzerland. Two important leaders of Congregationalism attended: John Robinson, pastor to the Pilgrim congregation that eventually immigrated to Plymouth, Massachusetts, and William Ames, a theologian very influential in shaping the Congregational way.

The synod considered many issues: the need for a new Bible translation; the need for catechetical preaching on a regular basis, so that the whole Heidelberg Catechism (see vol. 2:327–58) would be covered yearly; the issue of the baptism of children in the East Indies (they were not to be baptized until they had been properly instructed in the faith); the preparation of candidates for the ministry; and the misuse of the printing press.

It was not until the twenty-seventh session that the synod addressed the concerns of the Remonstrants. Unfortunately, although they were permitted to present their theses concerning the five articles, they were treated not as parties to a debate, but as heretics to be judged and condemned. As a result of the synod, over two hundred Remonstrant pastors were ousted from their positions, and many escaped into exile. (Later, after the death of Maurice, they returned and were restored to favor under the rule of his brother, Frederick Henry.)

The Canons of Dort became an important summary of Calvinist thinking. At the second meeting of the Coetus of German Reformed ministers in Philadelphia in September 1748, the American colonists embraced the canons with these words: "[we] do hereby affirm that we are devoted heart and soul to the Heidelberg Catechism and the Canons of the Synod of Dort of 1618 and 1619, and that we shall unalterably hold to them. . . ." At that meeting, all of the ministers signed except for Rev. J. B. Rieger, who said that he could not agree with the Canons' interpretation of the doctrine of predestination. A few years later (1752), however, his name does appear in a pledge to the acts of the Synod of Dort.[2]

A new English translation of the Canons of Dort has been produced by the Christian Reformed Church. It is printed here without the articles concerning the rejection of errors and the conclusions concerning the rejection of false accusations.[3]

Formally Titled
The Decision of the Synod of Dort on the Five Main Points of Doctrine in Dispute in the Netherlands

The First Main Point of Doctrine

The Judgment Concerning Divine Predestination Which the Synod Declares to Be in Agreement with the Word of God and Accepted Till Now in the Reformed Churches, Set Forth in Several Articles

Article 1: God's Right to Condemn All People

Since all people have sinned in Adam and have come under the sentence of the curse and eternal death, God would have done no one an injustice if it had been his will to leave the entire human race in sin and under the curse, and to condemn them on account of their sin. As the apostle says: *The whole world is liable to the condemnation of God* (Rom. 3:19), *All have sinned and are deprived of the glory of God* (Rom. 3:23), and *The wages of sin is death* (Rom. 6:23). [All quotations from Scripture are translations of the original Latin manuscript.]

Article 2: The Manifestation of God's Love

But this is how God showed his love: he sent his only begotten Son into the world, so that whoever believes in him should not perish but have eternal life.

Article 3: The Preaching of the Gospel

In order that people may be brought to faith, God mercifully sends proclaimers of this very joyful message to the people he wishes and at the time he wishes. By this ministry people are called to repentance and faith in Christ crucified. For *how shall they believe in him of whom they have not heard? And how shall they hear without someone preaching? And how shall they preach unless they have been sent?* (Rom. 10:14–15).

Article 4: A Twofold Response to the Gospel

God's anger remains on those who do not believe this gospel. But those who do accept it and embrace Jesus the Savior with a true and living faith are delivered through him from God's anger and from destruction, and receive the gift of eternal life.

Article 5: The Sources of Unbelief and of Faith

The cause or blame for this unbelief, as well as for all other sins, is not at all in God, but in man. Faith in Jesus Christ, however, and salvation through him is a free gift of God. As Scripture says, *It is by grace you have been saved, through faith, and this not from yourselves; it is a gift of God* (Eph. 2:8). Likewise: *It has been freely given to you to believe in Christ* (Phil. 1:29).

Article 6: God's Eternal Decision

The fact that some receive from God the gift of faith within time, and that others do not, stems from his eternal decision. *For all his works are known to God from eternity* (Acts 15:18; Eph. 1:11). In accordance with this decision he graciously softens the hearts, however hard, of his chosen ones and inclines them to believe, but by his just judgment he leaves in their wickedness and hardness of heart those who have not been chosen. And in this especially is disclosed to us his act—unfathomable, and as merciful as it is just—of distinguishing between people equally lost. This is the well-known decision of election and reprobation revealed in God's Word. This decision the wicked, impure, and unstable distort to their own ruin, but it provides holy and godly souls with comfort beyond words.

Article 7: Election

Election [or choosing] is God's unchangeable purpose by which he did the following:

Before the foundation of the world, by sheer grace, according to the free good pleasure of his will, he chose in Christ to salvation a definite number of particular people out of the entire human race, which had fallen by its own fault from its original innocence into sin and ruin. Those chosen were neither better nor more deserving than the others, but lay with them in the common misery. He did this in Christ, whom he also appointed from eternity to be the mediator, the head of all those chosen, and the foundation of their salvation.

And so he decided to give the chosen ones to Christ to be saved, and to call and draw them effectively into Christ's fellowship through his Word and Spirit. In other words, he decided to grant them true faith in Christ, to justify them, to sanctify them, and finally, after powerfully preserving them in the fellowship of his Son, to glorify them.

God did all this in order to demonstrate his mercy, to the praise of the riches of his glorious grace.

As Scripture says, *God chose us in Christ, before the foundation of the world, so that we should be holy and blameless before him with love; he predestined us whom he adopted as his children through Jesus Christ, in himself, according to the good pleasure of his will, to the praise of his glorious grace, by which he freely made us pleasing to himself in his beloved* (Eph. 1:4–6). And elsewhere, *Those whom he predestined, he also called; and those whom he called, he also justified; and those whom he justified, he also glorified* (Rom. 8:30).

Article 8: A Single Decision of Election

This election is not of many kinds; it is one and the same election for all who were to be saved in the Old and the New Testament. For Scripture declares that there is a single good pleasure, purpose, and plan of God's will, by which he chose us from eternity both to grace and to glory, both to salvation and to the way of salvation, which he prepared in advance for us to walk in.

Article 9: Election Not Based on Foreseen Faith

This same election took place, not on the basis of foreseen faith, of the obedience of faith, of holiness, or of any other good quality and disposition, as though it were based on a prerequisite cause or condition in the person to be chosen, but rather for the purpose of faith, of the obedience of faith, of holiness, and so on. Accordingly, election is the source of each of the benefits of salvation. Faith, holiness, and the other saving gifts, and at last eternal life itself, flow forth from election as its fruits and effects. As the apostle says, He chose us (not because we were, but) so that we should be holy and blameless before him in love (Eph. 1:4).

Article 10: Election Based on God's Good Pleasure

But the cause of this undeserved election is exclusively the good pleasure of God. This does not involve his choosing certain human qualities or actions from among all those possible as a condition of salvation, but rather involves his adopting certain particular persons from among the common mass of sinners as his own possession. As Scripture says, *When the children were not yet born, and had done nothing either good or bad . . . , she* (Rebecca) *was told, "The older will serve the younger." As it is written, "Jacob I loved, but Esau I hated"* (Rom. 9:11–13). Also, *All who were appointed for eternal life believed* (Acts 13:48).

Article 11: Election Unchangeable

Just as God himself is most wise, unchangeable, all-knowing, and almighty, so the election made by him can neither be suspended nor altered, revoked, or annulled; neither can his chosen ones be cast off, nor their number reduced.

Article 12: The Assurance of Election

Assurance of this their eternal and unchangeable election to salvation is given to the chosen in due time, though by various stages and in differing measure. Such assurance comes not by inquisitive searching into the hidden and deep things of God, but by noticing within themselves, with spiritual joy and holy delight, the unmistakable fruits of election pointed out in God's Word—such as a true faith in Christ, a childlike fear of God, a godly sorrow for their sins, a hunger and thirst for righteousness, and so on.

Article 13: The Fruit of This Assurance

In their awareness and assurance of this election God's children daily find greater cause to humble themselves before God, to adore the fathomless depth of his mercies, to cleanse themselves, and to give fervent love in return to him who first so greatly loved them. This is far from saying that this teaching concerning election, and reflection upon it, make God's children lax in observing his commandments or carnally self-assured. By God's just judgment this does usually happen to those who casually take for granted the grace of election or engage in idle and brazen talk about it but are unwilling to walk in the ways of the chosen.

Article 14: Teaching Election Properly

Just as, by God's wise plan, this teaching concerning divine election has been proclaimed through the prophets, Christ himself, and the apostles, in Old and New Testament times, and has subsequently been committed to writing in the Holy Scriptures, so also today in God's church, for which it was specifically intended, this teaching must be set forth—with a spirit of discretion, in a godly and holy manner, at the appropriate time and place, without inquisitive searching into the ways of the Most High. This must be done for the glory of God's most holy name, and for the lively comfort of his people.

Article 15: Reprobation

Moreover, Holy Scripture most especially highlights this eternal and undeserved grace of our election and brings it out more clearly for us, in that it further bears witness that not all people have been chosen but that some have not been chosen or have been passed by in God's eternal election—those, that is, concerning whom God, on the basis of his entirely free, most just, irreproachable, and unchangeable good pleasure, made the following decision:

to leave them in the common misery into which, by their own fault, they have plunged themselves;

not to grant them saving faith and the grace of conversion;

but finally to condemn and eternally punish them (having been left in their own ways and under his just judgment), not only for their unbelief but also for all their other sins, in order to display his justice.

And this is the decision of reprobation, which does not at all make God the author of sin (a blasphemous thought!) but rather its fearful, irreproachable, just judge and avenger.

Article 16: Responses to the Teaching of Reprobation

Those who do not yet actively experience within themselves a living faith in Christ or an assured confidence of heart, peace of conscience, a zeal for childlike obedience, and a glorying in God through Christ, but who nevertheless use the means by which God has promised to work these things in us—such people ought not to be alarmed at the mention of reprobation, nor to count themselves among the reprobate; rather they ought to continue diligently in the use of the means, to desire fervently a time of more abundant grace, and to wait for it in reverence and humility. On the other hand, those who seriously desire to turn to God, to be pleasing to him alone, and to be delivered from the body of death, but are not yet able to make such progress along the way of godliness and faith as they would like—such people ought much less to stand in fear of the teaching concerning reprobation, since our merciful God has promised that he will not snuff out a smoldering wick and that he will not break a bruised reed. However, those who have forgotten God and their Savior Jesus Christ and have abandoned themselves wholly to the cares of the world and the pleasures of the flesh—such people have every reason to stand in fear of this teaching, as long as they do not seriously turn to God.

Article 17: The Salvation of the Infants of Believers

Since we must make judgments about God's will from his Word, which testifies that the children of believers are holy, not by nature but by virtue of the gracious covenant in which they together with their parents are included, godly parents ought not to doubt the election and salvation of their children whom God calls out of this life in infancy.

Article 18: The Proper Attitude Toward Election and Reprobation

To those who complain about this grace of an undeserved election and about the severity of a just reprobation, we reply with the words of the apostle, *Who are you, O man, to talk back to God?* (Rom. 9:20), and with the words of our Savior, *Have I no right to do what I want with my own?* (Matt. 20:15). We, however, with reverent adoration of these secret things, cry out with the apostle: *Oh, the depths of the riches both of the wisdom and the knowledge of God! How unsearchable are his judgments, and his ways beyond tracing out! For who has known the mind of the Lord? Or who has been his counselor? Or who has first given to God, that God should repay him? For from him and through him and to him are all things. To him be the glory forever! Amen* (Rom. 11:33–36). . . .

• • •

The Second Main Point of Doctrine
Christ's Death and Human Redemption Through It

Article 1: The Punishment Which God's Justice Requires

God is not only supremely merciful, but also supremely just. His justice requires (as he has revealed himself in the Word) that the sins we have committed against his infinite majesty be punished with both temporal and eternal punishments, of soul as well as body. We cannot escape these punishments unless satisfaction is given to God's justice.

Article 2: The Satisfaction Made by Christ

Since, however, we ourselves cannot give this satisfaction or deliver ourselves from God's anger, God in his boundless mercy has given us as a guarantee his only begotten Son, who was made to be sin and a curse for us, in our place, on the cross, in order that he might give satisfaction for us.

Article 3: The Infinite Value of Christ's Death

This death of God's Son is the only and entirely complete sacrifice and satisfaction for sins; it is of infinite value and worth, more than sufficient to atone for the sins of the whole world.

Article 4: Reasons for This Infinite Value

This death is of such great value and worth for the reason that the person who suffered it is—as was necessary to be our Savior—not only a true and perfectly holy man, but also the only begotten Son of God, of the same eternal and infinite essence with the Father and the Holy Spirit. Another reason is that this death was accompanied by the experience of God's anger and curse, which we by our sins had fully deserved.

Article 5: The Mandate to Proclaim the Gospel to All

Moreover, it is the promise of the gospel that whoever believes in Christ crucified shall not perish but have eternal life. This promise, together with the command to repent and believe, ought to be announced and declared without differentiation or discrimination to all nations and people, to whom God in his good pleasure sends the gospel.

Article 6: Unbelief Man's Responsibility

However, that many who have been called through the gospel do not repent or believe in Christ but perish in unbelief is not because the sacrifice of Christ offered on the cross is deficient or insufficient, but because they themselves are at fault.

Article 7: Faith God's Gift

But all who genuinely believe and are delivered and saved by Christ's death from their sins and from destruction receive this favor solely from God's grace—which he owes to no one—given to them in Christ from eternity.

Article 8: The Saving Effectiveness of Christ's Death

For it was the entirely free plan and very gracious will and intention of God the Father that the enlivening and saving effectiveness of his Son's costly death should work itself out in all his chosen ones, in order that he might grant justifying faith to them only and thereby lead them without fail to salvation. In other words, it was God's will that Christ through the blood of the cross (by which he confirmed the new covenant) should effectively redeem from every people, tribe, nation, and language all those and only those who were chosen from eternity to salvation and given to him by the Father; that he should grant them faith (which, like the Holy Spirit's other saving gifts, he acquired for them by his death); that he should cleanse them by his blood from all their sins, both original and actual, whether committed before or after their coming to faith; that he should faithfully preserve them to the very end; and that he should finally present them to himself, a glorious people, without spot or wrinkle.

Article 9: The Fulfillment of God's Plan

This plan, arising out of God's eternal love for his chosen ones, from the beginning of the world to the present time has been powerfully carried out and will also be carried out in the future, the gates of hell seeking vainly to prevail against it. As a result the chosen are gathered into one, all in their own time, and there is always a church of believers founded on Christ's blood, a church which steadfastly loves, persistently worships, and—here and in all eternity—praises him as her Savior who laid down his life for her on the cross, as a bridegroom for his bride. . . .

• • •

The Third and Fourth Main Points of Doctrine
Human Corruption, Conversion to God, and the Way It Occurs

Article 1: The Effect of the Fall on Human Nature

Man was originally created in the image of God and was furnished in his mind with a true and salutary knowledge of his Creator and things spiritual, in his will and heart with righteousness, and in all his emotions with purity; indeed, the whole man was holy. However, rebelling against God at the devil's instigation and by his own free will, he deprived himself of these outstanding gifts. Rather, in their place he brought upon himself blindness, terrible darkness, futility, and distortion of judgment in his mind; perversity, defiance, and hardness in his heart and will; and finally impurity in all his emotions.

Article 2: The Spread of Corruption

Man brought forth children of the same nature as himself after the fall.

That is to say, being corrupt he brought forth corrupt children. The corruption spread, by God's just judgment, from Adam to all his descendants—except for Christ alone—not by way of imitation (as in former times the Pelagians would have it) but by way of the propagation of his perverted nature.

Article 3: Total Inability

Therefore, all people are conceived in sin and are born children of wrath, unfit for any saving good, inclined to evil, dead in their sins, and slaves to sin; without the grace of the regenerating Holy Spirit they are neither willing nor able to return to God, to reform their distorted nature, or even to dispose themselves to such reform.

Article 4: The Inadequacy of the Light of Nature

There is, to be sure, a certain light of nature remaining in man after the fall, by virtue of which he retains some notions about God, natural things, and the difference between what is moral and immoral, and demonstrates a certain eagerness for virtue and for good outward behavior. But this light of nature is far from enabling man to come to a saving knowledge of God and conversion to him—so far, in fact, that man does not use it rightly even in matters of nature and society. Instead, in various ways he completely distorts this light, whatever its precise character, and suppresses it in unrighteousness. In doing so he renders himself without excuse before God.

Article 5: The Inadequacy of the Law

In this respect, what is true of the light of nature is true also of the Ten Commandments given by God through Moses specifically to the Jews. For man cannot obtain saving grace through the Decalogue, because, although it does expose the magnitude of his sin and increasingly convict him of his guilt, yet it does not offer a remedy or enable him to escape from his misery, and, indeed, weakened as it is by the flesh, leaves the offender under the curse.

Article 6: The Saving Power of the Gospel

What, therefore, neither the light of nature nor the law can do, God accomplishes by the power of the Holy Spirit, through the Word or the ministry of reconciliation. This is the gospel about the Messiah, through which it has pleased God to save believers, in both the Old and the New Testament.

Article 7: God's Freedom in Revealing the Gospel

In the Old Testament, God revealed this secret of his will to a small number; in the New Testament (now without any distinction between peoples) he discloses it to a large number. The reason for this difference must not be ascribed to the greater worth of one nation over another, or to a better use of the light of nature, but to the free good pleasure and undeserved love of God. Therefore, those who receive so much grace, beyond and in spite of all they deserve, ought to acknowledge it with humble and thankful hearts; on the other hand, with the apostle they ought to adore (but certainly not inquisitively search into) the severity and justice of God's judgments on the others, who do not receive this grace.

Article 8: The Serious Call of the Gospel

Nevertheless, all who are called through the gospel are called seriously. For seriously and most genuinely God makes known in his Word what is pleasing to him: that those who are called should come to him. Seriously he also promises rest for their souls and eternal life to all who come to him and believe.

Article 9: Human Responsibility for Rejecting the Gospel

The fact that many who are called through the ministry of the gospel do not come and are not brought to conversion must not be blamed on the gospel, nor on Christ, who is offered through the gospel, nor on God, who calls them through the gospel and even bestows various gifts on them, but on the people themselves who are called. Some in self-assurance do not even entertain the Word of life; others do entertain it but do not take it to heart, and for that reason, after the fleeting joy of a temporary faith, they relapse; others choke the seed of the Word with the thorns of life's cares and with the pleasures of the world and bring forth no fruits. This our Savior teaches in the parable of the sower (Matt. 13).

Article 10: Conversion as the Work of God

The fact that others who are called through the ministry of the gospel do come and are brought to conversion must not be credited to man, as though one distinguishes himself by free choice from others who are furnished with equal or sufficient grace for faith and conversion (as the proud heresy of Pelagius maintains). No, it must be credited to God: just as from eternity he chose his own in Christ, so within time he effectively calls them, grants them faith and repentance, and, having rescued them from the dominion of darkness, brings them into the kingdom of his Son, in order that they may declare the wonderful deeds of him who called them out of darkness into this marvelous light, and may boast not in themselves, but in the Lord, as apostolic words frequently testify in Scripture.

Article 11: The Holy Spirit's Work in Conversion

Moreover, when God carries out this good pleasure in his chosen ones, or works true conversion in them, he not only sees to it that the gospel is proclaimed to them outwardly, and enlightens their minds powerfully by the Holy Spirit so that they may rightly understand and discern the things of the Spirit of God, but, by the effective operation of the same regenerating Spirit, he also penetrates into the inmost being of man, opens the closed heart, softens the hard heart, and circumcises the heart that is uncircumcised. He infuses new qualities into the will, making the dead will alive, the evil one good, the unwilling one willing, and the stubborn one compliant; he activates and strengthens the will so that, like a good tree, it may be enabled to produce the fruits of good deeds.

Article 12: Regeneration a Supernatural Work

And this is the regeneration, the new creation, the raising from the dead, and the making alive so clearly proclaimed in the Scriptures, which God works in us without our help. But this certainly does not happen only by outward teaching, by moral persuasion, or by such a way of working that, after God has done his work, it remains in man's power whether or not to be reborn or converted. Rather, it is an entirely supernatural work, one that is at the same time most powerful and most pleasing, a marvelous, hidden, and inexpressible work, which is not lesser than or inferior in power to that of creation or of raising the dead, as Scripture (inspired by the author of this work) teaches. As a result, all those in whose hearts God works in this marvelous way are certainly, unfailingly, and effectively reborn and do actually believe. And then the will, now renewed, is not only activated and motivated by God but in being activated by God is also itself active. For this reason, man himself, by that grace which he has received, is also rightly said to believe and to repent.

Article 13: The Incomprehensible Way of Regeneration

In this life believers cannot fully understand the way this work occurs; meanwhile, they rest content with knowing and experiencing that by this grace of God they do believe with the heart and love their Savior.

Article 14: The Way God Gives Faith

In this way, therefore, faith is a gift of God, not in the sense that it is offered by God for man to choose, but that it is in actual fact bestowed on man, breathed and infused into him. Nor is it a gift in the sense that God bestows only the potential to believe, but then awaits assent—the act of believing—from man's choice; rather, it is a gift in the sense that he who works both willing and acting and, indeed, works all things in all people produces in man both the will to believe and the belief itself.

Article 15: Responses to God's Grace

God does not owe this grace to anyone. For what could God owe to one who has nothing to give that can be paid back? Indeed, what could God owe to one who has nothing of his own to give but sin and falsehood? Therefore the person who receives this grace owes and gives eternal thanks to God alone; the person who does not receive it either does not care at all about these spiritual things and is satisfied with himself in his condition, or else in self-assurance foolishly boasts about having something which he lacks. Furthermore, following the example of the apostles, we are to think and to speak in the most favorable way about those who outwardly profess their faith and better their lives, for the inner chambers of the heart are unknown to us. But for others who have not yet been called, we are to pray to the God who calls things that do not exist as though they did. In no way, however, are we to pride ourselves as better than they, as though we had distinguished ourselves from them.

Article 16: Regeneration's Effect

However, just as by the fall man did not cease to be man, endowed with intellect and will, and just as sin, which has spread through the whole human race, did not abolish the nature of the human race but distorted and spiritually killed it, so also this divine grace of regeneration does not act in people as if they were blocks and stones; nor does it abolish the will and its properties or coerce a reluctant will by force, but spiritually revives, heals, reforms, and—in a manner at once pleasing and powerful—bends it back. As a result, a ready and sincere obedience of the Spirit now begins to prevail where before the rebellion and resistance of the flesh were completely dominant. It is in this that the true and spiritual restoration and freedom of our will consists. Thus, if the marvelous Maker of every good thing were not dealing with us, man would have no hope of getting up from his fall by his free choice, by which he plunged himself into ruin when still standing upright.

Article 17: God's Use of Means in Regeneration

Just as the almighty work of God by which he brings forth and sustains our natural life does not rule out but requires the use of means, by which God, according to his infinite wisdom and goodness, has wished to exercise his power, so also the aforementioned supernatural work of God by which he regenerates us in no way rules out or cancels the use of the gospel, which God in his great wisdom has appointed to be the seed of regeneration and the food of the soul. For this reason, the apostles and the teachers who followed them taught the people in a godly manner about this grace of God, to give him the glory and to humble all pride, and yet did not neglect meanwhile to keep the people, by means of the holy admonitions of the gospel, under the administration of the Word, the sacraments and discipline. So even today it is out of the question that the teachers or those taught in the church should presume to test God by separating what he in his good pleasure has wished to be closely joined together. For grace is bestowed through admonitions, and the more readily we perform our duty, the more lustrous the benefit of God working in us usually is and the better his work advances. To him alone, both for the means and for their saving fruit and effectiveness, all glory is owed forever. Amen. . . .

• • •

The Fifth Main Point of Doctrine

The Perseverance of the Saints

Article 1: The Regenerate Not Entirely Free from Sin

Those people whom God according to his purpose calls into fellowship with his Son Jesus Christ our Lord and regenerates by the Holy Spirit, he also sets free from the reign and slavery of sin, though in this life not entirely from the flesh and from the body of sin.

Article 2: The Believer's Reaction to Sins of Weakness

Hence daily sins of weakness arise, and blemishes cling to even the best works of God's people, giving them continual cause to humble themselves before God, to flee for refuge to Christ crucified, to put the flesh to death more and more by the Spirit of supplication and by holy exercises of godliness, and to strain toward the goal of perfection, until they are freed from this body of death and reign with the Lamb of God in heaven.

Article 3: God's Preservation of the Converted

Because of these remnants of sin dwelling in them and also because of the temptations of the world and Satan, those who have been converted could not remain standing in this grace if left to their own resources. But God is faithful, mercifully strengthening them in the grace once conferred on them and powerfully preserving them in it to the end.

Article 4: The Danger of True Believers' Falling into Serious Sins

Although that power of God strengthening and preserving true believers in grace is more than a match for the flesh, yet those converted are not always so activated and motivated by God that in certain specific actions they cannot by their own fault depart from the leading of grace, be led astray by the desires of the flesh, and give in to them. For this reason they must constantly watch and pray that they may not be led into temptations. When they fail to do this, not only **can** they be carried away by the flesh, the world, and Satan into sins, even serious and outrageous ones, but also by God's just permission they sometimes **are** so carried away—witness the sad cases, described in Scripture, of David, Peter, and other saints falling into sins.

Article 5: The Effects of Such Serious Sins

By such monstrous sins, however, they greatly offend God, deserve the sentence of death, grieve the Holy Spirit, suspend the exercise of faith, severely wound the conscience, and sometimes lose the awareness of grace for a time—until, after they have returned to the way by genuine repentance, God's fatherly face again shines upon them.

Article 6: God's Saving Intervention

For God, who is rich in mercy, according to his unchangeable purpose of election does not take his Holy Spirit from his own completely, even when they fall grievously. Neither does he let them fall down so far that they forfeit the grace of adoption and the state of justification, or commit the sin which leads to death (the sin against the Holy Spirit), and plunge themselves, entirely forsaken by him, into eternal ruin.

Article 7: Renewal to Repentance

For, in the first place, God preserves in those saints when they fall his imperishable seed from which they have been born again, lest it perish or be dislodged. Secondly, by his Word and Spirit he certainly and effectively renews them to repentance so that they have a heartfelt and godly sorrow for the sins they have committed; seek and obtain, through faith and with a contrite heart, forgiveness in the blood of the Mediator; experience again the grace of a reconciled God; through faith adore his mercies; and from then on more eagerly work out their own salvation with fear and trembling.

Article 8: The Certainty of This Preservation

So it is not by their own merits or strength but by God's undeserved mercy that they neither forfeit faith and grace totally nor remain in their downfalls to the end and are lost. With respect to themselves this not only easily could happen, but also undoubtedly would happen; but with respect to God it cannot possibly happen, since his plan cannot be changed, his promise cannot fail, the calling according to his purpose cannot be revoked, the merit of Christ as well as his interceding and preserving cannot be nullified, and the sealing of the Holy Spirit can neither be invalidated nor wiped out.

Article 9: The Assurance of This Preservation

Concerning this preservation of those chosen to salvation and concerning the perseverance of true believers in faith, believers themselves can and do become assured in accordance with the measure of their faith, by which they firmly believe that they are and always will remain true and living members of the church, and that they have forgiveness of sins and eternal life.

Article 10: The Ground of This Assurance

Accordingly, this assurance does not derive from some private revelation beyond or outside the Word, but from faith in the promises of God which he has very plentifully revealed in his Word for our comfort, from the testimony of *the Holy Spirit testifying with our spirit that we are God's children and heirs* (Rom. 8:16–17), and finally from a serious and holy pursuit of a clear conscience and of good works. And if God's chosen ones in this world did not have this well-founded comfort that the victory will be theirs and this reliable guarantee of eternal glory, they would be of all people most miserable.

Article 11: Doubts Concerning This Assurance

Meanwhile, Scripture testifies that believers have to contend in this life with various doubts of the flesh and that under severe temptation they do not always experience this full assurance of faith and certainty of perseverance. But God, the Father of all comfort, *does not let them be tempted beyond what they can bear, but with the temptation he also provides a way out* (1 Cor. 10:13), and by the Holy Spirit revives in them the assurance of their perseverance.

Article 12: This Assurance as an Incentive to Godliness

This assurance of perseverance, however, so far from making true believers proud and carnally self-assured, is rather the true root of humility, of childlike respect, of genuine godliness, of endurance in every conflict, of fervent prayers, of steadfastness in crossbearing and in confessing the truth, and of well-founded joy in God. Reflecting on this benefit provides an incentive to a serious and continual practice of thanksgiving and good works, as is evident from the testimonies of Scripture and the examples of the saints.

Article 13: Assurance No Inducement to Carelessness

Neither does the renewed confidence of perseverance produce immorality or lack of concern for godliness in those put back on their feet after a fall, but it produces a much greater concern to observe carefully the ways of the Lord which he prepared in advance. They observe these ways in order that by walking in them they may maintain the assurance of their perseverance, lest, by their abuse of his fatherly goodness, the face of the gracious God (for the godly, looking upon his face is sweeter than life, but its withdrawal is more bitter than death) turn away from them again, with the result that they fall into greater anguish of spirit.

Article 14: God's Use of Means in Perseverance

And, just as it has pleased God to begin this work of grace in us by the proclamation of the gospel, so he preserves, continues, and completes his work by the hearing and reading of the gospel, by meditation on it, by its exhortations, threats, and promises, and also by the use of the sacraments.

Article 15: Contrasting Reactions to the Teaching of Perseverance

This teaching about the perseverance of true believers and saints, and about their assurance of it—a teaching which God has very richly revealed in his Word for the glory of his name and for the comfort of the godly and which he impresses on the hearts of believers—is something which the flesh does not understand, Satan hates, the world ridicules, the ignorant and the hypocrites abuse, and the spirits of error attack. The bride of Christ, on the other hand, has always loved this teaching very tenderly and defended it steadfastly as a priceless treasure; and God, against whom no plan can avail and no strength can prevail, will ensure that she will continue to do this. To this God alone, Father, Son, and Holy Spirit, be honor and glory forever. Amen.

• • •

Notes

1. See J. Moltmann, "Dordrecht, Synode zu," *Evangelisches Kirchen-lexikon*, vol. 1 (Göttingen: Vandenhoeck, 1961), 968–69.
2. See H. M. J. Klein, *The History of the Eastern Synod of the Reformed Church in the United States* (Lancaster, Pa.: Rudisill and Smith, 1943), 39, 45.
3. See Johannes Pieter van Dooren, "Dordrechter Synode (1618–1619)," *Theologische Realenzyklopädie*, ed. Gerhard Krause and Gerhard Muller, vol. 9 (Berlin-New York: Walter de Gruyter, 1982), 140–47; Carl Bangs, *Arminius: A Study in the Dutch Reformation* (Nashville: Abingdon, 1971); and Philip Schaff, *Creeds of Christendom*, vol. 1 of *History of Creeds* (New York: Harper and Brothers, 1931), 508–23.

PART III

The English Reformation

Henry VIII, Edward VI, and the Elizabethan Settlement

24. The Book of Common Prayer

(1559)

The Book of Common Prayer is the enduring center of Anglicanism. According to one scholar, "On all hands it is acknowledged as the only surviving sixteenth-century liturgy in continuous use, and as the bond of union of the Anglican communion" around the world.[1]

Worship traditions of the United Church of Christ have been shaped by this book in at least three ways. First, the Book of Common Prayer gathers up some of the most important insights of the sixteenth-century reformers about worship, namely, the liturgical traditions of Ulrich Zwingli and Heinrich Bullinger (Zurich), Martin Bucer (Strasbourg), and John Calvin (Geneva). Second, the Book of Common Prayer was vigorously attacked by Puritans within the English Reformation because it did not completely repudiate all remnants of Romanism from Protestant worship. As such it greatly influenced Congregationalism, that expression of Puritanism that developed first in England and then spread to New England. Third, the Book of Common Prayer was valued highly by German Reformed theologians John W. Nevin and Philip Schaff, leaders in the nineteenth-century Mercersburg movement. Nevin and Schaff borrowed from the Book of Common Prayer in their preparation of the 1866 Order of Worship of the Reformed Church in the United States. In all of these ways, the Book of Common Prayer has had an important impact on the worship of the United Church of Christ.

SOURCE: William K. Clay, ed., *Liturgies and Occasional Forms of Prayer Set Forth in the Reign of Queen Elizabeth* (Cambridge: University Press, 1847).

The earliest versions of the Book of Common Prayer were shaped in 1549 and 1552 chiefly by Thomas Cranmer, who was archbishop of Canterbury under Henry VIII (1509–47) and his son Edward VI (ruled 1547–53). Although Henry VIII rejected the authority of the pope, he did not favor radical liturgical reform. Nevertheless, in 1544, a new litany for processions with suffrages, prayers of intercession, and supplication was approved. A bit later, under the reign of Henry's young son, Edward, and his protector, the duke of Somerset, additional moderate liturgical reforms were approved. A new Order of Communion was written in English early in Edward's reign and inserted into the Latin Mass following the Communion of the celebrant. Both of these rites were later incorporated into the Book of Common Prayer.

Reasons for the first Book of Common Prayer (1549) were set forth in its preface: (1) to provide a biblical and patristic form of worship in the English language; (2) to reduce the number of service books used by the priest to one (making it available to both priest and people for their common use); and (3) to bring uniformity out of the "great diversitie" of English usage.

The 1549 prayer book contained a balance of the old and the new—Catholic and Protestant. It included the Latin rite according to the use of Sarum, and English Scripture from the Great Bible translation (1539–40). It contained Lutheran church orders from Cologne and Brandenburg (already adopted in the Order of Communion), as well as some elements of the orthodox liturgy, notably, the prayer of Chrysostom and an epiclesis, *or invocation of the Holy Spirit in the prayer of consecration. It is also clear that the Catholic opposition to the Lutheran church order in Cologne, the* Antididagma *(against the teaching), had some influence on the liturgy.*[2]

The Communion liturgy of the 1549 prayer book followed the Catholic rite up to the Offering. At that point, instead of the people bringing bread and wine to the altar to be consecrated to God, the 1549 Book of Common Prayer called for an offering of alms, not to be set on the altar but placed into a chest in the choir. The motive for this change was to remove any hint of sacrifice. The Canon of the Mass was not abolished as Luther had done, but it was thoroughly cleansed of any notion of sacrifice. Although prayers for the dead and for the saints were retained, the prayer of consecration was greatly changed. All notion of the Mass as an ongoing sacrifice was expunged, and Christ's death as a one-time sacrifice was repeatedly underlined.

The prayer for the consecration of the elements combined the Eastern epiclesis, *calling on the Holy Spirit to consecrate the elements, with the*

Western formula, which repeated the words of institution: "With thy holy spirite and worde, vouchsafe to blesse and sanctifie these thy gyftes, and creatures of bread and wyne, that they maie be unto us the bodye and bloude of thy moste derely beloued sonne Jesus Christe." The prayer was not that the bread and wine may become the body and blood of Christ, but that they "maie be unto us the bodye and bloude" of Christ. Transubstantiation, that is, the belief that the elements were actually transformed into the body and blood of Christ, was ruled out, and the elevation of the host was omitted. The understanding of Christ's presence, however, remained ambiguous. If the "be . . . the bodye and bloude" of Christ was stressed, it upheld a more objective understanding. But the phrase "unto us" implied a subjective element that was closer to the Reformed interpretations of Zwingli or Calvin. Scholars agree that Thomas Cranmer did adopt a Reformed doctrine of the Eucharist between 1546 and 1548, but they do not agree as to whether he embraced a Zwinglian memorialist view or a Calvinist position stressing the spiritual, real presence of Christ in the sacrament.[3]

The seemingly compromising nature of the first prayer book was not enthusiastically received by either Catholics or Protestants. Certain continental reformers who had come to England in the late 1540s (such as Peter Martyr Vermigli, Martin Bucer, John Laski, and Valerand Pullain) pressed for more Protestant changes. "Churches of the Strangers" in London, made up of these Protestant refugees from the continent, used more Protestant liturgies. English advocates who wanted more thorough reform, such as John Hooper and Nicholas Ridley, also pushed Cranmer to revise the prayer book.[4]

Martin Bucer's detailed critique of the first prayer book was typical of their concerns. He argued for the removal of all vestments for the sake of apostolic simplicity. He rejected Communion in the side chapels. He made a case for the use of common leavened bread, for the sacrament to be placed in the hands of the people by the priest (rather than into their mouths), for the expunging of the commemoration of the dead in the intercessions, and for substituting, in the prayer of consecration, the words "Bless us and sanctify us by the Holy Spirit and word, that by true faith we may perceive in these mysteries the body and blood of thy Son" for "Blesse and sanctifie these thy gyftes. . . ."[5]

The second Book of Common Prayer (1552) shows that Cranmer took these and other criticisms into account, along with certain comments from a Catholic bishop named Stephen Gardiner, who had interpreted the first prayer book to be more Catholic than Cranmer intended. The revisions gave the 1552 edition a more Reformed Protestant flavor. For *example, the phrase "commonly called the Mass" was dropped from the title of the Order of Communion. The words "table" or "Lord's table" were everywhere substituted for "altar." Household bread was regarded as "sufficient," but not required. Communion bread was placed in the hands of the people. The Introit was left out, and the Kyrie Eleison and Gloria were replaced by the Ten Commandments. The Intercessions were taken out of the canon and placed after the Sermon and the Offertory. The commemoration of the dead and of the saints was removed from the Intercessions. With these revisions, Cranmer emphasized that there was no basis for thinking of the sacrament as a propitiatory sacrifice for the living and the dead, in spite of Bishop Gardiner's contention that those prayers did support such an interpretation.*

In the prayer of consecration, Cranmer followed Bucer in eliminating phrases concerning the sanctification of the elements by the Holy Spirit and the Word, which Gardiner considered orthodox. He replaced them, however, not exactly with Bucer's suggestion, but with "Graunt that wee, receuing these thy creatures of bread and wyne . . . in remembraunce of his death and passion, may be partakers of his most blessed body & bloud," followed immediately by the words of institution. Unfortunately, as later scholars have pointed out, this sequence unintentionally preserves the medieval belief that the consecration is caused by the repetition of the words of institution.[6]

A more Reformed, even Zwinglian, view of the Eucharist is most clearly evident in the words used for the administration of the elements. The 1549 edition stated "The body of our Lorde Jesus Christe whiche was geuen for thee, preserue thy bodye and soule unto everlasting lyfe." In 1552 these words were replaced by "Take and eate this, in remembraunce Christ dyed for thee, and feede on him in thy hearte by faythe, with thankes geuing." Words for the administration of the cup were similarly changed.

One controversial matter in the development of the prayer book concerned kneeling to receive communion. John Knox and other Reformed/Presbyterian leaders strongly protested. Kneeling seemed to suggest the adoration of the elements, which they regarded as a medieval superstition. In response to that objection, the new prayer book appended the so-called black rubric, stating that the practice of kneeling intends "the humble and gratefull acknowledgeynge of the benefites of Christe," not the adoration of the sacramental bread and wine, which "remayne styll in theyr naturall substaunces, and therfore may not bee adored."

The second Book of Common Prayer (1552) took effect for only one year. In July 1553 Edward VI died, and a Catholic, Mary Tudor, assumed the throne, immediately reviving the Catholic rite. A few years later, however, when Elizabeth I became queen, she restored the second rite. The Elizabethan prayer book, issued in April 1559, was essentially the 1552 prayer book with some significant modifications in the order of Holy Communion: (1) the black rubric was removed; (2) vestments were acceptable, conforming to the practice in the second year of Edward VI; and (3) the words of administration combined the language used in both earlier editions of the prayer book.

The "Order for Administration of the Lord's Supper or Holy Communion" from the 1559 Book of Common Prayer is a good example of the language and theology that has influenced many English-language services since the sixteenth century.

The Order for the Administration of the Lord's Supper, or Holy Communion

So many as do intend to be partakers of the holy Communion, shall signify their names to the Curate over night, or else in the morning, afore the beginning of morning prayer or immediately after.

And if any of those be an open and notorious evil liver, so that the congregation by him is offended, or have done any wrong to his neighbours by word or deed: The Curate having knowledge thereof, shall call him, and advertise him, in any wise not to presume to the Lord's Table, until he have openly declared himself to have truly repented and amended his former naughty life, that the congregation may thereby be satisfied, which afore were offended; and that he have recompensed the parties, whom he hath done wrong unto, or at the least declare himself to be in full purpose so to do, as soon as he conveniently may.

The same order shall the Curate use with those, betwixt whom he perceiveth malice and hatred to reign, not suffering them to be partakers of the Lord's Table, until he know them to be reconciled. And if one of the parties so at variance be content to forgive from the bottom of his heart all that the other hath trespassed against him, and to make amends for that he himself hath offended, and the other party will not be persuaded to a godly unity, but remain still in his frowardness and malice: The Minister in that case ought to admit the penitent person to the holy Communion, and not him that is obstinate.

The Table having at the Communion time a fair white linen cloth upon it, shall stand in the body of the Church, or in the Chancel, where Morning prayer and Evening prayer be appointed to be said. And the Priest, stand-

ing at the northside of the Table, shall say the Lord's prayer with this collect following.

ALMIGHTY God, unto whom all hearts be open, all desires known, and from whom no secrets are hid: cleanse the thoughts of our hearts by the inspiration of thy Holy Spirit, that we may perfectly love thee, and worthily magnify thy holy name: through Christ our Lord. Amen.

Then shall the Priest [1578, the Minister] rehearse distinctly all the .x. Commandments: and the people kneeling, shall after every Commandment ask God's mercy for their transgression of the same, after this sort.

Minister.

God spake these words, and said: I am the Lord thy God, Thou shalt have none other Gods but me.

People.

Lord have mercy upon us, and incline our hearts to keep this law.

Minister.

Thou shalt not make to thyself any graven image, nor the likeness of any thing that is in heaven above, or in the earth beneath, nor in the water under the earth. Thou shalt not now bow down to them, nor worship them: for I the Lord thy God am a jealous God, and visit the sin of the fathers upon the children, unto the third and .iiii. generation of them that hate me, and shew mercy unto thousands in them that love me, and keep my commandments.

People.

Lord have mercy upon us, and incline our hearts to keep this law.

Minister.

Thou shalt not take the name of the Lord thy God in vain: for the Lord will not hold him guiltless that taketh his name in vain.

People.

Lord have mercy upon us, and incline our hearts to keep this law.

Minister.

Remember that thou keep holy the Sabboth day: six days shalt thou labour and do all that thou hast to do, but the .vii. day is the Sabboth of the Lord thy God. In it thou shalt do no manner of work, thou and thy son and thy daughter, thy man servant, and thy maid servant, thy cattle, and the stranger that is within thy gates: For in .vi. days the Lord made heaven and earth, the sea, and all that in them is, and rested the seventh day: wherefore the Lord blessed the seventh day and hallowed it.

People.

Lord have mercy upon us, and incline our. &c.

Minister.

Honour thy Father and thy Mother, that thy days may be long in the land which the Lord thy God giveth thee.

People.

Lord have mercy upon us, and incline our. &c.

Minister.

Thou shalt do no murther.

People.

Lord have mercy upon us, and incline our. &c.

Minister.

Thou shalt not commit adultery.

People.

Lord have mercy upon us, and incline our. &c.

Minister.

Thou shalt not steal.

People.

Lord have mercy upon us, and incline our. &c.

Minister.

Thou shalt not bear false witness against thy neighbour.

People.

Lord have mercy upon us, and incline our hearts to keep this law.

Minister.

Thou shalt not covet thy neighbour's house. Thou shalt not covet thy neighbour's wife, not his servant, nor his maid, nor his ox, nor his ass, nor anything that is his.

People.

Lord have mercy upon us, and write all these thy laws in our hearts, we beseech thee.

Then shall follow the Collect of the day with one of these two Collects following for the Queen: the Priest [1578, Minister] standing up and saying.

Let us pray. *Priest* [1578, *Minister*].

ALMIGHTY God, whose kingdom is everlasting, and power infinite: have mercy upon the whole congregation, and so rule the heart of thy chosen servant Elizabeth, our Queen and Governour, that she (knowing whose minister she is) may above all things seek thy honour and glory: and that we her subjects, (duly considering whose authority she hath) may faithfully serve, honour, and humbly obey her, in thee, and for thee, according to thy blessed word and ordinance: Through Jesus Christ our Lord: who with thee and the Holy Ghost liveth and reigneth ever one God, world without end. Amen.

ALMIGHTY and everlasting God, we be taught by thy holy word, that the hearts of kings are in thy rule and governance, and that thou dost dispose and turn them, as it seemeth best to thy godly wisdom: we humbly beseech thee, so to dispose and govern the heart of Elizabeth, thy servant, our Queen and Governour, that in all her thoughts, words, and works, she may ever seek thy honour and glory, and study to preserve thy people committed to her charge, in wealth, peace, and godliness. Grant this, O merciful Father, for thy dear Son's sake Jesus Christ our Lord. Amen.

Immediately after the Collects, the Priest [1578, the Minister] shall read the Epistle beginning thus:

The Epistle written in the. Chapter of.
And the Epistle ended, he shall say the Gospel, beginning thus.
The Gospel, written in the. Chapter of.
And the Epistle and Gospel being ended, shall be said the Creed.

I BELIEVE in one God, the Father almighty, maker of heaven and earth, and of all things visible and invisible. And in one Lord Jesu Christ, the only begotten Son of GOD, begotten of his Father before all worlds: God of God, light of light, very God of very God: begotten, not made, being of one substance with the Father, by whom all things were made: who for us men and for our salvation came down from heaven, and was incarnate by the Holy Ghost of the virgin Mary, and was made man: and was crucified also for us, under Poncius Pilate. He suffered and was buried. And the third day he rose again according to the scriptures: and ascended into heaven, and sitteth at the right hand of the Father. And he shall come again with glory, to judge both the quick and the dead: Whose kingdom shall have none end.

And I believe in the Holy Ghost, The Lord and giver of life, who proceedeth from the Father and the Son, who with the Father and the Son together is worshipped and glorified, who spake by the Prophets. And I believe one Catholic and Apostolic church. I acknowledge one Baptism, for the remission of sins. And I look for the resurrection of the dead, and the life of the world to come. Amen.

After the Creed, if there be no sermon, shall follow one of the homilies already set forth, or hereafter to be set forth by common authority.

After such sermon, homily, or exhortation, the Curate shall declare unto the people whether there be any holy days or fasting days the week following: and earnestly exhort them to remember the poor, saying one or mo[re] of these sentences following, as he thinketh most convenient by his discretion.

LET your light so shine before men, that they may see your good works, and glorify your Father which is in heaven [Matt. 5:16].

Lay not up for yourselves treasure upon the earth, where the rust and moth doth corrupt, and where thieves break through and steal. But lay up for yourselves treasures in heaven, where neither rust nor moth doth corrupt, and where thieves do not break through and steal [Matt. 6:19–20].

Whatsoever you would that men should do unto you, even so do unto them: for this is the law and the Prophets [Matt. 7:12].

Not every one that saith unto me, Lord, Lord, shall enter into the kingdom of heaven: but he that doeth the will of my Father which is in heaven [Matt. 7:21].

Zache stood forth, and said unto the Lord: Behold Lord, the half of my goods I give to the poor, and if I have done any wrong to any man, I restore four fold [Luke 19:8].

Who goeth a warfare at any time of his own cost? who planteth a vineyard, and eateth not of the fruit thereof? or who feedeth a flock, and eateth not of the milk of the flock? [1 Cor. 9:7]

If we have sown unto you spiritual things, is it a great matter, if we shall reap your worldly things? [1 Cor. 9:11]

Do ye not know, that they which minister about holy things, live of the sacrifice? They which wait of the altar, are partakers with the altar. Even so hath the Lord also ordained, that they which preach the gospel, should live of the gospel [1 Cor. 9:13–14].

He which soweth little, shall reap little: and he that soweth plenteously, shall reap plenteously. Let every man do according as he is disposed in his heart, not grudging, or of necessity: for God loveth a cheerful giver [2 Cor. 9:6–7].

Let him that is taught in the word, minister unto him that teacheth, in all good things. Be not deceived, God is not mocked: for whatsoever a man soweth, that shall he reap [Gal. 6:6–7].

While we have time, let us do good unto all men, and specially unto them, which are of the household of faith [Gal. 6:10].

Godliness is great riches, if a man be contented with that he hath: for we brought nothing into the world, neither may we carry any thing out [1 Tim. 6:6–7].

Charge them which are rich in this world, that they be ready to give, and glad to distribute: laying up in store for themselves a good foundation against the time to come, that they may attain eternal life [1 Tim. 6:18–19].

God is not unrighteous, that he will forget your works and labour that proceedeth of love: which love ye have shewed for his name's sake, which have ministered unto saints, and yet do minister [Heb. 6:10].

To do good, and to distribute, forget not: for with such sacrifices God is pleased [Heb. 13:16].

Whoso hath this world's good, and seeth his brother have need, and shutteth up his compassion from him, how dwelleth the love of God in him? [1 John 3:17].

Give almose of thy goods, and turn never thy face from any poor man, and then the face of the Lord shall not be turned away from thee [Tobit 4:7].

Be merciful after thy power. If thou hast much, give plenteously: If thou has little, do thy diligence gladly to give of that little: for so gatherest thou thyself a good reward in the day of necessity [Tobit 4:8–9].

He that hath pity upon the poor, lendeth unto the Lord: and look what he layeth out, it shall be paid him again [Prov. 19:17].

Blessed be the man that provideth for the sick and needy, the Lord shall deliver him in the time of trouble [Ps. 41:1].

Then shall the Churchwardens, or some other by them appointed, gather the devotion of the people, and put the same into the poor men's box: and upon the offering[7] *days appointed, every man and woman shall pay to the Curate the due and accustomed offerings: after which done, the Priest [1578, the Minister] shall say.*

Let us pray for the whole state of Christ's Church militant here in earth.

ALMIGHTY and everliving God, which by thy holy Apostle hast taught us to make prayers and supplications, and to give thanks for all men: we humbly beseech thee most mercifully to accept our almose (If there be none alms given unto the poor, then shall the words of accepting our alms be left unsaid.) and to receive these our prayers which we offer unto thy divine Majesty: beseeching thee to inspire continually the universal Church with the spirit of truth, unity and concord: And grant that all they that do confess thy holy name, may agree in the truth of thy holy word, and live in unity and godly love. We beseech thee also to save and defend all Christian Kings, Princes, and Governours, and specially thy servant Elizabeth our Queen, that under her we may be godly and quietly governed: and grant unto her whole council, and to all that be put in authority under her, that they may truly and indifferently minister justice, to the punishment of wickedness and vice, and to the maintenance of God's true religion and virtue. Give grace (O heavenly Father) to all Bishops, pastors and Curates, that they may both by their life and doctrine set forth thy true and lively word, and rightly and duly administer thy holy Sacraments: and to all thy people give thy heavenly grace, and especially to this congregation here present, that with meek heart and due reverence they may hear and receive thy holy word, truly serving thee in holiness and righteousness all the days of their life. And we most humbly beseech thee of thy goodness (O Lord) to comfort and succour all them which in this transitory life be in trouble, sorrow, need, sickness, or any other adversity: Grant this, O Father, for Jesus Christ's sake our only mediator and advocate. Amen.

Then shall follow this exhortation, at certain times when the Curate shall see the people negligent to come to the holy Communion.

WE be come together at this time, dearly beloved brethren, to feed at the Lord's supper, unto the which in God's behalf I bid you all that be here present, and beseech you for the Lord Jesus Christ's sake, that ye will not refuse to come thereto, being so lovingly called and bidden of God himself. Ye know how grievous and unkind a thing it is, when a man hath prepared a rich feast, decked his table with all kind of provision, so that there lacketh nothing but the guests to sit down: and yet they which be called without any cause most unthankfully refuse to come. Which of you in such a case would not be moved? Who would not think a great injury and wrong done unto him? Wherefore, most dearly beloved in Christ, take ye good heed lest ye, withdrawing yourselves from this holy supper, provoke God's indignation against you. It is an easy matter for a man to say, I will not Communicate, because I am otherwise letted [hindered] with worldly business:

but such excuses be not so easily accepted and allowed before God. If any man say, I am a grievous sinner, and therefore am afraid to come: wherefore then do you not repent and amend? When God calleth you, be you not ashamed to say you will not come? When you should return to God, will you excuse yourself and say that you be not ready? Consider earnestly with yourselves how little such feigned excuses shall avail before God. They that refused the feast in the Gospel, because they had bought a farm, or would try their yokes of oxen, or because they were married, were not so excused, but counted unworthy of the heavenly feast: I for my part am here present, and according unto mine office, I bid you in the name of God, I call you in Christ's behalf, I exhort you, as you love your own salvation, that ye will be partakers of this holy Communion. And as the Son of God did vouchsafe to yield up his soul by death upon the Cross for your health: even so it is your duty to receive the Communion together in the remembrance of his death, as he himself commanded. Now, if you will in no wise thus do, consider with yourselves how great injury you do unto God, and how sore punishment hangeth over your heads for the same. And whereas you offend God so sore in refusing this holy banquet, I admonish, exhort, and beseech you, that unto this unkindness ye will not add any more. Which thing ye shall do, if ye stand by as gazers and lookers on them that do Communicate, and be no partakers of the same yourselves. For what thing can this be accounted else, than a further contempt and unkindness unto God? Truly it is a great unthankfulness to say nay when ye be called: but the fault is much greater when men stand by, and yet will neither eat nor drink this holy Communion with other. I pray you what can this be else, but even to have the Mysteries of Christ in derision? It is said unto all: Take ye and eat. Take and drink ye all of this: do this in remembrance of me. With what face then, or with what countenance shall ye hear these words? What will this be else but a neglecting, a despising, and mocking of the Testament of Christ? Wherefore rather than you should so do, depart you hence, and give place to them that be godly disposed. But when you depart, I beseech you ponder with yourselves from whom you depart: ye depart from the Lord's Table, ye depart from your brethren, and from the banquet of most heavenly food. These things if ye earnestly consider, ye shall by God's grace return to a better mind; for the obtaining whereof we shall make our humble petitions, while we shall receive the holy Communion.

And some time shall be said this also at the discretion of the Curate.

DEARLY beloved, forasmuch as our duty is to render to Almighty God our heavenly Father most hearty thanks, for that he hath given his Son our Saviour Jesus Christ, not only to die for us, but also to be our spiritual food and sustenance, as it is declared unto us, as well by God's word, as by the holy Sacraments [Sacraments: sacramental signs or representations] of his blessed body and blood; the which being so comfortable a thing to them which receive it worthily, and so dangerous to them that will presume to receive it unworthily: My duty is to exhort you to consider the dignity of the holy mystery, and the great peril of the unworthy receiving thereof, and so to search and examine your own consciences, as you should come holy and clean to a most godly and heavenly feast: so that in no wise you come but in the marriage garment, required of God in holy scripture; and so come and be received as worthy partakers of such a heavenly table. The way and means thereto is: First to examine your lives and conversation by the rule of God's commandments, and whereinsoever ye shall perceive yourselves to have offended, either by will, word, or deed, there bewail your own sinful lives, confess yourselves to Almighty God, with full purpose of amendment of life. And if ye shall perceive your offences to be such, as be not only against God, but also against your neighbours: then ye shall reconcile yourselves unto them, ready to make restitution and satisfaction according to the uttermost of your powers, for all injuries and wrongs done by you to any other: and likewise being ready to forgive other that have offended you, as you would have forgiveness of your offences at God's hand: for otherwise the receiving of the holy Communion doth nothing else but increase your damnation. And because it is requisite that no man should come to the holy Communion but with a full trust in God's mercy, and with a quiet conscience: therefore if there be any of you which by the means aforesaid can not quiet his own conscience, but requireth further comfort, or counsel; then let him come to me, or some other discreet and learned Minister of God's word, and open his grief, that he may receive such ghostly [spiritual] counsel, advice, and comfort, as his conscience may be relieved, and that by the ministry of God's word he may receive comfort and the benefit of absolution, to the quieting of his conscience, and avoiding of all scruple and doubtfulness.

Then shall the Priest [1578, the Minister] say this exhortation.

DEARLY beloved in the Lord: ye that mind to come to the holy Communion of the body and blood of our Saviour Christ, must consider what S. Paul writeth to the Corinthians, how he exhorteth all persons diligently to try and examine themselves, before they presume to eat of that bread, and drink of that cup: for as the benefit is great, if with a truly penitent heart and lively faith we receive that holy sacrament (for then we spiritually eat the flesh of Christ, and drink his blood, then we dwell in Christ and Christ in us, we be one with Christ, and Christ with us:) so is the danger great, if we receive the same unworthily. For then we be guilty of the body and blood of Christ our Saviour. We eat and drink our own damnation, not considering the Lord's body. We kindle God's wrath against us, we provoke him to plague us with divers diseases, and sundry kinds of death. Therefore, if any of you be a blasphemer of God, an hinderer or slanderer of his word, an adulterer, or be in malice or envy, or in any other grievous crime, bewail your sins, and come not to this holy Table, lest, after the taking of that holy Sacrament, the devil enter into you, as he entered into Judas, and fill you full of all iniquities, and bring you to destruction, both of body and soul. Judge therefore yourselves (brethren) that ye be not judged of the Lord. Repent you truly for your sins past, have a lively and stedfast faith in Christ our Saviour. Amend your lives, and be in perfect charity with all men, so shall ye be meet partakers of those holy mysteries. And above all things ye must give most humble and hearty thanks to God the Father, the Son, and the Holy Ghost, for the redemption of the world by the death and passion of our Saviour Christ both God and man, who did humble himself, even to the death upon the Cross for us miserable sinners, which lay in darkness and shadow of death, that he might make us the children of God, and exalt us to everlasting life. And to the end that we should alway remember the exceeding great love of our Master and only Saviour Jesu Christ, thus dying for us, and the innumerable benefits (which by his precious bloodshedding) he hath obtained to us, he hath instituted and ordained holy mysteries, as pledges of his love, and continual remembrance of his death, to our great and endless comfort. To him therefore, with the Father and the Holy Ghost, let us give (as we are most bounden) continual thanks: submitting ourselves wholly to his holy will and pleasure, and studying to serve him in true holiness and righteousness all the days of our life. Amen.

Then shall the Priest [1578, the Minister] say to them that come to receive the holy Communion.

YOU that do truly and earnestly repent you of your sins, and be in love and charity with your neighbours, and intend to lead a new life, following the commandments of God, and walking from henceforth in his holy ways: Draw near, and take this holy Sacrament to your comfort: make your humble confession to Almighty God, before this congregation here gathered together in his holy name, meekly kneeling upon your knees.

Then shall this general confession be made, in the name of all those that are minded to receive the holy Communion, either by one of them, or else by [1578, by the Minister himselfe, all] one of the ministers, or by the Priest himself, all kneeling humbly upon their knees.

ALMIGHTY God, Father of our Lord Jesus Christ, maker of all things, judge of all men: we knowledge [acknowledge] and bewail our manifold sins and wickedness, which we from time to time most grievously have committed, by thought, word and deed, against thy divine majesty; provoking most justly thy wrath and indignation against us: we do earnestly repent, and be heartily sorry for these our misdoings: the remembrance of them is grievous unto us, the burthen of them is intolerable: have mercy upon us, have mercy upon us, most merciful Father, for thy Son our Lord Jesus Christ's sake: forgive us all that is past, and grant that we may ever hereafter serve and please thee, in newness of life, to the honour and glory of thy name: through Jesus Christ our Lord. Amen.

Then shall the Priest [1578, the Minister. And so in the next four cases.] or the bishop, being present, stand up, and turning himself to the people, say thus.

ALMIGHTY God our heavenly Father, who of his great mercy hath promised forgiveness of sins to all them, which with hearty repentance and true faith turn unto him: have mercy upon you, pardon and deliver you from all your sins, confirm and strength you in all goodness, and bring you to everlasting life: through Jesus Christ our Lord. Amen.

Then shall the priest also say.

Hear what comfortable words our Saviour Christ saith to all that truly turn to him.

COME unto me all that travail and be heavy laden, and I shall refresh you. So God loved the world, that he gave his only begotten Son, to the end that all that believe in him, should not perish but have life everlasting.

Hear also what saint Paul saith.

This is a true saying, and worthy of all men to be received, that Jesus Christ came into the world to save sinners.

Hear also what Saint John saith.

If any man sin, we have an advocate with the Father, Jesus Christ the righteous, and he is the propitiation for our sins.

After the which, the priest shall proceed, saying.

Lift up your hearts.

Answer.

We lift them up unto the Lord.

Priest.

Let us give thanks unto our Lord God.

Answer.

It is meet and right so to do.

Priest.

It is very meet, right, and our bounden duty that we should at all times, and in all places, give thanks unto thee, O Lord holy Father, almighty everlasting God.

Here shall follow the proper Preface, according to the time, if there be any specially appointed, or else immediately shall follow: Therefore with Angels. &c.

Proper prefaces.

Upon Christmas day and seven days after.

BECAUSE thou didst give Jesus Christ, thine only Son, to be born as this day for us, who by the operation of the Holy Ghost, was made very man of the substance of the virgin Mary his mother, and that without spot of sin, to make us clean from all sin. Therefore. &c.

Upon Easter day, and seven days after.

BUT chiefly are we bound to praise thee, for the glorious resurrection of thy Son Jesus Christ our Lord: for he is the very Paschal Lamb, which was offered for us, and hath taken away the sin of the world, who by his death hath destroyed death, and by his rising to life again hath restored to us everlasting life. Therefore with. &c.

Upon the Ascension day, and seven days after.

THROUGH thy most dear beloved Son, Jesus Christ our Lord: who after his most glorious resurrection manifestly appeared to all his Apostles, and in their sight ascended up into heaven, to prepare a place for us, that where he is, thither might we also ascend, and reign with him in glory. Therefore with. &c.

Upon Whitsunday, and six days after.

THROUGH Jesus Christ our Lord, according to whose most true promise, the Holy Ghost came down this day from heaven, with a sudden great sound, as it had been a mighty wind, in the likeness of fiery tongues, lighting upon the Apostles, to teach them, and to lead them to all truth, giving them both the gift of divers languages, and also boldness with fervent zeal, constantly to preach the Gospel unto all nations, whereby we are brought out of darkness and error into the clear light and true knowledge of thee, and of thy Son Jesus Christ. Therefore with. &c.

Upon the Feast of Trinity only.

IT is very meet, right, and our bounden duty, that we should at all times, and in all places, give thanks to thee, O Lord, almighty and everlasting God, which art one God, one Lord, not one only person, but three persons in one substance: for that which we believe of the glory of the Father, the same we believe of the Son, and of the Holy Ghost, without any difference or inequality. Therefore with. &c.

After which preface, shall follow immediately.

THEREFORE with Angels and Archangels, and with all the company of heaven, we laud and magnify thy glorious name, evermore praising thee, and saying: Holy, holy, holy, Lord God of hosts: heaven and earth are full of thy glory; glory be to thee, O Lord most high.

Then shall the Priest [1578, the Minister] kneeling down at God's board, say in the name of all them that shall receive the Communion, this prayer following:

WE do not presume to [to come to this] this thy Table (O merciful Lord) trusting in our own righteousness, but in thy manifold and great mercies: we be not worthy so much as to gather the crumbs under thy table: but thou art the same Lord, whose property is always to have mercy: grant us therefore (gracious Lord) so to eat the flesh of thy dear Son Jesus Christ, and to drink his blood, that our sinful bodies may be made clean by his body, and our souls washed through his most precious blood; and that we may evermore dwell in him, and he in us. Amen.

Then the Priest [1578, the Minister] standing up, shall say as followeth:

ALMIGHTY God our heavenly Father, which of thy tender mercy didst give thine only Son Jesus Christ, to suffer death upon the cross for our redemption, who made there (by his one[8] oblation of himself once offered) a full, perfect and sufficient Sacrifice, Oblation, and Satisfaction for the sins of the whole world: and did institute, and in his holy Gospel command us to continue, a perpetual memory of that his precious death, until his coming again. Hear us, O merciful Father, we beseech thee: and grant that we receiving these thy creatures of bread and wine, according to thy Son our Saviour Jesu Christ's holy Institution, in remembrance of his death and Passion, may be partakers of his most blessed body and blood: who, in the same night that he was betrayed, took bread, and, when he had given thanks, he brake it, and gave it to his Disciples, saying: Take, eat, this is my body which is given for you. Do this in remembrance of me, Likewise after supper he took the cup, and when he had given thanks, he gave it to them, saying: Drink ye all of this, for this is my blood of the New Testament, which is shed for you and for many, for remission of sins: do this as oft as ye shall drink it in remembrance of me.

Then shall the minister first receive the Communion in both kinds himself, and next deliver it to other ministers, if any be there present (that they may help the chief minister,) and after to the people in their hands kneeling. And when he delivereth the bread, he shall say,

THE body of our Lord Jesus Christ, which was given for thee, preserve thy body and soul into everlasting life: and take and eat this in remembrance that Christ died for thee, and feed on him in thine heart by faith, with thanksgiving.

And the minister that delivereth the cup, shall say,

THE blood of our Lord Jesus Christ, which was shed for thee, preserve thy body and soul into everlasting life: and drink this in remembrance that Christ's blood was shed for thee, and be thankful.

Then shall the Priest [1578, the Minister] say the Lord's prayer, the people repeating after him every petition.

After shall be said as followeth.

O LORD and heavenly Father, we thy humble servants entirely desire thy fatherly goodness, mercifully to accept this our Sacrifice of praise and thanksgiving: most humbly beseeching thee to grant, that by the merits and death of thy Son Jesus Christ, and through faith in his blood, we and all thy whole church, may obtain remission of our sins, and all other benefits of his passion. And here we offer and present unto thee, O Lord, our selves, our souls, and bodies, to be a reasonable, holy, and lively Sacrifice unto thee, humbly beseeching thee, that all we which be partakers of this holy Communion, may be fulfilled with thy grace, and heavenly benediction. And although we be unworthy, through our manifold sins, to offer unto thee any sacrifice: yet we beseech thee to accept this our bounden duty and service, not weighing our merits, but pardoning our offences, through Jesus Christ our Lord: by whom and with whom, in the unity of the Holy Ghost, all honour and glory be unto thee, O Father Almighty, world without end. Amen.

Or this,

ALMIGHTY and everliving God, we most heartily thank thee, for that thou dost vouchsafe to feed us, which have duly received these holy mysteries, with the spiritual food of the most precious body and blood of thy Son our Saviour Jesus Christ: and dost assure us thereby of thy favour and goodness toward us, and that we be very members incorporate in thy mystical body, which is the blessed company of all faithful people, and be also heirs through hope of thy everlasting kingdom, by the merits of the most precious death and passion of thy dear Son: we now most humbly beseech thee, O heavenly Father, so to assist us with thy grace, that we may continue in that holy fellowship, and do all such good works as thou hast prepared for us to walk in, through Jesus Christ our Lord: to whom, with thee and the Holy Ghost, be all honour and glory, world without end. Amen.

Then shall be said or sung.

GLORY be to God on high. And in earth peace, good will towards men. We praise thee, we bless thee, we worship thee, we glorify thee, we give thanks to thee, for thy great glory. O Lord God, heavenly King, God the Father Almighty. O Lord, the only begotten Son Jesu Christ: O Lord God, Lamb of God, Son of the Father, that takest away the sins of the world, have mercy upon us: thou that takest away the sins of the world, have mercy upon us. Thou that takest away the sins of the world, receive our prayer. Thou that sittest at the right hand of God the Father, have mercy upon us.

For thou only art holy: thou only art the Lord: thou only, (O Christ,) with the Holy Ghost, art most high in the glory of God the Father. Amen.

Then the Priest [1578, the Minister] or the Bishop, if he be present, shall let them depart with this blessing.

THE peace of God which passeth all understanding keep your hearts and minds in the knowledge and love of God, and of his Son Jesu Christ our Lord: and the blessing of God Almighty, the Father, the Son and the Holy Ghost, be amongst you, and remain with you always. Amen.

Collects to be said after the Offertory, when there is no Communion: every such day one. And the same may be said also as often as occasion shall serve after the Collects, either of Morning and Evening Prayer, Communion, or Litany, by the discretion of the minister.

ASSIST us mercifully, O Lord, in these our supplications and prayers, and dispose the way of thy servants toward the attainment of everlasting salvation: that among all the changes and chances of this mortal life, they may ever be defended by thy most gracious and ready help: through Christ our Lord. Amen.

O ALMIGHTY Lord and everliving God, vouchsafe, we beseech thee, to direct, sanctify and govern both our hearts and bodies, in the ways of thy laws, and in the works of thy commandments: that through thy most mighty protection, both here and ever, we may be preserved in body and soul: through our Lord and Saviour Jesus Christ. Amen.

GRANT, we beseech thee, Almighty God, that the words which we have heard this day with our outward ears, may through thy grace be so grafted inwardly in our hearts, that they may bring forth in us the fruit of good living, to the honour and praise of thy name: through Jesus Christ our Lord. Amen.

PREVENT [precede] us, O Lord, in all our doings, with thy most gracious favour, and further us with thy continual help, that in all our works begun, continued, and ended in thee, we may glorify thy holy name, and finally by thy mercy obtain everlasting life: through Jesus Christ our Lord. Amen.

ALMIGHTY God, the fountain of all wisdom, which knowest our necessities before we ask, and our ignorance in asking: we beseech thee to have compassion upon our infirmities, and those things which for our unworthiness we dare not, and for our blindness we cannot ask, vouchsafe to give us for the worthiness of thy Son Jesus Christ our Lord. Amen.

ALMIGHTY God, which hast promised to hear the petitions of them that ask in thy Son's name: we beseech thee mercifully to incline thine ears to us, that have made now our prayers and supplications unto thee: and grant that those things which we have faithfully asked according to thy will, may effectually be obtained, to the relief of our necessity, and to the setting forth of thy glory, through Jesus Christ our Lord. Amen.

Upon the holy days, if there be no Communion, shall be said all that is appointed at the Communion, until the end of the Homily, concluding with the general prayer, for the whole state of Christ's church militant here in earth: and one or mo[re] of these Collects before rehearsed, as occasion shall serve.

And there shall be no celebration of the Lord's Supper except there be a good number to communicate with the priest [1578, the Minister], according to his discretion.

And if there be not above twenty persons in the Parish of discretion to receive the communion: yet there shall be no Communion, except four, or three at the least communicate with the priest [1578, the Minister]. And in Cathedral and Collegiate churches, where be many Priests [1578, Ministers] and Deacons, they shall all receive the Communion with the Minister every Sunday at the least, except they have a reasonable cause to the contrary.

And to take away the superstition which any person hath, or might have, in the bread and wine, it shall suffice that the bread be such, as is usual to be eaten at the Table with other meats, but the best and purest wheat bread, that conveniently may be gotten. And if any of the bread or wine remain, the Curate shall have it to his own use.

The bread and wine for the Communion shall be provided by the Curate, and the Churchwardens, at the charges of the parish, and the parish shall be discharged of such sums of money, or other duties, which hitherto they have paid for the same, by order of their houses every Sunday.

And note, that every Parishioner shall communicate at the least three times in the year: of which Easter to be one: and shall also receive the Sacraments, and other rites, according to the order in this book appointed. And yearly, at Easter, every Parishioner shall reckon with his Parson, Vicar or Curate, or his, or their deputy or deputies, and pay to them or him all Ecclesiastical duties, accustomably due, then and at that time to be paid.

Notes

1. See Horton Davies, *Worship and Theology in England From Cranmer to Hooker, 1534–1603* (Princeton: Princeton University Press, 1970), 165.

2. See Bard Thompson, ed., *Liturgies of the Western Church* (Cleveland: World Publishing Company, 1961), 233–34; and Davies, 167, 170–71, 179–81.

3. See Davies, 183–87; and Thompson, 228.

4. See Davies, 208–09.

5. See Thompson, 230–40.

6. See Davies, 206.

7. According to the editor, William K. Clay, "These had originally been Christmas, Easter, Whitsuntide, and the feast of the dedication of the parish church: but in 1536 Henry VIII. commanded the feast of the nativity of Saint John the Baptist, and that of Saint Michael, to be substituted for the last two."

8. According to Clay, "In 1597 we find 'own,' which reading existed, though by no means uniformly, for many years. Whether this was really an error, cannot easily be determined, since even in the earliest edition of the Prayer Book . . . the passage runs 'his awne oblacion.' "

25. The Geneva Bible

(1560)

The single most significant force in the English Reformation was the English Bible. William Tyndale (also spelled Tindal or Tindale), a scholar trained at Oxford (B.A. 1512, M.A. 1515) and at Cambridge, was probably inspired by Erasmus's Paraclesis *(see vol. 2:86–97) to make an English translation of Scripture. He is reported to have remarked to someone, "If God spare my life, ere many years I will cause a boy that driveth the plough shall know more scripture than thou doest."*

Originally he hoped that Erasmus's good friend, Bishop Cuthbert Tunstall, would support his efforts, but he was disappointed. Nevertheless, he did complete his translation of the New Testament in Germany and sought to have it printed in Cologne. Due to objections, he fled to Worms, where it was finally printed in 1526. Soon thereafter, in April 1526, copies appeared in England. Unfortunately, Tunstall and other bishops bought up as many copies as they could and had them destroyed.

Tyndale, however, was not to be stopped, producing revised editions in 1534 and 1535, without authorization in England. He also began work on the Hebrew Scriptures, publishing a translation of the Pentateuch in 1530, Jonah in 1531, and translating the Hebrew Scripture lessons for Communion. Before his death in 1536 in Belgium (he was strangled and then burned at the stake for heresy), Tyndale had finished his translation from Joshua through 2 Chronicles, although this work remained unpublished.

SOURCE: *The Geneva Bible*, a facsimile of the 1560 edition, Lloyd E. Berry, ed. (Madison: University of Wisconsin Press, 1969).

Tyndale's English translation of the New Testament (from the Greek) and the Old Testament (from the Hebrew) was the first of its kind. The Wycliffe English Bible, produced in the 1380s, was a translation from the Latin. Tyndale made use of Erasmus's 1519 and 1522 Greek editions of the New Testament, consulted Erasmus's Latin translation and Luther's German version, and exercised a great deal of independent judgment. By the standards of his times, Tyndale was an excellent Greek scholar and, even more remarkably, he handled Hebrew with skill.

In addition to his fine scholarship, Tyndale possessed an extraordinary sense of the everyday English language, portraying its power vividly and directly in his translations. The quality of Tyndale's work was such that much of it was incorporated into later translations, all the way to the King James (Authorized) Version of 1611.[1]

Ironically, although Tyndale translations were not authorized in England, before his death they appeared in the Coverdale Bible. In 1535, this Bible, produced by Miles Coverdale, became the first translation of the whole Bible ever printed in English. (Although it lacked formal authorization, it did claim the king's license.) Unlike Tyndale, Coverdale did not know Greek or Hebrew, but made use of various Latin versions, the German Bibles of Luther and Zurich, and Tyndal's translation.

In 1537 another English translation appeared. This Bible had the king's license and the strong recommendation of Archbishop Thomas Cranmer and Thomas Cromwell, a minister of the king with Protestant sympathies. It was known as the Matthew Bible. Thomas Matthew was the pseudonym of John Rogers, a colleague of Tyndale who produced a translation based largely on Tyndale's work and other aids. The Matthew Bible also incorporated a summary of the major doctrines of Scripture, prologues, and notes taken from Tyndale, Erasmus, Luther, and other continental reformers.

By 1537, although there were two English Bibles available, neither was wholly satisfactory. The Coverdale version was not based on Greek and Hebrew texts, and the Matthew version was offensive to conservatives because of its Protestantizing prologues and notes. For these reasons, in 1539 Cromwell, in cooperation with Cranmer, sponsored another translation and required it to be placed in every parish church. This was a large lectern-size volume, called the Great Bible. Its editor was Coverdale, but instead of basing it on his own version, he revised the Matthew Bible using Erasmus's Greek edition of the New Testament and Sebastian Münster's 1534–35 Hebrew-Latin Bible to improve the Old Testament. Coverdale dropped the offensive prologues and notes. For the second edition of the Great Bible (1540), Cranmer wrote an important preface, causing it thereafter to be known as Cranmer's Bible. It was the official Bible of the Anglican Church until the Bishops' Bible of 1568. Unfortunately, some of its Latinisms, which replaced the freshness of Tyndale's English, were carried later into the King James Version.[2]

The Geneva Bible of 1560 was never an official version, but it was the most popular English translation of the Bible from 1560 to until 1644, rivaling even the King James Version after 1611. The Geneva Bible was produced in Geneva, as its name suggests, by a group of English exiles who had escaped persecution under Mary I. William Whittingham, Anthony Gilby, William Cole, William Kethe, William Williams, and John Baron were all members of John Knox's English congregation in Geneva. It is unlikely that Knox himself had much to do with the translation.[3]

Beginning in 1557 William Whittingham had developed a New Testament translation that relied heavily on Tyndale's translation. In the same year a new translation of the Psalms had appeared, probably produced by Anthony Gilby, the best Hebraist in the group. The producers of the Geneva Bible stated in the preface that it was time for a fresh translation of the Bible, given the progress of scholarship in recent years. They made use of a 1551 Greek text printed by Robert Estienne; a 1557 Bible printed by Robert Estienne, which contained a Latin translation of the New Testament and notes by Theodore Beza (Calvin's colleague and successor); the Hebrew-Latin Bible of Sebastian Münster; the Latin versions of Leo Juda (1544) and Sebastian Castellio (1551); and the French Bible of Pierre Olivetan, as revised by John Calvin and Theodore Beza, printed by Estienne in 1553, and revised again by Calvin in 1558. Although the Geneva Bible translators used the Great Bible as their basis, they also translated directly from the Hebrew and the Greek and consulted other translations.[4]

The Geneva Bible further commended itself "to the [sisters and] brethren" because it contained several illuminating and convenient aids to understanding; was smaller in size than the Great Bible, and was thus easier to handle; was printed in clear Roman type, not in black Gothic; divided the English text into verses (for the first time); printed arguments for books and chapters; and contained marginal notes "upon all the hard places." Some of its arguments and notes reflect Calvinistic theology, as for example the argument on Romans and the notes on Rom. 9–11. In general, however, the notes in the 1560 Geneva Bible are more generally Protestant than specifically Calvinist.[5]

By the 1576 edition of the New Testament, new notes written by Puritan Lawrence Towson were blatantly Calvinistic. Towson's notes came in part from those of Joachim Camerarius, a disciple of Philip Melanchthon, but especially from the notes written by Theodore Beza for a New Testament (1574) edited and translated into French by Pierre L'Oisseleur, a Huguenot refugee in London. The Calvinistic character of the 1576 New Testament was further sharpened by the addition of strongly antipapal annotations by Franciscus Junius, a Dutch pastor and professor trained in Geneva. Calvin's catechism (1568–70) was eventually included in the Geneva Bible, and a catechism called "Certain Questions and Answers Touching the Doctrine of Predestination, the Use of God's Word and Sacraments" was bound with it beginning in 1579.[6]

The impact of the Geneva Bible on English Protestantism was enormous. In spite of the fact that the Great Bible (1539) and the Bishops' Bible (1568) were official Bibles of the church, the Geneva Bible was far more popular, undergoing numerous printings. From the beginning of the Reformation in Scotland in 1560, the Geneva Bible became its official version, although it was not even printed in Scotland until 1576. It was the favorite Bible quoted by Puritan clergy in their sermons, and in 1620 it was carried to Plymouth, Massachusetts, by the Pilgrims on the Mayflower. *It was regularly used by great authors, such as Shakespeare, Spenser, and Milton. The Geneva Bible translation also influenced many wordings and renderings in the later King James Version of the Bible authorized in 1611.*[7]

The epistle to Queen Elizabeth and the preface to the reader from the 1560 edition of the Geneva Bible, reprinted here, stress the centrality of the Word for the church and give the rationale for this translation.

The Bible and Holy Scriptures Conteyned in the Olde And Newe Testament.

Translated according to the Ebrue and Greke, and conferred with the best translations in divers langages.

With moste profitable annotations upon all the hard places, and other things of great importance as may appeare in the Epistle to the Reader.

At Geneva Printed by Rouland Hall 1560

TO THE MOSTE VERTUOUS AND NOBLE QUENE ELISABET,
Quene of England, France and Ireland, &c. Your humble subjects of the English Churche at Geneva, wish grace and peace from God the Father through Christ Iesus our Lord.

How hard a thing it is, and what great impedimentes let, to enterprise any worthie act, not only dailie experience sufficiently sheweth (moste noble and vertuous Quene) but also that notable proverbe doeth confirme the same, which admonisheth us, that all things are hard which are faire and excellent. And what enterprise can there be of greater importance, and more acceptable unto God, or more worthie of singuler commendation, then the building of the Lords Temple, the house of God, the Church of Christ, whereof the Sonne of God is the head and perfection?

When Zerubbabel went about to builde the material Temple, according to the commandement of the Lord, what difficulties and stayes daily arose to hinder his worthy indevours, ye bookes of Ezra & Esdras[8] playnely witnesse: how that not on ly he and the people of God were sore molested with foreyn adversaries, (whereof some maliciously warred against them, and corrupted the Kings officers: and others craftely practised under pretence of religion) but also at home with domestical enemies, as false Prophetes, craftie worldlings, faint hearted soldiers, and oppressors of their brethren, who aswel by false doctrine and lyes, as by subtil counsel, cowardies, and extortion, discouraged the heartes almoste of all: so that the Lords worke was not only interrupted and left of for a long tyme, but scarcely at the length with great labour and danger after a sort broght to passe.

Which thing when we weigh aright, and consider earnestly how muche greater charge God hath laid upon you in making you a builder of his spiritual Temple, we can not but partely feare, knowing the crafte and force of Satan our spiritual enemie, and the weakenes and unabilitie of this our nature: and partely be fervent in our prayers toward God that he wolde bring to perfection this noble worke which he hath begon by you: and therefore we indevour our selves by all meanes to ayde, & to bestowe our whole force under your graces standard, whome God hath made as our Zerubbabel for the erecting of this most excellent Temple, and to plant and maynteyn his holy worde to the advancement of his glorie, for your owne honour and salvation of your soule, and for the singular comfort of that great flocke which Christ Iesus the great shepherd hath boght with his precious blood, and committed unto your charge to be fed both in body and soule.

Considering therefore how many enemies there are, which by one meanes or other, as the adversaries of Iudah and Beniamin went about to stay the building of that Temple, so labour to hinder the course of this building (whereof some are Papistes, who under pretence of favoring Gods worde, traiterously seke to erect idolatrie and to destroy your maiestie: some are worldlings, who as Demas have forsaken Christ for the love of this worlde [2 Tim. 4:10]: others are ambicious prelats, who as Amasiah [Amos 7:12] & Diotrephes [3 John 9] can abide none but them selves: and as Demetrius

[Acts 19:24] many practise sedition to maynteyne their errors) we persuaded our selves that there was no way so expedient and necessarie for the preservation of the one, and destruction of the other, as to present unto your Maiestie the holy Scriptures faithfully and playnely translated according to the langages wherein thei were first written by the holy Gost. For the worde of God is an evident token of Gods love and our assurance of his defence, wheresoever it is obediently receyved: it is the trial of the spirits: and as the Prophet [Jer. 23:29] saieth, It is as a fyre and hammer to breake the stonie heartes of them that resist Gods mercies offred by the preaching of the same. Yea it is sharper then any two edged sworde to examine the very thoghtes and to iudge the affections of the heart, and to discover whatsoever lyeth hid under hypocrisie and wolde be secret from the face of God and his Churche. So that this must be the first fundacion and groundworke, according whereunto the good stones of this building must be framed, and the evil tried out and reiected.

Now as he that goeth about to lay a fundacion surely, first taketh away suche impedimentes, as might iustely ether hurt, let or difforme the worke: so is it necessarie that your graces zeale appeare herein, that nether the craftie persuasion of man, nether worldly policie, or natural feare dissuade you to roote out, cut downe and destroy these wedes and impedimentes which do not only deface your building, but utterly indevour, yea & threaten the ruine thereof. For when the noble Iosias entreprised the like kinde of worke, among other notable and many things he destroyed, not only with utter confusion the idoles with their appertinances, but also burnt (in signe of detestation) the idolatrous priests bones upon their altars, and put to death the false prophetes and sorcerers, to performe the wordes of the Lawe of God: and therefore the Lord gave him good successe & blessed him wonderfully, so long as he made Gods worde his line and rule to followe, and enterprised nothing before he had inquired at the mouth of the Lord [2 Kings 23:16–20; 2 Chron. 34:4–7].

And if these zealous begynnings seme dangerous and to brede disquietnes in your dominions, yet by the storie of King Asa it is manifest, that the quietnes and peace of kingdomes standeth in the utter abolishing of idolatrie, and in advancing of true religion: for in his dayes Iudah lyved in rest and quietnes for the space of fyve and thirtie yere, til at length he began to be colde in the zeale of the Lord, feared the power of man, imprisoned the Prophet of God, and oppressed the people: then the Lord sent him warres, & at length toke him away by death [2 Chron. 14:1–7; 15:15–19; 16:11–14; 1 Kings 15:23–24].

Wherefore great wisdome, not worldelie, but heavenly is here required, which your grace must earnestly crave of the Lord, as did Salomon, to whome God gave an understanding heart to iudge his people aright, and to discerne betwene good and bad. For if God for the furnishing of the olde temple gave the Spirit of wisdome & understanding to them that shulde be the workemen thereof, as to Bezaleel [Bezalel, son of Urison of Hur (Exod. 31:2)], Aholiab [Ohiliab, son of Ahisamach of tribe of Dan (Exod. 31:61)], and Hiram [Huram of Tyre (2 Chron. 2)]: how muche more wil he indewe your grace and other godly princes and chefe governours with a principal Spirit, that you may procure and commande things necessarie for this moste holy Temple, forese and take hede of things that might hinder it, and abolish and destroy whatsoever might impere and overthrowe the same?

Moreover the marvelous diligence and zeale of Iehoshaphat, Iosiah and Hezekiah are by the singuler providence of God left as an example to all godly rulers to reforme their countreys and to establish the worde of God with all spede, lest the wrath of the Lord fall upon them for the neglecting thereof. For these excellent Kings did not onely imbrace the worde promptely and ioyfully, but also procured earnestly and commanded the same to be taught, preached and maynteyned through all their countreys and dominions, bynding them and all their subiectes bothe great and smale with solemne protestations and covenantes before God to obey the worde, and to walke after the waies of the Lord. Yea and in the daies of Kyng Asa it was enacted that whosoever wolde not seke the Lord God of Israel, shulde be slayne, whether he were smale or great, man or woman [2 Chron. 15:13]. And for the establishing hereof and performance of this solemne othe, aswel Priests as Iudges were appointed and placed through all the cities of Iudah to instruct the people in the true knollage and feare of God [2 Chron. 17:7–9], and to minister iustice according to the worde, knowing that, except God by his worde dyd reigne in the heartes and soules, all mans diligence and indevors were of none effect: for without this worde we can not discerne betwene iustice, and iniurie, protection and oppression, wisdome and foolishnes, knollage and ignorance, good and evil. Therefore the Lord, who is the chefe governour of his Church, willeth that nothing be attempted before we have inquired thereof at his mouth. For seing he is our God, of duetie we must give him this preeminence, that of our selves we entreprise nothing, but that which he hath appointed, who only knoweth all things, and governeth them as may best serve to his glorie and our salvation. We oght not therefore to prevent him, or do any thing without his worde, but assone as he hath reveiled his wil, immediately to put it in execution.

Now as concerning the maner of this building, it is not according to man, nor after the wisdome of the flesh, but of the Spirit, & according to the worde of God, whose wais are divers from mans wais. For if it was not lawful for Moses to builde the material Tabernacle after any other sorte then God had shewed him by a patern, nether to prescribe any other ceremonies & lawes then suche as the Lord had expresly commanded: how can it be lawful to procede in this spiritual building any other waies, then Iesus Christ the Sonne of God, who is bothe the fundacion, head and chief corner stone thereof, hath commanded by his worde? And for asmuche as he hath established and left an order in his Churche for the building up of his body, appointing some to be Apostles, some Prophetes, others Evangelistes, some pastors, and teachers, he signifieth that every one according as he is placed in this body which is the Church, oght to inquire of his ministres concerning the wil of the Lord, which is reveiled in his worde. For thei are, saieth Ieremiah, as the mouth of the Lord: yea he promiseth to be with their mouth, & that their lippes shal kepe knollage, & that the trueth & the law shalbe in their mouth [Jer. 15:19]. For it is their office chefely to understand the Scriptures & teache them. For this cause the people of Israel in matters of difficultie used to aske the Lord ether by the Prophets, or by the meanes of the hie Priest, who bare Urim & Thummim [Exod. 28:30], which were tokens of light & knollage, of holines & perfection which shulde be in the hie Priest. Therefore when Iehoshaphat toke this order in the Church of Israel, he appointed Amariah [2 Chron. 19:11] to be the chief concerning the worde of God, because he was moste expert in the law of the Lord, and colde gyve counsel and governe according unto the same. Els there is no degre or office which may have that autoritie and priviledge to decise concerning Gods worde, except withall he hath the Spirit of God, and sufficient knollage and iudgement to define according thereunto. And as every one is indued of God with greater giftes, so oght he to be herein chefely heard, or at least that without the expresse worde none be heard: for he that hathe not the worde, speaketh not by the mouthe of the Lord. Agayne, what danger it is to do any thing, seme it never so godly or necessarie, without consulting with Gods mouth, the examples of the Israelites, deceived hereby through the Gibeonites: and of Saul, whose intention semed good and necessarie: and of Iosiah also, who for great considerations was moved for the defence of true religion & his people, to fight against Pharaoh Necho King of Egypt, may sufficiently admonish us [2 Chron. 35:20].

Last of all (moste gracious Quene) for the advancment of this building and rearing up of the worke, two things are necessarie, First, that we have a lyvely & stedfast faith in Christ Iesus, who must dwel in our heartes, as the only meanes and assurance of our salvation: for he is the ladder that reacheth from the earth to heaven: he lifteth up his Churche and setteth it in the heavenly places: he maketh us lyvely stones and buildeth us upon him selfe: he ioyneth us to him selfe as the mem bres and body to the head: yea he maketh him selfe and his Churche one Christ. The next is, that our faith bring forthe good fruites, so that our godly conversation may serve us as a witnes to confirme our election, and be an example to all others to walke as apperteyneth to the vocation whereunto thei are called: lest the worde of God be evil spoken of, and this building be stayed to growe up to a iust height, which can not be without the great provocation of Gods iuste vengeance and discouraging of many thousandes through all the worlde, if thei shulde se that our life were not holy and agreable to our profession. For the eyes of all that feare God in all places beholde your countreyes as an example to all that beleve, and the prayers of all the godly at all tymes are directed to God for the preservation of your maiestie. For considering Gods wonderful mercies toward you at all seasons, who hath pulled you out of the mouthe of the lyons, and how that from your youth you have bene broght up in the holy Scriptures, the hope of all men is so increased, that thei can not but looke that God shulde bring to passe some wonderful worke by your grace to the universal comfort of his Churche. Therefore even above strength you must shewe your selfe strong and bolde in Gods matters: and thogh Satan lay all his power and craft together to hurt and hinder the Lordes building: yet be you assured that God wil fight from heaven against this great dragon, the ancient serpent, which is called the devil and Satan, til he have accomplished the whole worke and made his Churche glorious to him selfe, without spot or wrincle. For albeit all other kingdomes and monarchies, as the Babylonians, Persians, Grecians & Romains have fallen and taken end: yet the Churche of Christ even under the Crosse hath from the begynning of the worlde bene victorious, and shalbe everlastingly. Trueth it is, that sometyme it semeth to be shadowed with a cloude, or driven with a stormie persecution, yet suddenly the beames of Christ the sunne of iustice shine and bring it to light and libertie. If for a tyme it lie covered with ashes, yet it is quickely kindeled agayne by the wynde of Gods Spirit: thogh it seme drowned in the sea, or parched and pyned in the wildernes, yet God giveth ever good successe for he punisheth the enemies, and delivereth his, nourisheth them and stil preserveth them under his wyngs. This Lord of lordes & King of kings who hath ever defended his, strengthen, comfort and preserve your maiestie, that you may be able to build up the ruines of Gods house to his glorie, the discharge of your conscience, and to the comfort of all them that love the comming of Christ Iesus our Lord. From Geneva. 10. April. 1560.

TO OUR BELOVED IN THE LORD THE BRETHREN OF England, Scotland, Ireland, &c.

Grace, mercie and peace, through Christ Iesus.

Besides the manifolde and continual benefites which almightie God bestoweth upon us, bothe corporal and spiritual, we are especially bounde (deare brethren) to give him thankes without ceasing for his great grace and unspeakable mercies, in that it hath pleased him to call us unto this mervelous light of his Gospel, & mercifully to regarde us after so horrible backesliding and falling away from Christ to Antichrist, from light to darcknes, from the living God to dumme and dead idoles, & that after so cruel murther of Gods Saintes, as alas, hathe bene among us, we are not altogether cast of, as were the Israelites, and many others for the like, or not so manifest wickednes, but receyved agayne to grace with moste evident signes and tokens of Gods especial love and favour. To the intent therefore that we may not be unmyndeful of these great mercies, but seke by all meanes (according to our duetie) to be thankeful for the same, it behoveth us so to walke in his feare and love, that all the daies of our life we may procure the glorie of his holy name. Now forasmuche as this thing chefely is atteyned by the knollage and practising of the worde of God (which is the light to our paths, the keye of the kingdome of heaven, our comfort in affliction, our shielde and sworde against Satan, the schoole of all wisdome, the glasse wherein we beholde Gods face, the testimonie of his favour, and the only foode and nourishment of our soules) we thoght that we colde bestowe our labours & studie in nothing which colde be more acceptable to God and comfortable to his Churche then in the translating of the holy Scriptures into our native tongue: the which thing, albeit that divers heretofore have indevored to atchieve: yet considering the infancie of those tymes and imperfect knollage of the tongues, in respect of this ripe age and cleare light which God hath now reveiled, the translations required greatly to be perused and reformed. Not that we vendicat any thing to our selves above the least of our brethren (for God knoweth with what feare and trembling we have bene now, for the space of two yeres and more day and night occupied herein) but being earnestly desired, and by divers, whose learning and godlynes we reverence, exhorted, and also incouraged by the ready willes of suche, whose heartes God likewise touched, not to spare any charges for the fortherance of suche a benefite and favour of God toward his Churche (thogh the tyme then was moste dangerous and the persecution sharpe and furious) we submitted our selves at length to their godly iudgementes, and seing the great oportunitie and occasions, which God presented unto us in this Churche, by reason of so many godly and learned men: and suche diversities of translations in divers tongues, we undertoke this great and wonderful worke (with all reverence, as in the presence of God, as intreating the worde of God, whereunto we thinke our selves unsufficient) which now God according to his divine providence and mercie hath directed to a moste prosperous end. And this we may with good conscience protest, that we have in every point and worde, according to the measure of that knollage which it pleased al mightie God to give us, faithfully rendred the text, and in all hard places moste syncerely expounded the same. For God is our witnes that we have by all meanes indevored to set forthe the puritie of the worde and right sense of the holy Gost for the edifying of the brethren in faith and charitie.

Now as we have chiefely observed the sense, and laboured alwaies to restore it to all integritie: so have we moste reverently kept the proprietie of the wordes, considering that the Apostles who spake and wrote to the Gentiles in the Greke tongue, rather constrayned them to the lively phrase of the Ebrewe, then entreprised farre by mollifying their langage to speake as the Gentils did. And for this and other causes we have in many places reserved the Ebrewe phrases, notwithstanding that thei may seme somewhat hard in their eares that are not wel practised and also delite in the swete sounding phrases of the holy Scriptures. Yet lest ether the simple shulde be discouraged, or the malicious have any occasion of iust cavillation, seing some translations read after one sort, and some after another, whereas all may serve to good purpose and edification, we have in the margent noted that diversitie of speache or reading which may also seme agreable to the mynde of the holy Gost and propre for our langage with this marke.

A gayne where as the Ebrewe speache semed hardly to agre with ours, we have noted it in the margent after this sort", using that which was more intelligible. And albeit that many of the Ebrewe names be altered from the olde text, and restored to the true writing and first original, whereof thei have their signification, yet in the usual names litle is changed for feare of troubling the simple readers. Moreover whereas the necessitie of the sentence required any thing to be added (for such is the grace and proprietie of the Ebrewe and Greke tongues, that it can not but ether by circumlocution, or by adding the verbe or some worde be understand of them that are not wel practised therein) we have put it in the text with another kynde of lettre, that it may easely be discerned from the common lettre. As touching the division of the verses, we have followed the Ebrewe examples, which have so even from the begynning distinct them. Which thing as it is moste profitable for memorie: so doeth it agre with the best translations, & is moste easie to finde out both by the best Concordances, and also by the cotations which we have dilygently herein perused and set forthe by this starre *. Besides this the principal matters are noted and distincted by this marke ¶. Yea and the argumentes bothe for the booke and for the chapters with the nombre of the verse are added, that by all meanes the reader might be holpen. For the which cause also we have set over the head of every page some notable worde or sentence which may greatly further aswel for memorie, as for the chief point of the page. And considering how hard a thing it is to understand the holy Scriptures, and what errors, sectes and heresies growe dailie for lacke of the true knollage thereof, and how many are discouraged (as thei pretend) because thei can not atteine to the true and simple meaning of the same, we have also indevored bothe by the diligent reading of the best commentaries, and also by the conference with the godly and learned brethren, to gather brief annotations upon all the hard places, aswel for the understanding of suche wordes as are obscure, and for the declaration of the text, as for the application of the same as may moste apperteine to Gods glorie and the edification of his Churche. Forthermore whereas certeyne places in the bookes of Moses, of the Kings and Ezekiel semed so darke that by no description thei colde be made easie to the simple reader, we have so set them forthe with figures and notes for the ful declaration thereof, that thei which can not by iudgement, being holpen by the annotations noted by the lettres a b c. &c. atteyn thereunto, yet by the perspective, and as it were by the eye may sufficiently knowe the true meaning of all suche places. Whereunto also we have added certeyne mappes of Cosmographie which necessarely serve for the perfect understanding and memorie of divers places and countreys, partely described and partely by occasion touched, bothe in the olde and newe Testament. Finally that nothing might lacke which might be boght by labors, for the increase of knowlage and fortherance of Gods glorie, we have adioyned two moste profitable tables, the one serving for the interpretation of the Ebrewe names: and the other conteyning all the chefe and principal matters of the whole Bible: so that nothing (as we trust) that any colde iustely desire, is omitted. Therefore, as brethren that are partakers of the same hope and salvation with us, we beseche you, that this riche perle and inestimable treasure may not be offred in vayne, but as sent from God to the people of God, for the increase of his kingdome, the comfort of his Churche, and discharge of our conscience, whome it hath pleased him to raise up for this purpose, so you wolde willingly receyve the worde of God, earnestly studie it and in all your life practise it, that you may now appeare in dede to be the people of God, not walking any more according to this worlde, but in the frutes of the Spirit; that God in us may be fully glorified through Christ Iesus our Lord, who lyveth and reigneth for ever. Amen. From Geneva, 10. April. 1560.

Notes

1. See David Daniell, ed., introduction to *Tyndale's New Testament* (New Haven: Yale University Press, 1989), xi–xiii, xvi–xxvii.

2. See S. L. Greenslade, ed., "English Versions of the Bible, A.D. 1525–1611," *The Cambridge History of the Bible: The West from the Reformation to the Present*

Day (Cambridge: Cambridge University Press, 1963), 152; and Daniell, xii–xiii, xxiv.

3. See Lloyd E. Berry, ed., introduction to *The Geneva Bible*, a facsimile of the 1560 edition (Madison: University of Wisconsin Press, 1969), 6.

4. See Berry, 11.

5. See Greenslade, 158; Berry, 16; and Dan G. Danner, "The Contribution of the Geneva Bible of 1560 to the English Protestant Tradition," *Sixteenth Century Journal* 12, no. 3 (1981), 5–18. Danner stresses that the notes reflect more the translators' own English Protestant tradition than any direct Calvinist influence from Geneva.

6. See Berry, 15–17. The Towson-Junius New Testament of 1607 has recently been made available in *The Geneva Bible: The Annotated New Testament, 1602 Edition*, ed. Gerald T. Sheppard (New York: The Pilgrim Press, 1989). For the strong influence of Beza on Towson's notes, see Irena Backus, *The Reformed Roots of the English New Testament* (Pittsburgh: Pickwick Press, 1980), 18–27.

7. See P. Marion Simms, *The Bible in America* (New York: Wilson-Erickson, 1936), 90.

8. Esdras was not recognized as canonical by Protestants or Roman Catholics, but it was placed in an appendix in the Latin Vulgate Bible.

The Rise of Puritanism

26. The Form of Prayers

(1556)

JOHN KNOX

The English community in Geneva in the late 1550s not only produced the Geneva Bible (see vol. 2:419–31) but also created a liturgy that strongly influenced Puritan worship in England for almost a hundred years. Known as the Form of Prayers, or John Knox's Genevan Service Book, it was adopted in Scotland as the standard liturgy. It was also known as the Book of Common Order, remaining in continuous use until the Westminster Directory was established in 1644. The English church in Geneva has rightly been called "the cradle of Puritanism."[1]

The Form of Prayers was used and printed for the first time in Geneva in 1556. It had been written by a committee consisting of John Knox (c. 1514–1572) and others at Frankfurt during the previous year. They were English exiles who had escaped to Frankfurt shortly after the Catholic Mary Tudor came to the English throne in 1553. They favored a form of liturgy closer to that of Calvin than to that of the Book of Common Prayer (see vol. 2:397–418).

Knox originally accepted the 1552 prayer book, after the black rubric gave kneeling a more Protestant interpretation. Later, however, like many Calvinists, he became very critical of it. Soon there was a conflict between Anglican Coxians (followers of Richard Cox) and Calvinist Knoxians over the correct form of liturgy. Knox and his colleagues were eventually banished from Frankfurt, and many of them fled to Geneva.

The Form of Prayers was heavily influenced by John Calvin.[2] The order for the Sunday morning service is as follows: confession of sins and pardon, singing of a psalm, prayer before the sermon, Scripture,

---

SOURCE: Bard Thompson, ed., *Liturgies of the Western Church* (Cleveland: The World Publishing Company, 1961). Used by permission of Harcourt, Brace & Company.

sermon, prayer for the whole estate of Christ's church followed by the Lord's Prayer, the Apostles' Creed (recited by the minister alone), a psalm sung by the people, and a closing blessing (either Aaronic or Apostolic). The Eucharist, which was supposed to be celebrated once a month (in Scotland, four times a year), consisted of the exhortation, the eucharistic prayer, the fraction, the delivery, the communion of the people during the Scripture reading, the post-communion thanksgiving, the singing of Psalm 103, and the blessing.

There were several noteworthy features of this service. It stressed confession of sin at the outset of the service, similar to Martin Bucer's and John Calvin's liturgies. Free prayer by the minister was permitted in place of a written general prayer after the sermon. At the beginning of the communion service, the words of institution were recited as a warrant for the celebration of the Eucharist, rather than being spoken in the communion prayer as part of the consecration of the elements. Furthermore, there was no epiclesis, *or calling upon the Holy Spirit to consecrate either the elements or the people. In later Puritan liturgies, such as the Westminster Directory and the Savoy Liturgy (1661) written by Richard Baxter, an* epiclesis *was restored.*[3]

The communion prayer in the Form of Prayers was an original composition not dependent on Calvin. It included words of thanksgiving for creation and redemption, as in the ancient church. In the exhortation prior to the Communion, a balance was achieved between the requirement that a worthy Communion be based on sincere faith, love, and discipline, and the need for the sacrament as "singuler medicine" for "poore sicke creatures." A sursum corda *("Lift up our hearts . . .") came at the end of the exhortation. The minister stood at the pulpit during the entire service until the moment of communion. Then, finding a place at "the holy table" and sitting alongside the communicants, the minister took the bread, gave thanks, and handed the bread to the communicants, who divided it among themselves. Unlike The Book of Common Prayer, there was no kneeling, which Knox found offensive. Sitting together at the table also gave expression to an understanding of the church as the family of God.*

Later Puritans of an Independent or Congregationalist persuasion tended to reject all fixed liturgies and written prayers. Yet Knox's Genevan Service Book and its successors—the Waldegrave and Middleburgh Liturgies (1586), the Westminster Directory, and the Savoy Liturgy—also show that many Puritans did not deny the tradition of liturgical worship.[4]

In fact, resistance to set forms of worship was characteristic only of the Separatists. The bulk of Puritans during the Elizabethan period would have preferred the Genevan Service Book to the Book of Common Prayer, but most of them were not so bold as to substitute it for the officially prescribed form. Generally speaking, Puritans used the Book of Common Prayer, adapting it variously according to their Puritan prejudices. Although the majority of Puritans agreed on such matters as making the sermon the center of the service, omitting vestments, not kneeling at communion, and refusing to use the sign of the cross in baptism or a ring in weddings, there was great variety among Puritans as to what portions of the Book of Common Prayer ought to be put into practice.[5]

THE FORME OF PRAYERS[6] AND MINISTRATION OF THE SACRAMENTS, &c. USED IN THE ENGLISHE CONGREGATION AT GENEVA: AND APPROVED, BY THE FAMOUS AND GODLY LEARNED MAN, IOHN CALVYN. GENEVA M.D.LVI.

• • •

THE PRAYERS.[7]

When the congregation is assembled, at the houre appointed, the minister useth one of these two confessions, or lyke in effect: exhorting the people diligently, to examine themselves, following in their hartes the tenor of his wordes.

A CONFESSION OF OUR SYNNES, FRAMED TO OUR TYME, OUT OF THE 9. CHAP. OF DANIEL.

O lord God which arte mightie, and dreadeful, thou that kepest covenant, and shewest mercie to theym that love thee, and do thy commaundementes: we have synned, we haue offended, we have wickedly, and stubburnely gone backe, frome thy lawes, and preceptes. We wolde never obey thy servantes the Prophetes that spake in thy name, to our kinges and princes, to our forfathers, and to all the people of our lande. O lord rightuousnes belongeth unto thee, unto us, perteyneth nothing but open shame, as it ys come to passe this day, unto our miserable contry of Englande, yea unto all our nation whether they be farr , or nere, through all landes, wherein they are scattered for the offences that they and we have committed against thee: so that the curses and ponishmentes which are wryten in thy lawe, are nowe powred upon us, and thou hast perfourmed those wordes wherwith thou didest menace us and our rulers, that governed us, in bringinge the same plagues upon us which before were threatened. And yet notwithstandinge bothe they, and we procede in our iniquitie and sease not to heape synne upon synne. For they which once were well instructed in the doctrine of thy gospel, are nowe gone backe frome the obedience of thy trueth, and are turned agayne to that moste abhominable Idolatrie, from the which they were once called by the lyvely preachinge of thy worde. And we alas, to this day do not earnestly repent us of our former wickednes, neither do we rightly consider, the heavynes of thy displeasure. Suche is thy iuste iudgementes (ò lord) that thou ponishes synne by synne, and man by his owne inventions, so that there can be no ende of iniquitie, except thou prevent [precede] us with thy undeserved grace. Therfore convert us (ò lord) and we shalbe converted: for we do not offer up our prayers trustinge in our owne rightuousnes, but in thy manifolde mercies. And althoghe thou haste once of thy especial grace delivered us from the miserable thraldome of error and blindnes, and called us many tymes, to the swet libertie of thy gospell which we notwithstandinge have moste shamefully abused, in obeinge rather our owne lustes, and affections, then the admonitions of thy prophetes: yet we beseche thee once agayne for thy nams sake, to powre some comfortable droppe of thy accustomed mercies upon us: incline thyne eares, and open thyne eyes, to beholde the grevous plagues of our contrie, the continuall sorrowes of our afflicted bretherne, and our wofull banishment. And let our afflictions and iuste ponishement be an admonition and warninge to other nations, emongest whome we are skattered that with all reverence they may obey thy holy gospell: lest for like contempte, in the ende, like, or wourse plagues fall upon theym. Wherfore ò lord heare us, ò lord forgive us, ò lord consider and tary not over longe, but for thy deare sonne Iesus Christe sake, be mercifull unto us, and delyver us. So shall it be knowen to all the worlde, that thou onely arte the selfe same God, that ever sheweth mercie, to all suche, as call upon thy holy name.

AN OTHER CONFESSION FOR ALL STATES AND TYMES.

O Eternall God and moste mercifull father, we confesse, and acknowlage, here before thy divine maiestie, that we are miserable synners, conceyved and borne in synne and iniquitie, so that in us there is no goodnes. For the fleshe evermoer rebelleth against the spirite, whereby we contynually transgresse thy holy preceptes, and commaundementes, and so purchase to our selves, through thy iuste iudgement, death and damnation. Notwithstandinge (ò heavenly father) forasmoche as we are displeased with our selves for the synnes, that we have committed against thee, and do unfeynedly repent us of the same: we moste humbly beseche thee, for Iesus Christes sake, to shewe thy mercie upon us, to forgive us all our synnes, and to increase thy holy spirite in us: that we acknowlaginge, from the botome of our hartes, our owne unrightuousnes, may from hensforth, not onely mortifie our sinfull lustes and affections, but also bringe forth suche fruites, as may be agreable to thy moste blessed wyll,[8] not for the worthynes thereof, but for the merites of thy dearely beloved sonne Iesus Christe our onely savyour, whom thou hast already given an oblation and offeringe for our synnes: and for whose sake, we are certainly persuaded, that thou wylt denye us nothinge, that we shall aske in his name, accordinge to thy wyl. For thy spirite doth assure our consciences, that thou arte our mercifull father, and so louest us thy childrene through hym, that nothinge is able to remove thy heavenlye grace, and favor, from us: to thee therfore ò father, with the sonne and the holy ghoste, be all honor, and glorye, worlde with owt ende. So beit.

This done, the people singe a Psalme all together, in a playne tune, which ended, the minister prayeth for thassistance of Gods holy spirite as the same shall move his harte, and so procedeth to the sermon,[9] U singe after the sermon this prayer following or suche lyke.

A PRAYER FOR THE WHOLE ESTATE OF CHRISTES CHURCHE[10]

Almightie God, and moste mercifull father we humbly submit our selves and fall downe before thy maiestie, besechinge thee frome the botome of our hartes, that this seede of thy worde, nowe sowen emongest us, may take suche depe roote, that neither the burninge heate of persecution, cause it to wither, nether the thorny cares of this lyfe, do choke it, but that as seede sowen in good grownde, it may bringe forth thirtie, sixtie, and an hundreth folde, as thy heavenly wisdome, hathe appointed. And becawse we have nede continuallie, to crave many thinges at thy handes, we humbly beseche thee (ò heavenly father) to graunt us thy holy spirite, to directe our peticions, that they may procede, frome suche a fervent mynde, as may be agreable to thy moste blessed wyll. And seinge that our infirmitie is hable to do nothinge, without thy helpe: and that thou arte not ignorant with how many, and greate temptations, we poore wretches, are on every side inclosed, and compassed: let thy strenghe (ò lord) susteyne our weaknes, that we beinge defended, with the force of thy grace, may be savely preserved, against all assaultes of Satan: who goeth abowte continually, like a roaringe lyon sekinge to devoure us. Encrease our faith (ò mercifull father) that we do not swarve at any tyme, frome thy heavenly worde, but augment in us, hope, and love, with a carefull kepinge of all thy commaundementes: that no hardnes of harte, no hypocrisie, no concupiscence of the eys, nor intysementes of the worlde, do drawe us away, frome thy obedience. And, seinge we lyve nowe in these moste perillous tymes, let thy fatherly providence defende us, against the violence of all our enemies, which do every where pursue us: but chiefely againste the wicked rage, and furious uproares of that Romyshe idoll, ennemie to thy Christe. Fordermore forasmoche as by thy holy Aposile we be taught, to make our prayers, and supplications for all men, we praye not onely for our selves here present, but beseche the also, to reduce all suche as be yet ignorant, from the miserable captivitie of blindnes and error, to the pure understandinge, and knowlage, of thy heavenly trueth: that we all, with one consent and unitie of myndes, may wourshippe thee our onely God and saviour. And that all Pastors, shepherds, and ministers, to whome thou hast committed the dispensation of thy holy woord, and charge of thy chosen people, may bothe in their lyfe and doctrine, be fownde faithfull: settinge onely before their eyes, thy glorie: and that by theim all poore shepe which wander and go astray, may be gathered, and broght home to thy foulde. Moreover, becawse the hartes of rulers are in thy hands, we beseche thee to direct, and governe, the hartes of all kinges, Princes, and Magistrates, to whome thou haste committed the sworde, especially (ò lord) accordinge to ourbondendutie, we beseche thee to mainteyne and increase, the honorable estate of this Citie, into whose defense we are receyved: the Magistrates, the counsell, and all the whole bodye of this common weale. Let thy fatherlye faver so preserve theym, and thy holy spirite so governe their hartes, that they may in suche sorte execute their office that thy religion may be purely mainteyned, manners refourmed, and synne ponished accordinge to the precise rule of thy holy woord. And for that we be all membres of the mysticall body of Christ Iesu, we make our requestes unto the (ò heavenly father) for all suche as are afflicted with any kinde of crosse, or tribulation, as warre, plague, famine, sickenes, povertie, imprisonement, persecution, banishement, or any other kinde of thy roddes: whether it be calamitie of bodie, or vexation of mynde, that it wold please thee, to gyve them pacience, and constancie, tyll thou send them full deliverance, of all their troubles. And as we be bownde to love, and honor our parentes, kinsfolkes, friendes, and contrye: so we moste humbly beseche thee, to shewe thy pitie, upon our miserable contrie of England, which once through thy mercie, was called to libertie, and now for their and our synnes, is broght unto moste vile slavery, and Babylonicall bondage. Roote owte from thence (ò lord) all raueninge wolves which to fyll their bellies, destroie thy flocke. And shewe thy great mercies upon those our bretherne, which are persecuted, cast in prison, and dayly condemned to deathe, for the testimonie of thy trueth. And thogh they be utterly destitute of all mans ayde, yet let thy swete comfort never departe frome them: but so inflame their hartes, with thy holy spirite, that thei may boldely and chearefully abide suche tryall, as thy godly wisdome shall appoint. So that at lenght [misprint: length] aswell by their deathe, as by their life, the kingdome of thy sonne Iesus Christ, may increase, and shyne through all the worlde. In whose name, we make our humble peticions unto thee, as he hath taught us.

Our father Which arte in heaven. etc.

Almightie and ever lyvinge God, vouchsave we beseche thee, to grant us perfite contynuance in thy lively faith, augmentinge the same in us dayly, tyll we growe to the full measure of our perfection in Christ, wherof we make our confession, sayinge.

I beleve in God. &c.[11]

Then the people singe a Psalme, which ended, the minister pronounceth one of these blessinges, and so the congregation departeth.

The lord blesse you, and save you, the lord make his face shyne upon you, and be mercifull unto you, the lord turne his countenance towardes you, and graunt you his peace.

The grace of our lord Iesus Christ, the love of God, and communion of the holie ghoste, be with you all: so be it.

It shall not be necessarie for the minister dayly to repete all these thinges before mentioned, but beginnynge with some maner of confession, to procede to the sermon, which ended, he either useth the prayer, for all estates before mentioned, or els prayeth, as the spirite of God shall move his harte: framinge the same, accordinge to the tyme and matter which he hath intreated of. And yf there shalbe at any tyme, any present plague, famine, pestilence, warre, or such like, which be evident tokens of Gods wrath: as it is our parte to acknowlage our synnes to be the occasion therof, so are we appointed by the scriptures to give our selves to mournynge, fastinge, and prayer, as the meanes to turne awaye Gods heavie displeasure. Therfore, it shalbe convenient, that the minister at suche tyme, do not onely admonyshe the people therof, but also use some forme of prayer, accordinge as the present necessitie requireth, to the which he may appoint, by a common consent, some severall daye after the sermon wekely to be observed.

THE MANER OF THE LORDES SUPPER

The day when the lordes supper is ministred which commonlye is used once a monthe,[12] *or so oft as the Congregation shall thinke expedient, the minister useth to saye as followeth.*

Let us marke deare bretherne, and consider how Iesus Christ did ordayne unto us his holy supper according as S. Paule maketh rehearsall in the 11. chapt. of the first Epistle to the Cor. I have (saith he) receyved of the lorde that which I have delivered unto you, to witt, that the lorde Iesus the same night he was betrayed toke breade, and when he had geven thankes, he brake it sayinge. Take ye, eate ye, this is my bodie, which is broken for you: doo you this in remembrance of me. Likewise after supper, he toke the cuppe, sayinge. This cuppe is the newe testament or covenant in my bloude; doo ye this so ofte as ye shall drinke therof, in remembrance of me. For so ofte as you shal eate this bread, and drinke of this cuppe, ye shall declare the lordes death untill his cominge. Therfore whosoever shall eate this bread, and drinke the cuppe of the lorde unworthely, he shalbe giltie of the bodye and bloud of the lord. Then see that everyman prove and trye hym selfe, and so let hym eate of this bread and drinke of this cuppe, for whosoever eateth or drinketh unworthelye, he eateth and drinketh his owne damnation, for not havinge due regarde and consideration of the lordes bodye.

This done, the minister proceadith to the exhortation.

Dearely beloved in the lorde, forasmoch as we be nowe assembled, to celebrate the holy communion of the body and bloud of our saviour Christ, let us consider these woordes of S. Paule, how he exhorteth all persons diligently to trye and examine them selves, before they presume to eate of that bread, and drinke of that cuppe. For as the benefite ys great, if with a truly penitent hart, and lively faith, we receyve that holy sacrament (for then we spiritually eate the fleshe of Christ, and drinke his bloude, then we dwell in Christ, and Christ in us, we be one with Christ, and Christ with vs) so is the daunger great, if we receyve the same unworthely, for then we be giltie of the bodye, and bloud of Christ our saviour, we eate and drinke our own damnation, not considering the lordes bodye: we kindle godes wrath against us, and provoke him to plague us with diverse diseases and sundry kindes of death. Therfore if any of you be a blasphemer of God, an hinderer or slaunderer of his worde, an adulterer, or be in malice or envie, or in any other grevous cryme, bewaylle your synnes, and come not to this holy table: lest after the takynge of this holy sacrament, the divell entre into you as he entred into Iudas, and fill you full of iniquities, and bring you, to destruction, bothe of bodye and soule. Iudge therfore your selves bretherne, that ye be not iudged of the lorde: repent you truly for your synnes paste, and have a lyvely and stedfast fayth, in Christ our saviour,[13] sekinge onely your salvation in the merites of his death, and passion, from hensforth refusinge, and forgettinge all malice and debate, with full purpose to live in brotherly amytie, and godlye conversation, all the dais of your lyfe. And albeit we fele in ourselves muche frailtie and wretchedness, as that we have not our faith so perfite, and constant, as we ought, being many tymes readye to distruste Godes goodnes through our corrupt nature, and also that we are not so throughlye geven to serve God, neyther have so fervent a zeale to set forth his glory, as our duetye requireth, felinge still such rebellion in our selves, that we have nede dayly to fight against the lustes of our fleshe, yet neuertheless seinge that our lorde hath dealed thus mercifully with us, that he hath printed his gospell in our hartes, so that, we are preserved from falling into desperation and misbeliefe: and seing also he hath indued us with a will, and desire to renownce and withstand our own affections, with a longing for his righteousenes and the keping of his commaundementes, we may be now right well assured, that those defautes and manifolde imperfections in us, shalbe no hinderance at all against us, to cause him not to accept and impute us as worthie to come to his spirituall table, For the ende of our comming thyther, is not to make protestation, that we are upright or iuste in our lives, but contrariwise, we come to seke our life and perfection, in Iesu Christ, acknowledging in the meane tyme, that we of our selves, be the children of wrath, and damnation. Let us consider then, that this sacrament is a singuler medicine for all poore sicke creatures, a comfortable helpe to weake soules, and that our lord requireth no other worthines on our parte, but that we unfaynedly acknowlege our noghtines, and imperfection. Then to the end that we may be worthy partakers of his merites, and moste comfortable benefits (which ys the true eatinge of his fleshe, and drinkinge of his bloud) let us not suffer our mindes to wander aboute the consideration of these earthlie, and corruptible thynges (which we see present to our eies and fele with our handes) to seeke Christ bodely presente in them, as if he were inclosed in the breade or wyne, or as yf these elementes were tourned and chaunged into the substaunce, of his fleshe and blood. [Transsubstantiation, Transelementation, Transmutation and Transformation as the papistes use them are the doctrine of divells.] For the only waye to dispose our soules to receive norishment, reliefe, and quikening of his substance, is to lift up our mindes by fayth above all thinges wordlye [misprint: worldlye] and sensible, and therby to entre into heaven, that we may finde, and receive Christ [the true eatyng of Christ in the sacrament], where he dwelleth undountedlye verie God, and verie man, in the incomprehensible glorie of his father, to whome be all praise, honor and glorye now and ever. Amen.

The exhortation ended, the minister commeth doune from the pulpet, and sitteth at the Table, every man and woman in likewise takinge their place as occasion best serveth, then he taketh bread and geveth thankes, either in these woordes followinge, or like in effect.

O Father of mercye and God of all consolation, seinge all creatures do knowlege and confesse thee, as governer, and lorde, it becommeth us the workemanship of thyne own handes, at all tymes to reverence and magnifie thy godli maiestie, first for that thou haste created us to thyne own Image and similitude: but chieflye that thou haste delivered us, from that everlasting death and danmation into the which Satan drewe mankinde by the meane of synne: from the bondage wherof (neither man nor angell was able to make us free) but thou (ò lord) riche in mercie and infinite in goodnes, haste provided our redemption to stande in thy onely and welbeloved sone: whom of verie love thou didest give to be made man, lyke unto us in all thynges, (synne except) that in his bodye he myght receive the ponishmentes of our transgression, by his death to make satisfaction to thy iustice, and by his resurrection to destroye hym that was auctor of death, and so to reduce and bring agayne life to the world, frome which the whole ofspringe of Adame moste iustly was exiled. O lord we acknowlege that no creature ys able to comprehende the length and breadthe, the depenes and height, of that thy most excellent love which moved thee to shewe mercie, where none was deserved: to promise and give life, where death had gotten victorie: to receve us into thy grace, when we could do nothyng but rebell against thy iustice. O lord the blynde dulnes of our corrupt nature will not suffer us sufficiently to waye these thy moste ample benefites: yet nevertheles at the commaundement of Iesus Christ our lorde, we present our selves to this his table (which he hath left to be used in remembrance of his death untyll hys comming agayne) to declare and witnes before the world, that by him alone we have receved libertie, and life: that by hym alone, thou doest acknowledge us thy chyldren and heires: that by hym alone, we haue entrance to the throne of thy grace: that by hym alone we are possessed in our spirituall kingedome, to eate and drinke at his table: with whome we have our conversation presently in heaven, and by whome, our bodies shalbe reysed up agayne frome the dust, and shalbe placed with him in that endles ioye, which thow (ò father of mercye) hast prepared for thyne elect, before the foundation of the worlde was layde. And these moste inestimable benefites, we acknowlege and confesse to have receaved of thy free mercie and grace, by thy onely beloved sonne Iesus Christ, for the which therfore we thy congregation moved by thy holy sprite render thee all thankes, prayse, and glorie for ever and ever.

This done, the minister breaketh the breade and delyvereth it to the people, who distribute and devide thesame amongst theim selves, accordinge to our saviour Christes commandement, and in likewise geueth the cuppe. Duringe the which tyme, some place of the scriptures is read, which doth lyvely set forth the death of Christ, to theintene that our eyes and senses may not onely be occupiede in these outwarde signes of bread and wyne, which are called the visible woorde: but that our hartes and myndes also may be fully fixed in the contemplation of the lordes death, which is by this holy sacrament representede. And after the action is done, he geveth thanckes, saing.[14]

Moste mercifull father,[15] we render to the all prayse thankes and glorie, for that thou hast vouchsafed to graunt unto us miserable synners so excellent a gifte and threasor, as to receave us into the felowship and company of thy deare sonne Iesus Christ our lorde, whome thou deliveredst to deathe for us, and haste given hym unto us, as a necessarie foode and norishment unto everlastynge life. And now we beseche the also (ò heavenly father) to graunt us this request, that thou never suffer us to become so unkinde as to forget so worthy benefittes: but rather imprint and fasten them sure in our hartes, that we may growe and increase dayly more and more in true faithe, which continually ys excersised in all maner of goode workes, and so moche the rather ò lord, confirme us, in these perelous daies and rages of satan, that we may constanly [misprint: constantly] stande and continewe in the confession of the same to the advancement of thy glorye, which art God over all things blessed for ever. So be it.

The action thus ended, the people singe the 103 psal. My soule give laud &c. or some other of thancks givynge, which ended, one of the blessings before mencionede is recitede, and so they ryse from the table and departe.

To the reader.

If parchaunce any wolde marvell why we followe rather this order, then any other in the administration of this sacrament, let him diligently consider, that first of all we utterly renownce the error of the papistes: secondly we restore unto the sacramentes theyr owne substaunce: and to Christe his proper place. And as for the wordes of the lordes supper we rehearce theym not bicawse they shuld chaunge the substaunce of the bread or wyne, or that the repeticion therof with the intent of the sacrificer should make the sacrament as the papistes falselie beleve; but they are read and pronownced to teache us how to behaue our selves in this action and that Christe might witnes unto owr faithe as it were with his owne mowthe, that he hath ordayned these signes for our spirituall use and comforte. wee do firste therefore examyne owr selves, accordyng to saint Pauls rule, and prepare our myndes that we may be worthie partakers of so high mysteries. Then takyng bread, wee give thankes, breake, and distribute it as Christe our savior hath taught us. Fynally, the ministration ended, wee gyve thankes agayne accordying to his example. So that without his woorde, and warrante, there is nothyng in this holy action attempted.

Notes

1. See William D. Maxwell, *John Knox's Genevan Service Book, 1556* (Edinburgh: Oliver and Boyd, 1931), 7.

2. See Maxwell, 17–18.

3. See *Liturgies of the Western Church*, ed. Bard Thompson (Cleveland: World Publishing Company, 1961), 369, 402.

4. See Horton Davies, *Worship and Theology in England from Cranmer to Hooker, 1534–1603* (Princeton, N.J.: Princeton University Press, 1970), 255–93.

5. See Patrick Collinson, *The Elizabethan Puritan Movement* (London: Jonathan Cape, 1967), 356–71.

6. Bard Thompson, the editor of the version reprinted here, notes the following: "The text has been reproduced exactly—spelling, punctuation, and paragraphing—from a microfilm of the original volume obtained from the National Library, Edinburgh. Marginal references to Scripture have been omitted, and the rubrics italicized." Spellings with "v" and "u," have been modernized, and where a line over the vowel required an "m" or "n" it has been added. Otherwise the original spelling is retained. The remainder of the notes come directly from Thompson.

7. In both Scottish and Puritan practice, a 'Reader's Service' was prefixed to the Sunday Morning Service. That office, conducted by a lay reader whom the elders appointed, preceded the main service by an hour or so, while the full congregation assembled; its purpose was to read through the Scriptures and engage the people in the singing of psalms. Readers were appointed in Scotland beginning in 1560.

8. To this point: Calvin's Prayer of Confession. For its origin, cf. Bucer's second Confiteor, which he himself composed.

9. 'Sermon' included both lesson and proclamation, as one inseparable element. The lesson was read 'in course.' Bucer permitted only the Gospels to be expounded on Sunday morning. . . . Calvin followed the same practice . . . , while Pullain allowed the entire New Testament to be used. . . . In accord with à Lasco . . . ,

Knox opened both Testaments to Sunday morning preaching, probably in Geneva . . . and certainly in Scotland according to the first *Book of Discipline*.

10. This is "an original composition, with some verbal resemblance to Calvin's Great Prayer."

11. This is "a prose version of the Creed, recited by the minister alone. In the Reformed Communion service, a metrical Creed was often sung by the people while the elements were brought to the table. . . . In the English congregation of Geneva, which apparently lacked a metrical version of the Creed, the elements were brought forward during the psalm that followed."

12. Thus monthly Communion was the practice of the English congregation in Geneva. The rubric remained unchanged in the Scottish editions; but it was overcome by the first *Book of Discipline*, which declared that 'four tymes a yeare' was 'sufficient' for the Eucharist. Permission was given 'to minister ofter,' granted there were 'reasonable causses.'

13. To this point, the Exhortation corresponds to that of the BCP [Book of Common Prayer], 1552, which was composed by Cranmer. . . . The remainder was taken directly from Calvin's Exhortation, or, more likely, from Huycke's translation of the same. The *Sursum corda*, at the end, can be traced ultimately to Farel's *La Maniere et fasson*.

14. The Fraction, conceived as a separate and distinct part of the action, was typical of Reformed practice at this time and has continued so in the Scottish church.

15. This is "adapted from Calvin, who in turn drew it from Bucer's second form of the Post-Communion thanksgiving."

27. The Art of Prophesying

(1592)

William Perkins

For Puritans, who stressed the Word of God as the fundamental authority for faith and practice (individual and communal), the preaching of the Word was the primary means of grace. Even as they emphasized preaching, however, they did not intend any rejection of the sacraments. In the beginning, both Puritans and loyal Anglicans held Word and sacrament together in a precarious balance. As tensions between the two parties heated up in the late sixteenth and seventeenth centuries, a gap developed between them regarding the relative importance of each vehicle of grace. Puritans laid the greatest stress on preaching, while loyal Anglicans focused on the sacraments.

The importance of preaching for the Puritans was underlined in the words of Philip Stubbes: "As the soul is the life of the body, . . . so the word of God preached is the life, . . . as well to the body, as to the soul. . . . Now certain it is, these things cannot be applied without the presence of the preacher; . . . and therefore is his absence from his flock a dangerous and perilous thing."[1] *Not only did Puritan preaching seek the conversion and the transformation of the individual soul, it extended to the transformation of the whole society. Not only did Puritans want sermons to be frequent, they wanted them to be solid, edifying, and uplifting.*

To provide for sound and frequent preaching, Puritans promoted two important institutions in the late sixteenth- and seventeenth-century English church: lectureships and prophesyings. Lecturers were usually

---

SOURCE: Ian Breward, ed., *The Work of William Perkins*, Courtenay Library of Reformation Classics, vol. 3 (Appleford, Abingdon, Berkshire, England: The Sutton Courtenay Press, 1970). Used by permission.

Puritan preachers appointed with a stipend by local parishes, town corporations, and even individual laypersons to supplement the work of parish priests. They arose when the preaching of the incumbents in the parishes ceased to be constant or edifying enough. Lecturers, appointed without the approval of the bishops, were a powerful instrument for the spread of Puritan doctrine.

Prophesyings were conferences of ministers, which arose in the market towns to train clergy in biblical exegesis and preaching as well as mutual admonition and correction. Though Puritans were the chief instigators of these meetings, the bishops sometimes encouraged them. The model was drawn from Reformed cities on the continent. Prophesying took place at Zurich as early as 1525, when ministers and candidates for ministry gathered for biblical study using the ancient languages and preached to the people in the vernacular. In England, prophesying provided a kind of seminary training in exegesis and the practical art of preaching, which exceeded learning at the university.[2]

William Perkins (1558–1602) of Cambridge was the first Puritan to write a major treatise on the art of preaching. It was entitled "The Art of Prophesying" (1592). A graduate of Christ's College, Cambridge, a center of Puritanism, Perkins became a lecturer at Great St. Andrews in Cambridge. His preaching ministry struck a responsive chord in the university and the community, and his reputation spread through his sermons and his theological and practical writings. Perkins stressed Scripture, the doctrine of original sin, the need for the assurance of grace, divine predestination, and an experiential piety. He gave detailed attention to the examination of conscience but remained rather indifferent to issues of polity. He did not agree with other Puritans, whether rabid Presbyterians or Congregationalists, that a particular form of church government necessarily led to Reformation. Perkins's writings profoundly influenced Presbyterians and Congregationalists as well as many other Reformed Protestants throughout the seventeenth century.[3]

Perkins believed that true preaching was based on Scripture as the Word of God. His treatise on the art of prophesying first explored the ground of scriptural authority as well as methods of scriptural interpretation. He made use of past humanist and Reformed exegetes, giving attention to the analogy of faith as the sum of Scripture and to "the circumstances of the place," showing the influence of Erasmus.[4]

In the application of doctrines derived from "the right dividing of the word," Perkins argued that the preacher must consider various ways of application according to the different conditions of people (as well as the kinds of application, mental or practical). He provided sound advice to the minister that when reproving sin, the preacher should "let the love of the person appear in the speeches" and "include himself (if he may) in his reprehension that it may be more mild and gentle."

When he wrote about sermon delivery, Perkins was concerned that there be no erudite or rhetorical display. He suggested that the preacher should leave philosophy, exegesis, and rhetoric in the study and strive for simplicity: Artis etiam celare artem, *"It is also a point of art to conceal art." Perkins believed that preaching should reveal by its gracious and simple speech and gesture, and by the minister's godly person, that it is the Holy Spirit speaking in and through the sermon. Finally, since Puritan ministers were commonly expected to preach without manuscript, Perkins also gave some suggestions as to how sermons could be committed to memory.*

Perkins's treatise, along with his own sermons, had an important impact on Puritan preaching in England and New England for many decades.

To the faithful ministers of the gospel: and to all that are desirous of and do labour for the knowledge of holy learning

THAT COMMONPLACE OF DIVINITY which concerneth the framing of sermons is both weighty and difficult, if there be any other throughout all that sacred science. For the matter which is to explicate and treat on is prophecy, an excellent gift indeed, whether we consider it in respect of dignity or of use. The dignity thereof appeareth in that like a lady it is highly mounted and carried aloft in a chariot, whereas all other gifts, both of tongues and arts, attend on this like handmaids, aloof off.

Answerable to this dignity there is also a twofold use: one in that it serveth to collect the church and to accomplish the number of the elect; the other, for that it drives the wolves away from the folds of the Lord. For this is indeed that *flexanima*, that allurer of the soul, whereby men's froward minds are mitigated and moved from an ungodly and barbarous life unto Christian faith and repentance. This is also that engine which as it hath shaken the foundations of ancient heresies, so it hath in these few by-past years cut asunder the sinews of that great Anti-christ. Whereof if it be demanded which is the most excellent gift of all, doubtless the praise must be given to prophesying.

Now by how much the more excellent everything is, by so much more the diligently it ought to be adorned with variety and plenty of precepts. Therefore, when I saw this commonplace so handled of many, as that it would remain naked and poor if all other arts should call for those things which are their own, I perused the writings of divines: and having gathered some rules out of them, I have couched them in that method which I have deemed most commodious, that they might be better for use and fitter for the memory. I do also publish them that they might be approved if they bring with them that which is good: if any evil, that they might receive their deserved punishment.

And whosoever thou art who pleasest to read them, where thou art persuaded of this order of preaching which here I handle, walk on with me: where thou standest at a stay, inquire with me: where thou perceivest thine own errors, return to me: where thou seest mine, call me back to thee. For that which now liketh me shall dislike me, if it like not godly and moderate-minded men. But if any man shall carp at this my travail, though very small, let him know that my only meaning is to benefit the church of God and that the conscience of my fact is a sufficient muniment against all calumnies. I do now betake you to God and this tractate of the art of prophesying both to you and to God.

Ann. 1592. Decemb. 12.
William Perkins

Chapter I

THE ART OR FACULTY OF PROPHESYING is a sacred doctrine of exercising prophecy rightly. Prophecy (or prophesying) is a public and solemn speech of the prophet, pertaining to the worship of God and the salvation of our neighbor (1 Cor. 14:3, 24; Rom. 1:9).

Chapter II

Of the preaching of the word

THERE ARE TWO PARTS OF PROPHECY: preaching of the word and conceiving of prayers. For in speaking there are only two duties of the prophet, that is of the minister of the word: to wit, preaching of the word and praying unto God in the name of the people (Rom. 12:6; Gen. 20:7). For this cause the word (prophecy) is given also to prayers (1 Chron. 25:1; 1 Kings 18:26, 29). And every prophet is partly the voice of God: to wit, in preaching; and partly the voice of the people in the act of praying (Jer. 15:19). Preaching of the word is prophesying in the name and room of Christ, whereby men are called to the state of grace and conserved in it (2 Cor. 5:19–20; 2 Thess. 2:13–14; Rom. 1:16; Prov. 29:18; Rom. 10:14).

Chapter III

Of the word of God

THE PERFECT AND EQUAL OBJECT OF PREACHING is the word of God (Luke 16:29; Matt. 23:2–3). The word of God is the wisdom of God concerning the truth which is according to godliness, descending from above (James 3:17; Titus 1:1). Admirable is the excellence of the word, which is evident partly by the nature thereof, partly by the operation. The excellence of the nature is either the perfection thereof, or the eternity. The perfection is either the sufficiency, or the purity. The sufficiency is that whereby the word of God is so complete, that nothing may be either put to it or taken from it, which appertaineth to the proper end thereof (Ps. 19:7; Deut. 12:32; Rev. 22:18–19). The purity thereof is whereby it remaineth entire in itself, void of deceit and error (Ps. 12:6). The eternity of the word is that whereby it abideth inviolable and cannot pass until all that which it commandeth be fully accomplished (Matt. 5:18). The excellence of operation is that whereby it is endowed with virtue, first to discern the spirit of man, secondly, to bind the conscience (Heb. 4:11; James 4:12; Isa. 32:22). To bind the conscience is to constrain it either to accuse us or to excuse us of sin before God.

The word is in the holy scripture. The scripture is the word of God written in a language fit for the church by men immediately called to be the clerks or secretaries of the Holy Ghost (2 Pet. 1:21). It is called canonical because it is, as it were, a canon, that is to say a rule or line of the master workman, by the help whereof the truth is both first to be found out and also afterwards to be examined (Gal. 6:16). Therefore the supreme and absolute determination and judgment of the controversies of the church ought to be given unto it.

The sum of the scripture is contained in such a syllogism or form of reasoning as this is which followeth.

The true Messaiah shall be both God and man of the seed of David; he shall be born of a virgin; he shall bring the gospel forth of his Father's bosom; he shall satisfy the law; he shall offer up himself a sacrifice for the sins of the faithful; he shall conquer death by dying and rising again; he shall ascend into heaven; and in his due time he shall return unto judgment. (Major)

But Jesus of Nazareth, the son of Mary, is such a one. (Minor)

He therefore is the true Messiah. (Conclusion)

In this syllogism, the major is the scope or principal drift in all the writings of the prophets and the minor in the writings of the evangelists and apostles. The scripture is either the New Testament or the Old. The Old

Testament is the first part of the scripture, written by the prophets in the Hebrew tongue, or at least in the Chaldee, unfolding chiefly that old covenant of works (Luke 16:29; 24:27). It is distinguished by books which are either historical, or dogmatic, or prophetic. . . . The New Testament is the second part of the scripture, written in the Greek tongue by the apostles, or at least approved of them, propounding plainly the doctrine of the new covenant (Eph. 2:20). . . . The New Testament containeth partly histories and partly epistles. . . .[5]

And thus the canonical scripture is distinguished by her books. Now there are very strong proofs which show that she alone is the word of God and no other besides. Of these proofs, one doth make a man certainly to know the same, the other doth but declare or testify it. Of the former kind there is only one, namely the inward testimony of the Holy Ghost speaking in the scriptures and not only telling a man within his heart, but also effectually persuading him that these books of scripture are the word of God (Isa. 59:21).

The manner of persuading is on this wise. The elect, having the Spirit of God, do first discern the voice of Christ speaking in the scriptures. Moreover, that voice which they do discern, they do approve and that which they do approve, they do believe. Lastly, believing they are, as it were, sealed with the seal of the Spirit (Eph. 1:13). The church also may bear witness of the canon, persuade she cannot. For by this means the voice of the church should be of greater force than the voice of God and the whole state of man's salvation should depend upon men; than which what can be said to be more miserable? . . .

The proof of declaration or testification is that which doth not demonstrate or persuade, but only testify, and by certain tokens approve the true canon. This proof is manifold. First, the perpetual consent of the church: of the ancient church of the Jews and of the new and later church from Christ and the apostles who cited testimonies forth of those books (Rom. 5:2). Secondly, from the fathers, . . . the consent in part made by the Gentiles and enemies, affirming the same things which are delivered in the holy scriptures. . . . Thirdly, the antiquity of the word, for it containeth in it a narration of things done from the beginning of the world. But the most ancient human history whatsoever was not written by any before the days of Ezra and Nehemiah, who were about the year of the world's creation three thousand and five hundred. Fourthly, the most certain accomplishment of the prophecies. . . . Fifthly, the matter thereof, which is of one true God, of the true worship of God and that God is the saviour. Sixthly, the consent of all the parts of scripture. Seventhly, the miraculous preservation of the scriptures in the perils of the church and in the time of general revolting. Eighthly, the operation thereof, for it converteth men, and though it be flatly contrary to the reason and affections of men, yet it winneth them unto itself. Ninthly, it is full of majesty in the simpleness of the words. Lastly, the holy penmen set down their own corruptions. . . .

Chapter IV

Of the interpretation of the scriptures

HITHERTO HATH BEEN SPOKEN OF THE OBJECT of preaching. The parts thereof are two—preparation for the sermon and the promulgation or uttering of it (Matt. 13:52). In preparation, private study is with diligence to be used (1 Tim. 4:13; 1 Pet. 1:10; Dan. 9:2). Concerning the study of divinity, this advice.

First, diligently imprint both in thy mind and memory the substance of divinity described, with definitions, divisions and explications of the properties. Secondly, proceed to the reading of the scriptures in this order. Using a grammatical, rhetorical and logical analysis, and the help of the rest of the arts read first the epistle of Paul to the Romans, after that the gospel of John (as being indeed the keys of the New Testament) and then the other books of the New Testament will be more easy when they are read. When all this is done, learn first the dogmatic books of the Old Testament, especially the Psalms, then the prophetic especially Isaiah, lastly the historical, but chiefly Genesis. For it is likely that the apostles and evangelists read Isaiah and the Psalms very much, for there are no more books of the Old Testament out of which we can read more testimonies to be cited than out of these. . . .

Thirdly, out of orthodox writings we must get aid not only from the latter, but also from the more ancient church, because Satan hath raised up from the dead the old heretics, that he might hinder the restoration of the church which is begun to be made in our time. . . . Fourthly, those things, which in studying thou meetest with, that are necessary and worthy to be observed, thou must put in thy tables or commonplace books, that thou mayest always have in a readiness old and new. Fifthly, before all these things God must be earnestly sued unto by prayer, that he would bless these means and that he would open the meaning of the scriptures to us that are blind (Ps. 119:18; Rev. 3:18). . . .

Preparation hath two parts: interpretation and right division or cutting. Interpretation is the opening of the words and sentences of the scripture, that one entire and natural sense may appear. The Church of Rome maketh four senses of the scriptures, the literal, allegorical, tropological and anagogical, . . . but this her device of the fourfold meaning of the scripture must be exploded and rejected. There is only one sense and the same is the literal. An allegory is only a certain manner of uttering the same sense, the anagoge and tropology are ways whereby the sense may be applied.

The principal interpreter of the scripture is the Holy Ghost (2 Pet. 1:20). Moreover, he that makes the law is the best and highest interpreter of the law. The supreme and absolute mean of interpretation is the scripture itself (Neh. 8:8). The means subordinated to the scripture are three: the analogy of faith, the circumstances of the place propounded and the comparing of places altogether.

The analogy of faith is a certain abridgment or sum of the scriptures, collected out of most manifest and familiar places. The parts thereof are two. The first concerneth faith, which is handled in the Apostles' Creed. The second concerneth charity or love, which is explicated in the Ten Commandments (2 Tim. 1:3).

The circumstances of the place propounded are these: who? to whom? upon what occasion? at what time? in what place? for what end? what goeth before? what followeth? The collation or comparing of places together is that where places are set like parallels one beside another, that the meaning of them may more evidently appear. But Saul increased the more in strength and confounded the Jews, confirming (that is conferring or conjoining places of scripture, as artificers being about to compact or join a thing together are wont to fit all the parts amongst themselves, that one of them may perfectly agree with each other) that this was the Christ (Acts 9:22).

Collation of places is twofold. The first is the comparing of the place propounded with itself cited and repeated elsewhere in Holy Writ. . . . The second collation is of the place propounded with other places and those again are either like or unlike. . . .

Chapter V

Of the ways of expounding

THE MANNER OR WAYS OF INTERPRETING are according to the places of scripture which are to be handled. Places are either analogical and plain, or cryptic and dark.

Analogical places are such as have an apparent meaning agreeable to the analogy of faith, and that at the first view. Concerning these places receive this rule. If the natural signification of the words of the place propounded do agree with the circumstances of the same place, it is the proper meaning of the place. . . . We must further know that every article and doctrine concerning faith and manners, which is necessary unto salvation, is very plainly delivered in the scriptures.

Cryptic or hidden places are those which are difficult and dark. For the expounding of them let this be thy rule and leader. If the native (or natural) signification of the words do manifestly disagree with either the analogy of faith, or very perspicuous places of the scripture, then the other meaning which is given of the place propounded is natural and proper, if it agree with like and contrary places, with the circumstances and words of the place, and with the nature of that thing which is intreated of. . . .[6]

Chapter VI

Of the right dividing of the word

HITHERTO WE HAVE SPOKEN OF INTERPRETING the word. We are now come to speak of the right cutting, or the right dividing of it. Right cutting of the word is that whereby the word is made fit to edify the people of God (2 Tim. 5:15). . . . The parts thereof are two—resolution, or partition, and application. Resolution is that whereby the place propounded is, as a weaver's web, resolved (or untwisted or unloosed) into sundry doctrines (Acts 18:28). Resolution is either notation or collection. Notation is when the doctrine is expressed in the place propounded (Rom. 3:9–11; Acts 2:24–27). Collection is when the doctrine not expressed is soundly gathered out of the text. This is done by the help of the nine arguments, that is of the causes, effects, subjects, adjuncts, dissentaries, comparatives, names, distribution and definition. . . .

In gathering of doctrines we must specially remember that an example in his own kind (that is an ethical, oeconomical, political, ordinary and extraordinary example) hath the virtue of a general rule in ethical, oeconomical, political, ordinary and extraordinary matters. The examples of the fathers are patterns for us (1 Cor. 10:11). And it is a principle in logic that the genus is actually in all the species and a rule in the optics that the general species of things are perceived before the particular. . . . That also I add, that collections ought to be right and sound; that is to say, derived from the genuine and proper meaning of the scripture. If otherwise, we shall draw any doctrine from any place. . . .

It shall be lawful also to gather allegories: for they are arguments taken from things that are like and Paul in his teaching useth them often (1 Cor. 9:9). But they are to be used with these caveats: let them be used sparingly and soberly; let them not be far-fetched, but fitting to the matter in hand; they must be quickly dispatched; they are to be used for the instruction of the life and not to prove any point of faith.

Any point of doctrine collected by just consequence is simply of itself to be believed and doth demonstrate (Acts 18:24, 28). From hence it followeth:

first, that human testimonies, whether of the philosophers or of the fathers, are not to be alleged. Yet with this exception—unless they convince the conscience of the hearer. Thus Paul alleged the testimony of Aratus (Acts 17:28–29). . . . And then also it must be done sparingly and with leaving out the name of the profane writer. Secondly, that a few testimonies of scripture are to be used for the proof of the doctrine and that sometimes there is need of none. Lastly, hence it follows that the prophets delivering their doctrines thus are not to be reproved of other prophets (1 Cor. 14:32, 37).

Chapter VII

Of the ways how to use and apply doctrines

APPLICATION IS THAT WHEREBY THE DOCTRINE rightly collected is diversely fitted according as place, time and person do require (Ezek. 34:15–16; Jude 22–23). The foundation of application is to know whether the place propounded be a sentence of the law or of the gospel. For when the word is preached, there is one operation of the law and another of the gospel. For the law is thus far effectual as to declare unto us the disease of sin and by accident to exasperate and stir it up, but it affords no remedy. Now the gospel, as it teacheth what is to be done, so it hath also the efficacy of the Holy Ghost adjoined with it, by whom being regenerated we have strength both to believe the gospel and to perform those things which it commandeth. The law therefore is first in order of teaching and the gospel second.

It is a sentence of the law which speaketh of perfect inherent righteousness, of eternal life given through the works of the law, of the contrary sins and of the curse which is due unto them (Gal. 3:10; Matt. 3:7, 10). A sentence of the gospel is that which speaketh of Christ and his benefits and of faith being fruitful in good works (John 3:16). Hence it is that many sentences which seem to belong to the law are by reason of Christ to be understood not legally, but with the qualification of the gospel (Luke 11:28; Deut. 30:11, 14). The sentence which is legal in Moses is evangelical in Paul (Rom. 10:8; Ps. 119:1–2; John 14:21, 23; Gen. 6:9; 17:1).

The ways of application are chiefly seven, according to the divers condition of men and people, which is sevenfold.

I. Unbelievers who are both ignorant and unteachable. . . .

II. Some are teachable, but yet ignorant. . . .

III. Some have knowledge, but are not as yet humbled. . . .

IV. Some are humbled. . . .

V. Some do believe. . . .

VI. Some are fallen. . . .

VII. There is a mingled people. . . .

Chapter VIII

Of the kinds of application

APPLICATION IS EITHER MENTAL OR PRACTICAL. Mental is that which respecteth the mind and it is either doctrine or redargution (2 Tim. 3:16–17). Doctrine is that whereby doctrine or teaching is used for the information of the mind to a right judgment concerning things to be believed. Redargution [refutation] is that whereby teaching is used for the reformation of the mind from error. In confutations which are made publicly before the assembly these cautions must be used. The thing that is determined, or the state of the question that is to be discussed, must be thoroughly understood. Let those errors only be reproved which trouble the church in which we live: all other being altogether let alone which do either lie dead, or are external, unless some danger be ready to ensue of them (Matt. 16:6). If the error be out of the foundation of faith, the confutation must not only be Christian-like, as it should be ever, but also a friendly, a gentle and brotherly dissension.

Practical application is that which respecteth the life and behaviour: and it is instruction and correction. Instruction is that whereby doctrine is applied to frame a man to live well in the family, commonwealth and church. To this place belong consolation and exhortation (Rom. 15:4). Correction is that whereby the doctrine is applied to reform the life from ungodliness and unrighteous dealing. Hitherto belongs admonition. This must be done first generally, the circumstances of the persons being omitted (2 Sam. 12; Acts 19:26, 35–37). Afterwards, if the former re-proof prevail not, it must be urged after a more special manner (1 Tim. 5:20). But always in the very hatred of sin, let the love of the person appear in the speeches and let the minister include himself (if he may) in his reprehension, that it may be more mild and gentle (Dan. 4:16–19; Gal. 2:15; 1 Cor. 4:6). Now these four kinds of application do offer themselves in every sentence of the scripture. . . .

Chapter IX

Of memory in preaching

BECAUSE IT IS THE RECEIVED CUSTOM for preachers to speak by heart before the people, something must be here annexed concerning memory. Artificial memory which standeth upon places and images will very easily without labour teach how to commit sermons to the memory, but it is not to be approved.

I. The animation of the image, which is the key of memory, is impious, because it requireth absurd, insolent and prodigious cogitations, and those especially which set an edge upon and kindle the most corrupt affections of the flesh.

II. It dulleth the wit and memory, because it requireth a threefold memory for one: the first of the places, the second of the images, the third of the thing that is to be declared.

It is not therefore an unprofitable advice, if he that is to preach do diligently imprint in his mind by the help of disposition, either axiomatical, or syllogistical, or methodical, the several proofs and applications of the doctrines, the illustrations of the applications and the order of them all: in the meantime nothing careful for the words which, as Horace speaketh, will not unwillingly follow the matter that is premeditated.[7] Their study hath many discommodities, who do con their written sermons word for word: it asketh great labour; he which through fear doth stumble at one word, doth both trouble the congregation and confound his memory; pronunciation, action and the holy motions of affections are hindered, because the mind is wholly bent on this—to wit, that the memory fainting now under her burden may not fail.

Chapter X

HITHERTO HATH BEEN SPOKEN OF THE PREPARATION or provision of the sermon. The promulgation or uttering of it followeth. In the promulgation two things are required: the hiding of human wisdom and the demonstration or showing of the Spirit. Human wisdom must be concealed, whether it be in the matter of the sermon or in the setting forth of the words, because the preaching of the word is the testimony of God and the profession of the knowledge of Christ and not of human skill: and again, because the hearers ought not to ascribe their faith to the gifts of man, but to the power of God's word (1 Cor. 2:1–2, 5).

If any man think that by this means barbarism should be brought into pulpits, he must understand that the minister may, yea and must, privately use at his liberty the arts, philosophy and variety of reading while he is framing his sermon, but he ought in public to conceal all these from the people and not to make the least ostentation. *Artis etiam celare artem*: it is also a point of art to conceal art.

The demonstration of the Spirit is when as the minister of the word doth in the time of preaching so behave himself that all, even ignorant persons and unbelievers, may judge that it is not so much he that speaketh, as the Spirit of God in him and by him (1 Cor. 2:4; 14:24–25; 4:19–20; Mic. 3:8). This makes ministry to be lively and powerful (Luke 11:27).

This demonstration is either in speech or in gesture. The speech must be spiritual and gracious. That speech is spiritual which the Holy Spirit doth teach and it is a speech both simple and perspicuous, fit both for the people's understanding and to express the majesty of the Spirit (1 Cor. 2:13; Acts 17:2–3; Gal. 3:1; 2 Cor. 4:2–4). Wherefore neither the words of arts, nor Greek and Latin phrases and quirks must be intermingled in the sermon. They disturb the mind of the auditors, that they cannot fit those things that went afore with those that follow. A strange word hindereth the understanding of those things that are spoken. It draws the mind away from the purpose to some other matter. Here also the telling of tales and all profane and ridiculous speeches must be omitted.

The speech is gracious wherein the grace of the heart is expressed (Luke 4:22; John 7:46). Grace is either of the person, or of the ministry. Grace of the person is the holiness of the heart and an unblamable life, which however it makes not a minister, yet it is very necessary. Because the doctrine of the word is hard both to be understood and to be practised, therefore the minister ought to express that by his example which he teacheth, as it were by a type (1 Pet. 5:3; 1 Tim. 4:12; Phil. 4:8–9). He that is not godly, howsoever he may understand the scriptures, yet doth he not perceive the inward sense and experience of the word in his heart (Ps. 25:8–9; Amos 3:7; Gen. 18:17–19). It is a thing execrable in the sight of God that godly speech should be conjoined with an ungodly life (Ps. 50:16–17). . . . It is an ecclesiastical secret that the minister ought to cover his infirmities, that they be not seen, for the simple people behold not the ministry, but the person of the minister (Mark 6:20). . . . For words make not such an impression in the soul as works do. A minister that is wicked, either openly or secretly, is not worthy to stand before the face of the most holy and the almighty God (Jer. 15:19; Isa. 6:6–8; Lev. 10:3). And hence it is that the judgments of God remain for wicked ministers to tremble at (1 Sam. 2:17, 25).

The parts of sanctity are especially:

1. A good conscience (2 Cor. 1:12; 1 Tim. 1:19; Acts 24:16). If this be wanting, the mouth of the speaker is shut (Isa. 56:10).

2. An inward feeling of the doctrine to be delivered. Wood that is capable of fire doth not burn unless fire be put to it: and he must first be godly affected himself who would stir up godly affections in other men. Therefore what motions a sermon doth require, such a preacher shall stir up privately in his own mind, that he may kindle the same in his hearers.

3. The fear of God, whereby being thoroughly stricken with a reverent regard of God's majesty, he speaketh soberly and moderately.

4. The love of the people (1 Thess. 2:7). And that affection may appear, the minister's duty is to pray seriously and fervently for the people of God (1 Sam. 12:23).

5. The minister must also be venerable, that is such an one as is to be reverenced for constancy, integrity, gravity and truth-speaking, who also knoweth how to perform reverence to others, either privately or publicly, as is befitting the persons of all his hearers.

6. He must be temperate, who restraineth inwardly his over-vehement affections and hath his outward fashions and gestures moderate and plain, by the which dignity and authority may be procured and preserved. Therefore he must be neither covetous, a lover of silver, a follower of wine, nor litigious, nor a striker, nor wrathful: and let the young men exercise themselves to godliness and fly the lusts of youth (1 Tim. 4:7).

The grace of the ministry is:

1. To be apt to teach (1 Tim. 3:2). Now Paul's meaning is that it is not only decent and laudable if this gift be had, but also that it is so necessary, as that may not be wanting. . . .

2. Authority, whereby he speaketh as the ambassador of the great Jehovah (Titus 2:15; 1 Pet. 4:11).

3. Zeal, whereby being most desirous of God's glory he doth endeavour to fulfil and execute the degree of election concerning the salvation of men by his ministry (Job 32:18–19; 2 Tim. 2:25; Col. 1:28–29).

Gesture is either in the action of the voice or of the body. The voice ought to be so high that all may hear (Isa. 58:1; John 7:37; Acts 2:14). In the doctrine he ought to be more moderate, in the exhortation more fervent and vehement. Let there be that gravity in the gesture of the body which may grace the messenger of God. It is fit, therefore, that the trunk or stalk of the body being erect and quiet, all the other parts, as the arm, the hand, the face and eyes, have such motions as may express and (as it were) utter the godly affections of the heart. The lifting up of the eye and the hand signifieth confidence, the casting down of the eyes signifieth sorrow and heaviness (2 Chron. 6:13; Luke 18:13). Concerning the gesture, other precepts cannot be delivered: only let the example of the gravest ministers in this kind be instead of a rule.

Chapter XI

Of the conceiving of prayer

HITHERTO HATH BEEN SPOKEN CONCERNING the preaching of the word. It remaineth now to speak of the conceiving of prayers which is the second point of prophesying, whereby the minister is the voice of the people in calling upon God (Luke 11:1; 1 Sam. 14:24).

Here are to be considered:

1. The matter thereof—first the wants and sins of the people and then the graces of God and the blessings they stand in need of (1 Tim. 2:1–2). The Lord's Prayer reduceth this matter to six heads, which are God's glory, kingdom and obedience, the preservation of the life, the remission of sins and the strengthening of the spirit.

2. The form thereof. Let there be one voice: and that the minister's alone, the people being in the meanwhile silent and showing their assent at the end by saying, Amen (Acts 2:24; Neh. 8:6; 1 Cor. 14:16). Let the voice be understood (1 Cor. 14:15). Let the voice be continued, not jagged and abrupt, that idle repetitions may be avoided (Matt. 6:7).

The parts which are three: consideration, ordering and uttering of it. Consideration is that whereby fit matter for the framing of prayers is diligently searched for. Ordering is that, whereby the matter being found out is disposed in the mind in a certain order. Prolation or uttering of it is that whereby it is orderly pronounced in public to the edifying of the people.

Tri-uni Deo gloria

The order and sum of the sacred and only method of preaching

1. To read the text distinctly out of the canonical scriptures.
2. To give the sense and understanding of it being read, by the scripture itself.
3. To collect a few and profitable points of doctrine out of the natural sense.
4. To apply, if he have the gift, the doctrines rightly collected to the life and manners of men in a simple and plain speech.

The sum of the sum

Preach one Christ by Christ to the praise of Christ.

The writers which lent their help to the framing of this *Art of Prophesying* are: Augustine, Hemmingius, Hyperius, Erasmus, Illyricus, Wigandus, Jacobus Matthias, Theodorus Beza, Franciscus Junius.[8]

Soli Deo Gloria

Notes

1. See Philip Stubbes, *The Second Part of the Anatomie of Abuses* (1583), cited and quoted by Paul S. Seaver, *Puritan Lectureships: The Politics of Religious Dissent, 1560–1662* (Stanford, Calif.: Stanford University Press, 1970), 18, 314.

2. See Patrick Collinson, *The Elizabethan Puritan Movement* (London: Cape, 1967), 168–76; and Horton Davies, *Worship and Theology in England, 1534–1603* (Princeton, N.J.: Princeton University Press, 1970), 297–300.

3. See Ian Breward, ed., introduction to *The Work of William Perkins*, Courtenay Library of Reformation Classics, vol. 3 (Berkshire, England: Sutton Courtenay Press, 1970), 3–131.

4. See John B. Payne, "Toward the Hermeneutics of Erasmus," in *Scrinium Erasmianum*, ed. J. Coppens II (Leiden: E. J. Brill, 1969), 13–49.

5. A summary of the scope of each book of the Bible is omitted. This and the following notes are based on Breward's notes, 329.

6. A long section of examples is omitted.

7. Horace, *Art of Poetry*, line 311.

8. Augustine, *On Christian Doctrine*, Bk. 4; N. Hemmingsen, *The Preacher*, 1576; A. Hyperius, *The Practis of Preaching*, 1577; D. Erasmus, *Ecclesiastae* [The Preachers], Basle, 1535; M. F. Illyricus, *Clavis Scripturae* [The Key to Scripture], Basle, 1567; J. Wigandus, *In XII Prophetas Minores Explicationes* [Explanations of the 12 Minor Prophets], Basle, 1566; T. Beza, *Tractationes Theologicae* [Theological Treatises], Geneva, 1570–82, together with the edition of the Bible in which he, Tremellius, and Junius collaborated. Cuno, *Franciscus Junius*, pp. 263 ff. gives a list of Junius's exegetical works. There was no book specifically on preaching. Matthias is possibly a reference to Matthaeus Richter who collaborated with Wigandus.

Separatist and Non-Separatist Perspectives

28. A Treatise of Reformation without Tarying for Anie

(1582)

ROBERT BROWNE

Robert Browne (c. 1550–1633) was the first English church leader to give clear and powerful articulation to a theory of church as covenantal community. In this respect he was an ancestor to Congregationalism, although it is doubtful that he had any direct influence on later Congregational thinking. During his brief career as a Separatist Congregationalist, he became an important exponent of "reformation without tarying for anie."

Robert Browne was not, however, the first to uphold a Separatist position. Already before him, underground Protestant groups had arisen in London reacting to Elizabeth I's efforts to enforce uniformity of ecclesiastical attire (the so-called vestiarian controversy). According to the queen's wish, Archbishop Matthew Parker issued the Advertisements of 1566, enjoining the use of the surplice by all parish clergy and the cope in cathedral and collegiate churches. In addition, the Advertisements insisted that people should kneel to receive communion, a practice rejected by Puritans. When Puritan clergy in London resisted these orders, many were deprived of their positions.

SOURCE: Albert Peel and Leland H. Carlson, eds., *The Writings of Robert Harrison and Robert Browne*, Elizabethan Nonconformist Texts, vol. 2 (London: George Allen and Unwin, 1953).

The bishop of London, Edmund Grindal, who leaned toward Puritanism, tried to persuade Puritan ministers that matters of clerical clothing were indifferent and should not be reasons for resistance to ecclesiastical law. Many agreed with his arguments, but some clergy refused to succumb and were arrested when they rented Plumbers' Hall for a meeting (or, say some, a wedding). They were accused by Grindal of gathering for worship in private assemblies apart from the parish. They responded through the voice of one of their leaders, John Smith. Smith admitted the truth of the accusation but explained that they had not held such gatherings as long as the sacraments were administered "without the preferring of idolatrous gear about it" and until "all our preachers were displaced by your law." He recalled that congregations had met in London during Mary I's reign and in Geneva, using a prayer book (John Knox's Form of Prayers, or Genevan Service Book) (see vol. 2:432–44) that was "most agreeable to the Word of God" in the administration of the sacraments and discipline.

It is significant that the Puritans interpreted their experience of repression in light of the persecution of a Protestant congregation in London during the time of Mary. Many Puritans (Separatist and Non-separatist) were deeply influenced by accounts of persecution that they read in John Foxe's Acts and Monuments *(see vol. 2:615–18) and other popular literature about martyrs.*

Whether the Plumbers' Hall group was truly Separatist is debatable, but it is likely that after the group's members were released from prison, some of them did form a gathered congregation distinct from the established church. Of the several sectarian groups in London at this time, the only one about which we have any information was known as Fitz's church, named after its principal leader, Richard Fitz. The covenant from this church sets forth an argument for withdrawal from the preachings "of them that have receaued these markes of the Romysh beast," that is, the vestments. Although Robert Browne was the first important exponent of the covenantal idea so central to later Congregationalism, it is not clear that Congregationalism can claim any exclusive connection to its "ultimate forebears in Plumbers' Hall or even in Fitz's church."[1]

In 1570 Robert Browne was a student at Corpus Christi College (Cambridge) when Thomas Cartwright, a passionate Puritan, was giving lectures on the Acts of the Apostles, insisting that Presbyterian order was the divinely established polity of the church. Although Cartwright was forced to go into exile in Geneva, in 1552 his disciples John Field and Thomas Wilcox published a treatise entitled the Admonition to Parliament, *arguing for the introduction of true apostolic order and discipline in the Church of England.*

During his studies at Cambridge, Browne was imbued with these Presbyterian Puritan views. Soon he called into question the authority of bishops. Upon accepting a call to preach at St. Benet's Church in Cambridge, he refused to obtain a license; when one was obtained for him by his brother, he destroyed it. By 1580 or 1581 he had joined a friend, Robert Harrison, in Norwich, having persuaded Harrison of the truth of a Separatist position. There, Browne, with Harrison and others of his disciples, organized a Separatist congregation grounded on "one covenant and fellowship" with one another and organized with its own officers and church order. Suffering persecution, they eventually left England and moved to Middelburg in the Netherlands.

From that vantage point, in 1582 Browne published A Treatise of reformation without tarying for anie, *a discussion of the proper relations between church and state and a plea for the immediate reformation of the church. In this treatise, Browne sought, first, to defend himself and his disciples from the charge of disloyalty by affirming the legitimacy of the civil power as exercised by the queen and Parliament. Second, he wished to stress the clear limits of the magistrate in relationship to the church. For Browne, the magistrate had no power over the church, because the church was ruled by Christ alone. In the rule of the church, pastors were superior to magistrates. Third, since the magistrate had no authority over the church, clergy did not need to wait for the magistrate to carry out reform, but should proceed to carry it out without delay. Finally, in his conviction that it was improper for the state to intrude into matters of the church, Browne upheld freedom of religion: "The Lord's people is of the willing sorte."*

Ironically, Browne, who at Norwich and Middelburg expounded radical Separatist ideas, did not remain a Separatist. After being alienated from Harrison in the congregation at Middleburg, Browne went to Scotland, eventually landing in prison. Once released, in 1585 he returned to the Church of England, where he remained for the rest of his life.

Although Browne's A Treatise of reformation without tarying for anie *initially made the Separatist case, the torch of Separatism was carried by John Greenwood and Henry Barrow, "the two founding fathers of Separatism."*[2]

SEEING in this Booke wee shewe the state of Christians, and have laboured also in good conscience to live as Christians, It is marvailed & often talked of among manie, why we should be so reviled and troubled of manie, & also leave our countrie.[3] *Forsooth* (say the enimies) *there is some hidden thing in them more then plainly appeareth: for they beare evill will to their Princes[s] Queene* ELIZABETH *and to their countrie, yea they forsake the church of God, & condemne the same, and are condemned of all, and they also discredit & bring into contempt the Preachers of the Ghospel.* To aunswere them, we say, That they are the men which trouble Israel, and seeke evill to the Prince, and not we. And that they forsake and condemne the Church and not we.

First concerning our faithfulnesse to our Prince and Countrie, and what our iudgement is of the civil authoritie, we aunswere as appeareth in this Treatise. For their other accusations and slaunders of forsaking and condemning the Church, &c. if our doings will not stoppe their mouthes, nor this booke which followeth of the state of Christians, we purpose by the grace of God, to shewe in an other booke, which shall hereafter come foorth, whether we or they be the rebellious children and a false seede. But for the Magistrate, howe farre by their authoritie or without it, the Church must be builded and reformation made, and whether anie open wickednesse must be tolerated in the Church because of them, let this be our aunswere. For chieflie in this point they have wrought us great trouble, and dismayed manie weakelings from imbracing the trueth. We say therefore, and often have taught, concerning our Souveraigne Queene Elizabeth, that neither the Pope, nor other Popeling, is to have anie authoritie either over her, or over the Church of God, and that the Pope of Rome is Antichrist, whose kingdome ought utterlie to be taken away. Agayne we say, that her Authoritie is civil, and that power she hath as highest under God within her Dominions, and that over all persons and causes. By that she may put to death all that deserve it by Lawe, either of the Church or common Wealth, and none may resiste Her or the Magistrates under her by force or wicked speaches, when they execute the lawes. Seeing we graunt, and holde thus much, howe doe they charge us as evill willers to the Queene? Surelie, for that wee holde all those Preachers and teachers accursed, which will not doe the duties of Pastors and teachers till the Magistrates doe force them thereto. They saye, the time is not yet come to builde the Lordes House [Hag. 1], they must tarie for the Magistrates and for Parliamentes to do it. They want the civill sworde forsooth, and the Magistrates doe hinder the Lordes building and kingdome, and keepe awaye his governement. Are they not ashamed thus to slaunder the Magistrate? They have runne their owne swordes uppon the Wall and broken them, and nowe woulde they snatche unto them the Magistrates sworde. In deede can the Lordes spirituall governement be no waye executed but by the civill sworde, or is this the iudgement that is written, Such honour shall be to all his Saintes? Is this to binde the Kinges in chaines, and the Nobles with Fetters of Iron [Ps. 149:7], by the highe actes of GOD in their mouthes, and a two edged sworde in their handes? Those bandes and chaines, which is the spirituall power of the Church, they have broken from them selves, and yet woulde they have Magistrates bounde with them, to beginne Discipline. They would make the Magistrates more then Goddes, and yet also worse then beastes. For they teache that a lawefull Pastour must give over his charge at their discharging, and when they withholde the Church governement, it ought for to ceasse, though the Church goe to ruine thereby. Beholde nowe, doeth not the Lordes kingdome give place unto theirs? And doe they not pull downe the heade Christe Jesus [Col. 1:18], to sett uppe the hande of the Magistrate? yea and more then this, for they firste proclaime the names and tytles of wicked Bishoppes and popishe officers, and the Lordes name after: Seeing also the Bishoppes must discharge the lawfull Preachers, and stoppe their mouthes, though the Lorde God have given them a charge for to speake, and not to keepe silence. The Lorde hath exalted Christe Iesus, and given him a name above everie name, that all thinges should bowe and serve unto him [Phil. 2:9–11], and yet have they exalted the power of wicked Bishoppes above him. Beholde a great and moste wholesome river, and yet their pudle water is preferred before it. Except the Magistrates will goe into the tempest and raine, and bee weather beaten with the haile of Gods wrath, they muste keepe under the roafe of Christes governement. They must bee under a Pastorall charge: They must obeye to the Scepter of Christe, if they bee Christians. Howe then shoulde the Pastor, which hath the oversight of the Magistrate, if hee bee of his flocke, bee so overseene of the Magistrate, as to leave his flocke, when the Magistrate shall uniustlie and wrongfullie discharge him. Yet these Preachers and teachers will not onelie doo so, but even holding their charge and keeping with it, will not guide and reforme it aright, because the Magistrates doo forbidde them forsooth. But they slaunder the Magistrate, and because they dare not charge them as forbidding them their dueties, they have gotten this shift, that they doo but tarie for the Magistrates authoritie, and then they will guide and reforme as they ought. Beholde, is not all this one thing, seeing they lift uppe the throne of the Magistrates, to thrust out the kingdome of Christe? For his governement or Discipline is wanting (saye they) but wee keepe it not awaye. And who then? For most of them dare not charge the Magistrates, but onelie closelie, and with manie flatterings, that they might still be exalted by the Magistrates. They leave their owne burthen, and crie out that it is not caried by faulte of the Magistrate. So they speake against them, and laye all the burthen on them: but they them selves will not moove it with one of their fingers. Yea they are bolde also some of them, in open places, so to charge the Magistrate. So they make them enimies, because they saye they witholde the Church governement: even enimies doo they make them to the Lordes kingdome and righteousnesse: and why then do they not wage that spirituall battell against them, whiche is to cut them of[f] from the Church? For the Scepter and kingdome of Christ is not of this worlde, to fight with dint of sworde, but it is a right Scepter [Ps. 45:6], which subdueth the people under us, and the Nations under our feete [Ps. 47:3]. Hee iudgeth the wicked, and by the rebuke of his worde, he filleth all places with the slaine, and smiteth the Heades over great countries [Ps. 110:6].

Now then if the Magistrates be enimies unto the Lords kingdome, why are not these men better warriars to upholde the same? For they give up the weapons of their warfare into the enimies handes, and then say, they can not doo withall. By their weapons I meane those whereof Paule doeth speake, that they are not carnall, but mightie through God [2 Cor. 10:3–4], to cast downe holdes, and so foorth: These weapons have they given from them, for they have not the Keyes of the Kingdome of heaven to binde and lose [Matt. 18:18], and to retaine or pronounce remitted the sinnes of men [John 20:23], seeing they graunt much open wickednesse incurable among them, and also avouche that it must needes be suffered. Yea they have given up these keyes to the Magistrates or to the Spirituall Courtes, and therefore have no right to call them selves the Church of God, or lawfull Pastors thereof. Christ is at the right hande of God, gone up into heaven saieth Peter [1 Pet. 3:22], to whom the Angels and powers and might are subiecte, howe then shoulde his kingdome tarie for the Magistrate, except they thinke that they are better able to upholde it then he. Yea we must presse unto his kingdome not tarying for anie, as it is written in Luke [Luke 16:16], & againe in Matthew [Matt. 11:12], The kingdome of God suffereth violence, and the violent take it unto them by force. In the throng which is made to escape a burning, would they tarie for the Magistrate to make them a waye, and should not they rather if they could, make a way for the Magistrate? They see that the kingdome of God is with strift and great labor, and yet they will have it with ease and the civill sworde must get it them. Ierusalem (saieth the Prophete) and the streetes and Wall thereof, shall be built even in a troublous time, and to tarie till it be built without troubles, is to looke for a conquest without going to battell, and for an ende and rewarde of our laboures which would never take paines. My kingdome, saith Christe, is not of this world, and they would shift in both Bishoppes and Magistrates into his spirituall throne to make it of this worlde; yea to stay the Church governement on them, is not onely to shift but to thrust them before Christ. Yet under him in his spirituall kingdome are first Apostles, secondlie Prophetes, thirdlie, teachers &c. [1 Cor. 12:28]. Also helpers and spirituall guides: But they put the Magistrates first, which in a common wealth in deede are first, and above the Preachers, yet have they no ecclesiasticall authoritie at all, but onely as anie other Christians, if so be they be Christians. Therefore hath God made these teachers fooles, and these spirituall professours as madde men. For woe unto you, ye Priestlie preachers and Doctours hypocrites, which are a snare to the people, and fill up their measure of iniquitie, while ye pretende the Magistrates authoritie. For will anie man else give over his calling, or abridge the full execution thereof, when the Magistrates forbid them, will they cease the teaching or due guiding of their housholdes and charge for their dischargings, and should the labourers in Gods spirituall husbandrie give over and ceasse. For it is Gods husbandrie and not theirs, the Church is his building and not theirs [1 Cor. 3:9]. They are but members thereof if they be Christians, and are not anie way to stay the building, neither is it to tarie or waite upon them. But these wicked preachers eate up and spoyle the Lords harvest them selves, and then set open the gapp, as though the Magistrates brake in like wild bores, and spoiled the harvest. They say, beholde we have a Christian Prince, and a mother in Israel: but can they be Christians, when they make them to refuse, or withstand the governement of Christ in his Church, or will not be subject unto it. If they therefore refuse and withstande, howe should they be taried for? If they be with them, there is no tarying: and if they be against them, they are no christians, and therefore also there can be no tarying. For the worthie may not tarie for the unworthie, but rather forsake them, as it is written [Matt. 10:14], Save your selves from this frowarde generation: and cast not pearles before Swine, nor holy things unto dogges [Matt. 7:6]: and rebuke not a skorner sayeth the wise man [Prov. 9:8–9], least he hate thee: and inquire who is worthie, sayeth Christ. He that will be saved, must not tarie for this man or that [Matt. 8:21–22]: and he that putteth his hande to the plowe, and then looketh backe, is not fitte for the kingdome of God [Luke 9:62]. Therefore woe unto you ye blinde guides, which cast away all by tarying for the Magistrates. The Lorde will remember this iniquitie, and visite this sinne upon you [Zach. 4:6]. Ye will not have the kingdome of God, to go forward by his spirit, but by an armie & strength forsooth: ye will not have it as Leaven hidde in three peckes of meale, till it leaven all [Matt. 13:33], but at once ye will have all aloft, by civill power and authoritie: you are offended at the baseness and small beginnings, and because of the troubles in beginning reformation, you will doe nothing. Therefore shall Christ be that rocke of offence unto you, and ye shall stumble and fall, and shall be broken, and shall be snared, and shal be taken. You will be delivered from the yoke of Antichrist, to the which you doo willinglie give your neckes, by bowe, and by sworde, and by battell, by horses and by horssemen, that is, by civill power and pompe of Magistrates: by their Proclamations and Parliamentes: and the kingdome of God must come with observation, that men may say, Loe the Parliament, o loe the Bishoppes decrees: but the kingdome of God shoulde be within you [Luke 17:21]. The inwarde obedience to the outwarde preaching and governement of the Church, with newnes of life, that is the Lordes kingdome. This ye despise. Therefore shall ye desire to see the kingdome of God, and shall not see it, and to enioye one day the Sonne of man, and ye shall not enioye it. For ye set aloft mans authoritie above Gods, and the Preacher must hang on his sleeve for the discharge of his calling. In the 32. of Iob, doth not Elihu holde his authoritie, and durst not account of mannes authorising, though learned, wise and aged, yea the Elders or Fathers of the Church, neither would he spare either Iob or them, or submitte him selfe to them in respecte of his calling. I will receive no mans person, saieth he, and I will use no title (or preface) before man, for I knowe not to use tytles, If I use them a little, he would take me awaye that made me [Job 32:21–22]. But these men name them selves, some the Bishoppes Chaplaines, some my Lordes Chaplaines, and some the Queenes Chaplaines, and call them their Maisters, to whom their calling and ministerie must serve at commaundement. Thus the Lordes spirituall message must be beautified with these tytles of men (*The right Honorable my Lorde. &c. who is my very good Lorde and Maister*,) Yet Christe him selfe saieth, that the Preachers nowe in his kingdome, have greater authoritie than Iohn Baptist, and Iohn Baptist greater then the Prophetes before him [Matt. 11:11]. Therefore if Ieremie was set over the Nations & over the Kingdomes, to plucke up and to roote out, and to destroye and throw downe, to build and to plante [Jer. 1:10], Then have we also an authoritie against which if the Kings and Nations doo sett themselves, we maye not be afraide of their faces, nor leave our calling for them. Howe long therefore will these men take the inheritance from the right heire, and give it unto the servaunt? For the spirituall power of Christe and his Church, and the Keyes of binding and losing, they take from Christe, and give to the Magistrate. The Magistrates have the civill sworde, and least they should strike them therewith, they give them the Ecclesiastical also. Hoe say they, If we were Prophetes, or if we were Apostles, then shoulde we preache though the Magistrate forbidde us, but wee are but bare Pastors or Preachers, and therefore we must feare their frowning and threates, and keepe silence thereat. But let them speake, Had not the Magistrates, as full and the same power over Apostles, as over other Pastoures, or were Apostles more exempted from their obedience to Magistrates, then other Preachers? For let everie soule be subject to the higher powers, saith the scriptures [Rom. 13:1]. Therefore as they coulde not displace, nor discharge Apostles from their office & calling, no more can they doo lawfull Pastours and Preachers: for whether it be right in the sight of God, to obeye men rather then God, let all men iudge. But to this they aunswere, that Peter saied this, being an Apostle: But in deede muste Apostles onelie followe their calling [Acts 4:19–20], though menne doo discharge them, and may not other doe it likewise? For as God hath distributed to everie man the gifte (saieth the Scripture) as the Lorde hath called everie one, so let him walke, and so ordained Paule in all the Churches [1 Cor. 7:17]. If then the Magistrate will commaunde the Souldiour to be a Minister, or the Preacher to give over his calling, and chaunge it for an other, they ought not to obeye him, for they have not the gifte, and God hath called them this way rather then that. Yet if the Magistrate call one of a lower calling to an higher, to the which he is fitt and prepared, he ought to obeye, for God hath calleth *[sic]* him thereunto. And in all thinges wee must first looke, what is the Lordes will and charge, and then what is the will of man. For we are bought for a price, saieth Paule, and we may not be servauntes to the unlawfull commaundings of men [1 Cor. 7:23–24]. And this freedome have all Christians, that they consider what is lawful and what is profitable, what they may doo and what is expedient, and in no case bee brought under the power of anie thing, as Paule teacheth us [1 Cor. 6:12]. What soever doth most edifie, that must we chuse, and avoide the contrarie [1 Cor. 10:23–24]: and what soever is most expedient, that must be done, and so we must applie our selves all unto all, that notwithstanding we holde our libertie. For if either Magistrate or other would take that from us, wee must not give place by yeelding unto them, no, not for an houre [Gal. 2:5], and this libertie is the free use of our callings and guiftes, as we see most agreeing to the worde of God, and expedient for his glorie. Therefore the Magistrates commaundement, must not be a rule unto me of this and that duetie, but as I see it agree with the worde of God. So then it is an abuse of my guifte and calling, if I cease preaching for the Magistrate, when it is my calling to preach, yea & woe unto me [1 Cor. 9:16], if I preach not, for necessitie is laied upon me, and if I doe it unwillinglie, yet the dispensation is committed unto me. And this dispensation did not the Magistrate give me, but God by consent and ratifying of the Church, and therefore as the Magistrate gave it not, so can he not take it away. Indeede if God take it away for my wickednesse and evill deserte, he may remove me from the Church, and withholde me from preaching: but if God doo it not, and his worde doeth approve me, as most meete for that calling, I am to preach still, except I be shut up in prison, or otherwise with violence withhelde from my charge. For the Magistrate so using me can not be a Christian, but forsaketh the Church: and howe then should my office in the Church depende on him which is none of the Church? And the welfare of the Church must be more regarded and sought, then the welfare of whole Kingdomes and Countries, as it is written: Because thou wast precious in my sight, and thou wast honourable and I loved thee, therefore will I give man for thee, and people for thy sake [Isa. 43:3]. And againe he saieth, I gave Egypt for thy raunsome, Ethiopia and Seba for thee. The Lorde shall therefore iudge these men, and cut them of[f] both heade & tayle, braunch and rushe in one day. The auncient and the honorable men, which take on them to put downe the Lordes authoritie, and to stoppe the mouthes of his messengers, they be the heade, and the wicked teachers which exalte men above God, they are the tayle. They are afrayde of the face of the Magistrate, & do flatter and currie favour with them, and they would have us also to doo the like. But ye the Lords faithfull servauntes trusse uppe your loines as Ieremie, which in your charges have greater authoritie than Ieremie, as we proved before. Arise and speake unto them, all that I commaunde you, sayeth the Lorde: Be not afrayde of their faces least I destroye you before them, sayeth the Lorde [Jer 1:17]. For I, beholde I have made you as defenced cities, and yron pillars, & walles of brasse, against the whole lande, against the Kinges and against the Princes, against the Priestes and against the people. For they shall fight against you, but they shall not prevayle, for I am with you to deliver you even to the ende of the worlde. Therefore yee vanishe in vanitie yee wicked Preachers: for knowe ye not, that they which have their full and sufficient authoritie and calling, are not to tarie for a further authorising. And hath not everie lawfull Pastor or Preacher his full authoritie? Are they not to teache the whole will of God, and guide accordinglie, and have they not then their whole authoritie? For herein was Paule free frem *[sic]* the bloode of all menne, because he had kept nothing backe [Acts 20:26–27], but hadde shewed them all the counsell of GOD. But (say they) Paule taught them in deede the whole counsell of God, and so maye wee, but we may not governe: we may tell the Magistrates, that governement is wanting, but we may not take uppon us, to be reformers. In deede, did not Paule both in worde and deede testifie his faithfulnesse, did he not in practise as well as in wordes, fulfill his calling? For (sayeth he) you knowe my manner of life: and addeth further, that in serving the Lorde, he kept backe nothing that was profitable [Acts 20:27]. Howe then shoulde hee keepe backe the governement of the Church, whiche is all in all. And in the 35. verse, he setteth himselfe for example, for I have sheweth *[sic]* you all thinges, saieth hee, howe that so labouring, ye ought to supporte the weake [Acts 20:35]. Noting that hee sheweth in worde and example, not that onelie, but all thinges else, for due guiding of the Church. And therefore let them not flee to their odde disti[n]ction of ordinarie ond *[sic]* extraordinarie, as though Paule might guide the Churche without tarying for the Magistrate and wee may not. For

Paule set downe him selfe for an example: and in the 28. verse [Acts 20:28], and in the 31 [Acts 20:31],. he applieth all unto them, that they shoulde followe him, that they shoulde watche night and daye in teaching and guiding the flocke as he did. Yea they must not onelie preache, but teache them the practise. They muste observe and doo all thinges which Christ hath commaunded [Matt. 28:19–20]. And the Lorde did not onelie shewe them the Tabernacle, but badde them make it [Exod. 25:8–9]. But these menne will not make it at all, because they will tarie for the Magistrate. Christe is before us and his Apostles: as Moses a figure of Christe was before them, and yet we must tarie for the Magistrates. And for what Magistrates? For those of our charge, trowe ye, or for those which are none of our charge? Muste wee not in all thinges looke duelie to our charge, and let them goe which are none of our charge? For wee shall not give accounptes unto God for them which are out of our charge. For we must take heede to our selves, sayeth the Scripture, and to all the flocke whereof the holie Ghoste hath made us overseers [Acts 20:28]. But these men teach, that we must let our charge alone, and lay from us the governement thereof, for their sakes which are none of our charge. Shal not these men be hurled out of their place and charge, whiche thus doe mocke with the Lord, and dallie with their charges? Yea the Lord shall take them awaye with a swifte destruction, and menne shall clappe their handes at them and hisse them out of their places. Everie Preacher must runne to the Queene and to the Counsaill forsooth, as though they were of their charge, and the Magistrates must plant & reforme al Churches at once. If they be of their flockes, why should they tarie for them? unlesse they will have the sheepe to force the sheepehearde unto his duetie. Indeede the Magistrate may force him, but it is his shame to tarie till he be forced. Be ashamed therefore ye foolish shepheardes, and laye not a burthen on the Magistrates, as though they should do that in building the Lordes kingdome, which the Apostles and Prophetes coulde not doo. They could not force Religion, as ye woulde have the Magistrate to do, and it was forbidden the Apostles to preache to the unworthie [Matt. 10:13–14], or to force a planting or governement of the Church. The Lordes kingdome is not by force, neither by an armie or strength [Zech. 4:6], as be the kingdomes of this worlde. Neither durst Moses, nor anie of the good Kings of Iuda force the people by lawe or by power to receive the church governement, but after they received it, if then they fell awaye, and sought not the Lorde, they might put them to death. For the covenaunte was firste made, as it is written, they made a covenant to seeke the Lord God of their fathers, with all their harte, and with all their soule. And then followe the next wordes which are to be understoode of them which made the covenaunt, for of them which so sware unto the Lorde, whosoever did not seeke the

Lorde God of Israel, should be slaine, whether he were small or great man or woman [2 Chron. 15:13]. And therefore did the whole Congregation of Israel gather them together, to warre against the children of Reuben and Gad, because they seemed to forsake the covenant [Josh. 22:11–12]. Yet woulde not Hezekiah fight against Israel, though they laughed him to skorne and mocked at his doings [2 Chron. 30:10], for they had not received the covenaunt, but their forefathers, and they were nowe called to the covenaunt againe [2 Chron. 15:12], which the Lorde had disannulled with their forefathers: as it is written, that for a long season Israel had bin without the true God, and without Prieste to teache, and without lawe. Nowe therefore let the wise understande these things, and the Lorde be mercifull, and deliver us from these unreasonable and evill men. For there is no ende of their pride and crueltie which ascende up and sit in the Magistrates chaire and smite the people with a continuall plague, and such of them as have not yet gotten the roume, do crie for Discipline, Discipline, that is for a civill forcing, to imprison the people, or otherwise by violence to handle and beate them, if they will not obeye them. But the Lorde shall bring them downe to the dust, and to the pitt, as abhominable carkasses, which would be above the cloudes, yea which dare presume into the throne of Christe Iesus, and usurpe that authoritie and calling in his Church, which is opposed and contrarie to his kingdom and governement. This shall appeare afterwarde: In the meane time let them knowe that the Lords people is of the willing sorte. They shall come unto Zion and inquire the way to Ierusalem [Jer. 50:5], not by force nor compulsion, but with their faces thitherward: yea as the hee goates shall they be before the flocke, for the haste they have unto Zion, and they them selves shall call for the covenaunt, saying, Come and let us cleave faste unto the Lorde in a perpetuall covenaunt that shall never be forgotten. For it is the conscience and not the power of man that will drive us to seeke the Lordes kingdome: as it is written againe, Remember the Lorde a farre of[f] and let Ierusalem come into your mindes [Jer. 51:50], for they see the fierce wrath of the Lorde, where the Lordes kingdome is not, and they flee from the same going and weeping as they goe, as the Prophete saieth, because he hath bin angrie so long. But nowe they have escaped his displeasure, they goe on and stande not still till they appeare before the Lorde in Zion. Yea and the Lords people shall come willinglie in the day of his assemblies, even his armies in holie beautie [Ps. 110:3]. Yet the frowarde wilbe frowarde still, for (say they) Moses and the kinges of Iuda did reforme the Church, and they were taried for, therefore we also must tarie for our Magistrates. Beholde nowe howe the shame of their faces doeth testifie against them, which dare against their consciences, make our Magistrates prophetes with Moses, yea high Priestes as he was and figures of Christ, as both he was and the Kings of Iuda also. Howe boldelie also dare they pervert the trueth, affirming that some which ought to reforme, did it not, because they would tarie for Moses or for the Kinges of Iuda. For did Zacharie (say they) or the Prophet Haggaie, builde of them selves, and not rather call on the civill Magistrates and tarie for them? But they knowe not (as men that are willinglie ignoraunt) that their building of the Temple stoode in outwarde furniture of timber, stone, cariage, and therefore had neede of the helpe of Zerubabel the Prince: but our spirituall provision, as the guiftes, callings, & graces of the Church neede not anie worldlie preparation in such outwarde cerimonies. Therefore we aunswere, that Zerubabel being a figure of Christ, as appeareth in Zacharie the 4. he was to be chiefe in the worke. Neither were they in that worke as civill Magistrates nowe a dayes, but as Spirituall guides, representing Christe and his spirituall kingdome. Neither did Haggaie or Zacharie tarie for the Magistrates, but went before them, for in the name of God they commaunded them to builde, and the test sayeth further, that they ioyned with them and helped them [Ezra 5:2]. So that neither by worde nor deede they taried and were behinde: yea when the King (whose subiectes they were) commaunded them to cease, they refused to give over the building. This appeareth in Ezra 4.23. and in Ezra 5.1. And before also, because they ceased and lingered the building, for that the Magistrates were against them, they were sharpelie reproved of Haggai, and it was a most grievous curse unto them [Hag. 2:15–16]. Yet dare these menne laye sinne upon the Prophetes, as tarying & lingering for the Magistrates. And wherefore? Forsooth they did not hewe timber, and carie stones first of all to further the worke. But in deede, were not they firste when they commaunded and the other obeyed, and when they ioyned with them & helped them? For otherwise might Salomon also not to be saied to builde the Temple, but to tarie for others, because he him selfe brought not the stones, neither hewed them, but commaunded others (as the text sayeth) and they obeyed and brought great stones, and costlie stones to make the foundation of the house [1 Kings 5:17]. But if Zacharie or Haggai had taried, it proveth not that we must tarie for our Magistrates. For both Iehoshua the high Prieste, and Zerubbabel the Prince, were figures of the high priesthoode and princedome of Christe, and also had an ecclesiastical governement over the Church, which our Magistrates have not. And further also, everie lawfull Preacher at this time hath that authoritie of building Gods Church equall with Zerubbabel and Iehoshuah, or rather superior, for they are compared with them, as the 11. of the Revelation, and the 4. of Zacharie will testifie, and in the 11. of Matthewe [Matt. 11:11], and the 3. to the Corinthes the second Epistle, they are preferred afore them. We knowe that Moses might reforme, and the Iudges and Kings which followed him, and so may our Magistrates: yea they may reforme the Church and commaunde things expedient for the same. Yet may they doo nothing concerning the Church, but onelie civillie, and as civile Magistrates, that is, they have not that authoritie over the Church, as to be Prophetes or Priestes, or spiritual Kings, as they are Magistrates over the same: but onelie to rule the common wealth in all outwarde Iustice, to maintaine the right, welfare, and honor thereof, with outward power, bodily punishment, & civil forcing of men. And therfore also because the church is in a commonwealth, it is of their charge: that is concerning the outward provision & outward iustice, they are to look to it, but to compell religion, to plant churches by power, and to force a submission to Ecclesiastical governement by lawes & penalties belongeth not to them, as is proved before, neither yet to the Church. Let us not therfore tarie for the Magistrates: For if they be christians thei give leave & gladly suffer & submit them selves to the church governement. For he is a christian which is redeemed by Christ unto holines & happines for ever & professeth the same by submitting him self to his lawes & government. And if they be not christians, should the welfare of the church or the salvation of mens soules, hang on their courtesie? But they aske how we prove that Moses & the kings of Iudah & the Iudges before them, were figures of Christ. They know it true, & dare not denie it, & yet to quarel & trifle with the trueth, they must have it proved. Yea they charge us as Anabaptistes & denying Magistrates, because we set not up them, nor the Magistrates above Christ Iesus and his glorius kingdome. How often have we proved by word &writing these matters. For the Scepter shal not depart from Iuda, saieth the Scripture, nor a law giver from betwene his feete, until Shiloe come [Gen. 49:10]. By these wordes Iacob did prophesie, that one should take the spiritual kingdom & be Lord thereof, namelie Christ Iesus, and ever more one of the tribe of Iuda & house of David, should foreshew the same as in figure, & sit also in the throne of iudgement, to declare it more livelie, and that the throne of David and the raigne of his children did so signifie, the Scripture declareth, as it is written, In mercie shall the throne be established, & he shal sit upon it in stedfastnes in the Tabernacle of David [Isa. 16:5], iudging and seeking iudgement and hasting iustice. And again it is written, In steade of thy fathers shal thy children be, whom thou shalt make Princes throughout all the earth [Ps. 45:16]. And this is spoken of the posteritie of Salomon, which as figures of Christ, were Lords of the world, though their dominion in wordly wise was not so large. For all that Psalm is to magnifie the kingdome of Christ which is his church, which was prefigured by Salomon & his posteritie, and by the mariage of Salomon, which shadowed the church & the children thereof. And againe it is written, that Christ shall sit upon the throne of his father David, & upon his kingdom, to order it & to stablish it with iudgement and with iustice for ever [Isa. 9:6]. Wherefore was it called the throne of David & his kingdom, but because in a continual course it shadowed out the kingdom of Christ till his comming. Therefore also are

David, Salomon, Iehoshaphat, Hezekiah, Iosiah, and others, set downe in the Scripture as figures. Yea and the evill Kings of Iuda, though not in their wickednesse, yet in that authoritie and calling whiche they should have rightlie used, were figures.

For they all had their entrance at the East gate of the Temple, at the which the people might worshippe, but not goe in: they might pray for the people, and by their sacrifices attonement might be made: as it is written, Let him remember all thine offerings, and turne thy burnt offerings into Ashes. And againe, Save Lord, let the King heare us in the daye that we call [Ps. 20:9]. Yea all those Kings were to looke to the Temple, to the building and restoring thereof when it was decayed, as did Iehoash, Iosiah, Hezekiah, and others.

Let them looke the 4. of Zacharie, the thirde of Hosea, and 5. verse, the 33 of Ieremie, and manie other places, especiallie in the Psalmes, and they shall finde David and his children after him, in the throne of iudgement to foreshewe the comming of Christ. And if the high Priestes and Kings of Iudah in their spiritual ministration were glorious, because they figured Christ Iesus, & for the glorie of their office were compared to two Olive trees, and two golden Candlestickes [Zech. 4:11–14], Then also must their ministration be glorious, to whom God shall give power in these latter dayes to be his witnesses. For they also stande before the God of the earth, as it is written Revel. 11. And if anie man, whether Magistrate or other, would hurt them, the fire of their message proceedeth out of their mouthes, and devoureth their enimies [Rev. 11:5]. Therefore is their authoritie of God and not of man, and much lesse doeth it depende on man, or on the Magistrate. For upon what man did the authoritie of Moses depende? yet Paule affirmeth, that the ministration of the spirite committed to all faithfull teachers at this time, exceedeth in glorie the ministration by Moses and the Prophetes before time [2 Cor. 3:7–11]. Yea the Church hath more authoritie concerning Church governement then Magistrates, as it is written, They shall followe thee, and shal goe in Chaines: they shall fall downe before thee, and make supplication unto thee [Isa. 45:14]. For who knoweth not, that though Magistrates are to keepe their civill power above all persones, yet they come under the censure of the Church, if they be Christians, and are openlie to humble them selves in unfained repentaunce, when they have openlie and grievouslie trespassed. They are in deede to keepe their Royal dignitie, yet keeping that they are to abase them selves unto God before the face of the Church. For all powers shall serve and obeye Christ, saieth the Prophete: and that kingdome and nation which will not also serve his Church (for so is the text) shall perishe, and the Nation shall be utterlie destroyed [Isa. 60:12]. And the daughters of Tyrus, saieth the Psalmist, with the riche of the people, shall do homage before thy face with presentes. And further it is written in Isai: Everie tounge that shal rise against thee in iudgement, shalt thou condemne, this is the heritage of the Lords servauntes, and their righteousnes is of me, saieth the Lorde [Isa. 14:15]. But all this would the adversaries shift of, with this aunswere, that concerning outwarde policie we must tarie for the Magistrate: See howe they grope for the wall, as menne without eyes. For when wee speake of spirituall power and authoritie in the Church, doo we speake of civile policie, trowe ye? So then they condemne them selves least wee should doo it, that the spirituall power and Ecclesiasticall reformation, must proceede without tarying, but to redress things civille, the civile Magistrate must meddle, and none is to take his authoritie from him. For we knowe that when Magistrates have bin most of all against the Church and the authoritie thereof, the Church hath most florished. Woe to you therefore ye blinde Preachers and hypocrites: for ye spread a vaile of darkenes upon the people, and bring upon them a cursed covering, because by your policie you hide them under the power of Antichrist, and keepe from their eyes the kingdome of Christe. The Lordes kingdome must waite on your policie forsooth, and his Church muste bee framed to your civill state, to supplie the wantes thereof: and so will ye chaunge the Lordes governement, and put your devises in stead thereof: but his shalbe alwayes the same, when yours shall chaunge with your wittes, his lawes shall alwayes abyde when yours shal turne in your hoodes, his hath the same offices, but yours have newe and renewed offices. Goe to therefore, and the outwarde power and civil forcings, let us leave to the Magistrates: to rule the common wealth in all outwarde iustice, belongeth to them: but let the Church rule in spirituall wise, and not in worldlie maner: by a livelie lawe preached, and not by a civill lawe written: by holinesse in inwarde and outwarde obedience, and not in straightnesse of the outwarde onelie. But these handsome Prelates, would have the Mase and the Scepter in their handes, and then having safetie and assurance by a lawe on their sides, they would make a goodlie reformation.

Beholde the Lorde hath seene this their villanie, and he hath made them despised and vile in the sight of the people. They have refused knowledge, and the Lorde hath refused them, they shall beare no more the name of his message.

Of their wicked aunswere, that they can not remedie things, and therefore they will tollerate.

Beholde, the Lorde hath cast dunge on their faces, even the dunge of their solemne feastes [Mal. 2:3], as of their Christmasse, and Easter, and Whit-suntide, and of all their traditions, receyved from Baal. For in their solemne meetings, then doeth their iniquitie most woefullie appeare. And they have saide plainlie (as in the dayes of Malachie) the table of the Lorde is not to be regarded [Mal. 1:7]. For though hogges and Dogges come thereto, yet who can redresse it: or why should the Communion be counted polluted unto us? Thus they pollute my name saieth the Lorde, and yet they say Wherein have we polluted thy name? In that ye suffer such wickednesse amongest you, saieth the Lorde, and say also that it is sufferable, and can no way be remedied. O goodlie teachers, which eate up the sinne of the people, and devoure seelie soules whyle they wil tollerate forsooth: For by tolleration, they make unlawfull things lawfull: and by a protestation they iustifie all iniquitie. Indeede they be evill say they, but yee must beare with them, for there is no remedie. So not onlie they practise and use them them selves, and drawe on others by their wicked example, but also commaunde and teache all men the like, yea hate and persecute all those which stande not with them. O notable Protestantes, whiche both witnesse evil & do the same. Darkenes hath certainlie covered us, and grosse darkenesse hath filled us, that we could not hitherto espie this great follie. For no wickednesse is tollerable, except for the hardnes of mennes hartes, we yeelde them uppe to their wickednesse. For the Lordes way sayeth the Scripture, is holy, and no polluted shall passe by it [Isa. 35:8]. And againe it is written, That the Lordes people (he speaketh of the Church) shal be all righteous [Isa. 60:21], that is, no open wickednesse shal so shew it selfe in the Church, that it shoulde be incurable. For either the parties which offende, shalbe separate, or else they shalbe reclaymed by due admonition. And therefore the Church is called the house of the living God, the piller and grounde of trueth [1 Tim. 3:15]. For by the due order therein, Religion and holinesse is uphelde, and all heresies, evill maners, and wicked examples put awaye. If then anie open wickednesse must needes be suffered, it is suffered in those which are none of the church: as it is written, What have I to doo to iudge them which are without, doe yee not iudge them which are within? for God iudgeth them which are without [1 Cor. 5:12–13]. Knowe ye not (saieth the Scripture) that a little leaven leaveneth the whole lumpe [1 Cor. 5:6]. Howe then shall we suffer but a little wickednesse, whiche indeede is not little if it can not be remedied. Yea Paule would not bee brought into bondage of the least thing that is, and it is horrible iniquitie to be servauntes to men, that is, when we are bought for so great a price to glorifie God as his free men, that we should be made servaunts to menne to suffer their wickednesse [1 Cor. 7:23]. Goe to therefore yee tolerating Preachers, this you get by your tolerating, to have no name amonge the righteous, nor to be of the bodie of the Church. For Ierusalem is called a citie of trueth, and the mountaine of the Lorde, the holie mountaine [Zech. 8:3]. But ye are unholie, in that ye saye, some pollutions can not bee clensed awaye, but muste needes be suffered among you. And this is a certaine trueth, that where anie open disorder is incurable, there is not the Lords Zion, to the which he is turned to dwell therein: that is, they are not the Lordes Church, over whom he doeth raigne to shewe his kingdome and governement. For the Lordes kingdome is not as mannes, and his rule in his church is not the rule of man. Man is not able to reforme al things, and in the commonwealthes manie thinges are suffered. But in the Church, though hypocrites which are called the tares, can not bee rooted out, yet no open disorder shall so spreade it selfe, that it can not be remedied. Else should not the Church be called the pillar and ground of trueth, the Lordes resting place, his holie habitation, his kingdome and glorious renowne. Therefore doth Paule call that parte of church governement, which is to separate the ungodlie, the power of our Lorde Iesus Christ [1 Cor. 5:4–5]. For thereby are the Kings bounde with chaines, and the Nobles with fetters of yron, that they may execute uppon them, the iudgement that is written [Ps. 149:8–9], Such honor bee to all his Saintes. And in deede this is a great honour we have, as Paule sayeth, that though we walke in the fleshe, yet we warre not after the fleshe [2 Cor. 10:3]. For the weapons of our warfare are not carnall, but mightie through God, to caste downe houldes, casting downe the imaginations, and everie high thing, that is exalted against the knowledge of God, & bringing into captivitie everie thought to the obedience of Christ. So then there is nothing which the Lorde will not breake, if it be against his glorie, neither anie wickednes which the governement of his Churche is not able to put downe. For the Scepter of Christ is a right Scepter [Ps. 45:6], hee will keepe in awe his people in this life, and put aparte from them the unrulie: he shall be Iudge among the Heathen, and fill all with dead bodies, and smite the heades over great Countries [Ps. 110:6], and after this life he hath made readie the last vengeance against all disobedience, when the obedience of his people is fulfilled. Howe then dare these menne teache us, that anie evill thing is tolerable in the Church, as though the church governement could not remedie it: yea and so tolerable, that all men should be brought into bondage thereby: yea into so foolishe bondage, that they should protest a thing to be evill, and so thinke they are excused to practise the same.

Notes

1. See C. Burrage, *Early English Dissenters*, vol. 2 (Cambridge: Cambridge University Press, 1912), 14; Patrick Collinson, *The Elizabethan Puritan Movement* (London: Cape, 1967), 84–91; and B. R. White, *The English Separatist Tradition from the Marian Martyrs to the Pilgrim Fathers* (Oxford: Oxford University Press, 1971), 20–33.

2. See Timothy George, *John Robinson and the English Separatist Tradition* (Macon, Ga.: Mercer University Press, 1982), 46.

3. The spellings with "v" and "u" have been modernized, and where a line over the vowel required an "m" or "n," they have both been added. Otherwise the original spelling is retained.

29. Principles and Foundations of Christian Religion

(1604 or 1605)

Henry Jacob

Henry Jacob (1563–1624) was a leading member of a group of Non-separatist Congregationalist Puritans who were forerunners of the Congregational way in England and New England. The others included William Bradshaw, Robert Parker, and William Ames. Jacob's importance is evidenced by the fact that Independent, or Non-separatist, Congregationalists in the early seventeenth century were known as Jacobites.

Educated in divinity at St. Mary's Hall, Oxford (1563–68), Jacob became precentor of the choir at Corpus Christi College, which had moved in a Puritan direction shortly before he arrived in December 1568.[1] *Although he served a parish in Kent, his activities remained obscure until 1599, when he wrote a treatise against Francis Johnson and the Separatists entitled* Defense of the Churches and Ministry of England.

At first Jacob tried to persuade Johnson and other Separatists that church government was not an essential matter of faith, and that episcopal hierarchy was an indifferent thing. By 1604, however, his treatise Reasons Taken out of Gods Word and the Best Humane Testimonies Proving a Necessitie of Reforming our Churches in England *took a*

SOURCE: Champlin Burrage, ed., *The Early English Dissenters in the Light of Recent Research (1550–1641)* vol. 2 (Cambridge: Cambridge University Press, 1912). Used by permission.

different point of view. Writing to the new king, James I, Jacob argued against episcopacy, insisting that Congregationalism was the only legitimate form of church government found in the New Testament. The external form of the church, he had come to think, was an essential matter of faith and doctrine, not a matter of indifference.

Jacob's dramatic change from 1599 to 1604 is differently evaluated by scholars. From 1604 until his last writing in 1616, Jacob made an increasingly strong argument for a Non-separatist form of Congregationalism, that is, a Congregationalism within, rather than apart from, the established Church of England.

In 1610 he wrote, "A true Visible and Ministerial Church of Christ is a nomber of faithfull people joyned by their willing consent in a spiritual outward society or body politike, ordinarily comming togeather into one place, instituted by Christ in his New Testament, and having the power to exercise Ecclesiasticall government and all Gods other spirituall ordinances [the means of salvation] in and for it selfe immediately from Christ." The important marks of a true church, understood this way, are voluntaryism (the church as "a nomber of faithfull people joyned by their willing consent"); localism (a body "ordinarily comming togeather into one place"); and independence (a society "having the power to exercise Ecclesiasticall government . . . in and for it selfe").

Jacob believed that the power and independence of the local congregation would be balanced by three factors: (1) Christ as the head to whom the congregation is to be obedient; (2) a consociation of congregations in synods for the purpose of mutual counsel and cooperation (although synods never have the power to impose their authority on neighbor congregations); and (3) ministers who exercise leadership responsibility for the congregation, even though ministers receive power and authority from the congregation. Ecclesiastical power lies with the congregation, but the use of this power is normally undertaken by the church officers—pastors, elders, deacons—who have been elected by the congregation for this purpose.[2]

Unlike the Separatists, Jacob did not think that his Congregational understanding of the church was incompatible with parish life in the Church of England. In spite of his rejection of the Church of England and its episcopal hierarchy as a whole, Jacob thought there were particular enclaves within the Church of England, voluntarily assembled, who were true, visible churches and whose ministers were true ministers. This position made Jacob a Non-separatist Congregationalist.

Not surprisingly, Jacob played a major role in the Puritan Millenary Petition of 1603, which urged James I to reform the worship and govern-

ment of the church. Many Puritans had hoped that James I, a Scottish king with a Calvinistic background, would lend a sympathetic ear to their requests. Unfortunately, they were greatly disappointed. At the Hampton Court Conference of 1604, James refused to accede to Puritan requests for changes in worship and church government. He is reported to have responded to their proposals with the words, "No bishop, no king." After the Hampton Court Conference, new canons were issued requiring subscription to the Book of Common Prayer (see vol. 2:379–418) and reaffirming the episcopacy. James, however, did agree to the Puritan request for a new English translation of the Bible, known after its publication in 1611 as the King James Version.

Not surprisingly, as a result of his radical Puritan views, Henry Jacob was imprisoned in London. Upon his release in 1605 or 1606, he left England for Holland and served a church in Middleburg. In 1616 Jacob returned to England, where he and several others founded a congregation in Southwark in south London. It is generally agreed that this was the first Non-separatist congregation in England, representing the organized beginning of Congregationalism in England and New England. Its covenant became a model for future Congregational churches. After "they made some confession of Profession of their Faith and Repentance. Then they Covenanted togeather to walk in all Gods Ways as he had revealed or should make known to them."[3]

John Robinson, the Separatist pastor to the pilgrims who settled in Plymouth, Massachusetts, acknowledged the Southwark congregation as a true church (see vol. 2:494–95). Apparently, while he was in Holland, Jacob (and William Ames) caused Robinson to modify his strict Separatist views. In the early 1620s, Jacob left England for Virginia, dying there in 1624.

Henry Jacob's unpublished catechism Principles and Foundations of Christian Religion *has been called "the earliest completely developed Independent, or Congregational Puritan (non-separatist) Catechism in existence."*[4] *It dates from 1604 or 1605, about the same time that Jacob published* Reasons Taken out of Gods Word, *which reflects his mature Congregational view. It has been recently pointed out that the former work is modeled closely on an earlier catechism of William Perkins. Jacob's* Principles and Foundations *is notable for its description of the covenantal basis of church membership, which is similar to the covenant that was the foundation of the Southwark congregation.*[5]

1. Concerning God.

Question.
What doest thou believe concerning God?

Answer.
I believe that There is one God Creator & Governor of all things; who is distinguished into the Father, the Sonne, & the Holy Ghost.

2. Concerning Man.

Question.
What doest thou believe concerning Man?

Answer.
All men by Nature are wholly corrupted with sinne through Adams fall; & so are become bond-slaves to Sathan, & subject to eternall damnation.

3. The Author & Principall Meanes of Salvation.

Question.
What meanes is there to escape this damnable estate?

Answer.
The holy & heavenly meanes of salvation given us[6] of God are of 2. sorts. Principall, & Instrumentall.

Question.
What is the Principall meanes?

Answer.
The Principall meanes is Iesus Christ, (yea indeed he is the whole Authour being the eternall Sonne of God & also true Man who perfitly alone by himselfe accomplisheth all things that are needfull for the salvation of mankind.[7]

4. The Instrumentall Inward meanes.

Question.
What are the Instrumentall meanes of Salvation?

Answer.

They are of 2. sortes: Inward, & Outward.

Question.

By what Inward meanes is a man made partaker of Christ & his benefits?

Answer.

A man of a contrite & humble spirit by Faith alone apprehending & applying to himselfe *[sic]* Christ in his 3. maine Offices (that is, as he is our Prophet, King, & Priest) with all his Merits in them, is justifyed before God & sanctifyed? *[sic]*

Question.

What is Christs Propheticall Office: or what did Christ for us as he is our Prophet & Teacher. *[sic]*

Answer.

He himselfe (in his owne word & Testament only) teacheth us all things Religious as properly belonging to the Church, both Outward & Inward. Wherein standeth his whole true Worship, & the meanes of our salvation.[8]

Question.

What is Christs Kingly Office. *[sic]*

Answer.

He himselfe alone ruleth & guideth us Spiritually. And this is called Christs Kingdom of grace.

Question.

How may we further know this his Kingdom of Grace?

Answer.

Christs Kingdom of Grace heere in this life is of 2. sorts: Inward & Outward. And this later is the meanes & ordinary cause of the former.

Question.

Wherein standeth Christs Inward spirituall Kingdom?

Answer.

In that he ruleth & guideth our hearts by his Spirit to the obedience of his Law, which is his word.

Question.

Wherein is his Outward Spirituall Kingdom?

Answer.

In that by himselfe or by his Spirit in his Apostles which is all one, (& by none other) he constituteth & injoyneth the forme of all his Visible Churches with their Ministeries, & admitteth (wheresoever) none other. Also in that he ordinarily ruleth, guideth, & blesseth us in them only by his owne Ministeries & ordinances, & by none other.

Question.

What is Christs Priestly Office?

Answer.

To offer unto God a Sacrifice allsufficient for all our sinnes, which he did by his infinit Sufferings [?] in this life, & to make Intercession for us in Heaven by vertue thereof for ever. And all this in his owne only person without any other with him whomsoever.

Question.

Doth not Christ save us only by his death & sufferings?

Answer.

No; He redeemeth us in deed only by his death & Sufferings: but he is our Saviour & mediator by his Doctrine teaching us, by his kingdom ruling us, & by his death once upon ye Gibbet. That is not by any one, but by all 3. his . . . & proper Offices apprehended & applyed to us by a true faith.

Question.

What use hath our Sanctification in this life?

Answer.

Our Sanctification, our Obedience to the Word, or our Good works have 2. uses./ 1. They are the fruits & sure witnesses of true faith justifying us. 2. They are the high way necessary for all men to walke in unto salvation.

5. The Instrumentall Outward Meanes.

Question.

What are the ordinary Outward meanes given by Christ for his outward true worship & for our obtayning of faith & salvation?

Answer.

The ordinary Outward meanes (which Christ as our Prophet & King gave us & sanctifyed for us) are of 2. sortes: Generall, & Speciall.

Question.
What is the ordinary Generall meanes?

Answer.
The ordinary Generall meanes is, to be joyned a Member in som true Visible or Ministeriall Church of Christ.

Question.
Are there many in the world, or is there only one Universall Visible Church?

Answer.
In the time of the Law there was only one Visible Church under one High priest of the Iewes. But since the Gospell went out of Ierusalem into all the world, by ye Divine ordinance there allwayes have ben & are many in nomber, & not only One Visible or Ministeriall Church of Christ, as the Catholiks do falsly believe.

Question.
How then do we say in the Creed; I believe the Catholik, yt is, the Universall Church?

Answer.
There we signify the Invisible Church Catholik, either Militant, or els the whole nomber of Gods Elect in Heaven & in Earth. It can not be contrary to ye Acts & Writings of ye Apostles, where a multitude of proper & distinct Ministeriall Churches are shewed us: one at Corinth, an other at Antioch, an other at Ephesus & many in Asia, many in Iudea, many in Galatia, Macedonia, &c. &c.

Question.
What is a true Visible or Ministeriall Church of Christ?

Answer.
A true Visible or Ministeriall Church of Christ is a particular Congregation being a spirituall perfect Corporation of Believers, & having power in it selfe immediatly from Christ to administer all Religious meanes of faith to the members thereof.

Question.
How is a Visible Church constituted & gathered?

Answer.
By a free mutuall' consent of Believers joyning & covenanting to live as

Members of a holy Society togeather in all religious & vertuous duties as Christ & his Apostles did institute & practise in the Gospell. By such a free mutuall consent also all Civill perfect Corporations did first beginne.[9]

Question.

If every particular Church be an intire Church & independent of any other, how shall Unitie be preserved & obedience to Magistrats?

Answer.

Unitie in conscience standeth not upon one Church or Pastor over the rest, but upon ye one Word & Testament of Christ taught ordinarily by that Church unto us whereof we are; as Gods Ordinance is. Also thus most easily may ye meanest next dwelling Magistrat rule any Church in outward peace; yea in peace & concord of Religion far more easily & more readily then otherwise.

Question.

What are the ordinary speciall meanes of faith?

Answer.

In speciall sort faith cometh only by ye preaching of the word, & increaseth dayly by it, as also by the administration of the Sacraments, Discipline, & Prayer. And heerein consisteth the whole true outward Worshipping of God.

Question.

What is the Word that is preached unto us. *[sic]*

Answer.

It is the Word of God. That is, his Will & Testament revealed & confirmed unto us in ye holy Scriptures only.

Question.

What is the effect & scope of the Scriptures?

Answer.

Their scope is to specify & shew most perfectly all the wayes of worshipping God a right, & so also ye whole meanes of our salvation.

Question.

Which are the holy Scriptures. *[sic]*

Answer.

The Bookes of ye Prophets & the Apostles, called the Old & New Testament.

Question.
From what authority com they?

Answer.
Those holy men of God (the Prophets & Apostles) writ them as they were inspired by ye Holy Ghost.

Question.
How know we that they have Divine authoritie, & were written by inspiration of the Holy Ghost?

Answer.
First the tradition of all times telleth us so much. Secondly & chiefly the Heavenly matter contained in them under such simplicity of words doth now assure us of it; with many other like reasons taken out of the Scriptures themselves.

Question.
What short Summe have we of all the holy Scriptures, as concerning any duty which we ought to do?

Answer.
The 2. Tables divided into 10. Commandements are a short & perfect Summe of all the Scriptures.

• • • [10]

Question.
Is there not then any outward thing Indifferent.

Answer.
Yea, there are many indifferent Civill matters. But of ye parts of Divine Service & Church use, there is nothing at all Indifferent. All such things are heere simply commanded or forbidden . . .

Question.
How many Sacraments are there; or holy Signes?

Answer.
Two; Baptisme, & the Lords Table. One other also may be reckoned as a holy Signe of lesse dignity & inferior nature; yt is, Laying on of hands. But beside these Christs Testament knoweth none.

Question.

Wherein standeth the Churches holy Government[?]

Answer.

In their Election of Ministers, & Their Spiritual Correction of offenders.

Question.

Is it Christs ordinance yt ye whole Church should Elect their Ministers, & Correct their Offenders?

Answer.

They are to do no more of necessity, & in their ordinary carriage, but freely to consen[t] to their Guides preparing & directing every matter.

Question.

What Ministers ought the Church to chose for her ordinary guidance & government.

Answer.

A Pastor or Bishop, with Elders, & Deacons.

Question.

What is ye Pastors Office?

Answer.

In Gods & in ye Churches Name to administer the Wo[rd, (?)] the holy Signes, the holy Government, & publik Prayer. Not any one, or so[me?] of these, but all.

Question.

What are the Elders?

Answer.

The Pastors assistants & coadjutors in ye holy government.

Question.

What are the Deacons?

Answer.

They are faithfull men trusted to gather & distribut ye Church[es?] publik treasure for Ecclesiasticall uses.

Question.

Wherein standeth ye Churches spirituall Correction of Offenders which is properly called the holy Discipline.

Answer.

In their Admonishing (twise or thrise at least) & Exhorting to repentance, & yen in cutting of & Excommunicating ye unrepentan[t.]

Question.

What is Prayer?

Answer.

A Calling upon God in our wants & necessities. Whereof ye Lords Prayer is a perfect rule & direction for us.

6. The End of all.

Question.

What is the estate of all men after death?

Answer.

All men shall rise againe with their owne bodyes to the last judgment. Which being ended, the godly shall possesse the Kingdom of heaven: but the Unbelievers & wicked shalbe in Hell tormented with the Divell & his Angells for ever.

[A detached Definition by Henry Jacob of a "true Visible or Ministeriall Church of Christ."]

A true Visible or Ministeriall Church of Christ is a constant & comple[te?] societie of Christians or spirituall Body politike ordayned by Christ in his word, which any one member the[re] of (having neede) may (& must on occasion) go unto, consult with, heare & obey intirely & wholly togeather & yet with keeping due order & distinction of degrees the[y] all of them being united under one Ecclesiasticall government with themselves & proper unto yem.

Notes

1. See Stephen Brachlow, *The Communion of Saints: Radical Puritan and Separatist Ecclesiology, 1570–1625* (Oxford: Oxford University Press, 1988), 58–59, n. 128.

2. See John von Rohr, "The Congregationalism of Henry Jacob," *Transactions of the Congregational Historical Society* 19 (1962): 107–17; and Brachlow, 136 ff., 185 ff.

3. See Champlin Burrage, ed., *The Early English Dissenters in Light of Recent Research (1550–1641)*, vol. 1 (Cambridge: Cambridge University Press, 1912), 314.

4. See Burrage, 153.

5. See Brachlow, 140.

6. The letter "v" is changed to "u" in conformity with modern spelling. Otherwise the original spelling is retained.

7. Scripture references in the margin of the original text have been placed in these endnotes. Heb. 12:2; 1 Tim. 2:5; 1 Cor. 3:10; Acts 4:12; John 14:6; Isa. 42:8; 1 Tim. 3:16.

8. John 4:25 and 16:13.

9. Matt. 18:19, 20.

10. "The portions here omitted are questions and answers concerning the Commandments," Burrage, 159 n. 1.

30. A Just and Necessary Apology

(1625)

John Robinson

John Robinson (c. 1576–1625), pastor to the pilgrims who settled in Plymouth, Massachusetts, in 1620, followed the Separatist movement as defined by Robert Browne. In spite of the 1593 deaths of a number of Separatist leaders—John Greenwood, Henry Barrow, and John Penry—the tradition was kept alive by Francis Johnson and Henry Ainsworth.

Francis Johnson, although imprisoned for a time for his views, was able to join his exiled congregation in Amsterdam in 1597. Unfortunately, his congregation suffered a series of controversies. First, a conflict arose between Johnson and his brother George, who objected to the fancy dress of Francis's wife. The objection was overruled when the congregation backed its pastor and excommunicated George. A second controversy developed in 1608, when John Smyth, a former student of Johnson's at Christ's College, Cambridge, came to Amsterdam. Smyth insisted on the use of original Greek and Hebrew Scriptures in worship rather than written translations; he promoted a democratic rather than an aristocratic form of church government (rule by the people rather than by the elders); and he rejected infant baptism in favor of believers' baptism. Henry Ainsworth, also a member of Johnson's church, was persuaded by Smyth's views on church government and eventually left Johnson's church along with some followers.

John Robinson held the opinions of Francis Johnson in high regard, especially the corporate confession of 1596 written by Johnson. Robinson called it "our Confession."

SOURCE: Robert Ashton, ed., *Works of John Robinson* (London: John Snow, 1851).

John Robinson, a native of Sturton-le-Steeple in Nottinghamshire, attended Cambridge University. When Robinson came in 1592 to Corpus Christi College, which Separatists Robert Browne and Robert Harrison had attended in the 1570s, Johnson had already been expelled in 1589 for preaching fiery Puritan sermons. By 1591 Johnson had become a Separatist.

While he was at Cambridge, however, there were no indications that John Robinson had any Separatist leanings. He was a devoted student of William Perkins, a staunch Puritan opponent of Separatism. In fact, one of Perkins's works carried to Plymouth on the Mayflower had the superscription "John Robinson's Book." From Perkins, Robinson imbibed the Calvinistic doctrine of election and later became an earnest defender of the Calvinistic decrees of the Synod of Dort.

In late 1603 or early 1604, John Robinson was called to St. Andrew's Church in Norwich, a congregation that had a history of Puritan independence. In spite of the great theological freedom he enjoyed at St. Andrew's, Robinson later wrote of two deficiencies that St. Andrew's shared in common with other English parishes: it lacked the capacity to discipline with the power of excommunication, and it could not dismiss its ministers without the approval of the bishop.

Robinson moved toward Separatism after James I ascended to the English throne in 1603. James tried to make the Puritans conform to new canons in 1604, excommunicating any who rejected the Book of Common Prayer (see vol. 2:397–418) or the episcopacy. Although the precise circumstances are unknown, it is probable that Robinson was suspended from his position in 1604 or 1605. He did not leave the established church immediately but struggled with his decision for some while.

Robinson's final decision to separate was shaped by the sermons of moderate Puritans Laurence Chaderton and Paul Baynes, whom he heard on a return visit to Cambridge. Their sermons did not counsel separation, but Robinson interpreted them as impelling him in that direction. He came to the conclusion that it was only through separation that the church as a disciplined community of the godly (as distinct from the wicked) might be realized.

By 1606 Robinson was the leader of a group of Puritan dissidents in the lower Trent valley at Scrooby. This group included William Brewster, the postmaster of Scrooby, who later became the ruling elder of the group. It also included a seventeen-year-old farmer's son, William Bradford, who later became the governor of Massachusetts. While they were still in England or soon after they moved to Holland to escape persecution, Robinson was elected pastor of the group.

Another group of Separatists, under the leadership of John Smyth, gathered at neighboring Gainsborough. The two groups had much in common, but they split when Robinson failed to go along with Smyth's refusal to share in private communion with Puritans who stayed within the established church.

In 1608 both groups went into exile in Amsterdam. Within a year, partially on account of the dissension within Johnson's church and the disagreement with Smyth's, Robinson's group moved to Leyden. In Leyden the small Scrooby congregation grew to around three hundred. Says one scholar: "It is a tribute to his [Robinson's] moderation and to the love he evoked from his followers that as long as he lived, alone of the Separatist churches in exile, the Leyden church was neither troubled nor rent by secession."[1]

In 1620 a portion of the Leyden congregation, with Robinson's blessing and charge, left Holland for America by way of Southampton and Plymouth, England. According to William Bradford, "They kne/w/ they were pilgrimes and looked not much on these thinges [the prospect of sailing to the "vast unpeopled Countryes of America"] but lifted up theire eyes to heaven; their dearest Country and quieted their speritts."[2] *Robinson kept in touch with his American flock, giving them wise counsel. He fully intended to join them in Plymouth, but died an untimely death in 1625.*

Robinson remained a Separatist to the end of his life, even though his views changed slightly under the influence of Non-separatist Puritans like Henry Jacob (see vol. 2:480–82) and William Ames (see vol. 2:521–51). The issue between Separatists and Non-separatists had not only to do with whether one should leave the Church of England or remain within it, but also whether the godly could fully exercise their religion within the established church and whether, from the Separatist side, it was permissible to have private or public communion with what they called the "the religious," or the Puritans still in the Church of England.

Generally speaking, Separatists like Robinson believed that there were faithful persons within the Anglican Church. At an early point in his career, Robinson permitted private but not public communion with these Christians. Ames took a position against Robinson, arguing that within the Church of England the godly should gather freely to carry on pious exercises and practice what he called "voluntary religion." It was important to hear Puritan preaching within one's parish and in other parishes, to gather in conventicles for catechism and prayer, and to practice fast days. Ames considered these exercises public, for they took place not only in homes but in public places. He questioned how Robinson could maintain his distinction between public and private. For Robinson, however, public *meant "by public authority." Robinson did not believe that such communion was permissible, because it implied agreement with episcopacy and the corrupt established church.*

Toward the end of his life, Robinson modified his earlier Separatist position to admit the legitimacy of private communion and also the hearing of sermons in the established church. In the words of Boston pastor John Cotton, Robinson "came backe [from separatism] indeed the one halfe of the way."[3]

John Robinson's A Just and Necessary Apology *was published first in Latin in 1619 and then translated into English by Robinson himself and published in 1625, the year of his death. In this treatise, Robinson defends his exiled congregation from slanderous reports about the faith and behavior of its members during its sojourn in Holland; he explains the commonalities and differences between their beliefs and practices and those of the Dutch Reformed Church; and finally, he defines their attitude toward the established Church of England. This tract is a full summary of Robinson's ecclesiology at the end of his life. The sections dealing with the nature of the church and its liturgy and government as well as the sections on the civil magistrate and the Church of England are the most important. In the following selection, sections are omitted that describe Robinson's view that baptism should be limited to the children of committed church members; that Sunday is the only holy day Christians are commanded to observe; that marriage is a civil matter, not a rite of the church; that prophecy or preaching is a gift not limited to the clergy, but one that may be exercised by any member of the community of faith; and that certain "things indifferent" are nonessential to faith and practice.*

Chapter I.

Of the Largeness of Churches.

And first, it is evident, that the most, especially city churches, are so great and populous, as that two or three divers temples are not sufficient for one and the same church to meet in at once. We on the contrary, so judge, that no particular church under the New Testament, ought to consist of more members than can meet together in one place; because,

1. The Holy Scriptures speaking definitely of the political, or ministerial, commonly called, visible church, instituted by Christ, and his apostles, by his power, understand none other than one congregation convening, and

coming together, ordinary at least, in one place. Matt. 18:17, 20, "gathered together in my name:" with 1 Cor. 5:4, "when you are come together." Acts 2:44, "All that believed were together:" and chap. 5:12, "They were all with one accord in Solomon's porch." Also chap. 6:2, 5; 13:1, 2; 14:23, 27; 15:4, 22, 25; Titus 1:5. So 1 Cor. 11:20, "When ye therefore come together in one," to wit, place, not mind, as some conceit, for from that the Corinthians were too far: and lastly, chap. 14:23, "If the whole church come together into some place."

2. There is then had the most full, and perfect communion of the body in the holy things of God, which is the next and immediate end of the visible church, when all the members thereof do convene, and assemble together in some one place, Acts 2:42; Heb. 10:25. And if nature, as philosophers teach, ever intend that which is most perfect, much more, grace. Now that the church, commonly called visible, is then most truly visible indeed, when it is assembled in one place; and the communion thereof then most full, and entire, when all its members inspired, as it were, with the same presence of the Holy Ghost, do from the same pastor, receive the same provocations of grace, at the same time and in the same place: when they all by the same voice, "banding as it were together," do with one accord pour out their prayers unto God: when they all participate of one, and the same holy bread, 1 Cor. 10:17; and lastly, when they all together consent unanimously, either in the choice of the same officer, or censuring of the same offender, no man admitting a due thought of things, can make doubt of.

3. We have the apostle Paul giving it in charge to the elders of every particular church, as was that of Ephesus, "that they take heed unto all the flock, whereof the Holy Ghost made them bishops," or overseers, "to feed the church of God, which he hath purchased with his own blood." Acts 20:17, 28. But surely, as that flock is very inordinate, if not monstrous, which for the largeness thereof, neither ever doth, nor possibly can feed together; so that shepherd of the Lord's flock seemeth not aright, and as he ought, to fulfil his charge, which doth not at the least, every Lord's day, minister unto the same, the wholesome food of God's Word. Add hereunto, that in these huge and vast flocks, the governors cannot take knowledge of the manners of the people, private or public; no, nor so much as of their presence at, or absence from the church assemblies; whereby what damage cometh unto true piety, any man may easily conjecture, and miserable experience makes too manifest in the reformed churches. I conclude therefore, since, as Junius saith, "it concerneth the pastor thoroughly to know the church committed unto him, the persons, their works and courses, without the knowledge of which things, he shall profit them no more than a tinkling cymbal," &c.,[4] that it were a point of good provision both for the

conscience of the officers, and edification of the people, that a division were made of the city churches, which by continual accession of members, are thus grown out of kind, into different, and distinct congregations, under their certain, and distinct pastors, and elders.

If any object, that there is one visible, and catholic church, comprehending as the parts thereof, all the particular churches, and several congregations of divers places; as there is one ocean, or sea, diversely called, according to the divers regions by whose shores it passeth; and that therefore this matter is not worth labour spending about it, I answer, first, that the catholic church neither is, nor can be called visible: since only things singular are visible, and discerned by sense: whereas universals, or things catholic, are either only in the understanding, as some are of mind; or as others think better, are made such, to wit, universals, by the understanding abstracting from them all circumstantial accidents, considering that the kinds intelligible have their existence in nature, that is in the individuals.[5]

4. The catholic church, with due reverence unto learned men be it spoken, is very unskilfully said to be one, as the sea is one. For, first, it is expressly said, Gen. 1:9, 10, that the waters which were under the heavens, were gathered into one place, or conceptacle, which God called sea, or seas. But the catholic church, which is said to comprehend all particular congregations in her bosom, is not gathered together into one place, nor ever shall be, before the glorious coming of Christ. 2. The ocean is a body so continued, as that all and every part thereof is continually fluent, so as the selfsame waters, which in their flux do make one sea, do in their reflux by contrary winds, make another, and so contrariwise. But thus to affirm of particular churches, and their material constitutive cause, were most absurd. 3. If some one particular sea were drawn dry, or should fail his course, a disturbance of all the rest would necessarily follow; but and if the sea should in divers places at once happen to be exhausted, or drawn dry, there would then be a failing of the ocean: neither were the waters now gathered into one place, neither made they one sea, and body of water, either continued or conjoined. But now, on the other side, upon the defection, or dissipation of this or that particular church, no such impediment should come in the way, but that the rest might hold their full course, as before. Yea, I add moreover, if all and every particular assembly in the world should languish, and fall away, one only excepted, that only one did still remain the true and entire church of Christ, without any either subordination, or co-ordination, or dependency spiritual, save unto Christ alone. The reason is plain, because this singular and sole assembly may, under Christ the head, use and enjoy every one of his institutions: the communion of saints combined together in solemn, and sacred covenant, the Word of God, sacraments, censures, and ministrations

whatsoever by Christ appointed, and therewith, the same Christ's most gracious presence.

And upon this ground it is, that the apostle Paul doth entitle the particular congregation, which was at Corinth, and which properly, and immediately he did instruct, and admonish, "the body of Christ," "the temple of God," and one "virgin espoused to one husband Christ." 1 Cor. 12:27; 2 Cor. 6:10; 11:2. We may not therefore under pretence of antiquity, unity, human prudence, or any colour whatsoever, remove the ancient bounds of the visible and ministerial church, which our right fathers, to wit, the apostles, have set; in comparison of whom, the most ancient of those, which are so called, are but infants, and beardless, as one truly, and wittily saith.

There is indeed one church, and as the apostle speaketh, "one body, as one Spirit, one hope of our calling, one faith, one baptism;" Eph. 4:4, 5; that is, of one kind, and nature; not one in number, as one ocean. Neither was the church at Rome in the apostles' days, more one with the church of Corinth, than was the baptism of Peter one with Paul's baptism, or than Peter and Paul were one. Neither was Peter or Paul more one, whole, entire, and perfect man, consisting of their parts essential and integral, without relation unto other men, than is a particular congregation, rightly instituted and ordered, a whole entire, and perfect church immediately and independently, in respect of other churches, under Christ.

To conclude, since the pastor is not a minister of some part of a church, but of the whole particular church, Acts 20:28. Attend to the whole flock, or church, "whereof the Holy Ghost hath made you bishops," &c., if the minister's office be to be confined within the circle of a particular congregation, then also the ministerial church itself. Now the pastor's office is either circumscribed within these bounds, or else "the angel of the church of Ephesus" was also "the angel of the church of Smyrna;" and so the pastor of this church is also the pastor of that; and by consequence, of all; that is, every pastor is an universal bishop, or pope by office; if not for execution, yet for power; according to which power, we are to judge of the office.

What then? will some man say. Is it not lawful for a pastor to execute his pastoral office but in the congregation over which he is set? I answer, with the apostle, "No man taketh this honour unto himself, but he that is called of God, as Aaron," Heb. 5:4. It is not lawful for thee, reverend brother, to do the work of a pastor where thou art no pastor, lest thou arrogate to thyself that honour, which appertains not unto thee. Thou are called, that is elected, and ordained a pastor of some particular church, and not of all churches. It is not only lawful, but requisite, that the pastor of one church, or rather he that is the pastor, and so any other member, impart the gift either spiritual, or bodily, which he hath received, to other churches, out of the common bond of charity in which he is obliged: not so, to execute a public office over them by the prerogative of authority, which he hath not but only over his own. We will illustrate this by a similitude. Any citizen of Leyden may enjoy certain privileges in the city of Delft, by virtue of the politic combination of the United provinces, and cities, under the supreme heads thereof, the States-general; which he is bound also to help and assist with all his power if necessity require; but that the ordinary magistrate of Leyden should presume to execute his public office in the city of Delft, were an insolent, and unheard of usurpation. The very same, and not otherwise, is to be said of pastors, and particular churches, in respect of that spiritual combination mutual under their chief and sole Lord, Jesus Christ.

• • •

Chapter III.
Of Written Liturgies.

We cannot but mislike that custom in use, by which the pastor is wont to repeat and read out of a prayer-book certain forms, for his and the churches' prayers, and that for these reasons.

1. Because this external mien and manner of worshipping God in prayer is nowhere found in the written Word, by the prescript whereof alone he is to be worshipped, whatsoever either the Jews' fable of the liturgy of Ezra; or the papists of St. Peter's, or St. James' liturgies. Isa. 29:13; Matt. 15:9; Col. 2:23. Yea, contrariwise, I add for overplus, that it did not seem good to the apostles, the last penmen of the Holy Ghost, that any such prescript form for such end should come in use, in the churches. And this seemeth unto me very clear, from the former epistle of Paul to Timothy, chap. 2:1, 2. The kings of the earth in those days, and such as were in authority under them, being, as it were, so many sworn enemies of the name of Christ, this conceit might easily, and it seems did, creep into the minds of divers Christians, that these kinds of men were rather to be prayed against, than for, by the servants of Christ. And now, what was the medicine prescribed by the apostle for this malady in that epistle written to Timothy for that very end, that he "might know how to converse in the church of God?" 1 Tim. 3:15. Did he now either send Timothy to any liturgy formerly set forth for his own and others' direction? Or did he himself frame any for the purpose, whose beaten troad the churches following afterwards should not err? Nothing less: although a more fit, and full occasion for that business scarce be

offered: which without doubt, Paul would no more have let slip, than did the other apostles, that which was more light, for the introduction of deacons, Acts 6:2, 3, if it had seemed good to the Holy Ghost, by whose finger he was guided in the ordering of the churches, that any such book-prayer should have come into use.

Three things especially are objected, which must here be cleared. The first is, that David, and other prophets penned the book of Psalms for the mother church of Israel. The second, that Christ himself delivered to his disciples a certain form of prayer, commonly called, "The Lord's Prayer." The third, that Moses from the Lord, Numb. 6, gave direction to Aaron, and his sons, in what form of words they should bless the children of Israel.

I answer first generally, that the consequence followeth not from the authority of Christ, and of Moses, and of the apostles, in ordaining these, and these forms of Divine worship, for the like authority in ordinary bishops, and pastors, to ordain other, and divers forms, for the same end. What can be spoken more insolently? Christ the Lord, Moses, the prophets, and apostles, being immediately and infallibly guided by the Spirit of Christ, have prescribed certain set forms of God's worship; therefore others, though not immediately and infallibly guided by the same Spirit, may also prescribe them. Why may they not by this argumentation, as well frame us a new canon of Holy Scriptures, considering that even these very forms, wherewith also they equalize their own, are parts, and portions of the same scriptures? More particularly, and first for Psalms. I deny that there is the same reason of a prayer, and of a Psalm; or (whereupon the difference hangeth) that singing and praying are all one. For the question is not, which I desire the reader once for all to bear in mind, either of the internal affection of him that singeth, or prayeth; or of the subject-matter of the song or prayer: but of the external act and exercise of praying and singing. Now these two exercises both the Holy Scriptures, and common sense in every man, that pleaseth but to open his eyes, and look upon them, do plainly difference.

For first, if to sing be to pray, then whosoever singeth prayeth: but how far from truth this is, the Psalms of David, 1, 2, and many others in which not the least parcel of prayer is to be found, do plainly evince.

2. "Is any man sad amongst you," saith the apostle, "let him pray; is he merry, let him sing." James 5:13. To pray then, and to sing, are not the same, nor which do agree, to wit primarily, with the same constitution of the mind.

3. In prayer the pastor's voice is only heard, unto which the people, as the apostle teacheth, 1 Cor. 14:14, 16, are to add their Amen: but in singing, all the multitude have as well their part for tuneable voice, as the pastor himself. Neither can divers possibly sing together, without confusion, but by a certain and set form, both of words and syllables, which yet may be done in church prayer, and is everywhere.

4. We have the same apostle elsewhere teaching us thus: "Speaking to yourselves in psalms, hymns, and spiritual songs." Eph. 5:19. And again, "Let the word of Christ dwell in you plenteously, with all wisdom, teaching and admonishing yourselves mutually in psalms and hymns." Col. 3:16. In singing then we do speak to ourselves, or one to another mutually: but in praying, neither to ourselves, nor to our brethren, but unto God alone. And the reason hereof is evident. Whenas we read or sing the Psalms of David (for what other thing is it to sing out of a book, than to read with a loud and harmonious voice? of which harmony singing is a kind): these selfsame psalms in this very use do still remain, and so are read or sung, as a part of the Word of God in the Holy Scriptures: and in which God speaketh unto us: whereas on the other side, we do speak unto God, in all our prayers, whether mental only, or vocal withal.

5. Even these very psalms, whose matter is prayer and thanksgiving, were framed and composed by the prophets into psalms, and spiritual songs, for this very end, that the men of God might in them teach us, as in the written Word of God, whereof they are parts, both what petitions they in their distresses put up to the Lord, and also what thanksgiving they returned upon their deliverance, that so we in reading and singing them, might instruct and admonish ourselves both publicly and privately, whether by way of doctrine, or admonition, or consolation, for the promoting of the glory of God in our hearts.

Lastly, That I may descend unto them, who are only taught by experience; if any going out of the temple, whilst the church were singing a psalm, either before or after sermon, being asked of one that met him, what the church were then doing, should answer that it were at prayer, would he not be judged by all men to tell a lie? but altogether without cause, if to sing, be to pray, as many imagine.

Touching the Lord's Prayer. We deny it to be the meaning of Christ, teaching his disciples, when they pray to say, "Our Father," &c., to bind them, and the Holy Ghost in them, Jude 20, by which they ought to pray, to a certain form of words and syllables, which they should repeat by heart, or, which is our question, read out of a book. Because, 1. The two evangelists, Matthew and Luke, of whom both the one and other did aright both understand and express the meaning of Christ, do not precisely keep the same words. 2. By these words, "when you pray," is meant, whensoever you pray: whereupon it should follow, that we were tied to this stint of words alone, and always: and so might lawfully use none other, except it be lawful for us sometimes to pray rather by the level of our own device, than of Christ's prescript. The words therefore of Cyprian[6] are good in a good sense. To pray otherwise than Christ hath taught, is not only ignorance, but guilt, seeing he himself hath said, you reject the precepts of God, that you may observe your own tradition. Matt. 6:6. 3. Amongst the many, and manifold prayers of the apostles to be seen in the Holy Scriptures, this form of words is not found: and yet can it not be denied, but they always prayed as they were taught in this place by their master Christ: whose meaning therefore it could not be to tie them necessarily to any such certain form of words. 4. It appears by the context, that the purpose of Christ is to speak of private, or rather secret prayer, and such as every Christian apart from others, and in his closet, with the door shut unto him, should pour out unto the Lord. Now that one alone, and by himself, should say, "Our Father," seems not very congruous. Lastly, Seeing of the like, there is the like consideration; if the apostle James in these words, "Go to now, ye that say, To-day or to-morrow we will go into such a city," &c., James 4:13; and verse 15, "For that ye ought to say, If the Lord will, we shall live, and do this or that," do neither simply find fault with the form of words, nor prescribe necessarily any other, but only (to use Calvin's words)[7] wakens them from their dream, who without respect of the Divine providence, will make themselves masters of a whole year, when there is not a moment in their power: so neither are we to conceive that our Saviour, Christ, Matt. 6 and Luke 11, doth enjoin unto his, any set words to pray in, but only shows whither all our prayers and vows ought to be referred, as with all other orthodox writers about this matter, the said author[8] speaketh: howsoever divers unskilful men cease not still to sing unto us, even to loathsomeness, the song, when you pray, say, as the papists do theirs, "This is my body:" as though the controversy were about the words, and not rather about the meaning of them.

• • •

2. We dislike all reading of prayer, in the act of praying, as inconvenient, yea, directly contrary unto that act? In prayer we do pour out matter, to wit the holy conceptions of the mind, from within to without; that is, from the heart to God: on the contrary, in reading, we do receive and admit matter from without to within; that is from the book, into the heart. Let him that prayeth do that which he doth, not another thing, not a divers thing. Let the whole man, and all that he is, both in soul and body, be bent upon God, with whom he converseth. The eyes of the mind are lifted to God in prayer; and why not the eyes of the body also? both which, he that prayeth, by intending them upon a book, both depresseth and averteth from God. The Apostle exhorteth, that "the men pray, lifting up pure hands to God in every place." 1 Tim. 2:8. In like manner, besides the reason of the thing, we have the patriarchs, prophets, Christ himself, with his apostles, and disciples, for ensamples of lifting up the eyes to heaven in prayer. Not that this

gesture of body is simply necessary but most convenient, save in some great temptation, and depression of mind, both to express and further the intention of a godly heart.

Let devout and learned men, if they please, commit to writing their holy meditations, and secret conferences with God, as did Austin [Augustine], and others amongst the ancients; and many of later times: which may be read, and that with no small benefit, both by pastor and people; but privately, and for better preparation unto prayer. Now the preparation unto prayer is very unseasonable at the self-same time of the solemn performance thereof; and unreasonable in and by the self-same act.

3. Seeing that "public prayer," as Bucanus saith,[9] "is a second part of the ministry;" as also that amongst the gifts of the Holy Ghost, wherewith the pastor is endued from above, that is not small, nor to be despised, by which he is able conveniently both for matter and form, to conceive a prayer according to the church's present occasion, and necessities; by the reading of this prescript form, that truly excellent gift, given of God for this end is made void, and of none use, and the Spirit, contrary to that which ought to be, extinguished. 1 Thess. 5:19. "The manifestation of the Spirit," saith the apostle, "is given to every one," especially to every pastor, "to profit withal." 1 Cor. 12:7. But he who reads a form of prayer conceived and consigned by another, doth not manifest the pastoral gift, (for of the internal affection our question is not) of the Spirit given to him to profit withal, but to that other by whom the form of prayer was indited.

4. If to read such a form of prayer be to pray aright, and pastor-like, no probable reason can be rendered, wherefore to read a sermon, or homily, is not as well to preach aright, and as is required of the pastor of the church. Which so being, small reason had the apostle, treating of the ecclesiastical ministry, which principally consists in these two exercises, Acts 6:4, to cry out, as he did, "Who is sufficient for these things?" 2 Cor. 2:16. For who is not sufficient even of the vulgar sort? who cannot read a liturgy, and an homily?

5. "The Spirit," saith the same apostle, speaking of all Christians, "helpeth our infirmities, for we know not what to pray, as we ought." Rom. 8:26. Yes, Paul, with your leave, right well; for we have in our prayer-book, what we ought to pray, word for word, whether the Spirit be present or not. What then is to be done in this business? That which Tertullian saith the Christians of his time did. "We pray," saith he, "without any to prompt us, because we pray from the heart."[10] But he who reads his prayers, or rather the prayers of him that penned them, and his lesson out of a book, hath one that prompts him, and that diligently, both what, and how much, and after what manner, and with what words and syllables he ought to pray.

Lastly, If it would be just matter of shame to any earthly father, that his child, who desired of him bread, fish, or an egg, should need to read out of a book, or paper, "Father, I pray you give me bread, fish, or egg;" how much more contumelious is it, to our heavenly Father, and his Holy Spirit, wherewith he furnisheth all his children, especially his ministers according to their place, that an help so unworthy, and more than babyish, and indeed the instrument of a "foolish shepherd," Rom. 8:26; Jude 20; Zech. 2:15; 7:10; namely a bare reader, with which kind of vermin Rome and England are pestered, should be used by such godly and learned pastors, as wherewith the reformed churches are furnished.

Chapter IV.

Of the Ecclesiastical Presbytery.

We do so acknowledge, and approve of, as divinely instituted, the presbyteries of the particular churches, as with all we judge them sundry ways defective. As first we require, that all received into the college, and company of elders, even those which are called governors, should be "apt to teach," 1 Tim. 3:2, and "able to exhort with sound doctrine," and "convince gainsayers," Titus 1:5, 7, 9, and that not only privately, or in the consistory, but in the public assembly also, as the nature of their public office requireth. I am not ignorant, what that learned man Gersom Bucer[11] in his late treatise hath published about this matter, neither do I unwillingly assent thereunto: provided only, that what he requires in those elders, that they be able to perform publicly, and in the church-assembly, if not exactly, yet competently.

A second defect, which we wish supplied is, that of annual or triennial or temporary, they might be perpetual, and for life, (except by some casualty, or occurrence they be disabled) as the pastors themselves. This term of years for the elders' administration in the reformed churches, the forenamed author in the same place doth not so much defend, as excuse; but it seemeth rather needful to have it reformed, which is also the desire of the said learned man, and that for these reasons.

1. The apostle Paul calling unto him the elders of the church of Ephesus to Miletus, doth pronounce of them all, as well the governors, as those that laboured in the Word, that they were made bishops or overseers of the same church, by the Holy Ghost. Acts 20:17, 28. Now the authority of that the appointer ought to work in the appointed great conscience, not lightly to relinquish that charge, which by the disposition of the Holy Ghost they had taken upon them.

2. The same apostle doth in the same place admonish and exhort the same elders that they should take heed unto themselves, and to all the flock, lest the same, after his departure should unhappily be damnified, either by "wolves entering in among them," or such as should "rise up from themselves speaking perverse things." Acts 20:28–31. Now if the date of their eldership and charge were shortly to be out, they might well think with themselves, that the apostle's admonition for after-times did not much concern them, whose term of office should so shortly be expired, and were perhaps to follow the apostle's departure at the heels.

3. It was sacrilege for the Levites being consecrated to the Lord, for the service of the tabernacle and temple, to retire from the office undertaken by them; although, age growing upon them, they were exempted from some the more laborious works of that ministration: how then is it lawful for the elders, or deacons (being now no more at their own disposing, but as the Levites of old, the Lord's sacred and consecrated ones) to withdraw so lightly from this special service? Numb. 8:24, 25. No man under the law might change a beast, if clean, no, not a better for a worse, if once hallowed to the Lord. Lev. 27:9, 10. How much less may the church, then, discharge her officers or they themselves, ministering faithfully, and as they ought!

Lastly, the apostle Paul instructing the church, in Timothy, to keep the commandment of Christ unrebukable until that his glorious appearing, doth not permit, no, not to the widows and deaconesses to relinquish the office once taken upon them, 1 Tim. 5:9–12, 21; 6:14; 1 Cor. 14:37; unto whom for that very cause he forbids marriage itself, otherwise permitted to all, and to some enjoined. How much less lawful is it for the elders, or deacons of the church, whose both condition and ministry is far more excellent, for far lighter causes, to look back, and relinquish their vocation, wherein Christ hath in such sort placed them!

A third thing there is, and that of most moment, viz. that the elders do not administer their public office publicly, as they should, but only in their private consistory. And first, the administration of every office doth in right follow the nature of the same; whether domestical in the family, or civil in the commonwealth, or spiritual in the church: the elders' office then being public, requires answerable and public administration. Not that it is unlawful for the elders to convene, and meet apart from the body, and to deliberate of such things as concerns the same, and so to do sundry things by virtue of their office; but because that is not sufficient, neither do they indeed fulfil their public and church-office, which in the Lord they have received, Col. 4:17; except as privately, and in their consistory, so also (and that specially) publicly, and in the face of the congregation, they execute the same.

2. The apostle beseecheth them of Thessalonica that they would in love highly esteem for their work's sake, not only them which laboured among them, to wit, in doctrine; 1 Thess. 5:12, 13; but them also, which were over them in the Lord, and admonished them. 1 Tim. 5:17. But of the work of their elders which govern, the reformed churches must needs be ignorant; neither do, or can they know, whether they be good, or bad. Their pastors they do prosecute with due love, and honour, out of their own certain knowledge of them and their work, but their elders only by hearsay.

Lastly, The same apostle warneth the elders of Ephesus, that they attend and take heed to the whole flock, in which they were made bishops. Acts 20:17, 28. But it cannot be, that he should ministerially, as he ought, feed the whole church, whose voice the greatest part thereof never so much as once heareth. To lead, or receive a sheep now and then into the sheepfold, to confirm one that is weak, or correct one that strayeth, and that apart from the flock, is in no wise to feed the whole flock, as the apostle requireth.

And that this point may be made the more plain, let us descend unto some such particulars, as in which the elders' office seemeth specially to consist. And they are, the admitting of members into the church, upon profession of faith made; and the reproving and censuring of obstinate offenders, whether sinning publicly, or privately with scandal. As we willingly leave the execution and administration of these things to the elders alone in the settled and well-ordered state of the church, so do we deny plainly, that they are, or can be rightly, and orderly done, but with the people's privity and consent.

• • •

2. If the elders in their consistory represent the church, then whatsoever they either decree or do, agreeing to the Word of God, whether respecting faith or manners, that also the church decreeth and doth, though absent, though ignorant both what the thing is which is done, and upon what grounds it is done by the elders; this being the nature of representations, that what the representing doth within the bounds of his commission, that the represented doth primarily, and much more, as but using the other for his instrument. Now how dissonant this is to true faith and piety, how consonant unto the papists' implicit faith, no man can be ignorant; and I had rather wise men should consider, than I, aggravate.

3. The constant and universal practice of the apostles and apostolic churches, do quite cross this consistorian course. The apostle Paul, well acquainted with the meaning of Christ, doth. 1 Cor. 5, so reduce into practice the rule and prescript of his Master, Matt. 18, or to use the words of the Bishop of

Chichester, "there commands to bring into practice this power, in the name of Christ, with his Spirit," as he seems to leave no place for doubting to him who with diligence, and without prejudice, will compare together these two places: what the Lord meaneth when he saith, "Tell the church." This our apostle doth in that place reprove, not the elders or governors alone, but with them also the whole commonalty and body, for tolerating the incestuous person amongst them. Which therefore, accordingly, as his authority apostolical and care for all the churches, 2 Cor. 2:28, did require; he admonisheth and directeth, that as mindful both of the sinner's repentance and salvation, and therewith of their own purity, they would exclude, by due order, that wicked man from their holy fellowship. And that by these words, "When ye are come together," the whole church is to be understood, many but heavy friends to the people's liberty, Jesuits, Prelatists, and others, do grant.

• • •

And surely, if it ever did, or could appertain to any church officers or governors whatsoever to represent the church assemblies, in elections, censures, and other ecclesiastical judgments, and occurrences; then without doubt unto the apostles in an eminent, and peculiar manner, especially living in that rude, and childish state of the church, considering both how superlative their office was, and how admirable their gifts, and endowments of the Holy Ghost, together with their incomparable both piety, and prudence; by which they were both most able, and willing, to promote the Christian faith in holiness. And although this constant and uniform both practice and institution of the apostles unto divers politic persons, swelling with pride of fleshly reason, despising apostolical simplicity, and who, as Irenaeus speaks,[12] would be rectifiers of the apostles, seem worthy of light regard, yet to us, who believe with Theodoret,[13] that we "ought to rest in the apostolical and prophetical demonstrations;" and who, with Tertullian, do adore the fulness of the Scriptures,[14] they seem of singular weight and moment.

And whilst I consider with myself, in the fear of God, how it was the apostles' duty to teach the disciples of Christ "to observe whatsoever he commanded them," Matt. 28:20; and how the apostle Paul testifieth, that even the things which he wrote, touching order and comeliness to be observed in the church exercises, were the commandments of the Lord, 1 Cor. 14:37; as also how the same apostle clearly professeth, that he and his fellow-officers were only to be reputed as ministers and ambassadors of Christ, 1 Cor. 4:1; 2 Cor. 5:20; to whom therefore in the execution of their office, it was not permitted to do, or speak the least thing, which they had not in charge from him; it is unto me a matter of great scruple, and conscience, to depart one hair-breadth, (extraordinary accidents ever excepted) from their practice, and institution, in anything truly ecclesiastical, though never so small in itself;—whatsoever, by whomsoever, and with what colour soever is invented and imposed;—touching the government of the church, which is the "house and tabernacle of the living God." 2 Tim. 3:15. And a partner in this faith I do hope to live, and die, and to appear before Jesus Christ, with boldness in that great and fearful day of his coming.

I add, that seeing the Christian congregation, as the spouse of Christ, free and ingenuous, hath the church officers whosoever, as Christ Jesus her husband's, so also her servants for Jesus' sake, whom, under Christ, she trusteth with her eternal salvation, and unto whom for their labour she oweth wages for relief and maintenance, 2 Cor. 4:5; 1 Tim. 4:16; 5:17, 18; considering also how much it makes both to whet on the diligence of the ministers, and to enforce the diligence of the people, whilst these on the one side consider with themselves, how they have them set over them, whom above others themselves have liked, and made choice of; and they on the other side, that they are set over those by whom they before others were made choice of, and elected: that which Cyprian hath,[15] seemeth most equal, and of institution moral, and unchangeable, that "the commonalty fearing God and keeping his commandments, should have the special hand either in choosing of worthy priests, or ministers, or of rejecting the unworthy: which also," saith he, "we see to be founded upon Divine authority."

The same is to be held of excommunication. Seeing that it behoveth the Christian multitude to avoid the fellowship of the excommunicated, not only in the course of religion, but even in common and familiar conversation, (the rights of nature, family, and commonwealth ever kept inviolated): and that whom yesterday I was to repute a brother near and dear in Christ, tomorrow I must hold as a "heathen and publican," and as, "for the destruction of the flesh, delivered to Satan," Matt. 18:17; 1 Cor. 5:5: who is so unequal a judge as not to think it a most equal thing, that the multitude should clearly, and undoubtedly, take knowledge both of the heinousness of the crime, and incorrigible contumacy of the person, after the use of all means and remedies for reclaiming him. This, if it be not done, then doth not the church herein live by her own, but by her officers' faith, neither are her governors to be reputed as servants, but lords unto her; neither do they exercise their office popularly in the church as they ought but tyrannically, as they ought not, by Chrysostom's verdict. His words are these:[16] "He who bears himself upon an external and worldly power, because he rules legally, and that men must of necessity obey him, doth ofttimes, and that not without cause, exercise authority against the will, and well-liking of his subjects. But on the other side, he who will be over those, who voluntarily submit unto him, and can him thank, and yet will presume to do things as himself liketh, and as if he were to give account to none other thereof, that man rather exerciseth his authority tyrannically than popularly."

The Lord God put it into the hearts of those who bear greatest sway in the reformed churches, to endeavour the furnishing of the same with such elders, as may both fully, and constantly, and popularly, discharge their place, for the peace of their own consciences before God, the edification of the churches over which they are set, as also for the abating, if not abolishing, of that contempt in which prelatists and supercilious persons use to hold these lay-elders, as they call them.

But now lest any should take occasion, either by the things here spoken by us, or elsewhere of us, to conceive, that we either exercise amongst ourselves, or would thrust upon others, any popular, or democratical church government: may it please the Christian reader to make estimate of both our judgment and practice in this point, according to these three declarations following.

First, We believe, that the external church government under Christ, the only mediator and monarch thereof, is plainly aristocratical, and to be administered by some certain choice men, although the state, which many unskilfully confound with the government, be after a sort popular and democratical. By this it appertains to the people freely to vote in elections and judgments of the church: in respect of the other, we make account it behoves the elders to govern the people, even in their voting, in just liberty, given by Christ whatsoever. 1 Cor. 12:28; 1 Tim. 5:17; Heb. 13:17. Let the elders publicly propound, and order all things in the church, and so give their sentence on them; let them reprove them that sin, convince the gainsayers, comfort the repentant, and so administer all things according to the prescript of God's Word: let the people of faith give their assent to their elders' holy and lawful administration: that so the ecclesiastical elections and censures may be ratified, and put into solemn execution by the elders, either in the ordination of officers after election, or excommunication of offenders after obstinacy in sin.

2. We doubt not but that the elders both lawfully may, and necessarily ought, and that by virtue of their office, to meet apart at times from the body of the church, to deliberate of such things as concern her welfare, as for the preventing of things unnecessary, so for the preparing, according to just order, of things necessary, so as publicly, and before the people, they may be prosecuted with most conveniency, and least trouble, that may be. Acts 20:18.

3. By the people whose liberty, and right in voting, we thus avow, and stand for, in matters truly public and ecclesiastical, we do not understand, as it hath pleased some contumeliously to upbraid us, women, and children; but only men, and them grown, and of discretion: making account, that as children by their nonage, so women by their sex are debarred of the use of authority in the church. 1 Cor. 14:34, 35; 1 Tim. 2:12.

• • •

Chapter XII.
Of the Church of England.

There remains one, and that a great matter of exception against us, and the same the fountain well-nigh of all our calamity: to wit, that we seem evil affected towards the Church of England, and so averse from the same, as that we do no less than make a plain secession and separation from it.

I answer, first, That our faith is not negative, as papists used to object to the evangelical churches; nor which consists in the condemning of others, and wiping their names out of the bead-roll of churches, but in the edifying of ourselves; neither require we of any of ours, in the confession of their faith, that they either renounce, or, in one word, contest with the Church of England, whatsoever the world clamours of us this way. Our faith is founded upon the writings of the prophets and apostles, in which no mention of the Church of England is made. We deem it our duty what is found in them to "believe, with the heart to righteousness, and to confess with the tongue of salvation." Rom. 10:10.

Secondly, We accord, as far as the Belgic and other reformed churches, with the Church of England in the Articles of Faith and heads of Christian religion, published in the name of that church, and to be found in the "Harmony of the Confessions of Faith."

Thirdly, If by the church be understood the catholic church, dispersed upon the face of the whole earth, we do willingly acknowledge that a singular part thereof, and the same visible and conspicuous, is to be found in the land, and with it do profess and practise, what in us lays communion in all things, in themselves lawful and done in right order.

But and if by the word church be understood a spiritual politic body, such as was in her time the Church of Israel: and in hers the Church of Rome, Corinth, the seven Churches of Asia, and others, with them, partaking of the same apostolical constitution, and as unto which do appertain the oracles of God, sacraments, censures, government and ministry ecclesiastical, with other sacred institutions of Christ: I cannot but confess and profess, though with great grief, that it is to us a matter of scruple, which we cannot overcome, to give that honour unto it which is due from the servants of Christ to the Church of Christ, rightly collected and constituted.

And, that there may be place left in the eyes of the prudent reader for our defence in this case, so far forth as equity and reason will permit, he must once and again be entreated by me, seriously to weigh with himself, and in his heart, this one advertisement following.

That a man may do a thing truly pleasing, and acceptable to God, it sufficeth not, that both the doer in his person be accepted of God, the thing done commanded by God, and that he do it with good and holy affection before God, except withal, and first, he be possessed of that state and condition of life, which may afford him a lawful calling to that work. That a man, though never so good, with never so good a mind, should exercise the office, or do (though the best) works of a magistrate, father of family, husband, steward, citizen, or messenger, except he were first lawfully called, and preferred to the state of a magistrate, master of family, husband, or the like: so far were he from deserving any praise for so doing, as on the contrary he most justly incurred the censure of great rashness, and violation of all order in family and commonwealth; as "taking unto himself that honour, unto which he was not called of God." Heb. 5:4. The same holdeth, and that specially in course of religion, which is the special state of man's life: so as if any either as a pastor dispense the holy things of the ministerial church, without a lawful pastoral calling going before; or participate in the same, out of a just and lawful church-state; neither that dispensation, nor this participation can be warranted, but both the one and other are usurpations, and which is seen not the use, but abuse of holy things, and confusion of order. And as it behoveth every person first to believe, and know, that he is truly a Christian, and partaker of the grace of Christ, before he can hope to please God in the performance of this or that particular Christian work; so doth it also concern every Christian to provide, that he be first possessed of a just and lawful church order, before he so much as touch with his least finger the holy things of the church thereunto proper and peculiar. Proper, I say, and peculiar, amongst which I do not simply reckon the hearing of the Word, which both lawfully may, and necessarily ought to be done, not only of Christians, though members of no particular church, but even of infidels, profane persons, excommunicates, and any others: as being that in which no communion spiritually passeth, either ecclesiastical or personal, between the teacher and hearer, but according to some union, ecclesiastical or personal, going before: seeing that Christian faith comes by hearing the gospel, by faith, union, and from union, communion.

This thus premised, I will speak a few things of the Church of England; not by way of accusation of it, but for our own purgation in the eyes of the godly and equal reader, of the imputed crime of schism, so far as truth and equity will bear.

And first, seeing that the people of God are materially, as they speak, the church of God, it is required to the constitution of a holy church of God, that the people be holy, or saints, and sanctified in Christ Jesus, Rom. 1:7; 1 Cor. 1:2; 2 Cor. 1:1: truly and internally in regard of God, and their own consciences; externally and in appearance in respect of others, whom it concerns to discern and judge of them, according to the Word of God and rule of charity. And considering that our question is about the church external, and visible, as it is called, we are not so fond, or rather frantic, as to require, in respect of others, other holiness in the members thereof, than that which is visible and external.

Now how marvellous a thing is it, and lamentable withal, that amongst Christians, any should be found so far at odds with Christian holiness, as to think that others than apparently holy at the least, deserved admittance into the fellowship of Christ's church, and therewith of Christ! Do, or can the gracious promises of God made to the church, the heavenly blessings due to the church, the seals of Divine grace given to the church, appertain to others than such? Are others to be admitted into the family of God, the kingdom of Christ, and as it were the suburbs of heaven? The church of God is by him called, and designated to advance his glory in the holiness of their lives, and conversations; what then have those to do with it, or it with those, who, as Calvin saith, in 1 Cor. 5, live not but with God's dishonour? For they, as the same author, on Rom. 2:24, both truly and holily affirmeth, who am called, and accounted the people of God, to bear as it were in their foreheads, Rev. 7:3, the name of God, whereupon it cannot but come to pass, that before men, even God himself, after a sort should be stained with their filth. And this I deem the rather to be observed, seeing that there are to be found, and these not a few, who would thrust upon the churches of our thrice holy Lord, a very stage-like holiness: stoutly striving to make it good, that to constitute a true and lawful member of the visible church, no more is required, than that a man with his mouth confess Christ, although in his works he plainly declare himself to be of the synagogue of Satan. But what saith the Holy Spirit of these impure spirits? "They profess they know God," saith the apostle, "but in their works they deny him, being abominable, and rebellious, and to every good work reprobate." Titus 1:16. Are abominable persons to be brought into the temple of God? rebellious persons into the kingdom of God? such as are reprobate unto every good work into the family of God, which is as it were the storehouse of all good works? "If any one that is called a brother, be a fornicator, or covetous, or idolater, or railer, or drunkard, or extortioner," 1 Cor. 5:11, or any way a wicked one, such a one by the apostle's direction, is to be expelled, and driven out of the church's confines. And seeing that, as one truly saith, "It is a matter of greater contumely to thrust out, than to keep out a guest," with what conscience can such plagues be received into the church, to the purging out whereof the same church, furnished for that end with the power of Christ, stands in conscience bound? or by what authority, I pray, can such persons be compelled into the bosom of the spouse of Christ, as for the expelling of whom far from her fellowship, and in embracing all authority ought to conspire? "He that saith he hath fellowship with God, and walks in darkness, is a liar, and doth not truly." 1 John 1:6. Profession of Christ therefore with the mouth, in those that work the works of darkness, and so by consequence, that by which a man is rather branded for a natural child of the devil, John 8:44, than marked for a true member of the church. Lastly, David, that holy man of God, and type of Christ, doth holily profess, that "he who works deceit, shall not continue in his house," Ps. 101:7. And shall the workers of deceit, and of all wickedness, not only be admitted, but even constrained into the house of the living God, which the church is? "O Jehovah, holiness becometh thine house to length of days." Ps. 93:5. Which notwithstanding (a sickness desperate of all remedy) that so it stands with the Church of England, no man to whom England is known, can be ignorant: seeing that all the natives there, and subjects of the kingdom, although never with strangers from all show of true piety, and goodness, and fraught never so full with many most heinous impurities and vices (of which rank, whether there be not an infinite, and far the greater number, I would to God it could with any reason be doubted,) are without difference compelled and enforced by most severe laws, civil and ecclesiastical, into the body of that church. And of this confused heap, a few, compared with the rest, godly persons mingled among, is that national church, commonly called the Church of England, collected and framed. And such is the material constitution of that church. But if now you demand of me, how it is formally constituted; and whether upon profession of faith and repentance, in word at least, made by them of years, any combination and consociation of the members into particular congregations, (which consociation doth formally constitute the ministerial church, and members thereof, as both the Scriptures and reason manifest) either is, or hath been made, since the universal and antichristian apostacy and defection in popery? Nothing less; but only by their parish perambulation, as they call it, and standing of the houses in which they dwell. Every subject of the kingdom dwelling in this or that parish, whether in city, or country, whether in his own or other man's house, is thereby, *ipso facto*, made legally a member of the same parish in which that house is situated: and bound, will he, nill he, fit, or unfit, as with iron bonds, and all his with him, to participate in all holy things, and some unholy also, in that same parish church.

If any object, that yet the minister of the parish may suspend from the Supper of the Lord flagitious persons, and so by complaint made to Mr. Chancellor, or Mr. Official, procure their excommunication; to let pass, that this is merely a matter of form for the most part, and a remedy as ill as the disease, I do answer, that even by this improved undeniably that which I intend: viz. that all these parishioners before mentioned, are not without, but within, and members of the church (and the same as before constituted) whom she judgeth. 1 Cor. 5:12, 13.

There is besides these a third evil in the way, and the same as predominant, and overtopping all other things in that church, as was Saul higher than all the rest of the people: and with whose Rehoboam-like finger we miserable men are pressed and oppressed: and that is, the hierarchical church-government in the hands of the lord bishops and their substitutes: the very same with that of Rome, the pope the head only cut off, upon whose shoulders also many, though not without notable injury, would place the supreme magistrate, and administered by the self-same canon law.

Now this vast and insatiable hierarchical gulf, swallowing up and devouring the whole order, and use of the presbytery, and therewith the people's liberty, and withal, by Mr. Parker's testimony, with whom "a bishop in England is the pastor of the whole diocese, and the priests or ministers, only his delegates and helpers,"[17] the very office of the pastors themselves, as did the seven lean and evil-favoured kine the seven fat, and the seven wizened ears the seven full that went before them, Gen. 41:20, 24; and so by consequence, not being of Christ the Lord, but of him rather, who opposeth and advanceth himself against whatsoever is called God, or is worshipped; 2 Thess. 2:4; so as he sits in the temple of God, as God, (for unto God alone dwelling in his temple it appertains to appoint the offices of the ministers, 1 Chron. 29:11–13, 19; and to prescribe the people's bonds) our hands are bound by that supreme, and sole authority of Jesus Christ in his churches, upon which both the order of presbytery, and liberty of people, and office of pastor are founded, and from whom as the one only Lord, 1 Cor. 5:4, all ecclesiastical power floweth, and by whom all ministries, 1 Cor. 12:5, 28, are instituted, from giving any the least honour or obedience to the same hierarchical exaltation in itself, or its subordinates, which, as philosophy teacheth, are one with it.

Wherein yet I would not so be understood, as if we were at any defiance with the persons of the bishops, much less with the king's civil authority whereof they are possessed, whether in matters civil or ecclesiastical. Of their persons, their own lords shall judge, to whom they stand or fall. Rom. 14:4. There have been of that rank, who in our Marian days have preferred the profession of the truth of the gospel before their lives: I hope there are also of their successors, who, if pressed with the same necessity (which God forbid) would give the same testimony, though at the same rate, unto the same truth of God revealed unto them.

Now as concerning their civil authority; albeit we do not believe, that the same is at all competent to the true ministers of the gospel, especially in that eminency, external glory, and pomp of this world, in which they far exceed many worldly princes, and rather seem to represent the triumphant, than the militant church; yet forsomuch as they both obtain the same, by the gift of the king, and exercise it in his name, we do not unwillingly yield honour and obedience unto it, and to his majesty in it.

But, whereas, it seems unto many, plain and evident, that we may adjoin ourselves to the Church of England without any subjection, or relation unto the spiritual government, and governors thereof; that is altogether beyond our capacities: neither can we comprehend it, how it may be that he who subjects and joins himself to any public and politic body, or community, whether spiritual or civil, becomes not in so doing, *ipso facto*, subject to the public government, and governors thereof, and undergoes not a relation and respect actually unto them. They rather are, with all seriousness, to consider, how faithfully and sincerely they quit themselves and their consciences before God and men, who contending, and proving in and by so many words and arguments, that the hierarchical government is papal and antichristian, do nevertheless submit themselves thereunto both in the respect, and relation political formerly mentioned, and also in acts properly ecclesiastical, into which the ecclesiastical government, and spiritual policy of the church doth necessarily diffuse itself. Now I do earnestly entreat thee, whosoever thou art, acquainted with Belgic, or rather Christian liberty, and either free from the mists of prejudice, or if any way prejudiced, "yet not choosing rather to serve a preconceived opinion, than to follow an apparent truth," that thou wouldest truly and ingenuously tell, whether if the magistrates here (from which they are far) should by public edict, under severe penalty constrain all and every the native subjects of the country into the bosom of the church, without any difference made, either in respect of faith or manners, according to the place of their habitation; and should set over this church so collected and constituted, an hierarchical bishop provincial or diocesan, in whose hands alone, with his officials, chancellors, commissaries, archdeacons, and other court-keepers, canonical authority should be placed, to constitute and depose ministers, excommunicate and absolve both ministers and people, yea, whole churches (yea, with the living, the dead that they may obtain Christian burial): whether now in this confused heap, and under this spiritual lordship, thou wouldst endure to remain either pastor or member. I suppose not. You, brethren, have not so learned Christ; whom you acknowledge both for the author of your faith, and instituter of your order ecclesiastical. Col. 2:5. Neither yet we, having learned otherwise by the grace of God. Christ the king doth gather and form unto himself another kind of kingdom amongst men, and the same to be administered by other officers, and according to other laws. And if no place upon the face of the earth should be free for us, poor creatures, refusing upon mere conscience of God, as thou God the judge and searcher of hearts knowest! to commingle, and prostitute ourselves in and unto this confusion and domination hierarchical, we have most assured hope, that heaven itself is open for us by Christ, who is the way, and whom in this duty also we do serve, in which we shall, at the length, be fully free from this, and all other incumbrances.

Our adversaries bear in hand not only others, but even us ourselves also, that we do for certain trifling matters, and as they speak, circumstantial corruptions, sequester ourselves from the Church of England. And as nurses use to lisp with children, so they, that they might descend to our capacities, do oft and much instruct us, that unworthy members must be born in the church, especially of private persons; that some corruptions at least in the discipline and external rites, are to be tolerated; that there may be the temple of God, though profaned; the holy city though without a wall; the field of the Lord, though the enemy sow tares amongst the wheat; also a heap of wheat, though much chaff commingled therewithal. And that we, dulbayards [i.e., persons dull in understanding] as we are, may at the length conceive those things, they very seriously inculcate and whet upon us in these and the like considerations: as that the Israelitish church in its time was stained with almost all enormities, both for manners and faith: that into the same all Israelites and Jews whatsoever without difference, were violently compelled by King Josiah and others; as also that in the parable, all were compelled to come to the marriage, good and bad, that the house might be filled. Lastly, that in the apostolic churches themselves, there were not wanting some who practised, and others who taught vile, and evil things: that in one place the discipline was neglected, in another the very doctrine of faith corrupted, and many the like matters, which it were too long to repeat.

Surely, foolish were we if we knew not these things, impudent, if we denied them to be true for the most part, and lastly, unequal, if we acknowledged not, that many the same, or like blemishes after a sort, will, and do creep into the churches of our days: which yet to disclaim as unlawful for the same, stood neither with wisdom, nor charity. But the prudent reader may plainly observe by the promises, that they are other matters, and of greater weight for the most part, wherewith we, and our consciences are pressed.

We do not judge it an evil intolerable, though greatly to be bewailed, that evil men should be suffered in the church; but that all of most vile, and desperate conditions that such, and so great a kingdom affords, should thereinto, will they, nill they, be compelled: nor that the discipline, as they call it, or ecclesiastical government instituted by Christ, is neglected or violated, but that another plain contrary unto it is set up by law, and fully and publicly everywhere exercised. Neither lies our exception against any personal, or accidentary profanation of the temple, but against the faulty frame of it, in respect of the causes constitutive, matter and form. Neither strive we about the walls of the city, but about the true and lawful citizens, the policy and government of the city of God, and essential administration of the same.

• • •

Lastly, It is objected, that in the Church of England lively faith, and true piety, are both begotten and nourished, in the hearts of many, by the preaching of the gospel there. God forbid! that we should not acknowledge that, and withal that infinite thanks for the same are due to God's great power and goodness, both in respect of ourselves and others; who, notwithstanding the great confusion both of persons and things, there to be found, vouchsafeth to his elect so plentiful grace; covering under the veil of his superabundant goodness and mercy, by their sincere faith in Christ Jesus, their sins and aberrations, whether of ignorance or infirmity. What, then, must be done? Should we continue in sin, that grace might abound? or, shall we against knowledge go on to walk inordinately, because in our ignorance God hath vouchsafed us of his grace in that disordered state of things? without the ministerial church, of which we speak, the preaching of the gospel both may, and useth to be had, and by it faith to be ingenerated, except Christian churches be to be gathered of infidels and unbelievers. Besides, what Minos, or Rhadamant will deny, that even in the bosom of the Romish church some faithful persons may be found? how much more in that of England, in which the main truths of the gospel, the most and greatest errors of popery being banished, are taught by so many godly and learned men, with such zeal and earnestness? Now what of these things? Is it therefore lawful for a Christian, either to content himself with himself, without joining to any Christian congregation; or to continue still in the bosom of the Church of Rome, as a member under the Pope, the head? I therefore conclude out of Mr. Brightman, on Rev. 2:20, whose words I had rather use than mine own, speaking of the government and ministry of the Church of England, "The fruit," to wit, of the word preached, "doth no more exempt from blame our corruptions, than a true child doth adultery."[18]

And here thou hast, Christian reader, the whole order of our conversation in the work of Christian religion, set down both as briefly and plainly as I could. If in any thing we err, advertise us brotherly, with desire of our information, and not, as our countrymen's manner for the most part is, with a mind of reproaching us, or gratifying of others: and whom thou findest in error, thou shalt not leave in obstinacy, nor as having a mind prone to schism. Err we may, alas! too easily: but heretics, by the grace of God, we will not be. But and if the things which we do, seem right in thine eyes, as to us certainly they do, I do earnestly, and by the Lord Jesus admonish and exhort thy godly mind, that thou wilt neither withhold thy due obedience from his truth, nor just succour from thy distressed brethren. Neither do thou endure, that either the smallness of the number, or meanness of the condition of those that profess it, should prejudice with thee the profession of the truth: but have in mind that of Tertullian,[19] "Do we measure men's faith by their persons, or their persons by their faith?" as also that of Austin,[20] "Let matter weigh with matter, and cause with cause, and reason with reason:" but especially that of the apostle, "My brethren, have not the faith of our glorious Lord Jesus Christ in respect of persons." James 2:1. But now, if it so come to pass, which God forbid, that the most being either forestalled by prejudice, or by prosperity made secure, there be few found, especially men of learning, who will so far vouchsafe to stoop, as to look upon so despised creatures, and their cause; this alone remaineth, that we turn our faces and mouths unto thee O most powerful Lord, and gracious Father, humbly imploring help from God towards those who are by men left desolate. There is with thee no respect of persons, neither are men less regarders of thee if regarders of thee for the world's disregarding them. They who truly fear thee, and work righteousness, although constrained to live by leave in a foreign land, exiled from country, spoiled of goods, destitute of friends, few in number, and mean in condition, are for all that unto thee (O gracious God) nothing the less acceptable. Thou numberest all their wanderings, and puttest their tears into thy bottles. Are they not written in thy book? Towards thee, O Lord, are our eyes; confirm our hearts, and bend thine ear, and suffer not our feet to slip, or our face to be ashamed, O thou both just and merciful God. To him through Christ be praise, for ever, in the church of saints; and to thee, loving and Christian reader, grace, peace, and eternal happiness. Amen.

Notes

1. See Michael R. Watts, *The Dissenters* (Oxford: Clarendon Press, 1978), 51.

2. See William Bradford, *Of Plymouth Plantation*, ed. Samuel Eliot Morrison (New York: Alfred Knopf, 1953), 47.

3. See Patrick Collinson, *Godly People: Essays on English Protestantism and Puritanism* (London: Hambledon Press, 1983), 543; and *The Religion of Protestants: The Church in English Society, 1559–1625* (Oxford: Clarendon Press, 1982), 278–80.

4. Franciscus Junius (1545–1602), *Ecclesiastici sive De natura et administrationibus ecclesiae Dei, libri tres, nunc primum in lucem editi [Church Officers or Concerning the Nature and Administration of the Church, Three Books Now Published for the First Time]* (Frankfurt: A. Wechelum, 1581).

5. Robinson shows himself here to be a philosophical nominalist who thinks that reality belongs only to particular things. Universals exist only as concepts in the mind and as terms or names (Latin *nomen*) in logical propositions.

6. Cyprian, *On the Lord's Prayer*, in *The Writings of Cyprian*, trans. Robert E. Wallis, vol. 1 (Edinburgh: T. & T. Clark, 1868), 408.

7. Calvin, *Commentary on James 4:13*, in *Commentaries on the Catholic Epistles*, trans. and ed. John Owen (Edinburgh: T. & T. Clark, 1855), 340.

8. Calvin, *Commentary on Matthew 6:7*, in *Commentary or a Harmony of the Gospels, Matthew, Mark, and Luke*, vol. 1, trans. and ed. William Pringle (Edinburgh: The Edinburgh Printing Co., 1845), 313.

9. Gulielmus Bucanus (fl. 1591–1608), *Gulielmi Bucani . . . in Dominicam orationem homiliae sylvae [William Bucan's Abundant Sermons on the Lord's Prayer* (Lausanne(?): Iacobus Storr, 1606).

10. Tertullian, *The Apology* 30, in *The Writings of Tertullian in Ante-Nicene Fathers*, ed. Alexander Roberts and James Donaldson, vol. 3 (New York: Charles Scribner's Sons, 1899), 42.

11. Gersom Bucerus (1598–1631), *Dissertatio de Gvberratione Ecclesiae maximeque de Presbyterio, & Episcopatv, praecipuas hujus argumenti controversias placide pertractans, amica collatione instituta cum Doctissim Clarissimique Viri D. Georgii Downami, S. Theologiae Doctoris Concionis quondam de hoc eodem subjecto Anglice editas nun vero in Latinum sermonem versa; non contentionis studio, sed justae defensionis causa, ad veritatis illustrationem suscepta, a Gersomo Bucero, verbi Administro in Ecclesia Veriana* [A Dissertation concerning the Government of the Church, Especially concerning Presbyterianism and Episcopacy, which Treats in a Calm Manner the Chief Controversies on this Subject, Furnished with a Friendly Discussion of the Discourse on the Same Subject by the Most Learned and Most Illustrious Gentleman, the Rev. George Downey (Once Published in English, Now Translated into Latin); Undertaken with the Desire Not for Strife, But for the Reason of Just Defense for Making Known the Truth, by Gersom Bucer, A Minister of the Word in the True Church] (Middleburg: Symon Moulert, 1618), 32–33, 44.

12. Irenaeus, *Against Heresies* III.2, *Ante-Nicene Christian Library*, ed. Alexander Roberts and James Donaldson, vol. 5 (Edinburgh: T. & T. Clark, n.d.), 259.

13. Theodoret, *Erasmistes etoi polymorphos* ("Beggar or Multiform"), *Dialogue* 1, *Patrologia cursus completus, series graeca . . .* , 83, ed. J. P. Migne (Paris: D'Amboise, 1864), 32.

14. Tertullian, *The Treatise against Hermogenes*, trans. J. H. Waszink, *Ancient Christian Writers* 24 (Westminster, Md.: Newman Press, 1956), 57.

15. Cyprian, Letter 67, in *The Letters of St. Cyprian or Carthage*, trans. and annot. G. W. Clarke, vol. 4 (New York: Newman Press, 1989), 23.

16. Chrysostom, *Homilies on the Epistle to Titus 2 (Nicene and Post-Nicene Fathers*, ed. Philip Schaff, vol. 13 (New York: Christian Literature Co., 1889), 525.

17. Robert Parker (1564?–1611), *De politeia ecclesiastica Chisti et hierarchica opposita libri tres, in quibus tam verae disciplinae fundamenta quam omnes fere de eadem controversiae summo cum judicio et doctrina methodice pertractantur* [Three Books Concerning Ecclesiastical Polity and the Opposed Hierarchy, in which the Foundations of True Discipline as well as All the Controversies concerning that Subject are Methodically Treated with Judgment and Learning] (Frankfurt: Godericus Basson, 1616).

18. Thomas Brightman, *A revelation of the Apocalypse, that is the Apocalypse of S. John illustrated with analysis and scolions where the sense is opened by the scripture, & and events of things foretold, shewed by histories* (Amsterdam: Thomas Stafford, 1644), 244. Robinson would probably have used the 1611 Amsterdam edition published by Hondius and Laurennss.

19. Tertullian, *On Prescription against Heretics* 3 in *The Ante-Nicene Fathers*, ed. Alexander Roberts and James Donaldson, vol. 3 (New York: Charles Scribner's Sons, 1899), 244.

20. Augustine, *Against Maximus, the Bishop of the Arians* 2.14, *Patrologia cursus completus, series latina . . .* , ed. J. P. Migne, 42 (Paris: J. P. Migne, 1841), 772.

31. The Marrow of Theology

(1629)

WILLIAM AMES

William Ames (1576–1633) was the English theologian who had the most influence on New England Puritanism. His The Marrow of Theology *was the principal theological textbook at Harvard and Yale Colleges well into the eighteenth century.*

Ames was born into a Puritan merchant family in 1576 at Ipswich, Suffolk. His parents died when he was a boy, and his maternal uncle sent him off to Cambridge for studies at Christ's College. At the college he was deeply influenced by Puritan theologian William Perkins.

Upon graduation, although Ames received a call to become the minister of the congregation at Colchester, he was prevented from accepting the position by the bishop of London. During his studies Ames had irritated church leadership by translating William Bradshaw's English Puritanism *into Latin and adding a supportive introduction. Soon thereafter, in 1610 he emigrated to the Netherlands along with his friend and fellow Puritan Robert Parker. In Rotterdam, he met John Robinson and tried to dissuade him from Separatist thinking. He was partially successful, causing Robinson to moderate some of his radical positions (see vol. 2:492–520). Like Bradshaw, Parker, and Henry Jacob, Ames was a Non-separatist Congregationalist, desiring to realize the congregational ideal within the established church.*

With the help of a Puritan sympathizer, Colonel Horatio Vere, Ames eventually obtained a position as chaplain to the English merchant

---

SOURCE: *The Marrow of Theology*, translated and edited by John D. Eusden from the third Latin edition, 1629 (Boston: Pilgrim Press, 1968). Used by permission.

community in the Hague. After several years as chaplain, however, he was dismissed due to pressure from the English authorities. The English officials also prevented him from obtaining a professorship at the University of Leyden. Fortunately, Ames was later appointed to a chair at the new University of Franeker in Friesland, where he remained for ten years.

During his years in Holland, Ames became involved in a lively dispute with the Arminians, or Remonstrants. Jacobus Arminius (1560–1609), an important Dutch theologian who opposed the strict Calvinist doctrine of predestination and advocated religious toleration, attacked the predestinarian position of Ames's revered teacher, William Perkins. Ames became well known through his tracts defending the orthodox Calvinist position against the Arminians. As a result, he was asked to be a consultant to the moderator of the Synod of Dort, 1618–19. Though Ames strongly asserted the priority of grace, he gave a greater place to human participation in the process of salvation than did his rigidly orthodox Dutch colleagues.

While teaching at the University of Franeker, Ames was a productive scholar in spite of some strained relations with other members of the faculty. Ames and his second wife (his first wife had died shortly after their marriage) carried on a lively correspondence with English friends who had emigrated to New England. In 1630 he wrote to John Winthrop, shortly after Winthrop's arrival in the Massachusetts Bay Colony, that he longed to join them. Unfortunately, his desire was never realized. As Cotton Mather wrote, he "was upon the wing for this American desert, but God took him to the heavenly Canaan."

After moving to Rotterdam to be co-pastor of an Independent congregation there, in October 1633 he died from exposure after the Maas River flooded the lower level of the house in which he and his wife were living. His wife eventually did emigrate to New England, settling in Salem in 1637.

Although William Ames the man never made it to New England, his thought was very influential in early America. When his library was brought over, it became an important part of the collection of the new Harvard College, influencing the minds of many New England clergy.

Two works by William Ames are of particular importance: Medulla Theologica *(*The Marrow of Theology*) and a book on Christian ethics called* De Conscientia *(*Concerning Conscience*).* The Marrow *was originally written for the children in an Amsterdam family whom Ames was tutoring in Leyden. It was not intended as an erudite treatise, but as a handy compendium summarizing the chief matters of Christian faith and life. It is divided into two major books with many chapters filled with numerous brief subsections. The style is simple, direct, and logical. His* *method and style reflect the influence of William Perkins and the work of a French Reformed philosopher, Petrus Ramus (1515–72), who was the creator of a new logic.*

For Ames, theology was not a speculative but a practical science: "Theology is the doctrine or teaching of living to God." It involves not only the head but also the heart. The study of theology should lead to transformed lives, demonstrating to human beings how "to live sober, upright, and godly lives in the world." Theology is divided into faith and observance. Both are necessary to right religion, but faith as "the resting of the heart on God, the author of life and eternal salvation," is the foundation of observance. Ames's work contains no simple moralism.

The sections of The Marrow of Theology *concerned with the doctrines of Scripture, covenant, church, ministry, and sacraments highlight the covenant of grace that Ames compares with the old covenant, sometimes called the covenant of works. According to Ames, the covenant of grace is the principal doctrine of Scripture. It is found in Genesis 3, with the promise that the seed of Eve, interpreted as Christ, will overcome sin and bring redemption. It is an unconditional covenant that God initiates, whereas the old covenant is a reciprocal one between partners on the same level. The covenant of grace determined Ames's view of redemption, the church, and the sacraments. The church is a community that has responded affirmatively to God's covenant of grace and whose members live in covenant with one another. The sacraments—the Baptism and the Eucharist—are signs and seals of the covenant of grace with the community and with each individual member.*

Although Ames grounded his concern for the covenant of grace in the Reformed tradition, he elaborated on it extensively. His views greatly influenced the covenantal theology and ecclesiology of New England Congregationalism as well as the later Reformed theology in the Netherlands.

Many years later, Douglas Horton, a leader in the Congregational Christian Churches and a major force in the shaping of the United Church of Christ, sparked renewed interest in Ames in the mid-twentieth century.[1]

• • •

XXIV. The Application of Christ

So much for redemption; we now consider its application.

1. Application is the making effectual, in certain men, of all those things which Christ has done and does as mediator.

2. This application, if specially designated, is attributed to the Holy Spirit. 1 Cor. 12:13, *By one Spirit we are all baptized into one body.* But it depends, first, upon the Father's decree and donation by which he has given Christ certain men to be redeemed and saved, John 6:39, *This is the will of my Father, that of those he hast given me I should lose nothing,* for those and only those whom the Father has given to Christ come to him, John 6:37. Second, upon the intention of Christ whereby he has made satisfaction for the good of those who have been destined for him by the Father. John 17:9, 11, 12, 19, *I pray for those whom thou hast given me because they are yours.* Third, upon the acceptance of the Father, or his ratification of the satisfaction given for the reconciliation and salvation of those persons. 2 Cor. 5:19, *God was in Christ reconciling the world to himself, not imputing their sins to them.*

3. The agreement between God and Christ was a kind of advance application of our redemption and deliverance of us to our surety and our surety to us. Upon that latter redemption, to be completed in us, it has the effect of a kind of an efficacious example; the former is a representation of the latter and the latter is brought into being by the former.

4. Thus our deliverance from sin and death was not only determined by the decree of God but also granted and communicated to Christ and to us in him before it was known by us. Rom. 5:10, 11, *We have been reconciled to God by the death of his Son . . . through whom we have now received a reconciliation.*

5. Both the Father and the Son are declared to send the Spirit to perform this application. John 14:16 and 16:7, *The Father shall give you an advocate . . . I will send him to you.*

6. Hence every good gift and every perfect good is said to come down from the Father from above, Jas. 1:17. All saving things are said to be communicated to us *In Christ,* as in the head, *Because of Christ,* as obtained by his merit, and *Through Christ*, as the one through whom they are effectually applied, Eph. 1:3, 5, 11.

7. Therefore, the application is the end result of the obtaining. Since the end is intended by God the Father and Christ the obtaining, as the means to that end, has a firm connection with it. If the redemption of Christ were of uncertain outcome, the Father would have appointed the Son to death and the Son would have undergone it without any certainty whether any would be saved by it or not, and all the fruit of this mystery would depend upon the free will of men.

8. The application plainly has the same latitude as redemption itself, i.e., redemption applies to all those and only to those for whom it was obtained by the intention of Christ and the Father. Yet because of them the same temporal benefits of Christ overflow also to others.

9. As for the intention of application, it is rightly said that Christ made satisfaction only for those whom he saved, though in regard to the sufficiency in the mediation of Christ it may also rightly be said that Christ made satisfaction for each and all. Because these counsels of God are hidden to us, it is the part of charity to judge well of every one, although we may not say of all collectively that Christ equally pleads the cause of each before God.

10. The application by which God fulfills with greatest firmness what was contained in a covenant formerly made and broken is called in the Scriptures the *New covenant*, Heb. 8:8, 10; *A covenant of life, salvation, and grace*, Rom. 4:16; Gal. 3:18. In the same sense it is also called the *Gospel*, Rom. 1:16; *The good word of God*, Heb, 6:5; *A faithful saying and worthy of all acceptation*, 1 Tim. 1:15; *A good doctrine*, 1 Tim. 4:6; *The word of life*, Phil. 2:16; *The word of reconciliation*, 2 Cor. 5:19; *The gospel of peace*, Eph. 2:17 and 6:15; *The gospel of salvation. The word of truth*, Eph. 1:13, *The arm of God*, Isa. 53:1; *The fragrance of life to life*, 2 Cor. 2:16.

11. It is called a covenant because it is a firm promise. In the Scriptures every firm determination, even though pertaining to lifeless things, is called a covenant. Jer. 33:20, 25, *My covenant with the day and my covenant with the night. . . . If my covenant be not with day and night, if I appoint not the statutes of heaven and earth.*

12. Yet because it is a free gift and confirmed by the death of the giver, it is more properly called a testament, not a covenant, Heb. 9:16. This sense is not found in a firm determination, which is not so properly called a testament as a covenant.

13. The new covenant differs from the old in many ways. First, in kind, for the old was a covenant of friendship, so to speak, between the creator and the creature, but this is a covenant of reconciliation between enemies.

14. Second, in the action, for in the former there was an agreement of two parties, God and man, but in the new only God covenants. For man being dead in sin has no ability to make a spiritual covenant with God. But if two parties are necessary in the strict sense of a covenant, then God is a party assuming and constituting and man is a party assumed.

15. Third, it differs in the object, for the old was extended to all men, but the new belongs in a special way only to certain men. Although from the human point of view it is often offered indiscriminately, by its nature it belongs and with special propriety is directed to those whom God intended, those who are called sons and heirs of the promise and salvation, Gen. 15; Acts 2:39 and 3:25; Rom. 4:16, 13 and 9:7, 8; Gal. 3:21, 29.

16. Fourth, in principle or in the moving cause, for in the old covenant God expressed his wise and just counsel in the form of sovereignty—but in

the new there is only mercy. A form of grace was shown in the old by the fixing of a reward for obedience, but it was not truly directed by grace. The new covenant, therefore (and not the old one), was complete, that is, it actually led man to happiness.

17. Fifth, in its basis, for the old was founded on the ability of man himself, but the new on Christ Jesus.

18. Sixth, in the matter or the goods promised, for in the old God promised only life but in this he promises righteousness and all the means of life. Man being dead, a restoration was necessary, not the continuance or perfection of life.

19. Seventh, in the conditions, for the old required perfect obedience of works to be performed by man of his own strength prior to the carrying out of the promise, which would then be in the form of a reward. But the present covenant requires no properly called or prior condition, but only a following or intermediate condition (and that to be given by grace as a means to grace), which is the proper nature of faith.

20. Eighth, in the effect, for the old teaches and shows what is righteous, but the new bestows righteousness in itself. In the old there was a dead letter which was death to a sinner, but in the new there is a quickening spirit.

21. Therefore, the former never wrought salvation to any man, neither could it bring anything to any sinner except death. But the present covenant does not in itself bring death or condemnation to any, but brings assured salvation to all those by whom it is received.

22. Ninth, in duration, for the old is antiquated for those who are partakers of the new. The present covenant is everlasting, both in its own duration, since it admits of no end or change in substance, and in its application, for the grace of this covenant continues forever with those who are once truly in it.

• • •

XXXI. The Church Mystically Considered

So much for the application of redemption considered in itself. Now we take up the matter of the subject to which and the way in which it is applied.

1. The subject is the church. Eph. 5:25–27, *Christ loved the church and gave himself for her, that he might sanctify her, being purified by him with the washing of water through the word, that he might make her glorious to himself, that is, a church without spot or wrinkle or any such thing, but rather holy and blameless.* Therefore, election, redemption, vocation, jus-

tification, adoption, sanctification, and glorification properly pertain to the same subject, i.e., to the individual men who make up the church. John 17:9–10, *Those whom thou hast given me, for they are thine*; Rom. 8:29, 30. *For those whom he foreknew he also predestined.*

2. The church is both the subject and an effect of redemption. For it is not first actually a church and later joined in union and communion with Christ; it is the church of Christ because it is united to Christ.

3. And this is the reason why we can neither explain nor understand the nature of the church unless we first perceive and explain the things which have to do with the application of Christ.

4. The elect, before they are grafted into Christ, are in themselves not of the church except in terms of that potentiality which in its own time will surely become actual because of God's intention and transaction with Christ. This remote potentiality in which all men are involved will certainly be made actual for the elect by God's determination.

5. Therefore, the orthodox who define the church as a company of the elect mean either those who are called according to election or the church not only as it exists now but also as it will exist hereafter.

6. The church is first of all constituted by calling, whence both its name and definition.

7. The church is indeed the company of men who are called. 1 Cor. 1:24 and 10:32, *Those who are called, both Jews and Greeks . . . to Jews, to Greeks, and to the church of God.* Because the end of calling is faith and the work of faith is a grafting into Christ, and this union brings with it communion with Christ, the church can be defined at once as a company of believers, a company of those who are in Christ, and a company of those who have communion with him.

8. Faith looks to Christ and through Christ to God; likewise the church which exists by faith looks to Christ as its head and through Christ to God. Therefore, the church is called the *Body of Christ*, Col. 1:24; the *Church of God*, 1 Cor. 10:32; the *Kingdom of Christ*, Col. 1:13; and the *Kingdom of God*, Rom. 14:17.

9. It is called a Company because it consists of a multitude joined in fellowship or a community of many (not a single person who is called), thus Eph. 4:16 where it is named a *Body joined and made up of diverse members*. Hence it is often called in Scripture a *House, family, city, kingdom,* or *flock*.

10. This company is limited to men because the good angels, although in a way they belong to the church because of their union with Christ and the saving grace communicated by him, are not the same as the members of the redeemed church.

11. The form or constituting cause of this church must be something found alike in all those who are called. This can only be a relationship, and the only relationship which has this power is that which comes from a primary and intimate affection toward Christ. In man this comes only by faith. Faith, therefore, is the form of the church.

12. Inasmuch as faith is in each believer individually it is the form of those that are called. But seen collectively in all, faith is the form of the company of those that are called, or the church.

13. The same believing men, on the one hand, are individuals called by God; on the other, they are collectively the company which is the church of God.

14. Therefore, all promises of God containing essential blessings which are made to the church in Scripture belong to each believer.

15. The relationship is so intimate that not only is Christ the church's and the church Christ's, Song of Sol. 2:16, but Christ is in the church and the church in him, John 15:4; 1 John 3:24. Therefore, the church is mystically called *Christ*, 1 Cor. 12:12, and the *Fullness of Christ*, Eph. 1:23.

16. The church is metaphorically called the bride and Christ the bridegroom; the church a city and Christ the king; the church a house and Christ the householder; the church the branches and Christ the vine; and finally the church a body and Christ the head.

17. But these comparisons signify not only the union and communion between Christ and the church but also the relation showing Christ to be the beginning of all honor, life, power, and perfection in the church.

18. This church is mystically one, not in a generic sense, but as a unique species or individual—for it has no species in the true sense.

19. It can, therefore, be called catholic, not as catholic signifies καθ' ὅλον, a genus of something general, but as it describes something uniquely universal (as when we speak of the world). This is so because it embraces believers of all nations, of all places, and of all times.

20. No part of the church can truly be called catholic unless it professes the faith of the catholic church. Thus the ancient authorities called not only that part of the church at Rome catholic but other churches as well. Our church at Franeker may rightly be called catholic since it professes the faith which belongs to the catholic church.

21. The church is divided according to the degree of communion it has with Christ. In this sense it is called either militant or triumphant.

22. The church militant is that which knows only of a communion begun and so still struggles with enemies in the battlefield of this world. 1 Cor. 13:9, 12, *We know in part and prophesy in part. For we see through a glass darkly*; 2 Cor. 10:4, *The weapons of our warfare*; Eph. 6:12, 13, *We wrestle. . . . Therefore take the whole armor of God.*

23. The church triumphant is that which is already perfected. Eph, 4:13, *Until we all come . . . to a perfect man, to the measure of the full stature of Christ*; 1 Cor. 15:46, *Afterwards comes that which is perfect.*

24. The militant church is both invisible and visible (that is, to outward sight or sense).

25. This distinction is not a division of genus into species, as if there were one church visible and another invisible, or of the whole into the members, as if one part of the church were visible and another invisible. It relates to phases of the same subject: Invisibility is a condition or mode of the church having to do with its essential and internal form; visibility is a condition or mode of the church having to do with its accidental or outward form.

26. The essential form is invisible both because it is a relation which cannot be perceived by the senses and also because it is spiritual, and so farther removed from sense perception than many other relations.

27. The accidental form is visible because it is an outward profession of inward faith, easily perceived by sense.

28. The visible profession is the manifest communion of the saints which they have with Christ and among themselves.

29. Their acts of the communion with Christ are those by which they present themselves to God in Christ to receive his blessings and to glorify him for those blessings.

30. Their acts of communion among themselves are all those in which they strive to do good to each other. These acts are especially those which directly further their communion with God in Christ.

31. Many acts of this kind are to be performed towards those who are not yet members of the church, for they ought to be judged as belonging to it potentially.

32. The church visible in itself, in comparative relation to others, is divided into the church hidden and manifest.

33. The manifest church is found where a greater number of saints exist and profession is freer and more public.

34. The hidden church is found where the number is fewer and profession less open. This is likely to occur in time of heresies, persecutions, or godless morality.

35. In the same way, the church is more pure or less pure as profession is more or less perfect.

36. Profession depends not only upon confession and the preaching of the word, but also upon the receiving of it and devout obedience to it.

37. Although the church is subject to changes of this kind and may relinquish any part of the world, yet from its gathering it never has totally failed nor shall it fail to the end of the world.

38. For Christ must always have his kingdom in the midst of his enemies until he makes his enemies his footstool.

39. The church never wholly ceases to be visible. Although sometimes there is scarcely a church pure enough to offer the same pure worship at all points, yet the church is still somehow visible in the very midst of the impurity of worship and profession.

XXXII. The Church Instituted

1. The church living upon earth, though it is not wholly visible, is visible in its parts both individually in its single members and collectively in its companies or congregations.

2. The first visibility is in the personal profession of men. This does not make a visible church, except as it exists in these particular members, i.e., it makes the church's members visible; the church itself, in its integral state, does not become visible in the same place. Acts 19:1, *Paul . . . came to Ephesus where he found certain disciples.*

3. That visibility which is in companies or distinct congregations not only makes a visible church, but, so far as outward form is concerned, also makes as many visible churches as there are distinct congregations. Rev. 1:4, *The seven churches*; 2 Cor. 8:1, 19, *The churches of Macedonia. All the churches.*

4. These congregations are, so to speak, similar parts of the catholic church and partake both of its name and nature.

5. Therefore a particular church, in respect of the nature it has in common with all particular churches, is a species of the church as a genus; but in respect of the catholic church, which has the nature [*ratio*] of a whole, it is a member made up of various individual members gathered together; and in respect of these members it is also a whole.

6. Such a congregation or particular church is a society of believers joined together in a special bond for the continual exercise of the communion of saints among themselves.

7. It is a society of believers because the same thing makes a church visible in profession which in its inward and real nature makes it a mystical church, namely, faith.

8. Because true faith has holiness joined with it, which it keeps effectual, Acts 15:9, and the profession of true faith cannot be separated from the profession of holiness, the church is variously but with the same meaning called a society of believers and a society of saints. Eph. 1:1, *To the saints which are at Ephesus and faithful in Jesus Christ*; 1 Cor. 1:2 compared with 2 Cor. 1:1; Rom. 1:7; and Col. 1:2.

9. Hence visible and particular churches are rightly said to be in God the Father and in the Lord Jesus Christ because of the faith which they profess, 1 Thess. 1:1; 2 Thess. 1:1.

10. Doubtless there is no particular church of this sort in which profession of the true faith is made but there are also to be found in it some true believers.

11. Those who are only believers by profession, while they remain in that society, are members of that church, as they are of the catholic church so far as outward status is concerned. In inward or essential status, they do not belong. 1 John 2:19, *They went out from us, but they were not of us.*

12. The children of those believers who are in the church are to be counted with the believers as members of the church, 1 Cor. 7:14, *Your children are holy.* For they are partakers with their parents of the same covenant and profession.

13. Yet children are not such perfect members of the church that they can exercise acts of communion or be admitted to all its privileges unless there is first a growth of faith. But they are not to be excluded from the privileges which pertain to the beginning of faith and entrance into the church.

14.Believers do not make a particular church, even though by chance many may meet and live together in the same place, unless they are joined together by a special bond among themselves. Otherwise, any one church would often be dissolved into many, and many also merged into one.

15. This bond is a covenant, expressed or implicit, by which believers bind themselves individually to perform all those duties toward God and toward one another which relate to the purpose [*ratio*] of the church and its edification.

16. Hence it is that in the Old Testament we very often read of the renewing of the covenant whenever any true reformation of the church is present.

17. Therefore, no one is rightly admitted into the church except on confession of faith and promise of obedience.

18. This joining together by covenant makes a church only as it looks toward the exercising of the communion of saints. For the same believing men may join themselves in covenant to make a city or some civil society when their immediate concern is for the common civil good. But they cannot make a church except as in its constitution they intend holy communion with God among themselves.

19. The same men may make a city or political society and not a church; or a church and not a city; or both a church and a city.

20. Therefore, those meetings that are formally ecclesiastical are said to be held in the name of the Lord, Matt. 18:20; 1 Cor. 5:4.

21. No sudden coming together and exercise of holy communion suffices to make a church unless there is also that continuity, at least in intention, which gives the body and its members a certain spiritual polity.

22. The church is instituted by God and by Christ. Heb. 3:3, 4, *He that built the house . . . For every house is built by someone*. In this sense it differs from the mystical church where the gathering is not prescribed to men but effected directly by divine operation. The gathering of an instituted church, however, is so effected by God that his command and man's duty and labor come first. Heb. 10:25, *Not forsaking the assembling of ourselves together.*

23. It is instituted by God and Christ alone because men have no power in themselves to institute or frame a church for Christ; neither is any such power committed to them by the revealed will of God. Their greatest honor is that they are servants in the house of God, Heb. 3:5.

24. Man, therefore, does not have power either to take away any of those things which Christ has given his church or to add things of like kind. Yet in every way he can and ought to make certain that the things which Christ has ordained are furthered and strengthened.

25. Christ has so instituted the church that it always depends upon him as the head—considered without Christ it is not a complete body.

26. Therefore, the church may not properly make new laws for itself for instituting new things. It ought to take care only to find out the will of Christ clearly and observe his ordinances decently and with order, with greatest edification resulting.

27. Since the ordinances of Christ always have God's blessing joined with them, various promises of God are made to the church about the presence of Christ, Matt. 18:20; 1 Cor, 5:4. So in a special way he is said to live and walk in the churches, Rev. 2:1; Isa. 31:9. And promises are made about the presence of the Holy Spirit, Isa. 59:21. Thus an ampler and surer blessing of God may be expected in the instituted church of God than is found in any solitary life.

28. Therefore, those who have opportunity to join the church and neglect it most grievously sin against God because of his ordinance, and also against their own souls because of the blessing joined to it. And if they obstinately persist in their carelessness, whatever they otherwise profess, they can scarcely be counted believers truly seeking the kingdom of God.

29. The profession of the true faith is the most essential mark of the church.

30. This profession may in some congregations precede the solemn preaching of the word and the administration of the sacraments.

XXXIII. The Extraordinary Ministers of the Church

1. So much for the subject of the application of redemption; now we consider the way of application.

2. The way of application consists of those means whereby the Spirit bestows Christ and all his benefits on us for our salvation.

3. The Spirit itself supplies all saving things to us internally, most intimately, and in its own way directly. No external means properly have the power to communicate grace to us in any real sense. Therefore, although external means naturally concur and operate in the preparation of man to receive grace, yet in themselves they do not properly confer grace. It is the Spirit that works together with them. 1 Cor. 3:7, *Neither is he that plants anything nor he that waters, but God who gives power to increase.*

4. The two principal means of this sort are the ministry and the holy signs (or symbols), to which some ecclesiastical discipline must be added.

5. The ministry is an ecclesiastical function in which a man, being singled out, is responsible by special right for holy things. 2 Cor. 4:1, *We have this ministry, having obtained mercy;* 1 Cor. 4:1, *Let a man account us as ministers of Christ and stewards of the mysteries of God.*

6. It is called the ministry because the power which is committed to the men of the church is a power of acting only by command of Christ and out of obedience to him alone, 1 Cor. 4:1, 2.

7. The spiritual or regal power of self-rule whereby one works in freedom and by his own choice does not belong to men, but to Christ alone.

8. Therefore, a minister of the church is bound to execute his office himself, as one who does not have power to appoint anyone in his place—for that would be an action of command, not of obedience.

9. The permanent minister of many churches where vicars must serve is not of God's ordaining, but of man's ambition and presumption.

10. Ministerial power is not absolute but relative, i.e., it is not an absolute power to do anything but consists of a right whereby one has due power to do lawfully what he could not do before. Therefore, it is called a power of right.

11. But it is a special right because it refers to special duties unlawful for others; and it undertakes certain common duties in a certain special way.

12. The right of ministry depends upon calling. Heb. 5:4, *No one takes this honor to himself except he that is called of God as was Aaron.*

13. Calling is an action which commits an office to someone with authority to minister.

14. Therefore, it is clearly ridiculous to ordain the calling of ministers but not give them power to preach the word without further permission.

15. A necessary part of calling is fitness for the ministry.

16. Those who are altogether unfit to do the work of the ministry, if they are called to it by men, are ministers of men and not of God. Hos. 4:6, *Because you have despised knowledge, I will also despise you so that you shall not be a priest to me*.

17. Fitness arises from a fit measure of gifts and a ready will to undertake and execute the office.

18. The ministry produces a third state of the church. As by faith it has its essential state and by gathering its integral state, so by the ministry it has a certain organic state. It is now made fit to do all the works which pertain to the good of the whole.

19. The course and direction of these operations is ecclesiastical polity.

20. The form of this polity is altogether monarchical in respect to Christ as the king and the head. But in respect to the visible system of administration, it is of a mixed nature: partly aristocratic, so to speak, and partly democratic.

21. Therefore, in the lawful ministry of the church, hierarchy or sacred rule has no place, but rather hieroduly or sacred service.

22. One minister is not subject to the power of another in his responsibility but each one depends directly upon Christ. So it is that the angels who are inferior in office to others are directly subject to God and not to other angels.

23. This ministry is either extraordinary or ordinary.

24. An extraordinary ministry is one which has a certain higher and more perfect direction than can be attained through ordinary means.

25. Such ministers always have extraordinary gifts and assistance so that they minister without error.

26. The authority of an extraordinary minister is given actually neither by man nor through man but by God alone through Jesus Christ and the Holy Spirit, Gal. 1:1.

27. Therefore, the calling to such a ministry is direct.

28. Yet an extraordinary calling is not so direct as to exclude all ministry of men, as appears in the calling of Elisha and Matthias. It excludes only the ministry which lacks infallible direction.

29. Such an extraordinary ministry was surely necessary for the church because that will of God to which living well to God is directed could not be discovered by human industry or any ordinary means used in other arts and sciences. But it required men who were stirred up and sent by God and to whom he manifested his will in order that they might be in the place of God himself for us. Exod. 4:15, 16, *And you be to him instead of God*.

30. God revealed his will to those extraordinary ministers in several ways. First, by direct speech, Rev. 1:10, to which was often added the

appearing and speaking of an angel or of Christ himself, such as the angel of the covenant. Second, by a vision in which the form of things to be declared was shown to the eyes of the vigilant along with the word. Third, by dreams through which like proposals were imparted to the minds of men asleep. Fourth, sometimes by a special familiarity, mouth to mouth, so to speak, without riddles. Num. 12:6–8, *If there be a prophet among you, I will make myself, the Lord, known to him in a vision and will speak to him in a dream. It is not so with my servant Moses. . . . With him I speak mouth to mouth and not in dark speeches; and the form of the Lord he beholds.*

31. The mode of this revelation was so powerful that it often took men into ecstasy: They were so caught up above themselves that they knew nothing but what was proposed, and not even that in all its circumstances, 2 Cor. 13:3, 4.

32. Yet it is certain that the divine truth of such revelation is always confirmed and sealed in a special way to those to whom it is revealed. Therefore, it does not need further confirmation. Gal. 1:17; 2:6, *Neither did I return to those who were apostles before me. . . . They who were of repute made no difference to me.* Sometimes, however, miracles are added for more abundant confirmation, Judg. 6:36–38.

33. This extraordinary ministry is either for the first instituting of a church, or for the special and extraordinary conservation of a church, or for the extraordinary restoring of a church which has collapsed.

34. The ministry of instituting a church is always accompanied by a testimony of miracles. Heb. 2:3, 4, *Which at first began to be spoken. . . . God also bearing witness with signs and wonders and many miracles and gifts of the Holy Spirit distributed according to his will.*

35. Yet miracles do not provide testimony to any doctrine in the sense that they immediately produce faith. For doctrine which does not agree with the known will of God ought not to be accepted, although it might seem to be confirmed with miracles. Deut. 13:1–3, *Although that sign or wonder come to pass which he foretold you, saying, "Let us go follow other Gods". . . do not harken to the words of that prophet; Gal. 1:8, Though we or an angel from heaven preach to you another gospel besides that which we have preached. . . . let him be accursed.*

36. The ministry of conserving and restoring a church although extraordinary and usually confirmed by miracles does not always or necessarily require a testimony of miracles. This appears in many places in the Old Testament and in John the Baptist.

37. The prophets, apostles, and evangelists were extraordinary ministers.

38. Wyclif, Luther, Zwingli, and the others who were the first restorers of the gospel were not, strictly speaking, extraordinary ministers.

39. Yet they are not wrongly called extraordinary by some. First, because they performed something similar to what was done by the extraordinary ministers of old. Second, because as occasion required they received gifts of special magnitude from God. This may also be affirmed of many of the more famous martyrs. Third, because they necessarily attempted some things out of the common course, since the order of the time was disturbed and decayed.

40. It is, therefore, ridiculous to require miracles of those men to confirm the doctrine which they propounded, when such an attestation was not necessary even among the extraordinary ministers.

• • •

XXXV. Ordinary Ministers and Their Office in Preaching

1. The ordinary ministry is that which receives all of its direction from the will of God revealed in the Scriptures and from those means which God has appointed in the church for its continual edification.

2. They are called ordinary because it is according to the order established by God that they may be and usually are called to minister.

3. In their service they have the will of God revealed earlier through the extraordinary ministers as a fixed rule; therefore, they ought not to propose or do anything in the church which is not prescribed to them in the Scriptures.

4. They depend upon the extraordinary ministers and are, so to speak, their successors. Although in manner and degree extraordinary ministers have no successors, ordinary ministers in their essential service perform the same office toward the church as the former once did.

5. The right to this ministry is regularly accorded by men and for that reason the calling of an ordinary minister is indirect.

6. But this is to be understood in the sense that the authority for administering divine things is directly communicated from God to all lawful ministers, though the appointing of persons upon whom the authority is to be bestowed is done by the church.

7. But the church cannot confer the necessary gifts for this ministry, and cannot prescribe for God those upon whom he should confer them. Therefore, the church can only choose those who appear to it in advance to be suitable. For ordinary ministers, unlike extraordinary ministers, are not made fit by their very calling when they were unfit before.

8. Therefore, in an ordinary calling it is required that a lawful examination precede the calling itself. 1 Tim. 3:10, *Let them be first tried then let them minister if they be blameless.*

9. The purpose of the ordinary ministry is to preserve, propagate, and renew the church through regular means.

10. There are two parts in this ministry: First, a minister must do those things which he does for the people in the name of God; second, he must do those things which he does for God in the name of the people.

11. Here the preaching of the word is of utmost importance, and so it has always been of continuous use in the church.

12. The duty of an ordinary preacher is to set forth the will of God out of the word for the edification of the hearers. 1 Tim. 1:5, *The end of preaching, παραγελλία, is love out of a pure heart, a good conscience, and faith unfeigned.*

13. Since first an earnest zeal for the church's edification is required, a man cannot be a fit preacher unless he has *Set his heart to study the law of the Lord and to do it, and to teach his statutes and ordinances in Israel*, Ezra 7:10. For one who teaches another ought before and while he teaches to teach himself, Rom. 2:21. Otherwise he is not prepared to edify the church.

14. This duty is to be performed not only for all hearers in common but also specifically for each status and age—for old men, young men, servants (Titus 2 and 3), teachers (2 Peter 1:12), yea, for each individual. 1 Thess. 2:11, *We exhorted, comforted, and charged each one of you not only publicly but privately*; Acts 20:20, *Publicly and from house to house*.

15. He ought always to have this aim of edification so clearly before his eyes as to take great care not to *Turn aside to vain discussion* (1 Tim. 1:6), *Striving about words* (2 Tim. 2:14), *Unprofitable controversies or speculations of what is falsely called knowledge* (1 Tim. 6:20). *He should hold fast to the faithful word which leads to teaching* (Titus 1:9), *And which cannot be condemned* (Titus 2:8).

16. Since to this end the will of God is to be set forth out of the word, no one is fit for the ministry who is not greatly concerned with the Holy Scriptures, even beyond ordinary believers, so that he might be said, with Apollos, to be mighty in the Scriptures, Acts 18:24. He must not put his trust in notes and commentaries.

17. In order that the will of God may be set forth fruitfully for edification two things are necessary: First, the things contained in the text must be stated; second, they must be applied to the consciences of the hearers as their condition seems to require. 1 Tim. 6:17, *Charge those that are rich in this world that they be not highminded or trust in uncertain riches.*

18. Ministers impose upon their hearers and altogether forget themselves when they propound a certain text in the beginning as the start of the sermon and then speak many things about or simply by occasion of the text but for the most part draw nothing out of the text itself.

19. In setting forth the truth in the text the minister should first explain it and then indicate the good which follows from it. The first part is concerned with doctrines and proofs; the latter with application or derivation of profit from the doctrines. 2 Tim. 3:16, *All the Scripture . . . is profitable for doctrine, for reproof, for correction, and instruction in righteousness.*

20. Those who invert and confuse these parts make it difficult for their hearers to remember and stand in the way of their edification. Their hearers cannot commit the chief heads of the sermon to memory so that they may afterwards repeat it privately in their families; and when this cannot be done, the greatest part of the fruit, which would otherwise be made available to the church of God through sermons, is lost.

21. A doctrine is a theological principle either in the express words of Scripture or deriving from them as a direct consequence.

22. A doctrine rightly must first be discovered and then discussed.

23. The discovery is made by a logical analysis in which rhetoric and grammar are utilized.

24. Analysis means principally observing the scope or purpose of the text and, by the art of logic, the means by which it is attained.

25. Confirmation must be added by interpreting the doubtful parts in the analysis. Manifest parts, clear in themselves, neither require nor permit needless interpretation.

26. The discussion of a doctrine consists partly in proofs, if it be questioned by the hearers (it is foolish to go to any length to confirm what all acknowledge), and partly in illustration of the things already well proved.

27. Proofs ought to be sought from the clearer testimonies of Scripture, with reasons being added where the nature of the thing will allow. But here the treatment must be adapted to the profit of the hearers.

28. Illustrations may be drawn from almost anywhere they may be found but the contrasting and comparing themes are the most important.

29. Each doctrine when sufficiently explained should immediately be applied to its use. Upon this part, unless there is some special reason against it, great insistence must be made, since this contains the conclusion and the good of the first part, and is closer to the chief purpose of the sermon, which is the edification of the hearers.

30. They sin, therefore, who stick to the naked finding and explanation of the truth, neglecting the use and practice in which religion and blessedness consist. Such preachers edify the conscience little or not at all.

31. Not all the doctrines which may be drawn out of the text are to be propounded or all the uses set forth but only those are to be selected which the circumstances of place, time, and person suggest as most necessary—and of these especially those which make for the stirring up or strengthening of the spirit of devotion.

32. They sin who do care little about what they say provided it may appear that they may have thought about and spoken many things. They do this frequently, forcing many things out of the text which are not in it and often borrowing for it from other places, bringing anything out of everything. The result is the ruin rather than the edification of the hearers, especially among the untutored.

33. Both doctrine and use ought to be structured, as far as possible, to have some connection between them and to manifest it. For the mind is not drawn from one thing to a different thing without loss; nor is there anything that helps the memory more than logical order.

34. A use is a theological principle deduced from a doctrine which shows the use, goodness, or end of it.

35. The logic of the deduction is to be explained, if it be not clear. To this should be joined a proof or illustration as the necessity of the hearers and the wisdom of the speaker suggests.

36. Use lies in the area of either of judgment or of practice, 2 Tim. 3:16.

37. In judgment it provides information and reformation of the mind.

38. Information is the proving of some truth.

39. Reformation is the refutation of some error.

40. Although every truth may be taught upon occasion, every error need not always come up for refutation. For heresies already buried are not to be dug up again just so that they may be refuted, nor wicked blasphemies glibly repeated. This troubles and offends, especially when all is declared, explained, and refuted in a solemn way.

41. Direction, needed in the practice of life, consists of instruction and correction.

42. Instruction is a setting forth of the life which ought to be followed.

43. Correction is a condemnation of the life which ought to be shunned.

44. After the declaration of a doctrine application should follow, and this is so like the derivation of uses that the two may often be made one.

45. To apply a doctrine to its use is to sharpen and make specially relevant some general truth with such effect that it may pierce the minds of those present with the stirring up of godly affections.

46. Men are to be pricked to the quick so that they feel individually what the Apostle said, namely, that the word of the Lord is a two-edged sword, piercing to the inward thoughts and affections and going through to the joining of bones and marrow. Preaching, therefore, ought not to be dead, but alive and effective so that an unbeliever coming into the congregation of believers should be affected and, as it were, transfixed by the very hearing of the word so that he might give glory to God. 1 Cor. 14:25, *The hidden things of his heart are disclosed; and so, falling down on his face, he will worship God and say that God is among you indeed.*

47. This application is either for an oppressed mind, in consolation, or one that is failing to follow up the good, or to avoid evil, in exhortation or admonition.

48. Consolation is the application of some point that either takes away or mitigates grief and oppressive fear.

49. In consolation, indications are profitably given to a man's conscience to assure him that he shares the benefits with which the minister comforts the conscience of believers. Thoughts to the contrary, which may arise in a pious and troubled mind, are dispelled and refuted.

50. Exhortation is the application of a point which begets, quickens, and excites some inward virtue or furthers the exercise of it.

51. In exhortation to virtue it is profitable to show the means which lead to the begetting of that virtue in us. But let each one be proved by places and examples from Scripture, or by reasons which have a firm foundation in Scripture.

52. Admonition is the application of a point to correct some viciousness.

53. In admonition, or exhortation against vices, remedies may be found from passages which are most likely to be effective against them.

54. The doing of all these things must have in it no show of human wisdom or mixture of carnal affections; it should manifest itself throughout as the demonstration of the Spirit. 1 Cor. 1:17; and 2:1, 4, 13, *Not with skill of speaking, lest the cross of Christ should have no effect. Not with excellence of speech or wisdom, not in persuading words of men's wisdom, but in spiritual and powerful demonstration. Not in words which man's wisdom teaches, but in that which the Holy Spirit teaches.* It is the word of the Spirit, the word of life, which is preached for the building up of faith in God. If anything be not fitly spoken or done to this end, it is as useless as hay and stubble, 1 Cor. 3:12.

55. Therefore, neither human testimonies, no matter what they be, nor stories known only to the learned ought to be mixed in, except on the rare occasions when urgent necessity or sure hope of good results seem to require it (and then the reason for so doing should be made clear). Much less should words or sentences in Latin, Greek, or Hebrew be used which the people do not understand.

56. The purity, perfection, and majesty of the word of God is violated when it is said to need the admixture of human words. And at the same time a disservice is done to hearers who get so accustomed to human flourishes that they often contract the disease of itching ears, begin to dislike the simplicity of the gospel, and will not endure sound teaching. 2 Tim. 4:3.

57. Consider Paul, who cites only a few, brief sayings of heathen poets, not naming the authors—and that incidentally and by the way—to convince the Gentiles to whom they were known and approved. His example

hardly supports those who "of necessity" or "to improve the sermon" frequently and purposely insert human testimonies, commending their authors with the same solemnity used in citing the names of the prophets. And such is done among Christians who only desire to hear Christ; the end result is only a show of learning.

58. Unnecessary and farfetched preambles and plausible words of orators ought not to be used. Nor should ministers indulge in digressions or excursions, for they smack of the human spirit, take time, and shut out other things more edifying.

59. If any introduction is used applying to the subject in hand, it should be either in announcing the text or applying it to use.

60. Speech and action should be completely spiritual, flowing from the very heart. They should show a man well versed in the Scriptures and in pious exercises, who has first persuaded himself and thoroughly settled in his own conscience those things to which he would persuade others, and in whom, finally, there is zeal, charity, mildness, freedom, and humility mixed with solemn authority.

61. Pronunciation must be natural, familiar, clear, and distinct so that it can be easily understood. It should fit the matter in such a way that the affections are moved. Gal. 4:20, *I wish now to be present with you and change my tone, for I am in doubt of you.*

62. There are two voices, among others, which are offensive. The first is heavy, slow, singing, drowsy in which not only the words are separated with a pause, as if by commas, but even the syllables in the same word, producing great hindrance to understanding.

63. The other voice which is most offensive in a sermon is hasty and swift, overwhelming the ears with so much speed that there is no distinct understanding of the subject.

64. Speech, pronunciation, and gestures which would be ridiculous in a senate, in courts of law, and the forum are the more to be avoided in a sermon.

65. The power of the Holy Spirit more clearly appears in the naked simplicity of words than in elegance and luster. Therefore, Paul calls himself ιδιώτης τῷ λόγῳ, unskilled in speaking, 2 Cor. 11:6. Yet if anyone has a certain outward forcefulness in speaking he ought to use it with genuine directness.

66. In proportion as affectation appears, effectiveness and authority are lost.

67. The sum of the matter is that nothing is to be allowed which does not contribute to the spiritual edification of the people, and nothing omitted by which we may surely reach that end.

68. A supplement to the sermon is prayer both before and after.

69. In the prayer before it, general matters ought to be set forth: the end and use of the word and of preaching, our wants, our unworthiness, and our duty, together with the gracious promises of God. All these should be brought to remembrance so that the minds of all will be stirred up humbly to seek and faithfully to observe the will of God.

70. In the prayer following, the giving of thanks should always be included and the chief heads of the sermon turned into petitions.

• • •

XXXVII. Ecclesiastical Discipline

Discipline is associated with the word and sacraments. In summary it has always been considered with them and, therefore, can be fitly treated in this place.

1. Holy discipline is an application of the will of God to persons through censure to guard against offenses or remove them from the church of God.

2. In the preaching of the word, the will of God is set forth and really applied to beget and increase faith and obedience. In the administration of the sacraments the will of God is applied to persons through the seals to confirm faith and obedience. In the exercise of discipline the will of God is also applied to persons in censure to remove the vices contrary to true faith and obedience.

3. Therefore, discipline is usually associated by the best theologians with the word and sacraments in the marks of the church. Although the relationship is not essential and reciprocal (nor is it in the case of the other two), yet it ought to appear in a full consideration of the church.

4. This discipline is ordained and prescribed by Christ himself, Matt. 16:19; 18:15–17. It is, therefore, plainly of divine right and may not be taken away, diminished, or changed by men at their pleasure.

5. Indeed, he sins against Christ, the author and ordainer, who does not do all he can to establish and promote this discipline in the churches of God.

6. It applies, without exception, to members of visible, instituted churches, Matt. 18:15; 1 Cor. 5:11; it does not apply to others, 1 Cor. 5:12. It pertains to all those, and only to those, who have the right to partake of the sacraments.

7. To such people it applies the will of God, i.e., those means of spiritual reformation which Christ alone has given to his churches, 2 Cor. 10:4. There-

fore, punishments and pains of body or purse have no place at all in ecclesiastical discipline.

8. Discipline has to do with sins and offenses in such people; it is a wholesome remedy for the wounds and diseases to which the sheep of Christ are subject, 1 Cor. 5:5.

9. It prevents and takes away offenses, effectually and personally applying the will of Christ, which attacks and abolishes them.

10. But because it effectually enforces obedience towards Christ, a great part of the kingship of Christ by which he visibly governs the church is placed, not without special reason, in this discipline by the best theologians.

11. The true reason why the discipline of Christ is solidly constituted and exercised with doctrine in so few churches is because most of those who would seem to know Christ and to hope in him refuse to receive the whole kingship of Christ and yield themselves completely to him.

12. As discipline is part of the kingship of Christ, so it is also part of the gospel. For it is the holy manner of promoting the gospel ordained by the gospel itself. Therefore, those who reject discipline accept neither the whole kingship of Christ nor the whole gospel.

13. Since every part of the kingship of Christ is necessary to us in its own way and especially that which effectually represses sin, men should not be well content in churches lacking discipline unless that public defect is made up by private watchcare over one another.

14. The parts of this discipline are brotherly correction and excommunication.

15. Discipline consists not only or even chiefly in the thunderbolt of excommunication and anathema, but primarily in Christian correction.

16. The proper end of reproof is not excommunication (although by chance that sometimes may happen) but the prevention of it, so that the sinner by timely repentance may be kept in the church.

17. The power of discipline (so far as the right to it is concerned) belongs to the whole church of which the offender is a member. Those who have the right to admit have the right to expel. The keeping or cutting off of members concerns the whole body equally, and is, therefore, to be carried out with the consent of the church, and not only with the church's permission but by its approval and determination.

18. The elders have the main role in the exercise and administration of discipline. This is not only in directing public action and pronouncing sentence but also in giving admonitions beforehand, making up for what they observe to be neglected by individuals.

• • •

XXXVIII. The Administration of the Covenant of Grace before the Coming of Christ

1. Although the free, saving covenant of God has been one and the same from the beginning, the manner of the application of Christ or the administration of the new covenant has not always been so. It has varied according to the times during which the church has been in process of being gathered.

2. In this variety there has always been a progression from the imperfect to the more perfect.

3. At first the mystery of the gospel was manifested in a general and obscure way and later more specifically and clearly.

4. The manner of administration of the covenant is twofold: One points to the Christ who will appear and the other to the Christ who has appeared.

5. The Old and New Testaments are reducible to these two primary heads. The Old promises Christ to come and the New testifies that he has come.

6. While Christ was still to appear, all things were more outward and carnal, afterwards more inward and spiritual. John 1:17, *The law was delivered by Moses; grace and truth came by Christ.*

7. The church then had a double aspect: first as an heir and second as a child. Gal. 4:1 ff., *So long as the heir is an infant he differs not at all from a servant, though he be lord of all.*

8. As an heir the church was free; as a child, in a certain way, not free, Gal. 4:1.

9. As an heir it was spiritual; as a child carnal and earthly, Heb. 9:10; Rom. 9:7.

10. As an heir it had the spirit of adoption, but as a child the spirit of fear and bondage. Rom. 8:15, *You have not received the spirit of bondage again to fear, but you have received the spirit of adoption.*

11. The manner of administration of the covenant, in respect to the coming of Christ, was one before Moses and another from Moses to Christ.

12. Before Moses the polity of the church was rude and loose, as it would be in its childhood. There were as many visible churches as there were families of godly people; the ministry was almost always an extraordinary one conducted by prophets. The masters of families and the firstborn had the right to administer certain holy things as ordinary ministers, according to the direction they received from the prophets.

13. And there was some difference of dispensation from Adam to Abraham from that of the time from Abraham to Moses.

14. From Adam to Abraham it should be noted, first, that redemption by Christ and the application of Christ was promised in general. It was to be carried out by the seed of the woman in order to banish the works of the

devil, or sin and death. Gen. 3:15; Rom. 16:20; 1 John 3:8, *The seed of the woman shall break the serpent's head. The God of peace will tread Satan under your feet shortly. The Son of God was manifested to dissolve the works of the devil.*

15. Second, calling was evident in the distinction between the seed of the woman and the seed of the devil, and between the sons of God and the sons of men, Gen. 6:2. Third, the way of justification was set forth by expiatory sacrifices offered and accepted for sins. Eph. 5:2, *Christ loved us and gave himself for us, an offering and sacrifice to God for a sweet-smelling savor.*

16. Fourth, adoption was indicated both by the title of sons, common to all the faithful at that time, and by the translation of Enoch into the heavenly inheritance, Gen. 5:24; Heb. 11:5.

17. Fifth, sanctification was expressly taught by the prophets and foreshadowed by typical oblations and rites of sacrifice, Jude 14; Rom. 12:1.

18. Sixth, glorification was publicly sealed by the example of Enoch and the saving of Noah and his family from the flood. 1 Peter 3:20, 21.

19. In this period the building and saving of the ark in the flood was an extraordinary sacrament, Heb. 11:7; 1 Peter 3:20, 21. There was no ordinary sacrament in those times, but in many sacrifices there was something like a sacrament, for those who sacrificed commonly partook of a holy banquet at a holy place with joy before God in their sacrifices, Exod. 18:12. This sealed to them in a certain way the grace of the covenant which is present in the sacraments.

20. From the time of Abraham the church chiefly consisted of his family and his posterity.

21. At that time the benefits of the new covenant were all more clearly and distinctly witnessed to than before.

22. First, election was set forth in the persons of Isaac and Jacob who were beloved before Ishmael and Esau, Rom. 9:11–13.

23. Second, redemption along with its application was majestically shown in the person and blessing of Melchizedek—also in the promise and covenant of blessing to come to all nations from the seed of Abraham.

24. Third, a calling came in the leading of Abraham from Ur of Chaldees to a certain new and heavenly country, Heb. 11:8–10.

25. Fourth, justification was illustrated by the express testimony of God that faith was reckoned to Abraham for righteousness, as the father and pattern of all who should believe. The sacrament of circumcision was also given, which was the seal of that righteousness.

26. Fifth, adoption was declared by giving God's name to Abraham and all the sons of the promises, and by assigning the inheritance to the sons of the promises, the family of the free woman through grace, Gal. 4:26, 28, 31.

27. Sixth, sanctification was prefigured by circumcism, which stood for the taking away and abolishing of the corruption of sin and the old man so that a new creature might come in their places, Col. 2:11; Deut. 30:6.

28. Seventh, glorification was pointed to in the blessing promised in the land of Canaan, which was a type of the heavenly country.

29. From the time of Moses to Christ, these same things were further adumbrated by extraordinary and ordinary means.

30. Redemption and its application were extraordinary. They were signified, first, in the deliverance from Egypt through the ministry of Moses, who was a type of Christ, Matt. 2:15, and by the entrance into the land of Canaan through the ministry of Joshua, another type of Christ. Second, in the brass serpent, by looking at which men who were about to die were restored to health, John 3:14; 12:32. Third, in the cloud which shielded the Israelites from all injuries from enemies and from the sky. They also had light provided day and night, along with a refreshing of their strength, 1 Cor. 10:2; Isa. 4:4–5. Fourth, in the passing through the Red Sea where a way was opened to the land of promise, their enemies being overwhelmed and destroyed, 1 Cor. 10:2. Fifth, in the manna from heaven and the water from the rock whence they received continual nourishment, so to speak, out of God's hand, 1 Cor. 10:3, 4; John 6:32, 33.

31. In the ordinary sense Christ and redemption were foreshadowed by the high priest, the altars and sacrifices for sins.

32. Justification was shown in many sacrifices and ablutions and in the sacrament of the Passover.

33. Adoption was shown in the dedication of the firstborn to God.

34. Sanctification was set forth in all the offerings and gifts as well as in the observances which had anything to do with cleanliness.

35. Glorification was shown in the inheritance of the promised land and the communion which they had with God in the holy of holies.

36. The church of the Jews instituted by Moses, in point of external coming together, was only one because the whole solemn communion prescribed at that time depended upon one temple and was exercised by public profession and rites.

37. The synagogues were not complete churches, for the total worship of God and the whole sacred communion prescribed at that time could not be exercised in them.

38. Therefore, the church of the Jews was a national church—though in some respect catholic or universal, inasmuch as the believing proselytes of every nation under heaven were bound to join themselves to that one church, Acts 2:5, 6, 8–11; 8:27.

39. The primary ministers were the priest of the family of Aaron in a continued line of succession, and to them were joined the other Levites, Num. 3:6–10.

40. Yet neither priests nor Levites were allowed to minister unless they were first examined, and passed the tests in body, age, and gifts of the mind.

41. The ecclesiastical discipline of that time was ceremonial to a large extent, but sufficient to keep pure all holy things of every kind.

XXXIX. The Administration of the Covenant from the Coming of Christ to the End of the World

1. The manner of administration of the covenant, now Christ has appeared, is twofold: the one lasting until the end of the world and the other at the end itself.

2. From the time of Christ to the end of the world there is an administration of one kind which is altogether new and is rightly called the New Testament.

3. It is of one kind without end or alteration because it is perfect; no other is to be expected to which it would give place as to the more perfect.

4. The testament is new in relation to what existed from the time of Moses and in relation to the promise made to the fathers. But it is new not in essence but in form. In the former circumstances the form of administration gave some evidence of the covenant of works, from which this testament is essentially different. Since the complete difference between the new covenant and the old appeared only in the administration which came after Christ, this administration is properly termed the covenant and testament which is new.

5. This differs also from the former administration in quality and quantity.

6. Its difference in quality is in clarity and freedom.

7. Clarity occurs, first in the more distinct expression than heretofore of the doctrine of grace and salvation through Christ and through faith in him (together with other kindred points of the doctrine). Second, it is expressed not in types and shadows, but in a most manifest fashion.

8. In both of these respects, Christ is said to have been set forth earlier under a veil but now to be offered with an open and unveiled face. 2 Cor. 3:12, *We use great evidence in speaking, being not like Moses who put a veil over his face so that the children of Israel could not see the end of that which was now taken away as unprofitable.*

9. Freedom comes, first, in doing away with government by law, or the

intermixture of the covenant of works, which held the ancient people in a certain bondage. The spirit of adoption, though never wholly denied to believers, is also most properly said to be communicated under the New Testament, in which the perfect state for believers most clearly shines forth. Gal. 4:4, 5, *After the fullness of time came, God sent forth his Son . . . that we might receive the adoption of sons*. Second, the yoke of ceremonial law is taken away in that it was a mortgage bond held against sinners, forbade the use of some things in their nature indifferent, commanded many burdensome observances of other things of the same nature, and veiled the truth itself with many carnal ceremonies. Col. 2:17, *Which are a shadow of things to come, but the body is of Christ.*

10. Those who force upon the Christian churches Jewish ceremonies or other similar religious and mystical ceremonies offend against the liberty which Christ has obtained for us. Divine ceremonies were not suppressed in order that human ones might supplant them. Nor is it likely that Christ would leave such mysteries to the will of men after his coming, when he permitted no such thing to his people before that. He might so easily have provided us religious and mystical ceremonies had he judged them necessary or profitable—that is, aside from the very few which he prescribed by name—or at least indicated in a last will to whom he granted such authority—but this he never did. Gal. 5:1, *Stand fast, therefore, in the liberty wherewith Christ has made you free and be not entangled with the yoke of bondage.*

11. In measure this administration differs from the former intensively and extensively.

12. It differs intensively, first, in that the application of the Spirit is more effectual and the gifts of the Spirit more perfect than they were ordinarily in the Old Testament. The old administration and the new are compared to each other as the letter and the Spirit, 2 Cor. 3:6. Second, the new administration produces a more spiritual life, 2 Cor. 3:18.

13. This administration differs extensively, first, in respect of place, because it is not confined to any one people as before, but is diffused through the whole world. It differs, second, in respect of time, since the duration of time before the consummation of the whole mystical church is not set. 2 Cor. 3:11; Eph. 4:13, *That which remains . . . until we all attain to . . . mature manhood, to the measure of the full stature of Christ.*

14. Since this new administration is so perfect, it follows that the communion of saints in the church instituted according to the New Testament should be most perfect.

15. Therefore, in every church of the New Testament the whole solemn and ordered worship of God and all his holy ordinances can and ought to be

observed in such wise that all the members of that church may find their communion in them at the same time.

16. It was once ordained of God, in the church of the Jews, that certain more solemn parts of divine worship should be celebrated in one place and others in other places. This is no longer true, for one particular church is ordained in which all holy offices are to be performed.

17. Therefore, all Christian churches together have one and the same right. One no more depends upon another than another upon it.

18. It is, therefore, fitting that a particular church should not consist of more members than may meet together in one place to hear the word of God, celebrate the sacraments, offer prayers, exercise discipline, and perform other duties of divine polity as one body.

19. In some larger cities there are more believers than can hold communion together. It is a gross error leading to all sorts of confusion not to distribute them into several churches, but let them overrun one to such an extent that the edification of individuals cannot be rightly taken care of and furthered.

20. The instituted church since Christ has appeared is not one catholic church in the sense that all believers throughout the world are joined with each other in one and the same outward bond, depending upon one and the same visible pastor or company of pastors. Rather there are as many churches as there are companies or particular congregations of people professing the faith who are joined together in a special bond for the continual exercise of the communion of saints.

21. The mystical church, as it exists in its members, has its divisions and subdivisions, as we might speak of the church of Belgium, of Britain, or of France, much as we name the sea from the shores it washes, i.e., the Belgian, the British, and the French, though it is one and the same sea. Yet the instituted churches are several different species or individuals participating in the same common nature, like several fountains, schools, or families. Many or all might perhaps be called one church because of the quality they have in common, just as many families of a certain noble stock are often designated by the name of one family, such as the family of the House of Nassau.

22. The church instituted by God is not rightly national, provincial, or diocesan. These forms were introduced by man from the pattern of civil government, especially Roman. Rather, it is a parochial church or a church of one congregation; the members are united with each other and ordinarily meet in one place for the public exercise of religion.

23. Such a company and no larger one is properly signified by the word ἐκκλησία, or church; nor does the word have a broader meaning in the

New Testament when it refers to a visible designated company. And so it is among more ancient profane authors.

24. Established congregations in the same country and province are, therefore, always called churches in the plural, never one church, even in Judea, which was once one national church, 1 Thess. 2:14; Acts 14:23; 15:41; Rom. 16:4, 5, 16; 1 Cor. 16:1, 19; 2 Cor. 8:1, 18, 19; Gal. 1:2, 22.

25. The particular churches mentioned in the New Testament were each accustomed to come together, επὶ τὸ αὐτὸ, Acts 2:46; 5:12; 14:27; 15:25; 21:22; 1 Cor. 5:4; 14:23, 26; 11:17, 33.

26. Nothing is read in all the New Testament about the establishment of any larger church upon which lesser congregations depend. Nor is any worship or holy ordinance prescribed which is not observed in each congregation. Neither is any ordinary minister ordained who is not committed to some one such company.

27. Yet particular churches, as their communion requires, and the light of nature and the rules of orderliness and examples from Scripture teach, may and often should enter into covenant relationship and mutual association in classes and synods in order to enjoy common agreement and mutual help as much as fitly may be, especially in matters of greater moment. But this combination does not constitute a new form of church nor ought it to take away or in any way diminish the freedom and authority which Christ has left to his churches. It should serve only to direct and promote that freedom and authority.

28. Ordinary ministers conform to the instituted church and are not ecumenical, national, provincial, or diocesan bishops, but rather elders of one congregation. In the same sense they are also called bishops in the Scriptures.

29. Those superior members of a hierarchy are merely human creations brought into the church without divine precept or example. They cannot fill the office of pastor in so many various congregations. They rob the churches of their liberty, while exercising a kind of regal or, rather, tyrannical dominion over them and their pastors. They have brought in with them the Roman Antichrist himself as the head, and as the tail of this wild beast the chancellors, suffragans, archdeacons, officials, and similar props of the hierarchy (whose very names are apocryphal and altogether unknown among the first churches) to the utter oppression of the churches of God.

30. The right of calling an ordinary minister is in the church itself which he must serve, Acts 14:23.

31. Yet the direction and help of the elders of the same church and usually of neighboring churches are needed.

32. The essence of the calling is in election by the church and acceptance by the one elected.

33. Preliminary to it comes an examination or test.

34. Consequent to it and consummating it comes ordination, which is nothing else than a solemn introduction of the minister already elected into the free execution of his responsibility. So it is that χειροτονία, the raising of hands to vote, and χειροθεσία, the laying on of hands, often mean the same thing among the ancients.

35. Episcopal ordination of a minister without title, i.e., without a church to which and in which he may be ordained is as ridiculous as trying to imagine a husband without a wife.

36. A minister called to one church cannot leave it of his choice nor be cast out without just cause. Neither can he undertake the like care of another church or neglect that which he has undertaken by voluntary nonresidence without a sacrilegious breaking of his covenant.

37. Ordinary ministers are either pastors and teachers or ruling elders with whom are associated those who take care of the poor, namely, deacons, deaconesses, or widows.

38. By these offices Christ has sufficiently provided for all the necessities of the members of the church, so that they may be instructed in the knowledge of the truth especially by the teachers, stirred up to the practice of piety chiefly by the pastors, preserved in the course of life and called back to repentance for sins by them and the ruling elders, and helped in their poverty by the deacons.

Note

1. See Douglas Horton, "Let Us Not Forget the Mighty William Ames," *Religion in Life* 19 (1960): 434–42; and his translations of early works on Ames, *William Ames by Matthew Nethenus, Hugo Visscher, and Karl Reuter* (Cambridge: Harvard University Press, 1965). See also the introduction to William Ames, *The Marrow of Theology*, ed. John D. Eusden (Boston: Pilgrim Press, 1968), 1–66; and Keith Sprunger, *The Learned Doctor William Ames* (Urbana: University of Illinois Press, 1972). On the covenant of grace, see John von Rohr, *The Covenant of Grace in Puritan Thought* (Atlanta: Scholars Press, 1986).

32. The Westminster Confession

(1646)

The Westminster Confession is the most influential confession of faith in the history of British and American Reformed Protestantism. Although it is well known among Presbyterians around the world, it is not so clearly understood that this confession, excluding its provisions on church government, was affirmed by Massachusetts Congregationalists in the Cambridge Platform (1648), by English Congregationalists (Independents) in the Savoy Declaration (1658), and by the Connecticut Congregational Synod at Saybrook (1708). The Westminster Confession, therefore, played a very significant role in the history of Congregationalism and in the wider American religious landscape. In 1844 Philip Schaff, an early German Reformed historian of American religion, recognized without exaggeration that "the reigning theology of the country is neither that of the Heidelberg Catechism (see vol. 2:327–58), nor that of the Augsburg Confession (see vol. 2:160–95), nor that of the Thirty-Nine Articles [the Anglican confession]. It is the theology of the Westminster Confession."[1]

The confession received its name from the place where it was formulated, Westminster Abbey. There, from 1643 to 1652, an assembly of church leaders met during the civil war between Charles I and Parliament. Charles and his main adviser, Archbishop William Laud, sought to impose episcopacy and the Book of Common Prayer (see vol. 2:397–418) on England and Scotland, only to meet strong resistance in both countries.

After Scotland's forces defeated the king's army in two battles and occupied northern England, Charles I was forced to turn to Parliament to get funds to pay the costs of the occupying Scottish army. He called into session what historians have called the Long Parliament (1640–52), dominated by Presbyterian Puritans. During this parliament, Archbishop Laud was imprisoned in the Tower of London. When the king used force

---

SOURCE: S. W. Carruthers, ed., *The Confession of Faith of the Assembly of Divines at Westminster from the Original Manuscript Written by Cornelius Burges in 1646* (London: Publishing House of the Presbyterian Church of England, 1946).

against some members of Parliament, civil war broke out. Eventually, as the armies of Parliament faltered on the battlefield against the king's forces, English parliamentary leaders called on Scotland for military help.

The Scots used this situation to their own advantage, requiring that the English Parliament make Presbyterianism the ruling religion of both countries. After some brief hesitation, in 1643 the English parliamentarians agreed to enter into a Solemn League and Covenant with Scotland.

Even before their agreement with the Scots, however, Presbyterian Puritans in the English Parliament had abolished the episcopacy and called on the Westminster Assembly to advise Parliament on the form of religion that should be established. The assembly, consisting of 121 ministers and 30 lay leaders from Parliament, was overwhelmingly Presbyterian, with a small contingent of Episcopalians and Congregationalists.

In the debates over church order within the assembly, Congregationalists Thomas Goodwin, Philip Nye, Sidrach Simpson, Jeremiah Burroughes, and William Bridge presented to Parliament An Apologetical Narration *(1643), which objected to the proposed Presbyterian system of church government.*[2] *Although Congregational views on church order were not incorporated in the final version of the confession as it was sent over to Parliament in late 1646, these Congregationalists had no objections to the theological substance of the confession. The Westminster Confession (the full title is* The Confession of Faith of the Westminster Assembly of Divines*) was finally approved by the assembly, after additional revisions, on June 20, 1648.*

In addition to a confession of faith, the Westminster Assembly presented Parliament with a directory of worship to replace the Book of Common Prayer, two catechisms (a longer catechism and a shorter catechism), and a directory for church government and discipline.

Actually, Congregationalists in England at that time did not need to worry about Presbyterianism. The commander of the New Model Army, Oliver Cromwell, was an Independent who opposed a Presbyterian establishment as much as he did an episcopal establishment. He favored a fair degree of toleration for all religious groups in England.

Cromwell was very successful on the military front, defeating the Scottish army when it joined the king's forces against him. In a dramatic expression of political power, he banished all Presbyterians from Parliament and had Charles I beheaded on January 30, 1649. Rule by Cromwell's parliamentary party did not last. With Cromwell's death in 1658 and the failure of his son Richard to rule wisely, the monarchy was restored. Charles II came to the throne in 1660, reestablishing episcopacy as the normative form of church order in England.

Ironically, the Westminster Confession and other recommendations of the assembly had little long-lasting impact on English religious practice, except among dissenting Presbyterians and Congregationalists. The work of Westminster, however, was highly valued in Scotland, and the confession became extremely influential in America. Philip Schaff called the confession "the clearest, strongest, most logical, and most careful symbolical statement of the Calvinistic scheme of faith."[3]

Among the most important doctrines declared in the Westminster Confession are the authority of Scripture (chapter 1); the doctrine of predestination (chapter 3); God's covenant with humanity (chapter 7); and affirmations regarding religious worship and keeping the Sabbath Day (chapter 21). The confession sets forth a twofold covenant: a covenant of works with Adam, and a covenant of grace with Christ. In spite of its historical importance, contemporary Christians in Presbyterian churches and the United Church of Christ rarely embrace all of its doctrines, especially the doctrine of double predestination set forth in chapter 3. The confession has also been criticized for promoting an overly legalistic and individualistic understanding of salvation.

Nevertheless, the first twenty-one chapters of the confession (which has thirty-three chapters) give a good summary of the theological position of early Congregationalism as well as Presbyterianism.

Chapter I.
Of the Holy Scripture.

Although the light of nature, and the works of creation and providence do so far manifest the goodness, wisdom, and power of God, as to leave men unexcusable; yet are they not sufficient to give that knowledge of God, and of His will, which is necessary unto salvation. Therefore it pleased the Lord, at sundry times, and in divers manners, to reveal Himself, and to declare that His will unto His Church; and afterwards, for the better preserving and propagating of the truth, and for the more sure establishment and comfort of the Church against the corruption of the flesh, and the malice of Satan and of the world, to commit the same wholly unto writing: which maketh the Holy Scripture to be most necessary; those former ways of God's revealing His will unto His people being now ceased.

II. Under the name of Holy Scripture, or the Word of God written, are now contained all the books of the Old and New Testament, which are these,

Of the Old Testament:

Genesis	2 Chronicles	Daniel
Exodus	Ezra	Hosea
Leviticus	Nehemiah	Joel
Numbers	Esther	Amos
Deuteronomy	Job	Obadiah
Joshua	Psalms	Jonah
Judges	Proverbs	Micah
Ruth	Ecclesiastes	Nahum
1 Samuel	The Song of Songs	Habakkuk
2 Samuel	Isaiah	Zephaniah
1 Kings	Jeremiah	Haggai
2 Kings	Lamentations	Zechariah
1 Chronicles	Ezekiel	Malachi

Of the New Testament:

The Gospels according to Matthew, Mark, Luke, John	Galatians	The Epistle to the Hebrews
The Acts of the Apostles	Ephesians	The Epistle of James
Paul's Epistles to the Romans	Philippians	The first and second Epistles of Peter
Corinthians 1	Colossians	The first, second, & third Epistles of John
Corinthians 2	Thessalonians 1	The Epistle of Jude
	Thessalonians 2	The Revelation of John
	To Timothy 1	
	To Timothy 2	
	To Titus	
	To Philemon	

All which are given by inspiration of God to be the rule of faith and life.

III. The books commonly called Apocrypha, not being of divine inspiration, are no part of the canon of the Scripture, and therefore are of no authority in the Church of God, nor to be any otherwise approved, or made use of, than other human writings.

IV. The authority of the Holy Scripture, for which it ought to be believed, and obeyed, dependeth not upon the testimony of any man, or Church; but wholly upon God (who is truth itself) the author thereof: and therefore it is to be received, because it is the Word of God.

V. We may be moved and induced by the testimony of the Church to an high and reverent esteem of the Holy Scripture. And the heavenliness of the matter, the efficacy of the doctrine, the majesty of the style, the consent of all the parts, the scope of the whole (which is, to give all glory to God), the full discovery it makes of the only way of man's salvation, the many other incomparable excellencies, and the entire perfection thereof, are arguments whereby it doth abundantly evidence itself to be the Word of God: yet notwithstanding, our full persuasion and assurance of the infallible truth and divine authority thereof, is from the inward work of the Holy Spirit bearing witness by and with the Word in our hearts.

VI. The whole counsel of God concerning all things necessary for His own glory, man's salvation, faith and life, is either expressly set down in Scripture, or by good and necessary consequence may be deduced from Scripture: unto which nothing at any time is to be added, whether by new revelations of the Spirit, or traditions of men. Nevertheless, we acknowledge the inward illumination of the Spirit of God to be necessary for the saving understanding of such things as are revealed in the Word: and that there are some circumstances concerning the worship of God, and government of the Church, common to human actions and societies, which are to be ordered by the light of nature, and Christian prudence, according to the general rules of the Word, which are always to be observed.

VII. All things in Scripture are not alike plain in themselves, nor alike clear unto all: yet those things which are necessary to be known, believed, and observed for salvation, are so clearly propounded, and opened in some place of Scripture or other, that not only the learned, but the unlearned, in a due use of the ordinary means, may attain unto a sufficient understanding of them.

VIII. The Old Testament in Hebrew (which was the native language of the people of God of old), and the New Testament in Greek (which, at the time of the writing of it, was most generally known to the nations), being immediately inspired by God, and, by His singular care and providence, kept pure in all ages, are therefore authentical; so as, in all controversies of religion, the Church is finally to appeal unto them. But, because these original tongues are not known to all the people of God, who have right unto, and interest in the Scriptures, and are commanded, in the fear of God, to read and search them, therefore they are to be translated into the vulgar language of every nation unto which they come, that, the Word of God dwelling plentifully in all, they may worship Him in an acceptable manner; and, through patience and comfort of the Scriptures, may have hope.

IX. The infallible rule of interpretation of Scripture is the Scripture itself: and therefore, when there is a question about the true and full sense of any Scripture (which is not manifold, but one), it must be searched and known by other places that speak more clearly.

X. The supreme judge by which all controversies of religion are to be determined, and all decrees of councils, opinions of ancient writers, doctrines of men, and private spirits, are to be examined, and in whose sentence we are to rest, can be no other but the Holy Spirit speaking in the Scripture.

Chapter II.

Of God, and of the Holy Trinity.

There is but one only, living, and true God, who is infinite in being and perfection, a most pure spirit, invisible, without body, parts, or passions; immutable, immense, eternal, incomprehensible, almighty, most wise, most holy, most free, most absolute; working all things according to the counsel of His own immutable and most righteous will, for His own glory; most loving, gracious, merciful, long-suffering, abundant in goodness and truth, forgiving iniquity, transgression, and sin; the rewarder of them that diligently seek Him; and withal, most just, and terrible in His judgments, hating all sin, and who will by no means clear the guilty.

II. God hath all life, glory, goodness, blessedness, in and of Himself; and is alone in and unto Himself all-sufficient, not standing in need of any creatures which He hath made, nor deriving any glory from them, but only manifesting His own glory in, by, unto, and upon them. He is the alone fountain of all being, of whom, through whom, and to whom are all things; and hath most sovereign dominion over them, to do by them, for them, or upon them whatsoever Himself pleaseth. In His sight all things are open and manifest, His knowledge is infinite, infallible, and independent upon the creature, so as nothing is to Him contingent, or uncertain. He is most holy in all His counsels, in all His works, and in all His commands. To Him is due from angels and men, and every other creature, whatsoever worship, service, or obedience He is pleased to require of them.

III. In the unity of the Godhead there be three persons, of one substance, power, and eternity: God the Father, God the Son, and God the Holy Ghost: the Father is of none, neither begotten, nor proceeding; the Son is eternally begotten of the Father; the Holy Ghost eternally proceeding from the Father and the Son.

Chapter III.

Of God's Eternal Decree.

God, from all eternity, did, by the most wise and holy counsel of His own will, freely, and unchangeably ordain whatsoever comes to pass: yet so, as thereby neither is God the author of sin, nor is violence offered to the will of the creatures; nor is the liberty or contingency of second causes taken away, but rather established.

II. Although God knows whatsoever may or can come to pass upon all supposed conditions, yet hath He not decreed anything because He foresaw it as future, or as that which would come to pass upon such conditions.

III. By the decree of God, for the manifestation of His glory, some men and angels are predestinated unto everlasting life; and others foreordained to everlasting death.

IV. These angels and men, thus predestinated, and foreordained, are particularly and unchangeably designed, and their number so certain and definite, that it cannot be either increased or diminished.

V. Those of mankind that are predestinated unto life, God, before the foundation of the world was laid, according to His eternal and immutable purpose, and the secret counsel and good pleasure of His will, hath chosen, in Christ, unto everlasting glory, out of His mere free grace and love, without any foresight of faith, or good works, or perseverance in either of them, or any other thing in the creature, as conditions, or causes moving Him thereunto: and all to the praise of His glorious grace.

VI. As God hath appointed the elect unto glory, so hath He, by the eternal and most free purpose of His will, foreordained all the means thereunto. Wherefore, they who are elected, being fallen in Adam, are redeemed by Christ, are effectually called unto faith in Christ by His Spirit working in due season, are justified, adopted, sanctified, and kept by His power, through faith, unto salvation. Neither are any other redeemed by Christ, effectually called, justified, adopted, sanctified, and saved, but the elect only.

VII. The rest of mankind God was pleased, according to the unsearchable counsel of His own will, whereby He extendeth or withholdeth mercy, as He pleaseth, for the glory of His sovereign power over His creatures, to pass by; and to ordain them to dishonour and wrath for their sin, to the praise of His glorious justice.

VIII. The doctrine of this high mystery of predestination is to be handled with special prudence and care, that men, attending the will of God revealed in His Word, and yielding obedience thereunto, may, from the certainty of their effectual vocation, be assured of their eternal election. So shall this doctrine afford matter of praise, reverence, and admiration of God; and of humility, diligence, and abundant consolation to all that sincerely obey the Gospel.

Chapter IV.
Of Creation.

It pleased God the Father, Son, and Holy Ghost, for the manifestation of the glory of His eternal power, wisdom, and goodness, in the beginning, to create, or make of nothing, the world, and all things therein whether visible or invisible, in the space of six days; and all very good.

II. After God had made all other creatures, He created man, male and female, with reasonable and immortal souls, endued with knowledge, righteousness, and true holiness, after His own image; having the law of God written in their hearts, and power to fulfil it: and yet under a possibility of transgressing, being left to the liberty of their own will, which was subject unto change. Beside this law written in their hearts, they received a command, not to eat of the tree of the knowledge of good and evil; which while they kept, they were happy in their communion with God, and had dominion over the creatures.

Chapter V.

Of Providence.

God the great Creator of all things doth uphold, direct, dispose, and govern all creatures, actions, and things, from the greatest even to the least, by His most wise and holy providence, according to His infallible fore-knowledge, and the free and immutable counsel of His own will, to the praise of the glory of His wisdom, power, justice, goodness, and mercy.

II. Although, in relation to the fore-knowledge and decree of God, the first Cause, all things come to pass immutably, and infallibly; yet, by the same providence, He ordereth them to fall out, according to the nature of second causes, either necessarily, freely, or contingently.

III. God, in His ordinary providence, maketh use of means, yet is free to work without, above, and against them, at His pleasure.

IV. The almighty power, unsearchable wisdom, and infinite goodness of God so far manifest themselves in His providence, that it extendeth itself even to the first fall, and all other sins of angels and men; and that not by a bare permission, but such as hath joined with it a most wise and powerful bounding, and otherwise ordering, and governing of them, in a manifold dispensation, to His own holy ends; yet so, as the sinfulness thereof proceedeth only from the creature, and not from God, who, being most holy and righteous, neither is nor can be the author or approver of sin.

V. The most wise, righteous, and gracious God doth oftentimes leave, for a season, His own children to manifold temptations, and the corruption of their own hearts, to chastise them for their former sins, or to discover unto them the hidden strength of corruption and deceitfulness of their hearts, that they may be humbled; and, to raise them to a more close and constant dependence for their support upon Himself, and to make them more watchful against all future occasion of sin, and for sundry other just and holy ends.

VI. As for those wicked and ungodly men whom God, as a righteous Judge, for former sins, doth blind and harden, from them He not only withholdeth His grace whereby they might have been enlightened in their understandings, and wrought upon in their hearts; but sometimes also withdraweth the gifts which they had, and exposeth them to such objects as their corruption makes occasions of sin; and, withal, gives them over to their own lusts, the temptations of the world, and the power of Satan, whereby it comes to pass that they harden themselves, even under those means which God useth for the softening of others.

VII. As the providence of God doth, in general, reach to all creatures; so, after a most special manner, it taketh care of His Church, and disposeth all things to the good thereof.

Chapter VI.

Of the Fall of Man, of Sin, and of the Punishment thereof.

Our first parents, being seduced by the subtilty and temptation of Satan, sinned, in eating the forbidden fruit. This their sin, God was pleased, according to His wise and holy counsel, to permit, having purposed to order it to His own glory.

II. By this sin they fell from their original righteousness and communion with God, and so became dead in sin, and wholly defiled in all the parts and faculties of soul and body.

III. They being the root of all mankind, the guilt of this sin was imputed; and the same death in sin, and corrupted nature, conveyed to all their posterity descending from them by ordinary generation.

IV. From this original corruption, whereby we are utterly indisposed, disabled, and made opposite to all good, and wholly inclined to all evil, do proceed all actual transgressions.

V. This corruption of nature, during this life, doth remain in those that are regenerated; and although it be, through Christ, pardoned, and mortified; yet both itself, and all the motions thereof, are truly and properly sin.

VI. Every sin, both original and actual, being a transgression of the righteous law of God, and contrary thereunto, doth, in its own nature, bring guilt upon the sinner, whereby he is bound over to the wrath of God, and curse of the law, and so made subject to death, with all miseries spiritual, temporal, and eternal.

Chapter VII.

Of God's Covenant with Man.

The distance between God and the creature is so great, that although reasonable creatures do owe obedience unto Him as their Creator, yet they could never have any fruition of Him as their blessedness and reward, but by some voluntary condescension on God's part, which He hath been pleased to express by way of covenant.

II. The first covenant made with man was a covenant of works, wherein life was promised to Adam; and in him to his posterity, upon condition of perfect and personal obedience.

III. Man, by his fall, having made himself uncapable of life by that covenant, the Lord was pleased to make a second, commonly called the covenant of grace; wherein He freely offereth unto sinners life and salvation by Jesus Christ; requiring of them faith in Him, that they may be saved, and promising to give unto all those that are ordained unto eternal life His Holy Spirit, to make them willing, and able to believe.

IV. This covenant of grace is frequently set forth in Scripture by the name of a testament, in reference to the death of Jesus Christ the Testator, and to the everlasting inheritance, with all things belonging to it, therein bequeathed.

V. This covenant was differently administered in the time of the law, and in the time of the gospel: under the law, it was administered by promises, prophecies, sacrifices, circumcision, the paschal lamb, and other types and ordinances delivered to the people of the Jews, all fore-signifying Christ to come; which were, for that time, sufficient and efficacious, through the operation of the Spirit, to instruct and build up the elect in faith in the promised Messiah, by whom they had full remission of sins, and eternal salvation; and is called the old Testament.

VI. Under the gospel, when Christ, the substance, was exhibited, the ordinances in which this covenant is dispensed are the preaching of the Word, and the administration of the sacraments of Baptism and the Lord's Supper: which, though fewer in number, and administered with more simplicity, and less outward glory, yet, in them, it is held forth in more fulness, evidence, and spiritual efficacy, to all nations, both Jews and Gentiles; and is called the new Testament. There are not therefore two covenants of grace, differing in substance, but one and the same, under various dispensations.

Chapter VIII.

Of Christ the Mediator.

It pleased God, in His eternal purpose, to choose and ordain the Lord Jesus, His only begotten Son, to be the Mediator between God and man, the Prophet, Priest, and King, the Head and Saviour of His Church, the Heir of all things, and Judge of the world: unto whom He did from all eternity give a people, to be His seed, and to be by Him in time redeemed, called, justified, sanctified, and glorified.

II. The Son of God, the second person in the Trinity, being very and eternal God, of one substance and equal with the Father, did, when the fulness of time was come, take upon Him man's nature, with all the essential properties, and common infirmities thereof, yet without sin; being conceived by the power of the Holy Ghost, in the womb of the virgin Mary, of her substance. So that two whole, perfect, and distinct natures, the Godhead and the manhood, were inseparably joined together in one person, without conversion, composition, or confusion. Which person is very God, and very man, yet one Christ, the only Mediator between God and man.

III. The Lord Jesus, in His human nature thus united to the divine, was sanctified, and anointed with the Holy Spirit, above measure, having in Him all the treasures of wisdom and knowledge; in whom it pleased the Father that all fulness should dwell; to the end that, being holy, harmless, undefiled, and full of grace and truth, He might be thoroughly furnished to execute the office of a mediator, and surety. Which office He took not unto Himself, but was thereunto called by His Father, who put all power and judgment into His hand, and gave Him commandment to execute the same.

IV. This office the Lord Jesus did most willingly undertake; which that He might discharge, He was made under the law, and did perfectly fulfil it; endured most grievous torments immediately in His soul, and most painful sufferings in His body; was crucified, and died, was buried, and remained under the power of death, yet saw no corruption. On the third day He arose from the dead, with the same body in which He suffered, with which also he ascended into heaven, and there sitteth at the right hand of His Father, making intercession, and shall return, to judge men and angels, at the end of the world.

V. The Lord Jesus, by His perfect obedience, and sacrifice of Himself, which He, through the eternal Spirit, once offered up unto God, hath fully satisfied the justice of His Father; and purchased, not only reconciliation, but an everlasting inheritance in the kingdom of heaven, for all those whom the Father hath given unto Him.

VI. Although the work of redemption was not actually wrought by Christ till after His incarnation, yet the virtue, efficacy, and benefits thereof were communicated unto the elect, in all ages successively from the beginning of the world, in and by those promises, types, and sacrifices, wherein He was revealed, and signified to be the seed of the woman which should bruise the serpent's head; and the Lamb slain from the beginning of the world; being yesterday and to-day the same, and for ever.

VII. Christ, in the work of mediation, acts according to both natures, by each nature doing that which is proper to itself; yet, by reason of the unity of the person, that which is proper to one nature is sometimes in Scripture attributed to the person denominated by the other nature.

VIII. To all those for whom Christ hath purchased redemption, He doth certainly and effectually apply and communicate the same; making intercession for them, and revealing unto them, in and by the Word, the mysteries of salvation; effectually persuading them by His Spirit to believe and obey, and governing their hearts by His Word and Spirit; overcoming all their enemies by His almighty power and wisdom, in such manner, and ways, as are most consonant to His wonderful and unsearchable dispensation.

Chapter IX.

Of Free-Will.

God hath endued the will of man with that natural liberty, that it is neither forced, nor, by any absolute necessity of nature, determined to good, or evil.

II. Man, in his state of innocency, had freedom, and power to will and to do that which was good and well pleasing to God; but yet, mutably, so that he might fall from it.

III. Man, by his fall into a state of sin, hath wholly lost all ability of will to any spiritual good accompanying salvation: so as, a natural man, being altogether averse from that good, and dead in sin, is not able, by his own strength, to convert himself, or to prepare himself thereunto.

IV. When God converts a sinner, and translates him into the state of grace, He freeth him from his natural bondage under sin; and, by His grace alone, enables him freely to will and to do that which is spiritually good; yet so, as that by reason of his remaining corruption, he doth not perfectly, nor only, will that which is good, but doth also will that which is evil.

V. The will of man is made perfectly and immutably free to good alone, in the state of glory only.

Chapter X.

Of Effectual Calling.

All those whom God hath predestinated unto life, and those only, He is pleased, in His appointed and accepted time, effectually to call, by His Word and Spirit, out of that state of sin and death, in which they are by nature, to grace and salvation, by Jesus Christ; enlightening their minds spiritually and savingly to understand the things of God, taking away their heart of stone, and giving unto them a heart of flesh; renewing their wills, and, by His almighty power, determining them to that which is good, and effectually drawing them to Jesus Christ: yet so, as they come most freely, being made willing by His grace.

II. This effectual call is of God's free and special grace alone, not from anything at all foreseen in man, who is altogether passive therein, until, being quickened and renewed by the Holy Spirit, he is thereby enabled to answer this call, and to embrace the grace offered and conveyed in it.

III. Elect infants, dying in infancy, are regenerated, and saved by Christ, through the Spirit, who worketh when, and where, and how He pleaseth: so also are all other elect persons who are uncapable of being outwardly called by the ministry of the Word.

IV. Others, not elected, although they may be called by the ministry of the Word, and may have some common operations of the Spirit, yet they never truly come unto Christ, and therefore cannot be saved: much less can men, not professing the Christian religion, be saved in any other way whatsoever, be they never so diligent to frame their lives according to the light of nature, and the laws of that religion they do profess. And, to assert and maintain that they may, is very pernicious, and to be detested.

Chapter XI.

Of Justification.

Those whom God effectually calleth, He also freely justifieth: not by infusing righteousness into them, but by pardoning their sins, and by accounting and accepting their persons as righteous; not for anything wrought in them, or done by them, but for Christ's sake alone; nor by imputing faith itself, the act of believing, or any other evangelical obedience to them, as their righteousness; but by imputing the obedience and satisfaction of Christ unto them, they receiving and resting on Him and His righteousness, by faith; which faith they have not of themselves, it is the gift of God.

II. Faith, thus receiving and resting on Christ and His righteousness, is the alone instrument of justification: yet is it not alone in the person justified, but is ever accompanied with all other saving graces, and is no dead faith, but worketh by love.

III. Christ, by His obedience and death, did fully discharge the debt of all those that are thus justified, and did make a proper, real, and full satisfaction to His Father's justice in their behalf. Yet, inasmuch as He was given by the Father for them; and His obedience and satisfaction accepted in their stead; and both, freely, not for anything in them; their justification is only of free grace; that both the exact justice, and rich grace of God might be glorified in the justification of sinners.

IV. God did, from all eternity, decree to justify all the elect, and Christ did, in the fulness of time, die for their sins, and rise again for their justification: nevertheless, they are not justified, until the Holy Spirit doth, in due time, actually apply Christ unto them.

V. God doth continue to forgive the sins of those that are justified; and, although they can never fall from the state of justification, yet they may, by their sins, fall under God's fatherly displeasure, and not have the light of His countenance restored unto them, until they humble themselves, confess their sins, beg pardon, and renew their faith and repentance.

VI. The justification of believers under the old testament was, in all these respects, one and the same with the justification of believers under the new testament.

Chapter XII.
Of Adoption.

All those that are justified, God vouchsafeth, in and for His only Son Jesus Christ, to make partakers of the grace of adoption, by which they are taken into the number, and enjoy the liberties and privileges of the children of God, have His name put upon them, receive the spirit of adoption, have access to the throne of grace with boldness, are enabled to cry, Abba, Father, are pitied, protected, provided for, and chastened by Him, as by a Father: yet never cast off, but sealed to the day of redemption; and inherit the promises, as heirs of everlasting salvation.

Chapter XIII.
Of Sanctification.

They, who are once effectually called, and regenerated, having a new heart, and a new spirit created in them, are further sanctified, really and personally, through the virtue of Christ's death and resurrection, by His Word and Spirit dwelling in them: the dominion of the whole body of sin is destroyed, and the several lusts thereof are more and more weakened and mortified; and they more and more quickened and strengthened in all saving graces, to the practice of true holiness, without which no man shall see the Lord.

II. This sanctification is throughout, in the whole man; yet imperfect in this life, there abiding still some remnants of corruption in every part; whence ariseth a continual and irreconcilable war, the flesh lusting against the Spirit, and the Spirit against the flesh.

III. In which war, although the remaining corruption, for a time, may much prevail; yet, through the continual supply of strength from the sanctifying Spirit of Christ, the regenerate part doth overcome; and so, the saints grow in grace, perfecting holiness in the fear of God.

Chapter XIV.

Of Saving Faith.

The grace of faith, whereby the elect are enabled to believe to the saving of their souls, is the work of the Spirit of Christ in their hearts, and is ordinarily wrought by the ministry of the Word, by which also, and by the administration of the sacraments, and prayer, it is increased and strengthened.

II. By this faith, a Christian believeth to be true whatsoever is revealed in the Word, for the authority of God Himself speaking therein; and acteth differently upon that which each particular passage thereof containeth; yielding obedience to the commands, trembling at the threatenings, and embracing the promises of God for this life, and that which is to come. But the principal acts of saving faith are accepting, receiving, and resting upon Christ alone for justification, sanctification, and eternal life, by virtue of the covenant of grace.

III. This faith is different in degrees, weak or strong; may be often and many ways assailed, and weakened, but gets the victory: growing up in many to the attainment of a full assurance, through Christ, who is both the author and finisher of our faith.

Chapter XV.

Of Repentance unto Life.

Repentance unto life is an evangelical grace, the doctrine whereof is to be preached by every minister of the Gospel, as well as that of faith in Christ.

II. By it, a sinner, out of the sight and sense not only of the danger, but also of the filthiness and odiousness of his sins, as contrary to the holy nature, and righteous law of God; and upon the apprehension of His mercy in Christ to such as are penitent, so grieves for, and hates his sins, as to turn from them all unto God, purposing and endeavouring to walk with Him in all the ways of His commandments.

III. Although repentance be not to be rested in, as any satisfaction for sin, or any cause of the pardon thereof, which is the act of God's free grace in Christ; yet it is of such necessity to all sinners, that none may expect pardon without it.

IV. As there is no sin so small, but it deserves damnation; so there is no sin so great, that it can bring damnation upon those who truly repent.

V. Men ought not to content themselves with a general repentance, but it is every man's duty to endeavour to repent of his particular sins, particularly.

VI. As every man is bound to make private confession of his sins to God, praying for the pardon thereof; upon which, and the forsaking of them, he shall find mercy; so, he that scandalizeth his brother, or the Church of Christ, ought to be willing, by a private or public confession, and sorrow for his sin, to declare his repentance to those that are offended, who are thereupon to be reconciled to him, and in love to receive him.

Chapter XVI.

Of Good Works.

Good works are only such as God hath commanded in His holy Word, and not such as, without the warrant thereof, are devised by men, out of blind zeal, or upon any pretence of good intention.

II. These good works, done in obedience to God's commandments, are the fruits and evidences of a true and lively faith: and by them believers manifest their thankfulness, strengthen their assurance, edify their brethren, adorn the profession of the Gospel, stop the mouths of the adversaries, and glorify God, whose workmanship they are, created in Christ Jesus thereunto, that, having their fruit unto holiness, they may have the end, eternal life.

III. Their ability to do good works is not at all of themselves, but wholly from the Spirit of Christ. And that they may be enabled thereunto, beside the graces they have already received, there is required an actual influence of the same Holy Spirit, to work in them to will, and to do, of His good pleasure: yet are they not hereupon to grow negligent, as if they were not bound to perform any duty unless upon a special motion of the Spirit; but they ought to be diligent in stirring up the grace of God that is in them.

IV. They who, in their obedience, attain to the greatest height which is possible in this life, are so far from being able to supererogate, and to do more than God requires, as that they fall short of much which in duty they are bound to do.

V. We cannot by our best works merit pardon of sin, or eternal life at the hand of God, by reason of the great disproportion that is between them and the glory to come; and the infinite distance that is between us and God, whom, by them, we can neither profit, nor satisfy for the debt of our former sins, but when we have done all we can, we have done but our duty, and are unprofitable servants: and because, as they are good, they proceed from His Spirit; and as they are wrought by us, they are defiled, and mixed with so much weakness and imperfection, that they cannot endure the severity of God's judgment.

VI. Notwithstanding, the persons of believers being accepted through Christ, their good works also are accepted in Him; not as though they were in this life wholly unblameable and unreprovable in God's sight; but that He, looking upon them in His Son, is pleased to accept and reward that which is sincere, although accompanied with many weaknesses and imperfections.

VII. Works done by unregenerate men, although for the matter of them they may be things which God commands; and of good use both to themselves and others: yet, because they proceed not from an heart purified by faith; nor are done in a right manner, according to the Word; nor to a right end, the glory of God, they are therefore sinful, and cannot please God, or make a man meet to receive grace from God: and yet, their neglect of them is more sinful and displeasing unto God.

Chapter XVII.

Of the Perseverance of the Saints.

They, whom God hath accepted in His Beloved, effectually called, and sanctified by His Spirit, can neither totally nor finally fall away from the state of grace, but shall certainly persevere therein to the end, and be eternally saved.

II. This perseverance of the saints depends not upon their own free will, but upon the immutability of the decree of election, flowing from the free and unchangeable love of God the Father; upon the efficacy of the merit and intercession of Jesus Christ, the abiding of the Spirit, and of the seed of God within them, and the nature of the covenant of grace: from all which ariseth also the certainty and infallibility thereof.

III. Nevertheless, they may, through the temptations of Satan and of the world, the prevalency of corruption remaining in them, and the neglect of the means of their preservation, fall into grievous sins; and, for a time, continue therein: whereby they incur God's displeasure, and grieve His Holy Spirit, come to be deprived of some measure of their graces and comforts, have their hearts hardened, and their consciences wounded; hurt and scandalize others, and bring temporal judgments upon themselves.

Chapter XVIII.

Of the Assurance of Grace and Salvation.

Although hypocrites and other unregenerate men may vainly deceive themselves with false hopes and carnal presumptions of being in the favour of God, and estate of salvation (which hope of theirs shall perish): yet such as truly believe in the Lord Jesus, and love Him in sincerity, endeavouring to walk in all good conscience before Him, may, in this life, be certainly assured that they are in the state of grace, and may rejoice in the hope of the glory of God, which hope shall never make them ashamed.

II. This certainty is not a bare conjectural and probable persuasion grounded upon a fallible hope; but an infallible assurance of faith founded upon the divine truth of the promises of salvation, the inward evidence of those graces unto which these promises are made, the testimony of the Spirit of adoption witnessing with our spirits that we are the children of God, which Spirit is the earnest of our inheritance, whereby we are sealed to the day of redemption.

III. This infallible assurance doth not so belong to the essence of faith, but that a true believer may wait long, and conflict with many difficulties, before he be partaker of it: yet, being enabled by the Spirit to know the things which are freely given him of God, he may, without extraordinary revelation, in the right use of ordinary means, attain thereunto. And therefore it is the duty of everyone to give all diligence to make his calling and election sure, that thereby his heart may be enlarged in peace and joy in the Holy Ghost, in love and thankfulness to God, and in strength and cheerfulness in the duties of obedience, the proper fruits of this assurance; so far is it from inclining men to looseness.

IV. True believers may have the assurance of their salvation divers ways shaken, diminished, and intermitted; as, by negligence in preserving of it, by falling into some special sin which woundeth the conscience and grieveth the Spirit; by some sudden or vehement temptation, by God's withdrawing the light of His countenance, and suffering even such as fear Him to walk in darkness and to have no light: yet are they never utterly destitute of that seed of God, and life of faith, that love of Christ and the brethren, that sincerity of heart, and conscience of duty, out of which, by the operation of the Spirit, this assurance may, in due time, be revived; and by the which, in the mean time, they are supported from utter despair.

Chapter XIX.

Of the Law of God.

God gave to Adam a law, as a covenant of works, by which He bound him and all his posterity to personal, entire, exact, and perpetual obedience, promised life upon the fulfilling, and threatened death upon the breach of it, and endued him with power and ability to keep it.

II. This law, after his fall, continued to be a perfect rule of righteousness; and, as such, was delivered by God upon Mount Sinai, in ten commandments, and written in two tables: the four first commandments containing our duty towards God; and the other six, our duty to man.

III. Beside this law, commonly called moral, God was pleased to give to the people of Israel, as a church under age, ceremonial laws, containing several typical ordinances, partly of worship, prefiguring Christ, His graces, actions, sufferings, and benefits; and partly, holding forth divers instruction of moral duties. All which ceremonial laws are now abrogated, under the new testament.

IV. To them also, as a body politic, He gave sundry judicial laws, which expired together with the State of that people; not obliging any other now, further than the general equity thereof may require.

V. The moral law doth for ever bind all, as well justified persons as others, to the obedience thereof; and that, not only in regard of the matter contained in it, but also in respect of the authority of God the Creator, who gave it. Neither doth Christ, in the Gospel, any way dissolve, but much strengthen this obligation.

VI. Although true believers be not under the law, as a covenant of works, to be thereby justified, or condemned; yet is it of great use to them, as well as to others; in that, as a rule of life informing them of the will of God, and their duty, it directs and binds them to walk accordingly; discovering also the sinful pollutions of their nature, hearts, and lives; so as, examining themselves thereby, they may come to further conviction of, humiliation for, and hatred against sin, together with a clearer sight of the need they have of Christ, and the perfection of His obedience. It is likewise of use to the regenerate, to restrain their corruptions, in that it forbids sin: and the threatenings of it serve to show what even their sins deserve; and what afflictions, in this life, they may expect for them, although freed from the curse thereof threatened in the law. The promises of it, in like manner, show them God's approbation of obedience, and what blessings they may expect upon the performance thereof: although not as due to them by the law as a covenant of works. So as, a man's doing good, and refraining from evil, because the law encourageth to the one, and deterreth from the other, is no evidence of his being under the law; and, not under grace.

VII. Neither are the forementioned uses of the law contrary to the grace of the Gospel, but do sweetly comply with it; the Spirit of Christ subduing and enabling the will of man to do that freely, and cheerfully, which the will of God, revealed in the law, requireth to be done.

Chapter XX.

Of Christian Liberty, and Liberty of Conscience.

The liberty which Christ hath purchased for believers under the Gospel consists in their freedom from the guilt of sin, the condemning wrath of

God, the curse of the moral law; and, in their being delivered from this present evil world, bondage to Satan, and dominion of sin; from the evil of afflictions, the sting of death, the victory of the grave, and everlasting damnation; as also, in their free access to God, and their yielding obedience unto Him, not out of a slavish fear, but a child-like love and willing mind. All which are common also to believers under the law. But, under the new testament, the liberty of Christians is further enlarged, in their freedom from the yoke of the ceremonial law, to which the Jewish Church was subjected; and in greater boldness of access to the throne of grace, and in fuller communications of the free Spirit of God, than believers under the law did ordinarily partake of.

II. God alone is Lord of the conscience, and hath left it free from the doctrines and commandments of men, which are, in any thing, contrary to His Word; or beside it, if matters of faith, or worship. So that, to believe such doctrines, or to obey such commands, out of conscience, is to betray true liberty of conscience: and the requiring of an implicit faith, and an absolute and blind obedience, is to destroy liberty of conscience, and reason also.

III. They who, upon pretence of Christian liberty, do practise any sin, or cherish any lust, do thereby destroy the end of Christian liberty, which is, that being delivered out of the hands of our enemies, we might serve the Lord without fear, in holiness and righteousness before Him, all the days of our life.

IV. And because the powers which God hath ordained, and the liberty which Christ hath purchased, are not intended by God to destroy, but mutually to uphold and preserve one another, they who, upon pretence of Christian liberty, shall oppose any lawful power, or the lawful exercise of it, whether it be civil or ecclesiastical, resist the ordinance of God. And, for their publishing of such opinions, or maintaining of such practices, as are contrary to the light of nature, or to the known principles of Christianity (whether concerning faith, worship, or conversation), or to the power of godliness; or, such erroneous opinions or practices, as either in their own nature, or in the manner of publishing or maintaining them, are destructive to the external peace and order which Christ hath established in the Church, they may lawfully be called to account, and proceeded against, by the censures of the Church, and by the power of the civil magistrate.

Chapter XXI.

Of Religious Worship, and the Sabbath Day.

The light of nature showeth that there is a God, who hath lordship and sovereignty over all, is good, and doth good unto all, and is therefore to be feared, loved, praised, called upon, trusted in, and served, with all the heart, and with all the soul, and with all the might. But the acceptable way of worshipping the true God is instituted by Himself, and so limited by His own revealed will, that He may not be worshipped according to the imaginations and devices of men, or the suggestions of Satan, under any visible representation, or any other way not prescribed in the holy Scripture.

II. Religious worship is to be given to God, the Father, Son, and Holy Ghost; and to Him alone; not to angels, saints, or any other creature: and, since the fall, not without a Mediator; nor in the mediation of any other but of Christ alone.

III. Prayer, with thanksgiving, being one special part of religious worship, is by God required of all men: and, that it may be accepted, it is to be made in the name of the Son, by the help of His Spirit, according to His will, with understanding, reverence, humility, fervency, faith, love, and perseverance; and, if vocal, in a known tongue.

IV. Prayer is to be made for things lawful; and for all sorts of men living, or that shall live hereafter: but not for the dead, nor for those of whom it may be known that they have sinned the sin unto death.

V. The reading of the Scriptures with godly fear, the sound preaching and conscionable hearing of the Word, in obedience unto God, with understanding, faith, and reverence, singing of psalms with grace in the heart; as also, the due administration and worthy receiving of the sacraments instituted by Christ, are all parts of the ordinary religious worship of God: beside religious oaths, vows, solemn fastings, and thanksgivings upon special occasions, which are, in their several times and seasons, to be used in an holy and religious manner.

VI. Neither prayer, nor any other part of religious worship, is now, under the Gospel, either tied unto, or made more acceptable by any place in which it is performed, or towards which it is directed: but God is to be worshipped everywhere, in spirit and truth; as, in private families daily, and in secret, each one by himself; so, more solemnly in the public assemblies, which are not carelessly or wilfully to be neglected, or forsaken, when God, by His Word or providence, calleth thereunto.

VII. As it is the law of nature, that, in general, a due proportion of time be set apart for the worship of God; so, in His Word, by a positive, moral, and perpetual commandment binding all men in all ages, He hath particularly appointed one day in seven, for a Sabbath, to be kept holy unto Him: which, from the beginning of the world to the resurrection of Christ, was the last day of the week; and, from the resurrection of Christ, was changed into the first day of the week, which, in Scripture, is called the Lord's Day, and is to be continued to the end of the world, as the Christian Sabbath.

VIII. This Sabbath is then kept holy unto the Lord, when men, after a due preparing of their hearts, and ordering of their common affairs beforehand, do not only observe an holy rest, all the day, from their own works, words, and thoughts about their worldly employments and recreations, but also are taken up, the whole time, in the public and private exercises of His worship, and in the duties of necessity and mercy.

• • •

Notes

1. See Philip Schaff, *The Principle of Protestantism*, trans. John W. Nevin, ed. Bard Thompson and George H. Bricker, Lancaster Series on the Mercersburg Theology, vol. 1 (Philadelphia and Boston: United Church Press, 1964), 147.

2. See Robert S. Paul, ed., *An Apologeticall Narration* (Philadelphia and Boston: United Church Press, 1963).

3. See Philip Schaff, *Schaff-Herzog Encyclopedia of Religious Knowledge* (New York: Fund and Wagnall, 1891), 2501.

PART IV

Lay Piety and Theology

33. Letter to the University of Ingolstadt

(1523)

Argula von Grumbach

Argula von Grumbach (1492–after 1563) was a German noblewoman who fearlessly proclaimed evangelical views, attacking clergy and monks in a series of pamphlets in the 1520s. Even as her boldness generated criticism from Catholic traditionalists, it also led to praise from Protestant reformers such as Martin Luther and Andreas Osiander of Nuremberg.

This courageous woman was born Argula von Stauffen of impoverished parents in a famous Bavarian noble family. Shortly before her parents died, they sent her to the court of the duke of Bavaria, where she came under the care of Kunigunde, sister of Emperor Maximilian I and mother of Duke William, who also promised to look after her.

Von Stauffen's father had given her a copy of a 1483 Koburger Bible when she was a child, and she read this Bible avidly along with other books of devotion provided by Kunigunde. As Luther's German writings appeared in the early 1520s, she read them with great interest. She corresponded with Luther in Wittenberg and Osiander in Nuremberg. In 1516, reaching the age of twenty-four, she married a poor noble named Friedrich von Grumbach and eventually gave birth to two sons and two daughters.

Argula von Grumbach came to public attention in 1523 when she published a letter to the faculty of Ingolstadt University on behalf of a young student, Arsacius Seehofer, who had been charged with teaching Lutheran heresy. Under threat of torture he had recanted, but he was subsequently locked up in a cloister.

SOURCE: Peter Matheson, ed., *Argula von Grumbach: A Woman's Voice in the Reformation* (Edinburgh: T. & T. Clark, 1995).

Arsacius Seehofer had studied in Wittenberg under Philip Melanchthon in 1521 and 1522. Although Seehofer did not have any direct contact with Luther (who was in hiding at the Wartburg Castle under the protection of Frederick the Wise), his views were decidedly Lutheran.

The letter by von Grumbach is a spirited defense of Seehofer and the teachings of Luther and Melanchthon, as well as a justification of her own rashness as a woman to enter the fray. Although she defends Luther in this letter, elsewhere she states: "I am said to be a Lutheran. I am not. I was baptized into the name of Christ, not of Luther." Along with other lay writers in the 1520s, she argues that she is simply an evangelical Christian, one who rests her faith on the teachings of Scripture rather than on human doctrines.

The university did not respond to the letter, but it sent a copy to Duke William. Von Grumbach also wrote a personal letter directly to the duke, reminding him of his promise to be not only a prince, but a father to her as well.

In her letter to the Ingolstadt faculty, von Grumbach pleaded not only for the case of Seehofer, but for the cause of the Reformation. Following the pattern of Luther's treatise To the Christian Nobility, *she urged the prince to reform the church, now beset by corrupt priests, monks, and nuns. She suggested that monasteries and parishes should be taxed to support the war with the Turks. The poor should receive relief, and the gospel should be preached to them.*

Von Grumbach was ridiculed by a student at Ingolstadt, who wrote a poem deriding her arrogance as a woman who thought she could assume the role of doctor to teach the faculty and the prince. A preacher in Ingolstadt accused her of being "an insolent daughter of Eve, a heretical bitch and confounded rogue." She responded in kind with a poem of her own, perhaps assisted by Hans Sachs. In her poem, she pointed out that God has not withheld God's Spirit from women, citing the biblical models of Judith and Deborah.

When von Grumbach's husband lost his job because of his wife's publications, he turned against her for a time. Writing to a cousin who apparently had advised the husband to lock her up, von Grumbach assured her cousin that her husband had done much to persecute Christ in her. But, she stated, obedience to Christ took precedence over obedience to her husband. Obedience to Christ required a willingness to forsake husband, family, and life. In the end, her family stayed together, although they experienced considerable financial hardship because of her husband's loss of job.

As early as 1522 von Grumbach began a correspondence with Luther and Osiander. She even paid a visit to Luther in 1530 at Coburg, where he was staying during the Diet of Augsburg. Luther wrote in a letter to a friend, "She [Argula von Grumbach] is a singular instrument of Christ. I commend her to you, that Christ through this infirm vessel may confound the mighty and those who glory in their strength."

After her husband died in 1532, she remarried the next year, but her second husband soon died. For the next thirty years, she passed from view. In May 1563 her feisty presence was once again noted when she was cited for having presided at funerals in cemeteries. Although the duke of Bavaria imprisoned her, she was released at the behest of the Nuremberg town council. Even in her old age, her spirit was redoubtable.[1]

THE LORD SAYS, JOHN 12 (46), 'I am the light that has come into the world, that none who believe in me should abide in darkness.' It is my heartfelt wish that this light should dwell in all of us and shine upon all callous and blinded hearts. Amen.

I find there is a text in Matthew 10 (32) which runs: 'Whoever confesses me before another I too will confess before my heavenly Father.' And Luke 9 (26): 'Whoever is ashamed of me and of my words, I too will be ashamed of when I come in my majesty', etc. Words like these, coming from the very mouth of God, are always before my eyes. For they exclude neither woman nor man.

And this is why I am compelled as a Christian to write to you. For Ezekiel 33 (8) says: 'If you see your brother sin, reprove him, or I will require his blood at your hands.' In Matthew 12 (31), the Lord says: 'All sins will be forgiven; but the sin against the Holy Spirit will never be forgiven, neither here nor in eternity.' And in John 6 (63) the Lord says: 'My words are spirit and life . . .'.

How in God's name can you and your university expect to prevail, when you deploy such foolish violence against the word of God; when you force someone to hold the holy Gospel in their hands for the very purpose of denying it, as you did in the case of Arsacius Seehofer? When you confront him with an oath and declaration such as this, and use imprisonment and even the threat of the stake to force him to deny Christ and his word?

Yes, when I reflect on this my heart and all my limbs tremble. What do Luther or Melanchthon teach you but the word of God? You condemn them without having refuted them. Did Christ teach you so, or his apostles, prophets, or evangelists? Show me where this is written! You lofty experts, nowhere in the Bible do I find that Christ, or his apostles, or his prophets put people in prison, burnt or murdered them, or sent them into exile. . . . Don't you know that the Lord says in Matthew 10 (28) 'Have no fear of him who can take your body but then his power is at an end. But fear him who has power to despatch soul and body into the depths of hell.'

One knows very well the importance of one's duty to obey the authorities. But where the word of God is concerned neither Pope, Emperor nor princes—as Acts 4 and 5 make so clear—have any jurisdiction.[2] For my part, I have to confess, in the name of God and by my soul's salvation, that if I were to deny Luther and Melanchthon's writing I would be denying God and his word, which may God forfend for ever. Amen.

Haven't you read the first chapter of Jeremiah (11, 13), where the Lord says to him: 'What do you see?' He says: 'I see a vigilant rod.' Says the Lord: 'You see correctly, for I am ceaselessly vigilant in order to bring my words to pass.' He asks him again: 'What else do you see?' 'I see a burning pot, and the face of God from midnight.' Says the Lord: 'You have seen correctly; for from midnight every evil will be revealed to every inhabitant of the earth.' The pot burns; and truly you and your university will never extinguish it. And neither the Pope with his decretals, nor Aristotle, who has never been a Christian, nor you yourselves can manage it. You may imagine that you can defy God, cast down his prophets and apostles from heaven, and banish them from the world. This shall not happen. I beseech you, my dear masters, let him stay; have no doubt about it: God will surely preserve his holy and blessed word. As he has hitherto declared; has done in the Old and New Testament, still does, and will continue to do.

God will fall upon you, as the prophet says, Hosea 13 (8): 'They puffed up their hearts and forgot me. I will be to them as a lion in their path. And will fall upon them like a bear who sees her young being stolen.' And Hosea 6 (5): 'I smote them with the words of my mouth. Woe to you! for you have made your counsel without me.' Isaiah 30 (1). And Ezekiel 13 (17, 19): 'Woe to the fools, to those who prophesy according to their own conceits. They see useless things, and teach lies. They say: "The Lord says" when I have neither spoken nor sent them. For a handful of barley and a piece of bread they kill souls which are not dying, and declare souls living which do not live. And they lie to my people, so that they believe their lies . . .'. And what does God say in Ezekiel 33 (32–33)? 'The warning of the Lord was like a cheerful ditty to them until the punishment came, for they did not know that a prophet was among them.' And Jeremiah 48 (27): 'God became the butt of their scorn, as if they had discovered him among thieves.'

Greed has possessed you; you would be much readier to suffer God's word if you did not profit from the publication of the Decretal. The gospel does not pull in so many dollars for its advisers. I have seen how my dear lord and father of blessed memory had to pay twenty gulden for a piece of advice four lines long; not that it did him a cent of good. But what does David say in Psalm 37(25)? 'I have been young and now am old and have yet to see the children of righteousness having to beg for bread.' I beseech you. Trust in God He will not desert us, for every hair on our heads is numbered and in his care, as Matthew 10 (30) says. I had to listen for ages to your Decretal preacher crying out in the Church of Our Lady: *Ketzer/ ketzer,* 'Heretic, heretic!' Poor Latin, that! I could say as much myself, no doubt; and I have never been to university. But if they are to prove their case they'll have to do better than that. I always meant to write to him, to ask him to show me which heretical articles the loyal worker for the gospel, Martin Luther, is supposed to have taught.

However I suppressed my inclinations; heavy of heart, I did nothing. Because Paul says in 1 Timothy 2 (12): 'The women should keep silence, and should not speak in church.'[3] But now that I cannot see any man who is up to it, who is either willing or able to speak, I am constrained by the saying: 'Whoever confesses me', as I said above. And I claim for myself Isaiah 3 (4, 12): 'I will send children to be their princes; and women, or those who are womanish, shall rule over them.' And Isaiah 29 (24): 'Those who err will know knowledge in their spirit, and those who mutter will teach the law.' And Ezekiel 20 (23ff.): 'I raise up my hand against them to scatter them. They never followed my judgements, they rejected my commandments, and their eyes were on the idols of their fathers. Therefore I gave them commandments, but no good ones; and judgements by which they could never live.' And Psalm 8 (2): 'You have ordained praise out of the mouth of children and infants at the breast, on account of your enemies.' And Luke 10 (21): 'Jesus rejoiced in the Spirit, and said: "Father, I give you thanks, that you have hidden these things from the wise, and revealed them to the little ones".' Jeremiah 3 (31–34): "They will all know God, from the least to the greatest." John 6 (45) and Isaiah 54(13) 'They will all be taught of God.' Paul in 1 Corinthians 12 (3): 'No one can say "Jesus", without the spirit of God.' Just as the Lord says of the confession of Peter in Matthew 16 (17): 'Flesh and blood has not revealed this to you, but my heavenly Father.'

Do you hear this? That it is God who gives us understanding, not any human being? As Paul, too, says in 1 Corinthians 2 (5): 'Your faith should not be in human wisdom . . .'. You, with your papal laws, will not be able to coerce us, not by a long chalk. We have witness enough from Scripture that they have no right to make laws without God's command, as Jeremiah 23 (32) says. Where, however, it is based in the Bible, the book which contains all God's commands, we will be happy and pleased to accept it. But where it is not, it has no validity for us at all. Or only in so far as it is my duty to spare my weak and foolish brother, until he, too, has been instructed. For God says, Deuteronomy 4 (2): 'Add nothing to my word, and subtract nothing from it.' And Proverbs 30 (6, 5): 'Add nothing to the words of God, lest you be reproved, and be found a liar.' Just before that we find: 'The word of God is a fiery shield to all who put their trust and confidence in him.' Isaiah (59:21) and Jeremiah (1:9): 'The word which I say to you, proclaim to them from my mouth . . .'.

How are the lawmakers and their representatives to endure if they invent laws out of their own heads and not from the counsel and the work of God? In my view the Lord is referring to them in Matthew 15 (7–9): 'O you hypocrites! You have made the command of God vain because of your impositions.' And declares that it is an empty honour if He is honoured by human commandments. And Luke 11 (46, 52): 'Woe to you who are wise in the law! You impose heavy burdens on people which they cannot bear but do not move a finger to carry them yourself.' And later in the same chapter: 'Woe to you who are wise in the law! You do not go in yourselves, and prohibit those who want to go in from doing so. You who have the key of knowledge and shut up the kingdom of heaven . . .'. Hear the Lord in Matthew 24 (49–51): 'If the wicked servant starts beating his fellow, when the hour comes unexpectedly he will be separated from the others and set among the hypocrites, and then there will be nothing but howling and gnashing of teeth', from which God defend us all.

My heart goes out to our princes, whom you have seduced and betrayed so deplorably. For I realise that they are ill informed about divine Scripture. If they could spare the time from other business, I believe they, too, would discover the truth that no one has a right to exercise sovereignty over the word of God. Yes, no human being, whoever he be, can rule over it. For the word of God alone—without which nothing was made—should and must rule.

If one could enforce faith why weren't all unbelievers given instructions to believe long ago? The difficulty is that it is the word of God which has to teach us, not flesh and blood. You won't be able to gain any such fame with Arsacius Seehofer, prettying him up with his coerced and dictated oath, calling him a Master of Arts. For you have forgotten one thing: that he is only eighteen years old, and still a child. Others won't forget. From the way in which the news has come to me from other places in such a short time, you will surely be notorious throughout the entire world.

What have our princes done to merit such conduct from you? Is this the reward for their frequent generosity, bestowing wealth on the poor among you? How do you make them look? Why do you make them and this university of yours, which they are rightly praised for founding, the laughing stock of the whole world? Ah, what loyalty you return for the good they have done you! What gratitude! How dare you?

For it is certain that they will soon become aware of the truth, and of your wicked and poisonous envy. God will give them a true understanding. That is my heartfelt, dutiful prayer. For they are the rulers of my fatherland, and I, too, was brought up for a while under their noble father and mother, my gracious lord and lady, and came to know their good living and godly fear. God be their reward, here in time and in eternity.

My heart goes out to them; for they have no one with enough integrity to tell them what is going on. And I realise very well that it is for their wealth, torn from them every day, that they are loved rather than for themselves. I am prepared to write to them in this vein, since, because of other business, they have no leisure to sit down and read for themselves. Although there is nothing more needful than the word of God, as the Lord says in Luke 10 (42): 'That is the best part—to listen to the word of God.' And what does he add in Luke 9 (25): 'If one were to win all this world, but lose one's soul, how could it be regained?' But they put their trust in you as the biblical scholars. That is why they installed you. And for this purpose you have no small revenue from the land and living of their poor subjects. This university was founded by their parents, to their great merit, and maintained at great expense.

I am quite convinced that if they knew the truth, they would not continue to act on your requests as they have now done with Seehofer and would not have given permission for him to be murdered, as indicated in his oath. May God be their reward eternally. I hope things will improve. Who knows why they gave such an instruction?

Have no doubt about this: God looks mercifully on Arsacius, or will do so in the future, just as he did on Peter, who denied the Lord three times. For each day the just person falls seven times and gets up on his feet again. God does not want the death of the sinner, but his conversion and life. Christ the Lord himself feared death; so much so that he sweated a bloody sweat. I trust that God will yet see much good from this young man. Just as Peter, too, did much good work later, after his denial of the Lord. And, unlike this man, he was still free, and did not suffer such lengthy imprisonment, or the threat of the stake.

A disputation is easily won when one argues with force, not Scripture. As far as I can see that means that the hangman is accounted the most learned. It's easy to see, though, that the devil has helped to arrange this fine hullabaloo. God will not put up with your ways much longer. In 2 Corinthians 11 (14) Paul says: 'the devil turns himself into an angel of light.' So it is no wonder that confidence tricksters turn themselves into apostles of Christ.

Remember Matthew 10(35) ‘There has to be conflict, the son against the father, the daughter against the mother, the bride against the mother in law, and one’s servants will become one’s enemies.’ And John 16 (2): ‘The time will come when they will kill you and think that they do God a service. For they know neither the Father nor me.’ And Paul in 1 Corinthians 11 (19): ‘Conflict must take place, so that those who are approved may be revealed.’ Also 2 Corinthians 4 (3): ‘If the Gospel is hidden, it is to those who are perishing . . .’.

What a fine way to observe the imperial mandate that has just been issued on 6 March! In which it is crystal clear that the Gospels are to be preached as God has commanded, together with the teachers approved by the Christian Church! Nothing at all is said about any Roman Church. I can find no word in the Bible about this Roman Church. I’d be glad if you could show me what God has said about the Roman Church. I have read in the histories of the saints that they were generally martyred by the same gathering. Find scant good said about it. May God better it!

Are you not ashamed that [Seehofer] had to deny all the writings of Martin, who put the New Testament into German, simply following the text? That means that the holy Gospel and the Epistles and the story of the Apostles and so on are all dismissed by you as heresy. It seems there is no hope of a proper discussion with you. And then there’s the five books of Moses, which are being printed too. Is that nothing? It would be easier, and more profitable, to engage in discussion with a Jew. I hear nothing about any of you refuting a single article [of Arsacius] from Scripture. What I do hear is that a learned lawyer came forward to him and asked: ‘Why was he crying? Wasn’t he a heretic?’ But jurisprudence is no value here.

I would have thought that you would have suspended your scholastic squabbles until the coming Council had been summoned, in pursuance of the imperial mandate which has been read out here publicly from the pulpit. The reason is obscure to me; up to now no one has been much worried by Luther. It doesn’t seem to worry our clergy. If some of them could at least read the Psalter that would be something.

Although I can’t discover anywhere else where it has been proclaimed. Nor in any other territory either. It seems those in Dietfurt have good ground to rejoice that they have led the way in this great matter which pertains to faith and eternal salvation. I would have thought it would have been proclaimed by the university. Especially to you in this diocese and territory; perhaps you think it is too lofty for any Christian to pronounce.

I beseech you for the sake of God, and exhort you by God’s judgment and righteousness, to tell me in writing which of the articles written by Martin or Melanchthon you consider heretical. In German not a single one seems heretical to me. And the fact is that a great deal has been published in German, and I've read it all. Spalatin sent me a list of all the titles. I have always wanted to find out the truth. Although of late I have not been reading any, for I have been occupied with the Bible, to which all of [Luther's] work is directed anyway—to bring us to read it. My dear lord and father insisted on me reading it, giving me it when I was ten years old. Unfortunately I did not obey him, being seduced by the afore-named clerics, especially by Observants who said that I would be led astray.

Ah, but what a joy it is when the spirit of God teaches us and gives us understanding, flitting from one text to the next—God be praised—so that I came to see the true, genuine light shining out. I don't intend to bury my talent, if the Lord gives me grace Matt. 25(18). 'The gospel', says Christ, Luke 7(22),'is preached to the poor, and blessed is the one who is not offended by me . . .'. As Paul said in 1 Corinthians 9 (18): 'I preach the unvarnished gospel, lest I abuse my power.' 'I speak truly to you of the light that shines again in the world'. Psalm 119 (130): 'As your word is disclosed it shines forth and gives understanding to the lowly.' Psalm 36 (9): 'In you is the well of life, and in your light we will see light.' John 2 (25): God sought no human witness, 'for he knew what was in everyone'. John 16 (13–15): 'The spirit will explain who I am.' John 14 (6): 'I am the way, the truth and life. No one comes to the Father except through me.' And in John 9 (39–41), the Lord says: 'I am come for judgment upon this world. So that those who do not see should see, and those who do see should be made blind. The Pharisees said: "Are we blind, then?" The Lord answers: "If you were blind you would be without sin. But if you say: We understand, then, your sin stands".' And John 8 (47): 'Whoever abides in my word is my disciple.' And in the same chapter: 'Whoever is of God, hears the word of God. Therefore if you do not hear it you are not of God . . .'. And John 10 (4): 'My little sheep know my voice, but a stranger's voice they do not know and so they do not follow him.' Matthew 24 (35): 'Heaven and earth will pass away. But my words will not pass away.' And Isaiah 40 (8): 'The word of God stands for ever.'

Now I don't find such promises from human beings, or papal laws or utterances. 2 Corinthians 1 (19): 'The word of God in his promises is a Yes which excludes any No.' 'From this word was made heaven and earth and all that is in it, and without nothing was made.' John 1 (3). And God was the word by which the dead were quickened, the sinner converted, the blind made to see, the lame made straight, the dumb to speak and so on. . . . That is a treasury of salvation, not a pit for cash, like the Decretals. Through it life is promised to us. Matthew 4 (23–24) and John 6 (40, 48–51) .

I cry out with the prophet Jeremiah, chapter 22 (29): 'Earth, earth, earth! Hear the word of the Lord.' I beseech and request a reply from you if you consider that I am in error, though I am not aware of it. For Jerome was not ashamed of writing a great deal to women, to Blesilla, for example, to Paula, Eustochium and so on. Yes, and Christ himself, he who is the only teacher of us all, was not ashamed to preach to Mary Magdalene, and to the young woman at the well (John 20:15–17; 4:7–20).

I do not flinch from appearing before you, from listening to you, from discussing with you. For by the grace of God I, too can ask questions, hear answers and read in German. There are, of course, German Bibles which Martin has not translated. You yourselves have one which was printed forty one years ago, when Luther's was never even thought of.

If God had not ordained it, I might behave like the others, and write or say that he perverts (Scripture); that it is contrary to God's will. Although I have yet to read anyone who is his equal in translating it into German. May God, who works all this in him, be his reward here in time and in eternity. And even if it came to pass—which God forfend—that Luther were to revoke his views, that would not worry me. I do not build on his, mine, or any person's understanding, but on the true rock, Christ himself, which the builders have rejected. But he has been made the foundation stone, and the head of the corner, as Paul said in 1 Corinthians 3 (11): 'No other base can be laid, than that which is laid, which is Christ.'

God grant that I may speak with you in the presence of our three princes and of the whole community. It is my desire to be instructed by everyone. Philosophy can avail nothing. As Paul says to the Colossians, chapter 2 (8): 'Be careful of philosophy and the lofty speech of those who are wise in the things of the world.' And what does he say in 1 Corinthians 1 (20): 'God has made human wisdom folly'? In 1 Corinthians 3 (19): 'All the wisdom of the world is folly to God.'

Jurisprudence cannot harm me; for it avails nothing here; I can detect no divine theology in it. Therefore I have no fears for myself, as long as you wish to instruct me by writing, and not by violence, prison or the stake. Joel 2 (12): 'Turn again; return to the Lord. For he is kind and merciful.' The Lord laments in the words of Jeremiah 2 (13): 'They have forsaken me, the well of living water, and have dug out broken cisterns which cannot hold any water.'

With Paul, 1 Corinthians 2, I say: 'I am not ashamed of the gospel which is the power of God to salvation to those who believe.'[4] The Lord says, in Matthew 10 (19): 'Should you be called forward do not worry about what you will say. It is not you who speak. In that same hour you will be given what you have to say. And the spirit of your Father will speak through you.'

I have no Latin; but you have German, being born and brought up in this tongue. What I have written to you is no woman's chit-chat, but the word of God; and (I write) as a member of the Christian Church, against which the gates of Hell cannot prevail. Against the Roman, however, they do prevail. Just look at that church! How is it to prevail against the gates of Hell? God give us his grace, that we all may be saved, and may (God) rule us according to his will. Now may his grace carry the day. Amen.

Dietfurt. Sunday after the exaltation of the holy Cross. The year of the Lord. . . . One thousand five hundred and in the twenty-third year.

My signature.
Argula von Grumbach,
von Stauff by birth

To the reverent, honourable, well-born, most learned, noble and esteemed Rector and general council of the whole University of Ingolstadt.

Notes

1. See Roland H. Bainton, *Women of the Reformation in Germany and Italy* (Minneapolis: Augsburg Press, 1971), 97–109; Paul A. Russell, *Lay Theology in the Reformation: Popular Pamphleteers in Southwest Germany*, 1521–1525 (Cambridge: Cambridge University Press, 1986), 191–201; and Peter Matheson, ed. *Argula von Grumbach: A Woman's Voice in the Reformation* (Edinburgh: T. & T. Clark, 1995), 1–71. Matheson is quite critical of the work of Bainton and Russell.
2. In his note here, Matheson points out that "Peter and John resist the rulers, elders, and scribes in Jerusalem; Acts 4:19f., 5:29."
3. But 1 Corinthians 14:34 more approximates her language.
4. Her reference is wrong. The text is Rom. 1:16.

34. A Conversation between an Evangelical Christian and a Lutheran in Which the Offensive Behavior of Some Who Call Themselves Lutherans Is Exposed and Admonished in a Brotherly Spirit

(1524)

HANS SACHS

Hans Sachs (1494–1576), a shoemaker and celebrated Meistersinger of Nuremberg, was an important lay pamphleteer who created effective propaganda to promote the Protestant Reformation. He wrote poems, hymns, and prose dialogues that were highly critical of the papacy, priesthood, and monks, and he praised Reformation teachings on the authority of the Bible and the priesthood of all believers. His impact went beyond his writings alone because he authored many texts to accompany woodcuts by Nuremberg artists that were published as broadsides, such as one depicting the papacy as the seven-headed beast in the Book of Revelation. In 1527 Sachs collaborated with an important Nuremberg reformer, Andreas Osiander, to publish A Miraculous Prophecy Concerning the Papacy. *This book contained thirty pictures with commentary by Osiander, and one hundred fifty verses by Sachs.*[1]

SOURCE: A. Keller and E. Goetze, eds., *Hans Sachsens Werke* (Tübingen: Literarischer Verein, 1870–1902), vol. 21. Translated by Elsbeth Duke.

Sachs's first literary work on behalf of the Reformation was a poem titled "The Wittenberg Nightingale" (1523). It described Luther as a prophet of a new day dawning after a long night of darkness. Nuremberg officially adopted the Reformation in 1525. During the previous year, Sachs had published a series of four dialogues.

In the first dialogue, Disputation between a Canon and a Shoemaker, *the shoemaker answers the canon, who had dressed him down for his attacks on clergy and the pope, by insisting on his right as a baptized Christian to name sin wherever he found it. The shoemaker maintains that it is his privilege to interpret Scripture for himself, and he argues for justification by faith without the works of law. Justification does issue in good works, not to win salvation but to benefit neighbors.*

In a second dialogue, A Conversation about the Fictitious Works of the Clergy and Their Vows by Which They Think They Will Be Saved but Which Blaspheme the Blood of Christ, *two lay leaders named Peter and Hans claim to be evangelical but not Lutheran, ridiculing the hypocrisy of the classic monastic vows of poverty, chastity, and obedience.*[2]

The last two dialogues of 1524 leave behind the faults of Catholic clergy and critique the evil behavior of Nuremberg citizens who had converted to the evangelical faith. In the third dialogue, A Dialogue Concerning an Argument of the Romanists against Profiteering and Other Public Evils of the Christian Community, *Romanus indicts the evangelical community of Nuremberg for a whole host of crimes: greed, adultery, drunkenness, blasphemy. He condemns profiteering by the merchants at the expense of the poor.*

In response, his adversary in the dialogue, Reichenburger, defends the Reformation in Nuremberg against these charges. He agrees with his Romanist opponent that excess profit and interest are evils, that workers should not be exploited, and that the poor should not be oppressed, but he does not think that they should be pampered by too generous charity. He insists that fair profit or interest does not run counter to evangelical law, nor are riches necessarily a barrier to the kingdom of God, especially if a rich person uses wealth in a charitable manner.

The attention given to economic injustice in this dialogue probably means that it was written against the backdrop of the incipient Peasants' War. One interpretation argues that Sachs's dialogue is a defense of the position and power of the burghers and the city council of Nuremberg on the eve of the rebellion.[3] *Another interpretation sees a dialogue written by "one who speaks for a movement that was trying to be realistic about people and society and cognizant of the disruptive consequences of unworkable moral, social and political ideals."*[4]

The fourth dialogue, A Conversation between an Evangelical Christian and a Lutheran in Which the Offensive Behavior of Some Who Call Themselves Lutherans Is Exposed and Admonished in a Brotherly Spirit, *is critical of Lutherans who abuse their Christian freedom, for example, by flaunting their eating of meat on Fridays and during Lent, even if it means offending their neighbor. Making abundant use of Scripture, the dialogue argues that Christian love toward neighbors should always take precedence over Christian freedom.*

It may be that Sachs, like other lay pamphleteers of the early 1520s, was less dependent on Lutheran ideas of reform than on late medieval mysticism and heretical movements (such as the Waldenses and the Hussites) (see vol. 2:10–11). He and other lay pamphleteers called for reformation on the basis of an evangelical law that exceeded Lutheran teachings.[5] Lay pamphleteers like Sachs regularly contrasted the terms evangelical *and* Lutheran. *Yet, in these dialogues, there is less criticism of Luther's teachings than there is of the abuse of Luther's teachings. Sachs urges Lutherans to remember that "although Luther has proclaimed the Christian freedom to release our poor captivated conscience, at the same time he has invariably warned in his writings and sermons . . . that we should keep ourselves from unchristian behavior . . . so as not to bring harm to the Gospel and the Word of God."*

Hans.

God bless you, dear brother in Christ!

Peter.

Blessings to you too, dear brother Hans! Where are you going? I say, you are a rare guest in my house.

Hans.

Well, to hear the sermon, as we have started doing just recently and get back my booklet on the Christian freedom. Did you read it to you father-in-law, the old Romanist?

Peter.

Oh no!

Hans.

How come? Is he not yet convinced?

Peter.

Well, this Friday a week ago I threw him out.

Hans.

Why so?

Peter.

Well, he showed up unexpectedly as we were just eating a veal roast. How he started to curse and admonish us, as if we had murdered someone! He behaved just like all the other Romanists! Since that time he has not spoken one word to me nor has he come to my house.

Hans.

Ah, indeed, you did wrong for you know that your father-in-law has not yet understood the evangelical freedom.

Peter.

What! Is eating meat now a sin? I think you are becoming hypocritical. Did not Christ call the people to him, Matt. 15 and said to them (10 f.):[6] "Hear and understand: not what goes into the mouth defiles a man," and Luke 10(8): "Whenever you enter a town and they receive you, eat what is set before you" and John 8(36): "So if the son makes you free, you will be free indeed," and Paul, 2 Cor. 3(17): ". . . where the Spirit of the Lord is, there is freedom." And Rom. 14(14): "I know and I am persuaded in the Lord Jesus that nothing is unclean in itself; but it is unclean for any one who thinks it unclean." And to Titus 1(15): "To the pure all things are pure, but to the corrupt and unbelieving nothing is pure; their very minds and consciences are corrupted." And again Rom. 14(22): ". . . happy is he who has no reason to judge himself for what he approves." Well, my dear, what do you say to these statements?

Hans.

You are right: to eat meat is not unclean in itself since it is from God free and unforbidden. Yet Paul says 1 Cor. 10(23f): "All things are lawful," but not all things are helpful. "All things are lawful" but not all things build up. Let no one seek his own good but the good of his neighbor. And 1 Cor. 8(9): "Only take care lest this liberty of yours somehow become a stumbling block to the weak." And to the Rom. 14(1f): "As for the man who is weak in faith, welcome him, but not for disputes over opinions. One believes he may eat anything, while the weak man eats only vegetables." And again in the same chapter (21): it is much better not to eat meat or drink wine or do anything that makes your brother stumble. The faith that you have, keep between yourself and God.

Peter.

It is also written in 1 Cor. 10(29): ". . . for why should my liberty be determined by another man's scruples? If I partake with thankfulness, why am I denounced because of that for which I give thanks?"

Hans.

Paul says in the text immediately following it (32 f.):"Give no offense to Jews or to Greeks or to the church of God. Just as I try to please all men in everything I do, not seeking my own advantage, but that of many, that they may be saved."

Peter.

I don't care about that. It is written in Galatians 5(1): "For freedom Christ has set us free; stand fast therefore, and do not submit again to a yoke of slavery." And Col. 2(16): Therefore let no one pass judgment on you in questions of food and drink or with regard to a festival. And again (20): If with Christ you died to the human regulations, why do you live as if you were still trapped by regulations such as: Do not touch such and such, do not eat or drink it, do not handle it. And still more clear in 1 Cor. 10(25): "Eat whatever is sold in the meat market without raising any question on the ground of conscience."

Hans.

My dear man, the text in 1 Cor. 10(28) continues: "But if someone says to you: This has been offered as to idols" (just as our forgoing of meat is a human law, not God's law). Paul's advice of not eating is for the sake of those who forgo eating and their conscience. And Rom. 14(15): "If your brother is being hurt by what you eat, you are not acting out of love. Do not let what you eat cause the ruin of one for whom Christ died." And 1 Cor. 8 (11f): "And so by your knowledge this weak man is destroyed, the brother for whom Christ died. Thus, sinning against your brethren and wounding their conscience when it is weak, you sin against Christ. Therefore, if food is a cause of my brother's falling, I will never eat meat." How do you like these statements by St. Paul?

Peter.

How good is our freedom if we can not make use of it?

Hans.

It is useful in a sense that we know none of the food is harmful to us. But for the sake of the weak we shall abstain, according to Rom. 15(1): "We who are strong ought to bear with the failings of the weak, and not to please ourselves;" as it is written in 1 Cor. 10(12): ". . . let one who thinks that he stands take heed lest he fall." I am afraid there are many who eat meat on Friday out of wickedness, inquisitiveness or lust, and yet they are not yet firmly rooted in faith and in the end will waver in their conscience. For Paul says in Rom. 14(23): "But he who has doubts is condemned if he eats because he does not act from faith; for whatever does not proceed from faith is sin."

Peter.

Oh, dear brother Hans, how long therefore shall we lie in the Babylonian captivity in Romanist chains and not use freely our Christian liberty regarding the eating of meat and in every other aspect?

Hans.

Dear brother Peter, be patient! Paul in Thess. 2(8) states: ". . . the Lord Jesus will slay him with the breath of his mouth and destroy him." Therefore, dear brother, let us, you and I and every one else be satisfied that our conscience is free and not bound by such human laws, regarding the salvation of the soul. Let us willingly bear such and similiar burdens with our brothers outwardly, just as other laws and social customs, as in Gal. 5–6(2): "Bear one another's burdens, and so fulfill the law of Christ."

Peter.

I quite understand that I again must treat certain foods differently, for the sake of old women and men, even though they have been condemned by Christ. Matt. 15(13): "Every plant which my heavenly father has not planted will be rooted up."

Hans.

Hear what Paul tells the Romans in chapter 14(17): "For the kingdom of God does not mean food and drink but righteousness and peace and joy in the Holy Spirit." And 1 Cor. 8(8): Eating does not improve us for the better. We are no worse off if we do not eat, and no better if we do. Well then, if we forgo meat for the sake of our brothers who do not know any better in their conscience, we do so out of faith and love, making acceptable in God's sight what had been abominable to him.

Peter.

So I am being told that I must again become a hypocritical Romanist and keep all their regulations and empty forms just like them.

Hans.

Well, what you can do in order not to cause offense to your brother, you may well do. We only ought to do what is not an offense to our brother. Therefore do as Paul in 1 Cor. 9(19): "For though I am free from all men, I have made myself a slave to all, that I might win the more. To the Jews I became a Jew, to the Gentiles I became a Gentile. To the weak I became weak, I have become all things to all men." And 2 Cor. 12 (11:29): "Who is weak, and I am not weak? And who is being offended and I am not indignant?" Therefore let us live according to the commandment of Christ. John 13(34): "A new commandment I give to you, that you love one another as I have loved you. By this all men will know that you are my disciples." Do you understand that love is a Christian's true test and not the eating of meat, for that dogs and cats can do as well.

Peter.

Dear man, it will do no good to try to spare them any longer, they will only get worse and more stubborn. Therefore, it is of no consequence whether to eat or forgo eating (of meat).

Hans.

Dear brother, you don't want to spare them even though the gospel and God's word is being defamed and called heresy by your eating of meat, since the eating of meat is the greatest scandal and offense in the evangelical teachings to the common man. May God enlighten their blindness with his Holy Word! Paul's statement in 2 Thess. 2(10f) has come true for them: ". . . because they refused to love the truth and be saved. Therefore God sends upon them a strong delusion to make them believe what is false, so that all may be condemned who did not believe the truth. . . ."

Peter.

Unfortunately, it is true. I have some neighbors who take it more to heart when someone eats a morsel of meat than if someone lies or cheats.

Hans.

Oh dear brother, it is right for you to avoid eating meat or to do it secretly so that no one will be offended.

Peter.

So be it. So far I had not given any thought to the fact that my ways could hurt someone.

Hans.

Well, now, the bells are ringing for the third time for the sermon.

Peter.

First, the other matter, my dear man, my father-in-law is coming, talk to him for the sake of the gospel.

Master Ulrich.

God bless you, you Lutheran people!

Hans.

Thank you! You are arriving at the right time. Dear Master Ulrich, come with us to hear our sermon.

Master Ulrich.

I wish that your preacher would be hanged, he is a heretic.

Hans.

Well, dear Master Ulrich why is that?

Master Ulrich.

My son-in-law here tells me when he visits: Our preacher says, we are no longer permitted to pray to and serve the saints, or to fast, confess, go on a pilgrimage, attend mass, keep vigil, hold mass for the dead, declare an Annual Feast Day, buy letters of indulgence, as well as that good works are useless for obtaining salvation. These and even greater antics, all of which my son-in-law and his companions then proceed to observe. He knows what I am talking about.

Hans.

Well, Peter, Peter! You are being unjust, you and your companions, in throwing such phrases at them: "our preacher says such and such" without giving the reason for them as well, as our preacher has told you. You ruin the doctrine for the common man, who in turn curses the Christian preachers and flees their sermons, which would tell them the real reason. They so defame the Holy Scriptures unknowingly by saying: "If that is the new teaching I will rather keep my old faith." Who is to blame? Only you rude guys. You and the likes of you, no matter whether they are dear to me or hostile toward me, one cannot tell the difference anyway. But when you become Christians you have to behave as such and tell the ignorant people the comforting word about Christ which you have heard from the preacher. That is to say, that the death of Christ is the only work for our salvation and that our heavenly father has given all authority in heaven and on earth to Christ. To Christ alone we ought to listen: what he tells us, we shall do; what he forbids, we shall abstain from; what he sets free, nobody shall restrain neither in heaven nor on earth, for the salvation of our souls. And if you tell this to the people, the hearts of the ignorant might be moved so that they also may come to listen to these sermons and hear for themselves the real reason and come to the true recognition of God's truth, causing all other human laws and trickery to collapse in itself.

Master Ulrich.

I too would appreciate much more if the good things were being pointed out; yet I hear very little of that from the Lutherans. Indeed, an entire table of Lutherans assembles at my son-in-law's and not one good Christian word can be heard from them. There they go, dressing down monks and priests, so that not even a dog would take a piece of bread from them. And whoever indulges in it the most, he is master among them. That's why your Lutheran ways don't attract me at all.

Hans.

Peter, Peter, that is against the love for your neighbor. Matt. 7(12): "So whatever you wish that men would do to you, do so to them." Well then, you don't want to be blamed, since they are so blind, poor and stubborn that it is more appropriate to have compassion and to pray to God for them, rather than shouting their disgrace, vices and injustices, and make fun of them at the table.

Peter.

Well, if they are allowed to do it, then they must be told so, for it is the truth.

Hans.

Listen to Paul whether it is right, Rom. 2(1): "Therefore you have no excuse, o man, whoever you are, when you judge another, for in passing judgment upon him you condemn yourself, because you are doing the very same things." Understand with your heart when you judge another.

Peter.

Dear man, they have pulled the wool over our eyes long enough, now we will pay them back with the same measure; according to Rev. 18(6): "Render to her as she herself has rendered, and repay her double for her deeds."

Hans.

Yet it is written in Matt. 5(44): "Love your enemies, bless those who malign you, do good to those who hate you and pray for those who insult and persecute you." And 1 Pet. 2(3:18): "Finally, all of you have unity of spirit, sympathy, love of the brethren, a tender heart and a humble mind. Do not return evil for evil or reviling for reviling, but on the contrary bless", etc.

Peter.

Should we then just dismiss it with a laugh? That would lead them to think we enjoyed it. I clearly see a new wave of defamation coming: how Christians for the sake of the gospel are being assaulted, fought, burned at the stake, expelled and forbidden to live here in the Babylonian Kingdom.

Hans.

Dear brother, everything that will happen to us has been prophecied by Christ. Read Matt. 10; Mark 12; Luke 21; and John 15: there you will find all about the persecution that is about to come upon Christians.

Peter.

It almost would be better, to punch them with our fists, according to the statement in Rev. 18(6f): Mix a double draught for her (that is to say the Babylonian whore) in the cup she mixed. As she glorified herself and played the wanton, so give her a like measure of torment and suffering."

Hans.

Oh no, it is written in Deut. 32(35): "Vengeance is mine, says the Lord." And Rev. 13(10): "If any one is to be taken captive, to captivity he goes and if any one slays with the sword, with the sword must he be slain." And Matt. 26(52): "All who take the sword will perish by the sword." And the Lord will find them out, according to 2 Pet. 2(12), they will be destroyed in the same destruction!—Therefore you be content and remain steadfast as a Christian. Luke 6(29): "To him who strikes you on the cheek, offer the other also; and from him who takes away your cloak do not withhold your coat as well."

Peter.

What? Should we then affirm their seductive deception?

Hans.

No, where ever you find yourself eye to eye with those who slander the evangelical truth do not keep silent but contradict their idle talk with the word of God. And do not react with making a row and shouting, for that is wrong and offensive to the common man.

Peter.

Well, has not Christ himself told us of these seductive wolves and also in their absence, namely in Matt. 7 and 24; Mark 13 and Luke 21. And Paul has written of them in 1 Cor. 15 and 2 Cor. 11; Gal. 5; Eph. 4; Phil. 3; Col. 2; 2 Thess. 2 and 1 Tim. 4 and 1 Tim. 2 as well as Saint Peter [has written] the same: 1 Pet. 5 and 2 Pet. 2; and also 1 John 4 and 2 John 1.

Hans.

Pay attention to what is written in Rom. 15(4): "For whatever was written in former days, was written for our instruction, that by steadfastness and by the encouragement of the scriptures we might have hope." Therefore we have been warned through Holy Scriptures to beware of them and their corruption, so that we may subject our conscience only and solely to the unchangeable word of God.

Peter.

Then why do our preachers also shout from the pulpit against the spiritually wrong, corrupt doctrine, worship, laws and behavior? Likewise, why do

Doctor Martin and many of his followers write about the aforementioned things for the Christian community? If it's right for them, so it's right for us.

Hans.

Yes, such teaching and writing are done from dutiful Christian love, for the sake of the common uneducated folk, so that they will be set free in their conscience from the seducers mentioned above. On the other hand, it is also for the good of these seducers, if God were to knock some down through his mighty word as he did to Paul before Damascus, Acts 9, and thereby make lambs of Christ out of the devil's wolves. However, if such teaching and writing stems from a bad character and not from Christian love, it is unjust and sinful, however useful and needful that work is in itself, according to the words in 1 Cor. 13(3): "If I give away all I have, and if I deliver my body to be burned, but have not love, I gain nothing." Here is a justified concern—when you sit and sip your wine and slander monks and priests, this takes place as a result not of Christian love but of insolence, envy, hatred or just bad habit which is clearly forbidden in Holy Scripture, namely in Eph. 4(29): "Let no evil talk come out of your mouth, but only such as is good for edifying as fits the occasion." And further (31): "Let all bitterness and wrath and anger and clamor and slander be put away from you. . . ." And Titus 3(2): "Remind them to speak evil of no one, to avoid quarreling, to be gentle and to show perfect courtesy toward all men." And in 1 Pet. 2(1): "So put away all malice and all guile and insincerity and hatred and all slander."

Peter.

They still would not comply with it, whether we sang sweet or bitter tunes; they are as obdurate as the Pharisees.

Hans.

Ah, indeed, so let them fare as the Gentiles. Matt. 18. For if you continue to disgrace and curse them, it does no good. And others who sit next to you, listening, will become angry and say: "All the Lutherans are doing is reviling the clergy, trying to beat and stab them; what good can therefore be behind their teachings and in their doctrine?" They think the devil has his hand in it and flee from the evangelical teachings altogether, and they remain in their old error. Such is the fruit of your badmouthing them. Therefore if you really want to be a true Christian, avoid such doings and spare other people. Furthermore, all of you, who call yourselves Lutherans, are seeking the protective cover of a pious man, namely Luther, for your impropriety, while you do not behave according to his teachings. For, although, Luther has proclaimed the Christian freedom to release our poor captivated conscience, at the same time he has invariably warned in his writings and sermons and still does again and again, that we should keep ourselves from deceitful, offensive, unchristian behavior, from rioting and raging like mad men, so as not to bring harm to the gospel and the Word of God by cursing and raging against the simple people. So do not disgrace Doctor Luther, a Christian man, whose intentions are so Christian and trustworthy, with your stupid behavior. For what kind of Christian mind, what faith and trust can those claim who outwardly pursue respectability and goodness, as spiritual beings in the flesh, but give offense to their brothers and neighbors by eating meat, just as these begin to become Christians? That kind of fruit clearly shows that the tree is bad and rotten, Matt. 7.[7]

Master Ulrich.

Yes, Master Hans, if only you were present when the Lutherans gather and let someone join them who is not Lutheran. You could hear for yourself how they spare him. It is like a carnival when they attack him, he is accused of being a Romanist, Papist, hypocrite and promoter of good works. They sneer at him, mock him so much that he sits there among them, feeling like a piper who spoiled the dance and does not know where to hide.

Hans.

Oh you blockheads! Your heart ought to rejoice (if you were truly Christians) when you come upon ignorant persons with whom you could share the word of God (the talent entrusted to you, Matt. 25) in brotherly love. Instead, you go about mocking them.

Peter.

Dear man, they don't understand the least bit of the Holy Scripture and go about it in such clumsy ways like a dog in a cart: we thus have to help them to it.

Hans.

Not at all, for Christ's sake! Spare the ignorant and weak consciences for they are not used to the word of God and you kitchen preachers have not made it clear to them, instead you have foisted on them your own fabrications. Furthermore, empty and mocking words are forbidden in Holy

Scripture. Eph. 5(4): Let there be no filthiness, nor silly talk, nor levity, which are not fitting. And 2 Tim. 2(16): "Avoid such godless chatter, for it will lead people into more and more ungodliness, . . ." instead as Paul says to the Col. 3(16): "Let the word of Christ dwell in you richly, as you teach and admonish one another in all wisdom."

Peter.

Dear man, there are many old and gray men who also boast that they know the gospel, yet they interpret it out of their own head. When questioned about the basics, it becomes clear they know about as much as cows know about chess. Now, should they not be laughed at and be punished?

Hans.

Hear Paul in 1 Tim. 5(1f): "Do not rebuke an older man but exhort him as you would a father; treat younger men like brothers, older women like mothers, younger women like sisters, in all purity." Note, here you have the way to sweetly and kindly instruct others.

Peter.

But there are some holy blusterers among them, who go from church to church, trying to buy their way into heaven with their good works. Whenever we tell them of the right kind of worship, they rise up on their hind lings, and nobody can get through to them.

Hans.

Ah, indeed, you have to point out their mistake in a kind way, as in Gal. 6(1): "Dear brethren, if a man is overtaken in any trespass, you who are spiritual should restore him in a spirit of gentleness."

Peter.

Well, yes, they do not accept that and tell us we ought to rebuke ourselves.

Hans.

That shows what I have always claimed: They are offended by your rough behavior.

Peter.

Should we then behave as hypocrites, like the monks?

Hans.

No, rather lead a Christian life, as Paul says in Rom. 13(13): "Let us conduct ourselves becomingly as in the day, not in reveling and drunkenness, not in debauchery and licentiousness, not in quarreling and jealousy." And Eph. 4(1): "I . . . beg you, dear brother, to lead a life worthy of the calling to which you have been called, with all lowliness and meekness, with patience, forbearing one another in love." And Paul describes the reason in Phil. 2(14): "Do all things without grumbling or questioning, that you may be blameless and innocent, children of God without blemish in the midst of a crooked and perverse generation."

Peter.

Yet they despise the Holy Scripture and want to adhere to their old habits. If we call something black, they say it is white. They question whether all the writings in the Bible is true and if we teach them the Christian doctrine with all diligence, what is their response? By the way, have you not seen my geese? How can we keep quiet in light of that?

Hans.

Paul writes in 2 Tim. 2(24): "And the Lord's servant must not be quarrelsome but kindly to everyone, an apt teacher, forbearing, correcting his opponents with gentleness. God may perhaps grant that they will repent and come to know the truth." And 1 Pet. 2(15f): "For it is God's will that by doing right you should put to silence the ignorance of foolish men. Live as free men, yet without using your freedom as a pretext for evil."

Peter.

Dear man, their conduct is too rough, they speak evil and accuse us of being heretical. If we don't bite back they will shout: "Hurrah, we won, we won!" Thus it is necessary to hit their shield with the blow of a rifle butt.

Hans.

Well, well, you claim to profess Christ and want to teach others and are not willing to endure evil words. How then will you be able to suffer beatings or even death? Hear Paul in Rom. 12(14f): "Bless those who persecute you; bless and do not curse them. Repay no one evil for evil, never avenge yourselves!" Here you are told to treat everyone with gentleness out of brotherly love and without any bitterness, so that your actions shall bear fruit. Do not treat others harshly, for this contributes greatly to turning many people away from the evangelical doctrine, who otherwise might come and accept the doctrine. Yet instead hostilities arise in the process of finding the true word of God and those who believe are called heretics and God's word, heresy. You alone are to be blamed for all of that, because of your eating meat, making a row, threatening, disgracing and slandering the clergy, besides all the ridiculing, suing, and despising of the simple folk. Thus many spit upon you when they see you and not only you but all who are pious Christians as well; those who are not like you but follow the gospel of Christ and lead a Christian life as is proper.

Peter.

Dear man, we know that some wish us evil and we know them quite well. We too are not exactly fond of them. Should it come to pass that we run into one another, it is likely that we will tear each other apart.

Hans.

Oh, I see, this is a waste of time. Just a lot of noise on your part and very little good will. If you do not love your brother, it is hard to recognize you as a fellow disciple of Christ.

Peter.

Why is that?

Hans.

It is written in 1 John 3(14): "He who does not love his brother remains in death. Any one who hates his brother is a murderer." And John 4 (1 John 4:20): "If any one says "I love God" and hates his brother, he is a liar; for he who does not love his brother whom he has seen, cannot love God whom he has not seen." That is why I am afraid, dear brother Peter, that as long as you and your gang harbor hostilities, you do not have the true Christian faith in Christ, a faith inspired by God. Col. 2. Your faith is a mere human fabrication of flesh and blood that is harmful to yourself and useless as well as offensive to others. For the mind that is set on the flesh is "hostile to God" says Paul in Rom. 8(8). "For all who are led by the spirit of God are sons of God," Rom. 8(14).

Peter.

How then can we recognize them?

Hans.

By their love alone, as Christ says in John 13(35): "By this all men will know that you are my disciples, if you have love for one another." And 1 John 4(7f): "Beloved, let us love one another; for love is of God and knows God. He who does not love, does not know God, for God is love." "He who abides in love, abides in God and God abides in him" [1 John 4:16]. Therefore I may well say to you as Christ said to the Jews, John 8(39): "If you were Abraham's children, you would do what Abraham did." That goes for you too: if you were evangelicals (as you claim), you would act according to the gospel, for the gospel is a wonderful, glad, and delightful message about Christ. Thus, if your mind were set on the gospel, you would proclaim the gospel to your brothers in Christ, lovingly and with all due respect and lead a God fearing life, like the apostles, who were well disposed toward others, as can be read in all their stories in every chapter.

Therefore, dear brother Peter, for God's sake listen to what I have said and tell your brothers too, even though they will think of me a hypocrite and apostate. That does not bother me, since I spoke the truth and the truth will always be persecuted by the godless. For God's sake I wish that all who call themselves Lutherans could have heard me. Perhaps by teaching only a part of the right doctrine, some might have succeeded in becoming good evangelical Christians.

Master Ulrich.

Peter, what do you think? If Master Hans came upon you, he could straighten you out. No doubt, if you Lutherans would lead such a chaste and non-offensive life, your teachings would be held in high esteem by all men. Those who now call you heretics would call you Christians; those who now curse you, would praise you; those who now badmouth you, would speak well of you; those who now avoid you, would seek you out and those who now despise you, would learn from you.

Yet with your eating of meat, making a row, dishonoring the clergy, quarrelling, scoffing, despising and other lewd behavior, you Lutherans yourselves have done a great disservice to the evangelical doctrine.

Hans.

Unfortunately, this is obviously true. May God bestow upon us his Holy Spirit that we may walk according to his holy will. They ring the bells for the third time: Let's go to hear the sermon.

Master Ulrich.

All right! You have made me feel like going to your sermon also; maybe I too might become a good Christian.

Hans.

With God's help!

Master Ulrich.

Amen.

Phil. 2:1 f.:

Dear brothers, "so if there is any encouragement in Christ, any incentive of love, any participation in the Spirit, any affection and sympathy, complete my joy by being of the same mind, having the same love, (being in full accord and one mind). Do nothing from selfishness or conceit, but in humility count others better than yourselves. Let each of you look not only to his own interests, but also to the interests of others."

Notes

1. See Robert Scribner, *For the Sake of Simple Folk: Popular Propaganda for the German Reformation* (Cambridge: Cambridge University Press, 1981), 100–104, 142–47.

2. See Steven Ozment, *Protestants: The Birth of a Revolution* (New York: Doubleday, 1992), 57–58, 76–78; and Paul Russell, *Lay Theology in the Reformation* (Cambridge: Cambridge University Press, 1986), 173–74.

3. See Bernd Balzer, *Bürgerliche Reformationspropaganda: Die Flugschriften des Hans Sachs in den Jahren 1523-25* (Stuttgart: n.p., 1973), 147, 151, 154–55, cited by Ozment, 235.

4. See Ozment, 86.

5. See Russell, 176–82.

6. The biblical quotes are not from the Sachs text but from the Revised Standard Version.

7. See Luther, *The Freedom of a Christian*, 111–12.

35. Katherine Schütz Zell's Foreword for Her Edition of the Hymnbook of the Bohemian Brethren

(1534–1536)

KATHERINE SCHÜTZ ZELL

Apart from Martin Luther's wife, Katherine von Bora, Katherine (Katharina) Schütz Zell was the most famous wife of a sixteenth-century Protestant pastor. Von Bora is remembered because of Luther's words about her, whereas Zell, although she was married to the lesser-known reformer Matthew Zell, of Strasbourg, achieved fame because of her own writings and actions.

The daughter of a carpenter, Katherine Schütz did not come into public view until her 1523 marriage to Matthew Zell. Zell was the fourth Strasbourg priest to break the vow of celibacy and get married during that year.

Faced with this rash of clergy marriages, the local bishop responded by taking away the benefices of the parishes (the endowments that supported clergy positions) and excommunicating the wayward priests. Katherine Zell took up her pen to defend her husband. In An Apology for her Husband, Matthew Zell *(1524), she claimed that the bishop did not want to permit the marriage of priests because of greed, namely, his desire to collect the fees paid by priests and monks who kept concubines, so that*

SOURCE: Elsie Anne McKee, "Reforming Popular Piety in Sixteenth-Century Strasbourg: Katharina Schütz Zell and Her Hymnbook," *Studies in Reformed Theology and History* 2:4 (Princeton, N.J.: Princeton Theological Seminary). Used by permission.

their sins might be remitted. She also contrasted the responsibility and mutual loyalty and affection of a clerical marriage with the sodomy of clerical concubinage.

Anticipating the charge that as a woman she had no business in speaking out on such matters, she stated: "You remind me that the Apostle Paul told women to be silent in church. I would remind you of the word of this same apostle that in Christ there is no longer male or female and of the prophecy of Joel: 'I will pour forth my spirit upon all flesh and your sons and your daughters will prophesy.'"[1]

Like Luther, whose writings she read, Katherine Zell was convinced of the truth of justification by faith, even as she struggled for assurance. However, her faith journey was never preoccupied with her own salvation, for she carried on a constant ministry to persons in need. In one situation, she supplied beds and food for eighty men from the town of Kenzingen, who had accompanied their pastor out of town when he was forced to flee. The men were then prevented from reentering the town by Austrian troops. In addition to making provision for the men, Zell wrote a letter to their wives, consoling them and strengthening their courage. The letter was published as a pamphlet.

Zell also took a leading role ministering to wounded survivors of the Peasants' War (1525) who sought refuge in the city of Strasbourg. She and her husband visited peasant camps outside the city walls and pleaded for peace.

Katherine Schütz Zell sought to overcome religious divisions by hospitality and love. For fourteen days in 1529 she entertained Ulrich Zwingli and Johannes Oecolampadius on their way to the Marburg Colloquy. Disappointed that no agreement was reached between Luther and Zwingli, she wrote Luther that love was more important than differences in doctrine. That principle also guided her work with persecuted Anabaptists (free church Protestants) who sought refuge in Strasbourg. She also befriended the Silesian nobleman Caspar Schwenckfeld, who taught that the body of Christ in the Lord's Supper was heavenly, not earthly. His views were sharply attacked by Luther.

It was perhaps through her friendship with Caspar Schwenckfeld that a Bohemian Brethren hymnbook produced in German translation by Michael Weisse in 1531 came into her hands. So impressed was she by the biblical quality of this hymnal that she was determined to reproduce it in the mid-1530s for the lay people of Strasbourg, so that they might have biblically sound and beautiful songs to sing not only in the church but also in their daily activities in the home. The purpose of her edition was not just to produce delightful hymns for the laity to sing; it was also catechetical, to teach them "the whole business of Christ and our salvation in song." Thus, she called the hymnbook "a teaching, prayer and praise book [rather] than a songbook." The hymnal was intended for the laity, especially women and children, so that "when they faithfully (in the faith) keep house, obey, cook, wash dishes, wipe up and tend children . . . , they can also turn to God with the voice of song." In so doing, "they please God much better than any priest, monk, or nun in their incomprehensible choir song." Here she pitted the priesthood of all believers and the Christian vocation of the laity over against the Catholic clergy. She emphatically included women among those who exercise their Christian calling in the daily rounds of their work: "A poor woman would so gladly sleep, but at midnight she must rock the wailing baby, and sing it a song about godly things."

Katherine Zell followed Weisse's instructions in his preface not to tamper with the words of the hymns, but she did alter its form of publication and change the music. Instead of publishing it as a single volume, she broke it into four small booklets that could be purchased cheaply even by the poor members of Strasbourg society. Either she or her musical assistant changed many of the tunes attached to the hymn texts. All the tunes except one were religious in origin, and they came from a variety of sources. In addition to its variety, Zell's hymnbook shows a concern for musicality and familiarity as well as intelligibility, for, like the Reformers, she was most concerned that the hymns be understood; otherwise, they could not teach. She was therefore careful to connect one word with one note and to have the words and music printed with clarity. So that the hymns might be better understood, Zell attached a series of her own annotations to the hymnbook in which her evangelical theology and her ideas for reform were still more clearly set forth.

Prior to Katherine Schütz Zell's hymnbook, the clergy in Strasbourg had given their primary attention to reform of the liturgy and the church's structure. They had not as yet stressed the reform of popular devotion. Sensitive as she was to the needs of the laity, Zell determined to fill this void with the publication of her hymnbook. By this action, and through her other writings and activities, she showed herself to be a remarkable lay reformer in her own right who made an important contribution to the popularizing of the Reformation.[2]

Out of special love and friendship a songbook was given to me to read. It was printed in Bohemia and sent to good people in Landskron and Fullneck by a godfearing man, indeed, a man who knows God. His name is Michael Weisse. I do not know him personally, but as the Lord says: "By their fruits shall you know them" [cf. Matt. 12:33]. When I read this book, I had to conclude that, so far as I understand the Scriptures, this man [Weisse] has the whole Bible wide open in his heart. Indeed, he has the same knowledge and experience as the two dear men Joshua and Caleb had of the promised land, when they had faithfully visited and walked through it by the command of the Lord given through Moses [cf. Numb. 13:1, 17, 30; 14:6–9].

I found such an understanding of the works of God in this songbook that I want all people to understand it. Indeed, I ought much rather to call it a teaching, prayer, and praise book than a songbook, although the little word "song" is well and properly spoken, for the greatest praise of God is expressed in song, as when Moses sang a glorious song of praise to God when the Lord brought him and His people through the sea, Exod. 15[:1–18]. And the holy Anna the same way sang thanks and praise to God the Lord when He had given her Samuel, 1 Kings 2 [1 Sam. 2:1–10]. As also David made so many glorious Psalm songs, and used often the expression: We should to sing to the Lord, and such like [cf. e.g., Ps. 95:1, 96:1, 2; 98:1, 5]. Thence have also come all the songs of the church, where they have been kept in the right way and with the right heart, as they were by the first singers.

Since, however, now so many scandalous songs are sung by men and women and also children throughout the world, songs in which all slander, coquetry, and other scandalous things are spread through the world by young and old—and the world likes to have such things sung! So it seemed to me a very good and useful thing to do as this man has done, that is, to convey the whole business of Christ and our salvation in song, so that the people may thus enthusiastically and with clear voices be exhorted regarding their salvation, and the devil with his songs may not have any place in them. Also so that good parents may say to their children: "Up till now we have all sung bad songs, to the scandal [vexation] of our souls and our neighbors' souls." But so that you may not complain: "So may we never sing? Must we become like sticks and stones?" Therefore now sing these songs, which express so admirably God's love towards us, and exhort us so faithfully not to neglect the salvation offered to us.

Wherefore also St. Paul teaches us such, in Eph. 5[:3, 4, 18–19] and Col. 3[:16], that we should not allow anyone to hear from us avaricious, insulting words, raillery, or foolish things, and should not be full of wine but full of the Spirit, and we should exhort one another with Psalms and hymns and spiritual songs. And St. James says, in the fifth chapter [verse 13]: whoever is anxious should pray, and whoever is in good spirits should sing Psalms, that is, all kinds of praise of God. As also this man of God has divided up the songs in his book into eighteen groups of songs about the works of God. This book was a concern to me [because of its size]; there were too many songs to be printed all together; that would be too expensive for people to buy. So I took the book in hand, for the use and service of children and the poor, and divided it into several small booklets costing two, three, and four pennies. However, in the first booklet I put a little index of the order and titles of all the songs of the whole book, and in the next booklet I indicated what follows in the other [book], so that if anyone wanted to buy all of them and put them together, in order in one book (until perhaps it is complete, as it has been printed), [that would be possible].

For there are to be found here many attractive songs about the feast days; the coming and the work of Christ, such as the angelic salutation, Christmas, Easter, Ascension, Pentecost, and so on, and the true dear saints. So that many good people may not complain: "the holy remembrances themselves will all be forgotten, if no one ever celebrates the feasts of Christ and the saints." Therefore, dear Christian, whoever you are, since you have until now allowed your children and relatives to sing false scandalous songs at the country dances and elsewhere, and even much more on the feasts of Christ and the saints! As on St. John the Baptist's Day, when it would be more fitting for all Christians to be sorrowful that things were in such bad shape in the world then—and are still so—that one who spoke and taught the truth [John the Baptist] had to die for doing so [cf. Matt. 14:3–12]. So now (in response to this clear call which God makes to the world) encourage them [your children and relatives] to sing godly songs in which they are exhorted to seek knowledge of their salvation.

And teach your children and relatives to know that they do not serve human beings but God, when they faithfully (in the faith) keep house, obey, cook, wash dishes, wipe up and tend children, and such like work which serves human life, and that (while doing this very work) they can also turn to God with the voice of song. And teach them that in doing this, they please God much better than any priest, monk, or nun in their incomprehensible choir song, as they [the clergy] lifted up some foolish devotion of useless lullaby to the organ. A poor mother would so gladly sleep, but at midnight she must rock the wailing baby, and sing it a song about godly things. That is called, and it is, the right lullaby (provided it is done in the faith) that pleases God, and not the organ or the organist. He is no child, and you may not silence Him with piping and singing! But silence yourself: He requires something else.

But the seven holy times, Mass, vespers, and matins, will be sung thus: the artisan at his work, the maidservant at her dishwashing, the farmer and vinedresser on the farm, and the mother with the wailing child in the cradle—they use such praise, prayer, and teaching songs, Psalms or other such like things, provided it is all done in the faith and the knowledge of Christ, and they devoutly order their whole lives with all faithfulness and patience towards everyone. These will also praise God with and in Christ the everlasting Priest, with His angels, before His [God's] throne [cf. Rev. 7:9–12]. But the others who only use scandalous knavish songs and rotten, wanton sayings, and so forth, and have let their children and relatives be taught these, and sing and say them, they will have to weep, wail, and gnash their teeth forever with the devil [cf. Matt. 8:12].

Here let each one choose which one he wants; he will receive final judgment according to that choice. But I wish for all people knowledge of the good, and everlasting salvation. Amen.

Notes

1. See Roland H. Bainton, *Women of the Reformation in Germany and Italy* (Minneapolis: Augsburg Press, 1971), 55; and Miriam Chrisman, "Women and the Reformation in Strasbourg 1490–1530," *Archiv für Reformationsgeschichte* 63 (1972), 152–53.

2. For a detailed analysis of the text and context of Katherine Schütz Zell's hymnbook, see Elsie Anne McKee, *Reforming Popular Piety in Sixteenth-Century Strasbourg: Katharina Schütz Zell and Her Hymnbook.*

36. The Sum of my examination before the King's Council at Greenwich and The Ballad which Ann Askew Made and Sang when she was at Newgate

(1546)

Anne Askew

Anne Askew was the most well known of the Protestant female martyrs in England during the reign of Henry VIII. The second daughter of Sir William Askew, she was married against her will to a gentleman by the name of William Kyme, who sent her away when he discovered that she held Reformed beliefs. Askew went on her own to London, becoming associated with the Reformist circle surrounding Henry's last queen, Catherine Parr. John Bale, a Protestant supporter, argued that she should be allowed to divorce her husband inasmuch as she had been released from her marital obligations by Paul's words about a faithful partner not being bound to an unbelieving spouse (1 Cor. 7:15).

Askew's Reformed view of the Eucharist created conflict with the authorities, especially the Catholic ministers of the king's council (Bishop Stephen Gardiner and Chancellor Thomas Wriothsley), who saw in her objections to accepted beliefs an opportunity to snare the queen herself, who was overly sympathetic to the reform movement. They insisted that any denial of the dogma of transubstantiation (which affirmed the actual change of bread and wine into the body and blood of Christ through

---

SOURCE: *Writings of Edward the Sixth, William Hugh, Queen Catherine Parr, Anne Askew, Lady Jane Grey, Hamilton and Balnaves*, British Reformers, vol. 3 (London: The Religious Tract Society, 1849).

priestly words of consecration) constituted heresy. Such heresy deserved the death penalty, according to the Six Articles.

Askew was clear about her theological position, giving a personal account of her two examinations in 1545, which were published by John Bale in 1546 with a preface and an interlinear "elucydacyon." Her description is "the rarest form of sixteenth century writing, the self-portrait."[1]

In contrast to Bale's picture of a frail woman strengthened by God's grace, Askew's "self-portrait" shows her to be confident and adroit in her answers and counter-questions before the bishop of London, Edmund Bonner, in 1545. She considered herself to be a match for her questioners in her knowledge of Scripture as well as in her skill at repartee. When the bishop's chancellor reminded her that St. Paul had forbidden women "to speak, or to talk of the word of God," she answered that she knew Paul's meaning regarding 1 Cor. 14 was "that a woman ought not to speak in the congregation by the way of teaching." Paul should therefore "find no fault in poor women, except they had offended against the law." But when her accusers sought to trap Askew into making a heretical statement by asking her to give her interpretation of a text of Paul, she retorted disarmingly that "it was against St. Paul's learning that I, being a woman, should interpret the scriptures, especially where so many wise learned men were."[2] *In the end, the bishop made her sign a statement affirming her belief in the real body and blood of Christ in the Eucharist.*

In the summer of 1546 she was arrested again and brought before the king's council at Greenwich, where she was interrogated by Wriothsley and Gardiner along with others of the king's ministers. This time, she clearly repudiated the bodily presence of Christ in the Eucharist, articulating a Zwinglian symbolic, or memorialist, view.

Convicted as a heretic at the Guildhall, she was sent to the Tower of London to await death. Her accusers, however, were not content with her execution. They wished to extract from her some words that might incriminate other women in the queen's court. Unable to get what they wanted through questioning, they placed her on the rack, but she steadfastly refused to cooperate. "And because I lay still and did not cry, my lord chancellor and master Rich took pains to rack me with their own hands till I was nigh dead." She was so crippled by this brutality that she had to be carried to the stake where she was burned. Such torture of a woman, especially a gentlewoman, was most exceptional.[3]

Anne Askew's resolute faith and courage before inquisitors and under torture were immortalized in her own writings and published by Bale and by John Foxe in his famous Acts and Monuments. *Their words of praise for "her glorious witness of the Lord" further endeared her to many Protestants. Her demeanor was a special inspiration to the scores of women martyred several years later when a Catholic, Mary Tudor, reclaimed the English throne from 1553 to 1558. About one-fifth of the Protestant martyrs under Mary were women.*[4]

Askew's writing is typical of the body of literature generated by and about Protestant martyrs in the sixteenth century.

The sum of my examination before the king's council at Greenwich.

Your request as concerning my prison fellows, I am not able to satisfy, because I heard not their examinations; but the effect of mine was this:—I, being before the council, was asked of M. Kyme. I answered that my lord chancellor knew already my mind in that matter. They with that answer were not contented, but said, it was the king's pleasure that I should open the matter unto them. I answered them plainly that I would not so do. But if it were the king's pleasure to hear me, I would show him the truth. Then they said, it was not meet for the king to be troubled with me. I answered, that Solomon was reckoned the wisest king that ever lived, yet misliked he not to hear two poor common women, much more his grace, a simple woman, and his faithful subject. So in conclusion I made them no other answer in that matter. Then my lord chancellor asked me of my opinion in the sacrament. My answer was this, I believe that so oft as I, in a christian congregation, do receive the bread in remembrance of Christ's death, and with thanksgiving, according to his holy institution, I receive therewith the fruits also of his most glorious passion. The bishop of Winchester bade me make a direct answer. I said I would not sing a new song of the Lord in a strange land. Then the bishop said, I spake in parables. I answered, it was best for him, for if I show the open truth, said I, ye will not accept it. Then he said, I was a parrot. I told him again I was ready to suffer all things at his hands, not only his rebukes, but all that should follow besides, yea and that gladly.

Then had I divers rebukes of the council, because I would not express my mind in all things as they would have me. But they were not in the mean time unanswered, which now to rehearse were too much, for I was with them there about five hours. Then the clerk of the council conveyed me from thence to my lady Garnish.[5]

The next day I was brought again before the council. Then would they needs know of me what I said to the sacrament. I answered, that I already had said what I could say. Then after divers words they bade me go by. Then came my lord Lisle, my lord of Essex, and the bishop of Winchester, requiring me earnestly that I should confess the sacrament to be flesh, blood, and bone. Then said I to my lord Parr and my lord Lisle, that it was great shame for them to counsel contrary to their knowledge. Whereunto in few words they said, that they would gladly all things were well.

Then the bishop said, he would speak with me familiarly. I said, so did Judas, when he unfriendly betrayed Christ. Then desired the bishop to speak with me alone. But that I refused. He asked me why? I said, that in the mouth of two or three witnesses, every matter should stand according to Christ's and Paul's doctrine, Matt. 18, 2 Cor. 13.

Then my lord chancellor began to examine me again of the sacrament. Then I asked him how long he would halt on both sides? Then would he needs know where I found that. I said in the scripture, 1 Kings 18. Then he went his way. Then the bishop said, I should be burnt. I answered, that I had searched all the scriptures, yet could I never find there, that either Christ or his apostles put any creature to death. Well, well, said I, God will laugh your threatenings to scorn, Psalm 2. Then was I commanded to stand aside. [Then came M. Paget to me with many glorious words, and desired me to speak my mind to him. I might, he said, deny it again if need were. I said that I would not deny the truth. He asked me how I could avoid[6] the very words of Christ; Take, eat, this is my body, which shall be broken for you. I answered, that Christ's meaning was there as in these other places of the scripture; I am the door, John 10. I am the vine, John 15. Behold the Lamb of God, John 1. The rock stone was Christ, 1 Cor. 10 and such other. Ye may not here, said I, take Christ for the material thing that he is signified by; for then ye will make him a very door, a vine, a lamb, and a stone, clean contrary to the Holy Ghost's meaning. All these indeed do signify Christ, like as the bread doth his body in that place. And though he did say there, Take, eat this in remembrance of me, yet did he not bid them hang up that bread in a box, and make it a god, or bow to it.[7] Then came to me doctor Cox and doctor Robinson. In conclusion we could not agree.

Then they made me a bill about the sacrament, willing me to set my hand thereunto, but I would not. Then on the Sunday I was sore sick, thinking no less than to die. Therefore I desired to speak with master Latimer, but it would not be. Then was I sent to Newgate in my extremity of sickness; for in all my life before was I never in such pain. Thus the Lord strengthen you in the truth. Pray, pray, pray.

The Ballad which Anne Askew made and sang when she was in Newgate.

Like as the armed knigh
Appointed to the field,
With this world will I fight,
And faith shall be my shield,

Faith is that weapon strong
Which will not fail at need;
My foes therefore among
Therewith will I proceed.

As it is had in strength
And force of Christ his way,
It will prevail at length
Though all the devils say, Nay.

Faith in the fathers old
Obtained righteousness,
Which makes me very bold
To fear no world's distress.

I now rejoice in heart,
And hope bids me do so,
That Christ will take my part,
And ease me of my woe.

Thou say'st Lord, Whoso knock
To them thou wilt attend;
Undo therefore the lock,
And thy strong power send.

More enemies now I have,
Than hairs upon my head,
Let them not me deprave,
But fight thou in my stead.

On thee my care I cast,
For all their cruel spite,
I set not by their haste
For thou art my delight.

I am not she that list
    My anchor to let fall,
For every drizzling mist;
    My ship's substantial.

Not oft use I to write,
    In prose, nor yet in rhyme,
Yet will I show one sight,
    That I saw in my time.

I saw a royal throne
    Where justice should have sit.
But in her stead was one
    Of moody, cruel wit.

Absorpt was righteousness
    As of the raging flood;
Satan in fierce excess
    Sucked up the guiltless blood.

Then thought I, Jesus, Lord,
    When thou shalt judge us all,
Hard is it to record
    On these men what will fall.

Yet Lord, I thee desire,
    For that they do to me,
Let them not taste the hire
    Of their iniquity.

Notes

1. See Elaine V. Beilen, "Anne Askew's Self-Portrait," in *Silent but for the Word: Tudor Women as Patrons, Translators, and Writers of Religious Works*, ed. Margaret P. Hannay (Kent, Ohio: Kent State University Press, 1985), 78.

2. See "The Examinations of Anne Askew," in *Writings of Edward the Sixth, William Hugh, Queen Catherine Parr, Anne Askew, Lady Jane Grey, Hamilton and Balnaves*, British Reformers, vol. 3 (London: The Religious Tract Society, 1849), 12, 16.2.

3. See Beilen, 89.

4. See Retha M. Warnicke, *Women of the English Renaissance and Reformation* (Westport, Conn.: Greenwood Press, 1983), 75–76.

5. Prison. (This explanation found in the Religious Tract Society edition.)

6. Make of no effect. (Noted in the Religious Tract Society edition.)

7. This statement respecting Paget is omitted in Foxe's *Acts and Monuments*. Paget was one of the principal ministers of state at that period. (Noted in the Religious Tract Society edition.)

37. Letter from John Careless to His Wife

From John Foxe's *Actes and Monuments*

(1556)

John Careless

John Careless was a weaver from Coventry whose courageous witness to the Reformed faith during the reign of the Catholic Mary Tudor from 1553 to 1558 brought him imprisonment and death. In his martyrdom, however, he gained immortal fame when many of his letters were published in a book by John Foxe entitled Actes and Monuments of these latter and perilous dayes touching matters of the Church *(1563), or Foxe's* Book of Martyrs, *as it was more popularly known.*

Next to the Bible, the Book of Martyrs *was the most widely read book in many Puritan households and Reformed assemblies for worship. It also had great influence on the English, especially in making Catholicism appear as a cruel and persecuting religion.*

Unlike some three hundred Protestant men and women during Mary's reign, John Careless was not actually burned at the stake. He died in prison. To justify including Careless in his book, Foxe offered the following rationale: "Though he [Careless] is no less worthy to be counted in honour and place of Christ's martyrs, than others that suffer most cruel torments, as well for that he was for the same truth's sake a long time imprisoned, as also for his willing mind and zealous affection he had thereunto, if the Lord had so determined it, as well may appear by his examination he had before Dr. Martin."[1]

SOURCE: *Acts and Monuments of John Foxe*, vol. 8 (New York: AMS Press, 1965). Used by permission.

In his inquisition before a Dr. Martin in the lord chancellor's house on April 25, 1556, while he was imprisoned at the King's Bench, Careless showed himself steadfast in his Protestant convictions and resistant to the examiner's efforts to get him to implicate his fellow prisoners. He boldly proclaimed his adherence to the Calvinist doctrine of predestination, to the Bible as the final rule of faith and practice, and to the second prayer book of Edward VI as in all respects conforming to the Word of God (this was the more Reformed of the two Edwardian prayer books).

His letters also show a strong Reformed faith and piety, made up of an acute consciousness of sin, an assured faith in divine providence and the promise of forgiveness for repentant sinners, a view of Word and sacrament as the two marks of the true church (which had existed during the rule of Edward VI), and a serene confidence in the prospect of eternal life and joy in the face of martyrdom.

The main purpose of Careless's letters, and those of other martyrs, was to encourage all men and women facing martyrdom—counseling and admonishing them to remain steadfast in Reformed faith and practice, without being tempted under duress to stray from it by attending a papist mass.

In his letter to his wife, Margaret, Careless prepares her for the prospect of his death by encouraging and admonishing her to behave herself in all her "doings, sayings, and thoughts, most thankfully unto our good God. . . ." He urges her to place her trust in God's providential care and, in case of necessity, to commend all, including her children, to God, who "will be a father and a mother, better than ever you or I could have been unto them."

As by the great mercy of God, at the time of his good-will and providence appointed, my dearly beloved wife, you and I were joined together in the holy and christian state of godly matrimony, as well to our great joy and comfort in Christ, as also to the increase of his blessed church and faithful congregation, by having lawful children by and in the same, with the which God of his mercy hath blessed us, praised be his name there-for: even so now by his merciful will and divine ordinance, the time is come (so far as I can perceive) wherein he will, for his glory and our eternal comfort, dissolve the same, and separate us asunder again for a time. Wherefore I thought it good, yea and my bounden duty, by this simple letter to provoke, stir, and admonish you, to behave yourself in all your doings, sayings, and thoughts, most thankfully unto our good God for the same. And therefore, my dear wife, as you have heartily rejoiced in the Lord, and oftentimes given God thanks for his goodness in bringing us together in his holy ordinance: even so now I desire you, when this time of our separation shall come, to rejoice with me in the Lord, and to give him most hearty thanks, that he hath (to his glory and our endless commodity) separated us again for a little time, and hath mercifully taken me unto himself, forth of this miserable world, into his celestial kingdom; believing and hoping also assuredly, that God of his goodness, for his Son Christ's sake,[2] will shortly bring you, and your dear children thither to me, that we may most joyfully together sing praises unto his glorious name for ever. And yet once again I desire you for the love of God, and as ever you loved me, to rejoice with me, and to give God continual thanks for doing his most merciful will upon me.

I hear say that you do oftentimes use to repeat this godly saying, "The Lord's will be fulfilled." Doubtless it rejoiceth my poor heart to hear that report of you, and, for the Lord's sake, use that godly prayer continually, and teach your children and family to say the same day and night: and not only say it with your tongues, but also with your heart and mind, and joyfully submit your will to God's will in very deed, knowing and believing assuredly, that nothing shall come to you or any of yours, otherwise than it shall be his almighty and fatherly good-will and pleasure, and for your eternal comfort and commodity. Which thing to be most true and certain, Christ testifieth in his holy gospel, saying, "Are not two little sparrows sold for a farthing, and yet not one of them shall perish without the will of our heavenly Father?" [Matt. 10:29] and he concludeth saying, "Fear not ye therefore, for ye are better than many sparrows." As though he should have said, If God have such respect and care for a poor sparrow, which is not worth one farthing, that it shall not be taken in the lime-twig, net, nor pitfall, until it be his good will and pleasure; you may be well assured, that not one of you (whom he so dearly loveth, that he hath given his only dear Son for you,) shall perish, or depart forth of this miserable life without his almighty good-will and pleasure.

Therefore dear wife, put your trust and confidence wholly and only in him, and ever pray that his will be fulfilled, and not yours, except it be agreeing to his will; the which I pray God it may ever be, Amen. And as for worldly things, take you no care, but be you well assured the Lord, your dear God and Father, will not see you nor yours lack, if you continue in his love and childly fear, and keep a clear conscience from all kind of idolatry, superstition, and wickedness, as my trust is that you will do, although it be with the loss and danger of this temporal life. And good Margaret, fear not them that can but kill the body (and yet can they not do that until God give them leave), but fear to displease him that can kill both body and soul, and cast them into hell-fire. Let not the remembrance of your children keep you from God. The Lord himself will be a father and a mother, better than ever you or I could have been unto them. He himself will do all things necessary for them; yea, as much as rock the cradle, if need be. He hath given his holy angels charge over them, therefore commit them unto him. But if you may live with a clear conscience (for else I would not have you to live), and see the bringing up of your children yourself, look that you nurture them in the fear of God, and keep them far from idolatry, superstition, and all other kind of wickedness. And for God's sake help them to some learning, if it be possible, that they may increase in virtue and godly knowledge, which shall be a better dowry to marry them withal, than any worldly substance. And when they be come to age, provide them such husbands as fear God, and love his holy word. I charge you take heed that you match them with no papists; and if you live and marry again yourself (which thing I would wish you to do, if need require, or else not), good wife take heed how you bestow yourself, that you and my poor children be not compelled to wickedness. But if you shall be able well to live God's true widow, I would counsel you so to live still, for the more quietness of yourself and your poor children. Take heed, Margaret, and play the wise woman's part. You have warning by others, if you will take an example. And thus I commit you and my sweet children unto God's most merciful defence. The blessing of God be with you, and God send us a merry meeting together in heaven. Farewell in Christ, farewell mine own dear hearts all. Pray, pray.

Notes

1. See *Acts and Monuments of John Foxe*, vol. 8 (New York: AMS Press, 1965), 163.1.

2. According to John Foxe, "Here is a true mark of a faithful christian, forsaking wife and children for Christ's sake."

38. *From the* Diary of Lady Margaret Hoby

(1599)

The diary of Lady Margaret Hoby is one of three extant diaries of late Elizabethan, or early Jacobean, women. It is the only one written by an obviously devoted Puritan.[1]

The daughter of Arthur and Thomasine Dakins of Linton, Yorkshire, Margaret was born in 1571 and reared in the strict Puritan household of the countess of Huntingdon, Catherine, wife of the earl of Huntingdon, Henry Hastings. The countess was the daughter of John Dudley, the duke of Northumberland and protector of Edward VI just before his death in 1553. Dudley sought to extend Edward's reign by supporting Lady Jane Grey's claim to the throne, but when the Catholic Mary Tudor, the first daughter of Henry VIII, gained the throne, Dudley and Grey went to the block.

As the only daughter and heiress of the estate of her wealthy father, Margaret Dakins was a most desirable marital partner. Before she was twenty-five, she had had three husbands. Her first husband was Walter Devereux, the brother of Robert, earl of Essex, and a later favorite of Elizabeth I. Margaret's father, the earl of Huntingdon, and the earl of Essex purchased Hackness Manor, in Yorkshire, for the young couple. The marriage lasted less than two years as Walter Devereux was killed in France in 1591.

With the assistance of the earl and duchess of Huntingdon again, Margaret next married Thomas Sydney, nephew of the duchess and brother of the famous poets Philip and Mary Sydney, both of whom were

---

SOURCE: Dorothy M. Meads, ed., *Diary of Lady Margaret Hoby (1599–1605)* (Boston: Houghton Mifflin, 1930), 62–75. The diary is Egerton MS 2614 in the British Museum.

militant Protestants. Margaret's second marriage was also brief; Thomas Sydney died in 1595.

Life for an unmarried woman was difficult, and within a year Margaret reluctantly married Thomas Posthumous Hoby, son of Sir Thomas and Lady Elizabeth Hoby. His father was a diplomat and his mother was one of the learned Cooke sisters, daughters of Anthony Cooke. Thomas Hoby's mother wrote long epitaphs in Latin and Greek verse on the family tombs in Bisham Church and Westminster Abbey. After the death of her first husband, Elizabeth Hoby married John Lord Russell.

Lady Russell was a formidable woman who was determined to find a good marriage for her poor son. She also had powerful connections that she did not hesitate to use. Her sister, Mildred, was married to William Cecil, Lord Burghley, who later became England's Lord Treasurer. Another sister, Ann, was the wife of Sir Nicholas Bacon and mother of Francis Bacon, the famous philosopher.

Upon the death of Margaret's first husband, Lady Russell had tried to win the hand of the young widow for her son, without success. At that time, the Huntingdons were convinced that their nephew, Thomas Sydney, was the proper choice. When Margaret was widowed a second time, Russell's success in promoting her son was facilitated by Margaret's need for legal help to preserve her inherited estate against claims put forward by a new earl of Huntingdon. Margaret's patron, the former earl, had been succeeded by his brother after his death.

Three years after her third and last marriage in 1596, Margaret Hoby began keeping a diary, which she sustained until 1605, almost ten years. These were very eventful years in English history: Elizabeth I died in 1603, and James I came to the throne; the Puritans presented their Millenary Petition to James in 1603, only to be rejected at the Hampton Court Conference in 1604.

Unfortunately, there is nothing in Margaret Hoby's diary about these or other public events. Even on a more private level, she does not reveal a great deal about her inner thoughts and feelings, and she does not write about her personal relationships.

What her diary does show are the activities of a lady of the manor at the turn of the seventeenth century. Since Margaret Hoby's husband was a justice of the peace and a member of Parliament, he was frequently absent, leaving her with the care of the estate. Her days are filled with managing servants and accounts, and serving the community as midwife and amateur physician, since no professional physician was available in the country.

Most significantly, the diary shows the religious activity of a typical strict Puritan household: daily private and public prayers, and regular attendance at services of worship dominated by long Puritan sermons. Margaret Hoby regularly practiced repetition, *the Puritan custom of writing down the main points of a sermon and studying them at leisure. She carried on the daily reading of Scripture and participated in the lector, a time when the Scripture would be read aloud in the household, either by Rhodes, a Puritan minister, or by Margaret or her husband. Rhodes served as the household chaplain and was Margaret Hoby's spiritual director.*

Hoby made constant notes in her Bible or in other notebooks to assist her with her daily meditations and self-examinations. She read, or had read to her, treatises by Puritan writers, such as Thomas Cartwright and William Perkins, in addition to Foxe's Book of Martyrs. *Although she had no children of her own, she assisted with the catechizing of her servants and the young women being reared in her household, just as she had been schooled in the home of the countess of Huntingdon. Beyond her religious concerns for her own household, Hoby engaged in religious conversation with other women in her region. Hoby's diary provides a valuable glimpse into the religious life of a dedicated Puritan lady and her household.*[2]

[Almost the whole of the first entry on this page is torn away.]

[Thursday]

. . . day was deadnes in praier, and my greatest offence was want of sorow for the same: the Lord of his mercie increase true and fervant mourninge unto god that he never take his spiritt from me amen amen

[Friday 10]

After I was redie I betooke my selfe to privat praier, wherin it pleased the Lord to deall mercifully (*page torn*): after, I went about the house, and instructed Tomson wiffe in som principles of relegion, and then eate my breakfast, and then walked abroad tell all most :11: of the Clock: and after I had read :2: chapters of the bible, I went to diner: after dinner I went to worke, at which (*page torn*) Contenewed tell :4:, then I took order for supper (*page torn*) went to praier and to writ som notes in my testament, from which I was Called to walk with Mr. Hoby, talkinge of sundrie busines, and so to supper: imediately after praer and Lector, for the diligent attencion of which the Lord did heare my praier by removing all wanderinges which use to hurt me so that I received much Comfort, I went to bed

[The entry for 11th August has disappeared completely, except for three words in the last two lines.]

[the Lordes day 12]

after I was redie, I went to privatt praiers, then to breakfast: then I walked tell church time [with] Mr Hoby, and after to dinner: after which I walked and had speech of no serious maters tell :2: a clock: then I wrett notes into my bible tell :3: and after :4: I came againe from the church, walk, and medetated a Litle, and againe wrett som other notes in my bible of that I had Learned tell :5: att which time I retourned to examenation and praier: and after I had reed some of bond of the suboth, I walked abroad: and so to supper, after to praers, and Lastly to bed.

[Munday 13]

In the Morninge after privat praiers and order taken for diner, I wrett some notes in my testament tell :10: a clock: then I went to walk, and, after I retourned home, I praied privatly, read a chapter of the bible, and wrought tell dinner time: after I walked a whill with Mr Rhodes and Then I wrought, and did som things about the house tell :4: then I wrett out the sarmon into my book preached the day before, and, when I had again gone about in the house and given order for supper and other thinges, I retourned to examination and praier: then I walked tell supper time, and, after Catichisinge, medetated awhill of that I had hard, with mourninge to god for pardon both of my omition and Commition wherin I found my selfe guilte, I went to bed.

[Teusday 14]

In the morning I praied privatly and wrett notes in *(page torn)* tement tell :7: a clocke: then I took order for divers thinges touchinge the house, and, after I had brekfast (*page torn*), I wrought tell dinner time and hard Mr Rhodes (*page torn*) tell dinner time: after dinner I walked with g (*page torn*) Younge tell 2: a clock, then I went to work tell (*page torn*): after I had praied and taken order for supper, (*page torn*) walked abroad tell after. 5: at which time I retourn ed (*page torn*) examenation and praier, at which time it pleased the Lord to give me sure testimonie of his favor in christ, his *(torn)* name evermore be praised, who sendeth not his empty away: tell super time I was busie in the graniry, and, after supper and praiers, I went to bedd:

[Wensday 15]

In the morninge at :6: a clock I praied privatly: that done, I went to awiffe in travill of child, about whom I was busey *(torn)* tell: 1 a Cloke, about which time, She bing delivered and I havinge praised god, returned home and betook my selfe to privat praier :2: severall times upon occasion: then I wrett the most part of an examenation or triall of a christian, framed by Mr Rhodes, in the doinge wher (*torn*) I againe fell to praier, and after continewed writing (*faded*) after 3: a cloke: then I went to work tell after 5, and then to examenation and praier: the Lord make me thankfull, who hath hard my praiers and hath not turned his face from me: then I taked with Mrs Brutnell tell supper time, and after walked a litle into the feeldes, and so to prairs, and then to bed:

[Thursday 16]

After I was readie in the morning I praied privatly and wrett out the rest of those possitions which I left uncopied the day before: then I went take order for dinner and went to work tell breakfast Came, and, after I had broken my fast, I examened that I had wreten with Mr Rhodes, read some thinge in the bible, and so to work tell Comringe.[3] Cam for dinner: then I went to pray and so came to dinner: after dinner I wrought and read tell 4, and then I walked a litle abroad and, after I Cam home, read and (*faded and torn*) tell all most 6: and then I went to praier (*faded and torn*) and examenation: after which, I walked tell supper time: that don,.I walked tell praiers, then hadd Mr Rhodes read a chapter, and so went to bed

[Friday]

After privat praiers I went about the house and read of the bible and wrought tell dinner time: and, after dinner, it pleased, for a Iust punishment to corricte my sinnes, to send me febelnis of stomak and paine of my head, that kept me upon my bed tell 5: a clock: at which time I arose, haveinge release of my sickness, according to the wonted kindnes of the Lord, who, after he had Let me se how I had offended, that so I might take better heed to my body and soule hereafter, with a gentle corriction let me feele he was reconsiled To me: at which time I went to privat praier, and praises, examenation, and so to work tell supper time: which done I hard the Lector and, after I had walked an Hower with Mr Hoby, I wente to bed

[Saterday 18]

After I was readie I praied privatly, and, because I was weak and had paine in my head, I wret litle but wound yearne and walked tell dinner time: after which I went about the house, and did walke abroad, workinge litle all that day because of my weaknes, least I should be disabled to keepe the Lordes day as I desired and am bound: before supper, I praied and examened my selfe, not so perteculerly as I ought to have don, which I beseech the Lord to pardon for his christs sack, and give me grace here after to be more carefull: then I walked tell supper time: after supper I taked with Mr Rhodes of the lordes praier, and, after lector, I medetated a litle of that I had hard, and so (*torn*) went to bed.

[the Lordes day 19]

After I was redie I betooke me privat praier: (*torn*) then, because Mr Hoby was not well, I kept him Kompanie tell the sarmon time, and did eate my breakfast: that done, I thank god who gave him will and abelitie, we went to church, where we received the sacrementes: after I came home I praied and so to dinner, att which, and after, both my selfe did talk and heare of more worldly mattres then, by godes assistance, I will here after willingly doe: tell :3: a Clock I was with Mr Hoby, not so Care full, the Lord forgive it me, as I ought, to medetate of what I hard, speakinge and thinking of many Idle mattres: then we went to Church and, after the sarmon, I walked tell 6: a clock, about which time I praied and examened my self, craving pardon for these my infirmities: after, I went to supper: after which, tell praier time, I walked and, after repeticion,[4] went to bed:

[Munday 20]

After I was readie I praied privatly: then I walked with Mr Hoby tell 8: a clock, at which time I brake my fast, and so to worke, and, at :11: of the Clock, I took a Lector of Mr Rhodes, and went to dinner: after dinner I wound yearn tell: 3, and then walked with Mr Hoby about the toune to spye out the best places where Cotiges might be builded: after I Came home I wrought tell :6: and gave order for supper, and then I betook me to privat praier and examenation, in which (*soiled*) I found my selfe a lackinge in performing my dutie I soune perceived, and, therfore, besought (*soiled*) Lord for pardon: then I went to supper, after which I walked a whill, and, because there (*torn and soiled*) not Mr Rhodes to pray publeckly, I praied privatly, and, after I had helped Mr Hoby to Looke over some papers, I went to bed:

[Teusday 21]

after I was readie I praied, and then I went awhile about the house and so to breakfast, and then to work, tell coveringe[5] came: then I went to privat praier but was interrupted: after I had dined I went to work tell 6:, and walked a little abroad, and then Came to examenation and praier: after, I walked a litle, and so to supper: after which I went to praiers, and, Nut long after, accordinge to my wonted use, to bed, save only I did not so deligently think of that I had hard, which I be seech the Lord to pardon, for Christ sack Annen Amen.

[Wensday 22]

after I was redie I praied, and, after I had gon a Litle about the house, I wrett out notes in my testement, and then brak my fast and walked abroad tell dinner: before which I praied, according to my wonte, and, after dinner, I was buisie dispacting one a way to Linton[6] tell :3: a Clock: then I wret notes out into my bible, and after went a walkinge with Mr. Hoby, and then returned into examination and praier: after, I reed of the bible, and walked alone, and then went into the kicthine, wher Mr Rhodes and my selfe had som speach with the poore and Ignorant of the som princeples of religion: and I had walked a litle after in the Court. Mr Hoby came, and so to supper and after to lector and then to bed.

[Thursday 23]

In the morninge I praied: then I took order for thinges about the house tell I went to breakfast, and sonne after I took my Coach and went to linton wher, after I had salluted my mother, I praied, and then, walkinge a litle and readinge of the bible in my Chamber, went to supper: after which I hard the Lector and sonne after that went to bed

[Friday 24]

In the morninge, beinge readie, I praied, then brak my fast with Mr Hoby, and so reed to church: after the sarmon I presently went to dinner, after which I passed the time in talk with some freinds, and then went to privat praier: that don I took the aire in the Coach with Mr Hoby, and so cam in and walked in the garden, medetatinge of the pointes of the sarmon and prainge tell hard before I went to supper: and after supper went to publeck praier and thence to bed:

[Saterday 25]

In the morning I praied and then I wreet a Letter to Doctor Brewer and so to breakfast: after which I taked privatly, with Mr Hoby, matters concerninge Conscience and our estates,[7] wch, beinge Concluded of betwene us, I took my Coache and Came home to Hacknes, wher, after I was well Comed, I praise god, I went to praier and medetation: then I went about the house tell supper time: after supper I talked with Mr Rhodes in the garden, and then to publect praiers, and sonne after to bed

[the Lordes day 26]

In the morninge, after privat praiers, I taked a litle with Mr Rhodes, and then to breakfast: sonne after which, I went to church, and, when the seermon was ended, I medetated of that I hard, and praied, tell allmost diner: after diner I taked a while with Mistress Brutnell, and then hard a Chapter wher of Mr Rhodes spake, and so to church, wher, at Caticising and sermon, I staied tell 4 a clock: then I cam hom and took order for supper, and wret out notes in my bible, and then went to walke: and after my Comminge home, praied, after which I went to supper and, sonne after that, to praers and thence to bed: this day, as ever, the divell laboreth to hinder my profittable hearinge of the word and callinge upon god, but the Lord, for his mercis sach strengten, his children to rissist and over Come

[Monday 27]

In the morninge after privatt praier I went a litle about the house, and then eate my breakfast, after which I wrett out a sermon that I was behind with, then I walked, and, sonne after, to dinner: after which I talked a little with Mr Cholmley, and then dispached a messhinger to my mothers, and to York to Mr Hoby, and then wrett out another sermon in my book: and so walked abroad, and, retourning hom, betook my selfe to privat praiers and medetacion: sonne after I went to supper, after which I walked a litle, and then to prairs: then I wret to Mr Hoby and so to bed:

[Tewsday 28]

In the morninge, after privat praier, I Reed of the bible, and then wrought tell 8: a clock, and then I eate my breakfast: after which done, I walked in to the feeldes tell: 10 a clock, then I praied, and, not long after, I went to dimer: and about one a clock I geathered my Apeles tell :4:, then I Cam home, and wrought tell almost :6:, and then I went to privat praier and examenation, in which it pleased the lord to blesse me: and besiech the lord, for christ his sack, to increase the power of his spirite in me daly Amen Amen: tell supper time I hard Mr Rhodes read of Cartwright,[8] and, sonne after supper, I went to prairs, after which I wrett to Mr Hoby, and so to bed.

[Wensday 29]

after privat praier I reed of the bible and wrought tell dinner time, before which I praied: and, after dinner, I continewed my ordenarie Course of working, reading, and dispossinge of busenes in the House, tell after 5:, at which time I praied, read a sermon, and examened my selfe: and then, goinge to super, it pleased god to send me ease of the tothache wher with I was troubled. sonne after I went to praers, and, after som talk with some of the sarvantes of houshould mattres, I went to bed.

[Thursday 30]

After privat praier in the morninge, I took order for dinner, and then wrought tell breakfast time: after that I walked, and then Came home and wrett of my Common place book:[9] then I praied, and so to dimer: after dinner I trifelde the time about the house and in the toune tell 2: a Clock, then I Came in, and wrought, and instructed som of my famelie:[10] at wch time I found my mind much and altogether eased of sume trouble it had before: then I was busie and hard Mr Rhodes Read his Catechismie tell 5:, then I went to privat praiers, medetation, and ordering som thing in the house, and so to supper: after that to Lector, and, no long after, to bed.

[Friday 31]

After privat prairs I I wrett notes in my testement after I had taken order in the house: then I eadt my break fast, and then wrought tell and walked tell dinner: then I praied privatly, and, when I had dined, wrought tell :3: a clock: then I went a little about the house and reed of the diatt of the soule tell :5:, and then returned to privat praier and medetacion, and so to readinge of the bible and walkinge tell supper: after which I hard of the sudden Death of Doctor Brewer, Procured by a medeson he minestred to him selfe to Cause him to sleep: I was much greved for it, because of the familiaritie I had with him, and good I had received from, but, after better advice, I found the mercie and power of god shewed in openinge his eies touchinge me, and shuttinge them against him selfe, by Causinge him to have great Care of ministringe unto me, and so litle for his owne saftie: therefore I may truly conclude it is the Lord, and not the phisision, who both ordaines the medesine for our health and orderethe the ministring of it for the good of his children, closinge and unclosinge the Iudgmentes of men at his pleasure: therefore let everie one phisision and pactente Call upon the Lord for a blessinge: and then, after Lector, I wen to bed:

[*September 1599, 1 Saterday]*

After praier in the morninge, I, beinge not well, did heare Mr Rhodes read of Gyffard upon the songe of Sallemon,[11] sone after I went to breakfast, and so walked allmost tell dimer time: then I Came in, and praied, and so to dimer: after which I walked about the house, barne, and feeldes, and, when I Came home, I praied privat with Mr Rhodes, wherin I had more comfort then ever I received in my Life before, I praise god: then I went to take my Beesse, and, after that, I returned to privat praier my selfe and examenation: then I went to se my Honnie ordered, and so to supper: after which I went to lector, and soone after to bed:

[the Lordes day 2]

After privat praier I brak my fast before I went to Church, and, when I Came home, I praied privatly, and so went to dimer: after which I talked tell :2: a Clock with som of my freindes, and then to Church: after I Cam home I wrett notes out into my bible, and then I went to privatt praier and examenation and so to supper: sonne after which I went to praers and then to bed.

[Munday 3]

In the morninge, after privat praier, I brake my fast: sonne after that I had hard som chapters of the bible read, I went abroad in to the feeldes in my Cotch, because my foot would not suffer me to goe: then I Came home and, havinge praied a litle, went to dinner: after which I walked abroad and, at my Cominge home, I took order for supper, and went to praier, and sonne after to supper: after which Mr Hoby Came home and, for that night, when he had eaten som thinge, I went to praiers, havinge no Lector, and so to bed.

[Tewsday 4]

when I had praied privatly I did read of the bible allmost untell dinner time: after dinner I walked to the Church wth Mr Hoby, and was then With him allmost tell :4: of the Clock: then I Came home and did studie my lector, and read a whill, and then, after talk with him of many thinges, I went to privat prair and examenation: after I went to supper, then to the lector, and so to Bed

[Wensday 5]

After privat praier I wret to my Lady Ewre:[12] then I went about the house and, having taken order for dinner, I walked and kept Mr Hoby Compenie almost tel dinner time: then I reed a litle, and praied, and so to dinner: after which I hilped to read of the book for the placing of the people in the church to Mr Hoby, and then we went to church: and after we Came home I taked with him, and Lay on my bed, not being able well to goe for my foot that was sore, tell allmost supper time: and then I praied and examened myself and, after I had supped, I reed of grenhame,[13] and so went to bed:

[Thursday 6]

after I had praied I did goe about in to the house, and then eate my breakfast, and after did see my hunnie ordered, and then to dimer: after which I wrought, and walked about with Mr Hoby, nothinge reading nor profiting my selfe or any, the Lord pardon my ommitiones and Commitions, and give me his spiritt to be wacthfull to redeme the time: then I went to privat praier and examenation, after to supper and lector, and so to bed:

[Friday 7]

After privat praiers I wrett my notes in my testement, which I geathered out of the Lector the night before: then I did eate my breakfast, then I walked abroad and talked of good thinges, so that I found much Comfort: after I Cam hom I wrett my sermon that was preached the saboth day before, then I went to privat praier, and so to dinner: after which I taked a litle with som of my frendes, and exercised my body at bowles a whill, of which I found good: then I Came home and wrought tell 4, then I praied with Mr Rhodes, and after walked abroad: and when I Came hom I praied privatly, and sonne after went to supper: after which I went to the Lector, and then to bed:

[Saterday 8]

after praier I went about and then eate my breakfast and then walked abroad: after, I wrett notes in my testement and reed of the bible, then to dinner: after wch I talked a litle, and then I wrought tell 3: then I walked with Mr Hoby tell 6:, then I came and wrowght awhill, and so to praier and examenation, then to supper, after to lecor, and then to bed

[the Lords day 9]

after privat praier I did eate my breakfast and so went to church: after the sarmon was done, I praied privatly and, after dinner, I kept Mr Hoby companie tell chuech time againe: after the sarmon I medetated a litle, and then I wrett out notes in my bible and, before supper, I praied, and, after supper and examenation, I went to bed:

[Munday 10]

After privat praers I went about the house, an then eate my breakfast: then I walked to the church with Mr Hoby: after that I wrougt a litle, and neclected my custom of praier, for which, as for many other sinnes, it pleased the Lord to punishe me with an Inward assalte: But I know the Lord hath pardoned it because he is true of his promise, and, if I had not taken this Course of examenation, I think I had for gotten itt: after dimer I walked with Mr Hoby and, after he was gon, I went to gett tithe aples: after I Came home, I praied wth Mr Rhodes, and, after that, privatly by my selfe, and tooke examenation of my selfe: and so, after I had walked a whill, I went to supper, after that to the Lector, and so to bed

[Tewsday 11]

After privat praier I went about the house, and then wrett som notes into my testement: after, I walked and, when I cam home, praied With Mr Rhodes: then I wrought a whill and praied privatly before diner: after, I walked, and took the aire in my Cocth, and when I Came home I wrought tell :6:, and then examened my selfe, and praied privatly, and reed of Grenhame tell supper time: after supper I went to praers and, sonne after, to bed:

[Wensday 12]

after privat praiers in the morning I, being not well, did walk a litle, and then eate my brecfast: then I wrought, and talked with such strangres as as Came to me tell 5: a clock att night, at which time I praed and examened my selfe: sonne after to supper, then to lector, and Not long after to bed.

[Thursday 13]

In the morninge, after privat praier, I wret some thinges touchinge Houshould mattres: then I did eate my breakfast, and did order diverse thinges in the granirie: sonne after Mr Hoby Came home, and I kept him Companie tell he went away againe: after diner I went to Birstall, and se him, who was not well, and his aples tithed: then I wrought tell almost :6:, and praied with Mr Rhodes, and privatly in my Closett: after medetation, I went to supper: after, I had reed of the bible, after to lector, and then to bed

[Friday 14]

After order taken for the house, and privat praers, I writt notes into my testement and then brak my fast: after, I wrought, and kept Mr. Hoby compenie tell allmost diner time: then I praied and, after dimer, I walked awhill and went to church Wth Mr Hoby, and when I Cam home wrought tell 6:, then I examened my selfe and praied, walked tell supper time: then I hard the Lector, and after wrought a whill, and so went to bed: Lord, for

Christs sack, pardone my drousenes which, with a neclegent mind, caused me to ommitt that medetation of that I had hard, which I ought to have had.

[Saterday 15]

when I had praied I wrought tell 9:, then I did eate my breakfast: after, I walked to the church wth Mr Hoby, and was there tell dimer time: then I praied, and, after dinner, I wrought and went a litle about the house tell :6:, then I went againe to the church wth Mr Hoby and, after I came home, I examened my selfe, and praied: after supper I examened papers, when lector was done, with Mr Hoby, and so went to bed:

[the Lordes day 16]

After I had praied privatly, I went to church and, from thence returninge, I praised god both for the inableinge the minister so proffetably to declare the word as he had, and my selfe to heare wth that Comfort and understanding I did: after dimer I walked wth Mr Hoby tell Catzhising was done, and then I went to church: after the sarmon I looked upon a poore mans Legg, and after that I walked, and reed a sarmon of Geferd upon the song of Salomon: then I examened my selfe and praied: after supper I was busie with Mr Hoby tell prair time, after which I went to bed:

[Munday the 17]

After privat praier I saw a mans Legg dressed, took order for thinges in the house, and wrough tell dinner time: after dinner I went about the house, and read of the arball:[14] then I tooke my Cocth and Came to Linton, wher, after I had talked a whill with my mother, examened my selfe and praied, I went to supper, and then praied publeckly, and so to bed:

[Tewsday the 18]

After I had praied privatly I went to breakfast and, sonne after, took my Cocth, and wente to malton to salute my Lady Ewre, with whom I staied about :2: howers: then Came to Rillington, and went to my Cossine Gates house, and so home to Linton to supper: after that to praiers, and then to bed

[Wensday the 19]

After praier I went to breakfast, and so tooke choch and Came to York, to Mr Skidmores house their, wher, after much time spent their with some freindes, I went to privat praier: and, havinge supped, I was at publeck praers very sicke: the Lord pardon the sinne for which I was so punished, it beinge the will of god often to punishe one sinne with another, for I had Litle proffet by that praier, by reasone of my sicknes: yet, presently, I was well with meanes, and so went to bed

[Thursday the 20]

After privat praier I went to the maner to doe my dutie to my Lady Borley,[15] wher I hard Commune sarvice, and diner: after which I had speech of some worldly matters, and then tooke Cocth with my Lady, and Cam home againe to supper with hir: before which we had sarvice and, about ten a clock, I came to my Lodginge, and so went to bed

[Friday the 21]

After privat praier I went to breakfast, and then I talked with a phesition which, I hope, the Lord hath provided for me in steed of Doctor Brewer, and some other gentelmen: after dinner I had companie of many gentllwemen that came to me, and Mr Fuller, my Lorde Burleys chaplen, who seemed a godly and relegous young man: then I went to vesitte my Cossin Bouser that lay ine, and thence returned to supper to Mr Skedmores, before which I praied privatly: after supper divers gentlemen cam in, who taried so late that we had no publeck praers, and so I went to bed, privatly Comending my self to god

[Saterday the 22]

After a privat praier I brake my fast and then talked with Mr lister:[16] then I took my Cotch and went to Bisshopthorpe to the Busship: their I dined, and talked with Mrs Hutten[17] of relegion tell I Came from thence: then I Cam to York, to Mr Skidmors House, wher, after I had praied, I went to supper to my Cossine Bousers howse, wher I had Conferrance with a relegious gintelwoman, and, thence Returninge, went to bed

[the Lordes day 23]

After privat praier I walked and did eate my breakfast: then I reed a chapter of the Bible to my mother, and repeted the Doctrins which from thence I had hard Mr Rhodes Colecte: then I went to the church, wher I hard Mr Pamer speak, but to small profitte to any: thence I returned and privatly praied, lamentinge the misirie of godes visible Church, and praisinge his goodnes to my selfee about others: then, sonne after, I went to diner: after that, I talked with Mr Hoby, and so went to my Cossine Bousers child christninge, and hard a sarmon, somthing better then that in the morninge: which ended, with all Ceremones, I returned to my lodginge, and examened my selfe and praid: then I went to supper to Mr Nevells:[18] after, I went to my lodging, and so went to bed

[Munday the 24]

After I had praed, I went to breakfast to my Cosins bousers house: after that I went to Gremston, to my Cossin Stanopes,[19] wher I praied privatly before supper, and sonne after went to bed

[Tewsday the 25]

After I had praied I walked in the garden tell break fast time: after breakfast I Came to York, then I went to the manner after I had praied privatly, and supped their, and took my leave of my Lady Burley, Came to my Lodginge and went to bed

[Wensday the 26]

After I had praied I brake my fast and then went to se a house in Yorke: and, after I had taken my leave of Certaine freindes, I Came to Linton, wher I praied privatly, went to supper, then hard a lector which Mr Nevill made, and so went to bed

[Thursday the 27]

After I had praied privatly I went to breakfast: I took my Cotch and Came home to Hacknes safe, I thanke god, and, after I had praied privatly and supped, I hard Mr Rhodes Caticize, and, sonne after, went to bed

[Friday the 28]

In the morninge, after privat praier, I tooke order for thinges about the house, and at 8: I did eate my breakfast: then I hard Mr Rhodes read tell allmost dinner time: after dinner I talked with Tho: Adesone about the purchassinge his owne farme: then I wrought tell allmost supper time and, after I had privatly praied, I went to supper: after that I walked tell Lector time, and after that I hard one of the men read of the book of Marters,[20] and so went to bed

[Saterday the 29]

After privat praier I did take order for thinges in the house, then I brak my fast and went to church: then I Came home and privatly praied: after I had dinned I wret to my mother and Mr Hoby, and dispacted one away to him, then I sawe some thinges done in the house: after, I wret notes in my bible, then I praied with Mr Rhodes, and then walked tell all most supper time, and then examened my selfe and praied

[the Lordes day 30]

After privat praier I went to church wher I hard the word preached, and received the sacrementes to my Comfort: after I had given thankes and dined, I walked a whill, and then went to church, whence, after I had hard Catchizising and sarmon, I returned home and wret notes in my bible, and talked of the sarmon and good thinges with Mrs Ormston: then I went to praier, after to supper, then to repetecion of the wholl daies exersice and praiers, hard one of the men reade of the book of marters, and so went to bed

• • •

Notes

1. The other two were by Lady Grace Mildmay and Lady Anne Clifford. See the introduction to *Diary of Lady Margaret Hoby*, ed. Dorothy M. Meads (Boston: Houghton Mifflin, 1930), 49–61; and Retha M. Warnicke, *Women of the English Renaissance and Reformation* (Westport, Conn.: Greenwood Press, 1983), 148–49.

2. See Meads, 1–39; and Diane Willen, "Women and Religion in Early Modern England," in *Women in Reformation and Counter-Reformation Europe*, ed. Sherrin Marshall (Bloomington: Indiana University Press, 1989), 148–52.

3. Perhaps the bailiff or steward.

4. According to Dorothy Meads, editor of the version reprinted here, "This probably means a repetition, by the assembled household, of the day's sermons and teaching, which, together with the 'lector' and catechizing, was Lady Hoby's method of training her household in religion, and was the usual procedure in a Puritan family. It may be concluded, perhaps, that she sometimes conducted the 'repeticion' and the 'lector' herself, unless Mr. Rhodes or Sir Thomas took the duty."

5. Perhaps the same name as in the entry for Thursday the 16th (of August).

6. The place where Lady Hoby was born, and where her mother still lived.

7. According to Meads, "It is not clear whether Lady Hoby here means their spiritual or material 'estates'. It is probably the latter, and this visit to her mother may have been upon family business, perhaps in connection with lawsuits concerning her inheritance."

8. This is Thomas Cartwright (1535–1603), a famous Puritan who taught briefly at Cambridge but had to flee to Geneva because of his outspoken Presbyterian views.

9. According to Meads, "A common-place book was, originally, one in which 'commonplaces', or passages important for reference, were collected, usually under general heads."

10. Lady Hoby refers to her household as her family, for she had no children.

11. This is a work by the Puritan divine George Gifford. Gifford dedicated this work to the Earl of Essex, Lady Hoby's brother-in-law."

12. According to Meads, this is "Mary, daughter of Sir John Dawnay of Sessay, co. York. She had married, in, or before, 1578, Ralph, Lord Eure, Sheriff of Yorkshire, 1593–4, and M.P. for the county 1584–6."

13. According to Meads, "Richard Greenham was a learned Puritan divine, active and zealous, a Fellow of Pembroke Hall, Cambridge, in 1564, and rector of Dry Drayton, 1570–91."

14. According to Meads, "This was probably the *New herball* of William Turner the reformer, who, having a garden at Kew, indulged in botany as a relief from ardent protestantism. His *herball* is considered to mark the beginning of the scientific study of botany in England."

15. Lady Dorothy Burghley and her husband, the second Lord Burghley, were cousins by marriage to Lady Hoby.

16. Probably her new physician.

17. Frances, widow of Marten Bowes, and third wife of Matthew Hutton, archbishop of York.

18. Ralph Nevell, "marcer," a York cousin of Lady Hoby.

19. According to Meads, this is "one of the sons of Sir Michael Stanhope, for long the Governor of Hull, and always on bad terms with the townsfolk. A keen partisan of Protector Somerset, Stanhope lost all his appointments on the latter's fall and his own execution followed that of Somerset in 1552."

20. On John Foxe's *Book of Martyrs*, see vol. 2:615–18.

Sources

Ames, William. *The Marrow of Theology*. Translated and edited by John D. Eusden from the third Latin edition, 1629. Boston: Pilgrim Press, 1968.

Askew, Anne. "The sum of my examination before the king's council at Greenwich" and "The Ballad which Anne Askew made and sang when she was in Newgate." In *Writings of Edward the Sixth, William Hugh, Queen Catherine Parr, Anne Askew, Lady Jane Grey, Hamilton, and Balnaves*. British Reformers, vol. 3. London: The Religious Tract Society, 1849.

"The Augsburg Confession." In *Book of Concord*, edited by Theodore G. Tappert. Philadelphia: Muhlenberg Press, 1959.

Berry, Lloyd E., ed. *The Geneva Bible*. A facsimile of the 1560 edition. Madison: University of Wisconsin Press, 1969.

"The Book of Common Prayer (1559)." In *Liturgies and Occasional Forms of Prayer Set Forth in the Reign of Queen Elizabeth*, edited by William K. Clay. Cambridge: University Press, 1847.

The Book of the Craft of Dying and Other Early English Tracts Concerning Death. London: Longmans, Green and Co., 1917; reprint, New York: Arno Press, 1977.

Browne, Robert. "A Treatise of reformation without tarying for anie." In *The Writings of Robert Harrison and Robert Browne*, edited by Albert Peel and Leland H. Carlson. Elizabethan Nonconformist Texts, vol. 2. London: George Allen and Unwin, 1953.

Bucer, Martin. "The Strasbourg Liturgy." In *Liturgies of the Western Church*, edited by Bard Thompson. Cleveland: World Publishing Company, 1961.

Bullinger, Heinrich. "Of the Word of God." Sermon One, Decade One in *The Decades of Henry Bullinger*, edited by Thomas Harding, translated by H. I. Cambridge: Cambridge University Press, 1849.

Calvin, John. "Draft Ecclesiastical Ordinances." In *Calvin: Theological Treatises*, edited by J. K. S. Reid. Library of Christian Classics, vol. 22. Philadelphia: Westminster Press, 1954.

———. "The Form of Church Prayers and Hymns with the Manner of Administering the Sacraments and Consecrating Marriage according to the Custom of the Ancient Church." In *Liturgies of the Western Church*, edited by Bard Thompson. Cleveland: World Publishing Com pany, 1961.

———. "The Law." *Institution of the Christian Religion (1536)*. Trans lated and annotated by Ford Lewis Battles. Atlanta: John Knox Press, 1975.

———. "For Us Our God Is Firm Support." In *The Piety of John Calvin*, edited by Ford Lewis Battles, music edited by Stanley Tagg. Grand Rapids, Mich.: Baker, 1978.

"The Canons of Dort." In *Ecumenical Creeds and Reformed Confessions*. Grand Rapids, Mich.: CRC Publications, 1987.

Careless, John. "To His Wife." In *Acts and Monuments of John Foxe*. Vol. 8. New York: AMS Press, 1965.

Erasmus, Desiderius. "The *Paraclesis*." In *Christian Humanism and the Reformation: Selected Writings of Erasmus*, edited by John C. Olin. 2d ed. New York: Fordham University, 1975.

Farel, William, and John Calvin. "The Geneva Confession" (1536). In *Calvin: Theological Treatises*, translated with introduction and notes by J. K. S. Reid. Library of Christian Classics, vol. 22. Philadelphia: Westminster Press, 1954.

Grumbach, Argula von. "Letter to the University of Ingolstadt." In *Argula von Grumbach: A Woman's Voice in the Reformation*, edited by Peter Matheson. Edinburgh: T. & T. Clark, 1995.

The Heidelberg Catechism. Translated by Allen O. Miller and M. Eugene Oster-haven. Philadelphia: United Church Press, 1962.

Hoby, Lady Margaret. *Diary of Lady Margaret Hoby (1599–1605)*, edited by Dorothy M. Meads. Boston: Houghton Mifflin, 1930.

The Imitation of Christ by Thomas à Kempis: A New Reading of the 1441 Latin Autograph Manuscript by William C. Creasy. Macon, Ga.: Mercer University Press, 1989.

Jacob, Henry. "Principles and Foundations of Christian Religion." In *The Early English Dissenters in the Light of Recent Research (1550–1641)*, edited by Champlin Burrage. Cambridge: Cambridge University Press, 1912.

Knox, John. "The Form of Prayers and Ministration of the Sacraments, etc., Used in the English Congregation at Geneva, and Approved by the Famous and Godly Learned Man, John Calvin." In *Liturgies of the Western Church*, edited by Bard Thompson. Cleveland: World Publishing Company, 1961.

Luther, Martin. "Formula of Mass and Communion for the Church at Wittenberg." In *Liturgies of the Western Church*, edited by Bard Thompson. Cleveland: World Publishing, 1961.

———."The Freedom of a Christian." In *Luther's Works: Career of the Reformer*, edited by Harold J. Grimm. Vol. 31. Philadelphia: Muhlenberg Press, 1957.

———."Out of the Depths I Cry to Thee." From the *Hymnal* of the Evangelical and Reformed Church. St. Louis: Eden Publishing House, 1941.

———."Small Catechism." In *Book of Concord*, edited by Theodore G. Tappert. Philadelphia: Muhlenberg Press, 1959.

"The Marburg Colloquy, 1529." In *Great Debates of the Reformation*, edited by Donald J. Ziegler. New York: Random House, 1969.

"The Palatinate Liturgy." Edited by Bard Thompson. *Theology and Life* 6, no. 1 (spring 1963): 49–63.

Perkins, William. "The Art of Prophesying." In *The Work of William Perkins*, edited by Ian Breward. Courtenay Library of Reformation Classics, vol. 3. Berkshire, England: Sutton Courtenay Press, 1970.

Robinson, John. "A Just and Necessary Apology." In *Works of John Robinson*, edited by Robert Ashton. London: John Snow, 1851.

Sachs, Hans. "A Conversation between an Evangelical Christian and a Lutheran in Which the Offensive Behaviour of Some Who Call Themselves Lutherans Is Exposed and Admonished in a Brotherly Spirit." In *Hans Sachsens Werke*, edited by A. Keller and E. Goetze. Vol. 21. Tübingen: Literarischer Verein, 1870–1902. Trans. by Elsbeth Duke.

"The Schleitheim Confession of Faith." Edited by John Wenger. *Mennonite Quarterly Review* 19, no. 4 (October 1945): 247–53.

Staupitz, John von. "Eternal Predestination and Its Execution in Time." In *Forerunners of the Reformation: The Shape of Late Medieval Thought*, edited by H. A. Oberman, translated by Paul L. Nyhus. New York: Holt, Rinehart and Winston, 1966.

[*The Westminster Confession*] *The Confession of Faith of the Assembly of Divines at Westminster from the Original Manuscript Written by Cornelius Burges in 1646*. Edited by S. W. Carruthers. London: Publishing Office of the Presbyterian Church of England, 1946.

Zell, Katherine Schütz. "Katharina Schütz Zell's Foreword for Her Edition of the Hymnbook of the Bohemian Brethren (1534–1536)." In Elsie Anne McKee, *Reforming Popular Piety in Sixteenth-Century Strasbourg: Katharina Schütz Zell and Her Hymnbook, Studies in Reformed Theology and History* 2:4 (Princeton, N.J.: Princeton Theological Seminary, 1994), appendix I, 65–67.

Zwingli, Ulrich. "Action or Use of the Lord's Supper." In *Liturgies of the Western Church*, edited by Bard Thompson. Cleveland: World Publishing Company, 1961.

———."Sixty-Seven Articles." In *Selected Works*, edited by Samuel Macauley Jackson, with introduction by Edwards Peters. Philadelphia: University of Pennsylvania Press, 1972.

Index

Scriptural Index

Old Testament

Apocryphal/Deuterocanonical Books